The American Political Landscape Series

Encyclopedia of Women in American Politics

Forthcoming Titles in the American Political Landscape Series

Encyclopedia of Religion in American Politics
Encyclopedia of Minorities in American Politics
Encyclopedia of Media in American Politics
Encyclopedia of Corruption in American Politics

The American Political Landscape Series

Encyclopedia of Women in American Politics

Edited by
Jeffrey D. Schultz
and
Laura van Assendelft

Foreword by
Helen Thomas

Oryx Press
1999

The rare Arabian Oryx is believed to have inspired the myth of the unicorn. This desert antelope became virtually extinct in the early 1960s. At that time, several groups of international conservationists arranged to have nine animals sent to the Phoenix Zoo to be the nucleus of a captive breeding herd. Today, the Oryx population is over 1,000, and over 500 have been returned to the Middle East.

Published by The Oryx Press
4041 North Central at Indian School Road
Phoenix, Arizona 85012-3397

Published simultaneously in Canada
Printed and bound in the United States of America

♾ The paper used in this publication meets the minimum requirements of American National Standard for Information Science—Permanence of Paper for Printed Library Materials, ANSI Z39.48, 1984.

Library of Congress Cataloging-in-Publication Data

Encyclopedia of women in American politics / edited by Jeffrey D. Schultz, Laura van Assendelft.
p. cm.—(The American political landscape series)
Includes bibliographical references and indexes.
ISBN 1-57356-131-2 (alk. paper)
1. Women in politics—United States—History—Encyclopedias.
I. Schultz, Jeffrey D. II. Van Assendelft, Laura A. III. Series.
HQ1236.5.U6E53 1999
320'.082—dc21 98-36327
CIP

Contents

Contributors

Academic Advisory Board

Janet M. Clark
State University of West Georgia

Janet M. Martin
Bowdoin College

Karen O'Connor
The American University

Georgia Sorenson
The University of Maryland

Contributors

[AM] Anne McCulloch
Columbia College

[AMD] Amy McCormick Diduch
Mary Baldwin College

[AMR] Amanda M. Rose
University of San Francisco

[BAW] Brian A. Weiner
University of San Francisco

[BLN] Barbara L. Neuby
State University of West Georgia

[BN] Bernadette Nye
Union College

[CGM] Cecilia G. Manrique
University of Wisconsin at LaCrosse

[CKC] Carole Kennedy Chaney
San Diego State University

[CW] Clyde Wilcox
Georgetown University

[EP] Elizabeth Purdy

[FC] Francis Carleton
University of Wisconsin at Green Bay

[GG] Gwen Gibson
Columbus State University

[GVS] Gratzia V. Smeal
St. Norbert College

[HNF] Heather N. Foust

[JAB] Judith A. Baer
Texas A & M University

[JAD] Julie A. Dolan

[JCS] Jonathan C. Smith

[JDG] Jean Donovan Gilman
Mary Baldwin College

[JEH] Jennifer E. Horan

[JG] Joyce Gelb
City University of New York

[JHT] Joan Hulse Thompson
Beaver College

[JJK] John J. Kennedy
Pennsylvania State University at Lehigh Valley

[JMC] Janet M. Clark
State University of West Georgia

[JMM] Janet M. Martin
Bowdoin College

[JS] Jean Schroedel
The Claremont Graduate School

[JW1] Jess Waters
The American University

[JW2] Jessamyn West

[KM] Karen McCurdy
Georgia Southern University

[LD] Lois Duke
Georgia Southern University

[LvA] Laura van Assendelft, Coeditor
Mary Baldwin College

[LW] Laura Woliver
University of South Carolina

[MAB] MaryAnne Borrelli
Connecticut College

[MB] Maria Bevacqua
Emory University

[MBS] M. Beth Stark
Georgetown University

[MEK] Martha E. Kropf
The American University

[MG] Maureen Gilbride

[MJR] Mark J. Rozell
The American University

[MP] Margaret Power

[NJM] N. Jane McCandless
State University of West Georgia

[NL] Nancy Lumpkin
The Claremont Graduate School

[PMF] Pamela M. Fiber
The Claremont Graduate School

[PS] Pamela Stricker
California State University at San Marcos

[RAJ] Roberta Ann Johnson
University of San Francisco

[RD] R. Darcy
Oklahoma State University

[RLP] Richard L. Pacelle, Jr.
University of Missouri at St. Louis

[RRT] Robert R. Thompson
Beaver College

[RW] Robin Wolpert
University of South Carolina

[SB] Sarah Brewer
The American University

[SD] Sue Davis
Grand Valley State University

[SJW] Sara Jane Williams
University of South Carolina

[SM] Susan Mezey
Loyola University

[ST] Sue Thomas
Georgetown University

[TGJ] Ted G. Jelen
University of Nevada at Las Vegas

[TSF] Terri Susan Fine
University of Central Florida

[VDD] Veronica D. DiConti

[WGC] Wendy Gunther-Canada
University of Alabama at Birmingham

Foreword

by Helen Thomas

I have always felt greatly privileged to have a ringside seat to instant history at the White House. But I realized after a preview of the Oryx Press encyclopedias on women, religion, and minorities that there are big gaps in my education regarding the role these humanistic trends have played in American politics.

I believe the essays in these volumes are informative, objective, and in-depth, with a wealth of material for scholars, students, and researchers of all kinds. Of course, I was first drawn to the *Encyclopedia of Women in American Politics* for both personal and professional reasons. I am still outraged that women did not get the vote until 1920. Often when I am walking into the White House I look at the big black fence on Pennsylvania Avenue and I think of the suffragettes who chained themselves to it to gain the right to vote.

The strides women have made in the last half of this century are awesome, but not enough. World War II was the defining moment, but it has been a long struggle and women have miles to go to achieve true equality in the workplace.

I have often heard quoted the letter from that remarkable woman, Abigail Adams, who wrote to her husband, John Adams, on March 31, 1776, while he was attending the Continental Congress.

> I desire you would remember the ladies and be more generous and favorable to them than your ancestors. Do not put such unlimited power in the hands of the husbands.

I was covering the White House in 1961 when John F. Kennedy created the President's Commission on the Status of Women by executive order. It was considered a great leap forward in those days and the panel included the most prominent women leaders of the times, those who had reached the top in their fields. Eleanor Roosevelt, who had worked for so many years on behalf of women, was chosen as the chair.

Two years later, the Commission wrote a report that documented "pervasive discrimination against women in state and national laws in work and at schools." State commissions later pursued the goals of equal opportunity for women and followed up on complaints of sex-based employment discrimination.

Women then began to focus their efforts on ratification of the Equal Rights Amendment, but they failed to achieve the necessary two-thirds of the states. I thought it was a very sad day for the Republic. Women began to venture forth afterward more strongly into the path of political acceptance, and, by the 1970s, the women's movement to empower females had gained great momentum. But the movement hit a plateau when President Ronald Reagan moved into the White House in 1981 and the country became more conservative.

So women have had their hills and valleys, which are vividly illustrated in the biographies and the other entries in the *Encyclopedia of Women in American Politics*.

Every student of American history has some insight into the role that religion has played in the founding of the United States and into the profound impact of religious groups on the politics of different eras, dating back to colonial times. School children learn of the flight of the Pilgrims from religious persecution in England. The *Encyclopedia of Religion in American Politics* is a gold mine of information. As its introductory essay explains,

> The story of religion in American politics is largely an account of the quest to harness the moral idealism of religion for political purposes while attempting to restrain the potential of religion for bigotry. The overwhelming success of that quest for a civic-minded religion can be seen in the thriving diversity of religious groups in the United States today.

Fortunately, the *Encyclopedia* shows that religions fostered in the United States have not been all-consuming, domineering, or fanatical, so as to nurture the kind of age-old religious-cultural hatreds that have torn apart Northern Ireland, Bosnia, and the Middle East. Every day, the United States is involved in seeking to bring peace to these lands, where religion is a tinder box.

Ministers in the colonial era used their tracts and sermons to lay the groundwork for the American Revolution. The founding fathers were mostly religious, but they also devoutly believed in religious freedom.

Almost from its beginning, the United States has had a multiplicity of religions and therefore an admirable tolerance. The First Amendment stipulated that "Congress shall make no law respecting an establishment of religion or prohibiting the free exercise thereof." The founding fathers, while trying to reconcile the influences of reason and revelation on moral law, believed strongly in the separation of church and state.

Politics in the new Republic depended on a shared morality rather than on a shared theology. The ministers of the post-colonial era fought the removal of the Cherokees from Georgia to the West, an infamous episode in American history known as the "Trail of Tears." The churches in the North were also leaders in the movement to abolish slavery, while religious institutions in the South played an equally important role on the other side of the controversy.

In this century, the best known minister in the struggle for civil rights was Martin Luther King, Jr., who first came to national attention when he spearheaded the boycott of segregated buses in Montgomery, Alabama, in 1955–56. Later, many religions banded together in support of the civil rights movement and it took a southern president, Lyndon B. Johnson, to push through Congress the Civil Rights Act of 1964 and the Voting Rights Act of 1965.

But the influence of religion in American politics during the twentieth century has swung from left to right. During the late 1970s and 1980s, the Moral Majority gained a foothold and, after its demise, was replaced by the Christian Coalition. The domestic agenda of the political conservatives includes restoring prayer in public schools and promoting family and pro-life values. Despite the strict wall that the Supreme Court has interposed between church and state in the past, recent years have seen a chipping away at that barrier with rulings permitting religious groups to gather and use schoolrooms and public facilities for their meetings.

Equally fascinating is the documentation in the *Encyclopedia of Minorities in American Politics* of the struggle for political rights of minorities, who have been historically under-represented in the American political system and who have had to fight to attain their rightful place as citizens. The discrimination against racial and ethnic groups is vividly chronicled in the *Encyclopedia's* biographies and historical references to past eras that were dominated by white males. Included among those discriminated against were blacks, Latinos, Asian Americans, and Native Americans. I can remember how often President John F. Kennedy was appalled to see signs at Boston job sites that read, "No Irish allowed." A sea change is occurring in the nation, and once-deprived groups are becoming increasingly involved in shaping the political dialogue in this country and in winning public office. Witness the number of big city black mayors currently holding office in the United States. Furthermore, no politician would dare to ignore the Cubans in Florida or the Hispanics in the Southwest and expect to get elected.

All this is to the good. It makes real the unity and validity of the melting pot and there is no question that these groups will have an even bigger voice in the future. My only hope and prayer is that they do not divide along ethnic and racial lines and forget that we are one people.

The three volumes in Oryx's American Political Landscape Series are a treasure trove for scholars and students, and provide the key to the significant historic trends that have made the United States great.

Helen Thomas is White House Bureau Chief for United Press International.

Preface

After all the hoopla surrounding the 1992 congressional elections, which were immediately proclaimed as "The Year of the Woman," I seriously began to ponder the issue of women in American politics. Were the political goals of women merely to increase their numbers in elected office? Are there any real issues that are women's issues? What impact have women made on the American political process? As an encyclopedist, I sought out a single source that could address my interests while answering the basics of who, what, where, when, and why. I was surprised to find that no reference work specifically addressed women in American politics. To be sure, there were encyclopedias on women's history, women's studies, and women's suffrage. However, there was not one that focused exclusively on the political trials and contributions of women from colonial times to the present. Therefore, I sought to produce a work that would fit the needs of students, researchers, scholars, and librarians.

In compiling this volume, the emphasis was placed upon being as comprehensive as the limitations of space would allow. The work contains over 700 alphabetically arranged entries written by more than 50 scholars that cover every woman who has served in a political capacity. The work contains biographies of leaders of the suffrage movement, as well as feminists and anti-feminists. It also has entries on significant events, court cases, and concepts. Most important are the entries that address specific political issues like abortion, welfare, education, and political participation (to name just a few). Written by leading scholars, these essays attempt to give context to current political issues and how they are faced by women.

Being a reference work, the *Encyclopedia* focuses on giving accurate information in a manageable dose. Because a good reference work must be able to lead the reader to more information, *every entry* in the *Encyclopedia* has a bibliography that can serve as a starting point for further research by the user of the volume. In addition to having bibliographies, entries are cross-referenced in two ways to aid the reader in successfully using the resources of the work. First, the work is internally cross-referenced through the use of **bold-faced** type. Bold-faced word(s) tell the reader that there is a separate entry on that person, event, concept, or issue. Second, many articles have *See also* listings at the end of the entry to offer other areas the reader may want to investigate. These two features in addition to the index will facilitate the user's ability to navigate the volume.

The *Encyclopedia* has several appendices. The first appendix reprints a selection of important documents and speeches, including the Nineteenth Amendment, the Declaration of Sentiments and Resolutions, and Title VII of the Civil Rights Act of 1964. The second appendix contains several tables of information, such as Women Members of Congress, First Ladies, and the like. The third appendix contains two directories. The first is a directory of women's organizations that are involved in politics either directly or indirectly; it contains contact information as well as brief descriptions of the missions. The second directory is a listing of political action committees (PACs) and donor networks, which offer sources of money for women interested in running for public office. The fourth and final appendix is a timeline of women in American politics. The four-column timeline begins with the Seneca Falls Convention of 1848 and runs to the present day. Events in American and world history are included to help give historical context to the events.

All in all, the volume attempts to be the most comprehensive single source on women in American politics. The *Encyclopedia* helps mark those events and people who have shaped the past and present, while looking forward to a political system in which women will play a growing part as shapers of public policy, voters, and elected officials.

Acknowledgments

A volume like the *Encyclopedia of Women in American Politics* requires many contributors to make it successful. Laura van Assendelft, my coeditor, gave tirelessly to making the volume better. She contributed throughout the project, from shaping entries to editing submissions for content and style. She did all of this while expecting her first child (Cady), who was born as the manuscript went to the publishers. In addition to her leadership, I owe much thanks to the Board of Advisors for their helpful comments, especially Karen O'Connor who not only wrote a wonderful introduction to the volume, but also originally put me in contact with Laura. The volume's many contributors rightly share in any praise the volume may find; their professionalism and knowledge have helped ensure the quality of this work.

Jeff Coburn and Nancy Schultz provided immeasurable help in aiding with research, fact checking, and typing. These two did yeomen's work on the volume. They lightened the load on my shoulders and allowed me to work on other areas of the volume by taking many of the mundane (though important) tasks from me.

Many people at The Oryx Press deserve my thanks for all their helpful comments and efforts in bringing the book to publication. Donna Sanzone guided me in the early stages and showed great faith in the volume as part of a larger series. The entire Oryx editorial team, especially Susan Slesinger, Anne Thompson, John Wagner, and Barbara Flaxman, was instrumental in making the volume better at every turn. And even when we all seemed frustrated, we persevered. The marketing staff led by Natalie Lang, who spearheaded the concept of the American Political Landscape Series, has given me an invaluable informal education in book publishing. In fact, all of my contact with the people at Oryx has made the volume better. I am grateful for having had the chance to work with them.

I would like to thank my agent, my advisor, and my friend George T. Kurian, who believed enough in my skills as an editor to help me move into full-time project management from the ivory towers of academia. He and his wonderful wife, Annie, have been undaunted supporters of this project, my family, and me.

Finally, I would like to acknowledge the intangible support of my wife Elena and our son Sasha. Both have been there to make me laugh and play when I needed to. Without them, there would have been no *Encyclopedia*.

Introduction: Women in American Politics

by Karen O'Connor

The Colonial and Early National Periods

On March 31, 1776, Abigail Adams wrote the following lines to her husband John, who was then in attendance at the Continental Congress:

> In the new Code of Laws . . . I desire you would Remember the Ladies, and be more generous and favourable to them than your ancestors. Do not put such unlimited power into the hands of the Husbands. Remember all Men would be tyrants if they could. If particular care and attention is not paid to the Laidies (sic) we are determined to foment a Rebelion (sic), and will not hold ourselves bound by any Laws in which we have no voice, or Representation.

Women were not remembered in the "new code of laws" (the Articles of Confederation) that established the United States or in the U.S. Constitution that followed it. The power to regulate elections and voting requirements were left to the states in Article I, Section 4, of the Constitution, and the power to legislate concerning the status of women, particularly in family relations and in the economic sphere, was largely left to the states with ratification of the Bill of Rights. The Tenth Amendment, in particular, leaves to the states "the powers not delegated to the United States by the Constitution, nor prohibited by it to the States." Moreover, although women were totally ignored in the Constitution, the rebellion predicted by Abigail Adams did not even begin for more than half a century and women played few overtly political roles.

Margaret Brent was one notable exception. An emigre to Maryland, Brent owned her own plantation and often appeared in court on her own behalf. From 1642 to 1650, she appeared in 134 separate court actions. A close friend of Lord Baltimore, the colonial proprietor, she was made his executrix and granted the power of attorney to handle his vast holdings. To avoid more legal confusion, Brent appeared before the Maryland assembly, becoming the first woman in recorded history to seek political recognition before a government body.

Unlike Brent, who took a public role, many colonial women were often keen behind-the-scenes participants in politics. They opposed royal taxes by boycotting goods as members of the Daughters of Liberty, they participated in public spinning bees to avoid cloth imports, and they participated in tea leagues to avoid the purchase of tea. Yet their contributions have been largely ignored.

Several women who participated in the Revolutionary War did have their service rewarded and heralded. Molly Hayes, known as Molly Pitcher, received a pension from Pennsylvania for her participation in the war effort, and her battlefield exploits were heralded in a well-known song. Deborah Sampson twice joined the American army disguised as a man and was even honorably discharged in 1783. Later, she went on the lecture circuit to tell of her exploits as a soldier and a spy, and, with the assistance of Paul Revere, received pensions from the Massachusetts and U.S. governments in recognition of her military service. A group of women from Groton, Massachusetts, became famous for dressing as men and taking several British soldiers captive the day after the fighting at Lexington and Concord. Although as many as 20,000 women may have participated in the Revolutionary War, their efforts have been largely forgotten today.

The few women who did participate in politics during the Revolutionary period did so under assumed identities. Mercy Otis Warren, for example, was the sister and wife of major colonial patriots (and the mother of five sons). Warren published several political tracts under assumed names, speaking out for independence from the Crown before it was popular to do so. During the Revolutionary War, she corresponded with most major American leaders about what form the new national government should take.

Other women also made significant contributions to the political life of the new nation. Abigail Adams has long been recognized as the most trusted political confidant and strategist of her husband John Adams, the first vice president and second president of the United States. Dolley Madison acted as President Thomas Jefferson's official hostess and then did the same for her husband James Madison, the fourth president. She is credited with participating in and facilitating political maneuvering in the new nation. However, after the Revolutionary War, politics was largely viewed as a "man's game" and thought to be unfit for respectable women. Moreover, prevailing social mores prevented women from speaking out publicly, which made the public participation of women in politics unlikely.

Historian Linda Kerber refers to this period as one that institutionalized the doctrine of "Republican motherhood." Women in the private sphere were to prepare men for the public sphere. Hence, a Republican mother had a "political purpose and . . . her domestic behavior had a direct political function in the Republic." This historically unique view of womanhood elevated a woman's role in the private realm, making it a substitute for formal political participation and justifing her exclusion from the public sphere.

The Antebellum Period

Not until the rise of the abolitionist movement in the 1830s did it become even marginally acceptable for women to speak out on political issues and to publicly commit themselves to some political course of action. Abolishing slavery was considered important enough to allow drastic political measures, including women speaking out against slavery from the pulpit. Angelina and Sarah Grimke of South Carolina, and Sojourner Truth, a freed slave, were among the first women to speak out against slavery. Similarly, the religious revival of the 1840s also contributed to the development of women's political consciousness. Women eventually took an active and vocal role in political causes despite the heated battles over their right to take action—especially within the more liberal branch of the anti-slavery movement.

By the mid-1800s, numerous local and national female anti-slavery societies were created. For the first time, women came together and had the opportunity to develop leadership and political skills. Just as important, participation in the anti-slavery movement made some women recognize that they were subject to discrimination simply because they were women. In 1840, this point was driven home for Lucretia Mott and Elizabeth Cady Stanton, who would later become the founding mothers of the women's rights movement in the United States. In that year, they traveled to London for a meeting of the World Anti-Slavery Society, but were not allowed to participate in the assembly. Male delegates debated whether or not to allow women into the meeting, and finally told Mott and Stanton they could participate only as observers from the balcony.

Stanton and Mott were stung by this rejection. They realized that they were nearly as devoid of political rights as the slaves they sought to emancipate. They vowed to return home and call a meeting of women to discuss their inferior situation. Both women, however, were still bound by many societal conventions, and both had families to raise. Thus, it was not until eight years later that they sent out a call for a meeting to discuss "woman's rights" in Stanton's hometown of Seneca Falls, New York. More than 300 women and men, including noted African-American journalist Frederick Douglass, attended the Seneca Falls Convention, as it has come to be called. (Seneca Falls is now the site of the National Women's Hall of Fame, and Stanton's home is maintained as a museum by the National Park Service.)

The women who attended the Seneca Falls Convention were primarily concerned with securing greater economic and social rights. The right to vote was initially only a secondary concern. Lucretia Mott, in particular, feared that a demand for the franchise would make women look "ridiculous" and urged her sisters to "go slowly." In spite of her caution, however, the ballot was demanded on the belief that women were first and foremost individuals and citizens and deserved not only the same political rights but also the same economic and social rights as men. Paraphrasing the Declaration of Independence, women at the Seneca Falls Convention issued a Declaration of Sentiments. They proclaimed: "We hold these truths to be self-evident: that all men and women are created equal; that they are endowed by their Creator with certain inalienable rights; that among these are life, liberty and the pursuit of happiness."

The Convention later passed a series of resolutions calling for the abolition of legal, economic, and social discrimination against women. These resolutions reflected the dissatisfaction of women with existing moral codes, divorce and criminal laws, and the limited opportunities for women to obtain an education, participate in the church, and enter professional careers. Since 1848, however, the pursuit of women's rights has been intermittent, and the involvement of women in politics, especially in the public arena, has been gradual, with both "highs" and "lows."

Some effort was made on the state level to change prevailing women's property acts, which often led to changes in women's rights concerning their inheritances or control of property they brought into their marriages. But in general, prior to the Civil War, women's rights activity was sporadic. Women had no formal national association to advance their own interests. Instead, they largely relied on anti-slavery associations to disseminate their ideas. Petition campaigns were also used by some women to demand suffrage or expanded rights within the family in their respective states. While these efforts brought about some legislative change in property and marital rights, they failed to result in woman suffrage in any state.

The Civil War and Its Aftermath

During the Civil War, work for women's rights stopped as energies were focused on the war effort and the campaign to end slavery via a constitutional amendment. During this time, women's rights activists again learned the dangers of putting their interests second. Fully expecting women's rights to be granted simultaneously with Negro rights, Susan B. Anthony and Elizabeth Cady Stanton actively participated in the political process and even helped form a woman's organization, the National Woman's Loyal League, to work for an amendment to end slavery.

Because they had worked so hard to end slavery and to support the Union during the Civil War, Stanton and Anthony were stunned to learn that Republican politicians, the major proponents of abolition, were abandoning the cause of woman suffrage. Republicans believed that linking woman suffrage to enfranchising Negroes would doom an amendment. Even the American Anti-Slavery Society rejected appeals to unite the two causes. This action prompted women, along with men who supported their cause, to form a new abolitionist organization. The stated purpose of the newly formed American Equal Rights Association (AERA) was universal suffrage for black persons and women.

The AERA, however, also abandoned the cause of woman suffrage. It supported the proposed Fourteenth Amendment on citizenship, which, for the first time, introduced the word male into the U.S. Constitution. Stanton and Anthony argued that women should not be left out of attempts to secure fuller rights for Negroes, who were freed from slavery by the Thirteenth Amendment to the Constitution in 1865. They also recognized that ratification of the Fourteenth Amendment might necessitate yet another constitutional amendment before women could vote in national elections. However, their arguments against the Fourteenth Amendment fell on deaf ears.

When the AERA announced its support of the proposed Fifteenth Amendment, Stanton and Anthony finally had enough. The Fifteenth Amendment, as proposed, specifically enfranchised Negro males by mandating: "The right of citizens of the United States to vote shall not be denied or abridged by the United States or by any State on account of race, color, or previous condition of servitude." Efforts to include the word "sex" proved futile; women again were told that the rights of Negro men must come first. Until passage of the Fifteenth Amendment, most commentators believed that the question of voter qualifications was a matter left to the individual states by the Constitution. The ratification of the Fifteenth Amendment made it apparent that an additional amendment to the U.S. Constitution would be necessary before women could vote in national elections.

Ratification of the Fifteenth Amendment made clear to Anthony and Stanton the need to alter their efforts to seek woman suffrage on a state-by-state basis. Angered by the actions of the AERA, they left it to found the National Woman Suffrage Association (NWSA) in 1869. The National Woman Suffrage Association's goals were reminiscent of the Seneca Falls resolutions; they included calls for greater rights for women in education, work, marriage, and the family and a national constitutional amendment to allow women to vote.

A more conservative group, the American Woman Suffrage Association (AWSA), was also founded the same year. The AWSA was headed by Lucy Stone, who had not given up her membership in the AERA. She and her followers believed that the NWSA's diverse goals were far too radical. They thought that pursuit of so many changes was likely to divert energies away from woman suffrage as well as bring negative publicity to their cause. And, unlike the NWSA, the AWSA continued to believe in the feasibility of a state-by-state route to woman suffrage. In its pursuit of that single goal, the AWSA also tried to avoid association with controversial issues that could cloud the suffrage issue.

Unlike the NWSA, which largely abandoned the abolitionist cause and the Republican Party, AWSA leaders continued to expect that abolitionists and Republicans would begin to advocate woman suffrage as soon as the Negro rights issue was resolved. This expectation and many of the strategies adopted to support it (the state-by-state route, for example, was proposed to leave the federal arena open for debate on Negro suffrage) were counter to everything Stanton and Anthony believed. They thought that a federal amendment was preferable to the AWSA's state-by-state approach and made little effort to establish state or local associational structures. This approach often resulted in the loss of potential members when state women's rights associations affiliated with the AWSA. State and local associations saw that their actions were more appreciated and that their efforts were more likely to have a greater impact in the AWSA.

From 1869 to 1890, these two national groups made little headway toward woman suffrage. Although they disagreed on how best to attain female suffrage, both groups believed that the dominance of men and the submission of women in the political order was arbitrary and not a result of any inherent differences in men and women. Influenced by the 1792 essay of British political theorist Mary Wollstonecraft, "A Vindication of the Rights of Women," they agreed that both sexes had natural rights and that it was not God's intention for women to be enslaved by men. Thus, they were angry at the unfairness of the existing system that kept women in personal, legal, and moral subjugation. Based on their belief in the natural equality of men and women, activists continued to press for women's rights, but with little success. Their views about the proper relationships between men and women and about women's natural abilities were simply seen as too radical by many.

Even when these women tried to work within the traditional legal and political processes, their efforts failed. Anthony, for example, orchestrated a massive female voter registration effort during the 1872 national elections in an effort to test the parameters of the Fourteenth Amendment. Several NWSA members, including one member of the U.S. Supreme Court, had suggested that the Fourteenth Amendment's privileges and immunities clause, which states that "No state shall make or enforce any law which shall abridge the privileges or immunities of citizens of the United States," could be construed to allow women to vote. Anthony and several other women in Rochester, New York, were jailed after they registered and voted. Anthony was later tried in federal district court and fined. Her case, however, was not the one ultimately heard by the U.S. Supreme Court. Instead, a case involving a close friend of Anthony's, Virginia Minor, was the vehicle by which the Court chose to address the issue of whether women already were enfranchised by the existing provisions of the Fourteenth Amendment.

In 1869, Francis Minor, the attorney-husband of Virginia Minor and president of the Missouri Woman Suffrage Association (MWSA), wrote persuasively about his belief that women citizens were entitled to vote under the Fourteenth Amendment. Minor believed that his legal theory could be used as the basis for litigation challenging the disenfranchisement of women. Moreover, he and Anthony believed that resorting to accepted political avenues of change, such as litigation, would lead the public to view suffrage much less frivolously. His wife was among those who, along with Anthony, tried to test his theory. Unfortunately, the Supreme Court disagreed with him.

Virginia Minor, with her husband as coplaintiff (as a married woman she had no right to sue in her own name), sued St. Louis voter registrar Reese Happersett after he refused to allow her to register to vote. They claimed that Virginia Minor's rights under the Fourteenth Amendment were violated because she was denied "the privileges and immunities of citizenship, chief among which is the elective franchise." That argument, however, was quickly rejected by the Missouri courts and the Minors appealed that decision to the U.S. Supreme Court. In *Minor v. Happersett* (1875), a unanimous Court upheld the Missouri court's ruling and maintained that suffrage was not a right of citizenship.

The Suffrage Movement (1890–1920)

While women on the east coast of the United States were battling for suffrage, women in the Wyoming Territory, which had applied for statehood in 1890, continued to go to the polls as they had since 1870. Although some senators opposed the admission of Wyoming solely because women were allowed to vote there, men in that territory refused to turn back the clock. Instead, they dared Congress by wiring it: "We may stay out of the Union for 100 years, but we will come in with our women." In spite of Wyoming's refusal to disenfranchise women, it was admitted to the Union by a narrow vote.

Soon other western states followed suit after it became clear that women voters not only helped community interests but also allowed smaller towns to fight the interests of big cities, which were often controlled by large businesses—especially the mining and liquor industries. In Colorado, for example, Carrie Chapman Catt led the campaign for woman suffrage. She pointed out the civilizing impact of women on polling places as well as the reform policies that began once women got the right to vote. She and those who went to the polls to support woman suffrage recognized the role that women's votes played in bringing law and order to what was previously called the Wild West.

Just as Wyoming was petitioning to become a state in 1890, the National and American Woman Suffrage Associations merged to become the National American Woman Suffrage Association (NAWSA) with the goal of woman suffrage. The National American Woman Suffrage Association's efforts for suffrage were also helped by the assistance of several other women's groups that joined its cause. The Women's Christian Temperance Union (WCTU), for example, was founded in the late 1870s. Although its major goal was abolition of the liquor trade, it eventually became a leading advocate of woman suffrage when its president, Frances Willard, convinced WCTU members that woman suffrage was a necessary antecedent to attaining prohibition. The Women's Christian Temperance Union's endorsement of suffrage was especially key in the South, where religious fundamentalists supported the cause. Adding WCTU members to the suffrage ranks, however, further exacerbated the NAWSA's conservative drift.

The tremendous growth of what is termed the "club movement" in the 1880s and 1890s also assisted the development of the suffrage movement. The General Federation of Women's Clubs (GFWC), for example, claimed a membership of over 2 million by 1910. A variety of clubs were affiliated with the GFWC. While some were book clubs, others were civic clubs designed to improve municipal services or to bring about political reform, and others were formed around specific issues, such as abolition of child labor or improved labor conditions for working women.

Within these clubs many women came to recognize their second-class political status and the need for the ballot. Without the vote, they saw little chance to enact government reform or legislation to improve the status of working women or children. This kind of thinking clearly buttressed the NAWSA's limited demand for the vote. While Stanton and Anthony had claimed that motherhood and marriage were only incidental roles for women with respect to any claim for rights, the new leaders of the suffrage movement viewed motherhood and marriage as an important basis for the right to vote.

Despite early suffrage victories in Wyoming (1890) and Colorado (1893), after Idaho and Utah entered the Union as suffrage states in 1896 no other states adopted suffrage until 1910. Although tremendous efforts were expended on state suffrage campaigns (historian Eleanor Flexner cites 480 efforts in 33 states and 17 actual referendum votes, but only two victories from 1870 to 1910), they went largely unrewarded. The West appeared unique and it became increasingly clear to NAWSA leaders that they could never win adoption of woman suffrage provisions in every state constitution.

Even the more conservative GFWC also came to that conclusion. In 1914, it decided to support the suffrage cause, and other organizations quickly followed suit. Still, in 1915, organized opposition contributed to the defeat of a suffrage referendum in four states in a period of a few weeks. These defeats and the growing organization of anti-suffrage forces finally led NAWSA leaders to recognize the need for a new strategy. The election of Carrie Chapman Catt as NAWSA president in late 1915 facilitated change, but even before she reorganized the NAWSA, a new suffrage strategy was being attempted.

In late 1912, the NAWSA board appointed Alice Paul, who had worked with the more militant English suffragists(ettes), to its Congressional Committee. She immediately went to work to build support for a federal constitutional amendment. Paul organized a spectacular media event in Washington, D.C., on the day before Woodrow Wilson's presidential inauguration. A parade of over 5,000 suffragettes dressed in white took to the streets. Although the NAWSA had obtained a parade permit, the police offered marchers no assistance when they were attacked by angry onlookers. The public was outraged at the violence directed at women and impressed by the size of the widely publicized parade. Capitalizing on this free, favorable publicity, the committee launched a national woman suffrage petition drive and began to send regular delegations to press President Wilson for a national solution.

In April 1913, Paul formed a new organization, the Congressional Union, to work exclusively for a national amendment. While she retained her chair on the NAWSA's Congressional Committee, a break with the larger organization was inevitable. At the NAWSA convention in 1913, Paul's insistence that a federal amendment be the sole target of suffrage forces was at odds with the beliefs of most NAWSA leaders, who continued to cling to the state-by-state approach. Not surprisingly, Paul was removed as chair of the Congressional Committee.

Paul then directed her efforts toward the Congressional Union and national suffrage. Following the lead of British suffragettes, the Congressional Union began to hold the "party in power," in this case the Democrats, responsible for failure to pass a suffrage bill, a political tactic strongly opposed by the NAWSA. In 1914, Union members actively campaigned against congressional candidates of the Democratic Party because it failed to endorse woman suffrage. The Union, later called the National Woman's Party (NWP), also pressed Congress for an amendment to the U.S. Constitution. Its effort resulted, at least, in a renewed interest in a suffrage amendment, a proposal that had been nearly dormant for over two decades.

Many NAWSA members began to see the utility of the NWP's single focus on a constitutional amendment. The newly elected Catt needed little convincing. After decisive state woman suffrage referenda defeats in 1916, she devised what she called a "Winning Plan"; its objective was to direct all of the NAWSA's resources and cooperating organizations toward the goal of achieving a woman suffrage amendment to the U.S. Constitution by 1922. A key component of the plan was national coordination whereby all activity of the state associations was to be geared toward the single goal of an amendment to the U.S. Constitution.

The Winning Plan was quite elaborate. Associations in states where female suffrage already existed were directed to lobby their legislators to request that Congress pass a constitutional amendment. Additionally, national officers handpicked a few states for new campaigns where passage of state amendments were deemed feasible. Other state associations were to channel their efforts toward presidential suffrage or voting rights for women in party primaries in states that allowed state legislatures to make those changes. Catt believed it was critical "to keep so much 'suffrage noise' going all over the country that neither the enemy nor friends will discover where the real battle is."

To keep the battle national in scope, Catt targeted southern and northern states for intense activity to break the spirit of suffrage opponents. And to speed up the process even more, Catt planned to have support for the suffrage amendment included in both party platforms by the presidential elections in 1920 to facilitate state ratification by 1922.

Slowly, Catt's plan began to produce results. The anti-suffrage "Solid South" was cracked in March 1917 when women in Arkansas won the right to vote in state primary elections. In addition, several states enacted laws allowing women to vote in presidential elections. And in the same year, New York voters approved the addition of a suffrage amendment to their state constitution. The noise was getting louder as women clamored for a federal suffrage amendment.

These events produced the enfranchisement of more and more women with no apparent ill results of the kind predicted by suffrage opponents. Yet strong suffrage opposition in the U.S. Senate prevented proponents from securing the necessary two-thirds majority required for a constitutional amendment. Southern senators steadfastly opposed the amendment and were joined by others from New England and some eastern states. Opposition was often justified on the rationale of "states' rights," but many women, particularly those in southern suffrage associations, rejected this claim. Southern senators, for example, supported a prohibition amendment and were not upset by the national government's intrusion into that arena. In fact, southern suffrage proponents believed that the true motive of Senate opponents was a combination of resistance to any change in a woman's role and fear of what female suffrage might do to the lucrative cotton industry in the South and Northeast. Manufacturers in both regions relied heavily on cheap, female labor. This labor was a resource that Senate suffrage opponents believed would be threatened should the amendment pass. They feared that women voters would use their ballot strength to secure passage and enactment of laws giving women equal pay or improving the working conditions of women and children.

National American Woman Suffrage Association leaders slowly came to the NWP's earlier conclusion that changes had to be made in the membership of the U.S. Senate before a suffrage amendment could garner the requisite two-thirds vote from that body. To that end, they began a campaign to defeat anti-suffrage senators who stood for re-election in 1918. The political clout of suffragists produced the defeat of two powerful opponents of the amendment. When this show of political force was coupled with the addition of several more states to the suffrage column— South Dakota, Michigan, Oklahoma, Iowa, Minnesota, Missouri, Ohio, Wisconsin, and Maine — quick passage of the Nineteenth Amendment in the Senate was virtually assured. Meeting in a special session in the spring of 1919, first the House of Representatives and then the Senate passed the suffrage amendment. Ratification by the necessary three-quarters of the states was completed in 1920, and the first national election with full woman suffrage occurred in November of that year. The fragile coalition that made up the suffrage movement soon disintegrated, however, when its diverse constituent groups could no longer agree on a new post-suffrage agenda.

After Suffrage: The 1920s to the 1950s

Once the Nineteenth Amendment was added to the Constitution, white women around the United States immediately gained the right to vote (black women in the South often faced the same obstacles as black men who were effectively disenfranchised by stringent literacy requirements or poll taxes). Legislators reacted quickly to pass laws of interest to women, such as the Sheppard-Towner Maternity Act, which provided federal funds to states to support maternity programs and reduce the high number of infant deaths in the United States. The Cable Act, which restored U.S. citizenship rights to women who married foreigners, was also passed. Women did not, however, use their votes to win changes in corrupt political systems as they had stressed in seeking the franchise; instead, they stayed home from the polls and politicians quickly took note. The first major study of women's electoral turnout found that in the 1923 Chicago mayoral election, three years after the amendment was ratified, nearly two-thirds of all men but only one-third of all eligible women actually went to the voting booths.

Although women had worked long and hard for the right to vote, it is now clear that they lacked the appropriate socialization to make the most of that opportunity. Prevailing societal notions about women's proper sphere made it clear that politics was a man's world and not one in which respectable women should engage. For example, the first nationwide public opinion polls conducted in the 1930s showed that public attitudes toward the participation of women in politics were decidedly negative. At a time when only a handful of women held public office, 60 percent of all citizens rejected the idea that "we need more women in politics."

People's aversion to women's participation in politics was particularly strong regarding elective office. Over half of those surveyed reported that they were opposed to the idea of a female governor or senator. When polled in 1937 about their willingness to vote for a qualified woman for president, only 27 percent of men and 40 percent of women answered positively.

These negative attitudes persisted through the next three decades. Compounding this problem was the fact that few women during this era entered the kinds of professions amenable to political involvement, especially the law. Numerous law schools either placed severe quotas on the admission of women students or excluded them altogether. Although a few women served in state legislatures or the U.S. Congress during this era, their participation as elected or appointed governmental officials was rare. Indeed, a woman was not appointed to a presidential cabinet until 1933, when Franklin Roosevelt appointed Frances Perkins secretary of labor.

The Second Wave: The 1960s to the 1980s

Historians and social scientists trace a renewed interest in the role of women in politics to the development of the women's rights movement in the 1960s. In 1961, President John F. Kennedy created the President's Commission on the Status of Women. Its report, which was issued in 1963, documented pervasive discrimination against women in state and national laws at work and in schools. Eventually, women active on the President's Commission, as well as the newly created state commissions, became angered when the Equal Employment Opportunity Commission (EEOC) failed to investigate complaints of sex-based employment discrimination as it was required to do under Title VII of the Civil Rights Act of 1964.

The National Organization for Women (NOW) was founded in 1966 when women at a national meeting of commissions on the status of women found that conference by-laws prohibited them from passing a resolution demanding that the EEOC treat sex-discrimination complaints seriously. In one of its first letters sent to prospective members, NOW explained its desire

> to initiate or support action, nationally or in any part of this nation, by individuals or organizations, to break through the silken curtain of prejudice and discrimination against women in government . . . the political parties, the judiciary . . . and in every field of importance in American society.

Because women and men generally enjoyed equal legal access in the political arena, NOW and other women's groups founded around the same time, such as the now defunct Women's Equity Action League, devoted most of their initial energies to alleviating discrimination in education and employment, and to the passage of the proposed Equal Rights Amendment (ERA). Many women believed that passage of the ERA was especially key because it would go a long way to mandating an end to state-based or state-enforced discrimination against women in all spheres.

The National Organization for Women's push for the Equal Rights Amendment and the quick support it garnered for its goals from most other women's groups provided the necessary cohesion to cement and focus the new movement. Its ability to gain final passage of the ERA in both houses of Congress in 1972 provided an emotional high to movement activists who then turned their energies to ratification. From 1972 until 1982, NOW focused most of its efforts toward passage of the ERA. Its leaders believed that passage of a constitutional amendment was a quick way to invalidate myriad discriminatory state laws and practices that affected women in the family, in schools, and in the workplace.

To fill the void left by NOW's concentration on the expansion of women's rights, especially through passage of the proposed ERA, the National Women's Political Caucus (NWPC) was created in 1971 to increase the number of feminist women elected at all levels of government. Its founders included leaders of many major women's organizations, such as writer and *Ms.* editor Gloria Steinem, Representative Bella Abzug (D-NY), Representative Shirley Chisholm (D-NY), and the author of *The Feminine Mystique* (1963), Betty Friedan. In 1972, Chisholm became the first African-American woman to run for president. *The Feminine Mystique* is credited with putting the discontent many women experienced about their inferior status into words.

The National Women's Political Caucus is unique in that it has a multipartisan base. However, to accommodate the needs of its members and to fulfill its commitment to increased representation in the political parties, it maintains special Democratic and Republican task forces. Since its creation, the NWPC has had a noticeable impact on Democratic Party rules.

The NWPC's goals include increasing support for women candidates and reforming party structures to assure equitable representation for women. Today, it also publicizes women's issues when they are at stake in elections, monitors the selection of women delegates to party conventions, and holds regional training sessions for women candidates and campaign workers throughout the United States.

Since 1976, the NWPC has also been at the forefront of efforts to increase the number of women appointed to high-ranking, policy-making federal jobs. After every presidential election, it convenes the Coalition for Women's Appointments, composed of representatives from more than 70 women's and public interest groups, to identify qualified female candidates, collect and forward their resumes to the White House, and then lobby for their appointment. In 1993, for example, after Bill Clinton was first elected, the coalition reviewed the credentials of nearly 1,000 women and nominated more than 600 to fill key positions. The coalition and the NWPC also work with the Federation of Women Judicial Lawyers Screening Panel and NOW to identify women qualified for appointment to the federal bench.

The media attention that aided development of the movement for women's rights and an expanded role in politics also contributed to the development of a counter movement. By the mid-1970s, some women came to perceive additional rights for women as a threat to their way of life. The proposed ERA and the legalization of abortion that occurred in 1973 when the Supreme Court decided *Roe v. Wade* were viewed as particularly ominous changes and threats to the social order. Using the organizational base of religious and other conservative groups, Phyllis Schlafly and other prominent conservatives created a counter movement that effectively mobilized to block passage of the Equal Rights Amendment. Women on the political right were, and continue to be, well organized on the local and state levels, which facilitated their ability to stop one-quarter of the states from ratifying the ERA. Schlafly's Eagle Forum was particularly effective in stopping passage of the Equal Rights Amendment, which was defeated in 1982. More recently, Concerned Women for America (CWA), headed by Beverly LaHaye, has effectively mobilized its members to stop or delay passage of many bills supported by the women's rights movement, including (until 1993) the Family and Medical Leave Act. Concerned Women for America is also active on the local level in school board elections, often running its members for school board posts where it believes it can play an important role in returning the schools to more traditionally based curricula.

These two rival women's movements continue to go head to head in the political arena—most notably in the area of reproductive rights. Prior to 1989, lacking the single unifying factor of the Equal Rights Amendment, the women's rights movement appeared in disarray. On July 3, 1989, however, the U.S. Supreme Court issued its opinion in *Webster v. Reproductive Health Services*. A few weeks before the decision, pro-choice supporters, galvanized by the threat that the Court might overrule *Roe v. Wade*, organized a march. Over 500,000 people participated— it was the largest march ever to occur in Washington, D.C. The Court's decision clearly acted as a catalyst for women's rights supporters and spurred women into greater political action on both sides of the abortion debate.

The hearings on the nomination of Clarence Thomas to the Supreme Court also spurred many women to political action. In 1991, women around the nation were aghast watching their television sets as the all-male Senate Judiciary Committee questioned Anita Hill, a former employee of Thomas's, for hours. Initially, his appointment to the bench had been fought by women's rights groups who believed that he would provide the fifth and deciding vote to overrule *Roe v. Wade* (1973). Then it was learned that while he was the head of the EEOC—the federal agency charged with investigating claims of sex discrimination, including sexual harassment—one of his young assistants claimed she had been the object of Thomas's improper sexual behavior. As white male senator after white male senator questioned law professor Hill's veracity, mental stability, and morals, women around the country were outraged. It was clear to many that most of the members of the all-male Judiciary Committee "just didn't get it."

Many women decided on the spot to run for public office; others decided to get involved in politics. Adding to this outrage were gaffes made by Republican Vice President Dan Quayle attacking a fictional television character (the unmarried Murphy Brown) for choosing to have a child. (Pro-choice advocates were quick to point out that Murphy was in a no-win situation with the Bush administration, which strongly opposed abortion for any reason except situations that endangered the life of the mother.) She was held up as a symbol of the decaying family. The collective impact of all of these events added fuel to the fire of women's desire for change. Women were also frustrated with 12 years of Republican administrations. In fact, the Bush administration, which used family values as its 1992 presidential nominating convention theme, vetoed the Family and Medical Leave Act.

Women's rights groups, especially EMILY's List, were able to capitalize on the anti-Congress sentiment. Encouraged by women's groups and the large number of open seats available in Congress—whether through retirement, redistricting, or electorally shaky incumbents—a record number of women sought elective office in 1992. Research reveals that the unique factors that came together in the 1992 elections heightened the perceptions of the electorate and of women voters for the need to elect more women to office. This interest in what some call the symbolic representation of women translated into more votes for women candidates.

The National Women's Political Caucus and EMILY's List provided training and support to many of these women candidates. EMILY's List stands for "Early Money Is Like Yeast (It Makes the Dough Rise)." It operates under the assumption that candidates—especially women—need large infusions of funds early in their campaigns to make them more viable candidates and to raise more funds later in their campaigns. EMILY's List contributes thousands of dollars to individual women candidates.

In 1989, Virginia Slims took a poll about whether people would be more, less, or equally likely to vote for a woman "if two people of equal qualifications were running for president of the United States." They found that 26 percent of women and 9 percent of men said they would be more likely to vote for a woman; 21 percent of women and 33 percent of men said they would be less likely; and 48 percent of women and 52 percent of men said that it would make no difference. Willingness to see a woman elected to lesser political offices, such as mayor or governor, has also increased. As early as 1975, more than 80 percent of the public reported that they would support a qualified woman for those positions. Similarly, in sharp contrast to the public's attitudes toward women judges in the 1930s (when three-quarters of those polled objected to a female Supreme Court justice), Sandra Day O'Connor's appointment to the Supreme Court in 1981 was approved by 87 percent of all women and 84 percent of all men.

In addition, Geraldine Ferraro's selection as the Democratic nominee for vice president in 1984 undoubtedly influenced public opinion about women running for office. For example, a 1984 Gallup poll found that 52 percent of the respondents indicated that a woman on the ticket would make no difference in how they voted. More importantly, of those who said it would make a difference, 26 percent said that a woman on the ticket would make them more likely to vote for that party. Nevertheless, analysis of the 1984 election results suggests the addition of Ferraro to the ticket had little effect, positive or negative, on the outcome.

The creation of both liberal and conservative women's groups since the 1960s has fostered the participation of women in politics in a variety of ways. Historically, women have been socialized to see politics as "unfeminine" or better suited for males. Nevertheless, since the 1960s, women have made astonishing progress in the political realm. Political activity for women, however, can take many forms. Initially, in the mid-1800s women held conventions to address and publicize their concerns. They also engaged in more direct forms of grassroots activity often signing petitions addressed to male legislators requesting the vote or changes in a wide array of laws that discriminated against women. Once women got the vote, they could expand their political participation.

Women in Politics in the 1990s

Women as Voters

Women did not get the right to vote in national elections until 1920. Still, it was not until 1980 that the proportion of eligible voting women exceeded the proportion of eligible men voting in elections. (The actual number of women voting has exceeded the number of men who vote since the 1964 presidential election.) Through the 1992 elections, women's political participation in the most basic act of citizenship, voting, rose during each presidential election year. It reached an all-time high in the 1992 presidential election when 62.3 percent of eligible women voters cast ballots. That year, the Republican incumbent, President George Bush, and Democratic challenger Bill Clinton held clearly different views on issues of concern to women voters, including health care, the Family and Medical Leave Act, and the continued legality of abortion.

Many women were aware of the Bush administration's hostile attitudes toward *Roe v. Wade* and went to the polls to keep abortion legal and safe. Others went to the polls to vote for the record number of women who sought elective office that year, the first election after the constitutionally mandated redistricting that must take place every 10 years. (Redistricting often results in new districts without incumbents, where women candidates fare best.)

Some of the increase in the percentage of voting women can be directly traced to the efforts of women's groups to "get out the vote" and to convince women that their votes count. In 1980, the Republican candidate was Ronald Reagan; his opposition to the ERA and his anti-abortion views were well known. In the 1992 presidential contest, abortion was again a major issue. Had Republican incumbent George Bush been re-elected, it was likely that the composition of the Supreme Court would change enough to overrule *Roe v. Wade,* thereby removing women's constitutional right to secure an abortion. When the National Abortion Rights Action League (NARAL), Planned Parenthood, NOW, and other women's rights groups invested millions of dollars to inform women about the importance of the presidential election to the long-term composition of the Supreme Court and its position on abortion, they were fairly successful. Several political commentators rated abortion as the number one issue that year, with liberal women's votes providing the margin of victory for the pro-choice Democratic presidential candidate, Bill Clinton. In fact, one political scientist summed up the vote in 1992 as "It's abortion, Stupid."

Far more women than men also report that they are registered to vote. As indicated by Table 1, 62.7 million women and 55.3 million men were registered to vote in 1994. Of those registered, only 44.6 million women and 40.4 million men reported that they voted that year according to figures compiled by the U.S. Census Bureau. Still, studies have found that the reasons men and women give for voting are similar. Voting evokes a sense of civic duty for both.

Table 1. Voter Registration, 1984–96

Number Reporting They Are Registered Voters		
	Women	**Men**
1996	67.9 million	59.6 million
1994	62.7 million	55.3 million
1992	67.3 million	59.3 million
1990	60.2 million	53.0 million
1988	63.4 million	55.1 million
1986	59.5 million	52.2 million
1984	62.1 million	54.0 million

Source: Center for the American Woman and Politics (CAWP), Eagleton Institute of Politics, Rutgers University.

The gender gap—a term used to describe the differences in voting behavior in men and women—also first appeared in the 1980 presidential election. In that year, women were far less likely to vote for the Republican presidential candidate than men—56 percent of men but only 47 percent of women voted for Ronald Reagan. (See Table 2.)

The gender gap continued to be evident into the most recent elections. In 1992, Bill Clinton was elected with 45 percent of all votes cast by women; George Bush got only 37 percent of women's votes.

In the 1994 national elections, women stayed away from the polls in record numbers. Their failure to go to the polls was a key reason that Republicans were able to win back control of both houses of the U.S. Congress in that year. While political pundits labeled it the year of the "angry white male," it could as easily have been called the year of the "overworked, disillusioned woman." The immediate threats to abortion were gone with the election of Bill Clinton in 1992, and Clinton and the Democratic Congress quickly enacted the Family and Medical Leave Act; these were key items of interest that had brought women to the polls in 1992. Thus, 59 percent of the women who voted in 1992 did not vote in 1994, while 41 percent of the men who voted in the presidential election year did not cast their ballots in the off-year election.

Table 2. Gender Gap in Presidential Elections

	Voter News Service*		ABC News Washington Post		CBS News/ New York Times		NBC News	
	Women	Men	Women	Men	Women	Men	Woman	Men
1996								
Bill Clinton	54%	43%						
Bob Dole	38%	44%						
Ross Perot	7%	10%						
1992								
Bill Clinton	45%	41%						
George Bush	37%	38%						
Ross Perot	17%	21%						
1988								
George Bush			50%	57%	50%	57%	51%	57%
Michael Dukakis			49%	42%	49%	41%	49%	43%
1984								
Ronald Reagan			54%	62%	56%	62%	55%	64%
Walter Mondale			46%	38%	44%	37%	45%	36%
1980								
Ronald Reagan			47%	53%	46%	54%	47%	56%
Jimmy Carter			42%	35%	45%	37%	45%	36%
John Anderson			9%	9%	7%	7%	8%	8%

*Voter News Service is the service which was known as Voter Research and Surveys until 1993.

The gender gap continues to be a major force in elections at the local, state, and national levels. In 1994, the Voter News Service found that 81 percent of the 63 races where it conducted exit polls had gender gaps of at least 4 percent. Women voters were more likely to vote for the Democratic candidate in 49 of the 51 campaigns that evidenced a gender gap. The Democratic Party clearly continues to be the major beneficiary of the gender gap (see Table 3). Study after study has demonstrated that women are more likely to affiliate with the Democratic Party and to vote for its candidates. The gender gap provided the margin of victory for six Democratic U.S. senators in 1994 as well as for two Democratic governors. In 1992, it helped elect three Democratic women to the U.S. Senate—Barbara Boxer, Carol Moseley-Braun, and Patty Murray.

This gender gap in party identification also affects how women view politicians. In July 1983, for example, a Gallup poll revealed that only 34 percent of women but 51 percent of men approved of the way Ronald Reagan was handling his job as president. This gender gap is also evident in support for President Clinton, with 57 percent of the women but only 47 percent of the men approving of the way he was handling his job in March 1996 (Table 4).

Women in some states vote much more often in presidential elections than do women in other states. Women's Vote '96, for example, found that over three-quarters of the women in Utah, Connecticut, and Wisconsin voted in the 1984, 1988, and 1992 presidential elections. In sharp contrast, less than 55 percent of the women in Georgia, Tennessee, and Kentucky cast their ballots in those same years.

Stung by the loss of the House and Senate to the Republicans in 1994 when so few women turned out to vote, some groups, most notably EMILY's List, the National League of Women Voters, and the American Association of University Women, began new initiatives to get more women back to the polls in 1996. Because women are overwhelmingly more likely to cast their votes for Democratic candidates in support of issues concerning women, the League in 1994 launched a comprehensive Election '96 campaign termed "Get Out the Vote." Included in this initiative was the effort to implement the new national Motor Voter Law, which made it easier to register to vote. The campaign's central focus was to achieve 85 percent voter registration and turn out rates among women. It worked in conjunction with the *Ladies Home Journal* magazine throughout 1996 to highlight issues of women's political participation and their consequences.

The League specifically targeted racial and ethnic minorities and 18-to-24-year-olds in its "Get Out the Vote" effort, partnering itself with MTV's "Rock the Vote." Because the League targeted young women, the American Association of University Women also got into the act. It saw the Republican-controlled 104th Congress as "threaten(ing) to devastate every initiative that AAUW" had supported for decades. Thus it launched the AAUW Voter Education Campaign in July 1995.

The AAUW campaign was divided into two parts. The first consisted of an organized nationwide fax campaign and e-mail network to inform women on how issues before Congress affected their lives. Biweekly "Get the Facts" alerts were produced in partnership with 43 organizations in a nonpartisan, issue-based coalition, the Women's Network for Change.

Table 3. Gender Gap and Party Identification

	Women	Men	Women	Men
April 1997*	36%	26%	26%	31%
June 1996	44%	33%	26%	29%
June 1995	31%	25%	29%	36%
June 1994	38%	34%	25%	29%
June 1993	38%	30%	28%	30%
June 1992	36%	29%	32%	34%
May 1991	38%	26%	28%	31%
May 1990	38%	28%	30%	32%
June 1989	36%	32%	31%	31%
May 1988	41%	32%	29%	31%
May 1987	44%	35%	30%	31%
June 1986	40%	35%	29%	28%
May 1985	38%	30%	31%	28%
April 1984	40%	37%	28%	31%
June 1983	43%	32%	21%	25%

Source: CBS News/New York Times
*Source for April 1997 figures is Gallup Report/CNN

Table 4. Women's Approval Ratings of Presidents Reagan, Bush, and Clinton

Approve of the way Clinton is handling his job as president

	Women	Men
April 1997	59%	50%
March 1996	57%	47%
December 1995	53%	49%
May 1995	53%	48%
January 1995	51%	43%
July 1994	43%	42%
June 1994	49%	42%
April1994	48%	48%
November 1993	49%	46%
July 1993	45%	38%
February 1993	61%	57%

Approve of the way Bush is handling his job as president

	Women	Men
July 1992	30%	33%
July 1991	69%	72%
July 1990	61%	66%
July 1989	61%	72%

Approve of the way Reagan is handling his job as president

	Women	Men
July 1988	43%	59%
July 1987	44%	54%
July 1986	58%	69%
July 1985	60%	65%
July 1984	49%	59%
July 1983	34%	51%
July 1982	38%	48%
July 1981	55%	63%

Source: Data taken from the Gallup Report. The table is taken from the Center for the American Woman and Politics (CAWP), Eagleton Institute of Politics, Rutgers University.

The second part of the campaign was a "Get Out the Vote" effort designed to organize AAUW members to encourage "drop off voters"—those who voted in 1992 but stayed home in 1994—to go to the polls in 1996. Members used phone banks to call nearly 1 million women in 50 key congressional districts.

Similarly, EMILY's List tried to mobilize women voters to vote for pro-choice female candidates. Its "Women Vote" project raised over $3 million used to turn out additional pro-choice women voters. In spite of these combined efforts, women's participation failed to go back to its record highs of 1992. Still, the women who did go to the polls again overwhelmingly cast their votes for Democratic candidates at all levels. Bill Clinton outpolled Republican challenger Bob Dole by being the beneficiary of the largest margin of victory ever recorded by exit polls in a presidential election—11 points.

Women as Campaign Activists

Women have long played behind-the-scenes roles in political campaigns. For years, women did "the licking and sticking"—stuffing envelopes, for example—in campaigns while men played more public roles. In 1988, Susan Estrich became the first woman to run a major party candidate's presidential bid when she headed Michael Dukakis's unsuccessful bid for president as the Democratic Party's candidate. The next presidential election saw Mary Matalin head George Bush's unsuccessful re-election effort.

Women today also play key roles as campaign operatives on all levels. Still, most women are less likely to engage in any kind of political activity. Research reveals that women are less likely to engage in political discussion or to try to influence another's vote even if they strongly support a particular candidate. Political scientist Susan B. Hansen, however, has found that women are more likely to discuss politics or proselytize about a candidate if that candidate is a woman. Her data show that women voters talked most about politics in 1984 when Geraldine Ferraro was the Democratic vice presidential candidate; in 1992, in states where women were candidates for the U.S. Senate; and in 1992 when the media paid so much attention to the "Year of the Woman" and record numbers of women actually sought office.

Women as Party Activists and Officials

The NWPC has sought to increase representation of women within the ranks of both political parties. Since its creation, the NWPC has had a noticeable impact on Democratic Party rules. At the 1976 Democratic National Convention, it championed a written guarantee that women would constitute 50 percent of the delegates at the 1980 convention. To prevent an embarrassing floor fight, soon-to-be-nominated candidate Jimmy Carter met with women's rights leaders to reach a compromise concerning women's representation at the convention. Carter promised to appoint women to high-ranking positions in his administration should he be elected, and a provision was to be added to the party rules to mandate that "future conventions shall promote equal division between delegate men and delegate women." The DNC also pledged to encourage the state parties to adopt rules to effect this goal. In 1978, the DNC actually passed a resolution that required that 50 percent of the future convention delegates be women. The NWPC has had only limited success in securing feminist reforms within the Republican Party.

Political Climate for Women Candidates in the 1990s

The combined impact of more women voters, campaign activists, and women's groups has gone a long way to change the climate for women candidates. Even with dramatic improvements in cultural beliefs, stereotypes continue to act as barriers to the full participation of women in politics. In 1991, for example, 19 percent of the public agreed that "women should take care of running their homes and children and leave running the country to men." Moreover, 27 percent of the public questioned agreed with the statement "most men are better suited emotionally for politics." When asked to list the reasons why there were not more women in public office, the public claimed one of the most important factors was "many Americans aren't ready to elect a woman to higher office."

Not only do segments of the public question whether women should hold political office, doubts also exist about how effective women are when they are elected. One 1990 survey revealed that when asked whether a woman in public office would do a better job, a worse job, or just as good a job as a man on a variety of public policy questions, the respondents indicated a number of areas where they believed a woman would do a worse job. Women were not expected to do as good a job in directing the military, conducting diplomatic relations with other countries, or making decisions on whether to go to war—the very policy areas one might expect a president to handle. President Clinton's selection of Madeleine Albright as secretary of state is likely to change those perceptions. Public opinion polls taken in 1997 reveal her to be one of the most admired women in the U.S. As more and more women are appointed to positions such as those held by Albright and Attorney General Janet Reno, myths about women's capabilities and appropriateness for high office will most likely be shattered.

Gender segregation at work also affects women's political attitudes. Women in traditionally male jobs are usually more liberal and more willing to talk about politics.

News Media

The treatment of women candidates has been the subject of considerable public and scholarly debate. In an era when candidates rely on the media to get their message out to voters, how women are portrayed is a critical issue in examining and trying to explain the fate of women politicians as well as the political climate for women candidates. Female state legislators, for example, are more likely to express dissatisfaction with media coverage. Research conducted about the 1980s by Kim Fridkin Kahn shows that female politicians were disadvantaged by the media in both the quality and quantity of newspaper reports. By the 1990s, however, newer studies of coverage of women candidates by the print media revealed that, overall, women candidates were reported about in a neutral tone whereas men were more likely to be written about in negative terms.

Studies concerning television coverage of female candidates in the 1990s also reveal little current bias in the way women candidates are treated. One study of the 1988, 1990, and 1992 election cycles found that women candidates may even enjoy a small advantage.

Political Action Committees (PACs)

In 1974, federal campaign laws were reformed in reaction to Watergate and other campaign abuses. Federal law now allowed for the creation of political action committees (PACs), designed to give money directly to political candidates. Several women's PACs were funded immediately, including the Women's Campaign Fund. Later, EMILY's List and two Republican Women's PACs—WISH List and RENEW—were created. All quickly became important sources of financial support for women candidates.

According to the Center for the American Woman and Politics (CAWP), by 1997, 58 PACs and donor networks existed as a source of funding for women's campaigns for public office. Eleven of these PACs were national in scope; the rest operated on the state or local level to support women candidates. Many have interesting names, such as the Susan B.

Anthony List, which is a pro-life women's PAC created to fund women running for national office; and PAM's (Power and Money for Choice and Change) List, which raises funds for pro-choice women running for the New Jersey legislature.

The largest of the women's political action committees is EMILY's List. It was founded in 1985 to support viable, pro-choice Democratic women running in congressional and gubernatorial races. Its goal is to raise money for pro-choice Democratic women candidates early in the election cycle to put more women in elective office. It tries to do this by putting them on its "list" and encouraging its members to support endorsed women. Each election cycle, members of EMILY's List agree to contribute no less than $100 to at least two of the recommended candidates on its list. (It costs $100 to become a member of EMILY's List.) Since 1988, EMILY's List has been the largest financial resource for women candidates. Unlike other PACs, whose boards decide how members' contributions are to be spent, EMILY's List members write their checks to the candidates of their choice. They are then bundled together and sent directly to the candidate by EMILY's List.

Aware that money was not enough, EMILY's List leaders recognized the tremendous opportunity presented by the 1990 reapportionment of the House of Representatives. In 1989, EMILY's List held a debriefing conference for the candidates it supported in 1988 and published "Campaigning in a Different Voice," a study of gender-related issues faced by female candidates for the House. In 1990, it commissioned a national poll on the abortion issue and how it affects female Democratic candidates. It also worked with the National Committee for an Effective Congress, using the committee's huge computer capacity to identify likely new congressional seats for 1992. Representatives from EMILY's List met with pro-choice Democratic women to brief them on ways to keep abreast of the potential district boundary changes and to suggest ways to keep their districts winnable. It also made an extensive search for viable candidates. Its efforts were key to women's successes in 1992, when EMILY's List donated more than $6.2 million to the campaigns of 55 women candidates, making it the largest PAC supporting congressional candidates—male or female. Most of the women elected in the "Year of the Woman" were supported by EMILY's List.

EMILY's List also provides professional training for candidates and their staffs, conducts surveys and issue research, and helps with campaign message development. It also contributed millions of dollars directly to candidates in 1996. Since 1994, it has been the single largest PAC in the United States.

The success of these liberal women's PACs led to the creation of WISH List (Women in the House and Senate) in late 1991. Like EMILY's List, viable candidates for the Senate, House, and governorships are recommended to members who send their checks directly to the group, where they are bundled. It supports Republican pro-choice women, including Governor Christine Todd Whitman (R-NJ) and Senator Kay Bailey Hutchinson (R-TX). In 1992, it raised over $400,000 from its 1,500 members. In 1994, it contributed $370,000 to 40 candidates, including the only pro-choice Republican woman elected that year.

The Republican Network to Elect Women (RENEW) is among the newest of women's political action committees. It was founded in 1993 to recruit, train, and help support Republican women candidates in local, state, and national elections. It supports Republican women candidates without regard to their position on abortion and, in general, focuses on state and local elections, deferring to the clout of WISH List in the national arena.

Women and Campaigns

Current research reveals that men and women run similar campaigns. Female candidates, however, are more likely to capitalize on their unique status as women. Yet differences in campaign styles have not been found to explain differences in election outcomes. Recent research reveals that when women run for office as challengers, incumbents, or open-seat candidates, they are just as likely, if not more likely, to win. While women are running for office in record numbers (see Table 5), many women opt not to run for office. The reasons for this unequal participation vary. Women report less interest in politics, a lack of motivation to seek elective office, family concerns, and other cultural factors.

Political scientists Susan Welch and Dudley Studlar have found that women are more likely to be candidates in less traditional constituencies, in more liberal political parties, and as challengers. Factors affecting success, however, appear to be the same for male and female candidates: incumbency and money. Similarly, others have found that in low-information campaigns, some voters use gender as a voting cue. Thus, uninformed voters perceive women candidates to be more liberal than male candidates.

Studies have concluded that women are generally less active in politics than men. Thus, it is not surprising that fewer women than men seek elective office. Statistically significant differences exist in men's and women's level of campaign contributions, working in the community, contacting government officials, and levels of participation in political organizations. Still, when researchers have controlled for differences in education and income, these differences largely disappear.

Elected Women

In spite of the evidence of some continued negative views of women as elected or appointed officials, record numbers of women are running for and winning elective office at all levels, often substantially helped by women's PACs.

For women to win elective office, they must first be willing to run for public office, an endeavor that is less attractive to many more women than men. Still, since 1992, record numbers of women have been seeking elective office. As Table 5 shows, many women must run to produce only a few elected

Table 5. Women Running for Office, 1996

U.S. Senate

	Total Filed	Won Primary	Won General	Incumbent Nominees	Challenger Nominees	Open Nominees	Incumbent Winners	Challenger Winners	Open Winners
Total	22	9	2	0	3	6	0	0	2
Democrat	12	5	1	0	1	4	0	0	1
Republican	10	4	1	0	2	2	0	0	1

U.S. House

	Total Filed	Won Primary	Won General	Incumbent Nominees	Challenger Nominees	Open Nominees	Incumbent Winners	Challenger Winners	Open Winners
Total	217	120	51	41	65	14	40	6	5
Democrat	136	77	35	27	41	9	27	5	3
Republican	81*	43*	16*	14	25*	4	13	1	2*

*Figures include Jo Ann Emerson (MO) who ran and won as an independent, but will serve as a Republican.

Governors

	Total Filed	Won Primary	Won General	Incumbent Nominees	Challenger Nominees	Open Nominees	Incumbent Winners	Challenger Winners	Open Winners
Total	9	6	1	0	3	6	0	0	1
Democrat	4	3	1	0	1	3	0	0	1
Republican	5	3	0	0	2	3	0	0	0

Source: Center for the American Woman and Politics (CAWP), Eagleton Institute of Politics, Rutgers University.

officials. In 1996, for example, 22 women filed to run for a U.S. Senate seat in their state. Of those women, nine won their primary bid, and only two won in the general election. Thus, only 10 percent of the women who initially sought election to the U.S. Senate in 1996 were elected. Both winners won in open seats where there was no incumbent. Similarly, 217 women sought election to the U.S. House in 1996. One hundred twenty won their primary bid and 51, or 23.5 percent of those who initially sought election, won seats in the House.

The number of women elected at the local, state, and national levels has skyrocketed since the 1970s, but has leveled off in the 1990s. In 1997, 59 women served in the U.S. Congress, making up 11 percent of that body. An all-time high of nine women, or 9 percent, served in the Senate and 50 served in the House, down from a record high of 51 in 1995. Senators from two states were exclusively women—Barbara Boxer and Diane Feinstein of California and Olympia Snowe and Susan Collins of Maine.

In the House, 50 women served from 20 states. This means, however, that over half of the states had no women in their state congressional delegations.

Three women were state governors in 1997 and 18 were state lieutenant governors, a position that often serves as a stepping stone to the governor's house. Women's numbers in state legislatures have remained stable in the 1990s and some states appeared to be disinclined to elect women to state office in particular. While in states such as Washington, Arizona, and Colorado, women make up over one-third of the elected state representatives, women have failed to make any meaningful inroads in other states—especially in the South (see Table 6). Many political pundits attribute this to the historically more conservative and traditional nature of the South—an area where state ERA ratification lagged substantially behind the rest of the nation.

The proportion of women mayors, another stepping stone for higher office, while up dramatically from earlier decades, has stagnated and even declined in recent years. In 1992, for example, there were 19 women mayors of the 100 largest cities in the United States. By 1997, only 12 of the 100 largest cities in the United States had female mayors. Similarly, in March 1997, 20.7 percent of the cities with populations over 30,000 had female mayors, up only 4 percent from 1992 according to CAWP.

Women in Appointive Positions

As of late 1997, 21 women have held cabinet or cabinet-level appointments in the 200-plus year history of the United States. Of the 41 men who have been president, only seven have appointed women to their cabinets. According to the Center for the Study of Women in Politics, only 4.3 percent of the 486 persons to hold cabinet positions have been women.

In 1933, Franklin D. Roosevelt, urged by his political activist wife Eleanor Roosevelt, became the first president to appoint a woman to his cabinet. He appointed Frances Perkins as secretary of labor (see Table 7). Patricia Roberts Harris became the first African-American woman appointed to the cabinet when she was named secretary of housing and urban development by President Jimmy Carter in 1977. (See Appendix 2 for a list of women who have served in presidential cabinets.)

Table 6. High and Low States for Women's Election to the State Legislature

States with highest percentages of women state legislators:

State	% Women
Washington	39.5
Arizona	37.8
Colorado	35.0
Nevada	33.3
Vermont	33.3
Minnesota	30.8
New Hampshire	30.7
Maryland	29.8
Kansas	29.7
Connecticut	28.9

States with lowest percentages of women state legislators:

State	% Women
Alabama	4.3
Kentucky	9.4
Oklahoma	10.1
Louisiana	11.8
Pennsylvania	12.3
Mississippi	12.6
South Carolina	12.9
Alaska	13.3
Tennessee	13.6
West Virginia	14.9

Source: Center for the American Woman and Politics (CAWP), National Information Bank on Women in Public Office, Eagleton Institute of Politics, Rutgers University.

Bill Clinton appointed a record number of women to his cabinet in 1993. Among them, Janet Reno became the first woman to be appointed as U.S. attorney general, making her the nation's chief law enforcement officer. When President Clinton nominated Madeleine Albright to be his secretary of state he shattered another glass ceiling for women. In 1997, women held two of the four most prestigious cabinet-level posts.

Who Runs for Office?

Early research on women who ran for and won elective office noticed how different they were from their male counterparts. Women elected to state legislatures, for example, were older when first elected, less likely to be married, and less likely to have children if they were married. Most were not professional and often had worked years for their political party. Over the years, these differences have narrowed. Women elected today are likely to be more educated than those in the past, younger, married, and from business or professional backgrounds—the traditional career paths for male politicians.

How Do Women Act as Politicians?

Getting more women elected to office has been at the forefront of the women's movement agenda since the early 1970s. It was only recently, however, that political scientists were able to conduct any rigorous scientific examinations to see whether or not the election of women candidates or the appointment of women judges made a difference to women. Research by political scientist Lyn Kathlene, which analyzes the conversational dynamics of committee members, witnesses, chairs, and bill sponsors, finds that significant sex differences among women and men exist. Male and female chairs not only conduct hearings differently, these differences appear to affect the behavior of witnesses and committee members. She also finds that as the number of women in a legislative body increases, male legislators become more verbally assertive as they try to control the hearings. Kathlene concludes that these findings may indicate that women will be unable to participate equally in legislative policy making.

Notwithstanding Kathlene's cautions, political scientist Sue Thomas has found that female state legislators prioritize and advance women's and family issues in state legislatures. Similarly, a comprehensive study of the 103rd Congress conducted by the Center for American Women in Politics (CAWP) found that women legislators were more likely to report that they had a special responsibility to represent women, and that they also used their positions in Congress to advance women's issues. Both Republican and Democratic women were more likely to vote for the Family and Medical Leave Act and the Conference Report on the Freedom of Access to (Abortion) Clinics Act.

The CAWP report also found a significant difference in the way Republican men and women legislators voted in the House of Representatives. Republican women were two to three times more likely to vote for what may be considered issues of interest to women and families than their Republican male counterparts.

Other studies reveal that women state legislators average two more requests per week for constituency services than their male counterparts, and they perceive that they get more requests than their male colleagues.

The Future of Women in American Politics

Women truly have come a long way in terms of their political participation at all levels. They not only register more than men (and are larger in numbers) but they also, at least in recent presidential elections, vote more than men. Women have begun to speak in a similar voice, at least at the polls. Evidence of a gender gap occurred in 1980 and continues to reveal itself in elections at all levels around the United States. Women not only vote for female candidates, they vote for candidates who they see as prioritizing women's issues, such as child care, family leave, gun control, or reproductive rights.

When women run today, they are more likely to be able to turn their gender into a plus at the polls, often with the help, or at least without the damage, of a negative press. Still, women hold less than 20 percent of all political offices in the United States. Until more women become interested in politics, begin to view it as a desirable career option, and actually run for office, their strength in the state houses and in the national government will continue to lag behind their contributions in other areas.

Bibliography

Abramowitz, Alan I. "It's Abortion, Stupid: Policy Voting and the 1992 Presidential Election." *Journal of Politics* 57, no. 1 (1995): 176–86.

Carroll, Susan. *Women as Candidates in American Politics.* Bloomington: Indiana University Press, 1985.

Center for the American Woman in Politics. *Voices, Views, Votes: The Impact of Women in the 103rd Congress.* New Brunswick, NJ: Eagleton Institute of Politics, 1995.

Dabelko, Kristen LaCour and Paul S. Herrnson. "Women's and Men's Campaigns for the U.S. House of Representatives." *Political Research Quarterly* 50 (March 1997): 121–35.

Duke, Lois Lovelace. *Women & Politics: Insiders or Outsiders?* 2nd ed. Upper Saddle River, NJ: Prentice Hall, 1995.

Flexner, Eleanor. *Century of Struggle.* Cambridge: Harvard University Press, 1975.

Friedan, Betty. *The Feminine Mystique.* New York: Dell, 1973.

Hansen, Susan B. "Talking About Politics: Gender and Contextual Effects on Political Proselytizing." *Journal of Politics* 59, no. 1 (February 1997): 73–103.

Hymowitz, Carol and Michaele Weissman. *A History of Women in America.* New York: Bantam Books, 1978.

Kahn, Kim Fridkin. *The Political Consequences of Being a Woman.* New York: Columbia University Press, 1996.

Kathlene, Lyn. "Power and Influence in State Legislative Policymaking: The Interaction of Gender and Position in Committee Hearings and Debates." *American Political Science Review* 88, no. 8 (September 1994): 560–76.

Koch, Jeffrey. "Candidate Gender and Women's Psychological Involvement in Politics." *American Politics Quarterly* 25, no. 1 (1997): 118–33.

McDermott, Monika. "Voting Cues in Low-Information Elections." *American Journal of Political Science* 41, no. 1 (1997): 270–83.

McGlen, Nancy E. and Karen O'Connor. *Women, Politics, and American Society.* 2nd ed. Upper Saddle River, NJ: Prentice Hall, 1998.

Norris, Pippa, ed. *Women, Media, and Politics.* New York: Oxford University Press, 1995.

Paolino, Philip. "Group Salient Issues and Group Representation: Support for Women Candidates in the 1992 Senate Elections." *American Journal of Political Science* 39 (May 1995): 294–313.

Richardson, Lillian E. and Patricia K. Freeman. "Gender Differences in Constituency Service Among State Legislators." *Political Research Quarterly* 48 (March 1995): 169–79.

Schlozman, Kay Lehman, Nancy Burns, and Sidney Verba. "Gender and the Pathways to Participation: The Role of Resources." *Journal of Politics* 56, no. 4 (November 1994): 963–90.

Schlozman, Kay Lehman, Nancy Burns, Sidney Verba, and Jesse Donahue. "Gender and Citizen Participation: Is There a Different Voice?" *American Journal of Political Science* 39 (May 1995): 267–93.

Thomas, Sue. *How Women Legislate.* New York: Oxford University Press, 1994.

Welch, Susan and Dudley Studlar. "The Opportunity Structure for Women's Candidacies and Electability in Britain and the United States." *Political Research Quarterly* 49, no. 4 (1996): 861+.

Encyclopedia of Women in American Politics

A

Grace Abbott (1878–1939)

Grace Abbott headed the **Immigrant Protective League (IPL)** from 1908 until 1917, at which time she joined the **United States Children's Bureau** and assisted in the passage of child labor laws. She was also active in the Chicago garment workers' strike in 1910–11, worked for Theodore Roosevelt's presidential campaign in 1912, participated in the Illinois woman **suffrage** campaign of 1913, and attended the International Congress of Women in 1915. Abbott then worked with the Illinois State Immigrants' Commission and again led the federal Children's Bureau until her retirement in 1934.

BIBLIOGRAPHY

Abbott, Edith. "Grace Abbott: A Sister's Memories." *Social Service Review* (September 1939).

Abbott, Grace. "What Have They Done?" *The Independent* 115 (October 24, 1925): 475–76.

Costin, Lela B. *Two Sisters for Social Justice: A Biography of Grace and Edith Abbott.* Urbana: University of Illinois Press, 1983.

Hazel Hempel Abel (1888–1966)

Hazel Abel was a delegate to Nebraska State Republican Conventions from 1939 to 1948 and from 1952 to 1956, as well as vice-chair of the State Republican Central Committee in 1954. She also served as a delegate to the White House Conference on Education in 1955, chaired the Nebraska delegation to the Republican National Convention in 1956, and served on the Theodore Roosevelt Centennial Commission from 1955 to 1959.

BIBLIOGRAPHY

"Lady from Nebraska." *Newsweek* 44 (December 20, 1954): 20.

Abolition

The abolition or anti-slavery movement, which began in the early 1800s, was based on a belief in the natural rights of men and women. Abolitionists opposed slavery because they believed it contradicted the fundamental principles upon which the United States had been founded. Despite the efforts of abolitionists, the existence of slavery failed to become a legitimate political issue. As a result, the movement was forced into other avenues of political agitation. Eventually, one of the movement's most important outlets became religion.

The meshing of religious righteousness with the issue of slavery brought women to the debate. While slavery was exclusively a political issue, women's participation was considered inappropriate. Locating the debate about slavery in a religious context allowed women a voice, as religious activity by women was both permissable and admired. Antislavery women such as the sisters **Angelina** and **Sarah Grimke** eventually became important figures in the abolition movement. One result of women's participation in the abolition movement was an increase in their awareness of their own limited political and social status. This awareness eventually led women to greater levels of political activism. Today, the abolition movement is widely considered to be one of the original sources of the women's movement. (JEH) **See also** Slavery and Women.

BIBLIOGRAPHY

Birney, Catherine H. *The Grimke Sisters.* Westport, CT: Greenwood Press, 1969.

Lutz, Alma. *Crusade for Freedom: Women of the Antislavery Movement.* Boston: Beacon Press, 1968.

Abortion

The issue of whether and when to permit women to terminate their pregnancies through abortion has become one of the most emotional and combative issues of contemporary gender politics. The issue has pitted opposing sets of women political activists against one another. Feminists argue that only the

Many women argue that abortion politics would be different if, as the sign says, "men got pregnant." National Archives.

women affected can make what is often a difficult moral judgment, and that the fetus is part of the woman's body until birth. Religious conservatives argue that the fetus is a baby with a soul from the time of conception, and that abortion is therefore murder. Thus, the abortion debate has been framed as a clash of absolute rights—the right to choose versus the right to life.

In early America, abortion was legal but dangerous, since most procedures posed significant risk to the life and health of the mother. In the late nineteenth century, most states criminalized abortion under pressure from organized groups of physicians, who argued that new medical evidence established that the fetus was a baby. By 1900, all states banned most abortions, although many states permitted abortion if a doctor would certify its need. In the late 1950s, many doctors and lawyers began to argue for liberalization of abortion laws. In 1962, abortion captured the public's attention when **Sherri Finkbine**, pregnant while taking **thalidomide**, sought a therapeutic abortion. Although thalidomide was primarily used outside the United States, pictures of children born with severe birth defects caused by the use of the drug during pregnancy appeared in major magazines. When Finkbine was forced to go to Europe to obtain an abortion, public support for the growing abortion reform movement swelled. By 1972, 17 states had liberalized their laws to allow abortion to protect the physical and mental health of the mother. These laws included a California law endorsed and signed by Govenor Ronald Reagan; four of the 17 states allowed abortion for any reason.

In 1973, the U.S. Supreme Court in ***Roe v. Wade*** struck down state and national laws regulating abortion. The Court ruled that in the first trimester of pregnancy, when abortion was generally safe, states could not restrict a woman's right to obtain an abortion. In the second trimester, when available procedures became somewhat more risky, states could regulate abortion to protect the health of the mother. In the final trimester, when the fetus was viable outside the mother's womb, the state could regulate or even ban abortions to protect fetal life. For many years after *Roe*, the Court consistently struck down state laws designed to limit access to abortion.

The *Roe* decision energized abortion opponents, who quickly formed a sizable social movement that became known as the pro-life movement. The Catholic bishops were the first to organize, but soon a number of evangelical Protestant churches announced their opposition to legal abortion. Within a few years, the pro-life movement was characterized by a sizable number of organizations with diverse constituencies, rationales, and strategies. Early efforts frequently focused on the passage of a **Human Life Amendment** to the U.S. Constitution that would protect fetal life, but it soon became clear that such an amendment had little chance of passing Congress, and did not command the support of the general public.

Many pro-life activists sought to reverse *Roe* by changing the composition of the Supreme Court. Working within the **Republican Party**, pro-life activists in 1980 became part of Ronald Reagan's electoral constituency, and succeeded in including a pro-life plank calling for a Human Life Amendment in the GOP presidential platform. Reagan and later George Bush had the opportunity to appoint a number of justices to the Court, replacing retiring liberals. By 1989 a more conservative Court ruled by a 5-4 margin in ***Webster v. Reproductive Health Services*** that certain state restrictions on abortion access were permissible, including tests for fetal viability and a ban on abortions in public hospitals. Four justices appeared ready to overturn *Roe*, but Reagan appointee **Sandra Day O'Connor** did not join this group to create a majority. In later rulings the Court elucidated a vague standard that states may enact regulations that do not pose an undue burden on a woman's ability to obtain an abortion. When Bill Clinton appointed two pro-choice justices, including **Ruth Bader Ginsburg**, pro-life hopes to change the composition of the Court and to thereby overturn *Roe* died.

As it became clear that strategies that sought to amend the Constitution or change the composition of the Court were unlikely to succeed, pro-life activists focused on two new tactics. Many sought to enact the kinds of restrictions the Court has permitted at the state level, including parental consent and notification, waiting periods, and tests for fetal viability. At the national level, pro-life activists sought to ban certain abortion procedures and to bar federal employees from obtaining abortions at military hospitals or through government-sponsored medical insurance. Other activists have rejected the incremental approach, and have instead resorted to more confrontational tactics. **Operation Rescue** has mounted a series of blockades of abortion clinics, trying to prevent providers and patients from entering. At the fringes of the pro-life movement, some activists have resorted to violence, firebombing clinics and even murdering abortion providers.

Pro-choice activists reacted to *Roe* by attempting to protect the status quo. The *Webster* case mobilized the pro-choice forces, which have mostly fought defensive actions against pro-life initiatives. Some have also sought to enact state laws guaranteeing freedom of choice, or to press test cases to state supreme courts that might guarantee abortion rights in the states based on state constitutions. In the early 1990s, pro-choice forces sought to pass a **Freedom of Choice Act**, but with the GOP takeover of Congress in 1994 this strategy is now on hold.

In response to *Webster* and later Court decisions, many states have moved to regulate access to abortion. A majority of states have passed laws requiring teen-aged girls to inform at least one of their parents, and in many cases to obtain their consent, before they can receive an abortion. Other states have imposed waiting periods, and the Court has upheld these even in states where abortion is only available in a few clinics, thus requiring substantial travel time. In Guam, the legislature, under strong pressure from the Catholic church, banned nearly all abortions, but the Court struck down that law, as it did severe restrictions in other states. In many states, such as Virginia, the state legislature has devoted great energy and time to debating parental notification—in Florida Governor Robert Martinez called the legislature into special session to consider only restrictions on abortion, which the legislature refused to pass.

Although activists have framed the abortion issue as a clash of absolute right, the majority of Americans are neither supportive of unlimited abortion rights nor opposed to all abortions. Instead, most Americans appear to value both personal choice and fetal life, and many weigh these rights and make relatively subtle distinctions based on the stage of fetal development and the circumstances surrounding the abortion decision. A substantial majority of Americans favor allowing abortions under circumstances that involve physical trauma—threats to the life or health of the mother, rape or incest, or fetal defect. A narrow majority would allow abortion for some, but not all social reasons—**poverty**, teenaged motherhood, and accidental pregnancies. In the 1990s, roughly 10 percent of Americans appear to oppose abortion in all circumstances, while approximately 40 percent favor allowing abortions for women who want them. Yet support for restrictions on abortion like waiting periods and parental notification is strong, even among those who want to keep abortion legal.

Although the abortion issue directly affects the lives of women and has been contested largely by groups of women activists, there is no real **gender gap** in support for legal abortion in the United States, although African-American women are somewhat more supportive of legal abortion than are African-American men. Although not conclusive, some evidence indicates that women may feel more intensely about abortion regardless of their position, and may be more likely to vote based on the abortion issue, but these differences are not substantial. Only on issues that directly affect paternal rights—such as spousal notification—have women been generally more liberal than men.

If the abortion issue has not divided Americans along gender lines, opinion has split along religious and class lines. Deeply religious citizens regardless of their faith are less supportive of legal abortion than those with little attachment to religion, and evangelical Protestants and Catholics are less supportive than mainline Protestants and Jews. Studies indicate that pro-life activists often have only average levels of education and income, but are strongly connected to religious communities. Pro-choice activists in contrast have only nominal ties to religion. Better educated and more affluent citizens are more supportive of legal abortion than are working class Americans.

Yet abortion has divided most religious denominations. Although the Catholic church has taken an unambiguous position in opposition to abortion, there are several organized groups of pro-choice Catholics. Most Protestant churches are likewise divided on abortion. Even feminists have not spoken with an entirely unified voice: Feminists for Life is an organization of feminists who oppose abortion.

In the 1980s, abortion became a litmus test issue for presidential campaigns for both Republican and **Democratic Party** nominations. GOP moderates such as George Bush adopted a pro-life position to appeal to pro-life delegates, and Democratic moderates such as Dick Gephardt and Jesse Jackson adopted pro-choice positions. Such litmus test issues are rare, especially for issues where the public does not fully support either position. The most likely explanation for such extreme platform positions on abortion is the impact of *Roe*, which essentially removed abortion from the realm of electoral politics, and left the parties free to appeal to the energies and monies of activists without risking the loss of votes from more moderate Americans. This was especially true of the Republicans, who benefited from the intensity of the pro-life activists without losing votes from moderate suburban Republicans.

The *Webster* decision changed the underlying partisan dynamics of the abortion issue. Suddenly it appeared that state legislatures could limit abortion rights, and that a politician's position on abortion might actually influence public policy. The immediate result was to energize the pro-choice community, which was numerically larger but had historically been less likely to vote their preference on abortion. In 1989, two key gubernatorial races were decided at least in part on the abortion issue, with pro-choice candidates winning. Pro-choice groups like **EMILY's List** and the National Abortion Rights Action League (NARAL) experienced surges in membership and contributions.

The longer-term consequence has led to internal debates in both parties, which may ultimately lead to more nuanced positions on abortion by Republicans and Democrats. Although the GOP presidential platform has endorsed a Human Life Amendment since 1980, in 1996 party delegates fought over whether to include the plank, and whether to amend it to call for tolerance of those with opposing views. When Christian conservatives managed to include the plank without the call for tolerance, GOP candidate Bob Dole announced that he had not read the platform. Many prominent Republicans called for the party to distance itself from the pro-life movement, including governors William Weld (MA), Pete Wilson (CA), and Christine Todd Whitman (NJ), and possible presidential candidate Colin Powell. Democrats have also debated their party's strong commitment to unlimited access to abortion, although the party is less divided on abortion than are the Republicans.

In the late 1990s, some activists began to seek increased dialog and perhaps common agreement on abortion. Bill Clinton's phrase that abortion should be "safe, legal, and rare" seemed to offer some possibility of common action to reduce the numbers of abortions through the actions of voluntary organizations. The Common Ground Network for Life and Choice was formed to explore common policy goals. Feminist writer Naomi Wolf and others called for a reexamination of the abortion issue, while insisting that abortion remain legal and a woman's choice. Although it seemed unlikely at the end of the 1990s that such efforts might lead to a resolution of the abortion issue, there was some hope that they might reduce the rancor and violence that the abortion issue has occasioned. (CW) **See also** Feminism; Reproductive and Contraceptive Technologies for Women; Reproductive Freedom Project (RFP); Right-to-Life Movement.

BIBLIOGRAPHY

Blanchard, Dallas A. *The Anti-Abortion Movement and the Rise of the Religious Right*. New York: Twayne, 1994.

Cook, Elizabeth Adell, Ted G. Jelen, and Clyde Wilcox. *Between Two Absolutes: Public Opinion and the Politics of Abortion*. Boulder, CO: Westview, 1992.

Craig, Barbara Hinkson and David M. O'Brien. *Abortion and American Politics*. Chatham, NJ: Chatham House, 1993.

Dodson, Debra L. and Lauren Birnbaum with Katherine E. Kleeman. *Election 1989: The Abortion Issue in New Jersey and Virginia*. New Brunswick, NJ: Eagleton Institute of Politics, 1990.

Goggin, Malcolm L. *Understanding the New Politics of Abortion*. Newbury Park, CA: Sage, 1993.

Granberg, Donald. "The Abortion Activists." *Family Planning Perspectives* 13 (1981): 158–61.

Luker, Kristin. *Abortion and the Politics of Motherhood*. Berkeley: University of California Press, 1984.

Staggenborg, Suzanne. *The Pro-Choice Movement: Organization and Activism in the Abortion Conflict*. New York: Oxford University Press, 1991.

Wolf, Naomi. "Rethinking Pro-Choice Rhetoric: Our Bodies, Our Souls." *The New Republic* (October, 16, 1995): 26+.

Abortion Control Act (1989)

In response to the Supreme Court's decision in ***Webster v. Reproductive Health Services*** (1989), which upheld Missouri's restrictive **abortion** regulations, Pennsylvania Governor Robert Casey (a pro-life Democrat) signed into law the Abortion Control Act. Under the Pennsylvania law, physicians were required to provide patients with mandated information, including the age and development of the fetus, the availability of state-funded social services programs, and the liability of the father to provide child support. The law also included a 24-hour waiting period, reporting requirements, spousal notification, and stringent parental consent rules. These restrictions were challenged in ***Planned Parenthood of Southeastern Pennsylvania v. Casey*** (1992). In *Casey*, the Supreme Court reaffirmed the "central holdings" of ***Roe v. Wade*** (1973), ruling that states could not pass restrictions that placed an "undue burden" on a woman seeking to obtain an abortion, nor could a state ban abortions in the early stages of pregnancy. The constitutionality of the restrictions contained in the Abortion Control Act was upheld, with the exception of the spousal notification requirement, because the Court did not consider them to place an undue burden on the woman seeking to obtain an abortion. (LvA) **See also** Reproductive and Contraceptive Technologies for Women.

BIBLIOGRAPHY

Drucker, Dan. *Abortion Decisions of the Supreme Court, 1973 through 1989: A Comprehensive Review with Historical Commentary*. Jefferson, NC: McFarland & Co., 1990.

O'Connor, Karen. *No Neutral Ground? Abortion Politics in an Age of Absolutes*. Boulder, CO: Westview Press, 1996.

Segars, Mary C. and Timothy A. Byrnes, eds. *Abortion Politics in American States*. Armonk, NY: M.E. Sharpe, 1995.

Bella Abzug (1920–1998)

Bella Abzug was born Bella Savitsky on July 23, 1920. After a successful private law practice, she was elected to the United States House of Representatives as a Democrat from a district in New York City. Serving in the House from 1970 to1976, she was an outspoken opponent of the Vietnam War and a tireless crusader for women's rights. She became famous for her confrontational style and trademark wide-brimmed hats.

In one of her signature hats, Bella Abzug (second from left) leads the procession into the 1977 National Women's Conference, which she chaired. Photo by Pat Field. National Archives.

In 1971 Abzug, along with **Shirley Chisholm**, **Betty Friedan**, and **Gloria Steinem,** founded the **National Women's Political Caucus (NWPC).** The caucus was dedicated to electing more women to government and to increasing women's representation at political conventions. Abzug resigned her House seat in 1976 to make a bid for the U.S. Senate. However, the increasingly conservative mood of the electorate in the late 1970s contributed to her losses in the Senate run, a 1977 mayoral run in New York City, and a 1978 House contest. President Jimmy Carter appointed Abzug to co-chair the National Advisory Committee for Women and abruptly fired her when the committee criticized him for cutting funding to women's programs. In 1984, Abzug co-authored a book in which she analyzed the emerging **gender gap** in voter choice. Abzug contended that the gender gap, in which women were more likely to vote for Democratic candidates than were men, was a result of the feminist movement's success in raising women's consciousness.

In the 1990s, Abzug continued to inhabit the public spotlight as a revered pioneer of second-wave **feminism** and for her work on environmental and women's concerns. Abzug was co-chair of the Women's Environment and Development Organization and opened the 1992 World Women's Congress for a Healthy Planet with a speech entitled, "Empowering Women."

She was also a prominent member of the U.S. delegation to the United Nation's Fourth World Conference of Women in Beijing in 1995. (CKC)

Bibliography

Abzug, Bella. *Bella! Ms. Abzug Goes to Washington.* New York: Saturday Review Press, 1972.

Abzug, Bella and Mim Kelber. *Gender Gap: Bella Abzug's Guide to Political Power for American Women.* Boston: Houghton Mifflin, 1984.

"Bella Abzug." *The Nation* 261, no. 7 (September 11, 1995): 230.

"'Empowering Women': Opening speech by Bella Abzug at the World Women's Congress for a Healthy Planet." *Women's International Network News.* 18, no. 1 (Winter 1992).

Roberta Achtenberg (1950–)

Roberta Achtenberg was the executive director of the National Center for Lesbian Rights in the 1980s. After she served on the San Francisco Board of Supervisors, President Bill Clinton appointed Achtenberg as assistant secretary of housing and urban development for fair housing and equal opportunity in 1993. She was the first open lesbian ever appointed to a high-ranking Cabinet position. (CKC)

Bibliography

Nominations of Kenneth D. Brody, Roberta Achtenberg, and Nicolas P. Retsinas: Hearing Before the Committee on Banking, Housing and Urban Affairs. United States Senate, April 29, 1993. Washington, DC: U.S. Government Printing Office.

Stoddard, Tom. "Man and Woman of the Year. (Tony Kushner; Roberta Achtenberg)." *The Advocate* no. 645 (December 28, 1993): 45.

Abigail Adams (1744–1818)

Married in 1764, Abigail and John Adams formed one of the most notable political partnerships in American history. Abigail was the rock of support for her ambitious and anxious husband, who was successively revolutionary, diplomat, vice president, and president. A coequal in his endeavors, she was his most trusted confidant. She was also one of the most notable and preeminent women of the early Republic, important in her own right as a writer, historian, and one of the country's first suffragettes.

On the eve of independence in 1776, Abigail Adams reminded her husband, John Adams, and his colleagues in the Continental Congress, to "remember the ladies." Library of Congress.

Abigail often lamented her lack of formal education. She matured in a family environment that imbued her with the traditional role of women as wives and mothers, but also encouraged a wide range of reading and learning. Consequently, Abigail became more broadly concerned that American women were denied the education available to men. She was an early proponent of women's rights, political as well as educational. On the eve of independence in 1776, she urged John, a member of the revolutionary congress, to "Remember the ladies," warning that women would not accept laws in which they had no voice. During her husband's often extended absences as congressman and diplomat, she had great success in managing the family farm and business affairs. She also spent time abroad with her husband, supervising his diplomatic households. When her husband became the nation's second president in 1797, Abigail was responsible for furnishing and managing the new, hardly habitable presidential mansion. She knew from experience that women were capable of fusing traditional with less conventional roles.

Abigail Adams was an unusual woman. The revolutionary moment, coupled with her husband's appreciation of her talents and abilities, enabled her to make a great impact on her era. She was a strong advocate for the recognition of women's intellect, education, and right to a political role in the new nation. At her death, her son John Quincy Adams, who would be sixth president of the U.S., noted, "Her life gave the lie to every libel on her sex that was ever written." (RRT) **See also** First Ladies.

Bibliography

Adams, Abigail. *New Letters of Abigail Adams 1788–1801.* Boston: Houghton Mifflin, 1947.

Akers, Charles W. *Abigail Adams—An American Woman.* Boston: Little Brown, 1980.

Butterfield, L. H. *The Book of Abigail and John—Selected Letters of the Adams Family 1762–1784.* Cambridge, MA: Harvard University Press, 1975.

Lee Levin, Phyllis. *Abigail Adams—A Biography.* New York: St. Martin's Press, 1987.

Louisa Catherine Adams (1775–1852)

In 1797, Louisa Catherine Johnson married John Quincy Adams, son of John and **Abigail Adams**, the early Republic's eminent couple. Often remembered only as the wife of the famous diplomat, congressman, and sixth president, she constructed a role that enabled her to move beyond her identity as an Adams wife. Louisa Adams was an accomplished writer, poet, and musician. She mitigated the negative impact of John Quincy Adams's stern personality. Her skills as a hostess facilitated his work in public and private, whether in Washington, or abroad in Berlin and St. Petersburg, Russia.

Louisa Catherine Adams, the wife of President John Quincy Adams, was an accomplished writer and musician. Library of Congress.

She suffered great physical and emotional distress in the White House during her husband's unpopular presidency. Still, despite illness, family trauma, and a dislike for "This great unsocial house," she more than met the expectations she faced as first lady. Louisa contributed much to John Quincy's career, and chafed at her secondary role. Like her mother-in-law Abigail Adams, she decried the suppression of women. She wrote, "I shall never consent to have our sex considered in an inferior point of light." On her death, in a tribute to her reputation, she became the first woman in whose honor Congress adjourned. (RRT) **See also** First Ladies.

BIBLIOGRAPHY

Nagel, Paul C. *The Adams Women*. New York: Oxford University Press, 1987.

Shepherd, Jack. *Cannibals of the Heart: A Personal Biography of Louisa Catherine and John Quincy Adams*. New York: McGraw Hill, 1980.

Jane Addams (1860–1935)

Social reformer and peacemaker, Jane Addams was born in Cedarville, Illinois, on September 6, 1860. She graduated at the top of her class from Rockford Female Seminary in 1882 and attended the Woman's Medical College of Pennsylvania for one year before deciding not to pursue a medical career. In 1889, after returning from a tour of Europe where she and a friend, Ellen Gates Starr, visited London's Toynbee Hall, a settlement house, Addams founded **Hull House** in Chicago. Hull House offered charitable services to the poor, including **child care**, medical services, job training, and legal aid. Addams's work at Hull House to protect immigrants and industrial workers led her into politics. She lobbied for social reforms, including child labor and worker safety laws. Addams wrote 10 books and more than 200 articles, gave hundreds of speeches in the United States and throughout the world, and was awarded 13 honorary degrees. Addams later became active in the **suffrage** movement, and served as the first vice president of the National American Women Suffrage Alliance from 1910 to 1914. In 1915, she was elected chair of the **Women's Peace Party** and president of the first International Congress of Women at the Hague at which the International Women's League for Peace and Freedom was founded. She was a founder of the American Civil Liberties Union and actively campaigned on behalf of African Americans, immigrants, and disadvantaged groups. In 1931, she became the first American woman awarded the Nobel Peace Prize. (GVS)

BIBLIOGRAPHY

McCree, M. ed. *The Jane Addams Papers*. Swarthmore College Peace Collection. Ann Arbor, MI: University Microfilms International, 1985.

Tims, M. *Jane Addams of Hull-House*. New York: Macmillan, 1961.

Bertha Adkins (1906–1983)

Bertha Adkins first began her political career by helping to rally women's votes for Dwight Eisenhower in her home state of Maryland during the 1952 presidential election. In 1953, Adkins served as executive director of the Women's Division of the Republican National Committee and eventually was appointed assistant national chair. In 1958, she became undersecretary of health, education, and welfare. In 1972, she was named executive vice-chair of the Older American Advisory Committee to HEW and the chair of the National Council on Aging.

BIBLIOGRAPHY

Adkins, Bertha. "Vote Republican." *Independent Woman* 35 (October 1956): 3, 34.

"Obituaries." *New York Times* (January 15, 1983): 11.

Adkins v. Children's Hospital (1923)

The Minimum Wage Act of 1918 created the Minimum Wage Board, an agency authorized to investigate the wages of women and minors and to establish a minimum wage. However, both the act and the board came into question in *Adkins v. Children's Hospital*, 261 U.S. 525 (1923). Several women who were employed at Children's Hospital, where they voluntarily worked for less than the minimum wage, lost their jobs due to intervention by the Minimum Wage Board. These women, who had been satisfied with their pay, hours, and working conditions, brought the suit to suspend the minimum wage law so they might take whatever jobs they desired.

In a vote of 5-3, the Supreme Court found the Minimum Wage Act in violation of the due process clause of the Fifth Amendment. The Court reasoned that the right to contract one's services was a part of the liberty of the individual, protected by the Fifth Amendment to the Constitution. This conclusion was based in great part on factors the Minimum Wage Board did not consider when setting a standard minimum wage, including the capacity and earning power of the employee, the number and frequency of hours worked, the character or circumstances of the surroundings, and the capabilities of a worker. Since the board focused solely on the presumed necessities of living and preservation of health for the women, not the individual freedom of the female employees, the case was decided in the workers' favor. However, this decision was overturned in 1937 by *West Coast Hotel Company v. Parrish*. **See also** Minimum Wage/Maximum Hours Laws.

BIBLIOGRAPHY

Cohen, Harry. "Minimum Wage Legislation and the Adkins Case." *New York Law Review* 2 (1925): 48.

Zimmerman, Joan G. "The Jurisprudence of Equality: The Women's Minimum Wage, the First Equal Rights Amendment and *Adkins v. Children's Hospital*, 1905–1923." *Journal of American History* 78, no. 1 (1991): 188–225.

Adolescent Family Life Act (1981)

The Adolescent Family Life Act amended the **Public Health Service Act** of 1970 to add Title XX, a program designed to prevent early sexual activity and adolescent pregnancy and to help adolescents with children improve their parenting skills, knowledge, and self-sufficiency. Establishing a partnership between community organizations and the federal government, the act provides grants to support services and research related to adolescent pregnancy and parenthood. The program includes such services as (1) pregnancy testing and maternity counseling; (2) adoption counseling; (3) health services, including prenatal and pediatric care; (4) education and family planning; and (5) other health, referral, and education services. While **abortion** counseling and referrals for abortion were permitted, funds could not be used to perform abortions.

Since its inception, approximately 196 care and prevention projects and 63 research projects have been supported by the program. Projects have examined factors that influence adolescent sexual, contraceptive, and fertility behaviors; the nature and effectiveness of services for pregnant and parenting adolescents; and reasons why adoption is rarely used as an alternative among pregnant adolescents. All care and prevention projects funded through the program are required to include an independent evaluation component. Research projects supported by the program are undertaken in an effort to improve understanding of the issues surrounding adolescent sexuality, pregnancy, and parenting. (JJK)

Bibliography

Collins, Carol C. and Oliver Trager, eds. *Abortion, The Continuing Controversy.* New York: Facts on File Publications, 1984.

Horan, Dennis J., Edward R. Grant, and Paige C. Cunningham, eds. *Abortion and the Constitution, Reversing Roe v. Wade Through the Courts.* Washington, DC: Georgetown University Press, 1987.

Affirmative Action

The generic term "affirmative action" refers to special programs, usually for admissions or hiring, that take some kind of initiative to increase, maintain, or promote within the larger group, certain group members usually defined by race or gender. The programs have been adopted to remedy past patterns and practices of race and gender discrimination. However, affirmative action programs are highly controversial because race and gender are usually thought to be irrelevant to employment and admissions decisions.

The origins of affirmative action are in the executive branch of government. The term "affirmative action" was officially used when President John F. Kennedy issued Executive Order 10925 on March 16, 1961, prohibiting government contractors from discriminating in their hiring practices and requiring them to take affirmative action. The requirement was more symbolic than real because enforcement was ineffective.

After many civil rights demonstrations, a shift in public sentiment, and as a legacy to President John F. Kennedy, Congress passed the **Civil Rights Act of 1964**. The act included **Title VII**, which prohibited discrimination on the basis of race, color, religion, sex, or national origin by employers or labor unions. Provisions of the act called for remedial steps, such as affirmative action, to undo past patterns of discrimination. The act created the **Equal Employment Opportunity Commission (EEOC)** for private sector enforcement of civil rights.

The real foundation for affirmative action programs was established in 1965 when President Lyndon B. Johnson issued Executive Order 11246 which prohibited discrimination on the basis of race, color, religion, or national origin by federal contractors and subcontractors. The executive order provided for enforcement by creating the Office of Federal Contract Compliance (OFCC) in the Department of Labor. The Department promised effective enforcement, required a demonstration of nondiscrimination, and threatened contractors with contract cancellation for noncompliance. In 1967, the executive order was amended by President Johnson in **Executive Order 11375** to expand coverage to women.

Contractors needed guidance as to how to comply with the executive order's affirmative action requirements. For several years, the OFCC worked at creating a model for industry standards by using African Americans in the Philadelphia construction industry as their trial target group. This effort became known as "the Philadelphia Plan." Based on this experience, the Department of Labor issued final guidelines, called Revised Order 4, in 1971. These guidelines required contractors to assess minority group numbers in the relevant employment pool, count the numbers of minorities employed in their own companies, and, if there was a disparity, establish for themselves hiring goals and timetables. Using these guidelines, underutilization of minorities and women was defined as "having fewer minorities or women in a particular job classification than would reasonably be expected by their availability."

Generally, Democrats supported affirmative action and Republicans did not. Under Democratic President Jimmy Carter (1977–1981), affirmative action efforts were consolidated and made more effective by an executive order he issued in 1978, which gave the OFCC complete responsibility rather than just overview responsibility for enforcement over all government contractors. However, Republican President Ronald Reagan (1981–1989) tried to weaken affirmative action during his eight years in office. He publicly criticized it and cut the budget and number of OFCC employees. Although less ideological than Reagan, Republican President George Bush (1989–1993) also opposed affirmative action. Democratic President Bill Clinton (1993–), while supporting it, has done so less aggressively than other Democratic presidents.

During much of this period, however, affirmative action was debated and decided in the courts. In the first Supreme Court affirmative action case, Allan Bakke sued the University of California, Davis, claiming that he had been turned down by their medical school when he applied for admission in 1973 because the university used racial quotas and admitted "less qualified" minority applicants.

On June 28, 1978, the Court rendered its decision in *Bakke v. University of California*. The judicial text consisted of six separate opinions and two separate majorities. By a 5-4 margin, the Court found the Davis Medical School affirmative action program, with its fixed number of seats for minorities, unacceptable. However, by a different 5-4 majority, the Court accepted race-conscious admissions and the principles of affirmative action as being consistent with the Constitution and with Title VI of the Civil Rights Act of 1964.

During the next decade, except when employee layoffs were involved, a divided Court rendered decisions that were generally in support of affirmative action. In 1979, in the *United Steelworkers v. Weber* case, it found acceptable the Kaiser Aluminum and Chemical Corporation's affirmative action program, which earmarked trainee openings for blacks. In 1980, in *Fullilove v. Klutznick*, the Supreme Court found permissible a congressional affirmative action 10 percent set-aside program for minority businesspeople.

In 1984 and 1986, when it came to employee layoffs, the Court did not support affirmative action goals. In the *Firefighters Local Union No. 178 v. Stotts* and in the *Wygant v. Jackson Board of Education* cases, the Court shifted from its more race-conscious permissive view because the seniority system could not be disregarded even if affirmative action goals and achievements were undone in the process of laying people off.

However, the Court again upheld affirmative action principles in two cases decided in 1987. In the *United States v. Paradise*, the Court affirmed Alabama's program of promoting one black state police trooper for each white trooper promoted. In ***Johnson v. Transportation Agency, Santa Clara County, California***, the Court affirmed what it called the moderate and flexible "case by case approach" of the Santa Clara County transit district's affirmative action program, which had promoted a woman who ranked third in examination scores over a man tied for second.

Eight years in the White House allowed President Ronald Reagan to appoint conservative justices as more liberal ones retired. By 1987, he had appointed three new justices, **Sandra Day O'Connor**, Antonin Scalia, and Anthony M. Kennedy, and had elevated conservative William H. Rehnquist to chief justice. Starting in 1989, the Supreme Court began reversing its majority pro-affirmative action position.

The Supreme Court opposed affirmative action principles during its 1989 session. In the *Richmond v. Crosen*, ***Wards Cove Packing Company v. Antonio***, and *Martin v. Wilks* cases, the Court broke with recent precedent. In the *Richmond* case, it ruled a 1983 Richmond, Virginia, affirmative action ordinance that channeled 30 percent of public works funds to minority-owned construction companies violated the Constitution. In *Wards Cove*, the Court reversed an 18-year precedent of prohibiting not only employment practices *intended* to discriminate, but also affirmative action, by ruling that whites may bring reverse discrimination claims against judge-approved affirmative action plans. This meant that consent decrees, which had settled many discrimination suits, could once again be opened and were vulnerable to future litigation.

In the 1990s, Congress and the business community would also get involved in determining the fate of affirmative action programs. In 1990, the Supreme Court decided another affirmative action case by a bare majority; it supported an affirmative action program in *Metro Broadcasting Inc. v. Federal Communications Commission*, defending the right of Congress to provide affirmative actions for minorities and women in issuing broadcasting licenses. But Supreme Court justices who had defended affirmative action principles were retiring. Five years later, only one of the five justices favoring affirmative action in this case, Justice John Paul Stevens, would still be on the Court.

The Democratic Congress tried to affect the fate of affirmative action by responding to the Supreme Court decisions. Many liberals in Congress, with the help of civil rights allies, began to prepare civil rights legislation designed to undo the anti-affirmative action Supreme Court decisions, especially the *Ward Cove* and *Martin* cases. The congressional sponsors, Senator Edward Kennedy (D-MA) and Representative Augustus Hawkins (D-CA), saw a Democratic congressional majority easily pass the bill in 1990 and Republican President George Bush veto it. Congress did not have the votes to override his veto.

Prominent leaders in the business community took the initiative in December 1990 and began working with civil rights advocates to save the bill. But the Bush administration actually worked to sabotage the business sector's efforts, fearing that a compromise bill would remove affirmative action as a partisan issue. **Republican Party** strategists believed that a Republican anti-affirmative action position would help get President Bush reelected in 1992. A surprising turn of events, however, reversed Bush's position on the civil rights bill.

David Duke, a self-described former Ku Klux Klan member and explicit racist, became the Republican candidate for Senate in Louisiana. The Republican Party wanted to disassociate itself from him. Continuing to support an anti-civil rights position became problematic for President Bush because such a position might seem too similar to Duke's. In 1991, Congress again passed a civil rights bill reinstating some features of affirmative action; this time, President Bush signed the bill into law.

While the Republican Party sought and failed to make affirmative action a pivotal issue in the 1996 presidential election, the Supreme Court continued to make decisions that struck down affirmative action programs without striking down the principle of affirmative action. In 1995, in *Adarand v. Pena*, the Court overturned its *Metro Broadcasting* decision. In *Adarand*, which decided the validity of a program that benefited minority- and women-owned highway construction businesses, the Court now set restrictive parameters declaring that treating a person differently because of race or ethnic origin is inherently suspect. Government can adopt affirmative action programs only when it can demonstrate a compelling interest to do so. It must prove that its programs correct real and present discrimination.

Some states have gone even further than the Supreme Court and have tried to outlaw affirmative action altogether. California's successful attempt, via a referendum, has been the most well-publicized. In November 1997, 54 percent of the California electorate voted in favor of Proposition 209, the California Civil Rights Initiative. The proposition prohibited the implementation of race- and gender-conscious affirmative action programs and banned such state-required programs in California. It is likely that many of the future changes in affirmative action will be made, like this one, on the state level. (RAJ)

Bibliography

Cahn, Stephen M. *Affirmative Action and the University: A Philosophical Inquiry.* Philadelphia: Temple University Press, 1993.

Greene, Kathanne W. *Affirmative Action and Principles of Justice.* New York: Greenwood Press, 1989.

Johnson, Roberta Ann. "Affirmative Action as a Women's Issue." In Lois Lovelace Duke, ed. *Women in Politics.* Upper Saddle River, NJ: Prentice Hall, 1996.

Maguire, Daniel C. *A New American Justice.* New York: Doubleday, 1980.

Mooney, Christopher F., S.J. *Inequality and the American Conscience.* New York: Paulist Press, 1982.

Oralns, Harold, and June O'Neill. "Affirmative Action Revisited." *Annals of the American Academy of Political and Social Science* 523 (September 1992): 144–58.

Rosenfeld, Michel. *Affirmative Action and Justice: A Philosophical and Constitutional Inquiry.* New Haven, CT: Yale University Press, 1991.

Sindler, Allan P. *Equal Opportunity: On the Policy and Politics of Compensatory Minority Preferences.* Washington, DC: American Enterprise Insitute for Public Policy Research, 1983.

Sowell, Thomas. *Civil Rights: Rhetoric or Reality?* New York: William Morrow, 1984.

Wilkinson, Harvey J., III. *From Brown to Bakke: The Supreme Court and School Integration.* New York: Oxford University Press, 1979.

Aid to Families with Dependent Children (AFDC)

The federal government created the Aid to Dependent Children (ADC) program, later renamed Aid to Families with Dependent Children (AFDC) program, as part of the Social Security Act of 1935. The ADC program was established "for the purpose of encouraging the care of dependent children in their own homes." Based on the philosophy behind Mothers' Pensions programs in the states, ADC enabled poor women to remain out of the workforce and stay home to rear their children. The law was designed to provide aid to needy children "deprived of parental support or care by reason of the death, continued absence from the home, or physical or mental incapacity of the parent."

AFDC was a joint federal-state cash grant program in which the federal government paid for approximately half to three-quarters of the costs; the federal share rose as the state's per capita income fell. The states retained the power to decide the level of benefits and, because AFDC benefits, unlike social security benefits, did not rise with inflation, their value steadily declined over time.

In 1967 and 1971, Congress placed more emphasis on encouraging AFDC recipients to work, creating Work Incentive Programs in which AFDC beneficiaries were required to accept jobs or enroll in work-training programs. In 1981, as part of the Omnibus Budget Reconciliation Act, Congress decreased the AFDC rolls by raising the eligibility levels, reducing the amount of income that could be earned by a family on AFDC, and lowering the deduction allowed for work-related expenses.

The **Family Support Act of 1988** required states to create programs to assist AFDC recipients to find jobs and leave the welfare rolls. The law also provided for transitional medical and **child care** benefits to women leaving **welfare** for work. The success of these programs was limited because states were unable to contribute enough money to it.

Based partly on President Bill Clinton's campaign promise to "end welfare as we know it," Congress repealed the AFDC program, replacing it with the Personal Responsibility and Work Opportunity Reconciliation Act of 1996. The most important part of the 1996 act is contained in the Block Grants to States for Temporary Assistance for Needy Families (TANF) program. Under TANF, recipients have to go to work within two years of receiving support, and there is a lifetime limit of five years during which recipients can collect benefits. (SM) **See also** Social Security.

Bibliography

Handler, Joel F. *The Poverty of Welfare Reform.* New Haven, CT: Yale University Press, 1995.

Piven, Frances Fox and Richard A. Cloward. *Regulating the Poor: The Functions of Public Welfare.* New York: Vintage Books, 1993.

Teles, Steven M. *Whose Welfare? AFDC and Elite Politics.* Lawrence: University of Kansas Press, 1996.

Akron v. Akron Center for Reproductive Health (1983)

In *Akron v. Akron Center for Reproductive Health,* 463 U.S. 416 (1983), the Supreme Court struck down an Akron, Ohio, city ordinance regulating abortions, ruling that the provisions unconstitutionally interfered with the right to an **abortion** established in ***Roe v. Wade*** (1973). The Akron city ordinance, entitled "Regulation of Abortions," included seven restrictions on abortions, five of which were challenged: (1) a requirement that abortions performed after the first trimester be performed in a hospital; (2) notification and consent by one parent 24 hours prior to an abortion performed on an unmarried minor; (3) a provision that physicians make certain statements to ensure informed consent, including "the unborn child is a human life from the moment of conception"; (4) a 24-hour waiting period after a woman has signed a consent form and before the abortion is performed; and (5) that fetal remains be disposed of in a "humane and sanitary" manner. In a 6-3 decision, the Supreme Court reaffirmed the *Roe* decision, which established a woman's fundamental, though not unqualified, right to an abortion. The potential life of the fetus and the health of the woman obtaining an abortion were recognized in *Roe* as interests that justified state regulations of abortion. The abortion regulations in the *Akron* case, however, were seen by the Court as a significant burden on the woman obtaining an abortion. Justice **Sandra Day O'Connor** dissented from the Court's opinion, arguing that *Roe* "is clearly on a collision course with itself" because the trimester framework does not resolve the conflict between individual rights, compelling state interests, and advancing medical technology. (LvA) **See also** Reproductive and Contraceptive Technologies for Women.

Bibliography

Craig, Barbara Hinkson and David M. O'Brien. *Abortion and American Politics.* Chatham, NJ: Chatham House Publishers, 1993.

Shapiro, Ian, ed. *Abortion: The Supreme Court Decisions.* Indianapolis: Hackett Publishing Company, Inc., 1995.

Madeleine Albright (1937–)

As the second woman to serve as U.S. ambassador to the United Nations, Madeleine Albright was an effective voice for U.S. foreign policy views. She was instrumental in facilitating UN action in both Bosnia and Haiti during President Bill Clinton's first term. In 1996, she became the first woman to serve as U.S. secretary of state. A Czech-born immigrant who lost her grandparents in the Nazi Holocaust, she is known for her hawkish views and her ability to negotiate a tough deal. Her prior political experience included serving on the staff of Senator Edmund Muskie (D-ME) from 1976 to 1978 as chief legislative assistant and as a staff member of the National Security Council. A loyal Democrat, Albright has served as foreign policy advisor to the presidential campaigns of Walter Mondale (1984), Michael Dukakis (1988), and Bill Clinton (1992, 1996). (JCS)

Bibliography

Blood, Thomas. *Madame Secretary.* New York: St. Martins, 1997.

Breslau, Karen, Carroll Bogert, and Arlyn Tobias Gajilan. "Bright Light." *Newsweek* 10 (February 1997): 23–29.

Alexander v. Yale University (1980)

In *Alexander v. Yale University,* 631 F.2d 178 (2d Cir. 1980), the federal courts recognized that sexual harassment of students violates **Title IX of the Educational Amendments of 1972**, the law banning **sex discrimination** in institutions receiving federal financial assistance. The case arose when female undergraduates and a male faculty member filed suit against Yale University on the grounds of sexual harassment. They argued that Yale violated Title IX because it had no policy against sexual harassment and had not instituted a grievance procedure to investigate complaints such as theirs. The lower court ruled against them and declined to order Yale to establish a grievance procedure for charges of harassment.

On appeal, the Second Circuit Court of Appeals upheld the trial judge. The appellate court held that the students had not proved their charges of sexual harassment against the university. Because they could not show that they had been harmed, they could not complain about the university's failure to establish a grievance procedure for receiving students' sexual harassment complaints.

Although the plaintiffs lost their suit because they lacked specific evidence of harassment, *Alexander* established the principle that sexual harassment of students is forbidden by Title IX. (SM)

Bibliography

Dziech, Billie Wright and Linda Weiner. *The Lecherous Professor: Sexual Harassment on Campus.* Boston: Beacon Press, 1984.

Alice Doesn't Day Strike (October 29, 1975)

Orchestrated by the **National Organization for Women (NOW)** to commemorate NOW's tenth anniversary, the Alice Doesn't Day Strike committee urged women to refrain from fulfilling their work, parental, and household duties for one day to demonstrate the enormous contributions women make to American society. "Alice Doesn't" was taken from *Alice Doesn't Live Here Anymore*, a film that dealt with a woman's move to escape an unhappy life. The strike was not nearly as successful as previous mass actions and resulted in as much media coverage of an antifeminist group, The National Coalition to Restore Women's Rights, who vowed to wear pink and bake cookies, as it did for feminists. **See also** Antifeminism; Feminism. (CKC)

Bibliography

Klemesrud, Judy. "Most of the Nation's 'Alice's' Stay on Job Ignoring NOW's Call for One-Day Strike." *New York Times* (October 30, 1975): 44.

Stephen, Beverly. "Evolution of the '75 Women's Strike Day." *San Francisco Chronicle* (October 30, 1975): 12.

Florence Ellinwood Allen (1884–1966)

Florence Allen was the first woman to serve on a state trial court, a state supreme court, and a federal court. Allen served on a general jurisdiction court in Ohio for two years before moving to the state supreme court in 1922, where she served two terms for a total of 12 years. Allen was appointed to the Sixth Circuit Court of Appeals by President Franklin Roosevelt in 1934. She served until her retirement in 1959. No other women were chosen to the federal courts until Lyndon Johnson

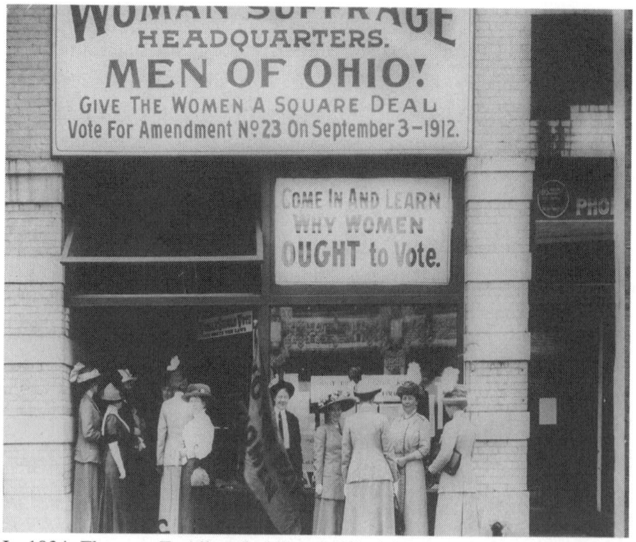

In 1934, Florence E. Allen (holding the flag) became the first woman appointed to a federal court; she is shown here at Woman Suffrage Headquarters in Cleveland, Ohio, in 1912. Library of Congress, National American Woman Suffrage Association Collection.

appointed **Shirley Hufstedler** to the Ninth Circuit in 1968. Allen had the further distinction of being the first woman seriously considered for the United States Supreme Court. She actively campaigned for the seat and made it to a short list. (RLP)

BIBLIOGRAPHY

Cook, Beverly B. "The First Woman Candidate for the Supreme Court." *Yearbook 1981 Supreme Court Historical Society*. 19–35.

______. "Women as Supreme Court Candidates from Florence Allen to Sandra O'Connor." *Judicature* 65, no. 6 (December-January 1982): 314–26.

Maryon Pittman Allen (1926–)

Maryon Allen, a Democrat, was appointed to her first political post in 1974 when she was made chairwoman of the Blair House Fine Arts Commission by President Gerald R. Ford. In 1978, Allen was appointed to the U.S. Senate, filling the vacancy created by the death of her husband James B. Allen. She served in the Senate for Alabama from June 8, 1978, until November 7, 1978, having failed to win renomination to fill out the term until 1981.

BIBLIOGRAPHY

Cohen, Richard. "Widows in Congress as Surrogate Males." *The Washington Post* (October 15, 1978): B1.

American Association of University Women (AAUW)

Founded in 1881, the American Association of University Women (AAUW) is a national organization dedicated to achieving educational equity for girls and women. It has over 150,000 members in over 2,000 local branches. Affiliated with the International Federation of University Women, a nongovernmental organization of the United Nations, AAUW was founded as an outlet for college-educated women, but it began admitting men in 1987. AAUW has focused attention on sexual harassment in schools and on promoting high self-esteem among girls through national and local initiatives.

Although active in a number of areas, the American Association of University Women focuses mainly on increasing educational opportunities for women. Photo by Marcia Fram. National Archives.

AAUW supports pro-choice policies and is a member of the Women's Network for Change. Headquartered in Washington, the organization publishes a bimonthly report, *AAUW Outlook*. (JHT) **See also** Educational Equity Act (1974).

BIBLIOGRAPHY

Costain, Anne N. *Inviting Women's Rebellion: A Political Process Interpretation of the Women's Movement*. Baltimore: Johns Hopkins University Press, 1992.

Slavin, Sarah, ed. *U.S. Women's Interest Groups: Institutional Profiles*. Westport, CT: Greenwood Press, 1995.

American Birth Control League

The American Birth Control League was established in 1939 by **Margaret Sanger** to address the nationwide debate of whether birth control should be accepted by the national government. The organization distributed information on birth control and physicians who would dispense birth control. In 1942, the league changed its name to the **Planned Parenthood Federation of America (PPFA)**, adding to its legislative agenda other services, including leadership coordination, information, and training programs in contraception, **abortion**, sterilization, and infertility services.

BIBLIOGRAPHY

Gordon, Linda. *Woman's Body, Woman's Right*. New York: Grossman, 1976.

Reed, James. *From Private Vice to Public Virtue*. New York: Basic Books, 1978.

American Woman Suffrage Association (AWSA)

The American Woman Suffrage Association (AWSA) was founded in 1869 at a convention in Cleveland, Ohio, led by **Lucy Stone**. The AWSA consisted largely of moderate feminists who disapproved of the tactics and programs of the more radical **National Woman Suffrage Association (NWSA)**, which was led by **Susan B. Anthony** and **Elizabeth Cady Stanton**. Drawing its membership mainly from New England, the AWSA sought a political alliance with the **Republican Party**, believing such a connection offered the most likely route to **suffrage**. The AWSA focused all its energies on the suffrage issue and concentrated its efforts at the state level. From 1870 to 1872, the AWSA published the ***Woman's Journal***, which was edited by Stone. In 1890, the AWSA and the NWSA merged to form the **National American Woman Suffrage Association (NAWSA)**.

BIBLIOGRAPHY

Blackwell, Alice Stone. *Lucy Stone, Pioneer of Woman's Rights*. Boston: Little Brown, 1930.

Hays, Eleanor R. *Morning Star: A Biography of Lucy Stone 1818–1893*. New York: Harcourt Brace & World, 1961.

Jessie Daniel Ames (1883–1972)

Jessie Ames worked with the Texas Equal Suffrage Association starting in 1916, eventually being elected treasurer in 1918. She also became the founding president of the Texas League of Women Voters in 1919 and was a representative for the organization at the 1923 Pan-American Conference. Ames served as a delegate at the 1920 and 1924 **Democratic Party** national conventions and as an alternate delegate in 1928. In 1930, Ames founded the **Association of Southern Women for the Prevention of Lynching (ASWPL)**. She served as director until the group disbanded in 1942.

BIBLIOGRAPHY

Hall, Jacquelyn Dowd. *Revolt Against Chivalry: Jessie Daniel Ames and the Women's Campaign Against Lynching.* New York: Columbia University Press, 1979.

Miller, Kathleen. "The Ladies and the Lynchers: A Look at the Association of Southern Women for the Prevention of Lynching." *Southern Studies* 17, no. 3 (Fall 1978): 221–40.

Eugenie Moore Anderson (1909–)

Eugenie Anderson began her political career in the 1930s when she joined the nonpartisan **National League of Women Voters**. In the 1940s, she ran the campaigns for the Democratic-Labor party candidate in her Minnesota district. Anderson worked for the Truman presidential campaign in 1948. In 1949, with the endorsement of influential Minnesota politicians, she was appointed U. S. ambassador to Denmark, a position she held from December 22, 1949, to January 19, 1953.

In 1962, Anderson became ambassador to Bulgaria, serving until December 6, 1964. Anderson took a number of other diplomatic assignments at the United Nations, including acting as U.S. representative to the United Nations General Assembly from 1965 to 1967, serving on the Trusteeship Council in the United Nations from 1965 to 1968, and working on the Economic Commission for Europe in 1966.

BIBLIOGRAPHY

Lesiser, E. "Denmark's American Sweetheart." *Saturday Evening Post* (May 5, 1951): 14–16.

McQuarters, Geneva F. "Representing United States—An American Family." *Independent Woman* 29 (January 1950): 2–4.

"U.S. Ambassadors." *Time* (December 31, 1951): 23–27.

Marian Anderson (1897–1993)

In 1939, renowned classical singer Marian Anderson became a voice in the civil rights movement when the **Daughters of the American Revolution** refused to rent Constitution Hall in Washington, DC, to her for a concert because she was African American. The situation was finally resolved when it came to the attention of First Lady **Eleanor Roosevelt** who invited Anderson to perform at the Lincoln Memorial to an audience of 75,000. Citing the incident, Anderson began speaking nationally on the injustices of discrimination and on the benefits of people working together.

BIBLIOGRAPHY

Black, Allida M. "Championing a Champion: Eleanor Roosevelt and the Marian Anderson 'Freedom Concert.'" *Presidential Studies Quarterly* 20, no. 4 (1990): 719–36.

Elizabeth Bullock Andrews (1911–)

In 1972, Elizabeth Andrews won the special election to fill the remaining portion of the U.S. House term belonging to her late husband, Alabama Representative George W. Andrews. The first woman elected to Congress from Alabama, Andrews served from April 4, 1972, until January 3, 1973.

BIBLIOGRAPHY

Chamberlin, Hope. *A Minority of Members.* New York: Praeger, 1973.

Susan Brownell Anthony (1820–1906)

An outstanding leader of the first women's rights movement, Susan B. Anthony worked tirelessly for more than half a century traveling, speaking, and campaigning on behalf of woman **suffrage**. Born in Adams, Massachusetts, on Febuary 15, 1820, Anthony grew up in a Quaker household and taught school in her early teens. Although she did not attend the 1848 **Seneca Falls Convention** with her parents and sister, she immediately became involved in the suffrage, **temperance**, and **abolition** movements. Remaining single, she was able to devote herself completely to these movements, most effectively working behind the scenes because she lacked natural speaking abilities. In 1852, when Anthony, as a woman, was denied the right to speak at a temperance rally in Albany, she and **Elizabeth Cady Stanton** founded the New York State Women's Temperance Society. Anthony and Stanton worked during the 1850s to improve the status of married women's property rights. In 1868, they formed the Working Women's Association. Throughout the Civil War, Anthony and Stanton worked with the abolitionist movement, however, when the Fifteenth Amendment did not include women in granting suffrage to slaves, they formed the **National Woman Suffrage Association (NWSA)** to work exclusively for woman suffrage. In 1868, Anthony began publishing the *Revolution,* a weekly newspaper advocating improvement in divorce laws, employment opportunity, and other women's rights. Anthony attempted to vote in the 1872 presidential election, but was arrested, tried without a jury, and fined $100, which she refused to pay. In 1881, she wrote the first volume of *History of Woman Suffrage*. When the NWSA merged with the **American Woman Suffrage Association (AWSA)** to form the **National Ameri-**

Working closely with Elizabeth Cady Stanton (seated), Susan B. Anthony (standing) was one of the most important leaders of the woman suffrage movement. Library of Congress, National American Woman Suffrage Association Collection.

can Woman Suffrage Association (NAWSA), Anthony served as president from 1892 to 1900. Although Anthony died March 13, 1906, before winning victory for woman suffrage, she predicted at the last women's rights convention she attended that, "Failure is impossible." (LvA)

BIBLIOGRAPHY

Barry, Kathleen. *Susan B. Anthony: A Biography of a Singular Feminist*. New York: New York University Press, 1988.

Harper, Ida Husted. *The Life and Work of Susan B. Anthony*. Indianapolis: Hollenback Press, 1898.

Sherr, Lynn. *Failure Is Impossible: Susan B. Anthony in Her Own Words*. New York: Time Books, 1995.

Antifeminism

As the feminist movement developed in the U.S., an organized antifeminist movement developed to counter it. Antifeminist organizations, such as Eagle Forum, **STOP ERA**, and **Concerned Women for America (CWA),** were organized by women. Many of these women held religious beliefs that kept them out of the paid labor force, and therefore they had significant time to devote to the movement. Antifeminist groups succeeded in blocking ratification of the **Equal Rights Amendment**, even though the majority of the population supported the amendment.

Antifeminist activists seek to promote traditional women's roles as wives and mothers. Antifeminist ideology holds that men and women are made by God to fulfill different roles, and thereby have different talents and weaknesses. Men are meant to work outside the home and to dominate the world of politics and business, while women have special nurturing talents that make them better able to deal with children and elder parents. Many antifeminists also believe that women should obey their husbands, and that men should make the major decisions in the family.

As a consequence, antifeminists oppose most policies that make it easier for women to play nontraditional roles; generally, they work against **affirmative action** plans for women, after-care programs in schools, adoption by lesbian mothers, and women in the military. They also tend to oppose laws that make it easier for men to abandon their responsibilities to support their families, and they seek to toughen divorce and child support laws. In some cases, antifeminists have joined with feminists in supporting anti-pornography legislation.

Studies of antifeminists reveal that they are atypical activists. Most have only a high school education or perhaps some college, are homemakers with modest incomes, and have little interest in politics. Initially, they differ from feminist activists in their deep and conservative religious beliefs and their close involvement in conservative churches, primarily in Protestant fundamentalist, pentecostal, and evangelical denominations. Ironically, many antifeminist leaders, such as **Phyllis Schlafly,** have spent much of their lives traveling the country organizing women politically while promoting the view that women should stay home with their children and husbands. (CW) **See also** Feminism.

BIBLIOGRAPHY

Faludi, Susan. *Backlash: The Undeclared War Against American Women*. New York: Crown, 1991.

Klatch, Rebecca. *Women of the New Right*. Philadelphia: Temple University Press, 1987.

Meylich, Tanya. *The Republican War Against Women*. New York: Bantam, 1996.

Wilcox, Clyde. "Religious Attitudes and Anti-Feminism: An Analysis of the Ohio Moral Majority." *Women & Politics* 7 (1987): 59–78.

Antisuffragism

Antisuffragism refers to the antisuffrage movement, an organized movement against the vote for women. Emerging in the late nineteenth century in response to the successes of the **suffrage** movement, it peaked between 1893 and 1907, but retained sufficient momentum to later cause significant opposition to ratification efforts for the **Nineteenth Amendment**. The movement died with the amendment's ratification in 1920 and many antisuffragists were among the first women to vote.

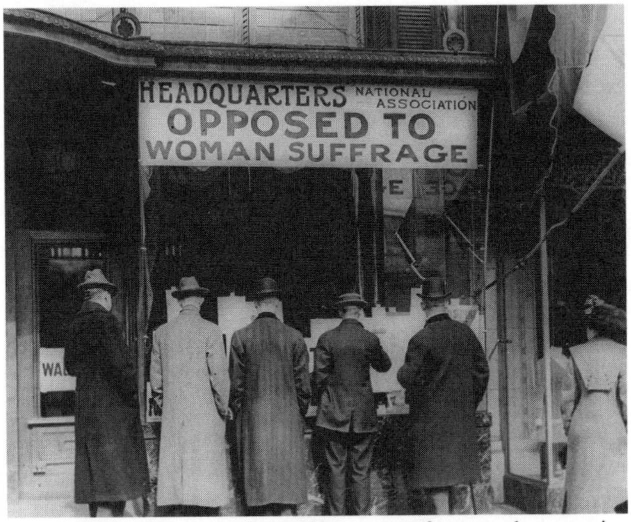

Not all women supported suffrage. Here a group of men are shown peering into the National Anti-Suffrage headquarters. Library of Congress, National American Woman Suffrage Association Collection.

Antisuffragists believed that the entry of women into politics would be disastrous for both women and society. They argued that women had no interest in politics and voting. Despite this perspective, antisuffragist women engaged in such activities as campaigning and lobbying, exactly the type of political behavior they wanted women to avoid. The leaders of the antisuffrage movement were wealthy, urban, Republican women who constituted the best organized element of the movement.

The achievement of suffrage makes it difficult to assess the effectiveness of antisuffragism. It did delay suffrage due to successful efforts at blocking critical pieces of legislation. Antisuffragists began to lose ground in 1917 when new leadership took over the movement and radicalized the political fight. The new leadership attempted to stigmatize suffragists as communists, socialists, or bolshevists. This approach succeeded in making antisuffragists appear to be out-of-touch radicals. After this point, the effectiveness of the movement became limited only to occasionally delaying the inevitable. (JEH)

Camhi, Jane Jerome. *Women Against Women: American Anti-Suffragism, 1880–1920.* Brooklyn: Carlson, 1994.

Jablonsky, Thomas J. *The Home, Heaven, and Mother Party: Female Anti-Suffragists in the United States, 1868–1920.* Brooklyn: Carlson, 1994.

Anne Legendre Armstrong (1927–)

Anne Armstrong gained her first major political position in 1972 when she became the first woman to co-chair a Republican National Convention. Armstrong went on to work in the White House for Richard Nixon, serving as counselor to the president from 1973 until 1974. While in Nixon's administration, Armstrong organized the first Office of Women's Programs on the White House, which brought over 100 women into the government. She acted as the president's expert on women's issues and took active roles during this time in the Organization of Government for the Conduct of Foreign Policy, the Council of Wage and Price Stability, and the Domestic Council. Armstrong also chaired the Federal Property Council and later served as U.S. ambassador to Great Britain and Northern Ireland from January 29, 1976, to March 3, 1977.

BIBLIOGRAPHY

Armstrong, Anne. "Women's Role in Politics." *National Business Women* 53, no. 5 (May 1972): 8.

Jean Spencer Ashbrook (1934–)

Jean Ashbrook was elected to the U.S. Congress as a Republican to fill the vacancy of her deceased husband John Milan Ashbrook. She served as representative for Ohio from July 12, 1982, until January 3, 1983.

BIBLIOGRAPHY

Women in Congress. Washington, DC: Government Printing Office, 1991.

Association of Southern Women for the Prevention of Lynching (ASWPL)

The Association of Southern Women for the Prevention of Lynching (ASWPL) was established by **Jessie Daniel Ames** in 1930. This group worked through church organizations and public demonstrations to prevent the lynching of African-American men. The ASWPL was both a proactive and a reactive organization. It pursued its cause to prevent general mistreatment of blacks, but it also felt a responsibility to act against lynchings because African-American males were often persecuted because white males inaccurately believed they had raped, hurt, or endangered white women. To clarify the mistaken reasons behind these lynchings, the ASWPL denounced bigoted thought during press conferences and other public speaking engagements. The group continued to fight for equality and an end to persecution until 1942, when it disbanded.

BIBLIOGRAPHY

Hall, Jacquelyn Dowd. "Women and Lynching." *Southern Exposure* 4, no. 4 (Winter 1977): 53–54.

Wells-Barnett, Ida. *On Lynching.* New York: Arno Press, 1969.

B

Caroline Lexow Babcock (1882–1980)

In 1904, Caroline Babcock helped organize the Collegiate Equal Suffrage League of New York, soon afterwards becoming president of the organization. She also served as executive secretary of the National College Equal Suffrage League in 1908 and as executive secretary, and then field secretary of **Harriot Stanton Blatch's Women's Political Union** in 1910. In 1919, Babcock became an executive board member of the Women's Peace Society and an organizer for the Women's Peace Union. She worked for the Women's International League for Peace and Freedom in 1935 before becoming executive secretary for the **National Woman's Party (NWP)** in 1938, a position she held until 1946.

Bibliography

Alonso, Harriet Hymen. *The Women's Peace Union and Outlawry of War, 1921–1942.* Knoxville: University of Tennessee Press, 1989.

Savell, Isabelle. *Ladies' Lib: How Rockland Women Got the Vote.* New York: The Historical Society of Rockland County, 1979.

Sarah G. Bagley (d. ca. 1847)

In 1844, Sarah Bagley founded and became first president of the Lowell Female Labor Reform Association, which prompted the Massachusetts legislature to set up a special committee to investigate the treatment of **Lowell Mill Girls**. Bagley testified in hearings for this committee, participating in the first governmental investigation of labor conditions in the United States. She also helped organize other branches of the Female Labor Reform Association in other New England mill towns and worked with labor reform newspapers, including the ***Voice of Industry*** and *Factory Tracts*. Due to her continued work, Bagley became a delegate to the 1946 National Industrial Congress held in Boston. **See also** Lowell Female Industrial Reform and Mutual Aid Society.

Bibliography

Josephson, Hannah. *The Golden Threads: New England's Mill Girls and Magnates.* New York: Russell & Russell, 1967.

Irene Baily Baker (1901–)

Irene Baker's first political appointment came when she served as Republican National Committeewoman for Tennessee, a post she held from 1960 to 1964. On March 10, 1964, Baker became a member of the United States House of Representatives, filling the vacancy created by the death of her husband Howard Baker. She served in Congress until January 3, 1965, when she retired from active politics.

Bibliography

Chamberlin, Hope. *A Minority of Members.* New York: Praeger, 1973.

Emily Greene Balch (1867–1961)

Emily Greene Balch received the 1946 Nobel Peace Prize for her contributions as a leader of the international women's peace movement. A founder of the Denison House Settlement in Boston and of the **National Women's Trade Union League**, Balch's pacifist beliefs precipitated her dismissal from the Wellesley College faculty in 1918 after 22 years of teaching. Balch was subsequently a founding member of the Women's International League for Peace and Freedom, serving as its first international secretary. Always a political activist, she also published extensively, including *Approaches to the Great Settlement* (1918) and *The Miracle of Living* (1941). (MAB) **See also** Pacifism

Bibliography

Randall, Mercedes M. *Improper Bostonian, Emily Greene Balch.* New York: Twayne, 1964.

Kate Barnard (1875–1930)

Kate Barnard was elected to the Oklahoma Commission of Charities and Corrections in 1907, becoming the first woman to win a statewide elective office in the United States. Barnard also served in a number of groups striving for union causes, including on President Woodrow Wilson's U.S. Commission on Industrial Relations in 1914 and as assistant director of the investigation service of the federal Department of Labor from 1918 to 1919.

Bibliography

Barnard, Kate. "Women for the Friendless." *The Independent* 63 (November 28, 1907): 1308.

Bryant, Keith L., Jr. "Kate Barnard, Organized Labor and Social Justice in Oklahoma During the Progressive Era." *Journal of Social History* 35, no. 2 (May 1969): 145–64.

Clara Barton (1821–1912)

Clara Barton worked in the Washington, DC, patent office from 1854 to 1857, making her one of the first appointed woman civil servants. Working independently in the 1860s, she provided medical supplies to wounded Civil War soldiers. In 1865, President Abraham Lincoln appointed her to manage the missing persons bureau, which she did until 1869. While in Europe in 1869, Barton became aware of the activities of the International Red Cross. She served with the Red Cross during the Franco-Prussian War. She returned home, and after a lengthy petition campaign in the United States, Barton began the American Red Cross in 1882 and acted as the organization's president until 1904.

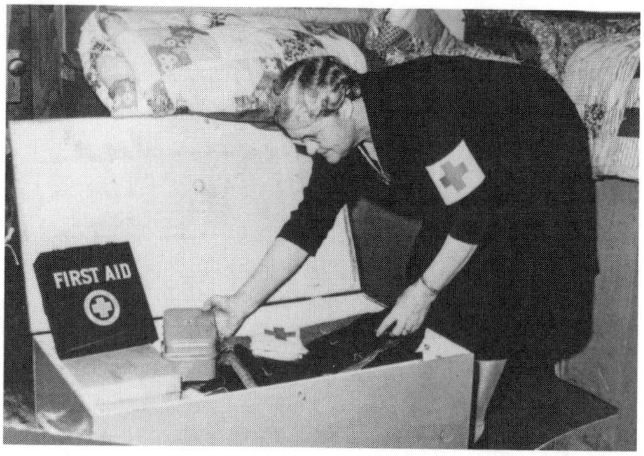

The American Red Cross was founded in 1882 through the lobbying efforts of Clara Barton. This photo shows a Red Cross worker in Turlock, California, in May 1942. Photo by Russell Lee. Library of Congress.

BIBLIOGRAPHY

Ross, Ishbel. *Angel of the Battlefield.* New York: Harper, 1956.

Williams, Blanche. *Clara Barton, Daughter of Destiny.* Philadelphia: Lippincott, 1941.

Charlotta Spears Bass (1880–1969)

From May 1912 until the early 1950s, Charlotta Bass edited the *California Eagle*, the oldest black issues newspaper on the West Coast. Bass supported Republican Wendell Willkie in the 1940 presidential campaign. In 1943, she was the first African-American grand jury member of the Los Angeles County Court. She was a representative to the Peace Committee of the World Congress in Prague in 1950 and ran for vice president on the Progressive Party ticket in 1952, becoming the first black woman to run for office.

BIBLIOGRAPHY

Gill, Gerald. "Win or Lose—We Win." In Sharon Harley and Roslyn Tenborg-Penn, eds. *The Afro-American Woman: Struggles and Images.* Port Washington, NY: Kennikat Press, 1978.

Beal v. Doe (1976)

At issue in *Beal v. Doe*, 432 U.S. 438 (1976), was whether Title XIX of the Social Security Act of 1965 required the state of Pennsylvania to fund nontherapeutic **abortion**s as part of its Medicaid program. Proponents argued that denial of the financial assistance was in violation of the Equal Protection Clause of the Fourteenth Amendment. However, Pennsylvania argued that the state should not have to fund nontherapeutic abortions for two reasons. First, when Congress passed Title XIX in 1965, there was no intent to cover nontherapeutic abortions, as most states prohibited these procedures. Second, the state argued that it had a compelling interest in promoting childbirth and protecting the possibility of life. The U.S. Supreme Court upheld the Pennsylvania law, stating that Title XIX could not have mandated nontherapeutic abortions as part of the legislation regarding Medicaid.

BIBLIOGRAPHY

Frakar, Susan. "Abortion: Who Pays?" Newsweek 83 (July 4, 1977): 12–13.

"New Abortion Debate: Decision on Medicaid Funding." *Commonweal* 103 (July 22, 1977): 451–52.

"Supreme Court Ignites a Fiery Abortion Debate." *Time* 10 (July 4, 1977): 6–8.

Mary Ritter Beard (1876–1958)

Mary Beard, a leading progressive writer and social activist, joined the **National Women's Trade Union League** in 1907. From 1902 to 1912, she edited *The Woman Voter,* a paper published by the **Woman Suffrage Party**. In addition she worked with the Wage Earner's League and the **National Woman's Party (NWP)** from the mid-1910s through the 1920s. An active member of the **Progressive movement**, Beard's lasting contribution to social reform and woman's rights was through her writing, including *On Understanding Women* (1931) and *Women: A Force in History* (1946). **See also** Suffrage.

BIBLIOGRAPHY

Beard, Mary R. *American Women Through Women's Eyes.* New York: Macmillan, 1933.

Bellotti v. Baird (1975, 1979)

The state of Massachusetts passed a statute that required unmarried women under the age of 18 to secure parental consent or the consent of a state court judge if they wanted to terminate a pregnancy. The law also created criminal penalties for any physician who performed an **abortion** without the proper consent. When the case originally entered the court system, a federal district court ruled that the law was unconstitutional because it assumed that all unmarried women under the age of 18 lacked the maturity to make a decision about abortion. However, the U.S. Supreme Court (*Bellotti v. Baird*, 428 U.S. 132 [1975]) vacated that judgment and ordered the case back to the Massachusetts Supreme Court for an interpretation of the law.

The Massachusetts Supreme Court ruled that the state had met the best interests standard because a parent's decision could be overruled by a judge if the judge believed the abortion was in the best interests of the minor. The court also ruled that the law offered no exceptions for mature minors even though they could consent to other forms of medical treatment.

The law was once again found unconstitutional in federal district court and the U.S. Supreme Court once again (*Bellotti v. Baird*, 443 U.S. 622 [1979]) heard the case on appeal. In a plurality decision, the justices found that the state did not take into enough consideration the privacy of the minor by allowing her to demonstrate that she was mature enough to make the decision of obtaining an abortion on her own. The Court's opinion stated three criteria by which to judge whether a judicial bypass procedure was proper. First, proper judicial bypass must allow an opportunity for the minor to show that she is mature enough to make the decision or that the abortion is in her best interests. Second, it must ensure the anonymity of the teenager. Finally, the process must allow for expedited appeals.

Bibliography

Paul, Eve W. and Harriet F. Pilpel. "Teenagers and Pregnancy." *Family Planning Perspectives* 11 (September/October 1979): 297–302.

Baer, Judith A. *Women in American Law*. New York: Holmes & Meier, 1996.

Alva Erskine Smith Vanderbilt Belmont (1853–1935)

In 1909, Alva Belmont, a wealthy socialite, used her influence and money to advance women's rights, especially **suffrage**. She established a headquarters for and funded the **National American Women Suffrage Association (NAWSA)** and the Political Equality League, the latter of which she served as president. In 1914, she financed a lecture tour for noted feminist, Christabel Pankhurst. Belmont served on the executive board of the **Congressional Union** in 1913 and on the board of its successor, the **National Woman's Party**. In 1917, she became president of the National Woman's Party, a post she held until 1921.

Bibliography

Belmont, Alva. "Are Woman Really Citizens?" *Good Housekeeping* 93 (September 1931): 99, 132, 135.

______. "Woman's Rights to Govern Herself." *North American Review* 190 (November 1909): 664–74.

Keeler, Rebecca T. "Alva Belmont: Benefactor for Women's Suffrage." *Alabama Review* 41 (April 1988): 132–45.

Helen Delich Bentley (1923–)

Helen Bentley, an influential maritime newspaperwoman, began her political involvement in 1966 when she supported Spiro T. Agnew's election as governor of Maryland. She went on to serve as staff advisor on shipping matters during Richard Nixon's 1968 presidential election. Because of her work, Bentley was chosen to be chair of the Federal Maritime Commission on August 9, 1969. Bentley was chair of this commission until 1975 and served in the U.S. House of Representatives from 1985 until 1995. She did not run for reelection in 1994.

Bibliography

McAllister, Bill. "Who Bentley Represents." *The Washington Post* 120 (October 2, 1997): A13.

______. "The Revolving Door." *The Washington Post* 120 (September 25, 1997): A23.

Mary McLeod Bethune (1875–1955)

Civil rights activist Mary McLeod Bethune was arguably the most influential black woman in the twentieth century. Born in the segregated South to former slaves, Bethune began her public career as a teacher. In 1904, she established the Daytona Normal-Industrial Institute, a school for black girls. Nineteen years later, the Institute became a coeducational college under the name of Bethune-Cookman College with Bethune as its president. Bethune's activities on behalf of black women earned her the presidency of the **National Association of Colored Women (NACW)** in 1924. In an effort to coordinate the activities of black women's groups, she created and became president of the **National Council of Negro Women (NCNW)** in 1935. Bethune is best remembered as a key advisor to First Lady **Eleanor Roosevelt** on issues of importance to blacks during the Franklin D. Roosevelt administration. Appointed to the National Advisory Committee to the National Youth Administration in 1935 and later becoming the head of the Division of Negro Affairs, Bethune was one of only two blacks who had access to the Roosevelt White House during the Great Depression. Although many New Deal programs suffered from discriminatory practices, Bethune promoted equality in the administration of education and job training programs. In 1936, Bethune organized the Federal Council of Negro Affairs, a group of government employees often referred to as the "black cabinet." Through her position, Bethune represented black interests to the administration, but also served as a spokesperson for Roosevelt in the black community. (BN)

Bibliography

Holt, Rackham. *Mary McLeod Bethune: A Biography*. New York: Doubleday, 1964.

Smith, Elaine M. "Mary McLeod Bethune and the National Youth Administration." In Mabel E. Deutrich and Virginia C. Purdy, eds. *Clio Was a Woman: Studies in the History of American Women*. Washington, DC: Howard University Press, 1979.

Clara Beyer (1892–1990)

From 1933 to 1945, Clara Beyer served as a confidential aide to Secretary of Labor **Frances Perkins.** Beyer also served as secretary of the Minimum Wage Board of the District of Columbia, helping to ensure equal pay for women. In 1928, Beyer began working for the **Children's Bureau** of the Labor Department, where she was teamed with Perkins and **Grace Abbott**. Beyer also helped pioneer a number of other New Deal reforms, including establishing worker safety, **minimum wages,** and Social Security.

BIBLIOGRAPHY

Beyer, Clara M. "What is Equality?" *The Nation* 116 (January 31, 1923): 116.

Blatch, Harriet Stanton and Clara M. Beyer. "Do Women Want Protection? Wrapping Women in Cotton Wool." *The Nation* 116 (January 31, 1923): 115–16.

Martin, George Madden. *Madam Secretary Frances Perkins, A Biography of America's First Woman Cabinet Member.* New York: Houghton Mifflin, 1976

"Obituary." *New York Times.* (September 28, 1990): A18.

Bill of Rights for Women (NOW)

The Bill of Rights for Women was created by the **National Organization for Women (NOW)** at its 1967 national conference in Washington, DC The Bill of Rights was a list of those political rights deemed most important for women to hold. Its formulation was controversial, as NOW's membership included female members of the United Automobile Workers (UAW) who feared the **Equal Rights Amendment (ERA)** would eliminate labor gains. NOW membership also included members of the **National Woman's Party (NWP)**, the organization that had originally proposed the ERA. Other controversial provisions included the call for day care and for the right to **abortion**.

As a result of the promulgation of the Bill of Rights for Women, NOW lost members from the UAW as well as members who opposed abortion. For supporters of the Bill of Rights and NOW, these issues were central to the goals of the organization and to the **women's movement** as a whole.

The Bill of Rights for Women calls for (1) passage of the Equal Rights Amendment, (2) enforcement of laws banning **sexual discrimination** in employment, (3) maternity leave rights in employment and in Social Security benefits, (4) tax deductions for home and **child care** expenses for working parents, (5) child day care centers, (6) equal and unsegregated education, (7) equal job training opportunities and allowances for women in **poverty**, and (8) the right of women to control their reproductive lives. (JEH) **See also** Social Security.

BIBLIOGRAPHY

Morgan, Robin, ed. *Sisterhood Is Powerful.* New York: Random House, 1970.

Wandersee, Winifred D. *On the Move: American Women in the 1970s.* Boston: Twayne, 1988.

Inez Milholland Biossevain (1887–1917)

Born in 1887, Inez Milholland Biossevain was a lawyer and war correspondent. An ardent feminist and member of the **National Woman's Party (NWP)**, she is most well known for leading a 1912 New York **suffrage** parade while riding a horse and wearing a white Grecian gown. She also penned the famous sign, "Mr. President, How Long Must Women Wait for Liberty?" which was displayed during a White House march on Woodrow Wilson's second Inauguration Day in 1917. Biossevain served as a war correspondent in Italy, but was expelled because of her pacifist views. She died of anemia in 1917 at the age of 30. (JW1) **See also** Pacifism.

BIBLIOGRAPHY

Irwin, Inez Haynes. *Up Hill with Banner Flying: The Story of the National Woman's Party.* New York: Harcourt Brace, 1921.

Shirley Temple Black (1928–)

Years after her career as a popular child actress ended, Shirley Temple Black overcame her starlet stigma to become a serious political influence. After losing a California congressional campaign to fellow Republican Paul McCloskey in 1967, Black remained active in California politics until being nominated as a member of the United States delegation to the United Nations in 1969. She served in this role until 1972. Black's next appointment came on December 6, 1974, when President Gerald Ford named her U.S. ambassador to Ghana, a position she held until July 1976. Later in 1976 she became the first woman to be named chief of protocol of the U.S. Department of State.

BIBLIOGRAPHY

Black, Shirley Temple. "Telling It Like It Is." *National Business Woman* 51, no 4. (May 1970): 8.

Alice Stone Blackwell (1858–1950)

Alice Stone Blackwell was the only child of suffragette **Lucy Stone**. After graduating from Boston University in 1881, Blackwell worked with her mother in the **suffrage** movement and wrote and edited *The Women's Journal*. She also started her own paper called the *Woman's Column* in 1887. A born negotiator, Blackwell played a pivotal role in uniting the **National Woman Suffrage Association (NWSA)** and the **American Woman Suffrage Association (AWSA)** in 1890. Blackwell served as secretary of the new united organization, the **National American Women's Suffrage Association (NAWSA),** for 20 years. She also helped found the League of Women Voters in Massachusetts and wrote a biography of her mother in 1930. **See also** National League of Women Voters. (CKC)

BIBLIOGRAPHY

McGlen, Nancy E. and Karen O'Connor. *Women, Politics, and American Society.* Upper Saddle River, NJ: Prentice-Hall, 1995.

Merrill, Marlene Deahl. *Growing up in Boston's Gilded Age: The Journal of Alice Stone Blackwell, 1872–1874.* New Haven, CT: Yale University Press, 1990.

Antoinette Louisa Brown Blackwell (1825–1921)

In 1846, Antoinette Brown enrolled in **Oberlin College**, one of the few institutions that admitted women to study theology. In 1853, Antoinette Brown Blackwell was the first woman to be ordained as a minister. She was an articulate supporter of the **abolition movement**, the **temperance movement,** and women's rights. An early suffragette, she served in a leadership capacity in several organizations, including the Association for the Advancement of Women and the **American Woman Suffrage Association (AWSA)**. **See also** Suffrage. (CKC)

BIBLIOGRAPHY

Cazden, Elizabeth. *Antoinette Brown Blackwell: A Biography.* New York: The Feminist Press, 1983.

Elizabeth Blackwell (1821–1910)

English-born Elizabeth Blackwell became the first woman physician in the United States. In 1849, she graduated at the top of her class from Geneva Medical College in New York after previously being rejected by every medical school in the country because of her sex. After graduation she entered the midwives course at La Maternité in Paris and worked at St. Bartholomew's Hospital in London. Blackwell returned to New York in 1851, but no hospital would hire her and she was even unable to rent quarters for private practice. In 1853, she opened a small dispensary in a New York slum district, which became the New York Infirmary for Women and Children in 1857. During the Civil War in the 1860s, Blackwell helped organize the Women's Central Association of Relief and the U.S. Sanitary Commission, and helped select and train nurses for war service. In 1868, she opened the Women's Medical College at the New York Infirmary. In 1869, she moved to England, where she helped establish the National Health Service in 1871. Blackwell was appointed professor of gynecology at the London School of Medicine for Women in 1875. (ST)

BIBLIOGRAPHY

Blackwell, Elizabeth. *Pioneer Work in Opening the Medical Profession to Women.* New York: Schocken Books, 1977.

Schleichert, Elizabeth. *The Life of Elizabeth Blackwell.* Frederick, MD: Twenty-First Books, 1991.

Emily Jane Newell Blair (1877–1951)

Emily Blair had a long career advocating women's **suffrage**. In 1914, she became editor of *Missouri Woman,* a monthly suffrage magazine that became the official organ of the state **Parent-Teacher Association** and the Federation of Women's Clubs. During World War I, she served as vice-chair of the Missouri Woman's Committee of the Council of National Defense, which led to her appointment to the national council. Blair was active in the founding of the League of Women Voters and joined the **Democratic Party** in 1920. Elected in 1921 to serve on the Democratic National Committee from Missouri, Blair was then elected to serve as vice-chair responsible for organizing women. Throughout her life, she continued to work for increased voting by women. **See also** National League of Women Voters.

BIBLIOGRAPHY

Blair, Emily. "Are Women a Failure in Politics?" *Harper's Magazine* (October 1925): 513–22.

———. "Why I am Discouraged about Women in Politics." *The Women's Journal* (January 1931): 14–15, 29.

Carroll, Mary. "Wanted—A New Feminist." *Independent Woman* (December 1930): 499, 544.

Hard, Anne. "Emily Blair 'Politician.'" *Women Citizen* (April 1926): 15–6.

Harriot Eaton Stanton Blatch (1856–1940)

Harriot Eaton Stanton Blatch was the daughter of **Elizabeth Cady Stanton** and Henry Brewster Stanton. She earned her B.A. from Vassar in 1878, graduated from the Boston School of Oratory in 1879, and earned an M.A. from Vassar in 1894. She co-authored with Stanton and **Susan B. Anthony** the *History of Woman Suffrage* (1881), was a contributor to *The Woman's Bible* (1895), and wrote *Mobilizing Woman-Power* (1918), *A Woman's Point of View* (1920), and *Elizabeth Cady Stanton, as Revealed in Her Letters, Diary, and Reminiscences* (1922). She lost her citizenship in 1882 when she married an Englishman, William Henry Blatch. In 1907, she returned to New York, where she organized the Equality League of Self-Supporting Women (later the **Women's Political Union**), the first **suffrage** association based on female factory and garment workers. (AM)

In this photo from around 1915, Harriot Stanton Blatch, the daughter of Elizabeth Cady Stanton, addresses a crowd of men on Wall Street in New York City. Library of Congress, National American Woman Suffrage Association Collection.

BIBLIOGRAPHY

Blatch, Harriot. *Challenging Years: The Memoirs of Harriot Stanton Blatch.* New York: G. P. Putnam's Sons, 1940.

DuBois, Ellen Carol. *Harriot Stanton Blatch and the Winning of Woman Suffrage.* New Haven, CT: Yale University Press, 1997.

Iris Faircloth Blitch (1912–1993)

Iris Blitch ran for her first political office—the Georgia State Legislature—in 1940 at the age of 28. While she lost that campaign, she began to build a grassroots organization that would serve her for years to come. She was successful in 1946 in her quest for a seat in the state legislature. A Democrat, she served one term in the house and two in the senate. During her time there, she championed many causes, including the right of women to serve on juries. In 1954, she was elected to the U.S. House of Representatives, having defeated the incumbent W. M. Wheeler in the **Democratic Party** primary. In the House, she voted with other southern representatives against the voting-rights amendment. Serving on the Public Works Committee, she was an environmental advocate and sponsored the Watershed Protection and Flood Prevention Act that provided funds for water-conservation projects. She retired from Congress in 1963 due to declining health.

BIBLIOGRAPHY

Chamberlin, Hope. *A Minority of Members*. New York: Praeger, 1973.

Women in Congress. Washington, DC: Government Printing Office, 1991.

Amelia Jenks Bloomer (1818–1894)

Amelia Jenks Bloomer was born May 27, 1818, in Homer, New York, to Anias and Lucy Webb Jenks. She married Dexter C. Bloomer on April 15,1840, in Seneca Falls, New York. The Woman's Rights Convention held in Seneca Falls in 1848 spurred her to publish *The Lily*, (1849–1855) the first newspaper published and edited by a woman for women. In 1851, Elizabeth Smith Miller, a cousin of **Elizabeth Cady Stanton**, visited Seneca Falls wearing a costume of short skirts over large Turkish pantaloons. Wearing the clothes herself, Amelia Bloomer advocated in *The Lily* the adoption of the costume to improve women's health and mobility. She spent most of her life writing and speaking for temperance and women's rights, yet Bloomer is best remembered for giving her name to "bloomers," a clothing fashion she only wore six to eight years. (AM) **See also** Seneca Falls Convention.

BIBLIOGRAPHY

Bloomer, D. C. *Life and Writings of Amelia Bloomer*. New York: Schocken Books, 1975.

Ella Reeve Bloor (1862–1951)

In the early 1900s, Bloor supported the **suffrage** and labor movements as a member of the **National Woman's Party (NWP)**, the Socialist Party, and the **Communist Party, USA**. She served as field organizer for the Worker's Defense Union during World War I and campaigned in the West and Midwest for the Communist Party in the 1930s. **See also** Socialism.

BIBLIOGRAPHY

Draper, Theodore. *The Roots of American Communism*. New York: Viking, 1957.

Nellie Bly (Elizabeth Cochrane Seaman) (1864–1922)

Under the pen name "Nellie Bly," Elizabeth Cochrane Seaman began working in 1885 as a journalist for the *Pittsburgh Dispatch*. Bly wrote on social and political issues, such as prostitution, prison conditions, and woman suffrage.While working for the paper, she was expelled from Mexico in 1887 after writing of the need for reform in that country. Seaman became a writer for the *New York World,* a newspaper headed by John Pulitzer, and traveled nationally and internationally covering social reform and suffrage issues.

BIBLIOGRAPHY

Emerson, Kathy. *Making Headlines*. Minneapolis: Dillon, 1989.

Ross, Ishbel. *Ladies of the Press*. New York: Harper, 1936.

Corrine "Lindy" Boggs (1916–)

Admired for her southern charm and political talents, Lindy Boggs (D-LA) won her late husband's congressional seat in 1973 and represented her New Orleans district until her retirement in 1990. In 1976, she presided over the Democratic National Convention in New York City, and became the first woman ever to chair a national party convention.

In Congress, Boggs secured legislation to prohibit discrimination against women in personal and commercial credit and to recognize the Women's Air Service Pilots from World War II. She served on the Appropriations Committee and helped found the **Congresswomen's Caucus**. After 1984, Boggs, with support from women of color, was the only white member from a majority African-American district.

As the wife of Democratic Whip Hale Boggs, who disappeared when his plane crashed in Alaska while he was campaigning for a fellow Democrat, Boggs had organized volunteer efforts for Presidents John F. Kennedy and Lyndon Johnson. She was a member of commissions to commemorate the 200th anniversary of the United States in 1976 and the Constitution in 1987. In 1997, Boggs was appointed the first female ambassador to the Vatican by President Bill Clinton.

Boggs' daughter, the late Barbara Sigmund, was mayor of Princeton, New Jersey, and her other daughter is ABC-TV and National Public Radio correspondent Cokie Roberts. Boggs believes that young women need to recognize that "equal opportunity and equal rights must constantly be exercised and protected or they are lost." (JHT)

BIBLIOGRAPHY

Boggs, Lindy with Katherine Hatch. *Washington Through a Purple Veil: Memoirs of a Southern Woman*. New York: Harcourt Brace & Co., 1994.

Peabody, Robert. *Leadership in Congress: Stability, Succession, and Change*. Boston: Little Brown & Co., 1976.

Veronica Grace Boland (1899–1982)

Veronica Boland was elected to the United States House of Representatives to fill the remainder of the term of her late husband Democratic Representative Patrick Boland. The first woman elected to Congress from Pennsylvania, she served from November 19, 1942, until January 3, 1943.

BIBLIOGRAPHY

Chamberlin, Hope. *A Minority of Members*. New York: Praeger, 1973.

Frances Payne Bolton (1885–1977)

The first woman elected to Congress from Ohio, Frances Payne Bolton used her position to further public health in the United States. Like many women in the early twentieth century, Bolton won a special election to serve out the term of her deceased husband Representative Chester C. Bolton. Running on her own as a Republican in 1940, Bolton opposed President Franklin D. Roosevelt and U.S. intervention in the war in Europe. Bolton was a strong champion of medical nurses, both those working at home and those in war zones. In 1943, she sponsored the Bolton Act, which created the U.S. Cadet Nurses

Corps. In her widely chronicled tour of U.S. military hospitals in 1944, Bolton became the first woman lawmaker to visit a war zone. Toward the end of her legislative career, Bolton was the ranking Republican on the House Foreign Affairs Committee. Bolton continued in the House until she was defeated in 1968. (BN)

BIBLIOGRAPHY

Loth, David. *A Long Way Forward: The Biography of Congresswoman Frances P. Bolton*. 1957.

U.S. House of Representatives, *Women in Congress 1917–1990*. Prepared by the Office of the Historian. 101st Cong., 2nd sess 1991. H. Doc. 101–238.

Mary Bono (1953–)

In 1998, Mary Bono was elected to fill the unexpired term of her late husband, Republican Sonny Bono of California. Bono, a political novice, easily won the election over her Democratic challenger, Ralph Waite, a 69-year-old actor best known for his role as Pa on the long-running television series, *The Waltons*. Bono has been awarded prime spots on important committees, including the House Judiciary Committee.

BIBLIOGRAPHY

Broder, David S. "Partisan Battle for House Seats." *The Times-Picayune* (17 March 1998): B5.

Bruni, Frank. "The Widow's Run." *The New York Times* (29 March 1998): 34.

Reva Zilpha Beck Bosone (1895–1983)

Reva Bosone, a Democrat, served as a member of Utah's House of Representatives from 1933 to 1935. From 1936 to 1949, she was a judge for Salt Lake City. During World War II, she served as chair of the **Women's Army Corps (WACs)** Civilian Advisory Committee of the Ninth Service Command. From 1947 to 1948, she was the first director of the Utah State Board for Education on Alcoholism. Bosone was elected to the U.S. House of Representatives in 1948 and reelected in 1950. In 1952 and 1956, she was a delegate to the Democratic National Convention. From 1957 to 1960, she was legal council to the Safety and Compensation Subcommittee of the House Committee on Education and Labor. She was appointed to her final government position in 1961 when she became a judicial officer for the Post Office Department, a role she filled until 1968.

BIBLIOGRAPHY

Bosone, Reva Beck. *Oral History Interview, Former Member of Congress Association*. Washington, DC: Manuscript Division, Library of Congress, 1978.

Clopton, Beverly B. *Her Honor, The Judge: The Story of Reva Beck Bosone*. Ames: Iowa State University Press, 1980.

"New Faces in Congress." *The New Republic* 120 (January 24, 1949): 9.

Bowers v. Hardwick (1986)

In *Bowers v. Hardwick,* 478 U.S. 186 (1986), a sharply divided (5–4) Supreme Court refused to extend the right of privacy to protect acts of consensual homosexual sodomy performed in private.

Hardwick was arrested for performing oral sex with another man in his bedroom. They were discovered by a police officer attempting to serve Hardwick with an arrest warrant for drinking in public. Georgia law made heterosexual and homosexual sodomy a felony punishable by a prison term of one to twenty years. Although Hardwick was not prosecuted, he challenged Georgia's sodomy law as a violation of the constitutional right to privacy.

Justice Byron White's majority opinion made a distinction between this case and earlier privacy cases regarding contraception (***Griswold v. Connecticut*, [1965]**; ***Eisenstadt v. Baird*, [1972]**) and **abortion** (***Roe v. Wade*, [1973]**). Those decisions encompassed rights integral to family relationships, procreation, and marriage. Since homosexual sodomy bore no resemblance to these things, it was unprotected by the Constitution. The majority of the Court was unwilling to agree that engaging in homosexual sodomy was a fundamental right. Fundamental rights are those "deeply rooted in this nation's history and tradition" or "implicit in the concept of ordered liberty." Since sodomy laws have been in force for centuries, the claim that homosexual sodomy was a fundamental right was "at best, facetious." The majority distinguished *Bowers v. Hardwick* from *Stanley v. Georgia* (1969), which protected from prosecution individuals possessing and reading obscene materials in the privacy of their homes. *Stanley* did not immunize conduct like sodomy simply because it occured in the home. The majority rejected Hardwick's claim that there was no rational basis for the sodomy law; popular belief that sodomy was immoral was a sufficient reason for upholding the law.

Justice Harry Blackmun, joined by Justices William Brennan, John Paul Stevens, and Thurgood Marshall, bitterly dissented. The Court's prior decisions regarding abortion and contraception established the right of privacy in intimate relationships. Their view was that precedent, therefore, protected intimate heterosexual conduct from state intervention and since Georgia's law prohibited both homosexual and heterosexual sodomy, it should be invalidated as an infringement on the right to privacy. The dissenters also found the core of Georgia's defense—that the sodomy law was consistent with the state's right to maintain a decent society—entirely unpersuasive. Although sodomy had been morally condemned for centuries, the minority on the court believed that this was not a sufficient reason to permit a state to ban it. (RW)

BIBLIOGRAPHY

Garrow, David A. *Liberty and Sexuality*. New York: MacMillan, 1994.

Jefferies, John C. *Justice Lewis F. Powell, Jr.* New York: Charles Scribner's Sons, 1994.

Posner, Richard A. *Sex and Reason*. Cambridge, MA: Harvard University Press, 1992.

"Sexual Orientation and the Law." *Harvard Law Review* 102 (1989): 1508–1671.

Eva Kelly Bowring (1892–1985)

Eva Bowring acted as vice-chair of the Nebraska Republican Central Committee from 1946 to 1954, as well as vice-chair of the State Midwest Vice Chairman's Association in 1954 and the director of the Women's Division of the **Republican Party** in Nebraska from 1946 to 1954. She served an interim appointment to the U.S. Senate from April 16, 1954, to November 7, 1954. A delegate to the Republican National Convention in 1954, she sat on the Board of Parole for the Department of Justice from 1956 to 1964. Bowring also served twice as a member of the National Advisory Council for the National Institutes of Health, from 1954, to 1958 and from 1960 to 1961.

BIBLIOGRAPHY

Donovan, Ruth Godfrey. "Lady from the Sandhill." *Independent Woman* 37 (June 1954): 204–06.

Barbara Boxer (1940–)

Barbara Boxer, a Democrat, was elected in 1992 to represent California in the U.S. Senate. She was born and educated in Brooklyn, New York, moving to California in 1965. Boxer began her political career in 1974 as a congressional aide to representative John Burton. Prior to being a senator, Boxer spent 10 years in the House of Representatives, from 1983 to 1992, working for her constituents in the San Francisco Bay area. Before that she spent six years on the Marin County, California, board of supervisors, serving as the first woman president of the board. Early in her term, Senator Boxer had a reputation for voting as a liberal, although that changed as she shifted from representing the decidedly liberal Bay area to the much more conservative state at large. In the middle of her term, Boxer supported several policies not usually associated with politically liberal positions, like tightening enforcement of immigration laws and strong anti-crime measures. However, Boxer's positions on the environment, women's rights, children's issues, and military reform are more typically liberal. Boxer's Senate term expires in January 1999. (KM)

BIBLIOGRAPHY

Boxer, Barbara and Nicole Boxer. *Strangers in the Senate: Politics and the New Revolution of Women in America.* Washington, DC: National Press Books, 1994.

Elving, Ronald D., Ines Pinto Alicea, and Jeffrey L. Katz. "Boxer and Feinstein Victories 'Year of the Woman'." *Congressional Quarterly Weekly Report* 50 (June 6, 1992): 1621–31.

Boylan et al. v. The New York Times (1974)

In 1974, seven women sued *The New York Times* for sexual discrimination under **Title VII of the Civil Rights Act of 1964**. Eventually, 550 women who worked for the *Times* joined the class-action suit, which was settled out of court in 1978. Former *Times* reporter Nan Robertson offers a first-hand account of *Boylan* in *The Girls in the Balcony*. Documenting extensive sexual discrimination at the *Times*, Robertson writes that the discrimination worsened as the suit progressed. Statisticians hired by Harriet Rabb, the women's lawyer, found that men averaged almost 100 dollars more a week than the women. Although never conceding defeat, the *Times,* as part of the settlement, created a temporary, monitored **affirmative action** plan and paid a small monetary award.

In her book, *Women in American Society* (1994), Virginia Sapiro maintains that journalism has historically been a "men's club." Female journalists formed their own clubs because the National Press Club, established in the nineteenth century, banned women from membership until 1971. Women journalists were relegated to the balcony of the ballroom of the National Press Club to cover events. In addition to the *Times* suit, sexual discrimination suits were also filed against other newspapers, magazines, and television stations. In 1976, the report of the National Commission on the Observance of **International Women's Year** suggested that there was a correlation between the absence of women in policy-making positions and sexist content in the media. (EP) **See also** News Media.

BIBLIOGRAPHY

National Commission on the Observance of International Women's Year. "*. . . To Form a More Perfect Union . . . :Justice for American Women.*" Washington, DC: National Commission on the Observance of International Women's Year, 1976.

Robertson, Nan. *The Girls in the Balcony: Women, Men, and The New York Times*. New York: Random House, 1992.

Sapiro, Virginia. *Women in American Society: An Introduction to Women's Studies.* Mountain View, CA: Mayfield, 1994.

Myra Colby Bradwell (1831–1894)

Lawyer and publisher Myra Colby Bradwell was born in Manchester, Vermont, on February 12, 1831. She married James Bolesworth Bradwell, a law student, in 1852. In 1854, they moved to Chicago where her husband was admitted to the Illinois bar and became a judge and state legislator. Myra Bradwell studied law under the tutelage of her husband and in 1868 published the first weekly of the *Chicago Legal News*, which became the most respected legal publication in the Midwest. In 1869, Bradwell passed the Illinois bar examination but was denied admission to the bar to practice law solely on the basis of gender. Under **common law**, women lost their legal identity upon marriage and therefore could not be recognized in a court of law. Bradwell appealed her case to the U.S. Supreme Court; however, in *Bradwell v. Illinois* (1873), the Court ruled that "proper timidity and delicacy evidently unfits (women) from many of the occupations of civil life." Bradwell served four terms as vice-president of the Illinois bar as an honorary member and supported women's issues through her editorials and writings. She helped organize the first **suffrage** convention in Chicago and the **American Woman Suffrage Association (AWSA)** in Cleveland in 1869. She also served on the executive committee of the Illinois Women Suffrage Association. In 1890, the Illinois Supreme Court admitted Bradwell to the bar and two years later she was admitted to practice before the U.S. Supreme Court. (GVS)

Bibliography

Kogan, H. "Myra Bradwell: Crusader at Law." *Chicago History* (1974–75): 132–40.

Bray v. Alexandria Women's Health Clinic (1993)

Bray v. Alexandria Women's Health Clinic, 113 S.CT. 753 (1993), challenged the rights of anti-abortion protesters to block **abortion** clinics. The lawsuit was filed by the **National Organization for Women (NOW)** and nine women's health clinics in an attempt to stop **Operation Rescue** from blockading abortion clinics. Using an 1871 civil rights law known as the "Ku Klux Klan" Act, 42 U.S.C. sec 1985 (3), the plaintiffs tried to demonstrate "class based animus," arguing that the abortion protesters interfered with their rights to obtain abortions and to travel interstate. The district court judge ruled in favor of the plaintiffs and issued an injunction prohibiting Operation Rescue from blockading the clinics. The decision was upheld by the appeals court. However, in a 6-3 decision, the Supreme Court disagreed with the lower courts, ruling that women obtaining abortions do not constitute a "class," and that Operation Rescue protesters had not demonstrated "invidiously discriminatory animus" against women as a class. Operation Rescue's protests were aimed at everyone involved at the abortion facilities, not solely the women seeking abortions. Writing the opinion of the Court, Justice Antonin Scalia concluded that existing federal statutes were insufficient to stop the protests, thereby calling into question the legality of similar injunctions against clinic protesters already in place in other states. (LvA)

Bibliography

Craig, Barbara Hinkson and David M. O'Brien. *Abortion and American Politics.* Chatham, NJ: Chatham House Publishers, Inc., 1993.

O'Connor, Karen. *No Neutral Ground? Abortion Politics in an Age of Absolutes.* Boulder, CO: Westview Press, 1996.

Sophonisba Preston Breckinridge (1866–1948)

An academic and social reformer, Sophonisba Breckinridge was the first woman to pass the Kennedy bar examination, earn a Ph.D. in political science and economics at the University of Chicago (1901), and earn a J.D. from the University of Chicago Law School (1904), a university she served from 1902 through 1942. She authored, co-authored, and edited a number of books that drew on her legal training to analyze the state's treatment of the disadvantaged. She was in the forefront of reform organizations, including those advocating the rights of women and the welfare of immigrants, African Americans, and children. She helped establish the academic discipline of social work and helped governments establish social service agencies. (RD)

Bibliography

Abbott, Edith. "Sophonisba Preston Breckinridge Over the Years." *The Social Service Review* 22, no. 4 (December 1948): 417–23.

Margaret Brent (1601–1671)

Margaret Brent acted as executor for Lord Baltimore, the proprietor of Maryland in the 1640s, helping maintain the state during Ingle's Rebellion, which resulted in the sacking of St. Mary's City by Richard Ingle and his rebellious followers. On January 21, 1647, she became one of the earliest feminists when she demanded two votes in the assembly, one as a freeholder and colonial landowner and another as the proprietor's attorney.

Bibliography

Chroust, Anton-Hermann. *The Rise of the Legal Profession in America.* Norman: University of Oklahoma Press, 1965.

Land, Aubrey C. *Colonial Maryland.* Millwood, NY: KTO Press, 1981.

Spruill, Julia. "Mistress Margaret Brent, Spinster." *Maryland History Magazine* (December 1934): 259+.

Corrine Brown (1946–)

Democratic Congresswoman Corrine Brown was born in Jacksonville, Florida, on November 11, 1946. She received a B.S. from Florida A & M University in 1969 and her masters degree in 1971. She holds an education specialist degree from the University of Florida and an honorary doctor of law degree from Edward Waters College. Brown worked as a faculty member and guidance counselor at Florida Community College in Jacksonville before she entered politics in 1982 as a member of the Florida House of Representatives. In 1992, she campaigned for the newly redrawn and controversial 3rd Congressional District of Florida, a district where minority groups are in the majority. Brown was elected to serve in the 103rd Congress by 64 percent of the vote. During her first term in office, Brown served on the Public Works and Transportation Committee and on the Veteran's Committee. She compiled a solid liberal record on a variety of issues, including the Head Start programs for children, the Earned Income Tax Credit for low income families, and the **Family and Medical Leave Act,** which provides workers with unpaid leave to care for newborn or ill children. She was elected to a second term in 1994 with 58 percent of the vote, and a third term in 1996 with 61 percent of the vote. (GVS)

Bibliography

Barone, Michael and Grant Ujifusa. *The Almanac of American Politics.* Washington, DC: National Journal, 1995.

Olympia Brown (1835–1926)

Olympia Brown was born in Prairie Ronde, Michigan, attended Mount Holyoke College, Antioch College, and the St. Lawrence Seminary at St. Lawrence University. A Unitarian minister, Brown was the first American woman to be ordained by full denominational authority. She founded the New England Woman Suffrage Association (1868) and the Federal Suffrage Association (1892) and served as president of the Wisconsin Woman Suffrage Association (1884–1912) and of the Federal Suffrage Association (1903–1920). She managed the *Racine Times* (1893–1900) after her husband's death. (AM)

BIBLIOGRAPHY

Cote, Charlotte. *Olympia Brown: The Battle for Equality*. Racine, WI: Mother Courage Press, 1988.

Greene, Dana, ed. *Suffrage and Religious Principles: Speeches and Writings of Olympia Brown*. Metuchen, NJ: Scarecrow Press, 1983.

Rita Mae Brown (1944–)

Rita Mae Brown began her political involvement in 1968 when she joined the **National Organization for Women (NOW)** and helped organize the 1969 White House picketing. However, Brown proved to be too radical for NOW especially on the issue of lesbianism. In 1969, she left NOW, and joined more radical groups like Redstocking and Radicalesbians. In 1970, she led the Lavender Massacre, a lesbian attempt to take over the second Congress to Unite Women. She advocated a separatist lesbian community as the only way to secure equal rights. When she was ousted from yet another radical group in June 1973, Brown turned to writing; her works have been praised by feminists and literary critics alike.

BIBLIOGRAPHY

Alexander, Dolores. "Rita Mae Brown: 'The Issue for the Future is Power.'" *Ms.* 3 (September 1974): 110–13.

Brown, Rita Mae. *Rubyfruit*. New York: Daughters, 1973.

——. *The Hand that Rocks the Cradle*. New York: New York University Press, 1971.

Koertge, Noretta. *Who Was that Masked Woman?* New York: St. Martin's Press, 1981.

Carol M. Browner (1955–)

President Bill Clinton appointed, Carol Browner the administrator of the Environmental Protection Agency in January 1993. Both environmental and business groups praised her appointment because she has been known as an environmental pragmatist, willing to accommodate business interests, but still protect the environment. Just before taking this position, she had served on the Clinton transition team at the behest of Vice President-Elect Al Gore, for whom she had served as legislative director from 1989 to 1991.

Before becoming head of the EPA, Browner held the position of secretary of Florida's Department of Environmental Regulation (1991–1992). She had also worked as a legislative aid to Senator Lawton Chiles (D-FL) from 1986 to 1989. (MEK)

BIBLIOGRAPHY

Freedman, Allan. "Browner Calls Superfund Bill a Step Backward." *Congressional Quarterly Weekly Report* 55, no. 10 (March 8, 1997): 586.

Gupte, Pranay B. and Bonner R. Cohen. "Carol Browner, Master of Mission Creep." *Forbes* 160, no. 9 (October 20, 1997): 170.

Kocheisen, Carol. "EPA Administrator Defends Tougher Air Standards." *Nation's Cities Weekly* 20, no. 7 (February 17, 1997): 1.

Lemonick, Michael D. "The Queen of Clean Air: EPA Chief Browner Wore Down Everyone, Right up to the President, in her Battle for Tougher Rules." *Time* 150, no. 1 (July 7, 1997): 32.

Michaels, James W. "The Curious Ecology of the EPA." *Forbes* 160, no. 9 (October 20, 1997): 14.

Vera Daerr Buchanan (1902–1955)

Vera Buchanan was elected to the House of Representatives as a Democrat from Pennsylvania on July 24, 1951, filling the vacancy caused by the death of her husband Representative Frank Buchanan. Despite her district being consolidated with another in the 1950 redistricting, she was reelected in 1952 and 1954, serving in Congress until her death in November 1955.

BIBLIOGRAPHY

"Women in Congress Now Number Eleven." *Independent Woman* 29 (October 1956): 311.

Mary Bunting (1910–)

Mary Bunting, a well-known scientific expert in atomic energy, was appointed to the United States Atomic Energy Commission and served from June 29, 1964, to June 30, 1965, becoming the first woman member of the commission.

BIBLIOGRAPHY

"Mary Bunting." *New York Post Magazine* (April 5, 1964): 19.

Yvonne Brathwaite Burke (1932–)

Elected to the U.S. House of Representatives in 1972, Yvonne Brathwaite Burke lived a life of firsts. She was the first woman member of Congress to give birth during her term in office, the first woman to chair the Congressional Black Caucus, the first African-American woman in the California legislature, and the first woman to serve as vice-chair of the Democratic National Convention, which she did in 1972. In Congress, as elsewhere, Burke concentrated on legislation dealing with community nutrition programs, displaced homemakers, funding for resettlement of Vietnamese refugees, full employment, and human rights. In 1978, Burke decided against another term in Congress. In addition to working as a lawyer, she later served on the Los Angeles County Board of Supervisors and the Board of Regents of the University of California.

BIBLIOGRAPHY

Gray, Pamela Lee. *Yvonne Brathwaite Burke: The Congressional Career of California's First Black Congresswoman, 1972–1978.* Ph.D. Dissertation, University of Southern California, 1987.

Sala Burton (1925–1987)

Succeeding her late husband as a U.S. representative from California in 1983, Democratic Congresswoman Sala Burton had years of experience in California **Democratic Party** politics, including membership on the State Democratic Central Committee. Representing San Francisco, she served on the Education and Labor Committee, where she opposed spending cuts, and on the powerful House Rules Committee. She belonged to the **Congressional Caucus for Women's Issues**, but died of cancer in 1987 after only four years in Congress. (JHT)

BIBLIOGRAPHY

Ehrenhalt, Alan, ed. *Politics in America, 1986*. Washington DC: Congressional Quarterly Inc., 1985.

Gertzog, Irvin N. *Congressional Women: Their Recruitment, Integration, and Behavior*. 2nd ed. Westport, CT: Praeger, 1995.

Barbara Bush (1925–)

The wife of Republican President George Bush, Barbara Bush was born in Rye, New York, on June 8, 1925. She attended Smith College for two years and later received numerous honorary degrees from American colleges and universities. She met her future husband at a dance during Christmas vacation when she was 16. They were married on January 6, 1946, and raised six children. She lived as a political wife, following her husband through 29 moves across the nation, and around the world. She selected the promotion of literacy as her special cause while her husband served as vice president, and as first lady continued her involvement by establishing and serving as honorary chair of the Barbara Bush Foundation for Family Literacy. Barbara Bush has been heavily involved in volunteer work throughout her life and has supported a variety of causes, including the homeless, the elderly, school volunteer programs, and AIDS. She has also served on the board of governors of Washington DC's Ronald McDonald House. Barbara Bush has been hailed and criticized for her devoted support to her husband's political career. With an 84-percent approval rating from the American public, Barbara Bush was often called the Bush administration's "greatest asset" and hailed as the most popular first lady. Her popularity ratings sometimes reached 30 points above her husband's ratings. Her grandmotherly image was often used to support the **Republican Party**'s political stance on family values. However, her strong support of President George Bush also prompted the "Wellesley Flap" in which 150 graduating seniors from Wellesley College protested the college's choice of Bush as a commencement speaker, claiming that she was not famous in her own right. Bush published *Barbara Bush: A Memoir* in 1994 and continues to work for the Barbara Bush Foundation. (GVS) **See also** First Ladies.

One of the most popular first ladies, Barbara Bush has volunteered her time to a number of causes, especially literacy. Photo by David Valdez. Library of Congress, Prints and Photographs Division.

BIBLIOGRAPHY

Bush, Barbara. *Barbara Bush: A Memoire*. New York: Charles Scribner's Sons, 1994.

Killian, Pamela. *Barbara Bush: A Biography*. New York: St. Martin's Press, 1993.

Radcliffe, Donnie. *Simply Barbara Bush*. New York: Warner Books, 1989.

Vera Cahalan Bushfield (1889–1976)

Vera Bushfield, a Republican, was appointed to the United States Senate for South Dakota, succeeding her deceased husband Harlan Bushfield. She served in the Senate from October 6, 1948, until her resignation on December 26, 1948, at which time Bushfield retired from active participation in national politics.

BIBLIOGRAPHY

Chamberlin, Hope. *A Minority of Members*. New York: Praeger, 1973.

Jane Burke Byrne (1934–)

Jane Burke Byrne started her political career in 1964 by working for Mayor Richard Daley of Chicago, a position that included her appointment to the chair of the 1972 Democratic Convention. After Daley's death, Byrne found employment in the Chicago mayor's office with Daley's successor, Michael Bilandic. Becoming dissatisfied with his politics, Byrne ran against Bilandic in the next campaign and beat him on April 16, 1979 to become the first female mayor of Chicago. She lost a tough re-election primary to Harold Washington and failed to retain the post through a write-in campaign.

BIBLIOGRAPHY

Alter, Sharon, R. "A Woman for Mayor?" *Chicago History* 15, no. 3 (1986): 52–68.

"Big Shoulders on the Lakefront." *U.S. News & World Report* 102 (March 8, 1987): 9.

Byrne, Jane. *My Chicago*. New York: Norton, 1992.

Kennedy, Eugene. "Mayor Jane Byrne of Chicago." In James David Barber and Barbara Kellerman, eds. *Women Leaders in American Politics*. Englewood Cliffs, NJ: Prentice Hall, 1986.

Masotti, Louis H. and Paul M. Green. "Battle for the Hall: A Ringside Guide to the Election That Will Determine the City's Future." *Chicago* 36 (February 1987): 104.

Leslie L. Byrne (1946–)

Leslie Byrne, a Democrat, became the only woman to serve in the U.S. House of Representatives from Virginia when she was elected in 1992. In her campaign in a northern Virginia district, Byrne stressed economic development and family issues like the proposed **Family and Medical Leave Act**. She was defeated for re-election in 1994 and withdrew from the 1996 race for the U.S. Senate. In August 1996, President Clinton named her director of the Office of Consumer Affairs in the Department of Health and Human Services. Prior to being elected to Congress, she served in the Virginia house of delegates from 1986 to 1993.

BIBLIOGRAPHY

Lipton, Eric. "Byrne Says Conviction of Purpose Drives Her Rough-and-Tumble Style. *Washington Post* (20 October 1994): C4.

Margolies-Mezvinsky, Marjorie. *A Woman's Place*. New York: Crown, 1994.

Beverly Butcher Byron (1932–)

Beverly Byron gained political influence through her family. Her husband, Goodloe E. Byron, and her father-in-law, William D. Byron, both represented Maryland's 6th District, as did her mother-in-law, **Katherine Byron**. Beverly Butcher Byron acted as treasurer of the Young Democrats in Maryland in 1962 and 1965, and helped manage her husband's campaigns until his death in 1978. She was elected to the U.S. House of Representatives as a Democrat from Maryland in 1978, for the first of seven terms. She lost her 1992 re-election bid. Byron was especially active in issues involving equality in the military.

Bibliography

Fulwood, Sam, III. "14-Year Incumbent Loses Congress Seat." *Los Angeles Times* (March 5, 1992): A15.

Wagner, Arlo. "Conservative Democrat Byron Formidable Foe for Fiotes." *Washington Times* (October 22, 1990): B3.

"Report: Pentagon Committed to Ending Sexual Harassment." *Boston Globe* (September 15, 1992): A5.

Katherine Byron (1903–)

After spending years supporting her husband Representative William D. Byron of Maryland in his political career, Katherine Byron began her own career in government upon his death. A Democrat, Byron won a special election to the House of Representatives to fill the unexpired term of her late husband. She served from May 27, 1941, until January 3, 1943. Byron also took an active role in beginning the political career of her daughter-in-law, **Beverly Butcher Byron**.

Bibliography

"Katherine Byron's Campaign for Congress." *Democratic Digest* 18, no. 5 (May 1941): 22, 31.

"Widow's Might." *Time* 37 (June 23, 1941): 16.

C

Cable Act of 1922

The Cable Act, passed by Congress on September 22, 1922, changed previous legislation which dictated that a woman's citizenship becomes the same as her husband's when marrying a man from another country. For years, women argued against the citizenship change, stating that many of them wished to remain U.S. citizens. **Jeannette Rankin**, the first woman to serve in the House of Representatives introduced a bill seeking to end the practice when she was in Congress. In 1917, the **National American Woman Suffrage Association** began championing the bill, eventually assisting its passage. Under the Cable Act, women were allowed to decide their own citizenship after marriage. In 1933, the act was amended to allow U.S.-born women of Asian ancestry to regain U.S. citizenship after divorce from a citizen of another country.

BIBLIOGRAPHY

Cable, John L. "The Citizenship of American Women Since 1830." *Atlantic Monthly* 145 (May 1930): 649–53.

Harrison, Gladys. "A Married Woman's Nationality." *The Woman's Journal* 15 (March 1930): 10–12, 39.

"Equal Nationality Rights for Women." *The New Republic* 77 (December 27, 1933): 179–80.

California Federal Savings and Loan v. Guerra (1987)

California Federal Savings and Loan v. Guerra, 107 S. CT. 683 (1987), involved a challenge to a California statute requiring employers to provide female employees a leave of absence for disability resulting from pregnancy. California Federal Savings and Loan contended that the law was in conflict with **Title VII of the Civil Rights Act of 1964,** which, as amended by the **Pregnancy Discrimination Act of 1978** prohibits employers from discriminating on the basis of sex, including disability. The Supreme Court upheld the statute, rejecting the bank's claim that the law constituted "special treatment" for pregnant women. Instead, the Court found that the law promotes equal opportunity for women in accordance with the spirit of Title VII. (MBS)

BIBLIOGRAPHY

Strimling, Wendy S. "The Constitutionality of State Laws Providing Employment Leave for Pregnancy: Rethinking *Geduldig* After *Cal Fed.*" *California Law Review* 77 (1989): 171–221.

California Judicial Council Advisory Committee on Gender Bias in the Courts

In April 1987, the California Judicial Council Advisory Committee on Gender Bias in the Courts met for the first time. After three years of research, the committee published a 680-page report citing widespread sexual bias in the justice system and including 65 recommendations for change. Following in the steps of the Supreme Court and several state justice systems, the 34-member advisory committee, known as the gender-bias task force, conducted public hearings, surveyed state judges, heard testimony from attorneys, and visited correctional facilities for women. The committee members also solicited reports from women's bar groups and investigated court employment practices. (MG)

BIBLIOGRAPHY

Cox, Gail Diane. "Reports Track Discrimination; Fourteen Volumes Chronicle How Women are Treated in Court: Gender-Bias Reports Find Common Thread." *The National Law Journal* (November 26, 1990): 1.

Slind-Flor, Victoria. "Rampant Sex Bias Cited in California: Texas Preparing for Similar Study of Judges, Lawyers." *Texas Lawyer* (April 2, 1990): 8.

Maria Cantwell (1958–)

Maria Cantwell, a Democrat, was elected to the U.S. House of Representatives from the state of Washington in 1992. A moderate who is both pro-business and pro-choice, she was elected by the party caucus to serve on the Democratic Caucus Steering and Policy Committee. In Congress, she served on the Foreign Affairs and the Public Works and Transportation Committees. She was defeated for re-election in 1994. Prior to serving in Congress, Cantwell served in the Washington House of Representatives from 1987 to 1993.

BIBLIOGRAPHY

Margolies-Mezvinsky, Marjorie. *A Woman's Place.* New York: Crown, 1994.

Lois Capps (1938–)

In 1998, Lois Capps was elected to the U.S. House of Representatives from California in a special election. She succeeded her late husband Democrat Walter Capps. Lois Capps had been a nurse for the Santa Barbara School District for 20 years and a health consultant for child development programs. When a serious car accident put her husband in the hospital in 1996, she campaigned for him and helped him win a second term.

BIBLIOGRAPHY

Broder, David S. "Partisan Battle for House Seats." *The Times-Picayune* (17 March 1998): B5.

Jones, Mary Lynn F. "It's Still Rep. Capps, But Now It's Lois, Not Walter." *The Hill* (18 March 1998): 1.

Hattie Wyatt Caraway (1878–1950)

Democrat Hattie Caraway was appointed to the United States Senate on November 13, 1931, to fill the vacancy left by the death of her husband, Arkansas Senator Thaddeus Horatius Caraway. She served in the Senate until January 3, 1945, having lost her reelection bid in the 1944 race. After leaving the Senate, Caraway was a member of the United States Employees' Compensation Commission (now the Bureau of Employees' Compensation) in 1945 and 1946, and served on the Employees' Compensation Appeals Board from July 16, 1946, until her death.

BIBLIOGRAPHY

Caraway, Hattie Wyatt. *Silent Hattie Speaks: The Personal Thoughts of Senator Hattie Caraway.* Westport, CT: Greenwood Press, 1979.

———. "Women in Congress." *State Government* 10, no. 10 (October 1927): 203–04.

Deutsch, Hermes B. "Hattie and Huey." *Saturday Evening Post* 205 (October 15, 1932): 6–7, 82–90, 92–93.

Liz Carpenter (1922–)

Co-founder of the **National Women's Political Caucus (NWPC)** and an **Equal Rights Amendment (ERA)** supporter, Liz Carpenter worked as a vice presidential aide to Lyndon Johnson from 1961 to 1963 and as press secretary to **Lady Bird Johnson** from 1963 until 1969. She was the first professional newswoman to become a press secretary. As a journalist, Carpenter witnessed the last days of the New Deal and the presidencies of Truman, Eisenhower, and Kennedy. In 1963, she wrote the words that Lyndon Johnson spoke upon landing in Washington after President John Kennedy's assassination. She later worked in the administrations of Gerald Ford and Jimmy Carter. (EP)

BIBLIOGRAPHY

Carpenter, Liz. *Getting Better All the Time.* New York: Simon and Schuster, 1987.

———. *Ruffles and Flourishes: The Warm and Tender Story of a Girl Who Found Adventures in the White House.* New York: Doubleday, 1970.

Julia M. Carson (1958–)

Julia Carson, a Democrat, was elected as an Indiana state representative in 1972 and 1974. She served as assistant minority caucus chair from 1973 until 1974. Prior to her tenure in the Indiana Legislature, she served as precinct committeewoman and as a member of the Democratic National Executive Committee. She went on to become a member of the Indiana State Senate, where she acted as ranking minority member. She was elected to the U.S. House of Representatives from Indiana in 1996.

BIBLIOGRAPHY

Jones, Joyce. "Out with the Old. . . . November Election marked by New Faces and, Hopefully, New Ideas." *Black Enterprise* 27, no. 6 (January 1997): 22.

"New Faces of 1997: First-Time Reps Bring Additional Color to U.S. House." *Ebony* 52, no. 3 (January 1997): 64.

Rachel Louise Carson (1907–1964)

A marine biologist, considered by many to be the "mother" of the modern environmental movement, Rachel Carson is the author of five widely read environmental books: *Under the Sea Wind*, *The Sea Around Us*, *Edge of the Sea*, *Silent Spring*, and *A Sense of Wonder.*

Carson's *Silent Spring* raised public awareness of the environmental damage caused by agricultural chemicals, particularly the effect of DDT on birds. She attempted to demonstrate how ecological damage to one creature could eventually harm all species, including humans. Carson's thesis was met with virulent attacks, specifically by the chemical industry, but President John Kennedy's Science Advisory Committee confirmed her findings in 1963. Honored by many scientific and environmental organizations, Carson was posthumously awarded the President's Medal of Freedom in 1980. (PS)

BIBLIOGRAPHY

Brooks, Paul. *The House of Life: Rachel Carson at Work.* Boston: Houghton Mifflin, 1972.

Carson, Rachel. *Silent Spring.* Boston: Houghton Mifflin, 1962.

Gartner, Carol. *Rachel Carson.* New York: Frederick Ungar Publishing, 1983.

McCay, Mary. *Rachel Carson.* New York: Twayne Publishers, 1993.

Lillian (Bessie) Carter (1898–1983)

Lillian Carter, mother of Jimmy Carter, the 39th president of the United States, gained much of her initial political experience by working with her son. Lillian Carter worked on a number of political campaigns in the 1960s and 1970s, including Lyndon B. Johnson's 1964 presidential run and Jimmy Carter's 1966 and 1970 campaigns for the governorship of Georgia. At the age of 68, she also served in the **Peace Corps** in India, challenging those who thought she was too old for such work. In February 1977, Carter returned to India as the official U.S. representative at the funeral of Indian President Fukhruddin Ali Ahmed. She also made peacemaking tours of Italy and West Africa in 1978.

BIBLIOGRAPHY

Spann, Gloria C. *Lillian Carter.* New York: Putnam, 1986.

Spann, Gloria C. and Lillian Carter. *Away from Home.* Boston: G.K. Hall & Company, 1978.

Rosalynn Smith Carter (1927–)

Wife of President Jimmy Carter, Rosalynn Carter was born in Plains, Georgia, on August 18, 1927. She started dating Jimmy Carter when she was 17 years old, and they were married in 1946. She traveled for several years, living the life of a "navy wife," until the couple finally settled in Plains in 1953 and took over the management of the Carter family peanut business. They had three sons and a daughter. Rosalynn Carter advised and supported her husband's professional and political endeavors from the beginning. When he entered politics in 1962, Rosalynn actively campaigned on his behalf, referring to herself as a "political partner," not a "political wife." In 1970, when Jimmy Carter was elected governor of Georgia, Rosalynn reluctantly increased her political involvement. She worked primarily on the issue of mental health, touring state facilities, giving speeches, and volunteering. As first lady from 1977 to 1981, Rosalynn Carter became actively involved in promoting the performing arts, and strongly supported programs to aid mental health and the elderly. She often represented her husband in various projects to resolve conflict, promote human rights, improve global health, and build democracy in Latin America. She was appointed honorary chair of the President's Commission on Mental Health in 1977, and was the recipient of several awards, including the Nathan S. Kline Medal of Merit from the International Commission Against Mental Illness in 1984 and the Dorothea Dix Award from the Mental Illness Foundation in 1988. After leaving the White House, Rosalynn Carter served as vice-chair of the Carter Center in Atlanta, which was founded to promote peace and human rights worldwide. In 1992, she received the Notre Dame Award for International Service, and the **Eleanor Roosevelt** Living World Award from Peace Links for her work on world peace. (GVS) **See also** First Ladies.

Referring to herself as a "political partner," Rosalynn Carter used her position to advocate mental health reforms. Library of Congress.

Bibliography

Arden, Davis Melic. *The Wives of the Presidents.* Hammond Incorporated, 1977.

Langford, Edna and Linda Maddox. *Rosalynn: Friend and First Lady.* Old Tappan, NJ: Fleming H. Revell Company, 1980.

Carrie Lane Clinton Chapman Catt (1859–1947)

President of the **National American Woman Suffrage Association (NAWSA)** following the death of **Susan B. Anthony**, Carrie Chapman Catt reinvigorated the **suffrage** movement, leading it through the final drive for ratification of the **Nineteenth Amendment**. Born in Ripon, Wisconsin, in 1859, Catt worked her way through Iowa State College, graduating to become a school principal and later one of the first woman superintendents. She became involved with the Iowa Woman Suffrage Association in 1887 upon the death of her husband. When she married George Catt in 1890, her prenuptial contract guaranteed her four months per year to work on suffrage activities. Described as the movement's best organizer, Catt served as president of the NAWSA from 1900 to 1904. Her husband's death in 1905 left her financially independent and therefore able to resume her full-time commitment to the suffrage movement. She worked with the New York Woman Suffrage Party, helping to win the vote in New York in 1917, and the International Woman Suffrage Alliance. Returning to the NAWSA in 1917, Catt's "Winning Plan" combined lobbying for a national constitutional amendment and efforts to win suffrage in individual states. In contrast to **Alice Paul's** strategy of holding all Democrats responsible for the failure of suffrage, Catt supported pro-suffrage Democrats and her diplomacy is credited with ultimately winning President Woodrow Wilson's support. Upon ratification of the Nineteenth Amendment, Catt founded the **National League of Women Voters**. She also renewed her interest in internationalism, founding the Committee on the Cause and Cure of War and helping Jewish refugees during World War II. Catt remained actively involved in women's rights and pacifist organizations until her death in 1947. (LvA)

One of the most important leaders of the suffrage movement, Carrie Chapman Catt also founded the National League of Women Voters. Library of Congress.

Bibliography

Fowler, Robert Booth. *Carrie Catt: Feminist Politician.* Boston: Northeastern University Press, 1986.

Peck, Mary Gray. *Carrie Chapman Catt: A Biography.* New York: Octagon Books, 1975.

Van Voris, Jacqueline. *Carrie Chapman Catt: A Public Life.* New York: Feminist Press, 1987.

Lynne Vincent Cheney (1941–)

Lynne Cheney is a distinguished fellow at the American Enterprise Institute where she continues to address educational curriculum and culture matters. A conservative, she served as chair of the National Endowment for the Humanities from 1986 to 1993. She is also a frequent guest on political talk shows and co-host of *Crossfire* on CNN. (KM)

Bibliography

Cheney, Lynne V. *Telling the Truth.* New York: Simon & Schuster, 1996.

Helen P. Chenoweth (1938–)

Congresswoman Helen P. Chenoweth first became involved in **Republican Party** politics in 1964 when she moved to Idaho. She served as state executive director of the Idaho Republican Party (1975–1977), and chief of staff for U.S. Representative Steven D. Symms (1977–1978). In 1994, she was elected to the 104th Congress. In 1996, she was reelected with 50 percent of the vote. Chenoweth presently serves on the Natural Resources, Agriculture, Veterans Affairs, and the Republican Policy Executive Committees in the U.S. House of Representatives from Idaho's 1st District as a Republican. (AM)

Bibliography

Bingham, Clara. *Women on the Hill.* New York: Times Books, 1997.

Child Care

Despite recent declines in fertility rates and a decrease in family size, the largest percentage of Americans will become parents. According to the *Statistical Abstract of the United States*, over 90 percent of all women between the ages of 18 and 34 expect to have children.

Every parent knows that children bring both happiness and stresses. Although raising children can be joyful, parenting today takes place in a social context that makes child rearing enormously difficult. Among the most difficult and challenging aspects of raising children is that of child care, the full-time care and socialization of children that is critically important for them to realize their full potential. However, securing child care is too often a frustration, leaving many parents wondering: Who will take care of the children?

There are many different circumstances to consider when addressing the issue of child care. If, for example, there is a two-parent family and only one parent works outside the home, the probability is the father is employed. In families with a single wage earner, the traditional pattern is that child care responsibilities fall solely upon the mother. While some authors argue that a small percentage of all families fall into the category of men as the sole breadwinner and women as the primary child care provider, many parents indicate that this is the preferred arrangement, especially when the child is young. The most obvious outcome of this type of arrangement is that often the role of the father in child care is limited by his occupational pursuits and the pressures associated with being the single financial provider. For the mother, staying out of the paid labor force can produce stress for her as well, because the role of homemaker is often devalued in light of the number of women in the paid labor force. If the mother was employed prior to the birth of her child and left her employment after the birth, returning to paid employment at a later date is often complicated by a loss of professional contacts or professional skills. However, not all families have two parents in the home and even among those that do, not all can financially afford to keep one parent out of the labor force for extended periods of time.

The majority of women with children are paid employees. Two-thirds of all children under the age of 6, and three-fourths of all children between the ages of 6 and 13 have mothers who are employed outside the home. Thus, obtaining high-quality and affordable child care is an important issue for employed parents.

Because the majority of children are cared for during the workday by a parent, an immediate option for the working parent is through the **Family and Medical Leave Act** of 1993, which allows a parent who is employed in an organization with 50 or more employees to take up to 12 weeks of unpaid leave following the birth or adoption of a child, or to care for a sick child. Since, on average, men have higher incomes than women, and women are socialized to be primary caregivers, it is most often the mother who uses the Family and Medical Leave Act. But not all women have this option because not all women are employed in organizations with 50 or more employees, and not all women can afford the loss of income, even for short periods of time. Consider, for example, the single, divorced, separated, or widowed parent, whose income is necessary for the survival of her family. Furthermore, the Family and Medical Leave Act does not solve the issue of child care on a long-term basis.

About 8 percent of all couples with both parent(s) working outside the home choose self-employment. When one or both parents are self-employed, the workday can be scheduled to be flexible enough to accommodate the needs of the children. In addition, almost 25 percent of all working women are employed on a part-time basis, which, like self-employment, allows one to better accommodate the tasks of child care. A third option includes shift work, an employment pattern found in another one-fourth of two-earner families. When a parent uses shift work, working hours are usually between 4:00 p.m. and 8:00 a.m. This schedule allows for the parent on a typical work week schedule to be at home with the children during the waking hours.

If self-employment, part-time jobs, or shift work are not options for the two-earner family, and not optimal for the single, divorced, separated, or widowed parent, the working parent is faced with the task of piecing child care together.

If the child is of school age, an employed parent might rely upon school attendance as a child care solution. Even though the average work week does not coincide with school hours or school vacations, school attendance remains a viable child care solution. But just as not all parents can or do use the Family and Medical Leave Act, not all children are of school age. Therefore, for many families, child care requires alternate, and sometimes creative, arrangements and accommodations.

The most frequent alternative for the parent who works outside the home on a full-time basis is to turn to a relative, neighbor, or nanny to care for the children. About two-thirds of all children with working parents are cared for by relatives or a hired caretaker. Day care centers have also become an option, in spite of their high cost, long waiting lists, and sometimes low quality. While only a minority of children under the age of 5 attend day care centers, the use of day care centers has increased, particularly within the past decade.

In all of the above cases, parents continue to face many difficulties. Some of the most obvious of these evolve from concerns with the quality of care that their children receive. Not only do parents want reassurance that the care their child receives is safe and free from potentially harmful occurrences, but most parents want their child's care to benefit the child intellectually and socially. Many parents continue to struggle with the question of what type of care is best and which setting is positively related to the child's intellectual and social development. Generally speaking, the answer to this question lies in the quality of care a child receives.

Struggles with the financial hardships associated with child care are involved as well. Suffice it to say that child care is expensive, requiring from 10 percent to as much as 35 percent of the family's financial resources. In some areas, domestic workers will not work for less than a salary that is compatible with clerical jobs. Further complicating the child care struggle are unique circumstances that too often leave the parent with no child care at all. For example, finding care that accommodates a parent's working schedule is not always easy. The hours of the caretaker may not always fit with the parent's working schedule, nor accommodate an early meeting or working after hours. Too often the only option is to leave children to care for themselves. Children who come home to an empty house and remain alone until a working parent returns are often referred to as "latchkey children." While many parents of latchkey children prepare their children for self-care by providing them with rules to be followed during the parents' absence and by maintaining regular telephone contact, not all parents can or do. Just as quickly as a changed working schedule can interfere with child care arrangements, so too can ordinary child illnesses or a change in the plans of the caretaker. Unfortunately, not even the best child care arrangements are infallible.

No doubt there are arguments suggesting that both employers and the federal government should provide options for quality child care. Some industries have become sensitive to the child care issue and have created child care options for their employees. Often we hear about flexible scheduling and on-site day care centers. Flexible scheduling is indeed a viable option; a parent can compress the work week into fewer days and fluctuate working hours. On-site day care centers also relieve parents of many of the burdens associated with child care, especially when the parent has the option to spend time with the child during breaks or the lunch hour. Unfortunately, few employees have these options.

In 1989, Felice Schwartz suggested that companies establish two career tracks for their female employees: one track for those women who are willing to commit themselves to their careers, "career-primary women," and a second track for those women who prefer to put the needs of their family before their career, "career-family women." By accommodating both types of women and their unique situations, businesses will profit. Not surprisingly, this recommendation, now referred to as the "mommy track," sparked heated debates. Some critics found the recommendation insightful, but others argued that such a proposal could do nothing more than track women into dead-end jobs, while at the same time reinforcing the traditional stereotype that child care is a woman's issue, not a parent's issue.

Both the states and the federal government have responded to the child care issue. Many states have subsidized child care, especially for poor families. The city of San Francisco set a precedent by requiring local developers to either create space for child care facilities in newly constructed buildings, or pay a penalty to a local child care trust fund. Michigan offers care for children attending Head Start programs whose parents work extended hours, and Alaska provides 24-hour care for children whose parents work on commercial fishing boats.

The response of the federal government has largely been in the form of tax credits that allow families to deduct some of their child care expenses from their annual income taxes. President Bill Clinton has also reaffirmed his support for Early Head Start, and has argued for a liberalization of the Family and Medical Leave Act. Wisconsin's Senator Herb Kohl has drafted a bill allowing companies a tax credit if such companies expand child care facilities and associated resources. One of the most hotly debated issues is a national child care policy. Authors continue to note that the United States remains one of the few industrialized countries that does not have a government-supported child care system. However, critics of a publicly funded day care program argue that the costs of such programs would be too burdensome. According to the Center for the Future of Children, universal, high-quality child care could be achieved by adding an additional $80 billion to the $40 billion already invested on an annual basis. Other critics argue that women should stay out of the workforce and care for their children, because women who choose to work outside the home are, in part, responsible for the weakening of the American family.

Still, these responses to child care burdens and stresses have been criticized for being too limited in nature. For example, Sweden's national policy on parental leave allows for 12 months (not 12 weeks) of paid (not unpaid) parental leave, and an additional three months of leave with pay, although the pay during the additional three months is at a lower rate. Furthermore, Sweden's policy allows a parent to use the leave at any time before the child enters school. In Denmark, day care facilities must be available to all children.

Child care will be an issue in years to come; the question of who will take care of the children has yet to be answered. (NJM)

Bibliography

Barnet, Ann and Richard Barnet. "Childcare Brain Drain?" *Nation* 264, no. 18 (May 1997) 6–7.

Hofferth, Sandra. "The Demand For and Supply of Child Care in the 1990s." In Alan Booth, ed. *Child Care in the 1990s: Trends and Consequences*. Hillside, NJ: Erlbaum, 1992.

Knox, David and Caroline Schacht. *Choices in Relationships: An Introduction to Marriage and the Family*. St. Paul, MN: West Publishing Co., 1994.

Lamanna, Mary Ann and Agnes Riedmann. *Marriage and Families: Making Choices in a Diverse Society*. Belmont, CA: Wadsworth, 1996.

Renzetti, Claire and Daniel Curran. *Women, Men, and Society*. Boston: Allyn and Bacon, 1995.

Reynolds, Larry "A Crisis in Childcare?" *HR Focus* 74, no. 5 (May 1997): 8.

Schwartz, Felice N. "Management Women and the New Facts of Life." *Harvard Business Review* 67, no. 1 (January/February 1989): 65–76.

Shehan, Constance and Kenneth C. W. Kammeyer. *Marriages and Families: Reflections of a Gendered Society.* Boston: Allyn and Bacon, 1997.

Statistical Abstract of the United States. (113 Ed.) Washington, DC: U.S. Bureau of the Census, 1993.

Tucci, Amy. "Child Care Initiatives in the States." *Public Welfare* 53, no. 4 (Fall 1995): 44–48.

Child Custody and Support

Divorce rates in the United States have reached an all-time high. In the late 1990s, as many as 50 percent of all marriages end in divorce. Complicating an already stressful situation is the fact that the majority of marriages that end in divorce include minor children. Current estimates indicate that approximately 53 percent of all children will experience the divorce of their parents and spend time in a single-parent family. As a result, two basic questions emerge when the issue of divorce and children is explored: (1) Which parent will assume primary responsibility for, and physical custody of, the child; and (2) How will divorced parents share in the costs associated with the care of their children?

The issue of child custody has changed considerably over the years. Under **common law**, upon the dissolution of a marriage, the father maintained primary responsibility for, and physical custody of, his children. During the time, when the patriarchal family was strongly enforced by both social norms and institutions, the mother's relationship with her children was established through her marriage to their father. The mother's role in the life of her children could then end upon divorce, if that was what the father desired. At the beginning of the twentieth century, as patriarchal authority began to weaken, so too did the father's control over his children during a divorce. During this time, a new thought emerged, one which established that the primary responsibility for, and physical custody of, the child belonged to the mother, as it was her caretaking and nurturing that was vital for the healthy development of the child.

Over the past 100 years even more changes have occurred in child custody. First, there has been an increase in the number of fathers gaining custody of their children. There is little empirical evidence to suggest that fathers cannot provide for the healthy development of their children. Some critics have argued that the small number of fathers obtaining physical custody of their children is a result of traditional stereotypes that link caretaking and nurturing with the role of the mother. Therefore, more fathers are gaining physical custody of their children and, sometimes, financial support from their ex-wives. Between 1970 and 1990, the number of single fathers raising their children increased from 275,000 to 1,355,000. As there has been an increase in single fathers gaining custody of their children, there has also been a corresponding increase in the number of mothers who choose to voluntarily relinquish custody of their children. Unfortunately, women who choose to live apart from their children often experience guilt and shame due, in part, to the negative reactions of others to their choice. Another change in child custody is the increase in gay or lesbian parents gaining custody of their children. The American Psychological Association has provided strong support for the rights of gay and lesbian parents in child custody cases, arguing that there isn't any difference between the children raised by gay or lesbian parents and the children raised by heterosexual parents. There has also been an expansion in the types of child custody arrangements. Today three types of child custody agreements generally prevail: (1) sole custody—when the child is in the sole custody of one parent, and visits the other; (2) joint legal custody—when both parents are given equal rights in making decisions about the child's welfare, but the child lives with only one parent; and (3) joint physical custody—when the parents share not only in decision making, but also in physical custody. In these cases, it is not unusual for the child to live with one parent one week and the other parent the next week. Still, in spite of all these changes, child custody is awarded to mothers in about 90 percent of all cases, with the most common custody arrangement being that of sole custody.

When a parent has only limited contact with a child, and sometimes none at all, it is not surprising to find that these same parents manipulate their child support—financial payments that are meant to provide for the care of their children. Sometimes the mother does not seek child support from the father. Almost 40 percent of all divorced women with children do not ask for child support. In these cases, the mother is too often unable to afford an attorney to represent her interests, and is not granted child support simply because she did not have the financial resources to seek legal counsel. Sometimes the mother exchanges child support payments for a financial settlement, or property, or both. In other cases, because the father did not provide financial support prior to the divorce, it is not in the mother's interest to try to receive something that was not provided during the marriage. Some women who have been subjected to physical and emotional abuse by their husbands choose not to deal with them for reasons of personal safety or fear of retaliation. On the other hand, many women want and need child support. For those mothers who are awarded child support by the judicial system, payments are too often not honored by the fathers. Recent estimates show that even when men are ordered to pay child support, which averages less than $3,500 per year, only a slight majority honor their responsibility. According to the U.S. Bureau of the Census (1991), among the 54 percent of custodial parents who were awarded child support, a little over one-half received the full amount of the support awarded; one-quarter received partial payment; and one-quarter received no payment at all.

There are a number of reasons given by fathers who do not pay their minimum child support payments. It is not unusual to find that when either of the parents remarry, child support payments decrease. In the case of the divorced father, upon a remarriage, new family obligations often interfere with such payments, particularly if there are more children. If the divorced mother remarries, a biological father will sometimes transfer his financial obligations to the new stepfather, assuming that he will provide for the stepchildren. There are also issues of unemployment, underemployment, and unforeseen circumstances, such as accidents and illnesses, which interfere with the father's ability to pay. About one-third of noncustodial fathers had low incomes, some close to the poverty level, and were simply unable to pay. However, the most common reason for the lack of child support payments by fathers is that they are rarely sanctioned for nonpayment. As a result, "deadbeat dads" have become a theme for discussion as **poverty** rates among their children have become a social concern. With almost 60 percent of all children under the age of 6, in single-parent, mother-headed households living in poverty, there is little choice for these women but to turn to the public **welfare** system to make ends meet.

In light of the relationship between high delinquency rates and unpaid child support, a number of changes have been made in child support and collection policies. Title IV-D of the Social Security Act, the Child Support Amendments of 1984, and the **Family Support Act of 1988** are some of the federal legislative changes made. With the passage of Title IV-D of the Social Security Act, each state was required to establish a child support enforcement agency to assist custodial parents, whose children receive public assistance, in the establishment of child support awards and collection of the payments from such awards. Families whose children do not receive public assistance can voluntarily seek the same services. The **Child Support Enforcement Amendment of 1984** and the Family Support Act of 1988 require states to revise and expand child support enforcement programs, and allow for states to withhold child support payments from the noncustodial parent's pay when his or her children are receiving federal financial assistance. Though once challenged on constitutional grounds, the Child Support Recovery Act of 1992 allows the federal government to punish parents who fail to pay child support to their children living in other states.

The focus of the federal government has been upon those children who receive federal cash assistance because the noncustodial parent has not made the necessary child support payments. Now that public assistance has a time limit, financial support for children is critical, and the new welfare reform law includes an additional set of changes to the child support enforcement system. The new law reinforces the belief that responsible parents should financially support their children. If the government must provide some of this support, then the parents should be working. Federal law now mandates that states have procedures to order the noncustodial parent into work if the parent is behind on child support. Wisconsin has gone a step further by targeting unemployed, noncustodial fathers regardless of whether or not their children receive federal assistance. The new federal welfare law will also require women to provide information about the child's father for the purposes of establishing paternity and pursuing child support payments.

Because these mandates from the federal government hold the states responsible for the implementation of these laws, states have spent millions of dollars and hundreds of hours of labor complying. All 50 states have implemented automatic wage withholding of child support when the child support payment is a result of a court order. States like Arkansas are electronically transferring such withholdings directly to the State Office of Child Support Enforcement, which can, after appropriate deductions, directly deposit the payment into the bank account of the custodial parent. Not only does such a system reduce costs associated with the processing of these transactions, but, most importantly, it allows the money to reach the custodial parent in a timely fashion.

The divorce rate in the United States will probably not decrease, and children will likely continue to be subjected to the separation of their parents. Therefore, child custody and child support will remain critical issues. (NJM) **See also** Social Security.

Bibliography

Cameron, Paul and Kirk Cameron. "Did the APA Misrepresent the Scientific Literature to Courts in Support of Homosexual Custody?" *Journal of Psychology* 131, no. 3 (May 1997): 313–32.

Grannan, Philip. "Automating Child Support Collection." *American City and County* 112, no. 2 (February 1997): 8.

Greif, Geoffrey. "Working with Noncustodial Mothers." *Families in Society: The Journal of Contemporary Human Services* 78, no. 1 (January 1997): 46–52.

Pearson, Jessica and Esther Ann Griswold. "Child Support Policies and Domestic Violence." *Public Welfare* 55, no. 1 (Winter 1997): 26–32.

Shehan, Constance and Kenneth C. W. Kammeyer. *Marriages and Families: Reflections of a Gendered Society*. Boston: Allyn and Bacon, 1997.

Sorensen, Elaine. "States Move to Put Low-Income Noncustodial Parents in Work Activities." *Public Welfare* 55, no. 1 (Winter 1997): 17–23.

U.S. Bureau of the Census. *Statistical Abstract of the United States.* Washington, DC: U.S. Government Printing Office, 1995.

Child Support Enforcement Amendment of 1984

The Child Support Enforcement Amendment was established in 1984 to help women secure court-ordered child support payments as part of Title IV-D of the Social Security Act. It also helped prosecute parents delinquent on payments from wherever they might reside and required states that received federal welfare funding to enforce all court-ordered child support payments.

Even though the amendment provided relief to divorced mothers and their children, delinquent payments and inadequate awards continued to exist. In 1994, the program established by the amendment was modified so child support cases with an average debt of $21,000 could be managed by the Internal Revenue Service, improving the possibilities of collection for delinquent payments. **See also** Social Security.

BIBLIOGRAPHY

Elrod, Linda D. "Congress Tackles Domestic Relations Issues— A Look at the Changes in Divorce Taxation and Child Support Enforcement." *The Journal of the Kansas Bar Association* 53 (Winter 1984): 283–94.

Roberts, Paula. "Additional Remedies Under the Child Support Enforcement Amendments of 1984." *Clearinghouse Review* 20 (May 1986): 17–24.

Shirley Chisholm (1924–)

Shirley Chisholm first entered politics when she was elected to the New York State Assembly in 1964. She was easily reelected in 1965 and 1966. In the assembly, she championed educational issues as well as those of domestic workers.

A Democrat, Chisholm became the first African-American woman elected to the U.S. House of Representatives in 1968 when she was chosen to represent the 12th District of New York. She served in Congress from 1969 until her retirement in 1983. While in Congress, Chisholm was an advocate of minority and women's rights. Originally appointed to the Agriculture Committee, Chisholm fought that appointment and sought a post on the Veteran's Affairs Committee where she thought she could better serve her constituency. In 1972, she was appointed to the House Education and Labor Committee where she was an effective advocate of an increased minimum wage and increased subsidies for day care centers. In 1976, she was appointed to the powerful House Rules Committee, becoming not only the first woman, but the first African American to serve on the committee.

In 1972, Chisholm sought the presidential nomination for the **Democratic Party**. She chose Cissy Farenthold of Texas as her running mate. She received 28.7 percent of the popular vote and commanded 158 delegates at the 1972 Democratic National Convention. Upon reflection, she noted that her campaign faced more hurdles because she was a woman than because she was African American. While she lost that bid, she became a leading spokesperson for women and minorities.

After Jesse Jackson's failed attempt to win the Democratic Party nomination in 1984, Chisholm helped form the National Congress of Black Women and served as the group's first president. In 1983, she embarked on a teaching career, accepting a post in political science at Mount Holyoke College, where she taught until 1987.

BIBLIOGRAPHY

Brownmiller, Susan. *Shirley Chisholm, A Biography.* Garden City, NY: Doubleday, 1971.

Chisholm, Shirley. *The Good Fight.* New York: Harper, 1973.

———. *Unbought and Unbossed.* Boston: Hougton Mifflin, 1970.

Haskins, James. *Fighting Shirley Chisholm.* New York: Dial, 1975.

Scheader, Catherine. *Shirley Chisholm: Teacher and Congresswoman.* Hillside, NJ: Enslow Publishers, 1990.

Donna Marie Christian-Green (1945–)

Donna Christian-Green, a Democrat, is the fourth elected and first woman delegate from the United States Virgin Islands to the U.S. House of Representatives. Christian-Green was a community health physician for the U.S. Virgin Islands Department of Health and served two terms as president of the Virgin Islands Medical Society as well as holding other medical and public health posts. Christian-Green was elected a member of the Democratic National Committee in 1984 and has served on the platform committee twice.

BIBLIOGRAPHY

Trafford, Abigail. "A Head Start on Health." *Washington Post* (September 16, 1997): H6.

Marguerite Stitt Church (1892–1990)

Succeeding her husband Ralph E. Church, who died in 1950, Marguerite Stitt Church, a Republican, served in the U.S. House of Representatives from Illinois from 1951 to 1963. While in office, Church introduced measures to implement recommendations made by the Hoover Commission that called for greater efficiency and economy in government. She also sponsored legislation that made it a federal offense to transport fireworks into states where they were prohibited.

BIBLIOGRAPHY

Church, Marguerite Stitt. *Oral History Interview, Former Member of Congress Association.* Washington, DC: Manuscript Division, Library of Congress, 1978.

Citizens Advisory Council on the Status of Women (1963)

Created by President John F. Kennedy in 1963, the Citizens Advisory Council on the Status of Women (CACSW) was intended to continue the work of the **President's Commission on the Status of Women (PCSW)**, an advisory body to the president on women's issues. The CACSW continued to advise presidents until 1977, when President Jimmy Carter replaced it with a similar advisory body that was eliminated from the administrations of Presidents Ronald Reagan and George Bush.

The February 7, 1970, CACSW report to President Richard Nixon endorsed the **Equal Rights Amendment (ERA)**. The CACSW reported that the Equal Rights Amendment would fill an important need in American society. The Council was the first governmental body to endorse the amendment. The CACSW was also important because of its enduring impact on the women's rights movement. This advisory council inspired the creation of similar bodies at other levels of the U. S. political system. These organizations worked to monitor the political and social status of women. Advisory councils modeled after the original existed in all 50 states. The result was the establishment of a network of information and experiences for women's rights activists. The fundamental impact of these commissions was to raise the political profile of women's issues across the nation at both the state and national levels. (JEH) **See also** Women's Movement

BIBLIOGRAPHY

Davis, Flora. *Moving the Mountain: The Women's Movement in America Since 1960.* New York: Simon and Schuster, 1991.

Tilly, Louise A. and Patricia Gurin, eds. *Women, Politics and Change.* New York: Russell Sage, 1990.

Civil Rights Act of 1964

The Civil Rights Act (CRA) of 1964 was intended to alleviate discrimination in employment, education, and public accommodations. Sent to Congress by President John Kennedy on June 19, 1963, the bill sought equal access to public accommodations, guarantees of desegregation in public schools, protection of **voting rights**, and an end to employment discrimination.

The most far-reaching section of the Civil Rights Act, **Title VII**, banned employment discrimination in private industry. As originally proposed, Title VII prohibited discrimination in employment on the basis of race, color, national origin, and religion. As the bill moved closer to passage, its opponents attempted to block it by inserting a prohibition against **sex discrimination** into it. They hoped this would create enough controversy to prevent the bill's passage. The plan backfired, and the Civil Rights Act was signed into law, with the ban on sex discrimination, by President Lyndon Johnson on July 2, 1964. The 1964 CRA has served as a model for equal employment statutes for other groups, such as the elderly and the disabled.

At first limited to private employers and labor unions with 25 or more employees, Title VII was expanded to apply to unions and companies with 15 or more employees as well as federal, state, county, and municipal workers and employees of educational institutions.

Another important section of the CRA, Title II, attempted to ban discrimination in public accommodations, such as theaters, hotels, motels, and restaurants. Title II prompted numerous demonstrations, termed "sit-ins," at segregated stores and restaurants. Enacted under congressional authority to regulate interstate commerce, its coverage is far-reaching, extending to all establishments that "affect commerce." In *Heart of Atlanta v. United States* (1964) and *Katzenbach v. McClung* (1964), the U.S. Supreme Court upheld the constitutionality of Title II against challenges that it interfered with the rights of private business owners.

The 1964 CRA also created the **Equal Employment Opportunity Commission (EEOC)** as an enforcement agency. At first the EEOC had only limited authority, but in 1972 Congress authorized it to file lawsuits against employers after unsuccessful attempts at voluntary conciliation. Also, beginning in 1974, it was given authority to bring "patterns and practice" lawsuits (suits charging systematic discrimination on an industry-wide or company-wide basis). It has been designated the "lead agency" in employment discrimination.

In the 1970s, the 1964 CRA, and especially Title VII, was at the heart of the controversy over **affirmative action**. Affirmative action refers to efforts by employers and educational institutions to reach the goals of equal opportunity by providing more diversity in the workplace or schools. The debate revolves around the question of whether Title VII of the CRA permits employers or universities to establish preferential hiring systems or admissions policies to achieve racial or sexual balance. One side argues that the goal of Title VII is a color-blind, gender neutral society and that equal employment opportunity will be achieved when gender and race are no longer relevant to employment decisions. The other side argues that until society is truly color-blind, race and sex have to be considered in employment decisions to eradicate racial and sexual inequality in the U.S. labor force. In *Adarand v. Pena* (1995), the U.S. Supreme Court adopted the view that employment decisions based on race are almost always unconstitutional. The concept of "affirmative action" is one upon which many Americans are divided. (SM) **See also** Equal Employment Opportunity Act.

BIBLIOGRAPHY

Adarand v. Pena, 515 U.S. 200 (1995).

Amaker, Norman. *Civil Rights and the Reagan Administration.* Washington, DC: Urban Institute Press, 1988.

Heart of Atlanta, Inc. v. United States, 279 U.S. 241 (1964).

Katzenbach v. McClung, 379 U.S. 294 (1964).

Maschke, Karen. *Litigation, Courts, and Women Workers.* New York: Praeger Publishers, 1989.

Civil Rights Act of 1991

The Civil Rights Act of 1991 was designed to reverse several U.S. Supreme Court decisions from 1989 that significantly limited the scope of federal anti-discrimination laws. These decisions included ***Wards Cove Packing Company v. Antonio***, 490 U.S. 642 (1989); *Patterson v. McLean Credit Union*, 491 U.S. 164 (1989); *Lorance v. AT&T Technologies*, 490 U.S. 900 (1989); ***Price Waterhouse v. Hopkins***, 490 U.S. 228 (1988); and *Martin v. Wilks*, 490 U.S. 755 (1989).

Among its provisions, the act calls for jury trials for cases of intentional discrimination and permits the recovery of compensatory and punitive damages. Prior to the act, issues of discrimination were decided by a judge. The act also places on employers the burden of proving that a challenged employment practice is a business necessity. Previously, the burden of proof had rested on the employee, and employers had only to produce evidence of a business justification for the practice. The Civil Rights Act of 1991 also provided the legislative basis for the formation of the **Glass Ceiling** Commission, which is charged with conducting ongoing studies and investigations of whether women and minorities are prevented by discrimination from rising to the highest levels of corporate America.

The U.S. Supreme Court ruled that the act could not be applied retroactively to cases filed before the act's passage. The Court ruled that it would be unfair to penalize an employer now for actions that were legal then. The Court also hinted, but did not rule, that the principle of retroactivity was probably unconstitutional.

BIBLIOGRAPHY

Brown, Barbara Berish. "The Civil Rights Act of 1991." *Employment Relations Today* 18 (December 22, 1991): 4.

Mann, Judith. "Feminism, Alive and Well." *Washington Post* (November 1, 1991): D3.

Savage David G. "Job Bias Law Not Retroactive." *Los Angeles Times* (April 27, 1994): D2.

Civil Rights Restoration Act (1988)

Through the introduction and passage of the Civil Rights Restoration Act, legislators attempted to clearly define **Title IX of the Education Amendments of 1972** and amend three additional civil rights statutes: Title VI of the **Civil Rights Act of 1964**, section 504 of the 1972 Rehabilitation Act, and the Age Discrimination Act of 1975. The bill enjoyed support and success in the House of Representatives but encountered opposition in the Senate. On April 12, 1984, House members introduced HR 5490 and senators introduced S 2568. The House Judiciary and House Education and Labor committees quickly sent the bill to the full chamber. The House by a wide margin (375–32) passed the civil rights legislation on June 26, 1984. The Senate's version, however, did not make it out of the Labor and Human Resources Committee. The bill reached the Senate floor when proponents of the Civil Rights Act offered it as an amendment to a continuing appropriations bill. The Senate subsequently tabled the civil rights amendment to House Joint Resolution 648 on October 2, 1984. Consequently, the civil rights measure did not survive congressional debate and died on the Senate floor.

Congress introduced the Civil Rights Act of 1984 in response to the Supreme Court's decision in ***Grove City College v. Bell***. On February 28, 1984, the Court narrowly interpreted **Title IX of the Educational Amendments Act of 1972**. The decision diminished the scope of a ban on **sex discrimination** in all federally aided schools and colleges. According to the Supreme Court, the anti-discrimination provision of Title IX applied only the program receiving federal funds and did not encompass the entire institution. The Civil Rights Act of 1984 sought to overturn this ruling and ensure that any institution receiving federal aid complied with non-discrimination laws.

Although the Civil Rights Act of 1984 failed to become law, civil rights activists did not abandon the campaign to protect women against discrimination. Civil rights advocates continued in their endeavors to overturn the *Grove City* ruling. On January 24, 1985, the House introduced a similar bill renamed the Civil Rights Restoration Act. Congress, however, did not succeed in broadening the scope of Title IX and other civil rights legislation until 1988 when both the House and Senate passed and overrode President Ronald Reagan's veto of the Civil Rights Restoration Act. (MG)

BIBLIOGRAPHY

Amaker, Norman C. *Civil Rights and the Reagan Administration.* Washington, DC: The Urban Institute Press, 1988.

Congressional Quarterly Almanac: 98th Congress 2nd Session. . 1984 Volume XL. Washington, DC: Congressional Quarterly Inc., 1984.

Hoff, Joan. *Law Gender and Injustice: A Legal History of U.S. Women.* New York: New York University Press, 1991.

Civil War Constitutional Amendments

Following the 1865 defeat of the Confederacy, the U.S. Congress passed three Civil War Amendments to the Constitution. The Thirteenth Amendment (1865) abolished slavery; the Fourteenth Amendment (1868) extended citizenship to all men born or naturalized in the United States; and the Fifteenth Amendment (1870) granted **voting rights** to former male slaves.

Although members of the **abolition** movement and the **Republican Party** fought for their passage, these amendments provoked controversy within the women's rights movements. As activists in the abolition movement, women had worked for decades to end the enslavement of African Americans. Their participation had afforded them previously unknown political experience and made them aware of male abolitionists' efforts to limit and control their activism. In the process, female abolitionists developed a deeper understanding of their own oppression as women and of the value of political activity to overcome it. Many women abolitionists drew parallels between the enslavement of African Americans and their own subjugation as women. Defining human equality as their goal, they believed that the emancipation of the slaves and of women should receive unqualified support from all members of the abolition movement and the Republican Party.

Feminist leaders who had been active in the abolition movement, particularly **Elizabeth Cady Stanton** and **Susan B. Anthony**, responded to the exclusion of women from privileges of citizenship and voting with dismay and anger. Their refusal to support either the Fourteenth or Fifteenth Amendments led to bitter arguments in the abolition movement and the dissolution of the **Equal Rights Association**. Declaring that the post-Civil War period was the "Negro's Hour," leading members of the Republican Party and the abolition movement (both men and women) believed that the most important fight, and the one most likely to succeed, was the enfranchisement of black men, not the enfranchisement of women. This argument for "political expediency" enraged Stanton, who responded with heretofore unsuspected racism. Arguing that white women were more qualified to vote than black men, she added that black women would be better off as "the slave of an educated white man, than of a degraded, ignorant black one." This controversy effectively ended the alliance between the abolition and women's rights movements. It also led to the formation of women's groups dedicated to female **suffrage**. (MP) **See also** Slavery and Women; Women's Movement.

BIBLIOGRAPHY

Clinton, Catherine. *The Other Civil War. American Women in the Nineteenth Century.* New York: Hill and Wang, 1992.

Foner, Eric. *Reconstruction. America's Unfinished Revolution 1863–1877.* New York: Harper & Row, 1988.

Griffith, Elizabeth. *In Her Own Right: The Life of Elizabeth Cady Stanton.* Oxford: Oxford University Press, 1984.

Marian Williams Clark (1880–1953)

Marian Clark was elected as a Republican from New York to the U.S. House of Representatives on December 28, 1933, to fill the vacancy of her deceased husband John Davenport Clark. She served in Congress until January 3, 1935, declining to run for reelection. In 1936, Clark was an alternate delegate to the Republican National Convention in Cleveland.

BIBLIOGRAPHY

Canning, Hazel. "She Represents New York." *Independent Woman* 14 (December 1934): 375, 402.

Frances Cleveland (1864–1947)

Wife of President Grover Cleveland, Frances Cleveland was born in Buffalo, New York, on July 21, 1864. She was the daughter of Grover Cleveland's law associate, Oscar Folsom. Cleveland became executor of the estate when Frances Folsom's father died. When she was just 21 years old and after she had graduated from Wells College, Frances and Grover Cleveland were engaged and married. She was the first woman to be married in the White House, and was always known for her loveliness, simplicity, and "infinite tact." She was extremely popular with the American public and was dedicated to her husband. While she did not make many public commitments, those that she engaged in were on behalf of African Americans. She attempted to found the Washington Home for Friendless Colored Girls and was the most visible member of the "Colored Christmas Club," a charity that provided food for poor children. She also ended the restriction that had barred African Americans from open houses and public receptions in the White House. She married Thomas Preston, Jr., a professor of archeology, five years after Grover Cleveland died in 1908. (GVS) **See also** First Ladies.

While first lady, Frances Cleveland lifted the ban preventing African Americans from attending open houses and public receptions at the White House. Library of Congress.

BIBLIOGRAPHY

Bassett, Margaret. *Profiles and Portraits of American Presidents and Their Wives.* Freeport, ME: The Bond Wheelwright Company, 1969.

Williams, Francis Howard. *The Bride of the White House.* Philadelphia: Bradley and Co., 1886.

Cleveland Board of Education v. LaFleur (1973)

In *Cleveland Board of Education v. LaFleur*, 414 U.S. 632 (1973), the U.S. Supreme Court struck down mandatory maternity leave policies in Cleveland, Ohio, and Chesterfield County, Virginia. The Court ruled that Cleveland's policy of requiring pregnant teachers to take unpaid leave five months prior to childbirth, remain on leave until the school semester after the child reached the age of three months, and require doctor's certification of the physical fitness of the teacher before returning to work, violated the Due Process Clause of the Fourteenth Amendment. The Court also ruled against Chesterfield County's similar policies.

The Court did not agree with the school board's argument that the leave policy was instituted to help insure a smooth instructional transition by allowing for the necessary administrative tasks to be completed, including the hiring of a substitute teacher. It found that the board's use of unwarranted presumptions in regard to a woman's health were too burdensome on her constitutional liberties.

BIBLIOGRAPHY

Bolmeier, Edward C. *Sex Litigation and the Public Schools.* Charlottesville, VA: Michie, 1975.

Goodman, Carl F. "Public Employment and the Supreme Court." *Civil Service Journal* 15 (July 1974): 18–22.

"Significant Cases in Labor Cases." *Monthly Labor Review* 97 (April 1974): 65–67.

Hillary Rodham Clinton (1947–)

Throughout her husband Bill Clinton's candidacy and presidency, Hillary Rodham Clinton has been one of the most admired and most criticized **first ladies** in American history. Specific criticism has centered around her role in Whitewater, a scandal concerning possible improper land dealings in Arkansas in the 1980s, and the claim that she has too much power for an unelected official, particularly her spear-heading of health care reform in 1993. Generally, she has received criticism for being nontraditional. Hillary Rodham Clinton believes that the harsh criticism of herself and her husband is due to the political and social transition from the 1980s to the 1990s. Through it all her approval ratings have remained remarkably resilient.

Hillary Rodham Clinton has been unlike most first ladies because she was powerful in her own right before she became first lady. As a partner in Arkansas' prestigious Rose Law Firm and a well-known advocate for children's rights and educational reform, she had already achieved a national reputation. As a young lawyer, she had served on the staff of the Nixon impeachment committee. At Wellesley College's 1969 commencement, Clinton became the first student to deliver a commencement address, and her speech was reported by *Life* magazine. At Yale Law School, she was chosen to the League of Women Voters' Youth Advisory Committee. While at Yale, she spent a lot of time traveling between New Haven and Washington attending congressional hearings on children and meeting with her mentor, Marian Wright Edelman, who heads the Children's Defense Fund. In 1997, Hillary Rodham Clinton became the first first lady to win a Grammy award for the audiotape version of her best-seller *It Takes a Village.* The title is based on an African proverb that says it takes a village to raise a child. (EP)

One of the most admired and most criticized first ladies, Hillary Rodham Clinton has been an important policy advisor to her husband. Library of Congress, Prints and Photographs Division.

BIBLIOGRAPHY

Radcliffe, Donnie. *Hillary Rodham Clinton: A First Lady for Our Times.* New York: Warner Books, 1993.

Truman, Margaret. *First Ladies: An Intimate Group Portrait of White House Wives.* New York: Random House, 1995.

Walker, Martin. *The President We Deserve: Bill Clinton: His Rise, Falls, and Comebacks.* New York: Crown Publishers, Inc., 1996.

Woodward, Bob. *The Agenda: Inside the Clinton White House.* New York: Simon and Schuster, 1994.

Club Movement

The Club Movement started in the late nineteenth century as a number of local organizations dedicated to women's and minority rights. Usually begun as social organizations, the groups quickly became involved in education and job reforms as well as political issues like women's **suffrage** and anti-lynching campaigns. Several clubs became national organizations like the **National Association of Colored Women (NACW)**, which was led by **Mary Church Terrell** and the **National Council of Negro Women (NCNW)** led by **Mary McLeod Bethune.**

BIBLIOGRAPHY

Giddings, Paula. *When and Where I Enter.* New York: Morrow, 1984.

Coalition for Women's Appointments

In 1969, the **National Federation of Business and Professional Women's Clubs** organized a coalition of women's organizations to contribute names to a talent bank. Intended for use in making presidential appointments, this resource was used by the Nixon administration. The term "talent bank" gradually became synonomous with efforts to advance women as credible appointees. The **National Women's Political Caucus (NWPC)** participated in these generalized initiatives until the 1976 presidential transition, when it established the Coalition for Women's Appointments to better focus lobbying efforts. The Coalition has subsequently been renewed in each presidential transition. (JMM; MAB)

BIBLIOGRAPHY

Borelli, MaryAnne. *Patterns of Opportunity, Patterns of Constraint: The Nomination and Confirmation of Women Cabinet Members in the United States.* Ann Arbor: University of Michigan Press, forthcoming.

Martin, Janet M. *A Place in the Oval Office: Women and the American Presidency.* Ann Arbor: University of Michigan Press, forthcoming.

Colautti v. Franklin (1978)

At issue in *Colautti v. Franklin*, 439 U.S. 379 (1978), was the Pennsylvania **Abortion Control Act** of 1974 that imposed criminal penalties on physicians who performed an **abortion** when the fetus was viable or if they had "sufficient reason to believe" it was viable. The act used the ***Roe v. Wade*** benchmark to define viability as the ability to survive outside the mother's womb.

The majority opinion of the U.S. Supreme Court struck down the law as unconstitutional. The majority stated that the ambiguity and vagueness of the physician's duty to the fetus if it was unclear whether the fetus was viable. Also, the majority stated that the effect of the law was to deny women in the second trimester an abortion because the most commonly used method—saline amniocentesis—could not be performed. Rather, more costly and more dangerous techniques would have to be used in its place.

The three-judge minority dissented by stating that the majority decision in this case went far beyond *Roe* and had "withdrawn from the States a substantial measure of the power to protect fetal life that was reserved to them."

BIBLIOGRAPHY

Boumil, Marcia Mobilia and Stephen C. Hicks. *Women and the Law.* Littleton, CO: Fred B. Rothman & Co., 1992.

Barbara-Rose Collins (1939–)

First elected in 1990, Democrat Barbara-Rose Collins served three terms in the U.S. House of Representatives representing Michigan's 15th District. She began her political career as a member of the Michigan state legislature, a position she fulfilled from 1975 to 1982. Collins next served on the Detroit City Council from 1982 to 1990. In Congress, Collins served on the Government Reform, Oversight, and Transportation and Infrastructure committees. She lost her reelection bid in 1996.

BIBLIOGRAPHY
"Black Caucus Loses Four Members After 104th Session of Congress." *Jet* 90, no. 23 (October 21, 1996): 4.
Wells, Robert Marshall. "Collins Loses to Kilpatrick." *Congressional Quarterly Weekly Report* 54, no. 32 (August 10, 1996): 2264.

Cardiss Hortaise Robertson Collins (1931–)

Cardiss Collins, a Democrat, was elected to the U.S. House of Representatives from Illinois on June 5, 1973, replacing her husband Representative George Collins, who died in a plane crash. With her election, she became the first African-American woman to serve the state in Congress. While in Congress, she sought to build unity in the Congressional Black Caucus. She served on a number of important committees, including the House Democratic Steering Committee, the Energy and Commerce committees, and the House Select Committee on Drug Abuse and Control. She did not run for reelection in 1996.

BIBLIOGRAPHY
Edward, Audrey. "Cardiss Collins: Do Your Votes Count?" *Essence Magazine* 11 (November 1980): 84–85, 102, 105, 107.
Reynolds, Barbara. "A Black Woman's Place Is in the . . . House of Representatives." *Ebony* 46 (January 1991): 104–105, 108, 110.
———. "Cardiss Collins, Chairperson." *Black Collegian* 9 (May–June 1979): 36–37.

Martha Layne Collins (1936–)

Martha Collins, a Democrat, served as lieutenant governor of Kentucky from 1973 to 1983, and acted as chair of the National Conference of Lieutenant Governors from 1982 to 1983. In 1983, Collins was elected governor of Kentucky, serving until 1987. While governor, she acted as secretary of the Kentucky Education and Humanities Cabinet from 1984 to 1987, and held membership on the federal government's Task Force on Drug and Substance Abuse in 1987. In 1984, many speculated that she might be tapped as a vice presidential candidate but the candidacy went to **Geraldine Ferraro**.

BIBLIOGRAPHY
Lynn, Frank. "Which Woman for the White House?" *50 Plus* 25 (February 1985): 24.
Rozen, Leah. "Kentucky's New First Family Includes Another Beauty Queen—But Martha Layne Collins Is the Governor." *People Weekly* 20 (November 28, 1983): 58.

Susan M. Collins (1952–)

Susan Collins was elected to the U.S. Senate from Maine to fill the seat being vacated by the retirement of William Cohen. Collins, a moderate Republican, served on Cohen's staff as an aide from 1975 to 1987 and had been active for a number of years in Maine politics. In 1994, she ran unsuccessfully for governor.

BIBLIOGRAPHY
Greenblatt, Alan. "Contest to Succeed Cohen Has a Familiar Cast." *Congressional Quarterly Weekly Report* 54, no. 24 (15 June 1996): 1709.
Winerip, Michael. "A Moderate's Moment." *New York Times Magazine* (July 20, 1997): 18.

Lucy Newhall Colman (1817–1906)

In 1853, Lucy Colman worked successfully for the end of segregated schools in the Rochester, New York, area and for an end to corporal punishment. Colman became a lecturer on anti-slavery issues, touring through New York, Pennsylvania, Michigan, Illinois, Indiana, and Ohio. After the Civil War, she worked at the National Colored Orphan Asylum in Washington, focusing her efforts on ensuring equal and humane treatment for the establishment's wards. She also served as superintendent for colored schools supported by the New York Aid Society. After 1873, Colman moved to the Syracuse area where she became active in the Spiritualist Society, joined the J.S. Mill Liberal League, and contributed to the *Truth Seeker*, a reform issues newspaper.

BIBLIOGRAPHY
Colman, Lucy. *Reminiscences.* Buffalo: H.L. Green, 1891.
May, John. *Danforth Geneology.* Boston: Pope, 1906.

Colored Woman's League

The Colored Woman's League was originally founded in 1896 to meet the educational, social, and civil rights needs of African-American women, many of whom were not allowed to join "white" female clubs. The Colored Woman's League met some initial success but gained greater influence a few years later when it merged with another group, the **National Federation of Afro-American Women (NFAAW)**, to form the National Association of Colored Women's Clubs, the title the group still goes by. The National Association of Colored Women's Clubs currently focuses on programs of civil service, education, and philanthropy, as well as state and national legislation for the betterment of others. The group also publishes its own quarterly newsletter, *National Notes*, which helps keep members abroad informed of relevant issues. **See also** Club Movement; National Association of Colored Women.

To advance their causes, many African-American women formed local and national clubs to act as a supportive network. Pictured here are the officers of the turn-of-the-century Colored Women's League of Newport, Rhode Island. Library of Congress.

BIBLIOGRAPHY

Davis, Elizabeth Linsay. *Lifting As They Climb.* Washington, DC: National Association of Colored Women, 1933.

Common Law

The common law is the traditional English unwritten code of law based on judicial precedent that forms the basis for the American legal system. Included in the common law tradition was the custom of **coverture**, which placed severe limitations on the rights of married women. Under the doctrine of coverture, a married woman lost her legal identity, becoming a *femme covert* — literally, a woman covered by a man. A married woman could not sign a contract, sue or be sued, keep her wages, or own property. In the event of a divorce, the father retained absolute right to custody of the children. Although dower rights insured the economic status of a woman entering marriage, there were no protections against a husband who might squander her property or inheritance. Women's rights activists lobbied state legislatures for reforms and the first **Married Woman's Property Act**s were passed in Mississippi in 1839 and New York in 1848, giving women the right to control their wages and to own property. Feminists continued to lobby to expand the reforms, which took decades to achieve on a state-by state-basis. The efforts of women's rights activists were joined by male legislators who sought to protect the inheritances of their married daughters. Although remnants of common law remained in the law books well into the twentieth century, the outmoded statutes were no longer enforced. (LvA)

BIBLIOGRAPHY

Kerber, Linda K. and Jane Sherron De Hart, Eds. *Women's America: Refocusing the Past.* Fourth Edition. New York: Oxford University Press, 1995.

McGlen, Nancy and Karen O'Connor. *Women, Politics, and American Society.* Englewood Cliffs, NJ: Prentice Hall, 1995.

Communist Party, USA

In the early twentieth century, American women began to take leadership roles in communist organizations in the United States. Communist philosophy paralelled the desire for equality that many women in the **suffrage** movement sought not only in politics but in all aspects of life. Labor activists like **Elizabeth Gurley Flynn** were instrumental in the success of communist organizations, like the International Workers of the World.

The Communist Party, USA, has a platform based on full equality and against all forms of racism, chauvinism, and discrimination. It supports full equality for all immigrants without regard to their legal status. It favors government-run health care, day care, and other family-oriented programs. The CPUSA has supported a number of female candidates for a variety of offices, including several for the presidency of the United States, among them **Angela Davis**. (SD)

BIBLIOGRAPHY

Klehr, Harvey. *The American Communist Movement.* New York: Maxwell MacMillan, 1992.

Comparable Worth

Comparable worth, or equal pay for equal work of equal value, aims to address the persistent gap between men's and women's compensation. Comparable worth differs from equal pay provisions in that it allows for comparisons across otherwise dissimilar job categories within the same firm. It is based on the allegation that much of the pay gap (women earned approximately 75 percent of what men earned in 1992) is explained by sex-based occupational segregation resulting from past or current discrimination. Female-dominated jobs (generally, jobs with 70 percent or more female workers) pay less than male-dominated jobs even when the skills required are fundamentally the same. Implementation of a comparable worth policy requires assignment of job evaluation point scores to predominantly male and female jobs by outside experts, statistical estimation of the economic worth of identified job skills, and adjustment of female wages to male wages when appropriate.

An early twentieth-century poster advocating higher wages for women workers. National Archives.

Opponents of comparable worth tend to focus on the economic effects of altering market-determined wages. Higher relative wages for women may result in increased unemployment for women. Labor shortages and surpluses created by comparable worth wage-setting would not be eliminated through the market mechanisms of increasing wages for jobs in demand and decreasing wages for those with too great a supply of workers. Moreover, opponents are concerned about the subjective nature of job evaluations. Proponents of comparable worth focus on labor market imperfections that interfere with market determination of wages, such as seniority provisions, statistical discrimination, unions, imperfect information, tradition, and barriers to occupational choice. Comparable worth, in this view, is the wage the market would pay without these imperfections. Institution of a comparable worth policy would benefit those women harmed by past market imperfections who are not in a position to change to jobs previously reserved for males.

Although the U.S. Supreme Court has not endorsed the principle of comparable worth, it did find in ***County of Washington v. Gunther* (1981)** that comparable worth comparisons were not precluded under **Title VII of the Civil Rights Act of 1964**. By 1984, 25 states had legislation relating to comparable worth and 10 had implemented or were about to implement comparable worth for public sector employees. The most serious attempts to implement comparable worth policies in the public sector have occurred in Minnesota, Iowa, and the state of Washington. (AMD)

Bibliography

England, Paula. *Comparable Worth: Theories and Evidence.* New York: Aldine de Gruyter, 1992.

Elizabeth Leslie Rous Comstock (1815–1891)

Elizabeth Comstock worked as a religious and social reform activist in the Quaker community. She championed **abolition**, peace, **temperance**, and **suffrage**. In the 1870s, she gave talks for the **Women's Christian Temperance Union (WCTU)** and in 1879 became secretary of the Kansas Freedmen's Relief Association.

Bibliography

Hare, Catherine. *Life and Letters of Elizabeth L. Comstock.* Philidelphia: Winston, 1895.

Jones, Rufus. *The Later Periods of Quakerism.* London: Macmillan, 1921.

Comstock Act (1873)

In 1873 at the behest of moral crusader Anthony Comstock (1844–1915), Congress passed the Comstock Act prohibiting the distribution of obscene materials through the U. S. mail. The law's definition of obscene included **pornography**, **abortion**, and "every article, instrument, substance, drug, medicine, or thing which is advertised or described in a manner calculated to lead another to use or apply it for preventing conception or producing abortions, or for any indecent or immoral purpose." The law forbade the importation or sale of birth control devices or literature about them across state lines. States responded by enacting their own versions of the Comstock Act, thereby prohibiting the distribution of contraceptives within states as well. Comstock ardently enforced the law through his Society for the Suppression of Vice and through his position as a U.S. postal inspector, which he used to seize mail and raid newspapers. Comstock went so far as to entrap physicians by writing under false names to request birth control information. In effect, the Comstock Act stalled the birth control movement. Although the law did not prevent the use of contraception, and educated, middle-class women were controlling *their* fertility, poor women continued to have large families. The prohibitions against birth control were not removed from the Comstock Act until 1971. (LvA) **See also** Margaret Sanger.

Bibliography

Back, Kurt W. *Family Planning and Population Control: The Challenge of a Successful Movement.* Boston: Twayne Publishers, 1989.

Chesler, Ellen. *Woman of Valor: Margaret Sanger and the Birth Control Movement in America.* New York: Simon and Schuster, 1992.

Concerned Women for America (CWA)

In the 1990s, Concerned Women for America (CWA) is the largest and best organized antifeminist organization in the United States. Founded by Beverly LaHaye in 1979, CWA claims several hundred thousand members, including anyone who has contributed money to the group or signed one of the organization's petitions. CWA is organized at the grass roots, with more than 2,500 local affiliates, many of which were initially formed as prayer and Bible study groups but which now prove especially effective in lobbying legislators in the local districts. The organization is dedicated to protect the family and preserve traditional Christian-American values. It also has a litigation and lobbying arm in Washington. (CW) **See also** Antifeminism.

Bibliography

Moen, Matthew. *The Transformation of the Christian Right.* Tuscaloosa: University of Alabama Press, 1992.

Rozell, Mark J. and Clyde Wilcox. *Second Coming: The Christian Right in Virginia Politics.* Baltimore: John Hopkins University Press, 1996.

Congressional Caucus for Women's Issues and Women's Policy, Inc.

Founded in 1977 as the **Congresswomen's Caucus**, the Congressional Caucus for Women's Issues, which adopted its current name in 1982, is a member service organization in the House of Representatives co-chaired by Republican **Nancy Johnson** of Connecticut and Democrat **Eleanor Holmes Norton**, the delegate from Washington, DC. An advocate for women's economic equity, family and medical leave, health equity, **affirmative action**, and freedom of choice, the caucus, under new rules passed by the Republican majority, was forced to sever itself from its staff operation in 1995. Affiliated congresswomen develop strategy and share staff, but status reports, formerly prepared by the caucus staff, are now available by subscription from Women's Policy, Inc. **See also** Economic Equity Act (1986); Freedom of Choice Act. (JHT)

Bibliography

Gertzog, Irvin N. *Congressional Women: Their Recruitment, Integration, and Behavior.* 2nd ed. Westport, CT: Praeger, 1995.

Hammond, Susan Webb. *Congressional Caucuses in National Policymaking.* Baltimore: Johns Hopkins University Press, 1997.

Congressional Union

The Congressional Union was formed by **Alice Paul** and **Lucy Burns** in 1914, with the goal of gaining **suffrage** for women through militant tactics and by campaigning against the party in power. It revived and led the fight for a suffrage amendment to the Constitution.

The Congressional Union began as a militant offspring of the **National American Woman Suffrage Association**'s Congressional Committee, which Alice Paul headed, and which she and Burns used to lobby Congress for suffrage in 1913. Paul and Burns left the NAWSA when their strategies for achieving suffrage were deemed '"radical"' by the organization's leadership. The newly formed Congressional Union campaigned against the party in power, the Democrats, as a means of holding that party accountable for the failure to pass a suffrage bill. The union also actively lobbied Congress for a constitutional amendment.

The **Nineteenth Amendment** to the Constitution ultimately was ratified in 1920. Reorganized as the **National Woman's Party (NWP),** in 1916, the Congressional Union attempted to lead the way after the passage of the Nineteenth Amendment by proposing an equal rights amendment. **See also** National American Woman Suffrage Association (NAWSA). (JEH)

BIBLIOGRAPHY

McGlen, Nancy and Karen O'Connor. *Women, Politics and American Society.* Englewood Cliffs, NJ: Prentice Hall, 1995.

Congresswomen's Caucus

In 1977, the women in Congress, led by **Elizabeth Holtzman** (D-NY), **Margaret Heckler** (R-MA), and **Shirley Chisholm** (D-NY), organized the Congresswomen's Caucus to devote special attention to women's issues in Congress. The caucus supported the **Equal Rights Amendment (ERA)** and under co-chairs Holtzman and Heckler, won enactment of an extension for ratification of the amendment. The caucus also proposed the **Economic Equity Act** in the House. In 1982, needing more financial and political resources after the election of President Ronald Reagan, the bipartisan caucus expanded to include congressmen and changed its name to the **Congressional Caucus for Women's Issues**. (JHT)

BIBLIOGRAPHY

Gertzog, Irvin N. *Congressional Women: Their Recruitment, Integration, and Behavior.* 2nd ed. Westport, CT: Praeger, 1995.

Slavin, Sarah, ed. *U.S. Women's Interest Groups: Institutional Profiles.* Westport, CT: Greenwood Press, 1995.

Consciousness Raising

Consciousness raising groups were an important element of the **women's movement** of the 1970s. The purpose of the groups was to gather women together to discuss their concerns as women. These groups soon comprised the basic unit of organization for the women's movement because of their success in stimulating interest and grass-roots participation. Originally, groups formed as a result of women meeting to talk about their lives and problems. Gatherings would focus on one particular topic, with members of the group taking turns to express their opinions and ideas. Men were explicitly prohibited from attending because women felt any male influence would likely be paternalistic in nature, thereby defeating the purpose of the meeting.

Consciousness raising not only increased the awareness of individual women, but it brought their shared problems to light. Women realized for the first time that their feelings of anger, inferiority, and frustration were shared. The impact of consciousness raising was widespread, particularly in motivating women to actively work for the women's movement. (JEH)

BIBLIOGRAPHY

Davis, Flora. *Moving the Mountain.* New York: Simon and Schuster, 1991.

Steinem, Gloria. *Outrageous Acts and Everyday Rebellions.* New York: Holt, Rinehart and Winston, 1983.

Ware, Cellestine. *Woman Power: The Movement for Women's Liberation.* New York: Tower Publishers, 1970.

Conservatism

In contemporary politics, commentators often refer to the crucial impact of "women's issues" in explaining the **gender gap** in electoral support for the two major political parties. In common parlance, "women's issues" refers most frequently to such issues as **abortion** rights, maternity and family leave, and equal pay for equal work. Indeed, public opinion polls confirm a gender gap caused in large part by the perception that Republican candidates, especially those associated with the dominant conservative wing of the party, are insensitive to the needs and wants of professional women in the modern world.

The relationship between politically active women and the conservative movement is not easily explained by relying upon evidence of a gender gap in elections. To better understand this relationship requires a recognition of the existence of a broad spectrum of political and social views among women and a review of the central tenets of conservative ideology.

The modern conservative movement in the United States has experienced considerable turmoil over exactly what it means to be "conservative." In the 1950s, when William F. Buckley wrote *God and Man at Yale* and founded the *National Review* magazine, there was little doubt about what it meant to be a conservative: one objected to big government and the welfare state as intrusions on liberty, was convinced of the virtues of capitalism, and supported an isolationist foreign policy. The New Deal was a travesty, in Buckley's words, "the way station on the road to 1984." Even as a public consensus developed in favor of active government, conservatives largely stood on the outside, denouncing government itself.

As times changed, so did the conservative movement. In the 1960s, many conservatives abandoned isolationism in favor of a policy of anti-communist containment. Those who had previously favored little or no government role domestically began to demand strong government action to preserve "law and order" in a society seemingly more and more prone to crime and disorder.

By the 1970s, the public consensus in favor of government action in the domestic sphere was so strong that the political scientist Theodore Lowi wrote that the major difference between liberals and conservatives no longer was over *whether* government had a role to play, but rather, the *ends* for which liberals and conservatives would use big government. The consensus in favor of an internationalist foreign policy was so strong that a formerly strident anti-communist president (Richard Nixon) opened U.S. relations with China and pursued a policy of détente with the former Soviet Union—actions universally praised despite some protest among old-line conservatives.

Perhaps a key event in defining the conservative movement in the United States was the controversial Supreme Court decision legalizing abortions, ***Roe v. Wade*** (1973). That decision had two major effects on the conservative movement: (1) it initiated the mobilization of many previously apolitical evangelical and born-again Christians, most of whom would later come to be known as a part of the Christian Right; and (2) it led to another significant split among more traditional conservatives over government's proper role.

Regarding the latter, opinion in the movement ranged from those such as Buckley, who denounced *Roe* as government sanctioned murder and the antithesis of the kind of humane society conservatives extolled, to those such as influential columnist James J. Kilpatrick, who proclaimed that the core principle of conservatism is the ultimate liberty of the individual, and that therefore women alone must be allowed to make the choice about their own pregnancy without any government intervention. That split in the movement not only continues, but is stronger than ever before, as evidenced in the breach in the GOP between the social conservatives and the economic conservatives.

In the late 1970s and throughout the 1980s, the "neo-conservative" movement formed another fissure on the Right. The neo-conservative movement consisted largely of former liberals, Marxists, and Trotskyites who had become disgruntled with the Left and later became leading conservative intellectuals and political figures. Among them were *Commentary* editor Norman Podhoretz and his wife **Midge Dector**, Georgetown professor and former U.N. ambassador **Jeane J. Kirkpatrick**, former counterculture figure David Horowitz, columnist George F. Will, and writer Irving Kristol.

What made the neo-conservatives unique to the movement was their ideology of pro-activist government in both the domestic and foreign policy spheres. They defended the welfare state and government intervention in the economy as consistent with a conservative philosophy and they enthusiastically defended the Reagan era defense buildup and military policies. Dector and Kirkpatrick argued that being both a feminist and a leader on the Right was perfectly consistent. Will and Kirkpatrick openly called themselves "big government conservatives." Although the more traditional conservatives lambasted the neo-conservatives as fraudulent, both sides were united in their pro-military and strident anti-communist views. That consensus broke down with the end of the Cold War in the early 1990s, and the conservative divide began to focus on the social issues.

The latest fissure on the Right specifically concerns the role of Christian social conservatives in the **Republican Party**. Because of substantial Christian Right control and influence on GOP state and local party committees, it is impossible to separate the Christian Right from the conservative movement today. The core constituency of the Christian Right consists of white, socially conservative, and politically active born-again and evangelical Christians. According to various surveys, this group comprises 11-15 percent of the voting population. In brief, Christian Right activists favor openly recited prayer in public schools and the elimination of abortion rights, and oppose such policies as government-mandated parental leave and extending spousal/partner benefits to gay and lesbian couples.

Because of the strong Christian Right influence in the GOP, the conservative movement today is widely regarded as favoring a number of policies that are unfriendly to the preferences of professional women. The Christian Right not only promotes policies that help stay-at-home mothers, but seeks to promote policies that would make it more difficult for other mothers to work and to advance in their careers. The Christian Right does not wish merely to protect its members' right not to choose abortions, it wishes to eliminate that option for other women as well.

Consequently, many commentators today perceive an incompatibility between being a politically active woman and a conservative. They characterize conservative stands on a range of issues as "anti-women" and to some extent this charge carries credibility for many female voters who have abandoned the Republican Party and contributed to the gender gap in elections. They also point to evidence that the family and workplace practices of social conservatives do not recognize the needs of women in modern society.

For example, one study examined the extent to which various organizations promoted "family-friendly" employment policies. Not surprisingly, socially conservative organizations that had openly opposed the **Family and Medical Leave Act** of 1993—e.g. the Christian Coalition, **Concerned Women for America**, Focus on the Family—lagged far behind more progressive organizations whose benefits included much more substantial maternity and paternity leave benefits. At the conservative Concerned Women for America, for example, women employees bearing a child receive no paid maternity leave and are generally expected to quit working for the organization. They receive the following note: "Congratulations! You've just gotten a promotion in life: being a full-time mom." By contrast, at the **National Organization for Women (NOW)**, women and men are entitled to three months full paid leave upon the birth of a child and they may also extend their leave with accumulated vacation and sick leave time.

Nonetheless, the feminist response to the modern conservative movement may be based on a rigid definition of what it means to be "pro-woman" as well as on a misunderstanding of the conservative movement. Members of the Concerned Women for America make a credible argument when they retort that their organization's membership has for years been more than double that of NOW and that it is patently unfair to characterize only the latter, much smaller group as "pro-woman" merely on the basis of ideology.

The conservative movement is highly diverse and cannot be defined as synonymous with the Christian Right. Polling data show, for example, that large majorities of Republican voters favor abortion rights, equal rights for women, the federally mandated family and medical leave policy, and other policies frequently labeled "pro-woman." Political consultant Ann Stone, the chair of Republicans for Choice, notes that even among the most conservative grouping of Republicans in the country—the delegates to the national party conventions that have adopted the pro-life plank since the 1980s—a majority have indicated that they support the pro-choice view on abortion. A strong feminist, Stone makes the point that there is no incompatibility between being a feminist and a conservative because the conservative movement and the Christian Right are not one and the same.

Former ambassador Kirkpatrick, one of the nation's leading conservative voices in the 1980s, also perceives no incompatibility between her **feminism** and her ideology. In her book *Political Woman,* Kirkpatrick praised "historic trends" leading toward a more "progressive inclusion of women" in political decision making. She advocated that government deny funding to institutions of higher learning that practice sexual discrimination and felt that government should intervene in private-sector employment practices when there is suspicion of discrimination.

Like Stone and Kirkpatrick, many leading professional and politically active women remain both wary of the social Right and committed to the Republican Party because of its views on the leading economic and foreign policy issues. They reject the oftentimes rigid definitions of many in the feminist movement of what it means to be "pro-woman."

Consequently, although the conservative movement is highly diverse and contains elements of social conservatism and social libertarianism, feminism and anti-feminism, pro-government and anti-government ideology, it is still widely perceived by many as at odds with the women's movement, and there is no sign that the GOP's gender gap is dissipating. Most political observers concede that the future success of the GOP will depend in large part on its ability to overcome its electoral gender gap. (MJR) **See also** Antifeminism; Comparable Worth; Democratic Party; Economic Equity Act; Family Leave/Mommy Track; Liberalism; Phyllis Schlafly; Right-to-Life Movement.

BIBLIOGRAPHY

Blumenthal, Sidney. *The Rise of the Counter-Establishment: From Conservative Ideology to Political Power*. New York: Harper and Row, 1988.

Buckley, William F., Jr. *Rumbles Left and Right*. New York: Putnam's Sons, 1963.

———. *God and Man at Yale*. Chicago: Regnery, 1951.

Bork, Robert H. *The Tempting of America: The Political Seduction of the Law*. New York: Simon and Schuster, 1990.

Himmelstein, Jerome L. *To the Right: The Transformation of American Conservatism*. Berkeley: University of California Press, 1990.

Hoeveler, David, Jr. *Watch on the Right: Conservative Intellectuals in the Reagan Era*. Madison: University of Wisconsin Press, 1991.

Kirkpatrick, Jeane. *Dictatorships and Double Standards: Rationalism and Realism in Politics*. New York: Simon and Schuster, 1982.

———. *Political Woman*. New York: Basic Books, 1974.

Rozell, Mark J. and James F. Pontuso, eds. *American Conservative Opinion Leaders*. Boulder, CO: Westview Press, 1990.

Rozell, Mark J., James F. Pontuso, and Clyde Wilcox. "The Past as Prologue" In *God at the Grass Roots: The Christian Right in the 1994 Elections*. Lanham, MD: Rowman and Littlefield, 1995.

Grace Anna Goodhue Coolidge (1879–1957)

Grace Coolidge taught deaf students at the Charlie Institute in North Hampton, Massachusetts, before marrying Calvin Coolidge in 1905. In 1921, she presided over the Senate Ladies Club after her husband became vice president of the United States. When Calvin Coolidge became president in 1923, Grace Coolidge began working for charitable organizations, especially those for veterans and the deaf. After she left the White House, she continued to be active in the **Republican Party** and on behalf of the deaf. **See also** First Ladies.

Grace Coolidge spent much of her life as a teacher and advocate for the deaf. Library of Congress.

BIBLIOGRAPHY

Caroli, Betty Boyd. *First Ladies*. New York: Oxford University Press, 1987.

Newman, O.P. "That Charm of Mrs. Coolidge." *Collier's* 78 (October 9, 1925): 8–9.

Ross, Ishbel. *Grace Coolidge and Her Era: The Story of a President's Wife*. New York: Dodd, Mead, 1962.

Midge Costanza (1933–)

Noted for her "candid-to-extremes" approach, Midge Costanza served as the head of the Office of Public Liaison in the Carter White House from 1977 to 1978. As the only woman on the White House senior staff, she was an effective advocate for gay rights and the **women's movement**. She became embroiled in controversy over a fund-raising dinner she hosted to pay off a 1974 campaign debt, and was soon demoted. She left the administration in August 1978.

BIBLIOGRAPHY

Glad, Betty. *Jimmy Carter: In Search of the Great White House*. New York: W.W. Norton, 1980.

"For Midge Costanza: New Job, Old Controversy." *U.S. News and World Report* 24 (April 1978): 72.

County of Washington v. Gunther (1981)

In *County of Washington v. Gunther,* 452 U.S. 161 (1981), the Supreme Court confronted the **comparable worth** issue for the first time. Although the 5–4 decision did not explicitly endorse comparable worth comparisons, women's groups believed that the Court's ruling had paved the way for future comparable worth claims.

The case involved female guards who claimed that the county of Washington evaluated the worth of their jobs as 90 percent of that of the male guards, yet paid them only 70 percent as much. The women contended that they were victims of sex-based discrimination and sought redress by filing a Title VII lawsuit. At issue in *Gunther* was whether Title VII protected the female guards.

The Supreme Court ruled on the assertion that the women were paid less than male guards based on intentional discrimination. In the majority opinion, Justice William Brennan declared that the Bennett Amendment to **Title VII of the Civil Rights Act of 1964** did not prevent this type of claim merely because the female guards did not perform work equal to that of the male guards. Hence, the Supreme Court asserted that Title VII provides a remedy if sexual discrimination is the motivating force behind the pay disparities between male and female jobs. (MG)

BIBLIOGRAPHY

Frankel, Ellen Paul. *Equity and Gender: The Comparable Worth Debate.* New Brunswick, NJ: Transaction Publishers, 1989.

Maschke, Karen J. *Litigation, Courts, and Women Workers.* New York: Praeger, 1989.

Coverture

When America was founded, communities and states adopted codes based on English **common law** principles. One of these principles, which became integrated into the American legal system, was coverture. Blackstone's eighteenth-century *Commentaries* described the legal status of married women under coverture as follows: "The very being or legal existence of the woman is suspended during the marriage." In other words, upon marriage women gave up all rights afforded individuals and were for all intents and purposes "civilly dead." In practical terms, it meant that in 1848, when the **Seneca Falls Convention** met, married women had no right to their property, earnings, or children and could not initiate a divorce. When a woman married a man, the couple became one entity and that one entity was the man.

Coverture, based on the belief that men inhabit the public sphere while women belong in the private sphere, became the legal basis for the complete subordination of women to men. The early suffragists placed marriage reform at the top of their agenda. Although there have been dramatic reforms in women's legal status, the lingering effects of coverture are still present in contemporary public policy debates over such issues as **domestic violence** and spousal consent for **abortion**s. (CKC) **See also** Suffrage.

BIBLIOGRAPHY

McGlen, Nancy and Karen O'Connor. *Women, Politics and American Society.* Englewood Cliffs, NJ: Prentice Hall, 1995.

Rhode, Deborah. *Justice and Gender.* Cambridge, MA: Harvard University Press, 1989.

Craig v. Boren (1976)

Craig v. Boren, 429 U.S. 190 (1976), declared state laws discriminating on the basis of sex to be constitutionally suspect. The case was filed in 1972 by Oklahoma State University student Mark Walker and Stillwater convenience store owner Carolyn Whitener. Their suit challenged Oklahoma's law permitting the sale of 3.2 percent beer to males at age 21 and to females at age 18. The plaintiffs claimed Oklahoma's **sex discrimination** violated the **Fourteenth Amendment**'s equal protection and due process clauses. Walker lost standing when he turned 21 as did his replacement, Curtis Craig, another student.

Previous Supreme Court decisions held classifications to be constitutional if the classification rationally related to a legitimate government function unless the classification denied a fundamental right or affected a suspect class, in which case the classification must be precisely tailored to serve a compelling government interest. Woman's rights advocates such as **Ruth Bader Ginsburg** had been trying to get the Supreme Court to rule sex a suspect classification. If the Supreme Court did this, then for all practical purposes state law that discriminated on the basis of sex would be unconstitutional. The Supreme Court, however, proved reluctant or unable to do this until *Craig v. Boren*.

Justice William Brennan delivered the 7–2 majority opinion. Brennan first settled the issue of beer vendor Whitener's standing by stating that "vendors and those in like positions have been uniformly permitted to resist efforts to restrict their operations by acting as advocates of the rights of third parties who seek access to their market or function." The next question concerned the constitutionally of Oklahoma's statute. For the first time, the Supreme Court articulated its intermediate scrutiny standard. "To withstand constitutional challenge . . . classifications by gender must serve important governmental objectives and must be substantially related to the achievement of those objectives." Brennan went on to declare "increasingly educated misconceptions concerning the role of females in the home rather than in the 'marketplace and world of ideas' were rejected as loose-fitting characterizations incapable of supporting state statutory schemes that were premised upon their accuracy."

The essential legal result of *Craig v. Boren* was to declare unconstitutional state laws that discriminated on the basis of sex. A political effect was to undermine the campaign for the **Equal Rights Amendment (ERA)**. (RD)

BIBLIOGRAPHY

Aikin, Wendy Lise. "Gender-Based Discrimination and Equal Protection: The Emerging Intermediate Standard." *University of Florida Law Review* 29, no. 3 (Spring 1977): 582–93.

Ginsburg, Ruth Bader. "The Burger Court's Grapplings with Sex Discrimination." In Vincent Blasi, ed. *The Burger Court: The Counter-Revolution that Wasn't.* New Haven, CT: Yale University Press, 1983.

Prudence Crandall (1803–1890)

In 1833, Prudence Crandall attempted to open a boarding and teacher-training school for black girls in Canterbury, Connecticut. As a result, Crandall was brought to trial for attempting to school African-American children, a crime at that time in Connecticut. She was eventually cleared of all charges and continued to fight for the education of black children.

BIBLIOGRAPHY

Yates, Elizabeth. *Woman of Courage.* New York: Dutton, 1985.

Mary Dent Crisp (1923–)

Pro-choice activist Mary Crisp is chair of the National Republican Coalition for Choice (NRCC). Crisp served as co-chair of the Republican National Committee in the late 1970s. However, she lost this position in 1980 probably due to her support of the **Equal Rights Amendment (ERA)** and her opposition to the Reagan administration's position on **abortion**. She founded the National Republican Coalition for Choice after the Supreme Court's 1989 ***Webster v. Reproductive Health Services*** decision signaled that the Court might eventually strike down the constitutional protection for abortion. The NRCC recruits and supports Republican challengers who advocate abortion rights to run against anti-abortion incumbents. Toward this goal, Crisp has built coalitions that cross party lines to include liberal groups. Her efforts have been met with great resistance by both the **Republican Party** leadership and Christian conservatives. However, the NRCC's efforts forced the Republican Party to re-evaluate their position on this issue. (GVS)

BIBLIOGRAPHY

"Mary Crisp." Working Woman. (April 1992): 24–25.

"True to the GOP in Her Fashion." *Newsweek* 98 (31 August 1981): 10.

Barbara Cubin (1946–)

Republican Barbara Cubin served in the Wyoming State Legislature from 1987 to 1994. In 1994, she was elected to the U.S. House of Representatives as the Wyoming Representative at Large. While in Congress, Cubin has voted along with the more conservative members. Re-elected in 1996, she serves on the Commerce and Resources Committees. (CKC)

BIBLIOGRAPHY

Babson, Jennifer, and Bob Benenson. "New Member Profile: Barbara Cubin." *Congressional Quarterly Weekly Report* 53 (7 January 1995): 105.

Lucille Atchingson Curtis (1895–1986)

Lucille Curtis made history when she became the first woman to serve in the U.S. Foreign Service; her appointment came in 1922 by President Warren Harding, for whom she served in France, Switzerland, Haiti, and Panama until her resignation in 1927. During World War I, Curtis worked along with Anne Morgan to help create the Society for Devastated France, as well as providing other relief work in France.

BIBLIOGRAPHY

"Obituary." *New York Times* (May 9, 1986): D 22.

D

Caroline Wells Healey Dall (1822–1912)

Caroline Dall was one of the earliest and most important authors on women's economic, legal and **educational policy**. Her writings helped explain how the lack of educational opportunities for women combined with limitations on the scope of career choices available to them to led to low pay. Dall argued that the dual limitations led to low pay because there was intense competition for "women's jobs." She argued that the only way to improve the plight of working women was to increase their educational opportunities and the types of jobs open to them. Among her works are *Woman's Right to Labor* (1860), *Woman's Rights Under the Law* (1862) and, perhaps her most important work, *The College, the Market, and the Court* (1867).

BIBLIOGRAPHY

Walter, Barbara. "The Merchant's Daughter: A Tale from Life." *New England Quarterly* 42 (March 1969): 3-22.

Danforth Amendment (1988)

Passed in 1988 as part of the **Civil Rights Restoration Act** of 1988 (CRRA), the Danforth Amendment bars federal funds recipients from treating health insurance, leave policy, and other services relating to **abortion** differently from services offered for pregnancy and childbirth. Named after the amendment's sponsor, Senator John C. Danforth (R-MO), the Danforth Amendment does not require federal funds recipients to pay for abortion benefits or services, but it prohibits discrimination against individuals seeking legal abortions. The net effect of the Danforth Amendment was to allow federally aided hospitals to refuse to perform abortions and to allow educational institutions to offer health and leave plans that did not cover abortions. Supporters argued that without this amendment, Title IX would have forced hospitals, including those affiliated with the Roman Catholic Church, to perform abortions. Although opponents of the Danforth measure rejected this contention, its inclusion delayed passage of the CRRA for more than three years. The CRRA was initially proposed in 1984 in an attempt to restore full coverage of Title IX provisions prohibiting **sex discrimination** in education. The legislation was proposed in response to the Supreme Court's decision in ***Grove City College v. Bell*** (1984), which held that only the program or activity of an entity receiving federal assistance, not the entire institution, was protected against discrimination. The CRRA ultimately passed in 1988 over President Ronald Reagan's veto. (JJK)

BIBLIOGRAPHY

Rubin, Eva R., ed. *The Abortion Controversy, A Documentary History.* Westport, CT: Greenwood Press, 1994.

Tribe, Laurence H. *Abortion: The Clash of Absolutes.* New York: W.W. Norton & Company, 1990.

Pat Danner (1934–)

Pat Danner, a Democrat, was first elected to the U.S. House of Representatives from Missouri in 1992. A moderate, she joined the Blue Dogs, the moderate-to-conservative Democrats also known as The Coalition. Prior to her election to Congress, she served 10 years in the Missouri state senate. From 1977 to 1981, Danner co-chaired the Ozarks Regional Planning Commission. Reelected in 1994 and 1996, she serves on the International Relations and Transportation and Infrastructure committees.

BIBLIOGRAPHY

Margolies-Mezvinsky, Marjorie. *A Woman's Place.* New York: Crown, 1994.

Merida, Kevin. "Many Democratic House Freshman Won't Be Returning." *Washington Post* (10 November 1994): A35.

Daughters of Bilitis (DOB)

The Daughters of Bilitis was founded in 1955 in San Francisco, California, as a social club for homosexual women. The group adopted its name from the erotic poem, "Songs of Bilitis." By 1960, the group had grown to include chapters in Chicago, Los Angeles, New York City, and Rhode Island. Over the years, the organization has evolved from its original purpose as a social and self-support group to include civil rights and educational issues in its focus. As a result, the DOB began hosting discussion groups in high schools, colleges, and through radio and television, as well as publishing its own newsletter, *The Ladder*. The group also sought legislative reform by working with leading homosexual and civil rights activists, like **Kate Millet,** and by supporting other civil rights groups, like the **National Organization for Women (NOW)**. The Daughters of Bilitis disbanded as a national organization in 1970.

BIBLIOGRAPHY

Damon, Gene. "The Least of These." In Robin Morgan, ed. *Sisterhood Is Powerful.* New York: Vintage, 1970.

D'Emilio, John. *Sexual Politics, Sexual Communities.* Chicago: University of Chicago Press, 1983.

Daughters of Temperance

While attending an 1852 mass meeting of the Sons of Temperance as representative of the Rochester Daughters of Temperance, **Susan B. Anthony** was informed she was not allowed to contribute to the proceedings because she was a woman. As a result, she began the national Daughters of Temperance to help women assist in seeking the abolition of alcohol. While with the group, Anthony came to realize that women would never be able to take an active enough role in reform movements without the right to vote. This realization prompted her involvement in the women's rights movement. The Daughters of Temperance grew in the mid-1800s to over 30,000 members, making it one of the largest female societies of the time. The group petitioned for legislation and held public displays of defiance in favor of temperance. **See also** Temperance Movement; Women's Movement.

BIBLIOGRAPHY

Levine, Harry Gene. "Temperance and Woman in Nineteenth-Century United States." In Oriana Josseau Kalant, ed. *Research Advances in Alcohol and Drug Problems, Volume S.* New York: Plevium, 1980.

Tyrnell, Ian R. "Woman and Temperance in Antebellum America, 1830–1860." *Civil War History* 28 (June 1982): 128–52.

Daughters of the American Revolution (DAR)

The Daughters of the American Revolution, a group still functioning throughout the United States, was originally founded in 1890 and consists solely of women descendants of Revolutionary War patriots. The organization conducts educational, historical, and patriotic activities and maintains a museum and archive of historical documents dating back to the Revolutionary War. The Daughters of the American Revolution, which has working affiliations with two groups with similar ideals, the National Defense Committee of the American Revolution and the National Society of Children of the American Revolution, also actively supports a number of children's causes.

BIBLIOGRAPHY

LaGanke, Lucille Evelyn. "The National Society of the Daughters of the American Revolution: Its History, Politics, and Influences, 1890-1949." Ph.D. dissertation, Western Reserve University, 1951.

Davey v. Turner (1764)

In 1764, in *Davey v. Turner*, 1 U.S. 11 (1764), the Supreme Court of colonial Pennsylvania upheld the joint deed system of *feme covert*, which required the consent of the woman in the transfer or sale of property that she had brought to the marriage. Prior to Pennsylvania's establishment of *feme covert*, all property owned by a woman became her husband's after their marriage; this included dowry possessions, holdings a widow had from her late husband, and any other family property a woman may receive. The system entailed a justice of the peace interviewing the woman after marriage to discern whether she agreed with or objected to the transfer of her holdings to her new husband. By establishing this procedure, a woman was protected from losing family holdings as well as her husband's property. More importantly, it marked one of the earliest cases where a higher court acknowledged the need for equality between males and females.

BIBLIOGRAPHY

Salvion, Marylynn. "Equality or Submission? *Feme Covert* Status in Early Pennsylvania." In Carol Ruth Berkin and Mary Beth Norton, eds. *Women of America: A History.* Boston: Houghton Mifflin, 1979.

Angela Davis (1944–)

A black militant communist and former acting assistant professor of philosophy at the University of California at Los Angeles, Davis suffered for her political views on several occasions. In 1970, Davis committed herself to working for the Soledad Brothers Defense Committee in its attempt to free inmates from charges and abuse brought upon them in a Soledad, California, prison. While court cases on the issue proceeded, Jonathan Jackson (brother of George Jackson, one of the inmates who had been murdered at Soledad) took guns that Davis had legally purchased and made a failed attempt at taking hostages and freeing three Soledad inmates from the Marin County Courthouse in San Rafael, California. As a result of the altercation, charges were brought against Davis because the guns Jackson used were registered in her name. Even though she claimed innocence, Davis went into hiding until she was extradited from New York back to California to stand trial. The trial opened on February 28, 1972, and ended June 4, 1972, with her full acquittal. Davis has gone on several national and international speaking tours promoting her political views.

BIBLIOGRAPHY

"Angela Davis." *Ebony* 27 (April 1972): 53+.

Davis, Angela Yvonne. *Women, Culture, and Politics.* New York: Random House, 1989.

Paulina Kellog Wright Davis (1813–1876)

Paulina Davis was the influential author and editor of the Boston publication ***Una*** from 1853 to 1855. Davis began the publication in response to the lack of a truly feminist periodical that advocated woman's equality in marriage, health, and the professions. She believed that the leading periodical of the day, ***Godey's Lady's Book***, did not address the concerns of women.

BIBLIOGRAPHY

The Una. vols. 1–3. Boston: Sayles, Miller & Simmons, 1853–55.

Dorothy Day (1897–1980)

Dorothy Day was a journalist and social reform activist who described herself as a "Christian anarchist" and led a life that reflected that description. Her first job as a journalist was reporting on labor unrest for the socialist newspaper, *Call*. She would later write for other radical papers, including *Masses* and *New Masses*. After her conversion to Catholicism in 1927, Day helped found the Catholic Worker Party and edited its journal, *Catholic Worker*.

Bibliography

Day, Dorothy. *The Long Loneliness*. New York: Harper, 1952.

Miller, William. *Dorothy Day: A Biography*. San Francisco: Harper & Row, 1982.

——. *A Harsh and Dreadful Love: Dorothy Day and the Catholic Worker Movement*. Garden City, NY: Doubleday, 1974.

Declaration of Sentiments and Resolutions

The Declaration of Sentiments and Resolutions sought to extend the democratic principles of liberty and equality that governed the relations among men in the United States to the relationship between the sexes. The declaration was authored by **Elizabeth Cady Stanton** and **Lucretia Mott** who modeled it after Thomas Jefferson's Declaration of Independence to underscore their radical intent to put women on an equal footing with men as citizens of the United States. The Declaration of Sentiments and Resolutions is also known as the Seneca Falls Resolution because it was the proposal put before the participants of the country's first women's rights convention held at the Wesleyan Chapel in Seneca Falls, New York, on July 19–20, 1848. The convention was attended by more than 300 people, including the former slave, Frederick Douglass, who spoke in favor of the resolution that women should exercise the franchise. The Declaration of Sentiments and Resolutions outlined the historical grievances that American women had experienced since the nation's founding. Stanton and Mott adapted Jefferson's natural rights arguments to their political purposes. They proclaimed that the equality of the sexes was a self-evident truth and that a woman had an inalienable right to pursue life, liberty, and happiness on her own terms. In the declaration, they took aim at what they considered to be a male tyranny institutionalized in the legal codes and the social customs of the country, emphasizing the role of ideology in perpetuating a moral double standard that reinforced women's material and spiritual subjugation to men. The resolutions addressed a broad range of cultural and political issues, focusing on how sexual inequality was maintained by gender inequities in educational opportunity, marriage law, and property rights. Targeting the tax revenues generated from the property of single women without the right to vote, Stanton and Mott echoed the colonial chant that in a free nation there should be "no taxation without representation." The Declaration of Sentiments and Resolutions examined the political consequences of women's second-class citizenship by linking civic duties to civil rights. Stanton and Mott argued that since the basis of democratic government was the consent of the governed, the barriers to women's civic participation must be removed or the continued coercion of half the population placed the future of American democracy in doubt. In all, 68 women and 32 men signed the Declaration of Sentiments and Resolutions. Many scholars date the organized **women's movement** in the United States to this first meeting in upstate New York. (WGC)

Bibliography

Flexnor, Eleanor. *A Century of Struggle: The Women's Rights Movement in the United States*. New York: Atheneum, 1974.

Declaration of the Rights of Women

The Declaration of the Rights of Women was written by **Matilda Joslyn Gage** and **Elizabeth Cady Stanton** as a political statement on the status of women during the celebration of the nation's centennial in 1876. The **National Woman Suffrage Association (NWSA)** planned and executed the presentation of the declaration, which was intended to highlight the noncitizen treatment accorded women by the social and political system and to demand equal rights with men.

On Independence Day in 1876, **Susan B. Anthony**, representing the NWSA, read the "Declaration of the Rights of Women." The declaration compared the political and social situation of women with men, highlighting women's lack of the civil rights and liberties guaranteed in the Constitution. The document claimed that because constitutional rights were extended only to men, the democratic system it purported to establish was a fraud. Because the rights that underlie the system were only selectively applied, the system could not be considered legitimate. Evidence of these "constitutional violations" included the right of trial by a jury of one's peers when women could not serve on juries, and taxation without representation because women were unable to vote. The document ends with the assertion of women's belief in self-government, women's equality with men in all ways, and a denial of the accepted status of women as subjects of men. Finally, the document asks the government to treat women equally with men.

Bibliography

Wagner, Sally Roesch. *A Time of Protest: Suffragists Challenge the Republic, 1870-1887*. Sacramento, CA: Spectrum, 1987.

Midge Decter (1927–)

After a long career as an editor, writer Midge Decter turned her focus in the 1970s to social issues, such as women's rights and the decline of family values. Besides supporting political activities in these areas, Decter also illustrated her conservative views in a number of works, including *The Liberal Woman and Other Americans* (1971), the *New Chastity* (1971), and *Liberal Parents, Radical Children* (1975).

Bibliography

Friedan, Betty and Midge Decter. "Are Woman Different Today?" *Public Opinion* 5 (April-May 1982): 20, 41.

Ada E. Deer (1935–)

Born on the Menominee Reservation in northern Wisconsin, Ada Deer became the first Menominee tribal member to graduate from the University of Wisconsin and the first Native American to receive a master's degree from the School of Social Work at Columbia University. Influential in obtaining restoration of the federal government's acknowledgment of tribal status for the Menominee, she became the first tribal chairperson after restoration in 1973. On July 16,1993, she became the first woman assistant secretary for Indian Affairs, a position she held until 1997. (AM)

BIBLIOGRAPHY

Deer, Ada with R. E. Simon, Jr. *Speaking Out*. Chicago: Children's Press, 1970.

Defense Advisory Committee on Women in the Services

The Defense Advisory Committee on Women in the Services, or DACOWITS, was created in 1950 as a result of women activists seeking appointment to emergency war committees during the Korean War. The group's initial objective was encouraging and increasing the enlistment of women in the services. The Defense Advisory Committee's agenda grew to include other issues, including providing women a voice on policy formation and assisting the secretary of defense on management issues pertinent to women in the military. During the late 1980s and early 1990s, DACOWITS turned its attention to amending armed services policies to allow women to participate in combat situations.

BIBLIOGRAPHY

Binkin, Martin and Shirley J. Boch. *Women and the Military.* Washington, DC: Brookings Institute, 1977.

Howes, Ruth and Michael Stevenson. *Women and the Use of Military Force.* Boulder, CO: Lynne Rienner, 1993.

Wilcox, Clyde. "Race, Sex, and Support for Women in the Military." *Social Science Quarterly* 73, no. 2 (June 1992): 310–23.

Diana L. DeGette (1957–)

Diana DeGette began her political career when she was elected to the Colorado House of Representatives in 1992 and reelected in 1994. A Democrat, she was elected to the U.S. House of Representatives in 1996 to the seat left open by the retirement of **Patricia Schroeder**. In Congress, she serves on the Commerce Committee and as the western regional whip for the Democratic House leadership.

BIBLIOGRAPHY

"The Rocky Mountains." *Washington Post* (November 3, 1996): A37.

"Election 1996 Results: US House." *Washington Post* (November 7, 1996): A38.

Rosa DeLauro (1943–)

Rosa DeLauro, a Democrat, was executive assistant to Mayor Frank Logue of New Haven, Connecticut, from 1976 to 1977 and executive assistant and development administrator for the city from 1977 to 1978. From 1980 to 1987, she was also chief of staff for Senator Christopher Dodd. On November 6, 1990, DeLauro was elected to the U.S. House of Representatives from Connecticut. An outspoken member of Congress, DeLauro has been reelected to each successive Congress.

BIBLIOGRAPHY

Mann, Judy. "Taking Another Crack at the Wage Gap." *The Washington Post* 120, no. 183 (July 2, 1997): D10.

_______. "Incidents and Law." *The Wall Street Journal* (March 31, 1997): A12.

Democratic Party

Though it is an oversimplification to speak of certain political issues as "women's issues," just as it is misleading to believe that all women are proponents of these issues, certain causes have been dominant concerns of **women's movements**. These causes include **suffrage**, equal rights, and reproductive rights. Historically, support of women's issues has not been consistently advocated by either of the mainstream, male-dominated political parties. Although the **Republican Party** initially supported women's suffrage, it has in more recent decades come out against both the **Equal Rights Amendment (ERA)** and **abortion**. Meanwhile, the Democratic Party has pushed anti-discrimination policies and supported equal rights and reproductive rights. And although Republican administrations put some of the first women in top government positions, the Democrats have been more aggressive in attempting to distribute these positions equally between men and women. In the 1980s, the Democratic Party sought to protect women who wished to lead nontraditional lives from the Reagan administration's "traditional family values" crusade that rolled back many advances of the women's movement. For these reasons, modern women's movements have come to expect support for their positions from the Democratic Party.

Campaign sheet music from the 1932 presidential campaign of Democrat Franklin D. Roosevelt. Library of Congress.

The Democratic Party's late arrival in support of women's movements stemmed from its opposition to women's suffrage. Although women's movements in the late nineteenth and early twentieth centuries advocated a great variety of causes, from **voting rights** to sexual liberation to freedom from the tyranny of pregnancy, family, or male domination, the one issue around which most women's movements could rally was universal and equal suffrage. Early in the suffrage movement, supporters gained the patronage of the Republican Party. During the 72 years between the first serious formulation of the demand for the enfranchisement of American women, the **Seneca Falls Convention** of 1848, and the passage of the **Nineteenth Amendment** in 1920, which granted women the vote, the Democratic Party staunchly opposed the extension of suffrage.

After 1896, when the Republican Party officially endorsed women's suffrage, Democrats consistently voted against granting women the vote. Of the 12 states that enfranchised women between 1896 and 1920, none had Democrat-controlled legislatures. In 1896, when a Republican senator introduced a proposed constitutional amendment to grant women the right to vote nationwide, the proposal was defeated in the Democrat-controlled Senate. The same measure was defeated three more times while control of Congress was in Democratic hands. When the measure finally passed, opposition was strongest among House Democrats, who comprised 72 of the 88 opposing votes. Democrat-controlled state legislatures also posed the most determined opposition to the amendment; of the nine states that voted against ratification, eight were controlled by Democrats.

This opposition to women's suffrage hurt the Democratic Party at the polls when women could at last cast their ballots. Although few women initially exercised their right to vote, those who did voted overwhelmingly Republican. However, with women's suffrage secured, the Republican Party did little to continue furthering the causes championed by women. In the ensuing decades, while that party was moving away from support of women's movements, the Democratic Party was moving away from its opposition to them. As the Democratic coalition came to include New Left movements, one of which was **feminism**, the Democratic Party became increasingly aware of the importance of women's issues. In the 1960 presidential election between John F. Kennedy and Richard Nixon, Democrats mobilized an increasingly conscientious women's vote, which helped Kennedy win one of the closest elections in American history.

Many women were angered, however, when Kennedy failed to appoint women to high government positions, particularly in the case of the Labor Department's Women's Bureau. In response, Kennedy created the **President's Commission on the Status of Women** for the purpose of combating "the prejudices and outmoded customs" that serve as "barriers to the realization of women's basic rights." The commission, following Kennedy's own position, rejected the ideas of the proposed Equal Rights Amendment, claiming that the rights of women were adequately protected by the Fifth and Fourteenth Amendments. The commission did, however, recommend a number of anti-discrimination measures, one of which was passed as the **Equal Pay Act** in 1963. This act, the first piece of federal legislation to prohibit discrimination on the basis of gender, required equal compensation for women and men who performed equal work.

Succeeding Democratic presidents were even more forceful in their support of women's rights. Lyndon Johnson pushed for passage of the Civil Rights Act. In an attempt to make passage of the act more difficult, Republican congressman Howard Smith of Virginia proposed that women should be included in the protected groups. The act passed anyway, and **Title VII** established the **Equal Employment Opportunity Commission (EEOC)** to help battle discrimination based on sex, color, race, religion, and national origin. Johnson also issued an executive order banning the federal government and any federal contractor from discrimination based on sex. In 1977, Democrat Jimmy Carter appointed renowned feminist **Bella Abzug** to chair the President's Commission on the Status of Women; he replaced other conservative Republican members appointed by Presidents Richard Nixon and Gerald Ford with liberal Democrats.

However, Carter and the Democratic Party were unable to secure passage of the ERA. Originally drafted by the **National Woman's Party (NWP)** and introduced in Congress in 1923, the ERA stated that "equality of rights under the law shall not be denied or abridged by the United States nor by any State on account of sex." For decades, the ERA was ignored by Republicans and Democrats alike, until the **National Organization for Women (NOW)**, formed in 1966, heightened awareness of women's issues and forced politicians to take notice of the ERA. The ERA was approved by the House of Representatives in 1971 and by the Senate in 1972. But despite the endorsement of three presidents, Republican as well as Democrat, and national polls indicating that a majority of Americans favored passage of the ERA, ratification eventually fell three states short. Carter did sign the Convention on the Elimination of All Forms of Discrimination Against Women, adopted by the United Nations in 1979, which would render the ERA unnecessary if ratified by the Senate. Though the convention has been before the Senate Judiciary Committee for a number of years, little action has been taken to secure its ratification.

In addition to supporting anti-discrimination laws and the ERA, the Democratic Party has also been a strong supporter of reproductive rights. Abortion, against the law in most states since the mid-nineteenth century, was legalized in one broad sweep in 1973, when the Supreme Court struck down a Texas abortion law in ***Roe v. Wade***. Although the original *Roe* Court was dominated by Republican-appointed justices (five of the seven justices in the majority belonged to the Republican Party), Democrats were firm supporters of *Roe* from the beginning. Carter, a deeply religious Southern Baptist who personally opposed abortion, was an exception. Carter's nomination by the Democratic Party in 1976 meant that the party's first post-*Roe* platform was a lukewarm concession to the prochoice forces within the party, reading "it is undesirable to amend the U.S. Constitution to overturn the Supreme Court decision [on abortion]." As the campaign progressed, Carter changed his position on the constitutional amendment, cutting the one thread that connected him to the abortion rights element of the Democratic Party.

As president, however, Carter did little either to legitimize or to oppose the ruling in *Roe*. He mainly restricted himself to fighting federal funding of abortion by supporting the **Hyde Amendment**'s restrictions on the use of Medicaid funds to pay for abortions. Carter maintained throughout his presidency that, though personally opposed to abortion, he had taken an oath to uphold the laws and Constitution of the United States, which included the Supreme Court's ruling in *Roe*. In 1980, pro-choice forces within the Democratic Party were more active than they had been at the 1976 convention. And though Carter was once again the Democratic presidential nominee, these forces managed to anchor the platform more strongly in support of abortion, recognizing "the belief of many Americans that a woman has a right to choose whether and when to have a child." This was a compromise between Carter's position and that of a faction of the Democratic Party, led by feminist **Gloria Steinem**, that had called for federal funding of abortions through Medicaid.

With the defeat of Carter and the victory of the dedicated anti-abortionist Ronald Reagan, the Democratic Party began adopting a stronger position on abortion, particularly in response to the Republican Party's denunciation of *Roe* and its calls for an amendment to overturn that ruling. The Democratic Party claimed that "reproductive freedom [is] a fundamental human right," a clause that would appear in Democratic platforms after 1984. Democratic members of the Senate were instrumental in opposing the Supreme Court nominations of the Reagan and Bush administrations. Democratic senator Joseph Biden, chairman of the Senate Judiciary Committee, spearheaded the successful opposition of Robert Bork, the controversial anti-abortion Reagan nominee. Though both Reagan and Bush called for the overturning of *Roe*, they were often forced to appoint moderate candidates to the Supreme Court because of this Democratic opposition. Still, by 1989, with William Rehnquist and Byron White, the original two dissenters in *Roe*, reinforced by three Reagan appointees, the Court began rolling back the 1970s rulings that supported the abortion right. In the case of ***Webster v. Reproductive Health Services*** (1989), the Court ruled by a 5-4 margin that some state-imposed restrictions on abortion were constitutionally permissible.

The Reagan and Bush appointments had succeeded in swinging the attitude of the Court, but when Bill Clinton became the first post-*Roe* Democratic president to make Supreme Court appointments (the one-term Carter made none), he quickly chose noted women's rights supporter **Ruth Bader Ginsburg**. Clinton failed to stick to this pattern with his second Supreme Court appointment, Steven Breyer, a moderate with no public stand on abortion prior to his nomination. Breyer, however, did contribute to the growing moderate element on the Court, and though not likely to be a strong supporter of women's rights, he seemed likely to be a sturdy bulwark against the overturning of *Roe* that Court-watchers thought was presaged by *Webster*.

In addition to helping reverse the anti-*Roe* drift of the Supreme Court, Clinton has been the strongest champion of women's rights ever to occupy the White House, appointing more women to his cabinet than any other president. His appointments include the first female attorney general, **Janet Reno**, and the first female secretary of state, **Madeleine Albright**. Further, Clinton instructed his secretary of defense, Les Aspin, to implement the congressional mandate on the assignment of women in the armed forces to all units excluding ground combat troops. He also supported the **Family and Medical Leave Act** of 1993, which required companies with 50 or more employees to grant up to 12 weeks of unpaid leave annually for the birth or adoption of a child or to care for a spouse or immediate family member with a serious health condition. Although not limited to women, this act greatly contributed to women's ability to balance family and career. In these ways, the Democratic Party in the late twentieth century has fought for women's rights and supported the causes of the women's movement. (JW2)

BIBLIOGRAPHY

Barone, Michael et al. *Almanac of American Politics*. Washington, DC: National Journal, 1996.

Brown, Dorothy M. *Setting a Course: American Women in the 1920s*. Boston: Twayne Publishers, 1987.

Clark, Judith Freeman. *Almanac of American Women in the 20th Century*. New York: Prentice Hall, 1987.

Hecker, Eugene A. *A Short History of Women's Rights*. Westport, CT: Greenwood Press, 1971.

Langley, Winston E. and Vivian C. Fox, eds. *Women's Rights in the United States: A Documentary History*. Westport, CT : Greenwood Press, 1994.

Le Veness, Frank P. and Jane P. Sweeney, eds. *Women Leaders in Contemporary US Politics*. Boulder, CO: Lynne Rienner Publishers, 1987.

Patterson, James T. *America in the Twentieth Century*. New York: Harcourt, Brace, Jovanovich, 1983.

Mary Coffin Ware Dennett (1872–1947)

Mary Dennett was an active suffragist and member of various peace movements. However, the main contribution she made to the women's movement was her founding of the National Birth Control League in 1915. Dennett was opposed to the more radical and confrontational style of **Margaret Sanger** and sought to work within the political system more effectively to achieve reproductive rights. The league was formed with the specific purpose of lobbying legislatures. Dennett focused much of her attention on overturning obscenity laws that prevented the distribution of information about birth control, as well as the adoption of sex education in schools. In 1918, the organization changed its name to the **Voluntary Parenthood League**. **See also** Suffrage.

BIBLIOGRAPHY
Dennett, Mary Ware. *Birth Control Laws*. New York: Hitchcock, 1926.
——. *The Prosecution of Mary Ware Dennett for Obscenity*. New York: ACLU, 1929.
——. *The Sex Education of Children*. New York: Vanguard, 1931.
——. *Who's Obscene?* New York: Vanguard, 1930.

Molly Dewson (1874–1962)

Molly Dewson headed the women's division of the **Democratic Party** from 1932 to 1937, after which she served from 1937 to 1938 as a member of the Social Security Board. The majority of Dewson's political career, however, was spent in service to President Franklin Roosevelt's New Deal legislation. A long-time friend of **Eleanor Roosevelt**, Dewson worked with the first lady in mobilizing thousands of female precinct workers while with the women's division of the Democratic Party in New York. She also worked in the National Consumers' League and helped **Frances Perkins** gain her appointment as secretary of labor and coordinate her activities as the first female cabinet member. One of Dewson's greatest influences was through her lobbying for the hiring of more women in government and for an increased presidential response to women's issues.

BIBLIOGRAPHY
Ware, Susan. *Partner and I: Molly Dewson, Feminism and New Deal Politics*. New Haven, CT: Yale University Press, 1987.

Nancy Dick (1930–)

Nancy Dick's political career began as **Democratic Party** treasurer of Pitkin County, Colorado, a position that enabled her to move quickly to the Democratic Party State Rules Committee. From there she went on to win the state representative's seat, where she was chairperson of the Governor's Commission on Rural Health/Manpower Solutions (1977), a member of the Colorado Medical Society Rural Health Committee (1975–1978), a member of the United States Oil Shale Environment Advisory Panel (1974–1978), and the finance chairperson for the Federation of Rocky Mountain States (1979). In 1979, she was named lieutenant governor of Colorado.

BIBLIOGRAPHY
Dean, Katie. "Nancy Dick, Colorado's New Lieutenant Governor." *Denver Post Enpine Magazine* (December 31, 1978): 12–19.
Priscilla, Marshall. "Smooth Transition." *Colorado Business Magazine* 22, no. 9 (September 1995): 115.

Sharon Pratt Kelly Dixon (1944–)

In 1976, Sharon Dixon was made a member at large in the District of Columbia State Committee. After this, she was elected Democratic national committeewoman for the District of Columbia in 1977, a position she held until 1985. During this time, she also worked on **Patricia Roberts Harris's** unsuccessful 1982 bid for mayor of Washington, DC, against Marion Barry. In 1984, Dixon was elected to the post of treasurer for the **Democratic Party**. On January 2, 1991, after a difficult campaign, Dixon gained her highest position when she was sworn in as mayor of Washington, DC She lost her reelection bid in 1994 to Marion Barry. She left office with the District in deep financial trouble.

BIBLIOGRAPHY
"Sharon Pratt Dixon: Rising to the Top in the DNC." *Focus* 14, no. 4 (April 1986): 3.

Doe v. Bolton (1972)

In a 7-2 decision, the U.S. Supreme Court struck down parts of a Georgia law that exempted therapeutic abortions from Georgia's criminal penalties as long as the **abortion** was necessary to save the life of the woman, the fetus was likely to have a serious mental or physical defect, or the pregnancy was the result of rape. In addition to meeting one of these three criteria, abortions had to be performed in an accredited hospital, be certified by three physicians, and have the approval of the hospital's abortion committee. Finally, the woman seeking the abortion had to be a resident of the state of Georgia.

The law was challenged when Mary Doe, who failed to meet the criteria, sued claiming that the Georgia law violated her Fourteenth Amendment rights. The Court agreed with Doe's reasoning that the requirements for hospital and physician approval, as well as for services to be performed in accredited hospitals, unduly restricted the woman's choice and served no legitimate state interest. The Court also ruled that the Georgia residency requirement violated the privileges and the immunities clause.

The decision in *Doe v. Bolton*, 410 U.S. 179 (1972), broke along the same lines as the decision in ***Roe v. Wade***, which was a companion case with *Doe*. The dissenters, Justices William Rehnquist and Byron White, argued that the Court's decisions were examples of judicial fiat and activism that created new rights for women while ignoring the state interest of protecting "the life or potential life of the fetus."

BIBLIOGRAPHY
Babcock, Barbara. *Sex Discrimination and the Law*. Boston: Little Brown, 1975.
Cox, Archibald. *The Role of the Supreme Court in American Government*. New York: Oxford University Press, 1976.

Elizabeth Hanford Dole (1936–)

Elizabeth Dole has dedicated more than 30 years to government and quasi-government service beginning in 1966 when she was a staff assistant to the assistant secretary for education at the Department of Health, Education, and Welfare. From 1967 until 1973, she held various positions on the President's Commission on Consumer Interests. She then served a six-year term as a commissioner on the Federal Trade Commission. When Ronald Reagan was elected president in 1980, Dole served as an assistant to the president for public liaison before being appointed secretary of the Department of Transportation in 1980. She served in that capacity until she left to be active in the 1987–88 presidential campaign of her husband,

Kansas senator Bob Dole. In 1989, President George Bush appointed her secretary of labor. She remained at that post until 1991 when she became the president of the American Red Cross. At the Red Cross, she has used her extensive Washington connections to secure the financial future of the organization and to give it lobbying strength.

Elizabeth Dole became familiar to the American public during the 1996 presidential campaign between President Bill Clinton and her husband. While Senator Dole lost, Elizabeth Dole made a dramatic impact on the American people. Some have speculated that she will run for the Republican nomination in 2000, while others believe that she is near the top of the list as a Republican vice presidential candidate. Dole describes herself as a mainstream conservative and is comfortable with all elements of the **Republican Party,** including the Religious Right. Where she stands on a number of issues is unclear because she has never run for elected office herself. While in the Reagan White House, she supported Reagan's alternative to the **Equal Rights Amendment (ERA)**. She has stated publicly that she is pro-life, but has never had to vote publicly or independently express her stance.

BIBLIOGRAPHY

Bumiller, Elisabeth. "Running Against Hillary." *New York Times Magazine* (October 13, 1996): 37.

Dole, Bob and Elizabeth Dole. *Unlimited Partners: Our American Story*. New York: Simon & Schuster, 1996

Franz, Douglas. "Blood Bank Politics." *New York Times* (May 30, 1996): A1.

Domestic Violence

It is estimated that 2–4 million women are abused by intimates each year and that two-thirds of all violence suffered by women in the United States occurs at the hands of partners or family members. The battered women's movement developed out of the increased activism by women in the 1960s and 1970s. The battered women's movement is characterized by the establishment of shelters, places of safety and refuge for battered women and their children, and the lobbying of the government and the public to increase awareness about domestic violence.

The number of shelters in the U.S. has greatly increased over the past 20 years to about 1,500. Shelters are primarily community-based, grassroots organizations that provide crisis intervention and safety for battered women and their children. Shelters also conduct a number of community outreach and education programs to increase the visibility of their services in the community and to increase the public's awareness of domestic violence. Shelters and other groups organized under the National Coalition Against Domestic Violence (NCADV) in 1979. The NCADV provides information networks for individual shelters and a support system for service professionals working with victims of domestic violence. The increased activity in the battered women's movement has led interested advocates and individuals in public service to seek to better understand the causes of domestic violence and its consequences.

Domestic violence researchers have presented three different models of the causes of domestic violence: (1) psychological, (2) sociological, and (3) feminist. The psychological model emphasizes the personal attributes of the batterer and the victim. Psychological model researchers begin their inquiry into the causes of domestic violence by focusing on the personal characteristics of the victim. Researchers initially concluded that victims were masochistic, taking a perspective that inherently blames the victim. More recent inquiries into the psychological makeups of battered women have revealed that these women do not possess specific personality traits or shared psychological problems, such as personality disorders.

In response to the one-sided nature of preliminary psychological research concerning victims, researchers shifted their focus to the psychology of batterers. This research began with inquiry into the levels of aggression of batterers. Research has found that batterers often exhibit a continuum of aggression, beginning with mild forms of violence that lead to severe beatings as a relationship continues. Researchers have yet to apply a consistent diagnosis to the levels of aggression exhibited by abusers. The major focus of this line of inquiry concerns whether or not batterers have a particular psychopathology. Feminists argue that psychological research detracts from abusers' accountability by blaming victims and labeling abusers' behavior as an illness.

The sociological model assumes that social structures influence individual behavior and analyzes how different social variables increase or decrease the presence of domestic violence. Sociologists have researched social factors such as age, position in the social structure, race and ethnicity, and the structure of the family to discover how these variables relate to domestic violence. Researchers have found that the rates of violence are highest for those individuals who are poor and unemployed, between the ages of 18 to 35, and African American or Hispanic. These findings did not suggest that domestic violence was isolated within these particular groups, however, which led researchers to focus on the family unit and the role of family structure in domestic violence.

Sociological researchers examined the structure of the family and concluded that domestic violence is not a result of pathological behavior but of a system of interaction between partners. Many researchers have focused on the interaction between men and women intimates and have developed theories of conflict tactics, which include mild forms of abuse, such as slapping and pushing, as well as more severe forms of violence, such as assault with a deadly weapon or rape. Feminists argue that sociologists' emphasis on conflict tactics fails to address the issue of power and control.

The feminist perspective stresses the role of the patriarchal culture in domestic violence. In a society that believes that a man is the "king of his castle" who should control his wife, domestic violence is believed to be generated out of these cultural expectations. The differences in power between the sexes in a patriarchal society contribute to the control tactics used by men in violent relationships. Feminists perceive domestic violence not as a result of conflict interaction but of the manifestation of power and control over women by their male intimates. Batterers use various forms of coercion to control their partners, the most prevalent being physical abuse. Power and control relationships also include verbal and mental abuse, as well as financial control.

In recent years, researchers have raised concerns about women's violence on their male partners. Despite the shift of perception, in 1994 the U.S. Department of Justice found that 95 percent of all domestic violence is perpetrated by men against their female intimates.

The consequences of domestic violence in society are far reaching. They affect women and their children in the areas of health and the workplace as well as the criminal justice system. Thirty percent of emergency room visits by women are the result of domestic violence. Medical expenses for domestic violence are estimated at between $3 billion and $4 billion a year. Women who seek medical attention for injuries suffered in domestic violence are more common than those who need medical help for auto accidents, rapes, and muggings combined. In addition to regular medical injuries, pregnancy is at high risk in domestic violence. Forty percent of women who have been assaulted report that physical abuse began during their first pregnancy. It is estimated that 17 percent of pregnant women suffer from abuse by their partners that results in premature births, low birth weight, miscarriages, and still births. In addition to the health risks of domestic violence, women victims often have been denied health insurance because they are considered to have "preexisting conditions."

In the late 1990s, health care providers are increasing their training to recognize and treat domestic violence more effectively. Health care professionals are often the only individuals who have access to women suffering in abusive relationships and need to be a powerful force in raising their patients' awareness about access to help. In 1996, the Family Violence Prevention Fund developed the National Health Initiative on Domestic Violence. This program was designed to train health care providers to better serve victims of domestic violence. The program included training for hospital staff to better assist battered patients, the development of a screening process to detect battered patients, resource materials for patients and staff, and the development of domestic violence protocols to guide the staff and institutions to effectively respond to incidences of domestic violence. In a report issued in 1991, the U.S. Department of Heath and Human Services proposed a national public health objective by the year 2000, which calls for 90 percent of emergency hospitals to have protocols for routinely identifying, treating, and referring victims of domestic violence and sexual assault.

Domestic violence has an enormous impact on the workplace. It is estimated that $100 million is lost annually to lost wages, sick leave, absenteeism, and nonproductivity because of domestic abuse; and 25 percent of workplace problems, such as absenteeism, low productivity, and high turnover, are attributed to domestic violence. In 1994, Roper Starch Worldwide conducted a survey of corporate leaders in the U.S. on behalf of Liz Claiborne, Inc. The survey found that 33 percent of the executives believed that domestic violence affects their businesses, and 66 percent believed that their businesses would benefit if the issue of domestic violence was addressed. However, only 12 percent believed that the businesses should be responsible for addressing the issue. Forty percent said they knew of an employee who was a victim of domestic violence, and 96 percent of these executives believed that the problem should be addressed by the family, not the businesses.

Fortunately, Liz Claiborne, Inc., has organized the Women's Work Program to raise American businesses' awareness of issues of domestic violence. In addition to this effort, October 1, 1997, was established as the first National Work to End Domestic Violence Day, and October was named Domestic Violence Awareness Month. As the kick off to Domestic Violence Awareness Month, FUND encouraged businesses across the country to hold seminars to educate employers and workers about domestic violence awareness and prevention.

In addition to domestic violence severely affecting the work of employed women, the most pressing concerns with domestic violence and the workplace are the new welfare-to-work programs being developed in many states in response to the federal welfare reform legislation passed in 1996. Three major components of this legislation have immediate effects on battered women and their children.

First, the elimination of **Aid to Families with Dependent Children (AFDC)** federal entitlements has immediate affects on battered women. Often, AFDC entitlements are the sole source of income for women who have just left their abusers. A 1992 survey in Washington State found that 60 percent of AFDC recipients were victims of domestic violence.

Second, the new legislation also requires battered women to establish paternity for social services to more rigorously pursue child support payments from fathers.When paternity is established, fathers can seek visitation rights or even custody, increasing the children's vulnerability to violence. In addition, when women who have been fleeing from their abusive partners disclose their location in compliance with the paternity requirement, they place themselves in potentially fatal danger.

The third major component of the welfare legislation that affects battered women is the welfare-to-work program's disregard for the experience of battered women. Many batterers sabotage their partners' attempts to become employed. Incidents of burning clothes, severely beating their partners, and turning off alarm clocks the night before a job interview or job training program are all attempts by batterers to continue to exert power and control over their partner. These tactics greatly interfere with women complying with the time requirements of the welfare-to-work legislation and getting the proper job training to make this transition. The Taylor Institute in Chicago found that from 50 to 60 percent of participants in welfare-to-work programs are past victims of domestic violence. The new legislation provides a hardship exemption for 20 percent of a state's average monthly case load, desperately falling short of being flexible enough to accommodate the women in the programs with histories of domestic abuse.

Protective legislation has been passed in recent years that directly addresses the needs of battered women. In 1994, the **Violence Against Women Act (VAWA)** was enacted by Congress. It increased the severity of criminal penalties for perpetrators of domestic violence and provided for increased funding for shelters and other intervention programs. The federal government is obligated to provide $800 million within five years of the act to assist states in restructuring their law enforcement responses to domestic violence.

In addition to providing financial support for domestic violence programs, VAWA made it unlawful for persons subject to restraining orders for harassing, stalking, or threatening an intimate partner to possess firearms. As a complement to this legislation, the Domestic Violence Offender Gun Ban of 1996 prohibited individuals convicted of domestic violence misdemeanors from purchasing or possessing guns. Interestingly, the gun ban has prevented several police officers, as well as military personnel, who have been convicted of domestic violence from carrying guns.

In recent years, the Battered Women's Syndrome (BWS) has been used in defense of women who have killed their abusive male partners. Battered Women's Syndrome is part of a recognized pattern of behavioral responses to intensely traumatic experiences known as Post Traumatic Stress Disorder (PTSD). Post Traumatic Stress Disorder is a psychological diagnosis characterized by exposure to intense trauma, memory distortions—either forgetting the event or experiencing recurring flashbacks—or flight symptoms such as blunted emotions, depression, or high avoidance. Battered Women's Syndrome is not congruent with previous psychological models of victims of domestic violence. Earlier models investigated whether particular personality traits or disorders were present in women who were victims of domestic violence, implying victim causality. Battered Women's Syndrome is a diagnosis about the psychological effects of domestic violence on women. Ninety percent of all the women in jail for killing men have been battered by those men and 60 percent of the women who killed were being assaulted at the time of the killing. The use of the BWS diagnosis assists the judge and jury in understanding the women's mental state and adds to her credibility about the abuse she suffered. The average prison sentence for men who kill their partners is two to three years. In contrast, women convicted of killing their male partners are sentenced to an average of 15 years.

Inevitably, questions arise as to why women do not leave their abusers. Many researchers have struggled to define the reasons why women remain in situations of tremendous abuse. Economic need alone is a great deterrent for women wishing to leave abusive situations. In a society that does not guarantee pay equity between men and women and that does not provide reasonable **child care**, women continue to be economically dependent on men. Over and above economic need, battered women are terrified to leave. Over 75 percent of calls for law enforcement intervention, over 75 percent of emergency room visits as a result of domestic violence, and half of all domestic violence homicides occur after separation.

Domestic violence knows no social or economic class boundaries in the United States. All the research on domestic violence suggests that this societal problem is pervasive; it occurs in every sort of family throughout the country. (SB) **See also** Feminism.

Bibliography

Dobash, R. Emerson and Russell Dobash. *Violence Against Wives: A Case Against the Patriarchy*. New York: The Free Press, 1979.

Dziegielewski, Sophia F. "Shelter-Based Crisis Intervention with Battered Women." In Albert R. Roberts, ed. *Helping Battered Women: New Perspectives and Remedies*. New York: Oxford University Press, 1996.

Gelles, Richard J. "Through a Sociological Lens: Social Structure and Family Violence." In Richard J. Gelles & Donillen R. Loseke, eds. *Current Controversies on Family Violence*. Newbury Park, CA: Sage Publications, Inc., 1993.

O'Leary, K. Daniel. "Through a Psychological Lens: Personality Traits, Personality Disorders, and Levels of Violence." In Richard J. Gelles & Donillen R. Loseke, eds. *Current Controversies on Family Violence*. Newbury Park, CA: Sage Publications, Inc., 1993.

Raphel, Jody. "Prisoners of Abuse: Policy Implications of the Relationship Between Domestic Violence and Welfare Receipt." *Clearinghouse Review*. (Special Issue 1996): 186–94.

Walker, Lenore E. "The Battered Women's Syndrome Is a Psychological Consequence of Abuse." In Richard J. Gelles & Donillen R. Loseke, eds. *Current Controversies on Family Violence*. Newbury Park, CA: Sage Publications, Inc., 1993.

Yllo, Kersti A. "Through a Feminist Lens: Gender, Power, & Violence." In Richard J. Gelles & Donillen R. Loseke, eds. *Current Controversies on Family Violence*. Newbury Park, CA: Sage Publications, Inc., 1993.

Dothard v. Rawlinson (1977)

Dothard v. Rawlinson, 433 U.S. 321 (1977), challenged an Alabama law that required all prison guards to meet a minimum weight requirement of 120 pounds and a minimum height requirement of five feet, two inches. Rawlinson's application for employment as a prison guard in Alabama was rejected because she failed to meet the miniumum weight requirement. While this case was pending, Alabama adopted additional requirements that prison guards in male maximum-security penitentiaries be male. She and others filed a class action suit against Alabama corrections officials challenging these provisions under **Title VII of the Civil Rights Act of 1964**.

In a 6-3 decision, the Supreme Court ruled that the superficially neutral height and weight requirements had a discriminatory effect on the selection of applicants for hire and therefore constituted unlawful **sex discrimination**. The Court found that Alabama offered no evidence that the height and weight requirements were related to the physical strength essential to efficient job performance. In a 7-2 decision, however, the Court upheld the requirement that positions in male maximum-security penitentiaries be filled by males, finding that the sex of the prison guard was a bona fide occupational qualification.

Alabama maintained a prison system where violence was common, inmate access to guards was facilitated by dormitory living arrangements, every correctional institution was understaffed, and substantial numbers of inmates were sex offenders. Using women guards, they said, would therefore pose a substantial security problem. The Court majority was not persuaded by evidence that other states employed women in all-male maximum-security prisons. (RW)

Bibliography

Baer, Judith A. *Women in American Law.* New York: Holmes and Meier, 1991.

Goldstein, Leslie Friedman. *The Constitutional Rights of Women.* Madison: University of Wisconsin Press, 1989.

Emily Taft Douglas (1899–1994)

Emily Douglas was a Democrat elected to the U.S. House of Representatives from Illinois in 1945. While in the House, she served as a member of the Foreign Affairs Committee, backing the creation of the United Nations. She introduced a bill to provide bookmobile libraries in rural areas, which later became the basis for the Hill-Douglas Act. After leaving Congress, Douglas was a moderator for the American Unitarian Association and an activist in the civil rights and **abortion** movements. **See also** Health Care Policy.

Bibliography

Douglas, Emily Taft. *Margaret Sanger: Pioneer of the Future.* New York: Holt Rinehart and Winston, 1970.

———. *Oral Interview, Former Member of Congress Association.* Washington, DC: Manuscript Division, Library of Congress, 1978.

Helen Gahagan Douglas (1900–1980)

In the 1920s and 1930s, Douglas was a Broadway actress and opera singer in New York. In 1940, Douglas became active in **Democratic Party** politics in California and established a close relationship with President Franklin Roosevelt and his wife **Eleanor Roosevelt**. Douglas was elected to the House of Representatives from an urban district in southern California in 1944. Douglas was a true liberal, championing labor and black civil rights in an era that was distinctly hostile to such causes. When Douglas ran for the Senate in 1950 against Richard Nixon, she was the subject of a vicious campaign that depicted her as a communist sympathizer, and her political career ended.

Bibliography

Scobie, Ingrid Winther. *Center Stage: Helen Gahagan Douglas, A Life.* New York: Oxford University Press, 1992.

Women in Congress, 1917–1990. Washington, DC: U.S. Government Printing Office, 1991.

Margaret Green Draper (1750–1807)

Succeeding her husband as publisher of the *Massachusetts Gazette* and *Weekly News-Letter*, Margaret Draper became one of the first American women to operate an independent business. As publisher and editor-in-chief, Draper continued her husband's loyalist policies of opposing American independence from Great Britain. Margaret Draper ceased the newspaper's publication and left America when British troops came to the colonies.

Bibliography

Stark, J. H. *The Loyalists of Massachusetts.* Boston: J.H. Stark, 1910.

Thomas, Isaiah. *The History of Printing in America.* New York: Franklin, 1967.

Abigail Jane Scott Duniway (1834–1915)

In 1871, Abigail Duniway began publishing the *New Northwest*, a paper dedicated to women's rights, and began lecturing on woman **suffrage**. In 1873, she founded the Oregon Equal Suffrage Association and became its president. She was elected vice president of the **National American Woman Suffrage Association (NAWSA)** in 1884. While working for the national suffrage, Duniway also practiced a state-by-state strategy. She was instrumental in securing the vote for women in the Washington Territory in 1883, in Idaho in 1896, and in Oregon in 1912.

A leading suffragist, Abigail Scott Duniway was instrumental in securing the vote in the Pacific Northwest. Library of Congress.

Bibliography

Duniway, Abigail Scott. *An Autobiographical History of the Equal Suffrage Movement in the Pacific Coast States.* New York: Schocken Books, 1971.

Moynhers, Ruth Barnes. "Of Women's Rights and Friends: Abigail Scott Duniway." In Karen J. Blair, ed. *Women in Pacific Northwest History: An Anthology.* Seattle: University of Washington, 1988.

Jennifer Dunn (1941–)

Jennifer Dunn, Republican of Washington State, became the highest ranking woman in the U.S. House of Representatives when she was elected vice-chair of the House Republican Conference. First elected to the House in 1992, Dunn, a conservative, serves on the powerful Ways and Means Committee. Reelected in 1994 and 1996, she has become a leading spokesperson for Republicans on the **gender gap** in American politics as well as on welfare reform and tax cuts. She served five terms as the Washington State Republican Party chair from 1981 until 1992. She has twice been a delegate to the United Nations Commission on the Status of Women, in 1984 and 1990.

BIBLIOGRAPHY

Oldenburg, Don. "The Gender Mind Bender." *Washington Post* (August 19, 1997): B5.

Merida, Kevin. "GOP Women Attack the Party's Gender Gap." *Washington Post* (May 25, 1996): A15.

Andrea Dworkin (1946–)

Andrea Dworkin became a leading spokesperson for the **women's movement** in 1974 with the publication of her book, *Woman Hating*. The book was considered by many feminists to be an important manifesto, especially for more radical feminists. With the publication of her book, *Pornography: Men Possessing Women* in 1981, she began a nearly two-decade campaign against **pornography** that has often aligned her with law professor **Catharine A. MacKinnon**. Her almost exclusive focus on pornography moved Dworkin to the fringe of the movement. In 1983, she wrote *Right Wing Women*, which attempted to explain why women supported the **Republican Party**; in 1987, she wrote *Intercourse*, which traced the roots of misogyny.

BIBLIOGRAPHY

"Andrea Dworkin" *Ms.* 16 (June 1988): 60.

Florence Dwyer (1902–1976)

Florence Dwyer, a Republican, was a member of the New Jersey legislature from 1950 to 1956. In 1956, she was elected to the U.S. House of Representatives, serving her district in New Jersey from 1957 until 1973. During her tenure in Congress, Dwyer also served on the United States Advisory Commission on Intergovernmental Relations from 1959 until 1973. From a densely populated district, she was especially concerned with issues of transportation and environmental impact, advocating the creation of the Environmental Protection Agency and the Department of Transportation.

BIBLIOGRAPHY

Chamberlin, Hope. *A Minority of Members*. New York: Praeger, 1973.

E

Amelia Mary Earhart (1897–1937)

In 1932, Amelia Earhart became the first woman and the second person to fly solo across the Atlantic. Earhart attempted to use her fame to demonstrate that women deserved an expanded role in public life. Earhart's last attempted flight was an around-the-world tour in 1937. Her plane disappeared during the last leg of the flight and her fate remains a mystery, though she is presumed dead. She was also an author who wrote about her experiences as a pilot in the following books: *20 Hrs., 40 Min.* (1928), *The Fun of It* (1932), and *Last Flight* (edited by her husband, 1938). (MEK)

BIBLIOGRAPHY

Burke, John. *Winged Legend: The Story of Amelia Earhart.* New York: Putnam, 1970.

Goerner, Fred G. *The Journey for Amelia Earhart.* New York: Doubleday, 1966.

Economic Equity Act (1986)

In 1985, a comprehensive bill of more than 20 provisions that addressed economic equity for women was placed on Congress's agenda. The bill's chief sponsor, Representative **Patricia Schroeder** (D-CO), championed the bill as a way to stem the so-called "feminization of **poverty**." In the end, only six of the 22 provisions were enacted into law and as the Economic Equity Act of 1986. Those six provisions included pension rights for military spouses and reforms of private pensions; increased **child care** services for low-income mothers; more funding for first-time college students; health insurance extension of coverage to widows, divorced spouses, and children; an increase in the tax deduction for single heads of households; and an increased earned income tax credit. (CGM)

BIBLIOGRAPHY

Gamarekian, Barbara. "Women's Caucus: Eight Years of Progress. *New York Times* (May 27, 1985): 20.

Educational Policy

For American women, the quest for educational opportunity has been a troubled crusade, largely because educational policymaking for women in the United States has been a policy of exclusion. For example, before the Civil War, women could not pursue higher education. After the Civil War, many women became teachers, often going into the South to fill teaching positions left vacant by men who had died in the war or who had left the region seeking opportunity elsewhere. After meeting certain standards to certify their qualifications, numerous women were offered sponsorship by various agencies. The most influential agency was the American Missionary Association (AMA), which recruited women to help educate freed slaves. According to the AMA, the freedmen needed much more than an education. They also needed to be taught how to find a place for themselves in society.

As a result of the increasing numbers of women in teaching, the idea of higher education for women gained popularity. If women were capable of teaching, they should also be offered higher education. However, because tradition and sexism would not allow for coeducation, parallel institutions for women, such as women's seminaries and colleges, were established.

The first women's college, Vassar Female College, opened on September 26, 1865, for women aged 14 to 24. Unlike men at other higher education institutions, women attending Vassar were not allowed to take electives because the administration believed women needed a high amount of structure in their daily lives. Despite these limitations, Vassar offered its students a full range of academic subjects, including math and physics.

Following Vassar's lead, other schools for women were established in the 1870s, including Troy Female Seminary—the first academy for upper-class women—Mount Holyoke, and Catherine Beecher's schools. These schools served women seeking preparatory education or to become teachers. All these schools established colleges for women that offered curricula comparable to that of men.

As the nineteenth century ended, many colleges remained single sex, for numerous reasons, including a widespread belief that women would distract males and lower standards in coeducational institutions. At the same time, however, in the nation's elementary and secondary schools, educational policy for female students would again change dramatically. The progressive school reform movement (1890-1940) brought numerous changes to the schools and the curriculum. For example, the comprehensive high schools, which built upon the common elementary school, had become the standard pattern of American secondary education. But after the turn of the century, the vocational high school began to spring up in the larger cities and the presence of such schools resulted in differentiation along social class lines, as did the vocational tracks within comprehensive high schools. Moreover, within the vocational schools and tracks, there was growing differentiation along gender lines, even in coeducational institutions. The most obvious example being the home economics courses that were seen during the first quarter of the century as preparing young women for their proper vocation, namely, homemaking.

Intellectual and political divisions did arise over the wisdom of such differentiation arrangements and debates over the education of women raged throughout the 1890s. Differences of opinion appeared within the National Society for the Promotion of Industrial Education over whether young women should be prepared for employment in industry or taught to care for their homes and their children. Liberals like Isaac T. Hecker argued for equality and maintained that women had the right to any position with duties and functions they had the intelligence and competence to fulfill. Conservatives, mainly in the Catholic Church, argued that women could find all the satisfaction they needed in the life of the Catholic home along with the other opportunities the Church had traditionally afforded for appropriate service. Catholic education, in turn, had the obligation to prepare them for the callings the Creator had patently intended them for, namely, that of wives and mothers.

Despite these limitations at the high school level, the turn of the century saw many changes promoting the education of women in coeducational colleges and increasing opportunities for women outside the realm of teaching. During the first half of the twentieth century, a strong sentiment in favor of the higher education of women spread throughout the growing nation. In the West, large state universities sprang up and were planned on a coeducational basis; in the East, the older and more conservative colleges reluctantly opened their doors to women.

It was not, however, a call for greater equality or educational opportunity that opened more colleges and universities to women. The most likely reason that women began to enroll in all higher education institutions in general and men's institutions in particular was the decreased number of men who were available to attend college during the Civil War and both World Wars. Men's colleges, such as Carleton, Yale, and **Oberlin**, chose to open their doors to women.

As the number of women attending coeducational institutions increased, a number of women's colleges became "nonviable." Some institutions, such as Harvard-Radcliffe and Hobart & William Smith, are the result of mergers of single-sex colleges. Today, only 84 all-female universities and colleges remain. Despite the dwindling numbers, the impact of women's colleges has been significant, especially at the classroom level. Studies have shown that women who attend women's colleges have higher levels of self-esteem than do their peers in coed institutions.

These studies demonstrated what came to be known as the "gender bias," an idea that began to take root at the start of the 1990s. Researchers argued that a gender bias could be found in American classrooms largely because most girls in first grade have skills and ambitions comparable to those of boys, whereas girls finishing high school have disproportionately less confidence in their academic abilities than do boys. In short, girls start life with the same ability as boys in the areas of reading, writing, and mathematics. The difference, some have argued, is not due to ability, but rather family, social, and cultural expectations.

In 1992, the **American Association of University Women (AAUW)** sought to find out why this difference existed. The AAUW commissioned a study that showed that teachers tend to pay more attention and to give more encouragement to boys, and that girls are frequently overlooked in particular courses of study. Those who studied the schools at the elementary and secondary level also found that a gender bias exists in the students' textbooks and that girls and boys receive unequal amounts of feedback and encouragement from their teachers. Surprisingly, the AAUW also found that teachers are usually unaware of their unequal and destructive bias.

The negative effects of differential treatment of women include limited education career goals, lowered self-esteem, and ambivalence about success and leadership. For example, one study conducted in local high schools found that the number of sophomore boys and girls enrolled in science courses were approximately equal, but by their senior year 150 boys and 46 girls were enrolled in physics. Other statistics show that boys outnumber girls two to one in physical science, and three to one in physics. Also, twice as many boys are enrolled in calculus classes. Clearly, girls are not interested in these fields of study in high school; therefore, this attitude carries over into college degrees and later career opportunities. To overcome this gap, the report recommended that teachers, administrators, and counselors must be prepared and encouraged to bring gender equity and awareness to every aspect of schooling.

Slowly, secondary schools and universities are developing programs to become more "female friendly," and incorporating tactics to help girls, such as confidence building, more hands-on activities, greater computer availability, and the teaching of gender equality at a young age. Elementary schools are also trying to bypass the gender stereotypes by educating parents and teachers about how to treat boys and girls equally. For example, parents are taught to not nurture the girls as much and to allow them more freedom to explore, play, and learn.

In addition to the problem of gender bias, discrimination in education against women has also been financial. For every dollar of financial aid that men receive, women receive 68 cents in work-study, 73 cents in grants, and 84 cents in loans. This is due, in part, to the inequalities found in college athletic programs. Due to these increasing inequalities, the Title IX amendment passed in 1972 stated that "no person in the

United States shall, on the basis of sex, be excluded from participation in, or denied the benefits of, or be subjected to, discrimination under any program or activity receiving federal aid." As a result of Title IX, women have increased their participation in athletics from 15.6 percent in 1972 to 34.8 percent in 1997.

While Title IX has helped to increase representation of women on the playing fields, there are still problems when it comes to enforcing the laws. Although the number of male participants is considerably greater, the women are still being shortchanged. On college campuses, the number of men and women are roughly equal, but men receive 70 percent of scholarship money, 77 percent of operating budgets, and 83 percent of recruiting money. Additionally, women college athletes receive 24 percent of the college sports operating budget and less than 18 percent of college recruiting money. This lack of funding takes away the opportunity for certain individuals to attain a college education.

Under **Title IX of the Education Amendments Act of 1972**, discrimination on the basis of sex is illegal in any educational program receiving federal funding. But federal enforcement of Title IX is complaint-driven, and, since its inception in the 1980s, the U.S. Office of Civil Rights has not actively pursued Title IX enforcement. Problems persist at the elementary and secondary level largely because educators do not perceive a problem in the policy. For example, in 1990, researchers who spent six months visiting 25 rural school districts in 21 states reported that 37 percent of the district administrators they interviewed saw no Title IX compliance issues in their districts. Some of these administrators expressed the view that it was "stupid" or "frivolous" to worry about equal opportunities for girls and boys. Furthermore, the research team reported that in some of the school districts where the administration perceived no problems, Title IX violations appeared to exist in terms of athletic opportunities and sex segregation in higher levels of mathematics and science classes. An additional 28 percent of the district administrators interviewed replied that they believed their districts were within the letter of the law but that they had not gone beyond equal access. A third group, 35 percent of the sample, reported that they were concerned that equal access in the narrow sense was not sufficient to provide genuine equal opportunity for girls and boys, but administrators in this latter group had been faced with **sex discrimination** suits or had attended equity workshops. (VDD)

BIBLIOGRAPHY

Arnot, Madeleine. *Race and Gender: Equal Opportunities Policies in Education.* New York: Pergamon, 1985.

Conway, M. Margaret. "Title IX and the Battle over Implementation." *Women in Public Policy.* Washington, DC: Congressional Quarterly Press, 1995.

Cremin, Lawrence A. *American Education: The Metropolitan Experience 1876-1980.* New York: Harper & Row, 1988.

Fishel, Andrew and Janice Pottker, eds. *National Politics and Sex Discrimination in Education.* Lexington MA: Lexington Books, 1977.

How Schools Shortchange Girls. The AAUW Report. The American Association of University Women Educational Foundation. New York: Marlowe & Company, 1992.

Katznelson, Ira and Margaret Weir. *Schooling for All: Class, Race, and the Decline of the Democratic Ideal.* New York: Basic Books, Inc., 1985.

Sadker, Myra. *Failing at Fairness.* New York: Charles Scribner's Sons, 1994.

Elaine Schwartzenburg Edwards (1929–)

Elaine Edwards, a Democrat, was appointed to the United States Senate from Louisiana by her husband Governor Edwin W. Edwards. The appointment filled the vacancy left by the death of Senator Allen Ellendor. Edwards served in the Senate from August 1, 1972, until her resignation on November 13, 1972.

BIBLIOGRAPHY

Chamberlin, Hope. *A Minority of Members.* New York: Praeger, 1973.

"Elaine Edwards." *Newsweek* 80 (August 14, 1972): 40.

India Edwards (1895–1990)

Born in Chicago in 1895, India Edwards dedicated her career to electing Democrats to political office and raising the status of women in political office. She worked in Chicago as a journalist before she entered politics as a volunteer during the Democratic presidential campaign of 1944. Shortly thereafter, she became executive secretary of the Women's Division of the **Democratic Party,** and its executive director in 1948. That year she also organized the "Housewives for Truman" movement in the presidential campaign. However, when Truman became president, she declined his offer to become chair of the Democratic National Committee, preferring to continue working for the Women's Division. She remained influential, however, and proposed women with exceptional records for specific vacant posts, publicly acknowledging President Truman once the appointments were made. During the Truman administration, 18 women were successfully nominated to positions that required Senate confirmation, and 200 women were appointed to other governmental posts. (GVS)

BIBLIOGRAPHY

Edwards, India. *Pulling No Punches: Memoirs of a Woman in Politics.* New York: Putnam, 1977.

Eighteenth Amendment

The Eighteenth Amendment (sometimes referred to as the Prohibition Amendment) was a nationwide ban on the production, sale, and consumption of alcohol. Prohibition is arguably the first political issue on which women successfully organized on a national scale. The **Women's Christian Temperance Union (WCTU)** was a national organization founded in 1874 to lead efforts to eliminate alcohol, in the United States. Women comprised a dramatic force in the movement against alcohol, as demonstrated by the rapid growth of the WCTU, which reached 150,000 members by 1892. Battling the corrupting forces of alcohol was seen as an important issue, for women were often victimized by male alcoholics.

As time passed, it became evident that women's inability to hold legislators accountable via the vote was an important barrier to achieving temperance goals. Once the need for **suffrage** became clear, the WCTU soon became an open advocate of women's rights. By 1898, the WCTU had relinquished its nationally dominant role on the issue of temperance and narrowed its focus to the liquor traffic. The Anti-Saloon League replaced it as the lead organization behind the **temperance movement**. The Eighteenth Amendment was ratified on January 16, 1919, but was repealed on December 5, 1933, by the Twenty-First Amendment to the Constitution. (JEH)

BIBLIOGRAPHY

Leonard, Priscilla. "Temperance and Woman Suffrage." *Harper's Bazaar* 44 (April 1910): 289.

Tilly, Louise A. and Patricia Gurin, eds. *Women, Politics and Change.* New York: Russell Sage, 1990.

Mamie Geneva Doud Eisenhower (1896–1979)

Mamie Doud took a chance when she married Second Lieutenant Dwight David (Ike) Eisenhower in 1916. Although a West Point graduate, his military future was uncertain. And successful or not, a military wife's life would be difficult. Their marriage followed a long road with difficult assignments and extended separations as Ike's career advanced. Ike returned from World War II a hero, and in 1952 he was elected president as a Republican.

Believing her role as first lady was private, Mamie Eisenhower did not publicly express her opinions on policy matters. Library of Congress.

Mamie never regretted marrying Ike, despite the difficulties and strains fame placed on their marriage over the years, including discomfort over his presidency. But as she wrote, Ike "was my whole life." She viewed her role as first lady as private and supportive, not public. Her opinions were strong, but she kept them to herself. She made no speeches, stating that "Ike speaks well enough for both of us." As first lady she ran the White House in a disciplined and frugal fashion, created a comfortable environment for those who worked there, and let Americans know they had, as she said, a "good friend" in the White House. (RRT) **See also** First Ladies.

BIBLIOGRAPHY

Eisenhower, Susan. *Mrs. Ike—Memories and Reflections on the Life of Mamie Eisenhower.* New York: Doubleday, 1978.

Neal, Steve. *The Eisenhowers—Reluctant Dynasty.* New York: Doubleday, 1978.

Eisenstadt v. Baird (1972)

In *Eisenstadt v. Baird,* 405 U.S. 438 (1972), the issue was whether a Massachusetts law limiting the distribution of a drug, medicine, instrument, or device for the prevention of contraception to married persons who had a valid prescription violated the rights of unmarried individuals under the Equal Protection Clause of the Fourteenth Amendment. The case began when a speaker at a lecture on contraception concluded his presentation to a group of students by distributing contraceptive foam in violation of the law.

In its arguments, Massachusetts stated that the law was necessary to regulate the distribution of contraceptives to ensure the health of the people receiving it. However, plaintiffs argued that the law was unconstitutional because it treated married and single people differently even though the situations were similar. Additionally, they argued that the ban violated a person's First Amendment right of free speech by limiting who could distribute and discuss contraceptives.

The U.S. Supreme Court held that the Massachusetts ban on providing contraceptives to unmarried people was a violation of the equal protection clause of the Fourteenth Amendment because it treated people in similar situations differently based upon their marital status.

BIBLIOGRAPHY

Carey, Eve and Kathleen W. Peratis. *Women and the Law*. Skokie, IL: National Textbook Company, 1977.

Kanowitz, Leo. *Sex Roles in Law and Society*. Albuquerque: University of New Mexico Press, 1973.

M. Joycelyn Elders (1933–)

Joycelyn Elders was born in Schaal, Arkansas, in 1933. Elders received her medical degree in 1960 from the University of Arkansas Medical School. In 1993, President Bill Clinton appointed Elders as U.S. surgeon general. Her confirmation by the Senate was a controversial affair due to her advocacy of condoms and sex education in the public schools and her support for **abortion** rights. She was confirmed and became the first African American and the second woman to serve as surgeon general. In 1994, while addressing the United Nations, Elders suggested that the public schools educate students about masturbation as a way of discouraging premarital sexual intercourse. The ensuing furor among conservatives resulted in her resignation. (CKC)

BIBLIOGRAPHY

Elders, M. Joycelyn. *Joycelyn Elders: From Sharecroppers' Daughter to Surgeon General of the United States of America.* New York: William Morrow, 1996.

Elizabethton, Tennessee, Strike of 1929

The Elizabethton, Tennessee, Strike began on March 12, 1929, after women in the inspection department of the American Glazstoff Rayon Plant walked out in protest over low wages. These women soon joined with female workers from the American Bemberg Plant in forming a local chapter of the

United Textile Workers in defiance of their employers. This group then began picketing the plants where they worked, even though this action violated court mandates against picketing and, subsequently, led to confrontations with National Guardsmen. The strikers were undaunted and continued to picket the factories. They marched through the streets draped in American flags and blockaded roads in protest. A settlement was finally negotiated on May 26, 1929. Although the strikers gained little wage compensation for their efforts, the strike did highlight the power that women held over policy and work conditions. The strike inspired a number of other strikes throughout the South during the 1930s.

BIBLIOGRAPHY

Hall, Jacquelyn Down, et al. *Like a Family: The Making of a Southern Cotton Mill World.* Chapel Hill: University of North Carolina Press, 1987.

Hodges, James. "Challenge to the New South: The Great Strike in Elizabethton, Tennessee, 1929." *Tennessee Historical Quarterly* 23 (December 1964): 343–57.

Trippet, Tom. *When Southern Labor Stirs.* New York: Jonathan Cape and Harrison Smith, 1931.

Sarah Barnwell Elliott (1848–1928)

Sarah Elliott served as a member of the Tennessee Equal Suffrage Association from 1906 to 1914, serving as president from 1912 until 1914. She participated in the 1913 march on Washington for a federal **suffrage** amendment. Her 1901 novel, *The Making of June* (1901), highlighted her feminist views. **See also** Feminism.

BIBLIOGRAPHY

Elliott, Sarah Barnwell. "The Sewanee Spirit." *Bulletin of the University of the South* (August 1918).

Taylor, A. Elizabeth. *The Woman Suffrage Movement in Tennessee.* New York: Octagon Books, 1957.

Jo Ann Emerson (1950–)

Jo Ann Emerson is the first Republican woman to represent the state of Missouri in the U.S. House of Representatives. She won her seat in a special election in November 1996 to fill the unexpired term of her late husband, Bill Emerson. She was simultaneously elected to a full term beginning in 1997. In Congress, she serves on the Agriculture, Transportation and Infrastructure, and Small Business committees.

BIBLIOGRAPHY

Grove, Lloyd. "The Congresswoman's House of Memories." *Washington Post* (November 27, 1996): B1.

EMILY's List

EMILY's List (an acronym for "Early Money Is Like Yeast"—it makes dough rise) was the first national partisan organization devoted to helping women candidates. Founded by **Ellen Malcolm** in 1985, EMILY's List serves as a donor network to assist female Democratic candidates who are pro-choice. Members choose from among endorsed candidates and contribute a minimum of $100 to two or more candidates. EMILY's List also conducts issue research, offers training seminars for candidates and campaign managers, and works to increase voter turnout among women. Today, EMILY's List has grown to over 45,000 members and has raised millions of dollars to continue increasing the number of women elected to office. (LvA)

BIBLIOGRAPHY

Burrell, Barbara C. *A Woman's Place Is in the House.* Ann Arbor: The University of Michigan Press, 1994.

Witt, Linda, Karen M. Paget, and Glenna Matthews. *Running As a Woman: Gender and Power in American Politics.* New York: The Free Press, 1995.

Karan English (1949–)

Karan English was elected to the U.S. House of Representatives from Arizona in 1992. A Democrat, she was unsuccessful in her bid for re-election in 1994. Prior to serving in Congress, English served in the Arizona state senate from 1991 to 1993. From 1987 to 1991, she served in the Arizona state house. The environment was the issue that first got her involved in politics when she was elected to the Coconino County Board of Supervisors in 1981. She served there until 1987, the last four years as board chair.

BIBLIOGRAPHY

Kaplan, Dave. "GOP Looks to Turn Tables on Two Female Freshman." *Congressional Quarterly Weekly Report* 52, no. 42 (October 29, 1994): 3096.

Margolies-Mezvinsky, Marjorie. *A Woman's Place.* New York: Crown, 1994.

Equal Credit Opportunity Act (ECOA) (1974)

The Equal Credit Opportunity Act (ECOA) was passed in 1974 after the issue of credit discrimination received national attention at the hearings of the National Commission of Consumer Finance in 1972. The law "prohibits discrimination on the basis of sex or marital status with respect to any aspect of a credit transaction." Support for the legislation was forthcoming from national women's groups, in particular the **National Organization for Women (NOW),** and the Center for Women Policy Studies, and female members of Congress. The Federal Reserve Board was charged with writing the regulations for the ECOA and opened the process to (then) unprecedented public hearings. The final regulations, which were issued in 1975 after a hard fought battle with creditors who opposed the measure, resulted in a partial victory for feminist forces. "Reg B" provides that creditors must provide written reasons for termination or credit refusal. By 1978, 80 percent of women surveyed had applied for credit in their own names during the prior two years; 56 percent felt that the ECOA had made it easier for women to obtain credit. Female home ownership has also increased, in part due to easier mortgage credit made possible by the ECOA. (JG)

BIBLIOGRAPHY

Conway, M. Margaret. Discrimination and the Law: The Equal Credit Opportunity Act." In Marian L. Palley and Michael Preston, eds. *Race, Sex and Policy Problems.* Lexington, MA: DC Health, 1979.

Gelb, Joyce and Marian L. Palley. "Women and Interest Group Politics: A Case Study of the Equal Credit Opportunity Act." *American Politics Quarterly* 5, no. 4 (July 1977): 331–52.

Equal Division Rule

Since 1968, quadrennial reform commissions of the Democratic National Party have recommended that party rules include affirmative steps to increase the number of blacks, women, and youths who serve as delegates to the national conventions, thus making conventions more representative of the voting public. In 1968, only 13 percent of the delegates to the Democratic National Convention were women. That percentage increased to 40 percent in 1972, but decreased to 33 percent in 1976. In response to the recommendations of reform commissions and the decline in the representation of women as delegates from 1972 to 1976, the Democratic National Committee (DNC) adopted a resolution at the 1976 convention to promote equal representation of women as delegates. In 1980, the DNC changed the **affirmative action** policy to require equal division of state delegations between men and women. The equal division rule went into effect at the 1980 convention, and as a result women represented 49 percent of the convention delegation. Since 1980, women have continued to represent approximately 50 percent of the delegates to Democratic National Conventions. Although the Republican National Party encourages its state affiliates to increase representation among women, it has not adopted comparable rules mandating affirmative action programs or equal division of the sexes in state delegations. (LvA)

BIBLIOGRAPHY

Bibby, John F. *Politics, Parties and Elections in America, Second Edition.* Chicago: Nelson-Hall Publishers, 1992.

Equal Educational Opportunities Act of 1972

The Equal Educational Opportunities Act is one of a series of pieces of educational legislation sponsored in Congress during the 1970s. The goal of this legislation was to remove the remaining elements of the previously legal, racially segregated systems of education based on race and to prohibit other types of discrimination as well. As a result, the act is a general ban on all types of discrimination, including, race, national origin, and sex, for state-funded educational activities.

Some scholars contend that this legislation is nothing more than a symbolic attempt to avoid court-ordered busing to further the cause of racial integration. For women, the act increases the legislative strength behind their efforts at achieving equal educational funding in academic and athletic programs. (JEH)

BIBLIOGRAPHY

Stetson, Dorothy McBride. *Women's Rights in the U.S.A.: Policy Debates and Gender Roles.* Pacific Grove, CA: Brooks-Cole, 1991.

Until relatively recently, women in the business world were largely confined to secretarial jobs and other low-wage positions. Library of Congress.

Equal Employment Opportunity Act (1972)

The Equal Employment Opportunity Act of 1972 was passed in response to political pressure to force the **Equal Employment Opportunity Commission (EEOC)** to follow its legislative mandate. The EEOC was created to enforce the provisions against job discrimination on the basis of race, color, religion, national origin, or sex in **Title VII of the Civil Rights Act of 1964**. However, as created, the EEOC had little actual power to enforce Title VII. Moreover, the commission demonstrated little inclination toward active enforcement of the legislation, repeatedly failing to investigate complaints. This situation was quickly identified by women's groups and a response came in 1966 with the formation of the **National Organization for Women (NOW)**, which organized to pass legislation that would increase the power of the EEOC and to improve enforcement of Title VII.

As a result of the efforts of NOW and other women's rights groups, the Equal Employment Opportunity Act became law in 1972. The act broadened the power of the EEOC to enforce Title VII by authorizing the commission to sue for compliance. Previously, the EEOC had been limited to pursuing only voluntary compliance. In addition, the act expanded the domain of the Civil Rights Act to include small businesses, federal and state employees, and educational institutions. (JEH)

BIBLIOGRAPHY

McGlen, Nancy E. and Karen O'Connor. *Women, Politics, and American Society.* Englewood Cliffs, NJ: Prentice Hall, 1995.

Equal Employment Opportunity Commission (EEOC)

The Equal Employment Opportunity Commission (EEOC) was created to enforce the provisions of **Title VII of the Civil Rights Act of 1964**. Title VII prohibits job discrimination on the basis of race, color, religion, national origin, or sex. The role of the EEOC was to oversee issuance of regulations for compliance and to respond to complaints of job-related **sex discrimination**. At the time, the EEOC was the only bureaucratic entity charged with any kind of enforcement of Title VII. Initially, the EEOC failed in its mandate, spurring other political activity aimed at guaranteeing enforcement of Title VII through the EEOC. One such initiative was to give the EEOC the power to sue employers who violated Title VII.

The powers of the EEOC remain limited. Under law, the commission cannot initiate investigations, thus as long as no employment-discrimination complaints are filed, employers can violate Title VII. The power of the EEOC lies with its ability to investigate complaints. However, even this role is restricted.

Upon receipt of a complaint, the EEOC notifies the employer and sends the complaint to a state or local agency for review and possible settlement. If resolution is not achieved, the EEOC conducts its own investigation. During this process, the EEOC arbitrates, attempting to facilitate an agreement between employer and employee. If this fails, the EEOC then has the option to sue the employer for violation of Title VII. (JEH) **See also** Equal Employment Opportunity Act.

BIBLIOGRAPHY

Hernardez, Aileen C. "EEOC and the Women's Movement, 1965–1975." Rutgers University Law School Conference, November 1975.

Zelman, Patricia G. "Development of Equal Employment Opportunity for Women as a National Policy, 1960–1967." Ph.D. dissertation, Ohio State University, 1980.

Equal Pay Act of 1963

After a 19-year debate over proposed changes, the Equal Pay Act was finally signed by President John F. Kennedy on June 10, 1963, amending the **Fair Labor Standards Act of 1938**. The new act required private sector employers to pay equal wages for equal work, regardless of an employee's gender. While the legislation did not cover women who were working in executive, professional, or administrative capacities, it helped to eliminate a large percentage of job-related discrimination. Because of legal and administrative complications, as well as further debate over the proposed changes, the Equal Pay Act did not go into effect until June 11, 1964, almost one year after Kennedy's approval. When it did finally go into action, however, the new act gained recognition as the first federal law to prohibit **sex discrimination**, a landmark event for women and civil rights activists.

BIBLIOGRAPHY

Berger, Caruthers Gholson. "Equal Pay, Equal Employment Opportunity and Equal Enforcement of the Law for Women." *Valparaiso Law Review* 5, no. 2 (Spring 1971): 326–73.

Vladek, Judith. "The Equal Pay Act of 1963." *Proceedings of the 18th New York University Conference on Labor.* Albany, NY: Bender, 1966.

Equal Rights Amendment (ERA)

The Equal Rights Amendment (ERA) is a proposed constitutional amendment intended to grant women explicit constitutional protection against **sex discrimination**. Drafted by **Alice Paul**, leader of the **National Woman's Party (NWP)**, the ERA was first introduced in Congress in 1923. It took nearly 50 years of debate before the amendment was approved by both Houses of Congress and sent to the states with a seven-year deadline for ratification. The final wording of the amendment proclaimed, "Equality of rights under the law shall not be denied or abridged by the United States or by any State on account of sex." Although Congress granted an unprecedented three-year deadline extension to June 30, 1982, the ERA fell three states short of the 38 needed for ratification.

Immediately following ratification of the **Nineteenth Amendment** granting women the right to vote, Alice Paul drafted the ERA, realizing that **suffrage** was necessary but insufficient to obtain equal rights for women. Many women's groups, including the **National League of Women Voters**, the National Consumers' League and the **National Women's Trade Union League**, opposed the amendment, fearing that equal protection for women would invalidate much of the **protective legislation**, including **minimum wage/maximum hour laws**, that they had fought for to ease the harsh conditions of women in the workplace. Major women's groups did not endorse the amendment until the 1960s, when, after passage of the **Equal Pay Act of 1963** and the **Civil Rights Act of 1964,** most protective legislation for women was ruled unconstitutional.

In 1961, President John F. Kennedy created a **Presidential Commission on the Status of Women**. Its 1963 report acknowledged the barriers women faced in the workplace and in politics, but failed to endorse the ERA. By the mid-1960s, states also established commissions on the status of women. Yet, despite mounting evidence, the federal **Equal Employment Opportunity Commission (EEOC)** continued to ignore gender discrimination cases. At the third annual meeting of the National Conference of State Commissions in the spring of 1966, women became frustrated when the conference was not allowed to pass resolutions urging the EEOC to act. Many of these women then met informally and founded the **National Organization for Women (NOW)** to lobby the national government about women's concerns. One year later, Alice Paul, then 82 years old, convinced the National Organization for Women to support the ERA, and thus began the modern campaign for the amendment.

Initially, failure of the ERA seemed unlikely; more than 450 national organizations supported the amendment and polls indicated that more than two-thirds of the public supported its passage. With NOW's support, the ERA finally passed the U.S. House of Representatives in 1971 and the Senate in 1972. Three-fourths of the states, a total of 38, are needed to ratify a national constitutional amendment. By the end of 1973, 30 states had ratified the ERA; however, additional states were slow to follow. In 1978, after intense lobbying, proponents of the ERA were able to get a three-year extension of the ratification deadline. By 1979, however, opponents of the ERA succeeded in convincing five states (Tennessee, Kentucky, Idaho, Nebraska, and South Dakota) to rescind their votes for ratification, thus raising a constitutional question. In December 1981, the U.S. District Court ruled that states had the right to rescind their ratification of constitutional amendments. ERA supporters were outraged and began the **ERA Countdown Campaign**, aimed at getting Oklahoma, North Carolina, Mississippi, Illinois, and Florida to pass the amendment. The 35th and final state to pass the amendment was Indiana in 1977. On June 30, 1982, the extended deadline expired and the ERA died. The unratified states were located primarily in the deep South and in western states dominated by the Mormon Church.

Controversy over the impact of the ERA on **family law**, including marriage, divorce, and **child custody and support** laws fueled opposition to the ERA early in the drive for ratification. Some argued that the ERA would require women to work and support their husbands. The fear of compulsory **military service** also became a controversial issue. Confidence in the ERA's success, however, led women's rights activists to ignore the increasing grassroots opposition to the amendment. The pro-ERA movement was also disorganized, lacking the national coordination and unified strategy that had led to success in obtaining woman suffrage decades before. The following three attempts at national organization failed due to insufficient funding, staffing, and coordination among affiliated members: (1) the National Ratification Council, formed shortly after the amendment was sent to the states for ratification; (2) the Operation Task Force, formed in the summer of 1973; and (3) ERAmerica, created in 1976 in response to a study by the Business and Professional Women (BPW). Lacking a unified voice, the drive for ratification was led by individual groups pursuing their own strategies.

The struggle between women's rights groups to dominate the process can be divided into three distinct stages. The first stage of the ERA ratification effort took place from 1972 through 1977 when NOW and the BPW both employed traditional lobbying tactics, including letter writing, testifying before Congress, and campaigning for pro-ERA candidates. After winning only five additional states after 1973, NOW embarked in 1977 on a more aggressive strategy, marking the second stage of the ratification movement. From 1979 to 1982, NOW called for an economic boycott of states that had not ratified the amendment. The American Political Science Association, for example, was persuaded not to hold its annual meeting in Chicago. NOW also organized intense lobbying of Congress to secure an extension of the ratification deadline. In 1979, NOW staged a march on Washington that attracted more than 100,000 women. Although Congress did not grant the full seven-year extension initially requested by NOW, the deadline for ratification was extended three years to 1982. This extension marked the beginning of the third stage of the ratification effort, in which NOW committed itself to a new national plan of action, including major donations to pro-ERA candidates, grassroots door-to-door canvassing in unratified states, a publicity campaign, acts of violent protest, and even a few cases of vandalism. NOW's attempt at national coordination occurred too late in the process, however, and the ERA ratification deadline expired in 1982.

The ERA's chances for success would have been much greater had it not been for the militant opposition of **Phyllis Schlafly**, who drew opposition to the amendment from both the religious and the political Right. Opponents of the ERA included fundamentalist Christian churches, the Moral Majority, the John Birch Society, the Mormon Church, and the American Farm Bureau, among others. Schlafly effectively publicized anti-ERA sentiments through the ***Phyllis Schlafly Report***. A 1972 edition of the newsletter stated, for example, "The laws of every one of the fifty states now require the husband to support the wife and children. . . . The Equal Rights Amendment will remove this sole obligation from the husband, and make the wife equally responsible to provide a home for her family, and to provide 50% of the financial support of her family." In 1972, Schlafly organized **STOP ERA** to mobilize grassroots opposition to the amendment. As the sole spokesperson for the organization, Schlafly became the symbol of the anti-ERA movement. She threatened that the ERA would abolish single-sex schools, eliminate separate cells for male and female prisoners, lead to a female draft, allow homosexuals to marry and adopt children, and even result in unisex toilets. To Schlafly and her followers, the ERA was anti-family, anti-children, and pro-abortion—a powerful message that was successful in convincing many homemakers that the ERA was a threat. The linkage made between the ERA and **abortion** rights following the Supreme Court's decision in ***Roe v. Wade*** (1973) gave these arguments further credibility and attracted additional opposition to the ERA, particularly among Catholics.

Because the impact of the ERA on homemakers was unclear, many turned against it. Homemakers felt threatened by feminists; their status in society as homemakers had declined as upper-class, well-educated women who least needed to work chose to enter the workforce. The divorce rate was increasing, alimony was decreasing, and feminists were seen as the enemy.

Both sides of the ERA debate claimed the amendment would have a universal impact. The ERA proponents promised educational, employment, and political equality for women. In abstract, these goals were supported by a majority of the public. Proponents of the amendment, however, failed to counterattack when threats were made about the specific impact of the ERA on family relationships. As a result, the anti-ERA forces were successful in defeating the amendment by raising concern about the potential impact of the ERA. While proponents of the ERA had to convince a total of 38 states to ratify the ambiguous amendment, opponents simply had to prevent the 38th state from ratifying the amendment. According to Jane Mansbridge, several lessons were learned from the failure of the ERA that made the effort worthwhile. Mansbridge explains that voluntary organizations encouraged ideological purity. Unwilling to compromise, the proponents of the ERA rejected clarifying amendments, even though they might have dispelled some of the fears concerning the ambiguity of the ERA. Mansbridge argues that the proponents of the ERA should have been more willing to listen to groups supportive of but not totally committed to the ERA. In the suffrage movement, it was not until conservative groups were convinced that they needed the vote to obtain their own goals that the movement was successful. Mansbridge also points out the failure of the proponents of the ERA to organize effectively at the state level. After almost 50 years of lobbying in Washington to coordinate passage of the ERA through Congress, there was little or no organization in place at the state level to facilitate ratification. Being "right" was not enough; the proponents needed to engage actively in grassroots mobilization. Although NOW led a renewed effort at grassroots mobilization for the ERA from 1979 to 1982, the third stage of the ratification movement, it was too little, too late to have an impact. The proponents of the ERA underestimated their opposition and should have met anti-ERA arguments of all kinds more forcefully. With 30 states ratifying the ERA by the end of 1973, it was perhaps too difficult to foresee the hard road ahead.

Feminists perhaps lost some credibility in failing to pass the ERA; however, the movement was successful in raising the consciousness of the public about women's issues, in helping women learn how to organize politically, and in stimulating legislative and judicial action to end gender discrimination. States have repealed much of their blatantly discriminatory legislation and the national government began enforcing such laws as **Title VII of the Civil Rights Act of 1964**.

On July 14, 1982, the ERA was reintroduced in Congress, however, efforts to regain congressional approval failed. A window of opportunity appears to have closed, as states today are more conservative and the opposition is organized. Suggestions have been made for an Equal Rights Act, which would be easier to pass than an amendment and could have its own amendments to explain its impact. However, legislation would also be easier to repeal than a constitutional amendment. Some people argue that the ERA is no longer necessary because many of the reforms that were arguments in favor of the ERA have passed. However, ERA supporters argue that the amendment would elevate gender discrimination to a heightened standard of review before the courts, making it easier for women to win battles in more concrete areas of reform. (LvA) **See also** Feminism; Last Walk for ERA.

Bibliography

Becker, Susan. *The Origins of the Equal Rights Amendment.* Westport, CT: Greenwood, 1982.

Berry, Mary Frances. *Why ERA Failed: Politics, Women's Rights, and the Amending Process of the Constitution.* Bloomington: Indiana University Press, 1986.

Boles, Janet K. *The Politics of the Equal Rights Amendment: Conflict and the Decision Process.* New York: Longman, 1979.

Hoff-Wilson, Joan. *Rights of Passage: The Past and Future of the ERA.* Bloomington: Indiana University Press, 1986.

Mansbridge, Jane J. *Why We Lost the ERA.* Chicago: University of Chicago Press, 1986.

McGlenn, Nancy and Karen O'Connor. *Women's Rights: The Struggle for Equality in the 19th and 20th Centuries.* New York: Praeger Publishers, 1983.

Whitney, Sharon. *The Equal Rights Amendment: The History and the Movement.* New York: Franklin Watts, 1984.

Equal Rights Association (ERA)

The Equal Rights Association (ERA) was founded in 1866 when the Woman's Rights Society adopted the call of **Elizabeth Cady Stanton** and **Susan B. Anthony** to work for the citizenship rights of both women and African-American men. The American Anti-Slavery Society had also been invited to merge into the ERA but declined. The linking of women's and African-American men's rights proved to be a difficult political strategy as forces fought internally over the direction the organization should take. At the third national convention in 1869, the group splintered. By 1869, the Fourteenth Amendment, which gave citizenship to African-American men, had been ratified and the Fifteenth Amendment, guaranteeing the vote to African-American men, had been approved by Congress. After the convention, Stanton and Anthony founded the **National Woman Suffrage Association (NWSA)** to pursue woman's **suffrage**. The ERA eventually became the **American Woman Suffrage Association (AWSA).**

Bibliography

DuBois, Ellen. *Feminism and Suffrage: The Emergence of an Independent Woman's Movement in America, 1848–1869.* New York: Cornell University Press, 1978.

Flexner, Eleanor. *Century of Struggle.* New York: Athaneum, 1968.

ERA Countdown Campaign

The ERA Countdown Campaign was the last 12-month effort to achieve ratification of the **Equal Rights Amendment (ERA)** by the states. Sponsored by the **National Organization for Women (NOW)**, the ERA Countdown Campaign officially began when **Betty Ford** accepted its chairmanship on June 30, 1981. At this time, the movement needed the support of only three more states to add the amendment to the Constitution. One year later the campaign ended unsuccessfully.

The campaign was intended to rally and crystallize support for the amendment before the deadline for ratification. The primary strategy of the campaign was to target key states, those viewed as being most likely to ratify in the last year. The targeted states included Florida, North Carolina, Oklahoma, and Virginia. The campaign used a variety of techniques to bring increased attention and support to the ERA. However, state and local chapters of NOW and other groups were unable to successfully coordinate their efforts. Finally, despite public support for equal rights in the abstract, the anti-ERA movement was able to focus attention on possible radical consequences of the ERA, such as subjection of women to the draft and unisex bathrooms. On June 30, 1982, the Equal Rights Amendment failed to be ratified by a margin of three states. (JEH)

BIBLIOGRAPHY

Kelley, Florence. "Why Other Women's Groups Oppose It." *Good Housekeeping* 78 (March 1924): 19, 162–65.

Williams, Roger M. "Women Against Women—The Clamor over Equal Rights." *Saturday Review* 4 (1977): 7–13, 46.

Anna Eshoo (1942–)

Democrat Anna Eshoo of California currently is serving her third term in the U.S. House of Representatives. Born on December 13, 1942, in New Britain, Connecticut, she obtained an A.A. degree from Canada College in 1975 and served for 10 years on the San Mateo County Board of Supervisors. She was elected to Congress in 1992, "The Year of the Woman," and served on the Science and Commerce Committee. In her first term, Eshoo was elected to serve as an at-large Democratic whip and co-chair of the House Medical Technology Caucus, and to serve on the Executive Committee of the Democratic Study Group. Eshoo has compiled a liberal voting record on cultural and foreign issues, but a more moderate one on economics. She was hesitant about supporting the 1993 Clinton budget and tax plan and only supported the NAFTA agreement after much hesitation. She was reelected by 61 percent of the vote in 1994 and by 51 percent in 1996. Currently, she serves on the Science, Business, and Ways and Means committees. (GVS)

BIBLIOGRAPHY

Cranford, John R. and Thomas Galvin, et. al. "Anna G. Eshoo, California." *Congressional Quarterly Weekly Report* 50, no. 44 (November 7, 1992): 24.

Willa McCord Blake Eslick (1878–1961)

During World War I, Willa Eslick served as the chair of the Giles County Council of National Defense and as a member of the Tennessee State Democratic Committee. Elected to Congress on August 4, 1932, she succeeded her deceased husband Edward Eslick. A Democrat, she served in Congress less than a year.

BIBLIOGRAPHY

Chamberlin, Hope. *A Minority of Members*. New York: Praeger, 1973.

Susan Estrich (1954–)

Susan Estrich received her law degree at Harvard where she was the first woman to edit the *Harvard Law Review*. At the age of 35, she became the first woman to manage a presidential campaign when she headed Massachusetts Governor Michael Dukakis' failed campaign in 1988. A law professor, Estrich is an expert in the field of feminist jurisprudence. (CKC)

BIBLIOGRAPHY

Estrich, Susan. *Real Rape*. Cambridge: Harvard University Press, 1987.

Toner, Robin. "Susan Estrich Brings Assurance and Toughness to Dukakis Drive." *New York Times Biographical Service* (May 1988): 508–09.

Executive Order 10980

President John Kennedy issued Executive Order 10980 on December 14, 1961, establishing the **President's Commission on the Status of Women (PCSW)**. **Esther Peterson**, director of the **Women's Bureau** and long associated with the labor movement and the protection of women workers, was influential in defining the membership of the commission and in shaping its agenda. Her role is most vividly illustrated in the commission's stated mandate to take "responsibility for developing recommendations for overcoming discriminations in government and private employment on the basis of sex and for developing recommendations for services which will enable women to continue their role as wives and mothers while making a maximum contribution to the world around them." Although the President's Commission issued reports documenting **sex discrimination** against women in the workplace, its failure to enforce the **Civil Rights Act of 1964** led to the formation of the **National Organization for Women (NOW)**. (JMM)

BIBLIOGRAPHY

Martin, Janet M. *A Place in the Oval Office: Women and the American Presidency.* Ann Arbor: University of Michigan Press, forthcoming.

Executive Order 11126

Based on the recommendation of the **President's Commission on the Status of Women** (PCSW), President John F. Kennedy issued Executive Order 11126 on November 1, 1963, creating the Interdepartmental Committee on the Status of Women (1963–1974), chaired by the secretary of labor, and a **Citizen's Advisory Council on the Status of Women** (1963–1977). The groups were created to review and assess progress in improving the status of women, as well as disseminate information on such efforts. While the Interdepartmental Committee only met once during the Nixon administration, the Citizen's Advisory Council played an influential role throughout the Nixon and Ford administrations in actively promoting the **Equal Rights Amendment (ERA)** and shaping other issues, including maternity leave and **sex discrimination** in education. In 1968, the council called for a repeal of all restrictive **abortion** laws. In 1970, it supported the ERA in its report to the president, rejecting the analysis of the original commission, which stated that the amendment was unnecessary. (JMM)

BIBLIOGRAPHY

Martin, Janet M. *A Place in the Oval Office: Women and the American Presidency.* Ann Arbor: University of Michigan Press, forthcoming.

Executive Order 11375

Issued by President Lyndon B. Johnson in October 1967, Executive Order 11375 amends Executive Order 11246 by prohibiting discrimination based on sex by most federal government contractors and subcontractors. Previous to Executive Order 11375, government contractors were prohibited from discriminating against employees because of race, creed, color, or national origin, but sex was not an included category. This executive order also requires contractors to "take **affirmative action** to ensure that applicants are employed, and that employees are treated, during employment, without regard to their race, color, religion, sex or national origin." The Office of Federal Contract Compliance is responsible for coordinating and overseeing compliance with the executive order. (JAD)

BIBLIOGRAPHY

Leonard, Jonathon S. "Women and Affirmative Action." *Journal of Economic Perspectives* 31, no. 1 (1989): 61–75.

Schmid, Gunter and Renate Wertzil, eds. *Sex Discrimination and Equal Opportunity.* New York: St. Martin's Press, 1984.

Zelman, Patricia G. *Women, Work and National Policy: The Kennedy-Johnson Years.* Ann Arbor, MI: UMI Research Press, 1980.

Executive Order 11478

Issued by President Richard Nixon in August 1969, Executive Order 11478 prohibits discrimination based on race, color, religion, sex, or national origin in employment within the federal government. In addition, it directs all federal agencies and departments to "establish and maintain an **affirmative action** program of equal employment for all civilian employees and applicants." Until it was abolished in 1978, the Civil Service Commission (CSC) had authority to hear complaints as well as issue regulations, orders, and instructions. Since then, the **Equal Employment Opportunity Commission (EEOC)** has had responsibility for investigating complaints and issuing guidelines and regulations. (JAD)

BIBLIOGRAPHY

Leonard, Jonathon S. "Women and Affirmative Action." *Journal of Economic Perspectives* 31, no. 1 (1989): 61–75.

Schmid, Gunter and Renate Wertzil, eds. *Sex Discrimination and Equal Opportunity.* New York: St. Martin's Press, 1984.

F

Fair Labor Standards Act of 1938

The Fair Labor Standards Act of 1938, the first national minimum wage law to pass a constitutional test, established a nominal minimum wage of $0.25 per hour (42 percent of the average manufacturing wage), banned oppressive child labor, and set 40 hours as the maximum number of hours of work per week without time-and-a-half overtime payment. In accord with President Franklin Roosevelt's New Deal program, its purpose was to protect the health, safety, and general well-being of workers without substantially curtailing employment. Both male and female workers were covered but only those enterprises engaged in interstate commerce were affected (to gain Supreme Court approval based on the interstate commerce clause). As a result, less than half of the private sector was covered initially. Congress has amended the act numerous times since 1938 to increase the minimum wage and extend coverage. Because Congress sets only the nominal value of the minimum wage, its real value falls during periods of inflation. As of September 1997, the minimum wage of $5.15 an hour again represented approximately 42 percent of the average manufacturing wage. Today, about 88 percent of workers are covered by the minimum wage requirement. Women make up 59 percent of all minimum wage workers and approximately 63 percent of minimum wage workers work part-time. **See also** Minimum Wage/Maximum Hours Laws. (AMD)

BIBLIOGRAPHY

Grossman, Jonathan. "Fair Labor Standards Act of 1938: Maximum Struggle for a Minimum Wage." *Monthly Labor Review* 101, no. 6 (June 1978).

Susan Faludi (1959–)

Susan Faludi is a journalist who emerged on the national **women's movement** scene in 1991 with the publication of her book, *Backlash: The Undeclared War Against American Women.* The book was received by leading women's advocates, like **Eleanor Smeal,** as a new feminist manifesto. However, critics of the book argued that Faludi wrote of a vast conspiracy that simply did not exist. The book itself sought to debunk three views of **feminism** that Faludi said existed in the mainstream. The first was that feminism was no longer needed because women had achieved their goal of equality. Second, Faludi argued that expanded roles of woman did not lead to increased unhappiness. Third, she argued that feminism had not caused the current predicament of woman as they struggled to balance career, family, and other commitments.

BIBLIOGRAPHY

"Susan Faludi." *People* 36 (November 11, 1991): 138.
"Susan Faludi." *Working Woman* (April 1992): 64.

Family and Medical Leave Act (FMLA) (1991)

On February 5, 1993, after just two weeks in office, President Bill Clinton signed into law the Family and Medical Leave Act (FMLA). The FMLA (PL 103-3) is a labor regulation that requires businesses with 50 or more employees within 75 miles of a work site to provide unpaid family or medical leave for full-time and some part-time employees. About 50 percent of the U.S. workforce, including government employees at all levels, are entitled to take up to 12 weeks of leave to care for a newborn baby, a newly adopted or foster child, a seriously ill child, a spouse or parent, or for their own serious health condition.

The law is gender neutral, applying to both women and men, because the women's groups and members of the **Congressional Caucus for Women's Issues** who first drafted it feared that a maternity-only benefit would be more likely to backfire, preventing women from being hired or promoted. The benefits were extended to males in an effort to garner wider support for the legislation. Key supporter of the bill, House Representative **Pat Schroeder** (D-CO) commented that she "liked the legislation because it challenged the commitment of conservative family proponents head on while not doing harm to women's rights."

In April 1996, a commission established by the FMLA reported to Congress that the law was accomplishing its goal of helping families balance the competing demands of employment and family responsibilities at minimal cost to employers.

The U.S. Chamber of Commerce and other employer groups opposed the new mandated benefit for fear that it would lead to a requirement that employers provide workers and their families with health insurance coverage. Some corporations spoke for the FMLA, arguing that it built employee loyalty and saved turnover expenses. The Women's Legal Defense

Fund and other women's groups, labor unions, senior citizen groups, and the U.S. Catholic Conference urged passage. The alliance between pro-life and pro-choice forces facilitated passage.

Regulations developed by the Labor Department state that employers are responsible for informing eligible workers about the FMLA. Leave is not generally available for minor illness that incapacitates the worker or a family member for more than three days and requires medical treatment or supervision or qualifies as a serious health condition. Workers can substitute accrued paid leave and take leave intermittently, when medically appropriate.

Several bills extending the FMLA have been introduced in Congress. The new proposals would cover employers with 25 or more workers, provide 24 hours of leave per year for school activities or routine medical appointments of family members, and assure that sick leave can be used to care for children. (JHT)

BIBLIOGRAPHY

Elving, Ronald D. *Conflict and Compromise: How Congress Makes the Law.* New York: Simon & Schuster, 1995.

Marcus, Richard L. *Family and Medical Leave Policies and Procedures.* New York: John Wiley & Sons, 1994.

Thompson, Joan Hulse. "The Family and Medical Leave Act: A Policy for Families." *Women in Politics: Outsiders or Insiders?* 2nd ed. Upper Saddle River, NJ: Prentice Hall, 1996.

Family Law

Family law is a broad term that encompasses a wide variety of subjects, including divorce (especially its impact on women and children), **domestic violence**, and the emerging issue of same-sex marriage (of particular relevance for lesbians). Family law, more so than any other branch of the law, involves deeply personal issues that can have a profound effect on the day-to-day lives of average citizens. It involves a range of external actors, be they judges, lawyers, social workers, police, or prosecutors, in the private lives of individuals. The conflicts are often extremely passionate, and the stakes are usually high. Divorce law goes back a long way in recorded human history, while the legal treatment of both domestic violence and same-sex marriage are fairly recent.

Divorce law in America was dominated from the start by *Blackstone's Commentaries on the Laws of England*, published in the late eighteenth century, which spelled out the conditions for male domination of women in marriage whereby a married woman became the property of her husband. Over time this patriarchal system was modified at both the federal and state levels, including by the **Married Women's Property Acts,** which were enacted at the state level between 1840 and 1900. These incremental reforms gave women more ability to escape from undesirable or intolerable marriages. Beginning in 1969, however, what many commentators have referred to as the "divorce revolution" occurred during which neither partner had to give cause or assign blame or, in some cases, get the other's assent to get a divorce. California passed the nation's first so-called no-fault reforms, and by 1986 every state had some form of such legislation. This "revolution" in divorce law has become the focus of academic scholarship.

Lenore Weitzman's landmark study of *The Divorce Revolution,* which came out in 1985, studied California's experience with **no-fault divorce** legislation. Weitzman examined approximately 2,500 cases decided between 1968 and 1977 to uncover the consequences of liberalizing access to divorce. Her primary finding was that the so-called "divorce revolution" did not improve the socioeconomic position of post-divorce women and children, and may have made it worse. She found that, on average, the living standard of women and children went down by about 73 percent in the wake of a divorce, while similarly situated men experienced a 43 percent increase. Weitzman argues that courts tend to award too little in child support payments, with lax enforcement of these awards. Women, it should be noted, get physical custody of the children about 90 percent of the time. Weitzman laments the fact that with no-fault reform came the assumption that women, upon divorce, could make their way in the world without assistance. This development, Weitzman argues, has systematically undercut the economic well-being of women and children.

One remedy to the vulnerable position of post-divorce women and children is to include workplace careers and educational degrees in the definition of property when it comes time to divide marital assets equally. This expanded conception of property would result in the honoring of women's traditional role as the subsidizer of men's careers and education. Benefits of no-fault divorce—such as the less accusatory and acrimonious divorce process—exist, but decry marriage as a purely contractual arrangement between competitive individuals that leaves the weaker party at a disadvantage when that contract is terminated.

Martha Fineman, in *The Illusion of Equality*, argues that contemporary divorce reform has been built upon the goal of the equal treatment of men and women. This devotion to abstract equality, she opines, has come at the expense of equity. Fineman advocates using the standard of fairness rather than formal equality to shape divorce law. She asserts that the goal of fairness is especially critical given the structural inequality of women in our society. Fineman emphasizes that the equal treatment of unequal individuals will exacerbate the impoverishment of women and children who experience divorce.

Fineman recommends greater support for divorced women, especially those with children, who have sacrified workplace careers to take primary care of the household and facilitate the male's career development. This could be in the form of larger alimony awards (which have declined since the no-fault revolution), child support payments, and governmental payments to post-divorce women and children who are economically vulnerable. Either way, Fineman believes, we must abandon the (admittedly attractive) allure of abstract equality and implement policies that will respond to the real needs of real people.

Herbert Jacob argues in *Silent Revolution* that the no-fault divorce reform movement was composed mostly of legal practitioners and accomplished its legislative goals largely below the political radar screen. Their goals were relatively narrow and technical, a fact often misunderstood by those who have criticized no-fault divorce law for not ameliorating the **poverty** of women and children who have been victimized by the breakup of families. No-fault divorce reform has, nevertheless, had a great impact on society at large, although it has also reflected deeper social changes that were taking place regardless of divorce law.

Jacob points out that the most important consequences of the divorce revolution were the dramatic rise in joint custody of children (previously a rare occurrence), a much greater role for the government in post-divorce families (an unintended consequence), and the toning down of bitter struggles during the divorce process. He also argues that no-fault laws have resulted in a more equitable distribution of property. On the basis of these criteria, the divorce revolution has been a success, although Jacob makes it clear that contemporary divorce law does not adequately address the real needs of women and children who are left impoverished by divorce.

Jacob believes that the next wave of divorce reform will be characterized by much more political conflict, media coverage, and public involvement and, instead of dealing primarily with relatively narrow and technical issues, will be set in the context of remedying socioeconomic inequalities.

The 1992 Family Violence Prevention Fund study showed that 13 percent of women involved in an intimate relationship with a man had been physically assaulted by that partner. The tragedy of such violence was not recognized by society until the 1960s, when the women's movement began to increase public awareness of this phenomenon. The battering of women by their male partners cuts across lines of race and class. In the last 25 years, a network of battered women's shelters has appeared in towns and cities across the United States, although many areas, especially rural, are underserved by these institutions. There has also been an explosion of local, state, and federal laws dealing with domestic violence; and judges, prosecutors, and the police have become more educated about this pressing issue.

Emerson and Russel Dobash provide in *Women, Violence & Social Change* a comparative study between Great Britain and the United States. They examine how the battered women's movement in each country produced social change over time. They look especially at such accomplishments as legislation, the creation of shelters, and broad changes in society at large. They argue that the criminal justice approach to domestic violence, which has been emphasized more in the United States than Great Britain, has been of some value in the struggle for social change. Such developments as mandatory arrest laws (whereby the police, upon being called to a scene of domestic violence, must arrest the aggressor, and the state must then prosecute the crime), the education of judges and prosecutors, and the federal **Violence Against Women Act** of 1994 are valuable weapons in the fight against domestic violence but must not be seen as the only possible response.

They Dobashs believe that shelters for victimized women are an absolutely crucial, and perhaps the most essential, part of the struggle for a safer future. In the United States, these shelters have tended to focus on changing individual women, whereas in Great Britain the shelters are much more focused on challenging the material and social circumstances that breed domestic violence. Great Britain has also been more progressive than the United States in establishing permanent housing for abused women to facilitate their escape from violence. The Dobashs are critical of the therapeutic approach to domestic violence, whether within or without shelters, since the focus of such efforts are on the individual, most often the victim, rather than the broad array of political, economic, and social forces that facilitate such behavior. They concede, however, that therapy can be a useful tool in some cases, especially if it focuses more on perpetrators and how they can participate in their own transformation.

In *Domestic Violence: The Changing Criminal Justice Response,* Buzawa and Buzawa focus on domestic violence. This edited volume critically analyzes how the criminal justice system, specifically judges, prosecutors, and the police, have dealt with domestic violence since the mid-1970s. The editors caution that each locality has developed its own, semi-autonomous legal response to domestic violence, and thus the issue cannot be too broadly generalized in discussions. Buzawa and Buzawa do point out that, in general, the criminal law has developed a much more effective response to domestic violence, although much remains to be done to effectively combat this phenomenon. They express concern that society has placed too much emphasis on a punitive, law-and-order approach to domestic violence rather than dealing with the underlying conditions that produce this crime.

The articles collected in Buzawa and Buzawa's book examine the criminal justice system's role in combating domestic violence from a range of angles: some empirical, others more theoretical. Authors provide analyses of this topic that cover, among other things, a feminist interpretation of how the police deal with 911 calls, the role public disapproval can play in minimizing this behavior, and the role that victims should play in the arrest and prosecution of perpetrators. We also find in this volume a trenchant critique of the battered woman syndrome.

Same-sex marriage has become an issue of great public moment since 1993, when the Hawaii Supreme Court ruled in *Baehr v. Lewin* that the denial of marriage licenses to gay and lesbian couples was in violation of that state's constitution. This case is currently on appeal to the United States Supreme Court. In the meantime, a movement has emerged to combat such a development. President Bill Clinton signed into law in 1996 the Defense of Marriage Act, and in many states legislation has been passed, or is pending, to forbid same-sex marriages and refuse recognition of any such marriages legalized elsewhere. Hawaii itself has recently proposed, as have various local governments and many private companies, something called domestic partnerships, which grant same-sex couples many of the same tangible benefits as married heterosexual couples.

William Eskridge was the first author to compile a book-length study of same-sex marriage. *The Case for Same-Sex Marriage*, published in 1996, argues that admitting gays and lesbians into the institution of marriage will prove a civilizing force for that community. Eskridge admits that domestic partnerships do provide many of the economic benefits of marriage, but sees in the latter the fostering of stable and long-lasting commitment, which he sees as the most valuable aspect of marriage. This institution, at its best, also promotes caring relationships and strong families. He believes that the Constitution's Fourteenth Amendment, with its equal protection and due process clauses, provides the legal basis for making marriage accessible to both gay and straight citizens.

Robert Baird and Stuart Rosenbaum collected in *Same-Sex Marriage: The Moral and Legal Debate* a series of essays that explore such topics as the Defense of Marriage Act, the emotional and philsophical dimensions of same-sex marriage, and the Hawaii Supreme Court case. Some of the entries are government documents—the full text of the Defense of Marriage Act and *Baehr v. Lewin*, for example—while others are drawn from newspapers, books, magazines, and scholarly journals. Baird and Rosenbaum take great care to provide the reader with a wide range of perspectives on this most controversial of issues from the libertarian federal appeals court judge Richard Posner, to conservatives like criminologist James Q. Wilson and commentator Cal Thomas, to liberals like the academic Richard Mohr and lesbian activist Paula Ettelbrick. The editors of this volume stress the heavily normative aspects of this issue and make it clear that understanding the many dimensions of same-sex marriage requires consideration of a diverse array of views.

Andrew Sullivan, a prominent gay conservative who was once editor of the magazine *The New Republic*, provides in *Same-Sex Marriage: Pro and Con* an eclectic and wide-ranging examination that draws from such sources as Plato, Michel de Montaigne, the Bible, Ann Landers, legislative debates, and court cases. Sullivan also includes in this book many of the same authors represented in Baird and Rosenbaum's volume. Sullivan is a conservative proponent of gay and lesbian marriage, and he makes this clear in his own selections. Sullivan argues that if gays are admitted to the heretofore heterosexual, mainstream institution of marriage, this will both symbolize and advance society's affirmation of gay and lesbian citizens.

Family law is an ever-changing field because it reflects societal changes. As divorce reform, spousal abuse awareness, and same-sex marriage continue to be political issues, the laws that govern them will continue to evolve to accommodate change. (FC)

Bibliography

Baird, Robert M. and Stuart E. Rosenbaum, eds. *Same-Sex Marriage: The Moral and Legal Debate*. Amherst, NY: Prometheus Books, 1997.

Buzawa, Eve S. and Carl G. Buzawa, eds. *Domestic Violence: The Changing Criminal Justice Response.* Westport, CT: Auburn House, 1992.

Dobash, R. Emerson and Russel P. Dobash. *Women, Violence & Social Change*. New York: Routledge, 1992.

Eskridge, William N., Jr. *The Case for Same-Sex Marriage: From Sexual Liberty to Civilized Commitment*. New York: The Free Press, 1996.

Fineman, Martha A. *The Illusion of Equality: The Rhetoric and Reality of Divorce Reform*. Chicago: University of Chicago Press, 1991.

Jacob, Herbert. *Silent Revolution: The Transformation of Divorce Law in the United States*. Chicago: University of Chicago Press, 1988.

Sugarman, Stephen D. and Herma Hill Kay, eds. *Divorce Reform at the Crossroads*. New Haven, CT: Yale University Press, 1990.

Sullivan, Andrew, ed. *Same-Sex Marriage: Pro and Con*. New York: Vintage Books, 1997.

Walker, Lenore E. *The Battered Woman Syndrome*. New York: Springer Publishing Company, 1984.

Weitzman, Lenore J. *The Divorce Revolution: The Unexpected Social and Economic Consequences for Women and Children in America*. New York: The Free Press, 1985.

Family Leave/Mommy Track

Family leave and "mommy track" policies are designed to deal with women who are trying to balance their careers with family obligations. The stated goal of family leave is "to promote the development of the family unit and to enhance worker productivity." The purpose of the "mommy track" is to allow female employees to choose whether family or work is a priority. Before the Civil War, few women worked outside the home; but as men joined the army, women filled essential vacancies. Industrialization further plunged women into the job market in unprecedented numbers. As higher education became available to women, they became professional workers. It was generally assumed, however, that women's work was temporary because the ultimate goal of all women was to have children. The Supreme Court upheld a limit of 10-hour working days for women in ***Muller v. Oregon*** in 1908.

World War I saw large numbers of women enter the job market, and some refused to leave. States passed laws forbidding married women to work. With World War II, women flooded the job market, and employers were forced to develop new policies. These policies generally centered around protecting women by limiting the hours they could work. In 1919, Illinois passed the first Mother's Aid Law, designed to allow widows with small children to remain at home, and other states followed. Sheila Kamerman, Alfred Kahn, and Paul Kingston note that in 1942 a joint effort by the Women's and Children's Bureau established guidelines for pregnant women, which included six weeks of prenatal—and eight weeks of postnatal—unpaid leave. The women's movement of the 1960s created a new environment for women in the workplace. Protecting maternity leave was among the initial goals of the **National Organization for Women (NOW)**.

Between 1947 and 1985, the number of women in the labor force increased 178 percent. By 1990, 58 percent of women were in the work world. Predictions for 2000 indicate that 62.6 percent of women will work, with slightly more white and black women working than Hispanic women. Current reports demonstrate that divorced mothers are still more likely to work than other mothers. Black women are more likely to work full-time than white mothers. It is estimated that 80 percent of women workers are of child-bearing age. Many of these women already have children: 53 percent of mothers with children under six years work outside the home, and the number rises to 68 percent for mothers with children under 18 years. Sara Rix contends that most women will spend 17 years caring for children and 18 years caring for older family members. Studies indicate that the average woman will lose seven years from her life to have and care for children. Many women work because they provide sole or partial support for their families. Two-thirds of mothers who work are heads-of-household, and those who live in two-parent homes provide from one-third to one-half of total income.

Until 1978, women who became pregnant often lost their jobs. Without jobs, they lost income at a time when medical care was essential; and many employee group plans did not cover pregnancy and pregnancy-related conditions. After giving birth, women were forced to search for new, lower-paying jobs and begin a new trek toward seniority. In 1978, in response to pressure from women's groups, Congress passed the **Pregnancy Discrimination Act**. Based on **Title VII of the Civil Rights Act of 1964**, the Pregnancy Discrimination Act banned pregnancy discrimination in hiring, firing, and seniority. The act forced employers to protect job security and to provide health coverage for pregnancy and pregnancy-related conditions.

Given the large numbers of women in the workforce who were dedicated mothers, companies began to attempt more flexible ways of designing positions. The most common method of flexible work is part-time, and two-thirds of part-time workers are women. This situation is ideal for mothers who want to work without committing to full-time schedules and who have husbands or partners who bring in sufficient income and provide medical care. Other mothers are not so fortunate; they have insufficient incomes and little or no insurance coverage. Flextime has also become common. This practice, arranged to fit employees' schedules, may involve full-time or part-time work and may or may not include benefits. Compressed work allows workers to work longer hours in a shorter workweek and is usually full-time with benefits. Compensatory time is based on overtime hours that hourly employees work, allowing them to take time off rather than receive overtime pay. A less formal method of compensatory time occurs with salaried employees who are free to leave work when necessary and who then work additional hours or take work home. Job sharing is a less common method of flexible work and usually involves two people with coordinated schedules sharing the same job.

The United States has traditionally lagged behind other countries in providing support for mothers who work and for those who choose to stay home with small children. All industrialized nations offer some sort of family leave, and many offer children's allowances, cash benefits at time of childbirth, and six months of income subsidies for new mothers. A French program, for example, allows mothers to remain at home until their youngest child is three years old with a subsidy equal to minimum wage. Contrarily, in the United States, a common practice has been to encourage women to retire from the job market without income or benefits. In the late 1980s, it was announced that women were doing just that when, in fact, both males and females were out of the job market because of the recession. A 1989 article in *Time* suggested that some women were choosing to stay home in response to the movie *The Hand That Rocks the Cradle*. Amid the emerging family values debate, the movie's psychotic nanny pierced the hearts of mothers who felt guilty for leaving their children to work. It was this environment that produced the "mommy track" debate.

In 1989, Felice Schwartz, feminist president and founder of Catalyst, a company that helped businesses prepare women for leadership, suggested in a January-February issue of the *Harvard Business Review* that companies should develop two tracks for women employees: career primary for those who elected commitment to work over family, and career-family for those who worked only because they needed to and who required flexible work schedules and less pressure to commit to jobs. Schwartz recommended that companies identify career-primary workers early, give them opportunities to grow, consider them valued members of the organization, and deal with on-the-job stresses such as sexist language and sexual harassment. Scwartz believed, however, that most women fell into the second category of career-family. She suggested that these women should be expected to work in mid-level positions and that companies should provide maternity leave and **child care**. Schwartz outraged feminists when she declared that hiring women was more costly than hiring men and asserted that the notion of a **glass ceiling** that prevented women from advancing in the corporate world was only a myth. Schwartz never used the phrase "mommy track," but the press immediately identified her proposal as such. A 1989 study revealed that 38 percent of working mothers would consider giving up work if money were no problem. A year later, the number of would-be stay-at-home moms rose to 56 percent.

The official feminist response to the Schwartz article appeared in the July-August 1989 issue of *Ms.* Barbara Ehrenreich and Deirdre English criticized Schwartz for attacking women who had been doing their best to make progress in the business world while being relegated to the bottom rungs. They contradicted Schwartz's claim that it was more costly to hire women and contended that no published data existed to support her arguments. They noted that on the average, women only used 5.1 sick days per year, favorably comparing to the 4.9 sick days per year for men. Ehrenreich and English attacked Schwartz's claim that working was optional for women and that it ignored single mothers and spouses of low-income males. A major part of the backlash against Schwartz dealt with her placing the burden for child rearing solidly on the backs of mothers—contrary to the feminist argument that it should be a responsibility shared with fathers.

The notion of a "daddy track" was bound to follow the backlash from the "mommy track." One of the effects of the women's movement was that fathers became more involved in child rearing. Patricia Aburdene and John Naisbitt cite a 1989 study in which 74 percent of the fathers surveyed maintained that they would prefer a "daddy track" to the current fast track demanded of most fathers. Forty-five percent of the men surveyed announced that they would prefer more family time to job advancement. **Patricia Schroeder**, a former Democratic congresswoman from Colorado and staunch supporter of women's rights, wrote in *Champion of the Great American Family* that a maternity leave bill would be a mistake because it would keep the responsibility for parenting with the mother. In early 1984, Georgetown law professors Wendy Williams and Sue Ross, along with attorney Donna Lenhoff, met with Schroeder's staff to develop the first family leave bill, called the Parental and Disability Leave Act of 1985. It included companies with at least 15 workers, and provided up to 18 weeks of leave to care for newborn, adopted, or seriously ill children and up to 26 weeks for disability leave. The proposed leave was unpaid but protected workers' jobs and health coverage.

In 1985, Schroeder held oversight hearings on parental leave and disability. Witnesses ranged from labor union president John Sweeney, who supported the bill, to antifeminist **Phyllis Schlafly**, who called the bill prejudicial to the majority of workers. In 1986, Schroeder introduced the Parental and Medical Leave Act, renamed the **Family and Medical Leave Act** in 1987. It soon became evident that attempting to cover companies with at least 15 workers was impossible. Opponents argued that small businesses could not afford to implement the policy. Even though some supporters believed that leave should be paid, it would have been impossible to win approval from conservative members of Congress, the president, and the powerful business lobby. Even with unpaid leave, opponents complained that the bill paved the way for future demands for paid leave.

The cost of family leave was a major issue in the debate over family leave. Joan Hulse Thompson reports that the Chamber of Commerce originally estimated the cost of implementing the bill at $16 billion, based on the assumption that all workers on leave would be replaced. Under pressure, the estimate was revised to $2.6 billion and subsequently dropped to $189 million after provisions of the bill were changed. According to Thompson, supporters believed that the final cost would be approximately $6.50 per year for each eligible worker. The **Congressional Caucus for Women's Issues** documented a cost of $607 million per year to families who lost their jobs without family leave and identified a cost of $108 million to taxpayers who were forced to provide assistance to the unemployed.

By 1990, the House of Representatives and the Senate agreed on provisions of the bill. Since a major controversy had erupted over whether to include small businesses in the mandate, it was determined that only those companies with 50 or more employees would be covered. Despite bipartisan support for the bill, George Bush vetoed it.

In 1993, President Bill Clinton signed the Family and Medical Leave Act into law, providing for up to 12 weeks of leave to care for a newborn, adopted, or foster child or for a seriously ill spouse, child, or parent or for personal illness. Under the new law, job security is assured and health benefits continue. Companies with 50 or more employees are covered, but employers may exempt the highest paid 10 percent of workers.

Response to family leave has been mixed. Supporters believe that it has provided job security for those who are most vulnerable. The inclusion of fathers is considered a major victory. A number of businesses are also lauding the success of the law, asserting that productivity is higher among employees who are free to deal with personal life changes and crises without loss of job security. Critics claim that the law caters to privileged workers who can afford to accept unpaid leave and that the law is exclusive. For example, lesbians cannot take leave to care for partners who are not considered "spouses." Another exclusion is women who live in extended or nontraditional families who cannot take leave to care for family members not identified in the law. Even though women are primary caretakers for elderly family members, a wife could not take leave to care for her husband's parent.

Deborah Rhode notes that current studies reveal significant noncompliance with family leave law. She cites one study in which two-thirds of workers reported that they had difficulty obtaining full leave and retaining benefits. A number of employees claimed that if they asked for leave, they were viewed as having an attitude problem or not being committed to their jobs. Those who were granted leave frequently said they were passed over for raises and promotions. The cost of government oversight is prohibitive, and employees are finding that they have little recourse.

In 1997, the Department of Labor determined that 58 percent of those who took leave were women between the ages of 35 and 49. The two most common reasons for taking leave were personal health and caring for ill family members. Half of those who took leave were away from their jobs no more than 10 days. Even though companies are required to post provisions of the law, many workers remain unaware of the availability of family leave. As more workers become aware of their rights, public awareness may help to improve enforcement. Some have suggested that fines would make compliance less expensive than noncompliance. (EP) **See also** Antifeminism; Feminism.

BIBLIOGRAPHY

Aberdene, Patricia and John Naisbitt. *Megatrends for Women.* New York: Villard Books, 1992.

Ehrenreich, Barbara and Deirdre English. "Blowing the Whistle on the 'Mommy Track.'" In Kurt Finsterbusch and George McKenna, eds. *Taking Sides: Clashing Views on Controversial Social Issues.* Guilford, CT: Duskin Publishing, 1991, 85-88.

Kamerman, Cheila B., Alfred J. Kahn, and Paul Kingston. *Politics and Working Women.* New York: Columbia University Press, 1983.

Littleton, Christine. "Does It Still Make Sense to Talk About 'Women'?" In Ralph Lindgren and Nadine Taub, eds. *The Law of Sex Discrimination, Second Edition.* Minneapolis/St. Paul: West, 1993.

Rhode, Deborah L. *Speaking of Sex: The Denial of Gender Inequality.* Cambridge, MA: Harvard University Press, 1997.

Rix, Sara E., ed. *The American Woman 1990-91: A Status Report.* New York: W.W. Norton, 1992.

Schroeder, Patricia, et al. "The Family and Medical Leave Act of 1987: Pros and Cons." In Kenneth Winston and Mary Jo Bane, eds. *Gender and Public Policy: Cases and Commentaries.* Boulder, CO: Westview Press, 1993.

Schroeder, Patricia, Andea Camp, and Robyn Lipner. *Champion of the Great American Family.* Thorndike, ME: Thorndike Press, 1989.

Schwartz, Felice. "Management Women and the New Facts of Life." In Kurt Finsterbusch and George McKenna, eds. *Taking Sides: Clashing Views on Controversial Social Issues.* Guilford, CT, 1991.

Thompson, Joan Hulse. "The Family and Medical Leave Act: A Policy for Families." In Lois Lovelace Duke, ed. *Women and Politics: Outsiders or Insiders?* Englewood Cliffs, NJ: Prentice Hall, 1992.

Family Protection Act (1979)

The failed Family Protection Act of 1979 sought to amend Title IV of the Social Security Act to offer fiscal relief to states and localities and improve the **Aid to Families with Dependent Children (AFDC)** program. In addition to the many technical amendments affecting AFDC benefit amounts and matching federal funds, the bill included several new sections. Among these was a section calling for additional federal funding for the development of statewide mechanized claims processing and information retrieval systems, as well as a section on the rights and responsibilities of AFDC applicants and recipients.

The most well-known and controversial parts of the bill had little to do with the **welfare** system, however. With the endorsement of **Phyllis Schlafly** and **Concerned Women for America,** the bill sought to deny federal funding to schools in states that prohibit voluntary prayer in public buildings. In addition, it sought the denial of federal funding for the purchase of textbooks that disparage the traditional role of women in society. While the bill as a whole was unsuccessful, California and Texas did subsequently adopt proposals aiming to extol classical female roles. (AMR) **See also** Social Security.

BIBLIOGRAPHY

Felsenthal, Carol. *Phyllis Schlafly: The Sweetheart of the Silent Majority.* Garden City, NY: Doubleday & Co., Inc., 1981.

McGlen, Nancy and Karen O'Connor. *Women, Politics, and American Society.* Englewood Cliffs, NJ: Prentice Hall, 1995.

Family Support Act of 1988

The Family Support Act of 1988 represents the culmination of a two-year bipartisan effort to overhaul the **welfare** system. Through revisions in the **Aid to Families with Dependent Children (AFDC)** program, amendments to Title IV of the Social Security Act, and other miscellaneous provisions, it attempts to prevent long-term welfare dependence.

Main features of the act include the creation of the Job Opportunities and Basic Skills (JOBS) Training Programs, which aim to provide training, education, and employment to welfare recipients. While the act makes participation in JOBS by able-bodied parents of children over three years mandatory, it requires states to provide participants with **child care** assistance. This assistance, as well as Medicaid benefits, are to be extended to families for up to 12 months after they cease to qualify for AFDC due to increased earnings.

Furthermore, the act calls for stricter child support enforcement, requiring states to implement immediate wage withholding for child support orders. It also creates performance standards in the determination of paternity for children of unwed mothers and limits the option of unwed minors to establish AFDC units separate from their parents.

Although the act met with wide popularity, passing through Congress easily, many liberals felt it discriminated against welfare recipients, and many conservatives felt it was insufficient to reduce their number. (AMR) **See also** Social Security; Child Custody and Support; Child Support Enforcement Amendment of 1984.

BIBLIOGRAPHY

"Welfare Reforms Advance: House Passes Bill, Sends it to Reagan." *The Sacramento Bee* (October 1, 1988): AA5.

Frances Tarlton (Cissy) Farenthold (1926–)

Frances Tarlton Farenthold, a Democrat, was the only woman to serve in the Texas House of Representatives from 1968 to 1972. In 1972, she became the first serious woman contender for the nomination of a major party for vice president on George McGovern's ticket. In 1974, Farenthold made an unsuccessful run for governor of Texas, losing in the primary.

BIBLIOGRAPHY

Farenthold, Frances T. "Are You Brave Enough to Be in Politics?" *Redbook* 147 (May 1976): 190.

———. "Women in Politics." *Saturday Evening Post* 246 (March 1974): 14–15.

Frappallo, Elizabeth. "The Ticket that Might Have Been." *Ms.* 1, no. 7 (January 1973): 74–76.

Harriet Farley (1813–1907)

Harriet Farley was the editor of the ***Lowell Offering*** from 1842 until 1845. As editor, she sought to remove the social stigma attached to women who worked in factories. Her paper worked to increase and showcase the intellectual and artistic sides of the workers. The *Offering* was criticized by some who thought that—as the most influential publication among woman workers—it should have taken stronger stands on issues like working conditions and wages. **See also** Lowell Mill Girls; *Voice of Industry.*

Bibliography

Robinson, Harriet Hanson. *Loom and Spindle*. Kailua, HI: Press Pacifica, 1976.

Mary Pruett Farrington (1898–1984)

A leading advocate of Hawaii statehood, Mary Farrington began her political career as the president of the National Federation of Women's Republican Clubs, serving from 1949 until 1953. Farrington served as the delegate to the U.S. Congress from the territory of Hawaii from 1955 to 1956, succeeding her husband Joseph R. Farrington.

Bibliography

"Obituary." *New York Times* (July 23, 1984): 16.

Women in Congress. Washington, DC: U.S. Government Printing Office, 1991.

Dianne Feinstein (1933–)

Dianne Feinstein, a Democrat, is a native of San Francisco, California, and the senior senator from that state since 1993. In her first four years in the Senate, she championed several pieces of legislation that had dim prospects of becoming law, including the ban on semi-automatic weapons, the California Desert Protection Act, and the Methamphetamine Control Act. She was the Democratic nominee and candidate for governor of California in 1990, losing to Pete Wilson whose unexpired term in the U.S. Senate she won in 1992 and still holds. She had serious difficulties in the 1994 election for the full Senate term, when Michael Huffington spent nearly $30 million on his campaign to unseat her.

Feinstein gained the stature to contest a statewide office and built a national reputation from her position as mayor of San Francisco, which she held from 1978 to 1988. During that time, Feinstein's administration focused attention on the city's neighborhoods and created the nation's first City Conservation Corps. The city was in the national spotlight when it hosted the 1984 Democratic National Convention, and Feinstein was considered as a potential vice presidential running mate for Walter Mondale. Feinstein came to the mayor's office in November, 1978, following the assassinations of Mayor George Moscone and board member Harvey Milk. Her first elected position was on the San Francisco Board of Supervisors, the city's legislative body on which she served from 1970 to 1978 (she served five of those years as board president).

Feinstein's political career began with service on the women's parole board from 1960 to 1966. Feinstein's career has been a series of firsts: first female president of the board of supervisors and mayor of San Francisco, first woman nominated by a major party in California as candidate for governor, and the first woman to represent California in the U.S. Senate. (KM) **See also** Barbara Boxer.

Bibliography

Elving, Ronald D., Ines Pinto Alicea, and Jeffrey L. Katz. "Boxer and Feinstein Victorious in 'Year of the Woman.'" *Congressional Quarterly Report* 50 (June 6, 1992): 1621–31.

Love, Keith. "Will Dianne Feinstein Play in Pacoima?" *Los Angeles Times Magazine* (February 25, 1990): 11–16, 18, 34–35.

Roberts, Jerry. *Dianne Feinstein: Never Let Them See You Cry.* San Francisco: Harper Collins, 1994.

Rebecca Latimer Felton (1835–1930)

Rebecca Felton supported women's **suffrage** and was active in Georgia politics. When a Georgia senator died in office in 1922, Felton was appointed by the governor to fill the seat. She traveled to Washington, and was sworn in as the first woman senator on November 21, 1922. Felton served for one day.

Bibliography

Tallmadge, John E. *Rebecca Latimer Felton: Nine Stormy Decades.* Athens: University of Georgia Press, 1960.

———. *Women in Congress, 1917–1990.* Washington, DC: U.S. Government Printing Office, 1991.

Feminine Mystique

The era of the feminine mystique usually refers to the two decades after World War II, when American women were restricted by a set of ideas that defined female happiness as total involvement in the role of wife and mother, thus extolling a woman's traditional role. Advertisers were said to have manipulated women into finding happiness in the latest vacuum cleaner model. The era romanticized women as gaily content in the world of bedroom and kitchen. In reality, many women, especially the college educated, felt disillusionment in these traditional roles.

In 1963, **Betty Friedan** captured these sentiments in her book, *The Feminine Mystique*, which became an immediate best seller and sold more than a million copies. As defined by Friedan and American feminists, the term denotes a set of attitudes and values that defines a woman solely as a function of someone else (her husband and children) or something else (her homemaking activities). The work stimulated many women to question the status quo, which eventually led to the birth of the modern **women's movement.** (CGM) **See also** Feminism.

Bibliography

Chafe, William Henry. *The American Woman.* New York: Oxford University Press, 1972.

Millstein, Beth and Jeanne Bodin. *We the American Women.* Chicago: Science Research Associates, Inc., 1977.

Feminism

Feminism, as it is understood today, is an ideology, a critical viewpoint, and a political movement. As an ideology, feminism focuses on the devaluation of women and their roles in society. As a critical viewpoint, it attempts to understand social arrangements—such as marriage, work, family, and politics—by examining them through gender politics. Feminists have worked toward altering structural imbalances that place women at a disadvantage in relation to men, and have advocated on behalf of women. People have embraced a wide variety of approaches, theories, and prescriptions for change, all in the name of feminism.

In *The Grounding of Modern Feminism*, historian Nancy Cott writes that the term feminism came into widespread use in the United States in the 1910s, although *feminisme* had been in use in France since the late nineteenth century. As a label, feminism often evokes strong and mixed reactions. It is paradoxical that while many people agree with, and benefit from, societal advances made by feminists on behalf of women, the majority of women do not consider themselves feminists. The popular press frequently questions feminism's validity, as **Susan Faludi** has documented in her popular book *Backlash*. Thus feminism has been marginalized in American society even though the concepts that feminism encompasses—such as equal pay for equal work and equal opportunities in education—are widely accepted. Much of this ambivalence can be traced to a common misunderstanding about feminism: many people believe that to be a feminist means to accept a single set of doctrines, when in fact a variety of feminist standpoints have emerged. A comprehensive understanding of feminism takes many perspectives into consideration.

Liberal feminism is perhaps the most recognizable form of feminism in practice today. It has its roots in the principles of classic **liberalism**—individualism, independence, self-determination—and applies them to women, concluding that women as well as men hold certain inalienable rights. For example, Mary Wollstonecraft, an eighteenth-century advocate of women's rights, decried the denial of women's basic humanity and intelligence by Enlightenment society. She argued that the failure to educate women for anything but providing pleasure for men fostered women's frivolity and ignorance. Human fulfillment, liberal feminists came to argue, can only result when all people are granted the same opportunities. This type of feminism seeks to create a level playing field on which women and men can compete together. The struggle to attain equal educational and workplace opportunities, legal equality, and reproductive rights for women has become the expression of modern liberal feminism.

In contrast to liberal feminism, which downplays gender differences, radical feminism asserts that gender is the defining human condition from which all oppression originates. Oppression based on other social identities—most notably race and class—are considered to be factors that stem from and aggravate gender oppression. Because gender inequity is inherent in the political system and deeply imbedded in society, radical feminists argue that simply granting women equal status within that system will not change women's subordination to men. Thus, liberal reforms, such as the attainment of economic opportunities within the existing economic system, are insufficient measures to address pervasive inequality. For radical feminism, the only changes worth pursuing are those that fundamentally change the social and political structure and root out its institutions, such as the family and the church. Radical feminist theorists frequently focus on women's sexuality and reproduction, which they view as exploited by male-dominated institutions, and violence against women, which they view as the ultimate symbolic and real expression of men's dominance.

Another significant thread in the feminist tapestry has been spun by black feminist thinkers. In her book *Black Feminist Thought*, Patricia Hill Collins identifies three arenas of oppression addressed by African-American feminists: economy (pervasive **poverty** and lack of economic opportunity); polity (virtual political disenfranchisement); and ideology (degrading images and beliefs about black women). Black feminist activity in the United States, which can be traced at least as far back as the early nineteenth century, responds to these multiple sources of oppression through strategies of workplace resistance, traditional and nontraditional political organizing, and the replacement of negative stereotypes with positive images of strength and beauty.

Feminists of color have also issued challenges to feminist ideologies that fail to consider the experiences of women of color and poor women of all races when issuing theoretical positions and prescriptions for change. They resist isolating different sources of oppression from one another, rejecting the argument that gender is a more definitive source of oppression than race. They have noted, for example, that a feminist platform focusing on making careers more accessible to women ignores the historical reality of the labor participation of African-American women, thus challenging the idea that paid work is necessarily liberating for women. Similarly, procreative issues have had different meanings for various groups of women. While some feminists have struggled to secure women's access to birth control and **abortion**, feminists of color have pointed out that poor African-American, Native American, and Hispanic women have been subjected to social policies that have restricted their ability to bear children, including involuntary sterilization. Thus, a feminist agenda that claims to represent the interests of all women must take historical experiences into account and acknowledge the ways in which some feminists have excluded or ignored women of color.

Much as black feminist theorists have argued that gender and race oppression work together to oppress women of color, so have socialist feminists theorized that the class and gender systems are simultaneously responsible for women's oppression. Socialist feminism, rooted in the Marxist ideology of class struggle, is critical of both Marxist claims that a working class revolution is all that is necessary to liberate women and of radical feminist claims that all women's oppression stems from male dominance.

Feminist ideologies have had a significant impact in two main arenas: the academic world of writers and teachers and the political world of activists and policy makers. Perhaps the most notable effect of feminism on the academy is the rise of women's studies as an area of study. This field is considered by some to be the academic "arm" of the women's movement. It is comprised of scholars who bring a feminist viewpoint to the traditional disciplines, such as history, literature, sociology, political science, and anthropology, and scholars who attempt to transform the disciplines and the academy itself through feminist research and teaching. Women's studies scholars frequently attempt to dismantle the sharp distinctions between student and teacher, between researcher and subject, and often between the disciplines themselves, referring to their methods as interdisciplinary or multidisciplinary. Women's studies has been accused by some of being too far removed from the reality of most women's lives to have much of an impact outside the university. But its presence has had an impact on the academy as women's studies degree programs have grown in strength, numbers, and visibility in the past three decades.

The **women's movement** in the United States has provided the political context in which feminism has taken shape as a social movement. Nancy Cott points out that the growth of a women's movement in the United States and the emergence of feminism, while not coterminous, were intimately linked in the early twentieth century. Most scholars of social movements trace the women's movement to the **abolition** movement of the nineteenth century, in which women became involved in large numbers. Through abolition, groups of activist women were able to meet and discuss their own circumstances. After years of work on this cause, many women activists concluded their position was not unlike that of the slaves whose liberation they sought. In 1848, **Lucretia Mott** and **Elizabeth Cady Stanton** launched an historic meeting at Seneca Falls, New York, an event that is considered by many to mark the beginning of the first wave of the women's movement in the United States. Women at the **Seneca Falls Convention** drafted the **Declaration of Sentiments and Resolutions**, a liberal feminist document modeled after the Declaration of Independence, which asserted women's equality with men, decried women's lack of freedom in both the public and private spheres, and demanded the right to vote. Stanton and **Susan B. Anthony** became the most vocal advocates for the changes necessary to correct the wrongs cited in the Declaration. Unfortunately, these activists often argued for women's rights at the expense of blacks' rights and might be perceived as racist. Woman **suffrage**, one of the most important goals of the nineteenth-century movement, was not achieved until the **Nineteenth Amendment** was passed in 1920 after decades of agitation by activists such as Mott, Stanton, Anthony, **Lucy Stone**, **Ida B. Wells**, **Carrie Chapman Catt**, and **Alice Paul**; and by groups such as the **National American Woman Suffrage Association (NAWSA)**, the **National Woman's Party (NWP)**, and the Alpha Suffrage Club. The amendment extended the right to vote to all women, but black women were still effectively disenfranchised by Jim Crow laws that often blocked African Americans' access to the polls.

Following the adoption of the Nineteenth Amendment, feminist activity declined. But the 1960s saw a renewal of feminist energy and activism that came to be known as the second wave of feminism. In 1966, **Betty Friedan**, **Pauli Murray**, and other politically active women founded the **National Organization for Women (NOW)**, one of the most visible liberal feminist groups in existence. The National Organization for Women and other liberal feminist groups formed what was called the "women's rights" branch or "older" branch of second-wave feminism by scholars of the movement.

According to its statement of purpose, NOW was founded "to bring women into full participation in the mainstream of American society now . . . in truly equal partnership with men." The National Organization for Women's efforts have focused on the attainment of educational, legal, and economic equality between women and men, including the attainment of reproductive rights for women and the struggle (ultimately unsuccessful) to ratify the **Equal Rights Amendment (ERA)** passed by Congress in 1972. The National Organization for Women membership grew rapidly in its early years, and the group now claims more than 250,000 members. Other liberal feminist organizations that have worked on political and legal change include the **Women's Equity Action League (WEAL)**, founded in 1968; the **National Women's Political Caucus (NWPC)**, founded in 1971; and **EMILY's List**, a political action committee that raises funds to support pro-choice female political candidates.

Around the same time that NOW was formed, women involved in the male-dominated radical protest movements of the 1960s—such as the civil rights, anti-war, and student movements—began to realize that the radical equality espoused by movement members did not extend to the relationship between women and men, in which traditional gender roles went unquestioned. Women around the country broke away from the male-dominated movements and began to organize what they called the women's liberation movement and were soon joined by women previously unaffiliated with the radical movements. These groups came to be called the "radical" or "younger" branch of the women's movement by social movement scholars.

Radical activists coalesced in small groups to organize political strategy and to work toward personal transformation. They used the strategy of **consciousness raising** to help each other arrive at a new political understanding of their personal lives. The groups took names such as Redstockings, Cell 16, and the Women's International Terrorist Conspiracy from Hell (WITCH), and they frequently engaged in nontraditional political organizing to call attention to the feminist cause and attract more members. This branch of the women's movement is responsible for such political developments as the anti-rape and battered women's movements. Many radical women of the late 1960s went on to enter academics and participate in the growth of women's studies as an academic discipline, although academic feminists have identified with both the women's rights and the radical feminist branches. Social movement scholars agree that the sharp distinctions between the branches have largely disappeared.

Numerous challenges face contemporary advocates of feminism, and a series of questions—and their answers—will undoubtedly affect the shape of feminism in the future: To what extent will ideological differences among feminists determine or possibly forestall political action? How will feminists pursue equality in the face of claims (often feminist claims) of women's difference? How will women committed to feminism be able to synthesize different women's experiences into a coherent feminist plan of action, in spite of competing needs? These questions have had salience since the earliest days of feminist activity, when women's everyday experiences became the basis of the women's movement. The resolution of these and other questions, therefore, will continue to shape women's lives well into the next century. (MB) **See also** Bella Abzug; Antifeminism; Economic Equity Act; Educational Equity Act; Equal Educational Opportunities Act of 1972; *MS* Magazine; Phyllis Schlafly; Gloria Steinem; STOP ERA; WISH List

BIBLIOGRAPHY

Cott, Nancy. *The Grounding of Modern Feminism.* New Haven, CT: Yale University Press, 1987.

Collins, Patricia Hill. *Black Feminist Thought: Knowledge, Consciousness, and the Politics of Empowerment.* New York: Routledge, 1991.

Davis, Flora. *Moving the Mountain: The Women's Movement in America Since 1960.* New York: Simon and Schuster, 1991.

Echols, Alice. *Daring to Be Bad: Radical Feminism in American 1967–1975.* Minneapolis: University of Minnesota Press, 1989.

Faludi, Susan. *Backlash: The Undeclared War Against American Women.* New York: Crown, 1991.

Freeman, Jo. *The Politics of Women's Liberation.* New York: David McKay, 1975.

Giddings, Paula. *When and Where I Enter: The Impact of Black Women on Race and Sex in America.* New York: Bantam, 1984.

Guy-Sheftall, Beverly, ed. *Words of Fire: An Anthology of African-American Feminist Thought.* New York: The New Press, 1995.

McGlen, Nancy E. and Karen O'Connor. *Women, Politics, and American Society.* Englewood Cliffs, NJ: Prentice Hall, 1995.

Tong, Rosemarie. *Feminist Thought: A Comprehensive Introduction.* Boulder, CO: Westview, 1989.

Millicent Fenwick (1910–1992)

After experience in the New Jersey legislature, Republication Millicent Fenwick was elected to the U.S. House of Representatives in 1974. As an elegant advocate of social justice, she inspired the comic strip character Lacey Davenport in "Doonesbury." A pipe-smoking multimillionaire, Fenwick preached strict ethical standards. After her 1982 defeat for the New Jersey Republican Senate nomination, President Ronald Reagan appointed her to a United Nations post dealing with food and agriculture. (JHT)

BIBLIOGRAPHY

Ehrenhalt, Alan, ed. *Politics in America, 1982.* Washington, DC: Congressional Quarterly Inc., 1981.

Gertzog, Irvin N. *Congressional Women: Their Recruitment, Integration, and Behavior.* 2nd ed. Westport, CT: Praeger, 1995.

Miriam Ferguson (1875–1961)

A two-term governor of Texas, Miriam Wallace Ferguson was born in Bell County, Texas, in 1875. After attending Salado College and Baylor Female College, she married James Edward Ferguson, a lawyer and banker in 1899. Her husband was elected governor in 1914. However, in 1917, he was impeached, convicted, and removed from office in the midst of a financial scandal. Since the Texas constitution prohibited a person removed from being elected again, Miriam "Ma" Ferguson ran for governor in 1924, promising "two governors for the price of one." There was no doubt that she was a "stand-in" for her husband. She won the election and became the second woman in the United States to be elected governor. She lost re-election in 1926, stayed out of the race in 1928, lost again in 1930, and was finally re-elected in 1932. A moderately progressive governor, she was a strong supporter of President Franklin D. Roosevelt during the Great Depression. She was successful at legalizing gambling, passing congressional redistricting legislation, and increasing taxes to benefit schools. The Fergusons actively opposed the Ku Klux Klan and publicly supported Catholics and Jews. Both of her terms, however, were tainted with accusations of corruption regarding pardons and paroles. (GVS)

BIBLIOGRAPHY

Calbert, Jack Lynn. "James Edward and Miriam Amanda Ferguson: The 'Ma' and 'Pa' of Texas Politics." Ph.D. dissertation, Indiana University, 1968.

Geraldine A. Ferraro (1935–)

Former congresswoman and cohost of CNN's "Crossfire," Geraldine Ferraro made history as the first woman candidate to be part of a major party presidential ticket. Chosen as Democratic presidential candidate Walter Mondale's running mate in 1984, Ferraro was hampered by President Ronald Reagan's popularity, Mondale's call for increased taxes, and a financial scandal involving Ferraro and her husband John Zaccaro. The Mondale/Ferraro ticket won only 41 percent of the vote.

Ferraro first won election to the U.S. House of Representatives from Queens, New York, in 1978 as a tough criminal prosecutor. She was a leader in the **Congressional Caucus for Women's Issues**, an advocate of **abortion** rights, and the sponsor of an **Economic Equity Act** provision on pension rights enacted in 1984. As a protege of House Speaker Tip O'Neill, Ferraro became secretary of the Democratic Caucus and a member of the Democratic Steering and Policy Committee. In 1983, she joined the House Budget Committee.

In 1984, she was appointed chair of the Democratic Platform Committee, the first woman to hold the post. The media coverage of her position elevated her status within the party, and she was considered as a possible vice presidential running mate. Ferraro was nominated to balance the ticket; a midwestern Protestant man at the top with an Italian-American Catholic woman from the East. Tickets had been balanced by region, religion, and ethnicity for decades, but the emerging **gender gap** in the early 1980s resulted in the first ever gender balancing. In a year of prosperity and peace, Mondale needed a way to attract attention, so he responded positively to the women's groups, labor unions, and elected officials who were urging him to select Ferraro. However, Democrats mistakenly assumed that simply having a woman on the ticket would mobilize female voters; Ferraro was even discouraged from discussing women's issues during the campaign.

New York Congresswoman Geraldine Ferraro was the first woman to run on a major party presidential ticket when she was selected to be the vice presidential running mate of Democrat Walter F. Mondale in 1984.

The Mondale staff downplayed Ferraro's candidacy, reporting that polls indicated that she was hurting the ticket. Controversy arose when questions were raised about the Ferraro/Zaccaro tax returns, about Ferraro's financial disclosure statement, and about Zaccaro's contributions to his wife's first campaign for Congress. Ferraro performed effectively in a lengthy press conference in August, but the conflict diverted energy from the campaign.

In 1992, Ferraro and **Elizabeth Holtzman** both lost the New York Democratic primary for the Senate in a bitter, four-way race. In 1994, Ferraro was appointed ambassador to the United Nations Human Rights Commission. She also served as vice-chair of the U.S. delegation at the Fourth World Conference on Women in Beijing in 1995. In 1997, Ferraro was the liberal voice on CNN's "Crossfire" and was considering another political race. (JHT) **See also** Democratic Party; News Media.

Bibliography

Ferraro, Geraldine with Linda Bird Francke. *Ferraro: My Story.* New York: Bantam Books, 1985.

Foerstel, Karen and Herbert N. Foerstel. *Climbing the Hill: Gender Conflict in Congress.* Westport, CT: Praeger, 1996.

Le Veness, Frank P. and Jane P. Sweeney, eds. *Women Leaders in Contemporary U.S. Politics.* Boulder, CO: Lynne Rienner Publishers, 1987.

Bobbi Fiedler (1937–)

California Republican Bobbi Fiedler served in the House of Representatives from 1981 to 1986. Fiedler honed her political skills through opposition to a Los Angeles busing plan to desegregate the public schools. Fiedler told *The New York Times* that although she supported President Ronald Reagan's conservative budget, she broke with the **Republication Party** line in her support for freedom of choice and the **Equal Rights Amendment (ERA)**. (EP)

Bibliography

Tolchin, Martin and Francis X. Clines. "The Lessons of Capitol Hill Life Are Not Wasted on the Young." *New York Times* (June 14, 1981): IV 5.

Abigail Powers Fillmore (1798–1853)

Born in Saratoga, New York, in 1798, Abigail experienced tragedy and **poverty** at an early age. Abigail's father died shortly after her birth, leaving the family in financial straits. Her mother consequently moved the family out West, educating Abigail and her brother at home with books from her husband's library. At the age of 19, Abigail met Millard Fillmore, and they were married in 1826 once his law practice was established. Abigail continued to teach for two years following their marriage. She first arrived in Washington in 1849 when Millard Fillmore was elected vice president on the Whig ticket. Upon the death of Zachary Taylor 16 months later, Millard Fillmore assumed the presidency. As first lady, Abigail Fillmore preferred to read, listen to music, or have quiet intellectual conversations in the family quarters of the White House rather than fulfill the social role expected of her. Pleading ill health, she delegated many of her social obligations to her daughter Mary Abigail. However, Abigail took an avid interest in issues related to her husband's career and the two openly discussed political matters. Millard Fillmore once wrote that he "never took any important step without her advice and counsel." Abigail stood by her husband's side at his successor's inauguration in 1853, after which she caught pneumonia and died shortly thereafter. Her most notable contribution as first lady was the establishment of a White House library. (LvA) **See also** First Ladies.

Bibliography

Caroli, Betty Boyd. *First Ladies, Second Edition.* New York: Oxford University Press, 1993.

Gould, Lewis L., ed. *American First Ladies: Their Lives and Their Legacy.* New York: Garland Publishers, 1996.

Sherri Chesson Finkbine (1933–)

In 1962, Sherri Finkbine, a mother of four and host of a local edition of the popular children's television show *Romper Room*, discovered that she had taken **thalidomide** for nausea while pregnant with her fifth child. Her husband had brought it home from a European business trip. Finkbine's doctor confirmed that it was the same drug linked to severe birth defects. Arizona permitted therapeutic abortions at the time, but to receive one Finkbine had to testify before a hospital therapeutic committee that having a fifth child would lead her to a nervous breakdown or perhaps even suicide. Finkbine's **abortion** was approved; however, before the scheduled surgery, her situation was leaked to the press and the publicity caused the Arizona hospital to cancel her abortion. The Finkbines traveled to Sweden where Sherri Finkbine had an abortion. The Finkbine episode occasioned a huge public debate about the wisdom of American abortion laws and their disparate impact on people without money to travel abroad. (LW)

BIBLIOGRAPHY

Craig, Barbara Hinkson, and David M. O'Brien. *Abortion and American Politics*. Chatham, NJ: Chatham House, 1993.

Garrow, David J. *Liberty & Sexuality: The Right to Privacy and the Making of Roe v. Wade.* New York: MacMillan Publishing Co., 1994.

Luker, Kristin. *Abortion & The Politics of Motherhood.* Berkeley: University of California Press, 1984.

Joan Finney (1925–)

Joan Finney, a conservative Democrat from Kansas, became the first female governor of the state in 1990 after upsetting incumbent governor Mike Hayden. As governor, she took controversial stances including signing a law requiring an eight-hour waiting period and parental notification for **abortion**. She retired from her position after one four-year term. Finney was also the first female state treasurer in Kansas; she held the office from 1975 through 1991. In 1996, Finney entered the primary race for the Kansas Senate seat vacated by Republican presidential candidate Bob Dole. Finney lost the primary. (MEK)

BIBLIOGRAPHY

"Bill Limiting Access to Abortion Is Signed by Governor of Kansas." *New York Times* (April 24, 1992): A17.

Farney, Dennis. "Gov. Finney of Kansas, Thwarted by Legislators, Is in Danger of Becoming an Irrelevant Populist." *Wall Street Journal* (May 1, 1991): A16.

Finney, Joan. "State of Kansas—Office of the Governor." *American Muslim Journal* 3 (May 3, 1991): 2.

First Ladies

The role of the first lady has changed over time from primarily a ritual and ceremonial one to one in which she may discuss politics, state private policy preferences, publicly influence appointments and nominations, attend policy meetings, act as a surrogate president, campaign on her husband's behalf, and lobby and testify in Congress. This changing role reflects the evolving role of women in society, as well as the increasingly complex political environment in which the first lady is always in the limelight.

Most studies of the presidency ignore the important political role played by first ladies. From **Abigail Adams**'s strong stand on slavery to **Nancy Reagan**'s leverage on White House staff, their influence has historically been underestimated because most first ladies preferred to adopt traditional roles in public. Furthermore, most first ladies chose to support causes that were perceived to be "appropriate" for women and only

Four first ladies at the opening of the Nixon Library in California in 1990—(from left to right) Nancy Reagan, Barbara Bush, Pat Nixon, and Betty Ford. Smithsonian.

in recent years have **Betty Ford**, **Rosalynn Carter**, and **Hillary Clinton** publicly adopted more controversial positions—with mixed results.

While the specific role that a first lady plays depends largely on her individual interests and strengths, the office of the first lady has dramatically grown in importance over the years. **Mary Lincoln** was the first to campaign with her husband, **Edith Roosevelt** was the first to travel abroad in an official capacity, **Helen Taft** was the first to attend cabinet meetings, **Eleanor Roosevelt** was the first to hold an official governmental position, Nancy Reagan was the first to address the United Nations as first lady, and Hillary Clinton was the first to be involved in a lawsuit over the definition of her duties. Clinton was also responsible for moving the office of the first lady to the west wing of the White House, closer to the office of the president. Today, first ladies not only have their own permanent staff, but they also have access to valuable and classified White House information with which they can intelligently affect policy outcomes.

The incursion of the first lady into nontraditional political roles has been viewed with suspicion because first ladies are not elected officials nor do they require Senate confirmation. Some scholars have concluded that the position of the first lady has evolved as much as it can without change in societal expectations of women's roles in leadership positions. **See also** entries for individual first ladies. (GVS)

BIBLIOGRAPHY

Anthony, Carl S. "Skirting the Issue: First Ladies and African-Americans." *American Visions* 7 (October-November 1992): 28–33.

Benze, James G., Jr. "Nancy Reagan: China Doll or Dragon Lady?" *Presidential Studies Quarterly* (Fall 1990): 777–91.

Gould, Lewis. "Modern First Ladies and the Presidency." *Presidential Studies Quarterly* (Fall 1990): 677–84.

O'Connor, Karen, Bernadette Nye, and Laura Van Assendelft. "Wives in the White House: The Political Influence of First Ladies." *Presidential Studies Quarterly* (Summer 1996): 835–54.

Flint Auto Workers' Strike (1936–37)

The Flint Auto Worker's Strike, which occurred in Flint, Michigan, was a 44-day sit-down strike that lasted from December 30, 1936, to February 11, 1937. The strike began over disagreements about speeding up assembly line production and employers' refusal to work with unions. Workers at three Fisher Auto Body Assembly Plants, subsidiaries of General Motors, went on strike; other area auto workers soon followed their actions.

Events became heated when, a few weeks into the strike, police were called in to prevent violence. The Women's Emergency Brigade was established as a result. This group of over 350 women volunteers formed picket lines between the police and strikers and helped deliver needed food and supplies to the workers. The group also helped band the strikers together after a January 21 confrontation with police in which 14 people were shot.

During the 44-day sit-down strike by Flint, Michigan, auto workers in 1937, women formed a barrier between police and strikers to prevent violence. Shown here are some of the wives of striking workers in January 1937. Photo by Sheldon Dick. Library of Congress.

As the strike dragged into February, a final push was made. In a mobilization that came to be known as "Women's Day," thousands of workers and several women's brigades, including groups from Lansing, Pontiac, and Detroit, descended on Flint. A few days later, the strike was settled. Wages were increased to compensate for the increased production. The United Auto Workers experienced a marked growth in membership, from 30,000 to 500,000.

Bibliography

Boyer, Richard and Herbert Morass. *Labor's Untold Story.* New York: United Electrical, Radio, and Machine Workers of America, 1974.

Fine, Sidney. *Sit-Down, The General Motors Strike of 1936–1937.* Ann Arbor: University of Michigan Press, 1969.

Elizabeth Gurley Flynn (1890–1964)

Elizabeth Gurley Flynn—known as "the rebel girl"—began her political involvement as a labor organizer for the International Workers of the World. She gained prominence during the **Lawrence Strike of 1912** as one of the lead organizers. Her Marxist ideology landed her in prison during the Red Scare of 1919. In 1920, she was one of the founding members of the American Civil Liberties Union and served on the board of directors until 1940 when she was expelled because of her support for communism. She was sent to prison again in 1926 for inciting violence at a protest of the execution of Sacco and Vanzetti. In 1952, she was convicted of sedition under the Smith Act. She died in 1964 on her first visit to the Soviet Union.

Bibliography

Baxandall, Rosalyn Fraad. *Words on Fire: The Life and Writings of Elizabeth Gurley Flynn.* New Brunswick, NJ: Rutgers University Press, 1987.

Flynn, Elizabeth Gurley. *The Rebel Girl: An Autobiography.* New York: International Publishers, 1973.

Jane Fonda (1937–)

Jane Fonda has used her position in Hollywood to advance her political ideology and various causes. She was active in the civil rights movement and in the anti-war movement of the 1960s. Her trip to North Vietnam during the Vietnam War earned her the moniker "Hanoi Jane" from those who believed that her liberal ideology was un-American. She has championed liberal causes and has been an outspoken supporter of the **Equal Rights Amendment (ERA)** and other women's issues. She has made controversial films like *Coming Home* (1978) and *The China Syndrome* (1979). Since her marriage to media mogul and philanthropist Ted Turner, who committed $1 billion to the United Nations in 1997, Fonda has led a more circumspect political life avoiding the spotlight.

Bibliography

Guiles, F.C. *Jane Fonda.* New York: Doubleday, 1982.

Elizabeth "Betty" Ford (1918–)

Betty Ford stands out among the **first ladies** for her openness about her mental and health problems and her ardent campaigning for women's rights. Born in Chicago in 1918 and raised in Grand Rapids, Michigan, Betty pursued a career in modern dance. Her first marriage at the age of 24 ended in divorce after five years, and she soon started dating Gerald Ford. Although she did not anticipate a political career when he proposed, they were married during his 1948 congressional campaign. Upon his election, they moved to Washington. Betty involved herself in the wives' clubs in Congress, worked in volunteer organizations, and raised four boys and one girl. In 1973, when Vice President Spiro Agnew resigned, Gerald Ford, then Republican minority leader of the House of Representatives, was selected to fill the vacancy. Richard Nixon subsequently resigned in 1974, and Gerald Ford moved into the presidency. Though unprepared for her role as first lady, she quickly embraced the opportunity to advance women's rights. At her first press conference, she announced her support for ratification of the **Equal Rights Amendment (ERA)** and subsequently had separate lines installed in her White House office to lobby for the amendment. In September 1974, she was diagnosed with breast cancer and her openness about the surgery publicized the issue of breast cancer awareness. Although polls indicated some controversy over Ford's willingness to discuss political and personal issues so candidly, her popularity as first lady was clearly demonstrated through buttons in the 1976 campaign that read "Betty's Husband for President." (LvA)

Bibliography

Caroli, Betty Boyd. *First Ladies, Second Edition*. New York: Oxford University Press, 1993.

Gould, Lewis L., ed. *American First Ladies: Their Lives and Their Legacy*. New York: Garland Publishers, 1996.

Abigail Kelley Foster (1810–1887)

Abigail Foster served as secretary of the Lynn (Massachusetts) Female Anti-Slavery Society from 1835 until 1837, as well as an officer in the Lynn Female Peace Society. She became a lecturer against slavery in 1839, speaking at such events as the 1840 convention of the American Anti-Slavery Society, and helped establish the *Anti-Slavery Bugle* in Salem, Ohio, in 1845. In the 1850s, Foster added **temperance** and **feminism** to her lecture topics, continuing to tour the nation for a number of years. **See also** Abolition; Slavery and Women.

Bibliography

Bacon, Margaret H. *I Speak for My Slave Sister.* New York: Harper Collins, 1974.

Benard, Joel. *Authority, Autonomy and Radical Commitment.* Cambridge, MA: Antiquarum Society, 1981.

Tillie Fowler (1942–)

Republican congresswoman for Florida's 4th District, Tillie Fowler was born in Milledgeville, Florida, on December 23, 1942. She received a B.A. in political science from Emory University in 1964 and a J.D. in 1967. After finishing law school, she worked for Georgia congressmen Robert Stephens as a legislative assistant, and as counsel for the White House Office of Consumer Affairs during the Nixon administration. In 1985, she was elected to the Jacksonville, Florida, City Council, and in 1992 to the 103rd Congress with 57 percent of the vote. During her first term, she served on the National Security Committee and was elected co-chair of the Freshman Republican Task Force on Reform. She introduced an eight-year term limit amendment that she modeled after Florida's "eight is enough" initiative. She disapproved of defense cuts and criticized President Bill Clinton's defense appropriation bill. She ran unopposed in the 1994 election and in her second term was elected to serve on the Republican Steering Committee, as a deputy whip, and as a member of the Executive Committee of the National Congressional Committee. She ran unopposed again in 1996 and currently serves on the National Security and Transportation and Infrastructure committees. (GVS)

Bibliography

Barone, Michael and Grant Ujifusa. *The Almanac of American Politics, 1996.* Washington, DC: National Journal, 1995.

Sheila Frahm (1945–)

Kansas governor Bill Graves nominated Republican Sheila Frahm to succeed Kansas senator Bob Dole when he resigned his seat in 1996 to devote more time to his presidential bid. With Frahm and Republican Senator Nancy Kassebaum, Kansas joined California in having a pair of female senators. Frahm subsequently lost the seat in a fractious primary to conservative Sam Brownback in the special election for the remaining two years of Dole's term. (MEK)

Bibliography

"Appointed, Sheila Frahm." *Time* 147, no. 23 (June 3, 1996): 21.

Kalb, Deborah. "Frahm Named Interim Successor to Resigning Sen. Dole." *Congressional Quarterly Weekly Report* 54, no. 21 (May 25, 1996): 1478.

———. "Party Divisions and Open Seats Have GOP Running Hard." *Congressional Quarterly Weekly Report* 54, no. 29 (July 20, 1996): 2066.

"Kansas Dust Storm." *U.S. News & World Report* 120, no. 24 (June 17, 1996): 26.

Barbara Hackman Franklin (1940–)

Barbara Franklin began her national political career in 1971 when she was nominated as an assistant on the White House staff for recruitment of women into government positions. From 1973 to 1979, she became vice-chair of the United States Consumer Product Safety Commission.

Franklin served as chair of the Task Force for Reform for the Advisory Committee on Trade and Policy Negotiations twice in her career, from 1982 to 1986 and from 1989 to 1992. She also served as advisor to the controller general of the United States from 1984 to 1992 and again starting in 1994. She was secretary of commerce in the Bush administration from 1992 to 1993.

Bibliography

"A New Strategic Framework for U.S. Policy: China: Friend or Foe?" *Vital Speeches* 62, no. 21 (August 15, 1996): 644.

Freedom of Access to Clinic Entrances Act (FACE) (1994)

The Freedom of Access to Clinic Entrances Act (FACE) was signed into law by President Bill Clinton on May 26, 1994. The act makes it a federal crime to use force, the threat of force, or physical obstruction, such as sit-ins, to interfere with, injure, or intimidate clinic workers or women seeking abortions or other reproductive health services. Violators are subject to imprisonment, fines, and civil remedies.

The Freedom of Access to Clinic Entrances Act was passed in reaction to the increasing number of blockades of **abortion** clinics by anti-abortion groups, such as **Operation Rescue**, and the inability or unwillingness of local law enforcement officials to protect them.

A Supreme Court ruling in ***Bray v. Alexandria Women's Health Clinic*** (1993) barred federal court judges from invoking a civil rights law to enjoin the protest activity that interfered with the work of the clinics. Reacting in part to the *Bray* decision, as well as to the growing violence of anti-abortion protestors, Representatives Charles Schumer (D-NY) and **Constance Morella** (R-MD) introduced FACE in the House of Representatives in February 1993. Before the bill was passed by Congress a year later, two physicians who performed abortions were shot—one fatally—by anti-abortion activists. (SM)

BIBLIOGRAPHY

Bray v. Alexandria Women's Health Clinic, 506 U.S. 263 (1993).

O'Connor, Karen. *No Neutral Ground? Abortion Politics in an Age of Absolutes.* Boulder, CO: Westview Press, 1966.

Freedom of Choice Act

In the wake of the Supreme Court's decision in ***Webster v. Reproductive Health Services*** (1989), Senator Alan Cranston (D-CA) and Representative Don Edwards (D-CA) introduced legislation that would prohibit states from enacting any **abortion** restrictions prior to fetal viability, and at any time if the abortion is necessary to protect the life or health of the woman. The Freedom of Choice Act was an attempt to codify the ***Roe v. Wade*** (1973) decision by writing into law abortion rights protected only by Supreme Court rulings. Opponents argued that the Freedom of Choice Act went far beyond *Roe* and would overturn abortion regulations upheld by the Supreme Court, including parental consent laws, 24-hour waiting periods, or requirements that abortions be performed in a hospital. First introduced in Congress in 1989, it was not until 1992 that the Freedom of Choice Act was approved at the committee stage. However, debate over amendments that might destroy the intent of the bill and a promised veto from President George Bush prevented the legislation from reaching the floor of the House or Senate for a vote. Prospects for passage of the Freedom of Choice Act improved following the 1992 election of President Bill Clinton and the election of 24 new pro-choice women in a Democrat-controlled Congress, but efforts to pass the legislation again failed as a result of divisions concerning regulations to be included in the bill. The House version included a judicial bypass clause and allowed parental consent for minors as long as the regulations included a judicial bypass clause and allowed private religious institutions to opt out of performing abortions on religious grounds, although public hospitals could not prohibit abortions. The Senate version also included an amendment that would allow states to refuse to use Medicaid funds to pay for the abortions of poor women. This issue divided pro-choice supporters between those who felt the government should not pay for abortions and those who believed that without public funding the legislation would discriminate against poor women seeking abortions. Ultimately supporters of the Freedom of Choice Act did not push the legislation towards a floor vote. Even with President Clinton's support, the bill was predicted to fail without amendments, yet amendments would defeat the purpose of the legislation. (LvA)

BIBLIOGRAPHY

Craig, Barbara Hinkson and David M. O'Brien. *Abortion and American Politics.* Chatham, NJ: Chatham House Publishers, Inc., 1993.

O'Connor, Karen. *No Neutral Ground? Abortion Politics in an Age of Absolutes.* Boulder, CO: Westview Press, 1996.

Jo Freeman (1945–)

Jo Freeman is a feminist scholar, lawyer, and activist who earned a Ph.D. in political science from the University of Chicago and a J.D. at New York University School of Law. Freeman was active in the younger branch of the Chicago **women's liberation** movement in the late 1960s. Her work in the movement and extensive research led to her first book, *The Politics of Women's Liberation*, which was awarded the American Political Science Association Annual Award for the Best Book on the Subject of Women and Politics in 1975. Freeman is a renowned authority on the subject of American women and politics and has published widely in the academic and popular press. (CKC)

BIBLIOGRAPHY

Freeman, Jo. *The Politics of Women's Liberation.* New York: McKay, 1975.

———. *Women: A Feminist Perspective.* Palo Alto, CA: Mayfield Publishing, 1975.

Betty Friedan (1921–)

Cofounder of the **National Organization of Women (NOW)** and a women's rights advocate, Betty Friedan wrote ***The Feminine Mystique*** (1963), which inspired thousands of women to initiate the modern women's rights movement beginning in the late 1960s. Born in Peoria, Illinois, on February 4, 1921, Friedan was influenced at an early age by her mother's unhappiness with having given up her career in journalism to become a housewife. Encouraged by her mother to pursue her interests in journalism, Friedan earned a degree from Smith College in 1942, graduating summa cum laude, and completed a year of graduate work at the University of California at Berkeley before moving to New York to work as a reporter. She married Carl Friedan in 1947 and took a one-year leave from her job upon the birth of her first child, but was fired when she became pregnant a second time. In response to a questionnaire her Smith College classmates filled out for their 15th anniversary celebration, Friedan attempted to describe in words "the problem that has no name." Although Friedan and her classmates graduated from college with degrees and visions of exciting careers, society expected them to assume the traditional roles of wife and mother. In *The Feminine Mystique*, Friedan questioned the "happiness" women were supposed to experience in these roles and urged women to refrain from becoming housewives. Thousands of women responded positively to Friedan's message, and she began giving lectures on feminist issues. Frustration at the 1966 Conference of the State Commissions on the Status of Women led Friedan to help organize NOW. She served as the organization's president until 1970, helped organize the 1970 Women's Strike for Equality in recognition of the 50th anniversary of the **Nineteenth Amendment**, and helped organize the **National Women's Political Caucus** in 1971. Friedan's writings and activism have had an immeasurable impact on the **women's movement**, and she continues to be active in feminist causes, especially on issues facing older women. **See also** Feminism. (LvA)

Bibliography

Behm, Barbara. *Betty Friedan: Speaking Out for Women's Rights.* Milwaukee: Gareth Stevens, 1992.

Friedan, Betty. *The Feminine Mystique.* New York: W. W. Norton, 1963.

———. *The Fountain of Age.* New York: Simon & Schuster, 1993.

———. *It Changed My Life: Writings on the Women's Movement.* New York: Random House, 1976.

———. *The Second Stage.* New York: Summit Books, 1981.

Frontiero v. Richardson (1973)

Frontiero v. Richardson, 411 U.S. 677 (1973), was an important early gender discrimination case. Air Force lieutenant Sharron Frontiero challenged regulations that forced servicewomen to prove their husbands were dependents to obtain benefits. Servicemen did not have to prove that their wives were dependents to receive similar benefits.

While the Supreme Court ruled 8-1 that the regulations unconstitutionally discriminated on the basis of gender, the case is significant because it triggered an internal debate on the standards that the Court should apply in future gender discrimination cases. Four justices supported characterizing sex as a suspect classification that would merit the use of strict scrutiny in discrimination cases. Under such a standard, the government can distinguish between the sexes only if it has a compelling rationale. Such a standard had only been adopted for cases involving racial discrimination of First Amendment rights. Justices William Brennan, William Douglas, Thurgood Marshall, and Byron White were unable to attract the fifth vote necessary to make sex a suspect classification. The other members of the majority supported the use of minimum scrutiny. Under the deferential standard, the law is deemed constitutional if has a rational basis. The government failed even that forgiving standard.

Justice Lewis Powell opposed the adoption of the strict scrutiny standard while the nation was debating the proposed **Equal Rights Amendment (ERA)**. He argued that such a decision would preempt the political debate. In ***Craig v. Boren*** (1976), the Court adopted a new intermediate standard, deciding that gender was a semi-suspect classification triggering moderate scrutiny. (RLP)

Bibliography

Epstein Lee and Thomas G. Walker. *Constitutional Law for a Changing America: Rights, Liberties, and Justice.* 2nd ed. Washington, DC: CQ Press, 1995.

Goldstein, Leslie F. *The Constitutional Rights of Women: Cases in Law and Social Change.* rev. ed. Madison: University of Wisconsin Press, 1988.

O'Brien, David M. *Constitutional Law and Politics: Civil Rights and Civil Liberties.* vol. 2. New York: Norton, 1997.

Full Employment and Balanced Growth Act of 1978 (Humphrey-Hawkins Act)

The Employment Act of 1946 required the federal government, including the Federal Reserve, to promote maximum employment, income, and output. Confronted with the policy dilemma of high rates of both inflation and unemployment in the mid-1970s, Congress responded with the Full Employment and Balanced Growth Act of 1978, commonly known as the Humphrey-Hawkins Act, for the primary sponsors. The legislation directs the federal government, including the president, Congress, and the Federal Reserve Board, to design and coordinate economic policies and programs to ensure full employment and balanced economic growth consistent with a stable price level. The act requires the chair of the Federal Reserve to report semiannually to Congress about the Federal Reserve's outlook on economic activity and inflation and to set and report targets for money growth. The law does not mandate specific practices for the Federal Reserve to follow and does not require that the Federal Reserve achieve its monetary goals. The act requires the president to submit an economic report by January 20 of each year that outlines monetary and fiscal policies, tax policies, employment goals, and legislative recommendations. (AMD)

Bibliography

Hadjimichalakis, Michael and Karma Hadjimichalakis. *Contemporary Money, Banking and Financial Markets.* Chicago: Richard D. Irwin, 1995.

_______. *Reducing Unemployment: The Humphrey-Hawkins and Kemp-McClure Bills.* Washington, DC: The American Enterprise Institute for Public Policy Research, 1976.

Margaret Fuller (1810-1850)

A feminist and transcendentalist writer, Margaret Fuller (known as Margaret Fuller d'Ossoli after her marriage in 1848) was born on May 23, 1810, in Cambridgeport, Massachusetts. Growing up under the strong tutelage of her scholarly and domineering father, she received a strict classical education and was reading Virgil, Ovid, and Horace by age 10. When her father died in 1825, she began to move in intellectual circles that included Ralph Waldo Emerson in Concord and Bronson Alcott in Boston. In 1839, she moved back to Boston and began holding her famous "conversations." These seminars centered on a variety of topics, including mythology, art, and ethics, and were attended by famous transcendentalists. From

1840 to 1842, she served as an editor of *The Dial*, a literary publication that she cofounded with Emerson and George Ripley. She also published *Woman in the Nineteenth Century,* which became an important contribution to classic feminist thought. In 1846, she traveled to Europe, where she met and married Giovanni Angelo Marchese d'Ossoli. She died in a shipwreck in 1850 with her husband and two-year-old son. **See also** Feminism. (GVS)

BIBLIOGRAPHY

Mason, Wade. *Margaret Fuller: Whetstone of Genius.* Clifton, NJ: Kelley, 1940.

Stern, Madeline. *The Life of Margaret Fuller.* New York: Greenwood, 1991.

Willa Lybrand Fulmer (1884–1968)

Willa Fulmer, a Democrat, was elected to the U.S. House of Representatives from South Carolina's 2nd District after the death of her husband Hampton P. Fulmer. She served in Congress from November 7, 1944, to January 3, 1945.

BIBLIOGRAPHY

Chamberlin, Hope. *A Minority of Members.* New York: Praeger, 1973.

Betty Furness (1916–1994)

In 1964, Betty Furness took her popularity as a screen and stage performer and used it to travel across the nation doing local TV and radio shows as a recruiter and promoter for VISTA and the Head Start federal programs. She also hosted several telethons for Democratic candidates and served President Lyndon B. Johnson as special assistant for consumer affairs. Furness headed New York State Consumer Board in 1970 and headed New York City's Department of Consumer Affairs. In 1973, she served on the board of the Consumers Union.

BIBLIOGRAPHY

"Obituary." *New York Times* (April 4, 1994): 16.

Elizabeth Furse (1936–)

A community organizer and activist for peace, justice, and human rights, Oregon Democrat Elizabeth Furse has served in the U. S. House of Representatives since 1992. Born in Nairobi, Kenya, in 1936, Furse earned a B.A. from Evergreen State College in Washington in 1974. Throughout the 1980s, she successfully lobbied Congress to pass legislation restoring legal status to three Oregon tribes and cofounded and directed the Oregon Peace Institute, an organization dedicated to teaching peace and nonviolent conflict resolution. In 1988, she organized the "citizen's train," which took hundreds of people to Washington, to educate Congress on the need for a "citizen's budget." She was first elected to Congress in 1992 and currently serves on the Commerce Committee. Furse has a liberal record on foreign and cultural issues and has voted moderately on economic issues. She helped pass legislation to increase trade opportunities for business, with emphasis on environmental technology. She has also worked to improve responses to **domestic violence**, to protect seniors, and to improve the quality of life of Oregon families. (GVS)

BIBLIOGRAPHY

Congressional Quarterly Weekly Report 50, no. 3 (January 16, 1993): 128.

G

Gag Rule

In 1988, the Reagan administration imposed restrictions on **abortion** counseling and referrals under Title X of the Public Health Service Act. The "gag rule," as the regulations came to be called, prohibited organizations receiving federal funding under Title X from offering any abortion services as part of their family planning projects, including counseling about the use of abortion or referrals for abortions. The purpose of the restrictions was to reduce the number of abortions performed by withholding funds from the organizations that provided abortion services. In effect, the number of abortions performed throughout the 1980s remained relatively constant, although private abortion clinics rapidly replaced public hospitals as the providers of abortions. The constitutionality of the gag rule was challenged in ***Rust v. Sullivan*** (1991); in a 5-4 decision the Supreme Court upheld the restrictions, ruling that the regulations did not violate freedom of speech, the right to privacy, or the intent of Title X. Both in 1991 and 1992, President George Bush vetoed congressional attempts to overturn the gag rule. The ban was ultimately lifted by President Bill Clinton on January 22, 1993, just two days after his inauguration, when he repealed the gag rule by executive order. **See also** Public Health Service Act, Title X. (LvA)

BIBLIOGRAPHY

Blank, Robert and Janna C. Merrick. *Human Reproduction, Emerging Technologies, and Conflicting Rights.* Washington, DC: Congressional Quarterly Press, 1995.

Craig, Barbara Hinkson and David M. O'Brien. *Abortion and American Politics.* Chatham, NJ: Chatham House Publishers, Inc., 1993.

Matilda Joslyn Gage (1826–1898)

An unsung hero of the **suffrage** movement, Matilda Joslyn Gage was born to Dr. Hezikiah and Helen Leslie Joslyn in Cicero, New York, in 1826 and educated at the Clinton Liberal Institute. At age 18, she married Henry H. Gage, a merchant; they had five children.

Gage entered public life in the 1850s, attending her first women's rights convention at the age of 26. Gage was a founder of the **National Woman Suffrage Association (NWSA)**, and the New York State Woman Suffrage Association. Gage lobbied Congress in 1875 on behalf of suffrage. During the 1880 elections, she attended the national party conventions to lobby delegates to make suffrage a campaign issue. She was a prolific author whose writings included newspaper articles, the *History of Woman Suffrage* (1881–1886), and the controversial *Woman, Church and State* (1893). In 1890, she formed the Woman's National Liberal Union in protest over the union between the NWSA and the **American Woman Suffrage Association (AWSA)**. Gage's organization promoted a broad agenda of women's issues; she served as president until her death in 1898. Gage's lifelong motto was: "There is a word sweeter than Mother, Home, or Heaven; that word is Liberty." (AM)

BIBLIOGRAPHY

Gage, Matilda Joslyn. *Woman, Church and State: A Historical Account of the Status of Woman Through the Christian Ages.* Watertown, MA: Persephone Press, 1980.

Helen Hamilton Gardner (1853–1925)

Helen Gardner began an active tour speaking on **feminism** in 1887. In 1888, she presented her study on the comparative size and function of the male and female brains, "Sex in Brain," to the International Council of Women. In 1890, she wrote a novel against legalized **prostitution** and low age of consent laws, *Is This Your Son, My Lord.*

In the early 1900s, Gardner became a suffrage lobbyist in Washington. She helped reorganize the Congressional Committee of the **National American Woman Suffrage Association (NAWSA)** in 1913, acting as vice president from 1917 until 1920. Gardner also served on the United States Civil Service Commission from 1920 until 1925.

BIBLIOGRAPHY

Papez, James. "The Brain of Helen H. Gardner." *American Journal of Physical Anthropology* (October-December 1927): 29-88.

Park, Maud Wood. *Front Door Lobby.* New York: Maud Wood Park, 1960.

"Obituary." *New York Times* (July 27, 1925).

Lucretia Rudolph Garfield (1832–1918)

Lucretia Garfield, the wife of President James A. Garfield, was born in 1832 in Hiram, Ohio. She was a scholarly woman who grew up under the tutelage of her father, Zeb Rudolph, a devout member of the Disciples of Christ. In 1851 she attended the Western Reserve Eclectic Institute where she met her future husband "Jim" Garfield. "Crete" and "Jim" married in 1858 and began a strong and happy marriage in which they shared intellectual interests and raised five children. When she became first lady in 1881, Lucretia Garfield spent long hours at the Library of Congress seeking historical documentation to guide her restoration of the White House. The first lady's moral and intellectual strength were well respected by the president, and he valued her opinion on political matters. In May 1881, James Garfield was shot by an assassin. Lucretia Garfield led a private life after she left the White House and survived her husband by 36 years. (GVS) **See also** First Ladies

After the assassination of her husband in 1881, Lucretia Garfield led a quiet life. Library of Congress.

BIBLIOGRAPHY

Blaine, Mrs. James G. *Letters of Mrs. James G. Blaine*. New York: Duffield and Co., 1908.

Smith, Theodore Clarke. *The Life and Letters of James Abram Garfield*. New Haven, CT:Yale University Press, 1925.

Elizabeth Hawley Gasque (1896–1989)

Elizabeth Gasque was elected in a one-party special election as a Democrat to the U.S. House of Representatives, filling the vacancy left by the death of her husband, Representative Allard H. Gasque. The first woman to be elected from South Carolina, she served in Congress from September 13, 1938, to January 3, 1939, at which time she retired from political life.

BIBLIOGRAPHY

Chamberlin, Hope. *A Minority of Members*. New York: Praeger, 1973.

Geduldig v. Aiello (1974)

The state of California established a self-supporting disability program for private employers that provided coverage for injuries and illnesses not covered by workman's compensation. The Unemployment Compensation Disability Fund set the contribution rate at 1 percent of the employee's salary, not to exceed an annual maximum of $85. Four women who were part of the plan filed suit in district court because the plan did not cover disabilities caused by pregnancy. The suit charged that the plan violated the equal protection clause of the Fourteenth Amendment. The district court agreed with the women.

On appeal to the U.S. Supreme Court, however, the decision was overturned (*Geduldig v. Aiello,* 417 U.S. 484 [1974]). The court's six-justice majority focused on the question of "whether the Equal Protection Clause requires such policies to be sacrificed or compromised in order to finance the payment of benefits to those whose disability is attributable to normal pregnancy and delivery." The majority found that the exclusion of pregnancy was within the scope of equal protection because the exclusion of women was not based upon sex, but rather condition. In the widely cited Footnote 20, Justice Potter Stewart, writing for the majority, justified the exclusion because "there is no risk from which men are protected and women are not. Likewise there is no risk from which women are protected and men are not." Stewart argued that the California disability fund "divided potential recipients into two groups—pregnant women and non-pregnant persons. While the first group is exclusively female, the second includes persons of both sexes." In the end, the Court upheld the plan as constitutional because the exclusion of pregnancy was related to the state's interest in maintaining the self-supporting structure of the plan and its discretion to include or not include any particular disability as long as it did not do so on the basis of sex.

BIBLIOGRAPHY

Levin, Betsy. "Woman's Place in the Constitution." *High School Journal* 59 (October 1975): 31–45.

Mezey, Susan. *In Pursuit of Equality*. New York: St. Martin's Press, 1992.

Williams, Wendy Webster. *Sex Discrimination and the Law*. Boston: Little Brown, 1978.

Gender Gap and Voting Patterns

Women in the United States received the universal right to vote much later than men. Although several states had granted women's **suffrage** earlier, the ratification of the **Nineteenth Amendment** in 1920 provided the first opportunity for American women in all states to vote and hold political office. At first women were less likely to use the franchise than men. The first gender gap noted in the United States referred to the lower rates of voting and political participation among women. For many years, women were less likely to vote, discuss politics, know political information, participate in interest groups, and hold public office than men. However, while women are still less likely than men to engage in many of these political activities, since 1980 the gap between the proportions of men and women voting has disappeared. The gender gap that is now widely discussed in the news media refers to the differences in candidate preferences between men and women. Public opinion polls and exit interviews have become the source of knowledge regarding voting behavior. Since the 1950s, polling information has been systematically gathered, and women have generally shown differing preferences from those of men. Over time, the direction of women's voting preferences has changed, and the causes of the gender gap have changed as well.

Table 1

Reported Voter Turnout by Sex, 1952–1994*

	% Men Voting	% Women Voting	Vote Gap**	% of Voters Who Were Women
1952	79.7%	69.3%	-10.4	—
1956	79.5	67.6	-11.9	—
1958	66.7	49.6	-17.1	—
1960	84.1	74.7	-9.4	—
1962	63.7	57.7	-6.0	—
1964	71.9	67.0	-4.9	51.5%
1966	58.2	53.0	-5.2	50.9
1968	69.8	66.0	-3.8	51.9
1970	56.8	52.7	-4.1	51.4
1972	64.1	62.0	-2.1	52.3
1974	46.2	43.4	-2.8	51.4
1976	59.6	58.8	-0.8	52.6
1978	46.6	45.3	-1.3	52.2
1980	59.1	59.4	0.3	53.0
1982	48.7	48.4	-0.4	52.7
1984	59.0	60.8	1.9	53.5
1986	45.8	46.1	0.3	52.8
1988	56.4	58.3	1.8	53.3
1990	44.6	45.4	0.7	52.8
1992	60.2	62.3	2.1	53.2
1994	44.4	44.9	0.6	52.5

*The data for elections 1952–1962 are from the National Election Studies. The data from 1964–1994 are from the U.S. Census Bureau. The Census figures were used because they have a lower nonresponse rate but were unavailable before 1964.

**A negative figure means men had the higher turnout rate; a positive figure means women had the higher rate.

The gender gap in voter turnout likely began when women first earned the right to vote but, because election results are not reported by sex, could not be documented until regular election polls were developed that asked men and women whether they voted. The earliest studies by the National Election Survey show approximately 10 percentage points less women than men voting in the 1950s, but the gap between men and women who voted declined gradually in the 1960s and 1970s. The U. S. Census Bureau indicates that by 1984 there was a tendency for larger proportions of women than men to vote. However, the closing of the turnout gap has not been the result of increased turnout by women voters as much as a decline in turnout among voters of both sexes. In the 1996 election, voter turnout was the lowest in a presidential election since 1924, with just under 50 percent of the eligible voters casting ballots. Yet the proportions of men and women voting were nearly the same. Moreover, since 1964 when the Census Bureau started asking questions about voting, women have been the majority of the electorate because of their greater numbers in the voting age population even though their turnout rate was lower than men's until the mid-1970s.

There are many possible reasons for the gender gap in voter turnout. The gap has been highest among older groups of voters. Therefore, it is possible that some women did not support the suffrage amendment and declined to exercise their new right. As this generation aged and gradually disappeared from the electorate, the difference in voter turnout began to decline. Aging itself may have a more negative impact on voting among women than among men since there continues to be a large gender gap in turnout between the oldest group of voters. Also, voter turnout increases with higher levels of education and income. Since the 1950s, women have gradually increased their levels of education relative to men's and have increased their participation in the job market. Employed women and those with a high school education or more are as likely as men to vote.

Now that the gender gap in voter turnout has closed, with women as likely as, or even more likely than, men to vote, attention has shifted to the voting patterns of women and men.

Table 2

The Gender Gap in Voting and Party Identification

Year	President Vote (% Dem)*	House Vote (% Dem)*	Party Identification** (% Rep)*	Party Identification** (% Dem)*
1952	-2	1	4	1
1956	-6	-10	8	-1
1960	-6	1	4	6
1964	4	0	2	3
1968	5	0	-1	5
1972	6	-1	1	7
1976	1	-1	5	5
1980	6	-3	2	7
1984	8	4	0	7
1988	7	0	-1	10
1992	10	5	-5	8
1994	--	4	-4	10
1996	11	9	--	6

*A positive gender gap means that women were more supportive; a negative one shows that men were more supportive.

**Unlike voting where only a minuscule percentage of Americans do not vote for either of the major parties, a substantial number do not identify with either party. Thus the gender gaps in Democratic and Republic identification do not have to be symmetrical (i.e., about the same size but in different directions).

Source: The author constructed the table using data from *The Public Perspective.* 1996, 39; Richard A. Seltzer, Jody Newman, and Melissa Voorhees Leighton. *Sex as a Political Variable: Women as Candidates and Voters in U.S. Elections.* Boulder, CO: Lynne Rienner Publishers, 1997, 37, 39, 41, 129, 131.

The gender gap in candidate preferences has received a large amount of media attention since the 1980s. However, it did not originate then. Evidence for the existence of a gender gap can be found in the election surveys of the 1950s, and it is likely that the gap in the voting preferences of men and women goes back to the 1920s when women first began to vote nationally. Nevertheless, the nature and size of the gender gap has varied over time.

In comparing the gender gap in voting preferences over time, it is important that consistent measures be used. The existence of a gender gap need not affect the outcome of the election since the gender gap can be large and yet have majorities of both sexes preferring a particular candidate or party.

The earliest voting studies showed that women were more likely than men to support the Republican candidate for president and to identify with the **Republican Party** in many of the elections until 1980. In regard to congressional elections, the gender gap tended to be smaller with the majority of both sexes preferring the Democratic candidates in most elections. Political analysts did not make much of these gender differences. Starting with the election of 1980, the political preferences of men and women underwent change, and interest in the gender gap grew. Women became more Democratic and liberal in their voting behavior and became less likely than men to support the Republican Party. Feminist organizations and leaders encouraged the news media to make this difference in voting patterns among women and men the focal point of their discussions of elections. They used this strategy to enhance the political power of women to gain more policy concessions and more public offices for female candidates. The media adopted the strategy to increase public interest in political coverage.

While the size of the gender gap has grown in recent presidential and congressional elections, it is not nearly as large as the differences in voting preference between most other demographic groups. For example, the difference in voting for President Clinton between women and men in 1996 was 11 points. The difference in voting for Clinton between blacks and whites was 41 points, and the difference in voting for Clinton between the lowest and highest income groups was 21 points. Of course, the difference in voting for Clinton between Democrats and Republicans was the highest of all at 67 percent. Nevertheless, the existence of a gender gap is important because women are the largest group of voters, comprising 52 percent of the electorate in 1996.

Many reasons have been adduced for the differences in candidate and party preferences between women and men. The more conservative position of women relative to men during the 1950s has been attributed to the differences in their occupations. At that time, most women tended to be housewives, while most men tended to work in blue collar jobs. Men's greater support for Democratic candidates may have been stimulated by their membership in trade unions. Housewives, on the other hand, were assumed to hold more conservative values; therefore, they would support the more conservative positions of the Republican Party.

Today, more information is available to help us analyze the causes of the current gender gap. Public opinion polls regularly ask many questions regarding political and economic attitudes and report the responses by gender and other demographic characteristics. In early opinion studies, only a few questions generated significant differences between the sexes. Women tended to be less inclined to support the use of force in international relations, and they were more likely to oppose harsh methods in dealing with those convicted of crimes. Yet women were more conservative than men regarding civil rights and moral issues. These early differences continue today but, in addition, other differences in attitudes have emerged. While both sexes are nearly equally distrustful of the government and supportive of equal roles for women in the political and economic spheres and for freedom of choice regarding **abortion**, there are large differences in women's and men's attitudes regarding the need for government programs providing a safety net for the economically disadvantaged and in attitudes regarding the health of the American economy. Furthermore, women and men tend to use different issues in deciding how to vote.

In recent elections, women have been fairly consistent in their level of support for the **Democratic Party** and its candidates. Men, on the other hand, have been moving away from allegiance to the Democrats since the 1960s. The change in men's voting preference began among white men in the South but has spread to other regions of the country. The issues associated with a Democratic vote today are support for government guarantees of an adequate standard of living for all Americans and holding a negative perception on the state of the American economy. Women are more likely than men to hold these opinions and to place a high priority on Medicare and education when selecting candidates. They perceive the Democratic Party as being more capable of solving these problems and providing a more equal share of economic benefits to all. In 1996, men gave a higher priority to foreign policy, taxation, and the budget deficit in their voting decisions. Despite the fact that both men and women were more likely to vote Democratic in 1996 than in 1994, there remained a significant voting gap for the Democratic Party in both the presidential and congressional elections of 11 percent and 9 percent, respectively.

The reason why more women have retained support for the Democratic Party in the face of men's increased vote for Republican candidates cannot be attributed to a single cause. The three reasons that have been developed are feminist consciousness, women's economic concerns, and women's sense of compassion. Pamela Conover first explained the gender gap by the rise of **feminism**, showing that the differences in attitudes existed mainly between women who were feminists and men. Feminists support liberal positions on many social and moral issues. Yet feminism alone cannot account for the current gender gap. Susan Carroll has explained the gap by pointing to the fact that more women are divorced and holding jobs in the labor force, making them more independent of men. The gap is slightly higher among singles than among those who are married. The fact that women who work full time on average receive less income than full-time male workers and that families headed by single women are more likely to be below the **poverty** level may also be related to the gender gap, since women are more likely to need government services and guarantees of an adequate standard of living. The size of the gender gap is somewhat influenced by factors associated with class, but class alone is not sufficient to explain it. The size of the gender gap tends to be largest among those who are employed, those in professional and managerial occupations, and those who have a college education—hardly likely to be those needing a safety net. Therefore, the third element causing the gender gap may be women's greater feelings of compassion for the less fortunate members of society, and their concern for the needs of children in particular. Carol Gilligan has noted that women approach moral issues in ways that differ from those of men. Women tend to think in terms of associations with others and community values while men tend to stress individual rights and responsibility.

The future of the gender gap in voting preferences depends on many factors. It may be that American politics will continue to polarize around gender. There has been an increase in political divisions among all demographic groups in the United States, including sex, in the 1990s. Yet the gender gap is relatively small, and the economic factors contributing toward it may slowly disappear. The earnings gap between men and women has been gradually narrowing. Women have improved their levels of education and are as likely to attend college as men. Women are making headway in many of the professions that have previously been dominated by men. Women's identification with the Democratic Party has been decreasing. In 1992, women were 10 percentage points less Democratic than in 1982, and by 1994 more women considered themselves to be Republican than in any of the seven previous elections. As the issues that dominate American elections change and the character of the candidates selected by the political parties varies, it is likely that the voting preference of both men and women will change as well. **See also** Conservatism, Liberalism, News Media. (JMC)

Bibliography

Carroll, Susan J. "Women's Autonomy and the Gender Gap: 1980 and 1982." In Carol M. Mueller, ed. *The Politics of the Gender Gap: The Social Construction of Political Influence*. Beverly Hills: Sage, 1988.

Clark, Cal and Janet Clark. "Whither the Gender Gap? Converging and Conflicting Attitudes among Women." In Lois Lovelace Duke, ed. *Women in Politics: Outsiders or Insiders*. 2nd ed. Upper Saddle River, NJ: Prentice Hall, 1996.

Conover, Pamela Johnston. "Feminists and the Gender Gap." *Journal of Politics* 50, no. 4 (November 1988): 985–1010.

Dougherty, Regina, Everett C. Ladd, David Wilber, and Lynn Zayachkiwsky, eds. *America at the Polls 1996*. Storrs, CT: The Roper Center for Public Opinion Research, University of Connecticut, 1997.

Gilligan, Carol. *In a Different Voice: Psychological Theory and Women's Development*. Cambridge, MA: Harvard University Press, 1982.

Pomper, Gerald M., Walter Dean Burnham, Anthony Corrado, Marjorie Randon Hershey, Marion R. Just, Scott Keeter, Wilson Carey McWilliams, and William G. Mayer, eds. *The Election of 1996: Reports and Interpretations*. Chatham, NJ: Chatham House Publishers, 1997.

The Public Perspective. 7, no. 3 (April-May 1996): 39.

Seltzer, Richard A., Jody Newman, and Melissa Voorhees Leighton. *Sex as a Political Variable: Women as Candidates and Voters in U.S. Elections*. Boulder, CO: Lynne Rienner Publishers, 1997.

General Electric Company v. Gilbert (1976)

In *General Electric Company v. Gilbert*, 429 U.S. 125 (1976), the U.S. Supreme Court answered the question of whether or not excluding pregnancy from disability plans was legal in light of **Title VII of the Civil Rights Act of 1964**, which barred **sex discrimination**. A class action suit was filed in federal district court claiming GE's exclusion of pregnancy from its expansive disability program was employment discrimination. The district court concluded that the exclusion violated Title VII. The decision was upheld in the court of appeals.

The U.S. Supreme Court, however, sided with GE and its arguments that the exclusion of one physical condition, in this case pregnancy, from a list of covered disabilities was an action within its prerogative in designing its benefits packages. The Court agreed that the exclusion was not based upon sex as it had been in ***Geduldig v. Aiello***, which challenged such exclusions on the equal protection clause of the Fourteenth Amendment. Justice William Rehnquist, writing for the majority, stated that "it is impossible to find any gender-based discriminatory effect in (GE's) scheme simply because women disabled as a result of pregnancy do not receive benefits; that is to say, gender-based discrimination does not result simply because an employer's disability-benefits plan is less than all-inclusive."

The decision in this case helped mobilize women's groups and Congress to pass the **Pregnancy Discrimination Act** of 1978. The act stated, in part, that "women affected by pregnancy . . . shall be treated the same for all employment-related purposes."

Bibliography

French, Larry L. "All Things Being Equal." *Journal of Law and Education* 7 (June 1978): 21–30.

Mezey, Susan. *In Pursuit of Equality*. New York: St. Martin's Press, 1992.

Williams, Wendy Webster. *Sex Discrimination and the Law*. Boston: Little Brown, 1978.

General Federation of Women's Clubs

The General Federation of Women's Clubs has been in existence for over 100 years, since its founding in 1890. This organization, which originally sought to unite numerous diverse local women's clubs to provide a greater influence over social and political services, currently functions as an international women's volunteer service organization that provides leadership training and development to women around the world. The organization also serves programs in a variety of areas, including the arts, conservation, international affairs, education, homelife, and public affairs and issues. On a national and international scale, the group focuses on women's history and achievement, maintaining the Women's History and Resource Center in Washington, D.C.

Bibliography

Wells, Mildred White. *Unity in Diversity: The History of the General Federation of Women's Clubs.* Washington, DC: General Federation of Women's Clubs, 1953.

Florence Reville Gibbs (1890–1964)

Florence Gibbs, a Democrat, served in the U.S. House of Representatives from October 1, 1940, until January 3, 1941, completing the term of her late husband William Benjamin Gibbs. The first woman from Georgia to serve in the House of Representatives, she retired from politics at the end of the 76th Congress.

Bibliography

Chamberlin, Hope. *A Minority of Members.* New York: Praeger, 1973.

Charlotte Perkins Gilman (1860–1935)

Charlotte Perkins Gilman, a social anthropologist and feminist author, espoused a radical restructuring of society that would allow women to more fully realize their potential. Among her more famous works were *The Yellow Wallpaper* (1892), a fictional account of Gilman's own mental breakdown, and *Women and Economics* (1898) in which she argues in favor of female economic independence. (JDG)

Bibliography

Berkin, Carol Ruth. "Private Woman, Public Woman: The Contradictions of Charlotte Perkins Gilman." In Carol Berkin and Mary Beth Norton, eds. *Women of America: A History.* Boston: Houghton Mifflin, 1979.

Ruth Bader Ginsburg (1933–)

Ruth Bader Ginsburg was an expert litigator on behalf of women's issues, and the second woman appointed to the United States Supreme Court. Joan Ruth Bader was born in Brooklyn on March 15, 1933. She learned of discrimination firsthand when after graduating at the top of her class from Columbia University School of Law she was unable to find a position commensurate with her abilities.

Ruth Ginsburg taught at a number of law schools and litigated for the American Civil Liberties Union (ACLU). She headed the litigation efforts of the **Women's Rights Project (WRP)** of the ACLU. Ginsburg has been credited with constructing a brilliant litigation history around cases involving discrimination against men. She adopted an incremental strategy in hopes of achieving enduring legal change. Ginsburg often selected cases that involved laws that favored women. She argued that men and women ought to be viewed as equal, and that men suffered discrimination when a system treated women as a special class. As a litigator, Ginsburg won five of the six cases she argued before the Supreme Court, erasing many of the legal distinctions between men and women. She has often been considered the "Thurgood Marshall of the women's movement."

Ginsburg was appointed to the contentious District of Columbia Circuit Court in 1980 in the waning days of the Carter administration. She served with distinction on the D.C. circuit court until President Bill Clinton appointed her to the Supreme Court to fill the vacancy created by the retirement of Justice Byron White in 1993. Her Supreme Court decisions have reflected her tenure on the Court of Appeals. She has been a moderate with respect for precedent and a sensitivity to the consequences of the case. (RLP)

Bibliography

Henry, Christopher. "Ruth Bader Ginsburg." In Leon Friedman and Fred I. Israel, eds. *The Justices of the United States Supreme Court: Their Lives and Major Opinions.* 5th ed. New York: Chelsea House Publishers, 1997.

Smith, Christopher, Joyce Ann Baugh, Thomas Hensley, and Scott Patrick Johnson. "The First Term Performance of Justice Ruth Bader Ginsburg." *Judicature* 78, no. 2 (September-October 1994): 74–80.

Girl Scouts of the United States

The Girl Scouts of the United States, an organization with more than 2 million girl members and close to 1 million adult members, was established in 1912 to help girls develop their potential as women and citizens in an all-girl setting. Juliette Gordon Low (1860–1927) began the first meeting of Girl Scouts with 18 girls. Low based her idea on the Boy Scout movement, which she had observed while in England.

The Girl Scout movement has been likened to "a roadmap of women's evolution." In 1913, the health badge asked girls not to chew gum or eat sweets. Now girls examine such issues as substance abuse, sexual harassment, and computers. (MEK)

Bibliography

Schultz, Gladys and Daisy Gordon Lawrence. *Lady from Savannah: The Life of Juliette Low.* Philadelphia: Lippincott, 1958.

Strickland, Charles E. "Juliette Low, the Girl Scouts, and the Role of American Women." In Mary Kelley, ed. *Woman's Being, Woman's Place.* Boston: G. K. Hall, 1977.

Glass Ceiling

The metaphor of the glass ceiling for women in management positions describes an invisible but impermeable structural barrier constructed by corporate leaders to impede and prevent women (and minorities) from reaching senior ranks in an organization. Women's upward mobility is impeded so that they do not rise beyond the middle levels of management. They are prevented from reaching the highest levels of the business world regardless of their accomplishments, experiences, capabilities, and merit. The term entered the sphere of public conventional usage and wisdom about a decade ago when in 1986 *The Wall Street Journal* used the term in its "Corporate Woman" column.

Various types of data point to the existence of the glass ceiling. As a result, the Glass Ceiling Act was enacted as Title II of the **Civil Rights Act of 1991**. This act established a bipartisan Glass Ceiling Commission chaired by the secretary of labor. The 21-member commission was given the task of conducting a study and preparing recommendations that would eliminate artificial barriers to the advancement of women and minorities to management and decision-making positions in business. The fact-finding report of the commission reinforces the appropriateness of the metaphor of a glass ceiling.

Women and minorities rarely penetrate this glass barrier to get to the highest levels of business. Thus, the data show that 97 percent of senior managers in American *Fortune 500* companies are white and 95 percent to 97 percent are male. In the *Fortune 2000* industrial and service companies, only 5 percent of senior managers are women, and of that 5 percent virtually all are white, showing the difficulty faced by women of color.

When women and minorities are in executive positions, their salaries are usually lower than those earned by white men. African-American men with professional degrees earn 79 percent of the amount earned by white males even though they hold the same degree and are in the same job category. And the evidence seems to suggest that this state of affairs is not a temporary phenomenon.

Between 1982 and 1992, the percentage of women holding the title of executive vice president rose from 4 to 9 percent and the percentage of those at the senior vice president level rose from 13 to 23 percent. Even though the data seem to show that advancement for white women appears to be taking place, the progress is slow and minority women are severely underrepresented in senior management positions in the private sector when compared to their white female peers.

Public hearings and private studies indicate the following major barriers to the achievement of senior management positions for women: clustering in pink-collar jobs (occupations traditionally held by women) that are low-paying, low-status, dead-end jobs; reluctance as well as resistance of middle level and upper level male managers to place women in line positions that will feed them into senior management positions; lack of mentoring; lack of visibility in jobs that will make their achievements stand out to be noticed; exclusion from informal communications networks; prevalence of bias, insensitivity, and incidents of sexual harassment; and lower compensation levels.

Some of these barriers are societal in nature. Stereotypes, prejudices, and biases play a role in preventing managers from widening the opportunities beyond people of the same gender and color; they want to be comfortable in the workplace, to be surrounded by persons like themselves. There are often perceptions that women are not senior management material because of the many popular stereotypes about women, including women are not as committed to their careers as men, women will not work long hours, women cannot or will not relocate, women lack quantitative skills, and women are warmer and more nurturing than men. However, private surveys like those conducted by Korn/Ferry International and Catalyst in 1989 and 1992 contradict such stereotypes. Women's commitment to their jobs are shown by their lower levels of leave-taking. Women worked the same number of hours as men did in the Catalyst survey. Because women are not asked to relocate as frequently as men this may reduce their chances at advancement. But of those asked to relocate in the 1992 Catalyst survey, only 14.1 percent refused relocation compared to 20 percent of their male counterparts. Thirty-three percent of men but only 18 percent of women in the surveys cited concern for people and nurturing skills as being important in their careers.

Some of the barriers are governmental. There is a lack of rigorous and consistent monitoring of legislation that prevents **sex discrimination** and provides for better opportunities for those who have been traditionally discriminated against by society in the past. Despite the fact that the government has tried to guarantee equality of opportunity through legislation and **affirmative action** programs, enforcement of the law is severely wanting. Sometimes the government is also guilty of inadequately reporting and disseminating information regarding glass ceiling issues.

Other barriers are internal to the business structure. They involve outreach and recruitment efforts. Major challenges to upward mobility are the so-called pipeline barriers. Women and minorities may feel isolated in a corporate world where there are few of them. The comfort level can only be achieved if a certain critical mass of women and minority corporate leaders can be reached. The resulting exclusion from white male groups is also discouraging, especially if one is always made to feel that she is "infiltrating" the "old boy network." Women often have to deal with the phenomenon of "tokenism" (the policy of making only a symbolic effort), whether actual or perceived. In addition, being the test case for future women places an unfair burden on those who make it up the corporate ladder, since they will be under constant scrutiny.

On top of all these barriers, many women have to walk the tightrope between work and home. Their responsibilities go beyond the board room and it is often a challenge in a household for a man and a woman to resist stereotyping females into sex roles determined by society.

How can women shatter the glass ceiling? Many positive approaches require a change in the corporate culture. Some of these might include providing for flexible working arrangements; providing for adequate **child care** through workplace nurseries, as well as making provisions for sick children and after-school care for children; and working out career adaptation schemes, so that there are adequate career opportunities for female managers. Some suggestions for career adaptation schemes include (1) career planning, counseling, and training; (2) providing senior management sponsorships in a mentoring relationship; (3) helping male managers if they happen to be biased and prejudiced come to terms with women managers through training programs designed to change male managers' views of their female counterparts; and (4) the creation of informal support networks for women managers. (CGM)

BIBLIOGRAPHY

Catalyst. *Catalyst's Study of Women in Corporate Management.* New York, 1990.

Davidson, Marilyn J. and Cary L. Cooper. *Shattering the Glass Ceiling: The Woman Manager.* London: Paul Chapman Publishing, 1992.

"Good for Business: Making Full Use of the Nation's Human Capital." A Fact-finding Report of the Federal Glass-Ceiling Commission, Washington, DC, March 1995.

Johnson, B. Kristine. "The Glass Ceiling Task Force Report." MN Planning, January 1995.

Korn/Ferry International and the John E. Anderson Graduate School of Management, UCLA. *Korn/Ferry International's Executive Profile 1990: A Survey of Corporate Leaders.* 1990.

Moore, Dorothy P. and E. Holly Buttner. *Women Entrepreneurs: Moving Beyond the Glass Ceiling.* Newbury Park, CA: Sage Publications, 1997.

Morrison, Ann, et al. *Breaking the Glass Ceiling.* Reading, MA Addison-Wesley, 1987.

A Report on the Glass Ceiling Initiative. Lynn Martin, Secretary of Labor. Washington, DC: Department of Labor, 1991.

Godey's Lady's Book

Godey's Lady's Book was the most important woman's publication of the latter half of the nineteenth century. The magazine was founded in 1830 by Louis A. Godey and Charles Alexander. Under Godey's editorship, the publication had little substance. In 1837, he secured the editorial skills of **Sarah Josepha Hale** who had been editor of the *American Ladies Magazine* (1828–1836). The magazine was a strong advocate of increased educational opportunities for women, but steadfastly avoided political references. Hale was criticized by more ardent activists for her refusal to address important political questions in *Godey's*. Hale remained editor until 1877.

BIBLIOGRAPHY

Finley, Ruth. *The Lady of Godey's.* Philadelphia, Lippincott, 1931.

Woodward, Helen. *The Lady Persuaders.* New York: Iva Oblensky, 1960.

Emma Goldman (1869–1940)

Emma Goldman was an active anarchist speaker and author. Nicknamed "Red Emma" because of her communist leanings, Goldman traveled extensively in the United States lecturing on **feminism** and sexual freedom and against the government and organized religion. In 1892, she was an accomplice in the assassination attempt on Henry Clay Frick, a steel executive involved in the Homestead Strike at Carnegie Steel. While she avoided future acts of violence, she was often harassed by police and officials, especially after the assassination of President William McKinley by anarchist Leon Czolgosz, who claimed that Goldman was his inspiration.

From 1906 until 1917, she served as editor of *Mother Earth*, a monthly publication that espoused her views on the oppressive nature of government and her socialist alternative. In 1908, she lost her citizenship when her former husband Jacob Kershner lost his. She was sentenced to two years in prison in 1917 for her anticonscription activities with the No-Conscription League, which she cofounded with her lover Alexander Berkman. When she and Berkman were released from jail, they were deported to Russia. Disappointed with the Bolshevik Revolution, Goldman became an outspoken critic of the totalitarian Soviet regime. She spent the remainder of her life touring Europe and Canada giving lectures and writing.

BIBLIOGRAPHY

Drinnon, Richard. *Rebel in Paradise: A Biography of Emma Goldman.* Boston: Beacon, 1961.

Goldman, Emma. *Living My Life.* New York: Knopf, 1931.

Wexler, Alice. *Emma Goldman: An Intimate Life.* New York: Pantheon, 1984.

Laura De Force Gordon (1838–1907)

In the 1860s, Laura Gordon lectured on spiritualism and women's rights. In 1870, she was influential in the founding of the California Women Suffrage Society. Serving as president in 1877 and from 1884 to 1894, she was nominated for state senator of California in 1871. **See also** Suffrage.

BIBLIOGRAPHY

Tinkham, George. *History of San Joaquin County.* 1923.

Jamie Shona Gorelick (1950–)

Jamie Gorelick worked for the United States Department of Energy in Washington from 1979 to 1980. She also served on the chairman's advisory council for the United States Judicial Committee from 1988 to 1993 and as general counsel to the Department of Defense from 1993 to 1994. In 1994, Gorelick was appointed deputy attorney general for the Department of Justice.

BIBLIOGRAPHY

Gorelick, Jamie S., Stephen Marzen and Lawrence Solum. *Deconstruction of Evidence.* New York: John Wiley & Sons, 1995.

Kathryn Granahan (1896–1979)

Democrat Kathyrn Granahan succeeded her husband William Granahan as a member of the House of Representatives for Pennsylvania, serving from 1956 to 1962. In 1959, she chaired the Postal Operations Subcommittee that focused on preventing unsolicited mail and the sale and distribution of **pornography** through the mail. Granahan was appointed by President John F. Kennedy as treasurer of the United States, the fourth woman to serve in that post. Due to her failing health, she resigned in 1966.

BIBLIOGRAPHY

Chamberlin, Hope. *A Minority of Members.* New York: Praeger, 1973.

Kay Granger (1943–)

Kay Granger, a Republican, was elected to the U.S. House of Representatives from Texas in 1996. Before her election to Congress, she served three terms as mayor of Ft. Worth. She was active in promoting the economic growth of the city, including aiding in the relocation of several new large employers. She also oversaw the first property tax reduction in 11 years. She also served on the city council and on the Zoning Commission. In Congress, she serves on the Budget Committee.

BIBLIOGRAPHY

Arndt, Randy. "Granger Wins House Seat." *Nation's Cities Weekly* 19, no. 45 (November 11, 1997): 1.

Svacina, Pat. "Fort Worth Uses 'Special Weapon' to Fight Crime." *Nation's Cities Weekly* 18, no. 17 (April 24, 1995): 7.

Warner, David. "A New Blend of Experience" *Nation's Business* 85, no. 6 (June 1997): 48.

Julia Dent Grant (1826–1902)

The wife of President Ulysses Grant, Julia Dent Grant was born in St. Louis on January 26, 1826. She met her future husband when she was 17 years old, and they married in 1848 against her father's wishes. Because of her husband's alcoholism, their married life was a difficult one. Ulysses Grant was often unable to provide for his wife and four children. Julia Grant remained emotionally supportive of her husband throughout his life and rarely left him alone. General Ulysses Grant returned a national hero from the Civil War and was elected president in 1868. For the following eight years, Julia Grant lived what she called "her bright and beautiful dream." She entertained lavishly and was well liked by Washington society. Even her husband's political scandals failed to affect her exuberant social life. When they left the White House, the Grants lost all they owned in stock market speculation. Still, Julia Grant was provided for by Ulysses Grant's *Memoirs*, which he wrote before he died of cancer in 1885. (GVS) **See also** First Ladies.

A strong emotional support for her husband throughout his career, Julia Grant entertained lavishly as first lady and was popular in Washington society. Library of Congress, Prints and Photographs Division.

BIBLIOGRAPHY

Ross, Ishbel. *The General's Wife: The Life of Mrs. Ulysses S. Grant.* New York: Dodd, Mead & Co., 1959.

Ella Grasso (1919–1981)

The first female governor of Connecticut and a two-term Democratic congresswoman, Ella Grasso was born in Hartford, Connecticut, on May 10, 1919. She received a B.A. in economics from Mount Holyoke in 1940 and an M.A. from the same institution in 1942. She served two terms in the Connecticut House of Representatives and chaired the Democratic State Committee for 12 years, from 1956 to 1968. In 1970, she was elected to the U.S. House of Representatives and served two terms. She compiled a strong liberal record, even though she opposed legalized **abortion** and **affirmative action**. She supported, but did not actively campaign for, the **Equal Rights Amendment (ERA)**. When she was elected governor in 1974, she was the first American woman elected state chief executive without succeeding her husband. She also never lost an election in 28 years in public office. As governor of Connecticut, she turned a budget deficit in the state into a surplus within four years. She resigned, due to ill health, in 1980, and died in 1981. (GVS)

BIBLIOGRAPHY

Bysiewicz, Susan. *Ella: A Biography of Governor Ella Grasso.* Old Saybrook, CT: Peregrine Press, 1984.

Dixie Bibb Graves (1882–1965)

Dixie Graves was president of the Alabama Division of the **United Daughters of the Confederacy** from 1915 to 1917, and vice president of the Alabama Federation of Women's Clubs in 1929. She was appointed as a Democrat to the U.S. Senate after the resignation of Hugo Black, who had been appointed to the Supreme Court. Her appointment was controversial because it was obvious the governor was appointing her to preserve the seat for himself in the next general election. She served from August 19, 1937, until January 10, 1938.

BIBLIOGRAPHY

Chamberlin, Hope. *A Minority of Members.* New York: Praeger, 1973.

Edith Starrett Green (1910–1987)

Edith Green, the Democratic candidate for secretary of state of Oregon in 1952, was a delegate at the Democratic National Conventions in 1956, 1960, 1964, and 1968, as well as serving as the chair of state delegations in 1960 and 1968. She was also the U.S. delegate to the 1958 Interparlimentary Conference in Switzerland, a congressional delegate to the 1959 NATO conference in London, and a member of the **President's Commission on the Status of Women (PCSW)**. Green was elected to the U.S. House of Representatives from Oregon, serving from January 3, 1955, until January 3, 1975. In her committee assignment to education and labor and her role as chair for the Subcommittee on Post-Secondary Education, she helped pass the Higher Education Acts of 1965 and 1967, as well as the Higher Education Facilities Act. Green also focused on work-study and grant programs for students and amendments to end discrimination in health, education, and Job Corps training.

BIBLIOGRAPHY

Dreifus, Claudia. "Women in Politics: An Interview with Edith Green." *Social Policy* 2 (January-February 1972): 16–22.

Green, Edith. *Oral History Interviews, Former Member of Congress Association.* Washington, DC: Manuscript Division, Library of Congress, 1980.

———. "School Busing: Are We Hurting the People We Want to Help?" *U.S. News and World Report* 67 (August 18, 1969): 72–73.

Wides, Louise. *Edith Green, Democratic Representative for Oregon.* Washington, DC: Grossman Publishers, 1972.

Isabelle Selmes Greenway (1886–1953)

Isabelle Greenway was elected as a Democrat to the U.S. House of Representatives from Arizona, serving from October 3, 1933, to January 3, 1937. After leaving Congress, she served as a member of the Mount Rushmore Memorial Commission.

BIBLIOGRAPHY

Gordon, Mildred Nixon. "Representing Arizona." *Independent Woman* 12, no. 11 (November 1933): 367, 391.

Martha Wright Griffiths (1912–)

Elected as the first woman lieutenant governor of Michigan in 1982 on the Democratic ticket with James Blanchard, Martha Griffiths served the citizens of the state in this capacity until her retirement in 1990. Griffiths is probably best known for her 20 years of service in the U.S. House of Representatives where she represented Detroit from 1955 until 1974. She was active in shaping social security, tax, and trade policy and was a tireless worker for women's rights. She is responsible for inclusion of the word "sex" in the U.S. **Civil Rights Act of 1964**, and for engineering the strategy that collected the 218 signatures necessary for a discharge petition to bring the **Equal Rights Amendment (ERA)** out of the House Judiciary Committee for a floor vote in June 1970. Griffiths also served in the Michigan legislature (1948–1952) and was appointed, and later elected, as recorder and judge of Recorders Court in Detroit (1953–1954). She graduated from the University of Missouri (B.A., 1934) and the University of Michigan Law School (J.D., 1940). (KM) **See also** Social Security.

Democratic Congresswoman Martha Griffiths of Michigan collected the necessary signatures on a discharge petition to bring the Equal Rights Amendment to a floor vote in 1970. She is shown here addressing an ERA ratification assembly. Photo by Betsy Segal. National Archives.

BIBLIOGRAPHY

George, Emily. *Martha W. Griffiths.* Washington, DC: University Press of America, 1982.

Angelina Emily Grimke (1805–1879)

Angelina Emily Grimke and her older sister **Sarah Moore Grimke** achieved fame and influence as outspoken activists in the abolitionist movement. Unable to live in the environment of the antebellum South, Angelina left her home in Charleston, South Carolina, to visit her sister Sarah in Philadelphia. Her involvement in the **abolition** debate began in 1829 when William Lloyd Garrison published in the *Liberator* a letter she had written testifying to the cruelty of slavery. As a southerner, Grimke's personal experiences fueled the debate. In an attempt to draw more women into the movement, Grimke published *Appeal to the Christian Women of the South* in 1836 and *Appeal to Women of the Nominally Free States* in 1837. In these pamphlets, Grimke argued that slavery harmed white women by condoning adultery between married males and their slaves. Although condemned for their public speaking, the Grimke sisters attracted thousands of men and women to their lectures. In 1838, Angelina married abolitionist Theodore Weld; her health deteriorated after bearing three children in six years. Together with her sister and her husband, she wrote *Slavery As It Is: Testimony of a Thousand Witnesses* (1839), the most popular anti-slavery tract of its time. Although they continued to lecture occasionally, Weld and the Grimke sisters largely retired from public life in 1840. (AM) **See also** Slavery and Women.

BIBLIOGRAPHY

Birney, Catherine H. *The Grimke Sisters: Sarah and Angelina Grimke, the First American Women Advocates of Abolition and Woman's Rights.* New York: Haskell House, 1970.

Lerner, Gerda. *The Grimke Sisters from South Carolina, Rebels against Slavery.* New York: Oxford University Press, 1997.

Sarah Moore Grimke (1792–1873)

The older of the two famous Charleston abolitionist sisters, Sarah Moore Grimke, was born to John Faucheraud Grimke, a South Carolina patriot of Huguenot heritage, and Mary Smith Grimke. Two years following a trip to Philadelphia with her father in 1819, Grimke left home to join the Society of Friends, a Quaker organization. While attempting to speak against slavery at a Quaker meeting in 1836, she was silenced because **abolition** was considered too divisive an issue for pacifists to champion. Grimke left Philadelphia to join her sister in the anti-slavery movement in New York. Although a pastoral letter of the Congregational Ministerial Association of Massachusetts condemned public speaking, the Grimke sisters continued to lecture against slavery. In *Letters on the Equality of the Sexes* (1838), Grimke compared enslavement to the oppression of women. After her younger sister married in 1838, Sarah joined their household and coauthored *Slavery As It Is: Testimony of a Thousand Witnesses* (1839), a documentary of southern newspaper articles describing the realities of slavery. Grimke continued teaching and lecturing until her retirement from public life in 1840. (AM) **See also** Slavery and Women.

Bibliography

Birney, Catherine H. *The Grimke Sisters: Sarah and Angelina Grimke, the First American Women Advocates of Abolition and Woman's Rights*. New York: Haskell House, 1970.

Lerner, Gerda. *The Grimke Sisters from South Carolina, Rebels against Slavery*. New York: Oxford University Press, 1997.

Griswold v. Connecticut (1965)

In *Griswold v. Connecticut,* 381 U.S. 479 (1965), the Supreme Court struck down a Connecticut law banning the provision of contraceptives to married couples. Over the previous two decades, the Supreme Court had refused to consider the constitutionality of this Connecticut law, claiming that the law was seldom enforced and thus past plaintiffs lacked standing. Estelle Griswold, the executive director of the Planned Parenthood League, opened a birth control clinic in violation of an 1879 Connecticut law that prohibited the use of contraceptives and her arrest brought the issue before the Court. The *Griswold* decision found a right to privacy inherent in the Constitution. In addition, the Court ruled that the right to privacy was a fundamental right, meaning that attempts to abridge it by the government would trigger strict scrutiny. Under strict scrutiny, the government must have a compelling or paramount interest to enforce a law.

In a plurality opinion for the Court, Justice William Douglas argued that the right to privacy was found in the shadows or penumbras of the First, Third, Fourth, Fifth, and Ninth Amendments to the Constitution. Three justices (Goldberg, Warren, and Brennan) felt the Ninth Amendment was a sufficient basis for the right to privacy. Two justices (Harlan and White) felt that the due process clause of the Fourteenth Amendment was the appropriate rationale.

The dissenters (Black and Stewart) and critics of the decision argued that there was no constitutional basis for the right to privacy. Justice Potter Stewart argued that this was an uncommonly silly law and should not be the vehicle for the creation of a new constitutional right. Critics claim that *Griswold* was an extreme example of judicial activism. The dissenters charged that Douglas was invoking a new form of substantive due process, a controversial doctrine in disrepute that allows the unelected courts to substitute their judgment for those of the elected legislators.

The *Griswold* landmark became the basis of a number of other privacy connected rights, most notably reproductive rights in ***Roe v. Wade*** (1973). Because the right to privacy is not explicitly stated in the Constitution, attempts to extend that right have been difficult. More recently, the Court has refused to extend that right to gays and lesbians and to countenance the right to die. **See also** Planned Parenthood Federation of America. (RLP)

Bibliography

Emerson, Thomas I. "Nine Justices in Search of a Doctrine." *Michigan Law Review* 64 (1965): 219–34.

Friendly, Fred W. and Martha J. H. Elliot. *The Constitution— That Delicate Balance.* New York: Random House, 1984.

Grove City College v. Bell (1984)

Grove City College v. Bell, 465 U.S. 555 (1984), was an important case involving Title IX of the Federal Education Act (1972), which prohibits **sex discrimination** in any program that receives federal funds. Title IX authorizes the withholding of all federal funds from institutions that impermissibly engage in gender-based discrimination. Grove City College argued that it had no legal obligation to certify its compliance with Title IX because the institution received no direct federal assistance. Grove City College did acknowledge some federal aid but it was in the form of a student loan program, which went directly to the students.

Interpreting a narrow construction of Title IX, the Court ruled in a 6-3 majority that sex discrimination is banned only in specific programs that directly receive federal aid. The decision effectively gutted Title IX and raised the ire and opposition of Congress. Over the next four years, legislation designed to overturn the decision was introduced each year. For three years, the bill died in Senate filibusters. In 1987, both houses of Congress passed the **Civil Rights Restoration Act** to overturn the *Grove City College* decision. President Ronald Reagan vetoed the act, but Congress mustered the super majorities necessary to override the veto, thus overturning the *Grove City College v. Bell* decision. The Civil Rights Restoration Act broadened Title IX to reflect the original intent of Congress: if an institution discriminated on gender grounds, it would lose all its federal funding.

The Civil Rights Restoration Act strengthened Title IX and has been responsible for greater equality for women's programs, most notably funding for college athletics. It has not been the end of the Title IX litigation, however. More broadly, *Grove City* was one of a number of narrow equal protection decisions by the Supreme Court during the Reagan administration that were overturned by congressional statutes. **See also** Title IX of the Educational Amendments Act of 1972. (RLP)

Bibliography

Goldstein, Leslie Friedman. *The Constitutional Rights of Women: Cases in Law and Social Change*. Madison: University of Wisconsin Press, 1988.

Hoff, Joan. *Law, Gender, and Injustice: A Legal History of U.S. Women.* New York: New York University Press, 1991.

H

Sarah Josepha Buell Hale (1788–1879)

Sarah Hale became editor of the *Ladies' Magazine* (the *American Ladies' Magazine* after 1834) in January 1828, often focusing her duties on women's issues. She also took up editorship of another women's issues magazine, ***Godey's Lady's Book***, in January 1837 and continued to focus on equality between the sexes until her retirement from editing in December 1877.

Besides her editorial duties, Hale backed a number of organizations dedicated to women's issues; she worked as secretary of the Ladies Medical Missionary Society of Philadelphia in the 1850s and as head of the Woman's Union Missionary Society in the 1860s.

BIBLIOGRAPHY

Finley, Ruth E. *The Lady of Godey's.* North Stratford, NH: Ayer Company, 1974.

Fryett, Norma R. *Sarah Josepha Hale.* New York: Dutton, 1975.

Okker, Patricia. *Our Sister Editors.* Athens: University of Georgia Press, 1995.

Katie Beatrice Hall (1938–)

Katie Hall began her political career in 1974 when she was elected as a Democrat to the Indiana House of Representatives, where she served until 1976. She then served in the Indiana state senate from 1976 to 1982. On November 2, 1982, Hall was elected to the United States House of Representatives and remained there until January 3, 1985. She failed to be re-elected to the 99th Congress in 1984.

BIBLIOGRAPHY

Catlin, Robert A. "Organizational Effectiveness and Black Political Participation: The Case of Katie Hall." *Phylon* 46 (September 1985): 179–92.

Julia Butler Hansen (1907–1988)

Julia Hansen began her political career as a member of the Cathlamet, Washington, City Council, serving from 1938 to 1946. She also worked as chairperson of the Western Interstate Committee on Highway Policies from 1951 to 1961 and acted as a member of the Washington House of Representatives from January 1939 to November 1960, serving as speaker pro tempore from 1955 to 1960. Hansen, a Democrat, served in the United States House of Representatives from November 8, 1960, to January 3, 1973. In 1975 she was appointed to the Washington State Toll Bridge Authority and State Highway Commission and served until 1981, the last two years as chair.

BIBLIOGRAPHY

Darmstader, Ruth. *Julia Butler Hansen, Democratic Representative from Washington.* Washington, DC: Grossman Publishers, 1972.

Hansen, Julia Butler. *Oral History Interview, Former Member of Congress Association.* Washington, DC: Manuscript Division, Library of Congress, 1979.

Cecile Murray Harden (1894–1984)

Cecile Harden was named Republican national committeewoman from Indiana in 1944 and in 1948. In 1948, she was elected to the first of five terms in the U.S. House of Representatives. A highlight of her tenure was a 1957 bill assuring equal pay for women. From 1959 to 1961, Harden acted as the special assistant for women's affairs for the postmaster general. In 1970, she also served on the National Advisory Committee for the White House Conference on Aging.

BIBLIOGRAPHY

Chamberlin, Hope. *A Minority of Members.* New York: Praeger, 1973.

Florence Kling Harding (1860–1924)

The wife of President Warren G. Harding, Florence Kling Harding was born in Marion, Ohio, on August 15, 1860. She married Warren Harding, a newspaper publisher, in 1891 against her father's wishes. Florence Harding took over the management of the Marion *Star* and effectively helped her husband develop a successful political career. She closely supervised his political campaigns and once said, "I have only one real hobby—my husband." When he became president in 1921, "The Duchess"—as she was called— opened up the White House to tourists and guests. While she

Known as "the Duchess," Florence Harding was a key political and campaign advisor to her husband. Library of Congress.

was well received by the press, there was much negative speculation about her and her husband's relationship to the "Ohio Gang," a group of close associates who were accused of bribery, blackmail, and graft. In the summer of 1923, in the midst of scandal and disrepute, Florence and Warren Harding embarked on a cross-country trip called "Voyage of Understanding." He died of an apoplectic stroke on August 2, 1923, in San Francisco. After his death, Florence Harding recklessly burned all the correspondence that could have implicated or exculpated her husband. (GVS) **See also** First Ladies.

BIBLIOGRAPHY

Adams, Samuel Hopkins. *Incredible Era: The Life and Times of Warren Gamaliel Harding*. Boston: Houghton Mifflin, 1939.

Jane Harman (1945–)

Jane Harman, a Democrat, has represented California's South Bay in the U.S. House of Representatives since 1993. A fiscal conservative, she has supported both a balanced budget amendment and the line-item veto. A proponent of congressional term limits, Harman has supported campaign finance reforms endorsed by several groups including Common Cause and the League of Women Voters. Prior to entering Congress, she served in several staff positions in the U.S. Senate and in the White House before going into private law practice. **See also** National League of Women Voters.

BIBLIOGRAPHY

"The Dirty Dozen." *Mother Jones* 21, no. 5 (September-October 1996): 40.

Bartlett, Roscoe G. and Jane Harman. "Should the Military Return to Gender-segregated Basic Training?" *The American Legion* 143, no. 2 (August 1997): 10.

Florence Jaffray Hurst "Daisy" Harriman (1870–1967)

Daisy Harriman began her political career in 1912 when she chaired the National Wilson and Marshall Association. Her efforts earned her an appointment by President Woodrow Wilson to a four-year term on the Federal Industrial Relations Commission. In 1922, she led the National Consumers' League in opposition to the **Equal Rights Amendment**. In that year, Harriman also cofounded the Women's National Democratic Club. She was appointed to the Democratic National Committee in 1924 and remained on the committee for 32 years. In 1937, Harriman became the second American woman to be named an ambassador when President Franklin D. Roosevelt appointed her minister to Norway, where she served until 1940 when she was evacuated from Sweden. In 1963, she received the Presidential Medal of Freedom from President John F. Kennedy.

BIBLIOGRAPHY

Harriman, Florence. *From Pinafores to Politics*. New York: Holt, 1923.

———. *Mission to the North*. London: G.G. Harrap & Co., 1941.

Louchheim, Katie. *By the Political Sea*. Garden City, NY: Doubleday, 1970.

Pamela Harriman (1920-1997)

After a long and illustrious life at the center of international politics, Pamela Harriman served as American ambassador to France. Born and raised in England and educated in France, Harriman, the daughter of a British baron, adopted the United States as her home. After rising to prominence as a leading **Democratic Party** fund-raiser and activist, Harriman was appointed ambassador in 1993 by President Bill Clinton. Almost as well known for the men in her life as for her political clout, Harriman first married Randolph Churchill, becoming a long-time friend and aide to her father-in-law, Sir Winston Churchill. Her last husband, Averill Harriman, was a former diplomat and governor of New York. (MBS)

BIBLIOGRAPHY

Forbes, Malcolm S., Jr. "The Democrats' Dazzling Diplomat, Pamela Harriman." *Forbes* 155, no. 9 (April 24, 1995): 24.

La Donna Crawford Harris (1931–)

La Donna Crawford Harris is a member of the Comanche tribe and a consultant and nationally known speaker on Indian issues. Born to William and Lily Crawford in Temple, Oklahoma, Harris attended Oklahoma public schools and in 1949 married Fred Harris, who later (1970) became a U.S. senator from Oklahoma. She is the founder and president of the Americans for Indian Opportunity, an organization that works for the equality of Indians, especially Indian women. (AM)

BIBLIOGRAPHY

Schwartz, Michael. *La Donna Harris*. Austin, TX: Raintree Steck-Vaughn, 1997.

Patricia Roberts Harris (1924-1985)

Patricia Harris served as U.S. ambassador to Luxembourg from 1965 to 1967. She then spent time at a prominent Washington law firm and served on a number of boards of large corporations. From 1973 to 1977, she served as the District of Columbia's Democratic national committeewoman. From 1977 to 1979, Harris served in the Carter cabinet as secretary of the United States Department of Housing and Urban Development. During this time, she oversaw creation of the Urban Development Action Grants, which were designed to stimulate private investment in urban development projects. On July 27, 1979, Harris was named secretary of the Department of Health, Education, and Welfare, a post she held until 1981. In 1982, Harris ran unsuccessfully for mayor of Washington, DC.

BIBLIOGRAPHY

Nye, Peter. "Conversation with Patricia Roberts Harris." *Nation's Cities* 15, no. 8 (August 1977): 10-13.

"Patricia Harris, Our Lady in Luxembourg." *Sepia* 14 (December 1965): 18-22.

Harris v. Forklift Systems, Inc. (1993)

In *Harris v. Forklift Systems, Inc.*, 114 S. CT. 367 (1993), the United States Supreme Court broadened the legal definition of **sexual harassment** to include a hostile work environment without proof of extreme emotional distress. Lower courts had disagreed over whether actionable hostile environment sexual harassment cases needed to prove serious psychological harm or other injury. In reviewing the *Harris* case, the Supreme Court reaffirmed the precedent set by ***Meritor Savings Bank v. Vinson*** (1986), in which harassment simply had to create an abusive working environment.

In the *Harris* case, the plaintiff, Teresa Harris, worked as a rental manager for Forklift Systems in Nashville, Tennessee, from April 22, 1985, until October 1, 1987. Charles Hardy, the president of the company, continually told dirty jokes and made sexual references in front of Harris, and even asked her to negotiate a pay raise with him in a hotel room. Hardy would throw objects on the ground for Harris and other female employees to retrieve, as he commented on their clothes and the size of their breasts. Hardy also asked Harris to retrieve coins from his front pants pocket. Hardy's actions made Harris's job stressful to the point where she began crying frequently and drinking, and her relationship with her family became strained. Harris confronted Hardy in August 1987. Despite his promise to stop the harassment, he continued to insult Harris in front of customers and other employees, referring to her as stupid and suggesting that she traded sexual favors for customer accounts. Consequently, Harris quit her job on October 1, 1987, and filed a Title VII action against Hardy for creating an "abusive work environment."

The case was dismissed by the United States District Court for Middle Tennessee on the grounds that while a "reasonable person" might find Hardy's actions offensive, they did not create an abusive work environment. Although the 6th Circuit Court of Appeals upheld the lower court's decision, the Supreme Court overturned the case, interpreting the Title VII definition of hostile work environment to include "discriminatory intimidation, ridicule and insult." In the written opinion of the Court, Justice **Sandra Day O'Connor** clarified that an abusive work environment need not lead to psychological harm or injury; any harassment that detracts from job performance or career advancement violates Title VII. The Supreme Court's decision in the *Harris* case has eased the burden of proof on victims of Title VII **sex discrimination**. (LvA) **See also** Title VII of the Civil Rights Act of 1964.

Bibliography

Stockdale, Margaret S. *Sexual Harassment in the Workplace: Perspectives, Frontiers, and Response Strategies.* Thousand Oaks, CA: Sage Publications, 1996.

Harris v. McRae (1980)

The Social Security Act of 1965 established the Medicaid program to provide federal assistance to states by reimbursing some medical costs for the poor. In 1976, Congress enacted the **Hyde Amendment**, named after chief sponsor Representative Henry Hyde (R-IL). The amendment limited the use of federal money to reimburse **abortion**s. The act was challenged in federal district court as a violation of the religious clauses of the First Amendment, the due process clause of the Fifth Amendment and Title XIX of the Social Security Act. The district court ruled that the Hyde Amendment violated the First, Fifth, and Fourteenth Amendments.

On appeal to the U.S. Supreme Court (*Harris v. McRae*, 448 U.S. 297 [1980]), however, the Court overturned the lower court's decision. The Court stated that "although government may not place obstacles in the path of a woman's exercise of her freedom of choice, it need not remove those not of its own creation. . . . The financial constraints that restrict an indigent woman's ability to enjoy the full range of constitutionally protected freedom of choice are the product not of governmental restricts . . . , but rather of her indigency." In effect, the Court stated that all women had the right to abortions, but the government could not be forced to pay for them. **See also** Freedom of Choice Act; Social Security.

Bibliography

Mendelson, June E. and Serena Domollay. "Courts and Elective Abortion under Medicaid." *Social Service Review* 54 (March 1980): 124–34.

Mezey, Susan. *In Pursuit of Equality*. New York: St. Martin's Press, 1992.

Neuhaus, Richard J. "Hyde and Hysteria." *Christian Century* 97 (September 10, 1980): 849–52.

Anna Symmes Harrison (1775–1864)

Most of Anna Symmes Harrison's political career involved assisting her husband, President William Henry Harrison, in his political career. Anna Harrison served as an advisor and hostess in conjunction with William Harrison's positions as first governor of the Indiana Territory, commander of the Army of the Northwest in the War of 1812, and U.S. congressman and senator from Ohio. Because of poor health and her husband's death after only one month in office, Anna Harrison had little impact as first lady. **See also** First Ladies.

Because her husband died after only one month in office, Anna Harrison had little impact as first lady. Library of Congress, Prints and Photographs Division.

Bibliography

Feinberg, Barbara S. *America's First Ladies.* New York: Franklin Watts, 1998.

Caroline Lavinia Scott Harrison (1832–1892)

The wife of President Benjamin Harrison, Caroline Harrison was born in Oxford, Ohio, on October 1, 1832. "Carrie" and "Ben" Harrison met when they were both teenagers and mar-

Founder of the Daughers of the American Revolution in 1890, First Lady Caroline Harrison was also responsible for the installation of electricity in the White House. Library of Congress, Prints and Photographs Division.

ried in 1853. While her husband pursued his legal career, Caroline Harrison cared for their two children and pursued her own interests, which included active service for the First Presbyterian Church and volunteer work.

Benjamin Harrison came back from the Civil War a hero and started his national political career, which culminated in the White House in 1889. As first lady, Caroline Harrison started a renovation project that would bring modern updates to the mansion, including electricity and additional bathrooms. She was also responsible for starting the presidential china collection and founding the **Daughters of the American Revolution** in 1890. She died in the White House on October 24, 1892, from an infectious disease. (GVS) **See also** First Ladies.

Bibliography

Sievers, Harr J. *Benjamin Harrison*. vol. 1. New York: University Publishers, 1959–60.

Hartford Accident and Indemnity Company v. Insurance Commissioner of the Commonwealth of Pennsylvania (1984)

In *Hartford Accident and Indemnity Company v. Insurance Commissioner of the Commonwealth of Pennsylvania*, 482 A. 2nd 542 (1984), the Supreme Court of Pennsylvania ruled that the state's equal rights amendment banned **sex discrimination** in automobile insurance. Male policyholders argued that it was unconstitutional for them to pay higher rates than females because the categories were based on accident statistics and not on individual driving records and experience. The insurance companies had asked that the insurance commissioner's actions be examined in the light of the "state action" doctrine, arguing that the commissioner had no power to apply federal constitutional standards to private activity. The court, however, determined that the "state action" doctrine was irrelevant.

Automobile insurers typically develop classifications of drivers based on age, sex, marital status, and scholastic achievement. However, research has shown that these standards do not actually identify drivers who will create greater losses. The differences in treatment of males and females is particularly striking for young males who pay more for automobile insurance and for older females who pay a price for living longer. After the passage of **Title VII of the Civil Rights Act of 1964**, which banned discrimination on the basis of sex, pressure was placed on insurance companies to end classifications based on sex. Most states now have laws banning differential treatment in insurance, even though the United States Congress failed to pass the Nondiscrimination in Insurance Bill. *Hartford* is the first case in which a state supreme court applied a equal rights amendment to sex discrimination in insurance. (EP) **See also** Equal Rights Amendment (ERA).

Bibliography

Bamburger, Ruth. "Sex at Risk in Insurance Classifications? The Supreme Court as Shaper of Public Policy." In Lois Lovelace Duke, ed. *Women in Politics: Outsiders or Insiders?* Englewood Cliffs, NJ: Prentice Hall, 1993.

Cheney, Karen. "How Women Pay More Than Men for *Less* Health Coverage." *Money* (April 1997): 29.

Maroney, Patrick and Frank A. Vickory. "Discrimination in Automobile Insurance: Issues and Remedies." *American Business Law Journal* 24 (1986): 269–91.

Hatch Amendment (1983)

In early 1983, Senator Orrin G. Hatch (R-UT) proposed a constitutional amendment that began with the words: "A right to **abortion** is not secured by this Constitution." The amendment would have overturned ***Roe v. Wade*** (1973), returning abortion law to its pre-1973 status and thus allowing both states and Congress to pass restrictions on abortion.

Ultimately, by a vote of 49-50, with Senator Jesse Helms (R-NC) voting "present," the Hatch Amendment fell 18 votes shy of the two-thirds majority needed for a constitutional amendment. The vote was a defeat for President Ronald Reagan, an anti-abortionist who had lobbied senators extensively on the issue. Helms opposed the amendment because it failed to recognize "the unborn child's inalienable right to life." Helms and others within the pro-life movement instead threw their support behind a bill sponsored by Senator Roger W. Jepson (R-IA). Aimed at protecting the fetus, the bill encouraged states to pass new anti-abortion laws, made permanent the temporary ban on federal funding for abortion, and created a federal policy to prevent withholding food or medical treatment from deformed infants. A statute, unlike a constitutional amendment, would have required only a majority vote to pass. However, amendment supporters believed that a constitutional amendment was required to overturn the *Roe* decision and that any outright ban on abortion, such as the Jepson bill, would never clear Congress.

Opponents of the constitutional amendment also included those on the "pro-choice" side who, led by Senator Robert Packwood (R-OR), portrayed their argument as one of choice for women. Packwood charged that the amendment would not prevent abortion but would simply drive it underground, forcing women to risk their lives obtaining illegal abortions. (JJK)

Bibliography

Butler, J. Douglas and David F. Walbert, eds. *Abortion, Society and the Law, Third Edition.* New York: Facts on File Publications, 1986.

Horan, Dennis J., Edward R. Grant and Paige C. Cunningham, eds. *Abortion and the Constitution, Reversing* Roe V. Wade *through the Courts.* Washington, DC: Georgetown University Press, 1987.

Tribe, Laurence H. *Abortion: The Clash of Absolutes.* New York: W. W. Norton & Company, 1990.

Paula Fickes Hawkins (1927–)

Children's rights advocate and former U.S. senator from Florida Paula Fickes Hawkins was born in Salt Lake City, Utah. She attended Utah State University (1944–1947) until she married Walter Eugene Hawkins. In 1972, she became the first Republican public service commissioner in Florida since Reconstruction serving in the past until 1979. In 1980, she was elected to the United States Senate where she championed the cause of missing children. She was defeated in her re-election bid in 1986. (AM)

Bibliography

Hawkins, Paula. *Children at Risk, My Fight against Child Abuse: A Personal Story and a Public Plea.* Bethesda, MD: Adler and Adler, 1986.

Mary Garrett Hay (1857–1928)

In 1895, Mary Hay, a committed **suffrage** activist, joined the Organization Committee of the **National American Woman Suffrage Association (NAWSA)** as its director. From 1910 to 1912, she served as president of New York's Federation of Women's Clubs, and from 1914 to 1918 as director of the **General Federation of Women's Clubs**. In the 1920s, Hay worked for the New York League of Women Voters and the Women's Committee for Law Enforcement. **See also** Club Movement; National League of Women Voters.

Bibliography

Hay, Mary Garrett and Mrs. George Buss. "In What of the Two Big Parties Will You Enroll?" *Woman's Home Companion* 46 (November 1919): 10–11.

Lucy Webb Hayes (1831–1889)

Lucy Webb Hayes is best known for her courageous stance against alcohol, which earned her the moniker "Lemonade Lucy" while she occupied the White House with husband President Rutherford B. Hayes. The first presidential wife to hold a college degree, Lucy Hayes was a politically active partner, though some were disappointed by the traditional subjects she addressed. After becoming the first lady of Ohio in 1868, for example, Hayes used her position to lobby the legislature for a home for Civil War orphans. While her husband sought the presidency, she was described as a "student of politics." Though Hayes was interested in a variety of reform issues, including **feminism** and woman **suffrage**, she muted her interests once in the White House. In addition to the symbolic politics of the liquor ban, Lucy Hayes tackled the pressing issues of American inner cities. As first lady, she served as the honorary president of the Women's Home Missionary Society and pressured Congress to address urban needs. She also frequently listened to debates in the House of Representatives. Lucy Hayes's activities made her so popular as first lady that advertisers used her image to promote household products. (BN) **See also** First Ladies.

Nicknamed "Leomonade Lucy" because of her strong temperance stand, Lucy Webb Hayes was active in many reform causes, including suffrage. She is shown here at her Ohio home in 1888.

Bibliography

Caroli, Betty Boyd. *First Ladies*. New York: Oxford University Press, 1995.

Truman, Margaret. *First Ladies*. New York: Random House, 1995.

Health Care Policy

Health care policy, like the health care system in the United States, is extremely broad and complex. This complexity is reflected, in part, by the size of its expenditures, which amounted to $988.5 billion or 13.6 percent of the gross domestic product (GDP) in 1995. The role that public policy plays in shaping the health care system in this country is more limited than in other Western nations, however, since the majority of health care provision and its financing is carried out by the private sector. Public health care policy encompasses a broad array of functions, including health care financing, delivery, and research, as well as the regulation of many aspects of health care, including private insurers, health care institutions, and professionals. The relevance of health care to policymakers has been increasing during the past several decades, especially at the federal and state levels, because of the relentless growth in health care expenditures and projections of even greater demand for public financing in the future. The percentage of national health care expenditures financed by the public sector has increased over the past decade, while that of the private sector has diminished. Health care financing has become the largest single item in state budgets.

The U.S. health care financing and delivery system has been undergoing especially rapid change for the past 15 years. The increased role of market forces among providers and insurers has been one of the most dramatic developments as evidenced by the growth of managed care and for-profit institutions, as well as the increase in consolidations and mergers among health care institutions. This trend has also been accompanied by a growing number of persons without health insurance (approximately 40 million in 1995). Many factors have been influential in shaping the health care system, including the demand for greater accountability from consumers and insurers, technological growth and innovation, an increase in the elderly and minority populations, the changing professional labor supply, globalization of the economy, and the revolution in information management.

In addition to these influences, public sector policies have also been important in shaping the health care system. During the 1980s, in an attempt to curb the relentless increase in health care costs, a number of initiatives at the national level were adopted to promote the growth of market forces. One of the most significant of these was the congressional decision in 1983 to switch from an inflationary cost-based Medicare reimbursement system to a prospective payment method involving Diagnosis Related Groups (DRGs). Other policies in 1987 forced the long-term care industry to institute a number of new policies to improve quality of care. Changes in Medicaid eligibility and benefits throughout the 1980s and early 1990s extended services to millions of new recipients and contributed to greatly increasing health care expenditures.

While public health care policy has been important in helping to shape the U.S. health care system, public sector policy making in this country is fraught with problems. Health care policy is fragmented and lacks clearly defined goals. Furthermore, lines of responsibility are blurred, with different levels of government and institutions within the same level of government sharing responsibility for various health care functions. This makes it difficult for policymakers to plan and address health care issues comprehensively, such as balancing the goals of providing access to care, controlling rising health care expenditures, and ensuring quality of care.

These characteristics of health care policy emerge from several sources. One of the most important is the fragmentation and complexity of our government institutions themselves. This fragmentation arises, in part, from the structures outlined in the Constitution. The principle of federalism (the balance of power between a central authority and its constituent units), one of the hallmarks of this country's government, ensures that the state and federal governments will both exert a role in shaping public policy. States (and the larger local governments) have historically assumed the lion's share of responsibility for providing care to those not served by the private sector—the poor, mentally ill, and chronically ill—through health departments and mental and other long-term care institutions. In addition, states help finance Medicaid (the medical assistance program for categories of the poor), medical education, and public health programs; they also regulate the insurance industry, license facilities and personnel, and establish health codes. However, since the mid-1960s the federal government has exerted an increasingly important role as the financier of health care for certain groups. It is responsible for Medicare (the health insurance program for the elderly and disabled) and shares financing with the states for Medicaid, the federal health insurance program for the poor. In addition, it sets standards for Medicare providers, determines the safety and efficacy of pharmaceuticals and medical equipment, and conducts health-related research.

Because responsibility for financing health care for different groups is assigned to different levels of government, the generosity of benefits awarded to those groups differs markedly. While federal Medicare standards for eligibility and benefits are universal throughout the nation for the elderly no such standards exist among the states in their treatment of the poor through Medicaid.

Another constitutional principle that promotes fragmentation in policy making in this country is the "separation of powers." Along with federalism, this structure of governing ensures that multiple sources of decision making will occur at each level of government—executive, legislative, and judicial. Furthermore, the decentralized committee structure within Congress creates further obstacles to formulating unified health care policy within that institution. More than 14 committees and subcommittees in the House and 24 in the Senate, along with over 60 other legislative panels, have some direct or indirect responsibility over health legislation. In the context of such institutional fragmentation and the absence of strong political parties or other centralizing forces, formidable barriers exist for policymakers seeking to gain consensus when defining health care goals and policies.

Federal election laws and the need for legislators to raise large sums of money to finance their election campaigns are other features of our political system that help determine health care policy. This arrangement promotes the influence of wealthy, well-organized health care interest groups over those that are poorly organized, such as consumers. The number of health care organizations with a Washington office has grown from 117 in 1979 to more than 740 in 1992. Over the same period, more than 370 health care industry political action committees (PACs) contributed more than $150 million to congressional campaigns. While such resources have not assured that these interests consistently win legislation in their favor, it has assured them a higher level of access to policymakers than the average citizen. Furthermore, such groups are positioned to monitor what is happening within the congressional committees and to help prevent legislation that may be harmful to them.

Their influence poses a serious obstacle to health care policy makers seeking to create a rational, coordinated health care system, which might adversely affect one or more of these private sector groups. The most obvious case occurred in 1993 when health-related special interests—including the American Medical Association (AMA), the Health Insurance Association of America, the Pharmaceutical Manufacturers Association, and many others—spent more than $100 million to defeat President Bill Clinton's proposed Health Security Act, an ambitious piece of legislation to comprehensively redesign the health care system.

Yet another influence on health care policy making is the projection of dramatically increased entitlement expenditures—especially Social Security and Medicare—as the baby boomers retire. Predictions of insolvency in the Medicare trust fund occurring shortly after the turn of the century, along with political pressures to balance the federal budget, have heightened the significance of health care to policymakers and have contributed to greater partisan conflict within Congress.

Throughout the 1990s, members of Congress have struggled with politically acceptable means of curtailing the growth of Medicare. While the private sector health care expenditures have slowed considerably, Medicare continues its troubling climb.

The political culture in the United States, with its preference for the use of the private sector and for limitations on government's role, also helps to shape health care policy. Such distrust of "big government" helped to defeat the 1993 Health Security Act, which called for a much stronger role for the federal government. Such a philosophy has paved the way for the private sector, including health care think tanks such as the Jackson Hole Group, to exert great influence and take the lead in creating new delivery and financing structures.

In recent decades the health care system has come under criticism from a variety of sources for the way in which it relates to women. Feminists have claimed that the health care system systematically demonstrates bias against women. They point out areas such as gender imbalance in employment in the health care sector, the male dominance in the choice of topics for research, and the exclusion of females as subjects of research. Using a variety of political strategies, such as pursuing these issues in the courts, lobbying for legislative changes, and cultivating public opinion, women's groups have succeeded in gaining ground in each of these arenas.

A major criticism of the health care system is that women dominate the lowest levels of health care related employment, such as nursing, nutrition, and housekeeping, with little power, status, or financial compensation. By contrast, men hold most of the positions of authority, e.g., physicians, trustees, and hospital administrators. In 1971, the **women's movement** spawned a class action suit against all medical schools in the nation, which highlighted the extent of **sex discrimination** in admission policies and earned women more equitable consideration of their applications. Subsequently, the number of women admitted to medical schools mushroomed; and now approximately 41 percent of all medical students are women. The less influential health care related positions, however, continue to be overrepresented by women.

Health care research is another important area in which women have successfully use the political process to achieve significant gains. Beginning in the mid-1980s, the Task Force on Women's Issues of the Public Health Service began holding public hearings on the issue of women's health. Their report in 1985 warned that the lack of medical data on women was inhibiting the understanding of women's health problems. The following year, a National Institutes of Health (NIH) advisory committee recommended that women be included in all NIH-sponsored clinical trials unless a legitimate reason existed to exclude them. (NIH represents the major publicly funded research institution of this country.) As late as 1990, a group of prominent women scientists, well aware that this NIH policy was being routinely ignored, formed the Society for the Advancement of Women's Health Research. They then brought their concerns to the **Congressional Caucus for Women's Issues**. With the support of Henry Waxman (D-CA), chair of the House Subcommittee on Health and the Environment, the Women's Caucus requested the General Accounting Office to conduct an audit of NIH's adherence to this policy of including women. The damning evidence from this study, widely publicized by women's groups during the summer of 1990, helped to gain widespread support for improving research related to women's health. Within months, the NIH created the Office of Research on Women's Health (ORWH), and Congress ensured its continued existence and financial stability in 1993 with the adoption of the NIH Revitalization Act. Currently, the ORWH is undertaking the Women's Health Initiative—the largest clinical trial ever conducted—to uncover some of the major questions related to women's health, including menopause, cancer, heart disease, and aging.

Despite these gains, a number of problems remain for women in their attempt to receive adequate health care. Among the most troubling is the financial vulnerability women face. While women are more likely than men to have some form of health insurance, they are also more dependent on a spouse's employment-related insurance or on some public form of insurance (Medicaid or Medicare). Divorce or the death of a spouse leaves many women uninsured. Furthermore, Medicaid is not widely accepted by physicians, and Medicare requires expensive copayments and contains significant gaps in its coverage. Inadequate health insurance is most acute for elderly women. Since women live on average seven years longer than men and are more likely to need long-term care services, this situation disproportionately affects women.

Another potential problem, given the rapid transition to managed care, is the uncertain impact this may have on women. Although public policy guarantees that women enrolled in managed care organizations will have access to both a primary care physician and an obstetrician/gynecologist, early research indicates that women's health care needs, especially for mental health services, may not be adequately met. This concern, along with other complaints about the quality of care delivered to women in general, has prompted a widespread debate within the health care community about the advisability of establishing a women's health specialty akin to the formulation of the pediatric specialty for children.

Although much progress has been made in highlighting shortcomings in the health care system for women, many challenges remain. The impending financial crisis facing the Medicare program and the projected pressures on the federal budget suggest that women will face an uphill battle in winning further concessions from the public sector to meet their unique needs. (JDG) **See also** Social Security.

Bibliography

Friedman, Emily, ed. *An Unfinished Revolution: Women and Health Care in America*. New York: United Hospital Fund, 1994.

Kovner, Anthony R. *Health Care Delivery in the United States*. 5th ed. New York: Springer Publishing Co., 1995.

Litman, Theodor J. and Leonard S. Robins. *Health Politics and Policy*. 3rd ed. Albany, NY: Delmar Publishers, 1997.

Longest, Beaufort B. *Health Policymaking in the United States*. Ann Arbor, MI: AUPHA Press/Health Administration Press, 1995.

Johnson, Haynes and David S. Broder. *The System: The American Way of Politics at the Breaking Point*. Boston: Little, Brown and Co., 1996.

Mann, Thomas E. and Ornstein, Norman J., eds. *Intensive Care: How Congress Shapes Health Policy*. Washington, DC:American Enterprise Institute and the Brookings Institution, 1995.

Margaret M. Heckler (1931–)

Margaret Heckler, a Republican, began her political career by serving on the Massachusetts Governor's Council, a position she held from 1962 to 1966. On January 3, 1967, Heckler began her tenure in the United States House of Representatives, where she served until 1983. During her time in Congress, she served on the Government Operations Committee and the Veterans Affairs Committee, as well as the Banking and Currency, Science and Technology, Agriculture, and Joint Economic committees.

In January 1983, Heckler was named secretary of the Department of Health and Human Services to help oversee Social Security, Medicare entitlement programs, medical research, food and drug safety, and public health projects; she served in this capacity until 1985. On December 17, 1985, Heckler was appointed by President Ronald Reagan as ambassador to Ireland. **See also** Social Security.

BIBLIOGRAPHY

Belonzi, Arthur A. "Margaret M. Heckler; Student Legislator to Ambassador." In Frank P. LeVeners and Jane P. Sweeney, eds. *Women Leaders in Contemporary U.S. Politics.* Boulder, CO: Lynne Rienner, 1987.

Lawson, Peggy. "Three Congresswomen: What Makes Them Run." In *Few Are Chosen: American Women in Political Life Today.* Boston: Houghton Mifflin, 1968.

Anna Hedgeman (1900–1990)

Anna Hedgeman began her political career as assistant to New York City mayor Robert P. Wagner from 1954 to 1958, becoming the first African-American woman to serve in the city cabinet. Hedgeman served as the executive director of the National Council for a Permanent Fair Employment Practices Commission and as assistant to Oscar R. Ewing, administrator of the Federal Security Agency, now a part of the Department of Health and Human Services. In 1953, she served with Ambassador Chester Bowles in India as a representative for the State Department. Hedgeman also dedicated her time and energy to the National Urban League, the National Association for the Advancement of Colored People (NAACP), the Young Women's Christian Association, and the Commission on Religion and Race of the National Council of Churches.

BIBLIOGRAPHY

"Obituary." *New York Times* (January 26, 1990): D18.

Walker, Jesse H. "Anna Hedgeman Made History During Her Time." *Amsterdam News* 16 (February 10, 1990): 1.

Wilma Scott Heide (1921–1985)

Wilma Scott Heide, a former chair of the **National Organization for Women (NOW)** board of directors, worked for maternity choice rights starting in the 1970s. In February 1970, Heide disrupted Senate activities in Washington with demands that the hearings commence to review the **Equal Rights Amendment (ERA)**; the Senate complied. These hearings, which were held from May 5 to May 7, were the first ERA hearings conducted since 1956. Heide also became president of NOW in the 1970s, helping expand the organization's **sex discrimination** and women's rights platform to include other women's issues, such as prison reform. In 1969, she helped initiate *Pittsburgh Press v. Human Relations Commission* (1973), a case in which the Supreme Court decreed that segregated ads were illegal.

BIBLIOGRAPHY

Haney, Eleanor Humes. *A Feminist Legacy: The Ethics of Wilma Scott Heide and Company.* Buffalo, NY: Margaretdaughters, Inc., 1985.

Dorothy Irene Height (1912–)

From 1952 to 1955, Dorothy Height served on the United States Department of Defense's Advisory Committee on Women in the Service. She also served as president of the **National Council of Negro Women** in 1957, on New York's Social Welfare Board in 1958, and on the Council to the White House for International Minority Rights in 1966. Also in 1966, Height was a delegate to the United Nation's Educational, Scientific, and Cultural Organization Conference on Women's Rights, and in 1975 she participated in the tribunal for the **International Women's Year** Conference. In 1986, Height organized the Black Family Reunion Celebration, an annual event that reaffirms the bonds of family and the African-American community.

Dorothy Height (left), pictured here with California Democratic congresswoman Maxine Waters, has been active in both the women's rights and the civil rights movements. National Archives.

BIBLIOGRAPHY

Height, Dorothy. "Speech Delivered at the First African-American Summit." *Vital Issues* 2 (1992): 44–45.

Alexis M. Herman (1948–)

At the age of 29, Alabama native Alexis Herman was appointed by President Jimmy Carter to head the Women's Bureau of the U. S. Department of Labor. Herman also served for four years as the White House director of public liaison during President Bill Clinton's first term. In 1997, Clinton appointed Herman as secretary of labor. She has come under investigation for possible influence peddling in connection with Clinton's re-election compaign in 1996.

BIBLIOGRAPHY

"Herman Performance Appears to Assure Confirmation." *Congressional Quarterly Weekly Report* 55, no.12 (March 22, 1997): 709.

Margaret Hickey (1902–1994)

During World War II, Margaret Hickey chaired the Women's Advisory Committee in the Federal War Manpower Commission. After the war was over, she turned her attention to guaranteeing the rights of women in the workplace. From 1964 to 1966, Hickey chaired the Presidential Advisory Council on the Status of Women for President Lyndon B. Johnson.

BIBLIOGRAPHY

Little, Joan. "Miss Hickey: Her Life's Work was in Helping Women." *St. Louis Dispatch* (December 11, 1994): C1.

"Obituary." *New York Times* (December 10, 1994): 52.

Emily Hickman (1880–1947)

In her political career, Emily Hickman served as a member of the National Peace Conference as well as participating in a number of other causes dedicated to world peace. She also acted as chair of two other organizations, the Committee on Participation of Women in Postwar Planning and the Educational Committee of the Woman's Action Committee.

BIBLIOGRAPHY

Alonzo, Harriet Hyman. *Peace as a Women's Issue.* Syracuse, NY: Syracuse University Press, 1993.

Louise Day Hicks (1919–)

In 1961, Louise Hicks was nominated to Boston's School Committee and won re-election in 1963 and 1965. She unsuccessfully ran for the Democratic nomination for Massachusetts state treasurer in 1964 and lost by about 10,000 votes in an election for mayor of Boston in 1967. Hicks won a position in the Boston City Council on November 7, 1969, and in 1970 was elected to a single term in the United States House of Representatives. In 1972, she again ran unsuccessfully for mayor of Boston. On November 6, 1973, Hicks was re-elected to the Boston City Council.

BIBLIOGRAPHY

"Breeze That Whispered Louise." *National Review* 22 (October 6, 1970): 1038.

Goodman, Ellen. "People: Louise Day Hicks—'When They Call Me a Racist, I Don't Listen . . .'." *Ms.* 4, no. 7 (June 1976): 99–103.

Kuriansicy, Joan. *Louise Day Hicks, Democratic Representative from Massachusetts.* Washington, DC: Grossman Publishers, 1972.

Anita Faye Hill (1956–)

After earning a law degree at Yale University in 1980, Anita Hill worked for Clarence Thomas for two years at the **Equal Employment Opportunity Commission (EEOC)**. In 1991, Hill was subpoenaed to testify at the U.S. Senate confirmation hearing regarding Thomas's alleged **sexual harassment** toward her. Following her testimony, Hill became a *cause celebre* among feminists, although Thomas was confirmed for his position as a U.S. Supreme Court justice by a vote of 52-48. (CKC) **See also** Thomas Confirmation Hearings.

BIBLIOGRAPHY

"Anita Hill." *Current Biography Yearbook*. New York: The H. W. Wilson Co., 1995.

Mayer, Jane and Jill Abramson. *Strange Justice: The Selling of Clarence Thomas.* Boston: Houghton Mifflin, 1994.

Carla Anderson Hills (1934–)

Carla Anderson Hills entered politics in 1959 as an assistant U.S. attorney. In 1962, she joined her husband in private practice; 12 years later, she was appointed assistant attorney general in the Civil Division of the Department of Justice. President Gerald Ford subsequently appointed her Housing and Urban Development secretary, a position that she held from 1975 to 1977. Hills returned to private practice in 1978, and in 1989 she was appointed U.S. trade representative. When Hills rejoined the private sector in 1993, she founded a consulting firm specializing in international trade. (MAB)

BIBLIOGRAPHY

Borrelli, MaryAnne. *Patterns of Opportunity, Patterns of Constraint: The Nomination and Confirmation of Women Cabinet Members in the United States.* Ann Arbor: University of Michigan Press, forthcoming.

Ross, Irwin. "Carla Hills Gives the Woman's Touch a Brand New Meaning." *Fortune* 92 (December 1975): 120–23.

Oveta Culp Hobby (1905–1995)

Parliamentarian of the Texas legislature (1925–1931, 1939–1941), Oveta Culp Hobby married newspaper publisher and former Texas governor William Pettus Hobby in 1931. She became the Houston *Post* publisher in 1952. In 1941, her political career moved to Washington; she was appointed director of the War Department's Women's Interest Section. In 1942, she was appointed director of the Women's Auxiliary Army Corps (later the **Women's Army Corps**). She retired in 1945, the first woman to receive the Distinguished Service Medal. A member of Citizens for Eisenhower, Hobby also founded Democrats for Eisenhower. She was subsequently appointed head of the Federal Security Administration, which was reorganized in 1953 as the Department of Health, Education, and Welfare. The second woman Cabinet secretary, Hobby served for 31 months. (MAB)

BIBLIOGRAPHY

Borrelli, MaryAnne. *Patterns of Opportunity, Patterns of Constraint: The Nomination and Confirmation of Women Cabinet Members in the United States.* Ann Arbor: University of Michigan Press, forthcoming.

Crawford, Ann Fears and Crystal Sasse Ragsdale. "Mrs. Secretary, Oveta Culp Hobby." In *Women in Texas*. Austin: State House Press, 1992.

Hodgson v. Minnesota (1990)

In 1981, Minnesota enacted a law that required that both parents be notified if their minor child sought an **abortion** and that after notification the doctor must wait 48 hours before performing the procedure. The law excluded the following circumstances: when the minor had been a victim of abuse by her parents, when there was an emergency, or when a "reasonably diligent effort" to contact the parents had failed. The law also provided for a judicial bypass procedure if the two-parent notification section of the act were ruled unconstitutional.

The law was declared invalid in district court in 1986 when a coalition of doctors, clinics, minors, and parents filed suit alleging that the law violated the equal protection and due process clauses of the Fourteenth Amendment. The decision was reversed when the entire panel of the 8th Circuit reheard the case. On appeal to the U.S. Supreme Court, the requirement to notify both parents was struck down by a 5-4 decision that included Justices John Paul Stevens, Thurgood Marshall, William Brennan, Harry Blackmun, and **Sandra Day O'Connor**. However, in *Hodgson v. Minnesota*, 497 U.S. 417 (1990), by a 5-4 decision that included Justices O'Connor, Anthony Kennedy, Antonin Scalia, Byron White, and Chief Justice William Rehnquist, the Court held that the 48-hour waiting period was constitutional.

Bibliography

Baer, Judith A. *Women in American Law*. New York: Holmes & Meier, 1996.

Boumil, Marcia Mobilia and Stephen C. Hicks. *Women and the Law*. Littleton, CO: Fred B. Rothman & Co., 1992.

Jane Marguerreta Hoey (1892–1968)

After helping to form the Bureau of the United States Social Security Administration, Jane Hoey became its director in 1936. She served the bureau until November 3, 1953, when she was removed by President Dwight D. Eisenhower. During her tenure, she was responsible for administrating the Social Security Act of 1935. Hoey also served on the Executive Committee of the National Council on Social Work Education and the National Welfare Assembly. **See also** Social Security.

Bibliography

Axinn, June and Herman Levin. *Social Welfare: A History of the American Response Need.* New York: Mead Dodd, 1975.

Hoey, Jane M. "The Federal Government and Desirable Standards of State and Local Administration." *National Conference of Social Work Proceedings*. 1937.

Mohler, Dorothy. "Jane Hoey and Agnes Regan, Women in Washington." *Catholics in America.* 1976.

Anna Rosenberg Hoffman (1902–1983)

Anna Hoffman served as the New York State regional director of the National Recovery Administration in 1935 and of the War Manpower Commission from 1942 to 1945. She was also sent to Europe on fact-finding missions by President Franklin D. Roosevelt in 1944 and President Harry S. Truman in 1945. Hoffman served as assistant secretary of defense from 1950 through 1953, the highest Pentagon position ever held by a woman.

Bibliography

Hudson, Lynn. "The Confident Confidante." *50 Plus* 21 (August 1981): 56.

"Obituary." *New York Times* (May 19, 1983): 25.

Jeanne Marjorie Holm (1921–)

Jeanne Holm served as director of Women in the Air Force from 1965 to 1973. Holm continued her service to the U.S. military in 1973 when she was named secretary of the Air Force Personnel Council; she maintained this position until 1975. Holm went on to serve as special assistant to the president from 1976 to 1977. She has lectured and written extensively on workforce issues and women serving in the military. She has become a leading expert and advocate for an expanded role for women in the military. **See also** Military Service.

Bibliography

Holm, Jeanne M. *Women in the Military: An Unfinished Revolution.* new ed. Novato, CA: Presidio Press, 1992.

Marjorie Sewell Holt (1920–)

In 1971, Marjorie Holt, a long-time lawyer became counsel for the Maryland State Federation of Republican Women, a role she maintained until 1972. Holt also was a member from 1970 to 1972 in the Maryland Governor's Commission on Law Enforcement and the Administration of Justice. Holt was a four-time delegate to the National Republican Convention, attending gatherings in 1968, 1976, 1980, and 1984. She was nominated in 1973 to the United States Congress and served until July 1987. At that time, President Ronald Reagan nominated her for membership on the General Advisory Committee on Arms Control and Disarmament.

Bibliography

Holt, Marjorie. *Case Against the Reckless Congress.* New York: Jameson Books, 1976.

Elizabeth Holtzman (1941–)

The media called Elizabeth Holtzman (D-NY) a "giant killer" after she defeated incumbent Emanuel Cellar in a 1972 congressional race in New York. She subsequently served four terms in the U.S. House of Representatives as the representative from the 16th District. A liberal feminist, Holtzman was instrumental in the formation of the **Congresswomen's Caucus** in 1977, serving on a steering committee to discuss the services such a group could offer. (In 1981, the group was reorganized into the **Congressional Caucus for Women's Is-**

sues.) Holtzman also served as one of the first co-chairs of the Congresswomen's Caucus. She resigned her House seat in 1980 to launch an unsuccessful bid for Republican Senator Alfonse D'Amato's seat.

In 1992, Holtzman was one of four people who were vying for the Democratic nomination for a New York Senate seat. Holtzman drew fire from both the media and some prominent feminists for launching attacks at the front-runner—another well-known woman, **Geraldine Ferraro**. After the race, Holtzman was dubbed the "town witch," and the race a "cat fight." Ferraro came in second in that primary, and Holtzman last, after Reverend Al Sharpton. (MEK)

BIBLIOGRAPHY

Lamson, Peggy. "Elizabeth Holtzman and the Impeachment of Richard Nixon." In James David Barker and Barbara Kellerman, eds. *Women Leaders in American Politics.* Englewood Cliffs, NJ: Prentice Hall, 1986.

Rimmerman, Craig A. "Why Women Run Against Women." In Elizabeth Adell Cook, Sue Thomas, and Clyde Wilcox, eds. *The Year of the Woman.* Boulder, CO: Westview, 1994.

Nan Wood Honeyman (1881–1970)

Nan Honeyman served as president of the 1933 Oregon State Constitutional Convention, which ratified the Twenty-First Amendment to the Constitution. She also served as a member of Oregon's state house from 1935 to 1937 and as a delegate in the 1936 and 1940 Democratic National Conventions. Honeyman was a member of the U.S. Congress from 1937 to 1939, a representative of the Pacific Coast Office of Price Administration from August 1941 to May 1942, and the customs collector for Portland, Oregon, from 1942 to 1953.

BIBLIOGRAPHY

Honeyman, Nan Wood. "Government Needs Viewpoint of Both Men and Women." *Democratic Digest* 14, no. 1 (January 1937): 6.

Isabelle Beecher Hooker (1822–1907)

In 1868, Isabelle Hooker helped found the New England Woman Suffrage Association. Hooker also spoke at the second conference of the **National Woman Suffrage Association (NWSA)** in 1870. Her work for a federal **suffrage** amendment helped institute Senate Judiciary Committee hearings in 1872, as well as a number of other investigative hearings in her lifetime.

BIBLIOGRAPHY

Farhan, Anne. "Isabelle Beecher Hooker, 'Shall Woman Be Allowed to Vote Upon the Sale of Liquor and in School Matters?'" *Connecticut History Society Bulletin* 36 (April 1971): 41–51.

Stouse, Lynman Beecher. *Saints, Sinners, and Beechers.* Indianapolis: Bobbs-Merrill, 1934.

Darlene Hooley (1939–)

Darlene Hooley, a Democrat, was elected to the U.S. House of Representatives from Oregon in 1996. She serves on the Banking and Financial Services and Science Committees. Prior to her election to Congress, she was a Clackamas County commissioner from 1987. In 1980, she was elected to the Oregon state house, serving until 1986. Hooley defeated an incumbent Republican Jim Bunn, but had to outspend him nearly 2-1. She was aided in her effort by **EMILY's List**.

BIBLIOGRAPHY

"Democrat Wins Race in Oregon." *Chicago Tribune* (November 10, 1996): 8

Jessie Annette Jack Hooper (1865–1935)

In 1900, Jessie Hooper joined the Wisconsin Woman Suffrage Association and from 1915 to 1919, served as legislative chair and the first vice president for the organization. In 1919, Hooper became director of the **National American Woman Suffrage Association (NAWSA)** and the president of the Wisconsin League of Women Voters in 1920. In 1928, she held her last political position, serving as chair of the international relations department of the **General Federation of Women's Clubs**. **See also** National League of Women Voters.

BIBLIOGRAPHY

Hooper, Jessie and Anna Dickie Olesen. "Path Finders to the U.S. Senate." *The Woman Citizen* 7 (December 2, 1922): 22, 25–26.

"Obituary." *New York Times* (May 9, 1935).

Lou Henry Hoover (1874–1944)

The best and most traveled first lady of her time, Lou Hoover was an active supporter of increased opportunities for women. Born in Iowa on March 29, 1874, she attended public schools until her family moved to California in 1884. After hearing a public lecture on geology, she was inspired to enroll at Stanford University where she became the first woman to major in geology. After graduating in 1898, she married Herbert Hoover one year later and his position in a mining firm took them around the world. Together the Hoovers translated the difficult mining text *De Re Metallica* from Latin to English, earning the Gold Medal of the Mining and Metallurgical Society. While abroad, the Hoovers became involved in relief efforts, first in China during the Boxer Rebellion and then in England at the start of World War I. As first lady, from 1929 to 1933 Lou Hoover was the first to give radio broadcasts from the White House. She exercised considerable influence over her husband's appointments of seven women to high-level administrative positions and 35 others to government commissions. She served as national president of the **Girl**

Lou Hoover was the first presidential wife to make radio broadcasts from the White House. Library of Congress, Prints and Photographs Division.

Scouts of America and used her talents as an outstanding organizer and fund raiser to advance social causes. Lou Hoover is not ranked among the most popular **first ladies**, partly because of her poor relationship with the media, her inattentiveness to her appearance, and the anonymity of much of her generosity. She died in 1944. (LvA)

BIBLIOGRAPHY

Gould, Lewis L., ed. *American First Ladies: Their Lives and Their Legacy*. New York: Garland Publishers, 1996.

Mayer, Dale C. ed. *Lou Henry Hoover: Essays on a Busy Life*. Worland, WY: High Plains, 1994.

Joan Kelly Horn (1936–)

Joan Horn, a Democrat, represented the 2nd District of Missouri in the U.S. House of Representatives during the 102nd Congress (1991–1992). She defeated a two-term Republican incumbent in one of the closest congressional races of the 1990 elections but lost the seat in 1992. The Democratic majority in her district was severely diminished by redistricting following the 1990 census apportionment. (KM)

BIBLIOGRAPHY

Bingham, Clara. *Women on the Hill*. New York: Times Books, 1997.

Margolies-Mezvinsky, Marjorie. *A Women's Place*. New York: Crown Publishers, 1994.

Julia Ward Howe (1819–1910)

In 1853, Julia Howe worked with her husband, Samuel Grindley Howe, on his free-soil (anti-slavery) journal *Commonwealth*. In February 1862 the *Atlantic Monthly* published Howe's "Battle Hymn of the Republic," which, by 1864, swept the North as a unifying song. In 1868, she became founder of the New England Women's Club and of the New England Woman Suffrage Association, where she served as president from 1868 to 1877 and from 1893 to 1910. She also served as president of the Massachusetts Woman Suffrage Association from 1870 to 1878 and from 1891 to 1893. Howe was a founder in 1870 of the ***Woman's Journal,*** a magazine that focused on women's issues. She contributed to the magazine as an editor and writer for 20 years. **See also** Abolition; Suffrage.

Best remembered as the author of the "Battle Hymn of the Republic," Julia Ward Howe was also a leading suffragist. Library of Congress, National American Woman Suffrage Association Collection.

BIBLIOGRAPHY

Hall, Florence Howe. *Julia Ward and the Woman Suffrage Movement*. New York: Arno Press, 1969.

Howe, Julia Ward. "The Case for Woman Suffrage." *Outlook* 91 (April 3, 1909): 780.

Representative Women of New England. Boston: New England Historical Publishing Co., 1904.

Hoyt v. Florida (1961)

Hoyt v. Florida, 368 U.S. 57 (1961), challenged a Florida statute that declared women would not be called for jury service unless they volunteered to serve. Seventeen other states and the District of Columbia allowed similar exemptions for women, and in three states women were not permitted to serve on a jury. Hoyt, the appellant, was convicted of second-degree murder of her husband. Hoyt claimed that her trial by an all-male jury violated her constitutional rights under the Fourteenth Amendment. The United States Supreme Court ruled that the statute was not unconstitutional because it did not deliberately exclude women from jury service and that Hoyt's rights were not violated. Justice Harlan wrote that the Constitution "does not entitle one accused of a crime to a jury tailored to the circumstances of the particular case, whether relating to sex or to her conditions of the defendant." He further reasoned that the Florida statute should stand, as the state was "acting in pursuit of general welfare . . . [because] a woman is still regarded as the center of home and family life." (JW1)

BIBLIOGRAPHY

Mahoney, Anne Runkir. "Women Jurors: Sexism in Jury Selection." In Laura L. Crites and Winifred L. Hepperle, eds. *Women, the Courts and Equality*. Beverly Hills, CA: Sage, 1987.

Weisbrod, Carol. "Images of the Woman Juror." *Harvard Women's Law Journal* 9 (Spring 1986): 59–82.

Winnifred Sprague Mason Huck (1882–1936)

Republican Winnifred Huck was elected to fill the vacancy in the U.S. House of Representatives left by her father, Illinois representative William Ernest Mason. The third woman elected to Congress, she served from November 7, 1922, until March 3, 1923. She left Congress and began a successful career as a journalist and lecturer.

BIBLIOGRAPHY

Huck, Winnifred. "What Happened to Me in Congress." *Woman's Home Companion* (July 1923): 3.

Richardson, Anna Steese. "What About the Ladies?" *Collier's* (September 27, 1924): 18–19, 39.

Shirley Mount Hufstedler (1925–)

Shirley Mount Hufstedler initiated her political career after practicing law for 10 years. Appointed to fill an unexpired term on the Los Angeles County Superior Court in 1961, she was elected to the bench in the following year. In 1966, Hufstedler was appointed to the California State Court of Appeal for the 2nd District; in 1968, she was appointed to the U.S. Court of Appeals, 9th Circuit. Always interested in judicial reform, she served on numerous task forces. In 1979, President Jimmy Carter appointed Hufstedler secretary of education. She returned to private legal practice in 1981. (MAB)

BIBLIOGRAPHY

Borrelli, MaryAnne. *Patterns of Opportunity, Patterns of Constraint: The Nomination and Confirmation of Women Cabinet Members in the United States*. Ann Arbor: University of Michigan Press, forthcoming.

Sarah T. Hughes (1896–1985)

Sarah Hughes was a member of the Texas state legislature from 1931 to 1935. From 1950 to 1952, she acted as president for the **National Federation of Business and Professional Women's Clubs**. Hughes was appointed federal district judge for the northern district of Texas by President John F. Kennedy in 1961, and in 1963 she administered the presidential oath of office to Lyndon B. Johnson after Kennedy's assassination.

BIBLIOGRAPHY

Hughes, Sarah T. "Now I Can Throw Away That Speech." *Independent Woman* 34 (February 1955): 63–64.

Moses, Carolyn H. "Miss Sally, Texas' District Judge." *Independent Woman* 17 (April 1938): 107, 118–19.

Hull House

After buying an abandoned Chicago mansion, Charles J. Hull, **Jane Addams**, and Ellen Gates Starr remodeled the building; in 1889, they dedicated Hull House as a settlement house to serve the city's poor, underprivileged, and immigrant populations. Hull House offered a number of services, including arts and crafts classes, education and job programs, and nursery, playground, and boarding house facilities. It also provided artistic outreaches for the community, including a gallery, a theater, and a music school, and provided instruction to poor and immigrant families on a number of levels, including lessons on American middle-class values for new citizens, kindergarten for younger children, and adult education programs for parents and workers.

Hull House also sponsored the Jane Club, a group created by Addams on May 1, 1891. The Jane Club sought to provide housing for young working women by offering room and board for only $3 a week. Besides this, Hull House members were active in lobbying for a number of reforms, including eight-hour work days for women, better working conditions in factories, and other labor issues. In doing so, it gained support from well-known activists such as **Florence Kelley** and Charlotte E. Carr, who managed Hull House in 1938 after Addams's death.

BIBLIOGRAPHY

Addams, Jane. *Twenty Years at Hull House.* New York: Macmillan, 1911.

———. *The Second Twenty Years at Hull House.* New York: Macmillan, 1930.

Scott, Anne Firor. "Jane Addams and the City." *Virginia Quarterly Review* 43, no. 1 (1967): 53–62.

Human Life Amendment

When the U.S. Supreme Court struck down state laws restricting access to **abortion** in 1973 in the ***Roe v. Wade*** decision, anti-abortion forces led by the Roman Catholic Church sought to amend the Constitution to ban abortions. More than 20 "Human Life Amendments" were introduced, although none passed either the Senate or House. The version supported by many activists declared that "The paramount right to life is vested in each human being from the moment of fertilization without regard to age, health, or condition of dependency." Nearly all versions of the amendment would have banned abortion under all circumstances. The National Committee for a Human Life Amendment (NCHLA), organized by the Catholic bishops in 1973, mobilized Catholic women activists at the local level. Although various proposed amendments attracted substantial media and interest group attention, all fell far short of passing Congress by the requisite two-thirds majority, much less ratification by the states. The reasons for these failures were simple: polls showed that substantial majorities of Americans opposed each of the proposed amendments. Although similar amendments have been introduced in Congress in recent years, the pro-life movement has generally abandoned the strategy of amending the Constitution. A human life bill was introduced in the Senate by Jesse Helms (R-NC) and in the House by Henry Hyde (R-IL) in 1981, but with opposition from the **National Organization for Women (NOW)** and other women's groups, the bill was unsuccessful. (CW) **See also** Right-to-Life Movement.

BIBLIOGRAPHY

Blanchard, Dallas A. *The Anti-Abortion Movement and the Rise of the Religious Right.* New York: Twayne, 1994.

Cook, Elizabeth. "National Committee for a Human Life Amendment." *Women's Interest Groups.* Westport, CT: Greenwood Press, 1996.

Muriel Buck Humphrey (1912–)

Democrat Muriel Humphrey entered national politics when she was appointed to the United States Senate by Minnesota's governor to fill the vacancy left by the death of her husband Herbert Horatio Humphrey II. She served in this capacity for Minnesota from January 25, 1978, to November 7, 1978. She did not run for re-election in 1978.

BIBLIOGRAPHY

"Senator Muriel: Following in a Tradition." *U.S. News & World Report* 84 (February 6, 1978): 50.

Humphrey-Hawkins Act. *See* Full Employment and Balanced Growth Act of 1978

Anne Hutchinson (c. 1591–1643)

Hutchinson settled in Boston in the Puritan colony of Massachusetts Bay in 1634. When she began preaching doctrines that contradicted Puritan belief, she was tried for "traducing" the authority of the Puritan clergy, a serious charge, especially against a woman. Although Hutchinson's preaching had been popular, drawing listeners from throughout the colony, she was convicted of the charges and banished from Massachusetts Bay in 1637, the colonial authorities fearing her doctrines, her fanatical approach, and her growing influence. She and her family then settled in Rhode Island Colony. Hutchinson and her family were killed by Indians in 1643.

BIBLIOGRAPHY

Cameron, Jean. *Anne Hutchinson, Guilty or Not?* Boston: Peter Lang, 1994.

Williams, Selma R. *Divine Rebel.* New York: Henry Holt, 1981.

Kay Bailey Hutchison (1943–)

Currently serving as a Republican senator from Texas, Kay Bailey Hutchison has been active in government since 1972. She was elected to the Senate in 1993, replacing the retiring Lloyd Bentsen, a Democrat. Hutchison is the first woman to represent Texas in the U.S. Senate. An unconventional Republican, she is known for her pro-choice stance and her belief that women have to work harder than men to succeed. In the U.S. Senate, Hutchison serves on the Armed Services; Small Business; Intelligence; and Commerce; Science; and Transportation committees. She also serves as deputy majority whip.

Prior to her tenure in federal government, Hutchison was active in Texas state politics. She served in the Texas house from 1972 to 1976 before returning to private life. She also served as Texas state treasurer from 1991 to 1993. She was later indicted for violations of the state ethics and open-records laws. The allegations contended that she had misused her office to further her political career, but she was acquitted in 1994. Her current term in the Senate expires in 2001. (JCS)

BIBLIOGRAPHY

Burka, Paul. "The Trials of Senator Sweet." *Texas Monthly* 21 (November 1993): 134–35.

Gregory, Sophfronia Scott. "Hasta la vista, Bobby." *Time* (June 14, 1993): 31.

Jarboe, Jan. "Sitting Pretty." *Texas Monthly* 22 (August 1994): 80–83.

"Kay Bailey Hutchison." *Congressional Yellow Book.* Winter 1996. Washington, DC: U.S. Government Printing Office, 1996, I-74.

Hyde Amendment

The Hyde Amendment refers to language originally included in the Appropriations Act of 1977 and subsequent appropriations acts that excludes federal reimbursement to states for the costs of abortions. Named after Representative Henry J. Hyde (R-IL), the clause limits federal funds to state Medicaid programs for the costs of both therapeutic and nontherapeutic abortions. Before enactment of the Hyde Amendment in 1976, Congress appropriated funds through Title XIX of the Social Security Act of 1965 to pay the federal portion of the costs for **abortion** services covered under state Medicaid plans. Since the passage of the amendment, Congress has restricted funds either by amendment to the annual appropriations bill for the Department of Health, Education, and Welfare (subsequently the Department of Health and Human Services) or by joint resolution.

Although the original language stated "None of the funds contained in this Act shall be used to perform abortions except where the life of the mother would be endangered if the fetus were carried to term," some Congresses have passed versions that allowed funding in cases of rape or incest.

In 1980, the Supreme Court upheld the constitutionality of the amendment in ***Harris v. McRae***. The appellees charged that the amendment violated the equal protection clause of the Fifth Amendment's due process clause and the free exercise clause of the First Amendment, and abridged the right to choose abortion as granted in ***Roe v. Wade*** (1973). The Court held that states have the right to encourage childbirth and cannot be compelled to fund abortions once federal funds are withdrawn.

In 1994, President Bill Clinton signed into law the least restrictive version of the Hyde Amendment. The appropriations act for the Department of Health and Human Services included the following: "None of the funds appropriated under this Act shall be expended for any abortion except when it is made known to the Federal entity or official to which funds are appropriated under this Act that such procedure is necessary to save the life of the mother or that the pregnancy is the result of an act of rape or incest." The provision was re-enacted unchanged for fiscal years 1995 and 1996. (PMF; JS)

BIBLIOGRAPHY

Millsap, D'Andrea. "Sex, Lies and Health Insurance: Employer-provided Health Insurance Coverage of Abortion and Infertility Services and the ADA." *The American Journal of Law and Medicine* 22, no. 51 (1996).

Oleszek, Walter J. *Congressional Procedures and the Policy Process.* Washington, DC: Congressional Quarterly Inc., 1996.

I

"I Am Woman"

"I Am Woman" was a popular music hit in 1972, written and recorded by Helen Reddy. The song was included in the soundtrack of a Columbia movie on the women's liberation movement entitled *Stand Up and Be Counted.* The lyrics to the song begin, "I am woman, hear me roar, in numbers too big to ignore." The song quickly became the unofficial anthem of the women's liberation movement. Eighty percent of the records were sold to women. In 1973, Reddy won a Grammy award for best female pop vocal for the song. (CKC) **See also** Women's Movement.

Bibliography

Current Biography Yearbook. New York: H.W. Wilson Co., 1975.

Immigrant Protective League (IPL)

The Immigrant Protective League was founded in 1908 in Chicago by a committee of the Women's Trade Union League. This new organization was the result of a study by the Women's Trade Union League on the dangers facing immigrant women who traveled alone from Ellis Island to Chicago. According to the study, 29 percent of the women never made it to Chicago and many became victims of abuse, murder, or forced **prostitution**.

The IPL was led by **Jane Addams**, **Sophonisba Breckinridge**, and **Grace Abbott**, the latter of whom served as director of the organization for most of its existence. Under the guidance of these three women, the IPL provided escorts for immigrant women during their trip from Ellis Island. The IPL also helped immigrant women improve language skills and obtain employment. As the number of immigrants making the trip declined, so did the need for the IPL. By 1921, due in part to declining immigrant numbers caused by the First World War, the group had only two paid staff members. In 1958, the IPL changed its name to the Immigrant Service League, and in 1967 it merged with the Chicago's Traveler's Aid Society and ceased independent functions.

Bibliography

Buroker, Robert L. "From Voluntary Association to Welfare State: The Illinois Immigrant's Protective League, 1908–1926." *Journal of American History* 58 (December 1971): 643–60.

Leonard, Henry B. "The Immigrant Protective League of Chicago, 1908–1921." *Journal of the Illinois Historical Society* 66 (1973): 271–84.

International Ladies' Garment Workers Union (ILGWU)

The International Ladies' Garment Workers Union (ILGWU) was formed in 1900 to organize the rapidly expanding women's ready-to-wear industry. Women represented one-half of the 50,000 members in 1912. Successful strikes in 1920 gave the union recognition as the bargaining agent for most workers in women's clothing. Early contracts delivered safety and sanitation standards in addition to a more equitable pay system. The industry adopted the "union label" following strikes in 1958 and the ILGWU initiated the "Look for the Union Label" campaign in 1975 to educate consumers about the location of manufacture. In 1995, the ILGWU merged with the Amalgamated Clothing and Textile Workers' Union to form the Union of Needletrades, Industrial and Textile Employees (UNITE). (AMD)

Bibliography

Foner, Philip Sheldon. *Women and the American Labor Movement.* New York: Free Press, 1982.

International Union of Electrical, Radio and Machine Workers v. Westinghouse Electric (1980)

In *International Union of Electrical, Radio and Machine Workers v. Westinghouse Electric,* 631 F. 2d 1094 (3d Cir., 1980), the 3rd Circuit Court of Appeals held that plaintiffs were not required to demonstrate they worked at substantially equal jobs to bring suit under **Title VII of the Civil Rights Act of 1964** for wage discrimination.

The case arose when the International Union of Electrical, Radio and Machine Workers (IUE) filed suit against Westinghouse for setting wages in female-dominated job classifications lower than in male-dominated job classifications. Under a plan established in 1965, women's jobs were given a lower grade that the men's jobs and women were paid less than men. Under this plan, with just one exception, all workers in the four lowest grades were women and no women were in the highest four grades.

The district court had dismissed the suit because it interpreted Title VII to require plaintiffs to show that men and women performed equal work. The appellate court reversed the decision to dismiss, pointing out that the lower court ruling would allow employers to discriminate on the basis of sex where they could not on the basis of race, religion, or national origin. (SM)

BIBLIOGRAPHY

Mezey, Susan Gluck. *In Pursuit of Equality: Women, Public Policy and the Federal Courts.* New York: St. Martin's Press, 1992.

International Women's Day

International Women's Day is observed on March 8. It commemorates one of the first organized actions by working women in the world in 1857, when hundreds of women workers in garment and textile factories in New York City staged a strike against low wages, long working hours, and inhumane working conditions.

The United Nations did not begin officially celebrating March 8 as International Women's Day until 1975—during **International Women's Year**. The observance is based on the belief that peace, social progress, full human rights, and fundamental freedoms require the active participation, equality, and development of women. The day is also an acknowledgement of the contributions of women to the strengthening of international peace and security. For women all over the world, the day symbolizes how far women have come in their struggle for equality. (CGM)

BIBLIOGRAPHY

Lawrence, Pamela. "How International Women's Day Began." *Business and Professional Women's Bulletin* (February 1994).

International Women's Year

In a general assembly resolution of December 18, 1972, the United Nations proclaimed the year 1975 as International Women's Year (IWY). A group of women's nongovernmental organizations, having consultative status with the United Nations Economic and Social Council, conceived the idea of International Women's Year. To commemorate the event, an International Women's Year conference was held in Mexico City, Mexico, from June 19 to July 2, 1975. The designation of such an International Women's Year would intensify the action required to advance the status of women, a milestone for the transnational **women's movement**. The designation prompted a number of governments to revise parts of their legal codes, pass new legislation, or establish institutions to attend to women's issues.

The World Conference of the International Women's Year was the first United Nations conference devoted specifically to the interests of women and was also the first UN conference where a majority of delegates were women. In attendance were 1,300 delegates representing 133 nations, seven intergovernmental organizations, 21 UN bodies and specialized agencies, eight liberation movements, and 114 nongovernmental organizations with consultative status with the United Nations.

Three of the major accomplishments of the IWY conference were: (1) the World Plan of Action, which called upon the United Nations to proclaim the decade 1976–1985 as the **United Nations Decade for Women**, Equality, Development, and Peace; (2) the conference set a mid-decade target date of 1980 for a second world conference, the World Conference of the UN Decade for Women, 1980; and (3) Resolution 26, subsequently endorsed by the UN General Assembly, which called for the establishment of an International Research and Training Institute for the Promotion of Women—now entitled the International Research and Training Institute for the Advancement of Women (INSTRAW). (CGM) **See also** *International Women's Day.*

BIBLIOGRAPHY

United States Delegation to the World Conference of the United Nations Decade for Women: Equality, Development, and Peace, 1980, Copenhagen, Denmark. *Report of the United States Delegation to the World Conference on the UN Decade for Women, Equality, Development, and Peace, Copenhagen, Denmark, July 14–30, 1980.* Washington, DC: U.S. Department of State, 1981.

Whittick, Arnold. *Woman into Citizen: The World Movement towards the Emancipation of Women in the Twentieth Century with Accounts of the Contributions of the International Alliance of Women, the League of Nations and the Relevant Organizations of the United Nations.* New York: Athenaeum, Distributed by Muller, 1979.

Winslow, Anne. *Women, Politics, and the United Nations.* Westport, CT: Greenwood Press, 1995.

Patricia Ireland (1945–)

American feminist and president of the **National Organization for Women (NOW)**, Patricia Ireland was born on October 19, 1945, in Oak Park, Illinois. As a college student in Indiana, Ireland became pregnant and went to Japan to have an **abortion**. Her feminist views were reinforced during her second marriage. She was hired as a flight attendant by Pan-Am and soon learned that her health insurance did not cover her husband, although wives were covered. She took action against the policy and it was changed in 1969. Empowered by the experience, she studied law at the University of Miami Law School where she became increasingly aware of the gender discrimination in law. After graduation in 1975, she worked as a corporate attorney for 12 years and also became increasingly active in NOW. She became the vice president of NOW in 1987 and president in 1991. She has tried to expand the image of NOW to appeal to a broader section of American women. Her book, *What Women Want* (1996), coincided with the 30th anniversary of NOW; in it, she tells of her own development as a feminist, which she defines as "the freedom to live our lives as we please, and to reinvent the world as we do so." (GVS) **See also** Feminism.

BIBLIOGRAPHY

Blow, Richard. "What Patricia Wants." *Mother Jones* 21, no. 5 (September 1996): 70–71.

Kristol, Elizabeth. "Song of Myself." *Commentary* 102, no. 3 (September 1996): 83–84.

J

Virginia Ellis Jenckes (1882–1975)

Virginia Jenckes began her political career as secretary of the Washbash Maumee Valley Improvement Association in Indiana, serving in this capacity from 1926 until 1932. Jenckes, a Democrat, was elected as a member of the United States House of Representatives, serving from 1933 until 1939, and as U.S. delegate to the Interparliamentary Union in Paris in 1937.

BIBLIOGRAPHY

Jenckes, Virginia Ellis. "Ladies and Legislation." *Democratic Digest* 8, no. 5 (May 1933): 12–13, 27.

Richel, Virginia. "A Hoosier Congresswoman at Home and Abroad." *Democratic Digest* 14, no. 11 (November 1937): 14, 39.

_______. "What American Women Expect from Congress." *Democratic Digest* 14, no. 1 (January 1937): 8, 31.

Claudia Alta ("Lady Bird") Johnson (1912–)

Claudia Johnson helped finance the successful congressional campaign of her husband, Lyndon B. Johnson, in 1937. She later managed Johnson's congressional office in Washington from 1941 to 1942 while he was in the Navy, as well as assisted in his 1948 campaign for the United States Senate. When Lyndon B. Johnson had a heart attack in 1955, Claudia Johnson acted as liaison so he could continue his Senate position.

An active campaigner, Lady Bird Johnson was an important political advisor to her husband. Library of Congress, Prints and Photographs Division.

In 1960, when her husband was the vice presidential candidate on the Democratic ticket, Claudia Johnson went on a series of speaking tours. During the campaign, she traveled abroad with him on goodwill visits, sponsored fund-raising drives for various organizations, and cultural and humanitarian events for which she served as patroness—including heading the Senate Ladies' Red Cross Unit.

When Lyndon Johnson became president in 1963, Claudia Johnson took active interest in social, political, and economic problems. These activities included touring depressed and impoverished areas of Pennsylvania as well as the Appalachian region of the United States in January 1964. She also held White House luncheons honoring successful women and spoke in tribute of **Eleanor Roosevelt** at the first annual anniversary of the Eleanor Roosevelt Memorial Foundation in New York in April 1964. **See also** First Ladies.

BIBLIOGRAPHY

Flynn, Jean. *Lady: A Biography of Claudia Alta (Lady Bird) Johnson.* Austin, TX: Eakin Press, 1992.

Gould, Lewis L. *Lady Bird Johnson and the Environment.* Wichita: University of Kansas, 1988.

Eddie Bernice Johnson (1935–)

Eddie Bernice Johnson began her career in public office in 1972 when she won election to the Texas legislature. In her second legislative term, she became the first woman in the history of the state to chair a major committee (labor). In 1977, she was appointed by President Jimmy Carter as regional director of the Department of Health, Education, and Welfare, a post she held until 1981. Johnson was elected to the Texas state senate in 1986, becoming the first woman and the first African American to represent Dallas since Reconstruction. Elected to the U.S. House of Representatives in 1992, she has been a strong advocate of women's and minority issues. Reelected in 1994 and 1996, Johnson serves on the Transportation and Infrastructure Committee and is a **Democratic Party** deputy whip.

BIBLIOGRAPHY

Gill, LaVerne. *African American Woman in Congress.* New Brunswick, NJ: Rutgers University Press, 1997.

Margolies-Mezvinsky, Marjorie. *A Woman's Place.* New York: Crown, 1994.

Eliza McCardie Johnson (1810–1876)

Eliza McCardie Johnson, wife of President Andrew Johnson, was limited in her political activities because she managed the family's affairs during her husband's long absences and she had periodic bouts with a form of tuberculosis. From 1835 to 1861, Eliza Johnson cared for the family's five children and

Because of her poor health, Eliza Johnson left most of the responsibilities of White House hostess to her daughter Martha. Library of Congress.

maintained the estate while Andrew Johnson engaged in politics, serving in the state legislature, in the U.S. House of Representatives, as governor of Tennessee, and as a U.S. senator. She joined her husband in Nashville in 1862 when President Abraham Lincoln named him military governor of the state. Her eldest daughter, Martha, performed most of the hostess duties in the White House during Andrew Johnson's presidency because of Emma Johnson's poor health. **See also** First Ladies.

BIBLIOGRAPHY

Caroli, Betty Boyd. *First Ladies.* New York: Oxford University Press, 1987.

Winston, Robert. *Andrew Johnson: Plebeian and Patriot.* Norwalk, CT: Easton Press, 1987.

Nancy L. Johnson (1935–)

First elected in 1982, Republican Nancy L. Johnson (R-CT) is the U.S. House representative for the 6th District of Connecticut. Currently, she serves on the Ways and Means Committee and is chair of the oversight subcommittee. She has also served as a co-chair of the **Congressional Caucus for Women's Issues**. Johnson also served in the Connecticut senate from 1977 to 1983. (MEK)

BIBLIOGRAPHY

Bingham, Clara. *Women on the Hill.* New York: Times Books, 1997.

Johnson v. Transportation Agency, Santa Clara County, California (1987)

In *Johnson v. Transportation Agency, Santa Clara County, California*, 480 U.S. 616 (1987), the U.S. Supreme Court ruled 5-4 that the plan adopted by the transit authority to increase the number of women and minority workers in jobs in which they were underrepresented did not violate the rights of Paul Johnson, who was bypassed for a promotion in favor of an equally qualified woman. *Johnson* was the first case that ruled on the use of **affirmative action** for women. Justice William Brennan wrote in the majority opinion that **Title VII of the Civil Rights Act of 1964** was passed with the purpose of "eliminating the effects of discrimination in the workplace, and that Title VII should not be read to thwart such efforts." Additionally, the Court relied heavily on its decision in *United States Steelworkers v. Weber* in assessing the transit authority's plan. The plan passed muster, according to the majority, because it used a number of factors, including gender, rather than being based solely on gender. The Court also observed that the plan was a temporary measure designed to aid the agency in obtaining a labor mix that more closely reflected the area labor market; also, the plan was reviewed annually and would be eliminated when a more equitable balance had been achieved.

BIBLIOGRAPHY

Baer, Judith A. *Women in American Law.* New York: Holmes & Meier, 1996.

Boumil, Marcia Mobilia and Stephen C. Hicks. *Women and the Law.* Littleton, CO: Fred B. Rothman & Company, 1992.

Johnson v. University of Pittsburgh (1973, 1977)

In *Johnson v. University of Pittsburgh*, 539 F. Supp. 1002 (1973), 435 F. Supp. 1328 (1977), Dr. Sharon Johnson, an assistant professor and biochemist at the University of Pittsburgh, sued the university after being denied tenure. Even though she had published several papers, been admitted to the prestigious American Society of Biological Chemists, worked with graduate students, and performed other professional duties without being notified that her work was unacceptable, Dr. Johnson's tenure was denied on the grounds that she was an ineffective teacher and that her research was irrelevant. Her tenure was denied in a meeting of which she had received no notification, and her teaching ability was judged on four observations of her classroom. She was unsuccessful at locating another position within her time constraints and was notified that she would lose her outside research grant if she was not hired by another university.

Herma Hill Kay notes that *Johnson* was the first time **Title VII of the Civil Rights Act of 1964** had been used to issue an order for an academic professor. This preliminary injunction allowed Johnson to remain at Pittsburgh until the case was reheard in 1977. At that time, it was determined that she had not shown sufficient evidence of **sex discrimination**, while the university had adequately demonstrated her ineffectiveness. Even though the courts and the **Equal Employment Opportunity Commission (EEOC)** had been slow to react to sex discrimination, the Supreme Court decision in ***Reed v. Reed*** in 1971 had created an environment that demanded careful examination of charges of sex discrimination.

Studies show that women in higher education cluster in lower levels of rank in all kinds of universities, but particularly in those with four-year programs and graduate schools. The more male-dominated the field, such as science or mathematics, the fewer the women in the top ranks. According to Virginia Sapiro, of the 60 new scientists accepted to the National Academy of Sciences in 1991, only five were female. Mary Frank Fox maintains that women in academia are constrained by the predominant "male culture" in which men accept, support, and promote one another. The Report of the National Commission on the Observance of International Women in 1976 states that the number of women faculty in higher education remained constant from 1924 to 1975, and that the proportion of women to men actually declined at the ranks of professor and associate professor. They also report that while 60 percent of males had tenure, only 42 percent of females had achieved that status. As late as 1990, reports indicate that women make up only 12 percent of full professors and 25 percent of associate professors at all institutions of higher education. (EP)

BIBLIOGRAPHY

Fox, Mary Frank. "Women and Higher Education: Gender Differences in the Status of Students and Scholars." *Women: A Feminist Perspective.* Mountain View, CA: Mayfield, 1989, 217–35.

Kay, Herma Hill. *Sex-Based Discrimination: Text, Cases, and Materials.* 3rd ed. St. Paul, MN: West, 1988.

Sapiro, Virginia. *Women in American Society: An Introduction to Women's Studies.* 3rd ed. Mountain View, CA: Mayfield, 1994.

"To Form A More Perfect Union...Justice for American Women." *National Commission on the Observance of International Women's Year.* Washington, DC: National Commission on the Observance of International Women's Year, 1976.

Mary Harris "Mother" Jones (1830–1930)

Mary Harris was born of Irish immigrant parents in 1830. She married George Jones, a union organizer, and had four children. In 1867, a yellow fever epidemic claimed her husband and all four children. She went on to become a labor organizer and got the sobriquet "Mother Jones" in 1897 while organizing mine workers in West Virginia. Mother Jones was a petite, white-haired, and profane woman who was able to mobilize workers with her fighting words and brave spirit. One of her many exploits included organizing a "women's army" of striking miners' wives who attacked the scabs and surrounded the mine, bringing the strike to an end and their husbands back to work. (CKC)

BIBLIOGRAPHY

Foner, Philip S. *Mother Jones Speaks: Collected Writings and Speeches.* New York: Monad Press, 1983.

Nies, Judith. *Seven Women: Portraits from the American Radical Tradition.* New York: The Viking Press, 1977.

Paula Corbin Jones (1967–)

Paula Jones was thrust into the national spotlight on May 6, 1994, when she filed a federal civil lawsuit against President Bill Clinton. Jones alleged in her suit that Clinton, while governor, had propositioned her for sex on May 8, 1991, at a Little Rock, Arkansas, hotel. At the time of the incident, Jones was an employee of a state economic development office. She has received little support from the women's groups who came to the aid of **Anita Hill** when she accused Supreme Court nominee Clarence Thomas of sexual harassment. In 1998, an Arkansas judge dismissed the case for lack of evidence. **See also** Jones v. Clinton; Thomas Confirmation Hearings.

BIBLIOGRAPHY

"The Complaint Against the President." *Wall Street Journal* (June, 26 1996): A18.

Ellis, David. "The Perils of Paula." *People* 41, no. 19 (May 23, 1994): 88–94.

Walsh, Kenneth. "The Case that Keeps on Hurting." *U.S. News and World Report* 122, no. 2 (January 20, 1997): 29.

Jones v. Clinton

In June 1994, **Paula Corbin Jones** filed a sexual harassment case against President Bill Clinton. Jones, a former administrative assistant for Arkansas's Industrial Development Commission, claimed in her suit that Clinton, while governor, propositioned her for sex at an economic development conference in Little Rock. Jones declined to have sex with Clinton and said that she was eventually forced to leave state employment because of her inability to earn raises and promotions.

Clinton retained Washington power attorney, Bob Bennett, to lead his defense. Bennett filed a motion on behalf of Clinton seeking immunity from the case for Clinton while he is president. The case reached the U.S. Supreme Court in 1997, and by a 9-0 vote the Court ruled that Clinton did not have immunity from suit. However, in 1998 a lower court ruled that there was insufficient evidence to support Paula Jones's allegations. Jones has appealed the ruling.

In addition to the claim of immunity, the case has been marked by several interesting events. First, few women and women's organizations have come to the defense of Jones as they did for **Anita Hill** when she accused Supreme Court nominee Clarence Thomas of sexual harassment. More importantly, the case has embroiled Clinton in possible perjury and obstruction of justice charges that are being investigated by Special Prosecutor Kenneth Starr, because of Clinton's testimony about an alleged affair with a White House intern, Monica Lewinsky. **See also** Thomas Confirmation Hearings.

BIBLIOGRAPHY

Cohen, Adam. "Will She Have Her Day in Court?" *Time* 149, no. 3 (January, 20 1997): 32–34.

O'Rourke, Jason J. "Jones v. Clinton." *Creighton Law Review* 30 (May 1997): 913–47.

Walsh, Kenneth. "The Case that Keeps on Hurting." *U.S. News & World Report* 122, no. 2 (January 20, 1997): 29.

Williams, Glenn T. "Temporary Immunity." *Nova Law Review* 21 (Spring 1997): 969–1018.

Barbara Charline Jordan (1936–1996)

Barbara Jordan was born in Houston, Texas, in the Fifth Ward, an African-American neighborhood with much **poverty**, strong families, and many churches. Her father was a Baptist minister, and her mother was a domestic worker. She went to Boston University Law School, graduated in 1959, and soon thereafter became involved in Texas politics. She achieved many "firsts." In 1966, she became the first African American since 1883 to be elected to the Texas senate and the first African American to chair a major committee in the state senate. In 1972, she was elected from the 18th Congressional District of Texas, and became the first woman and the first African American elected to Congress from Texas. Congresswoman Jordan made a memorable stance for the rule of law, the sanctity of the United States Constitution, and the ideal that no person was above the law as a member of the House Judiciary Committee during the 1974 hearings and votes on the articles of impeachment against President Richard Nixon. Jordan's simple yet elegant reminder that "we the people of the United States" made the government that derives its powers from the people resonated with many Americans then and now. She explained when casting her "yes" vote for the impeachment articles, "My faith in the Constitution is whole, it is complete, it is total, and I am not going to sit here and be an idle spectator to the diminution, the subversion, the destruction of the Constitution." Jordan's page one obituary in *The New York Times* noted how her resonant voice had mesmerized and "stirred the nation with her Churchillian denunciations of the Watergate abuses of President Richard M. Nixon."

Jordan spoke as one of the people of "we the people." In political office, she resisted being categorized as a woman or an African American, and often insisted that she was in office as a citizen, like everyone else. As both a state and national elected official, she worked to ease the burdens of poverty for people. She sponsored legislation to extend provisions of the 1965 Voting Rights Act to Mexican Americans. Health problems linked to multiple sclerosis pushed her to retire from the House of Representatives in 1978. She went on to a long and distinguished second career as a visiting professor at the University of Texas at Austin's Lyndon B. Johnson School of Public Affairs. Jordan was a keynote speaker at the 1976 and 1992 Democratic Conventions. (LW)

Bibliography

Clines, Francis X. "Barbara Jordan, A Lawmaker of Resonant Voice, Dies at 59." *The New York Times* (January 18, 1996): 1.

Jordan, Barbara and Shelly Hearn. *Barbara Jordan: Self Portrait.* Garden City, NJ: Doubleday, 1979.

Pitre, Merline. "Barbara Charline Jordan." In Darlene Clark Hine, Elsa Barkley Brown, Rosalyn Terborg-Penn, eds. *Black Women in America: An Historical Encyclopedia.* Bloomington: Indiana University Press, 1993.

K

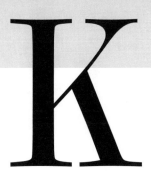

Florence Prag Kahn (1866–1948)

Florence Prag Kahn was born in Salt Late City, Utah, on November 9, 1866. She married Julius Kahn, a Republican congressman for California's 4th Congressional District on March 19, 1899, and for the next 25 years she closely followed his political career and studied law under his tutelage. When he died after a long illness in 1924, she campaigned successfully for his seat in the special election held in February 1925.

As a congresswoman, she distinguished herself with her ability to "hold her own in a male-dominated Congress." She also moved beyond the label of "widow's succession" to make a name for herself in her own right as an intelligent, sharp, and "all-around first rate legislator." Although originally named to the Indian Affairs Committee she finally succeeded in being assigned to the Military Affairs Committee, where her husband had distinguished himself during his lifetime. She also served on the Appropriations Committee and campaigned vigorously for financing for the San Francisco Bay Bridge, and for increasing the military budget so California might benefit from military installations. She served consecutively from the 69th Congress through the 74th Congress and was finally defeated in the 1936 election.

Past the age of 70, she continued to work for the **Republican Party** and sought to increase women's interest in national politics. Throughout her life, she was active in the **American Association of University Women** and the Council of Jewish Women. (GVS)

BIBLIOGRAPHY

Gilfond, Duff. "Gentlewomen of the House." *American Mercury* (October 1929): 18.

Keyes, Frances Parkinson. "The Lady from California." *Delineator* (February 1931): 14, 40, 64, 67, 68.

Marcy Kaptur (1946–)

Democrat Marcy Kaptur, once an advisor to President Jimmy Carter, has represented Toledo, Ohio, in the U.S. House of Representatives since 1982. With strong labor union support, she has opposed free trade agreements that cost manufacturing jobs in her district. Although a member of the **Congressional Caucus for Women's Issues**, Kaptur opposes federal funding of **abortion**s. Currently serving her eighth term, Kaptur is a member of the House Appropriations Committee. (JHT)

BIBLIOGRAPHY

Ehrenhalt, Alan, ed. *Politics in America, 1996.* Washington, DC: Congressional Quarterly Inc., 1995.

Gertzog, Irvin N. *Congressional Women: Their Recruitment, Integration, and Behavior.* 2nd ed. Westport, CT: Praeger, 1995.

Nancy Landon Kassebaum (Baker) (1932–)

Republican Nancy Kassebaum served as United States senator from Kansas from 1979 to 1997. In the 104th Congress, her final term, she chaired the Senate Labor and Human Resources Committee where she cosponsored the Health Insurance Reform Act with the ranking minority member, Senator Edward Kennedy (D-MA). This bill was a major revision of the health insurance system guaranteeing health care portability. Kassebaum favored similar major overhauls in welfare programs, Medicaid, and job training programs that returned the power and responsibility for setting public policy to state legislatures. Kassebaum took what were considered moderate positions on social issues and conservative positions on economic issues. Influential in foreign affairs, she pushed for sanctions in South Africa while apartheid was in place and played a key role in scaling them back as apartheid was dismantled. She was also an important supporter of family planning projects, both domestically and internationally. When Kassebaum was seated in the 96th Congress, she was the only woman in the chamber; by the time she retired, she was one of eight women in the Senate. Kassebaum went to Washington in 1975 as an aide to Senator James B. Pearson and ran for his seat when he retired in 1978. While her four children were young, she served in local elective and state appointive positions: the Maize School Board (1972–1975), Kansas Governmental Ethics Commission (1975-1976), and Kansas Committee for the Humanities (1975-1979). Senator Kassebaum's personal life is marked by two prominent male Republican politicians: her father, Alfred E. Landon, governor of Kansas from 1933 to 1937 and the 1936 Republican presidential candidate; and Howard H. Baker, former chief of staff in the Reagan administration and former senator from Tennessee, whom she married in 1996. (KM)

Bibliography

Richter, Linda K. "Nancy Landon Kassebaum: From School Board to Senate." In Frank P. Leveness and Jane P. Sweeney, eds. *Woman Leaders in Contemporary U.S. Politics.* Boulder, CO: Lynne Rienner, 1987.

Maude Elizabeth Kee (1895–1975)

In May 1951, Elizabeth Kee became the first woman in the United States House of Representatives from West Virginia when she was appointed to fill the vacancy left by the death of her husband, Democrat John Kee. She won re-election in 1952, and served another term in Congress. During her second term, she sat on the House Committee on Veteran's Affairs and went on a self-financed peace tour through South America.

Bibliography

Hardin, William H. "Elizabeth Kee: West Virginia's First Woman in Congress." *West Virginia History* 45, no. 1–4 (1984): 109–23.

Florence Kelley (1859–1932)

A social reformer, Florence Kelley wrote "Our Toiling Children," a pamphlet denouncing child labor in 1889. In 1892, she convinced the Illinois Bureau of Labor Statistics to hire her to investigate the garment industry's labor practices and to conduct a survey of living conditions in city slums. In 1893, she contributed to the passage of a factory act by the Illinois legislature that limited women's work hours, prohibited child labor, and controlled tenement sweatshops. From 1893 to 1897, Kelley served as chief factory inspector. Kelley continued her crusade in 1899 when she was appointed general secretary of the National Consumers' League. In addition to serving in this position, Kelley also helped establish the New York Child Labor Committee in 1902, the National Child Labor Committee in 1904, the **Children's Bureau** in 1912, the National Association for the Advancement of Colored People (NAACP) in 1909, and the Women's International League for Peace and Freedom in 1919.

Bibliography

Blumberg, Dorothy Rose. *Florence Kelley: The Making of a Social Pioneer.* New York: A. M. Keeley, 1966.

Kelley, Florence. "Women and Social Legislatures in the United States." *Annals of the American Academy of Political and Social Science* 56 (November 1914): 62–71.

Sklar, Katheryn Kish. *Florence Kelley and the Nation's Work: The Rise of Women's Political Culture, 1830–1900.* New Haven, CT: Yale University Press, 1995.

Edna Flannery Kelly (1906–)

Edna Kelly was appointed associate research director of the **Democratic Party** in the New York State legislature in 1943; a year later she became chief research director, a role she filled until 1949. First elected in 1948 to the U.S. House of Representatives from Brooklyn, New York, Kelly was re-elected until redistricting placed her against another incumbent, Emanuel Allen, in 1968. During her tenure in Congress, she was a strong advocate of civil rights and Social Security. Kelly participated as a delegate in a number of Democratic State Conventions from 1944 to 1968 and Democratic National Conventions from 1948 to 1968.

Bibliography

Chamberlin, Hope. *A Minority of Members.* New York: Praeger, 1973.

Kelly, Edna Flannery. *Oral History Interview, Former Member of Congress Association.* Washington, DC: Manuscript Division, Library of Congress, 1976.

Sue W. Kelly (1936–)

Sue Kelly's was elected to the U.S. House of Representatives from New York in 1994. A Republican, she has voted consistently as a fiscal conservative, seeking a balanced budget, greater opportunities for small businesses, and an end to the capital gains tax, while also protecting such social programs as Meals on Wheels. Kelly was re-elected in 1996 and serves as vice-chair of the Railroads Subcommittee.

Bibliography

Kiely, Kathy. "The New(t) Women in Congress." *Working Woman* 20, no. 4 (April 1995): 12.

Rosin, Hanna. "Sister Sledgehammer." *The New Republic* 214, no. 26 (June 24, 1996): 6.

Barbara Bailey Kennelly (1936–)

Raised in a political family and experienced in public office, Democrat Barbara Kennelly was elected to the U.S. House of Representatives from Connecticut in 1982. A member of the **Congressional Caucus for Women's Issues** and the Ways and Means Committee, she sponsored economic equity laws improving child support collection and revising the Social Security tax provisions for domestic workers. Kennelly was the first woman appointed to the Select Intelligence Committee. In 1994, she was elected vice-chair of the Democratic Caucus. Although she is the highest ranking woman in the Democratic leadership, Kennelly maintains that no woman has achieved real power in the House. (JHT) **See also** Economic Equity Act (1986); Social Security.

Bibliography

Foerstel, Karen and Herbert N.Foerstel. *Climbing the Hill: Gender Conflict in Congress.* Westport, CT: Praeger, 1996.

Gertzog, Irvin N. *Congressional Women: Their Recruitment, Integration, and Behavior.* 2nd ed. Westport, CT: Praeger, 1995.

Martha Elizabeth Keys (1930–)

Democrat Martha Keys served in the U.S. House of Representatives from Kansas. Keys served in Congress from January 3, 1975, until January 3, 1979. In February 1979, she was made a special advisor to the secretary of the Department of Health, Education, and Welfare, a post she held until May 1980. In June 1980, she was appointed assistant secretary of education, serving until January 1981. After this, Keys worked from 1981 to 1984 as a consultant in Washington on government and education issues. She also served as director of the Center for a New Democracy from 1985 to 1986.

Bibliography

Kuttner, Robert. "What's the Bid Idea? Inside Democratic Think Tanks." *The New Republic* 193 (November 18, 1985): 23.

———. "Who's Who in the Carter Administration." *Washington Monthly* 24 (June 1980): 47.

Carolyn Cheeks Kilpatrick (1945–)

Carolyn Kilpatrick, a Detroit Democrat, was elected to the U.S. House of Representatives in 1996. In addition to being named the interim vice-chair of the Democratic Freshman Caucus, Congresswoman Kilpatrick has been appointed to the House Banking and Financial Services Committee and also appointed a Democratic whip. Prior to her election to Congress, she served 18 years, beginning in 1978, in the Michigan house of representatives.

Bibliography

Jones, Joyce. "Racing Toward the Finish Line." *Black Enterprise* 27, no. 4 (November 1996): 20.

"New Faces of 1997" *Ebony* 52, no. 3 (January 1997): 64.

Wells, Robert Marshall. "Collins Loses to Kilpatrick." *Congressional Quarterly Weekly Report* 54, no. 32 (August 10, 1996): 2264.

Coretta Scott King (1922–)

American civil rights leader, Coretta Scott King, was born in Marion, Alabama, and was educated at Antioch College in Ohio where she received an A.B. degree in 1951. She left for Boston in 1951 to attend the New England Conservatory of Music where in 1952 she met Martin Luther King, a postgraduate student working on a Ph.D. in systematic theology. They were married in 1953. King closely followed her husband's career as a civil rights activist and rejoiced in the success of the **Civil Rights Act of 1964** and the Voting Rights Act of 1965. Throughout those years, King gave concerts across the nation in support of the civil rights movement. She also worked for the antinuclear lobby and participated in the protest movement against the Vietnam War. After Martin Luther King's assassination in 1968, she was made a symbol for her husband's struggles by both the black and white communities and continued his job as a civil rights leader. She received numerous awards in his name and eventually was recognized as a civil rights leader in her own right. In 1969, she published a memoir, *My Life with Martin Luther King*, and in 1971, she inaugurated the Center for Non-Violent Social Change in Atlanta in memory of Martin Luther King. King is a strong believer in nonviolent action, including protest demonstrations, economic withdrawal campaigns, and voter registration and education drives. She has distinguished herself as a writer, a lecturer, and an activist. She has led an exemplary life of public service and her numerous responsibilities have included serving as the president of the Martin Luther King Jr. Foundation, a trustee of the Robert F. Kennedy Memorial Foundation, and a member of the board of directors of the Southern Christian Leadership Conference. King has also worked as a commentator for CNN in Atlanta since 1980. (GVS)

Bibliography

Henry, Sondra and Emily Taitz. *Coretta Scott King: Keeper of the Dream.* Hillside, NJ: Enslow Publishers, 1992.

Huggins, Nathan I., ed. *Coretta Scott King: Civil Rights Leader.* New York: Chelsea House, 1995.

Wheeler, Jill C. *Coretta Scott King.* Edna, MN: Abdo & Daughters, 1992.

Jeane Kirkpatrick (1926–)

The first woman to serve as U.S. ambassador to the United Nations, Jeane Kirkpatrick served the Reagan administration in that position from 1981 to 1985. Considered by many to be a forceful and principled woman, she continued to advise the Reagan administration on foreign policy issues even after she left her UN post.

Fiercely anticommunist, Kirkpatrick is one of the academic founders of the neo-conservative movement. Her decision to switch her party affiliation from Democrat to Republican in 1985 led to speculation that she might be a candidate for political office. Kirkpatrick first rose to political prominence with the publication of her 1979 commentary article, "Dictatorships and Double Standards," in which she argued that the United States ought to prefer authoritarian regimes to totalitarian ones. Many credit this article as the reason Reagan chose her for the UN post. A Columbia University graduate, she is the author of several books, including *Dictatorship and Double-standards: Rationalism and Reason in Politics* (1982), *Legitimacy and Force* (1988), and *Political Woman* (1974). She is currently director of the American Enterprise Institute and teaches at Georgetown University. (JCS)

Bibliography

Harrison, Pat. *Jeane Kirkpatrick.* New York: Chelsea House, 1991.

Ward, Cynthia. "Outstanding Woman on the Bush List." *Conservative Digest* 14 (July 1988): 83–85.

Virginia Knauer (1915–)

In 1956, Virginia Knauer founded the Northeast Council for Republican Women and served as its president until 1964. She was also nominated vice-chair of the Philadelphia County Republican Committee and president of the Philadelphia Congress of Republican Councils in 1958. In 1959, Knauer became the first Republican woman to be elected to the Philadelphia City Council; this achievement was followed in 1963 by her appointment as director of the Pennsylvania Council of Republican Women and membership in the Pennsylvania Bureau of Consumer Protection. On April 9, 1969, Knauer was appointed by President Richard Nixon as special assistant for Consumer Affairs.

Bibliography

"Has Reagan Forgotten the Consumer?" *U.S. News & World Report* 91 (October 5, 1981): 58.

Knutzen, Erik. "Consumer Activists: A Few Middle-aged Americans are Fighting Back. What About You?" *Dynamic Years* 15 (September-October 1980): 32.

Warren, Vicki. "Conspicuous Consumer." *50 Plus* 21 (July 1981): 64.

Coya Gjesdal Knutson (1912–)

In 1950, Coya Knutson was elected to the Minnesota house of representatives where she served two terms. On May 2, 1954, Knutson, the Democratic-Farmer-Labor Party candidate, won a seat in the United States House of Representatives and served in Congress until 1959. During her tenure, she sat on the House Committee on Agriculture.

Bibliography

Beito, Gretchen Urnes. *Coya Come Home: A Congress Woman's Journey.* Los Angeles: Pomegranate Press, 1990.

Biographical Directory of the American Congress, 1774–1989. Washington, DC: U.S. Government Printing Office, 1989.

"Out of Andy's Inn." *Time* 71 (May 19, 1958): 17–18.

"When a Mom Goes Into Politics: Mrs. Knutson." *U.S. News & World Report* 45 (September 5, 1958): 42–43.

Elizabeth Duncan Koontz (1919–1989)

In 1965, Elizabeth Koontz was appointed to the National Advisory Council on the Education of Disadvantaged Children by President Lyndon B. Johnson because of her work in special education. She was also the first African-American president of the National Education Association, serving from 1968 to 1969. She resigned from her position to head the United States Labor Department's **Women's Bureau**. Koontz supervised nutritional programs for the North Carolina Department of Human Resources from 1973 until 1975. In 1975, she was appointed to the United Nations Commission on the Status of Women, and she served as North Carolina's assistant state school superintendent from 1975 until 1982.

Bibliography

Koontz, Elizabeth Duncan. "Women as a Minority Group." In Mary Lou Thompson, ed. *Voices of the New Feminism.* Boston: Beacon, 1970.

———. "Women's Bureau Looks to the Future." *Monthly Labor Review* 93 (June 1970): 3–9.

Juanita Morris Kreps (1921–)

Juanita Morris Kreps received a Ph.D. in economics from Duke University in 1948. She returned to the university in 1955; in subsequent decades, she advanced to full professor and held various high-ranking administrative posts. Her extensive publications focused on aging and women workers. In 1976, Kreps served as an economic advisor during the Ford-Carter presidential transition. She was appointed commerce secretary by President Jimmy Carter when the post was declined by Jane Cahill Pfeiffer. Kreps returned to Duke University in 1979, when her husband's poor health prompted her retirement from the Cabinet. (MAB)

Bibliography

Borrelli, Mary Anne. *Patterns of Opportunity, Patterns of Constraint: The Nomination and Confirmation of Women Cabinet Members in the United States.* Ann Arbor: University of Michigan, forthcoming.

Kreps, Juanita Morris. *Women and the American Economy: A Look to the 1980s.* Englewood, NJ: Prentice Hall, 1976.

Lamson, Peggy. "Juanita Morris Kreps, Secretary of Commerce: In the Vanguard." *Six American Women in Public Life.* Boston: Houghton Mifflin, 1979.

Mary Anne Krupsak (1932–)

Mary Anne Krupsak, a Democat, was elected to the general assembly of New York in 1968 and served two terms. While in the assembly, she advocated the liberalization of **abortion** legislation and the restructuring of marriage and divorce laws for women. On November 7, 1972, Krupsak was elected to the state senate, a position she held until her election as lieutenant governor of New York on November 5, 1974. She did not run for re-election as lieutenant governor. Instead, she choose to run against Governor Hugh Carey in the 1978 Democratic primary. She lost that race and was replaced as lieutenant governor by Mario Cuomo. In 1980, she ran unsuccessfully for the U.S. House of Representatives. While not ruling out a return to politics, Krupsak has remained in the private sector since her loss in 1980.

Bibliography

Hernandez, Raymond. "Lieutenant Governors, Take a Back Seat." *The New York Times* 145 (June 4, 1996): B6.

Madeleine May Kunin (1936–)

After serving three terms as a state legislator and two terms as lieutenant governor, Democrat Madeleine Kunin was elected in 1984 as the first female governor of Vermont and the seventh female governor in the history of the United States. She was re-elected to two additional terms before announcing her retirement in 1990.

In her autobiography, *Living a Political Life*, Kunin describes her initial run for political office as an accident. In 1972, she attended a local Democratic caucus meeting to point out that there had never been any women elected to the Burlington Board of Aldermen. She was subsequently nominated, but lost by 16 votes. That fall she was elected to the Vermont house of representatives.

As governor, Kunin was committed to placing women in key positions within her administration. Approximately 40 percent of the appointees in her second term were women, and she named the first woman to the Vermont Supreme Court. Throughout her tenure as an elected official, Kunin focused her energies on education and environmental policy. President Bill Clinton appointed her deputy secretary for education in 1993. (JAD)

Bibliography

Kunin, Madeleine. *Living a Political Life.* New York: Alfred A. Knopf, Inc., 1994.

L

Ladies Association of Philadelphia

The Ladies Association of Philadelphia, founded in 1780 by Esther De Berdt Reed, was one of the earliest women's relief organizations in the United States. Attracting women who wished to gain a voice in the formation of the country, the group included such influential individuals as Martha Wayles Jefferson, Thomas Jefferson's wife. The group began its efforts by providing clothing and supplies to George Washington's men during the American Revolution and sponsoring national sewing and fund-raising efforts for the war. Because of its dedication to George Washington's army, the Ladies Association of Philadelphia gained the nickname "George Washington's Sewing Circle." After Reed's death, Benjamin Franklin's daughter Sarah Franklin Bache assumed leadership of the association, which renewed its dedication to fostering liberty in a growing United States by cementing the role of women within the new society.

BIBLIOGRAPHY

Bruce, H. Addington. *Women in the Making of America.* Boston: Little Brown, 1928.

Norton, Mary Beth. *Liberty Daughters.* Boston: Little Brown, 1980.

Mary Landrieu (1955–)

The victory of the first woman senator elected from Louisiana was marred by her Republican opponent's allegations of voter fraud. Democrat Mary Landrieu defeated Louis "Woody" Jenkins in the controversial 1996 Senate election. Only 5,788 out of 1.8 million votes separated the two in the contest to replace Senator J. Bennett Johnston. Landrieu retained her seat after the Senate investigation of the allegations fizzled. Her term expires in January 2003. Landrieu was also state representative of Louisiana from 1979 to 1987 and state treasurer from 1987 to 1995. (MEK)

BIBLIOGRAPHY

Bingham, Clara. *Women on the Hill.* New York: Times Books, 1997.

Katherine Gudger Langley (1888–1948)

Katherine Langley was vice-chair of the Republican State Central Committee of Kentucky from 1920 to 1922 and served as the first chair of the Kentucky Woman's Republican State Committee in 1920. An alternate delegate to the 1920 Republican National Convention, she was a delegate to the 1924 convention. Langley was elected to the U.S. House of Representatives in 1926, serving from March 4, 1927, until March 3, 1931. From 1939 to 1942, she acted as railroad commissioner in Kentucky.

BIBLIOGRAPHY

"Kentucky's First Congresswoman." *Literary Digest* 90 (August 21, 1926): 14–15.

"Will It Be Congresswoman Langley?" *Literary Digest* 88 (June 30, 1926): 9.

Last Walk for ERA

On August 22, 1981, **Equal Rights Amendment (ERA)** supporters conducted rallies and walkathons in over 100 U.S. cities to raise funds and publicize the breadth of approval for the constitutional amendment. The walks were held to commemorate the passage in August 1920 of the **Nineteenth Amendment**, which gave women the right to vote. This event came at a critical time for the ERA: three more states were needed to ratify the proposed amendment before the June 1982 deadline. The largest walk was in Los Angeles where 6,000 people, including celebrities like former first lady **Betty Ford**, Maureen Reagan, Lily Tomlin, and Ed Asner, joined the activists. (MP)

BIBLIOGRAPHY

Berry, Mary Frances. *Why ERA Failed.* Bloomington: Indiana University Press, 1986.

Julia Clifford Lathrop (1858–1932)

Julia Lathrop worked at **Hull House**, the famous **settlement movement** house founded by **Jane Addams** in Chicago, from 1890 to 1901 and from 1905 to 1909. In 1893, she was appointed to the Illinois Board of Charities and became a charter member of the National Committee for Mental Hygiene in 1909. Lathrop was also head of the **Children's Bureau** from 1912 to 1921, president of the Illinois League of Women Voters from 1922 to 1924, and an assessor on the Child Welfare Committee of the League of Nations from 1925 to 1931. **See also** National League of Women Voters.

BIBLIOGRAPHY

Addams, Jane. *My Friend, Julia Lathrop.* New York: Macmillan, 1935.

Lass-Taylor, May Madeleine, and Molly Taylor. "Hull House Goes to Washington: Women and the Children's Bureau." In Noralee Frankel and Nancy S. Dye, eds. *Gender, Class, Race and Reform in the Progressive Era.* Lexington: University Press of Kentucky, 1991.

Parker, Jacqueline K. and Edward M. Carpenter. "Julia Lathrop and the Children's Bureau: The Everguise of an Institute." *Social Service Review* 55, no. 1 (1981): 60–77.

Lawrence Strike of 1912

A strike began in Lawrence, Massachusetts, on January 12, 1912, when employers lowered wages and demanded more production because the state had cut the work week from 56 to 54 hours. Over 23,000 workers from 27 different ethnic backgrounds united against their employers, putting aside any race, religion, or gender issues to fight for a common cause. The local division of the Industrial Workers of the World soon joined the workers' cause by sending several of its members, including Joe Ettor, Arturo Grovannitti, **Elizabeth Flynn**, and Bill Haywood, to help with leadership tasks.

The strike gained national attention when Flynn and **Margaret Sanger** assisted women workers involved in the proceedings to find temporary housing for their children. The Children's Crusade brought national attention and sympathy for the strikers and the plight of their children. Even though the strikers met opposition from the American Federation of Labor, who refused to sponsor the strike, the united workers of the Lawrence Strike finally gained an appropriate settlement in the form of a 20-percent wage increase. The strike officially ended on March 1, 1912. The success of the Lawrence Strike influenced garment unions and textile factory workers around the country to use strikes as a means of achieving better pay and working conditions.

Bibliography

Brooks, Thomas E. *Toil and Trouble: A History of American Labor.* New York: Delaconte, 1964.

Foner, Philip S. *Women and the American Labor Movement.* New York: Macmillan, 1979.

Mary Elizabeth Clyens Lease (1853–1933)

In 1884, Mary Lease formed the Hypatia Society, a women's discussion group, which she used as a springboard for a public speaking tour in 1885. In 1889, she helped found the labor newspaper, *The Colorado Workman.* From 1890 to 1894, Lease worked as a speaker for the Farmer's Alliance and the People's Populist Party, helping both attain the national spotlight.

Bibliography

Blumberg, Dorothy Rose. "Mary Elizabeth Lease, Populist Orator: A Profile." *Kansas History* 1, no. 1 (1978): 1–15.

Stiller, Richard. *Queen of Populists: The Story of Mary Elizabeth Lease.* New York: Dell, 1970.

Barbara Lee (1946–)

In 1998, Barbara Lee was elected to fill the unexpired term of long-time California Congressman Ron Dellums, who retired at mid-term. A Democrat like Dellums, Lee was easily elected by the district that includes Oakland. Prior to her election to Congress, she served in the California assembly where she worked with Dellums on a number of policy issues. She will continue to work on such issues as the conversion of military bases to civilian use and child care.

Bibliography

Del Vecchio, Rick. "Ron Dellums' Replacement Is Raring to Go." *The San Francisco Chronicle* (April 9, 1998): A15.

Sheila Jackson Lee (1950–)

Sheila Jackson Lee, a Democrat from Texas, was first elected to the U.S. House of Representatives in 1994 and re-elected in 1996. A champion of women's and minority rights, Lee has used her post on the Judiciary Committee to defend **affirmative action**, **voting rights** legislation, and gay rights. As a member of the 104th Congress, Lee was elected president of the Democratic freshman class, and was appointed to serve as the freshman member of the House Democratic Steering and Policy Committee. Before her election to Congress, she served two terms as a member of the Houston City Council.

Bibliography

"Congresswomen Lead Campaign for Summer Jobs for Black Youth." *Jet* 89, no. 22 (April 15, 1996): 39.

Dite, Lloyd. "The South's New Gen. Lee." *Black Enterprise* 25, no. 11 (June 1995): 32.

Gill, LaVerne. *African American Women in Congress.* New Brunswick NJ: Rutgers University Press, 1997.

Lemons v. City and County of Denver (1980)

In *Lemons v. City and County of Denver*, 620 F. 2d 228 (10th Cir., 1980), the Tenth Circuit Court of Appeals upheld a lower court ruling that had dismissed a suit for wage discrimination brought by Denver nurses. The nurses had claimed that Denver's pay plan violated **Title VII of the Civil Rights Act of 1964** because it sought to base the wages of city employees on the wages of similar jobs in the private sector, making the salaries of city nurses comparable to the salaries of other nurses in the community. The nurses maintained that they did not want their pay based on the pay of private sector nurses because nurses have historically been subject to discrimination. They argued that because nursing is a predominantly female occupation, nurses have traditionally been undervalued and underpaid. They urged that the city be prevented from perpetuating this pattern of discrimination and that it instead base nurses' wages on comparable positions or job titles that were equally valued by the city itself.

The apellate court rejected the nurses' claims on two grounds. First, the court stated that wages are based on a number of factors, including supply and demand, and are simply a reflection of the economic value of the jobs involved. This type of difference, said the court, was not discrimination as banned by Title VII. More fundamentally, the court held that the plaintiffs failed to make a valid Title VII claim of wage discrimination. In making such a ruling, the court used a narrow interpretation of Title VII, in which plaintiffs complaining of wage discrimination have to show that they are being paid less than those performing substantially equal jobs, not just less than employees who might have the same level of skill or responsibility.

The court stated that Congress had not intended Title VII to require employers to pay equal wages for comparable jobs. In essence, the court would only allow Title VII to be used to remedy pay differentials in situations in which men and women worked at substantially equal jobs. In ***County of Washington v. Gunther*** (1981), the U.S. Supreme Court ruled that the plaintiffs were not required to satisfy substantially the equal work requirement in a Title VII wage claim. **See also** Comparable Worth; Sex Discrimination. (SM)

Bibliography

Bergmann, Barbara. *The Economic Emergence of Women*. New York: Basic Books, 1986.

County of Washington v. Gunther, 452 U.S. 161 (1981).

Mezey, Susan Gluck. *In Pursuit of Equality: Women, Public Policy and the Federal Courts*. New York: St. Martin's Press, 1992.

Katherine F. Lenroot (1891–1982)

Katherine Lenroot, one of the leading women government officials of her time, teamed with **Grace Abbott** and **Clara Beyer** to form the backbone of a decision-making body within the **Children's Bureau** that dealt with New Deal legislative matters, including the child-labor provisions of the Fair Labor Standard Act. In 1934, Lenroot was named chief of the United States Children's Bureau where she carried out New Deal reforms and emergency programs. Lenroot took these actions a step further when in August 1941 she proposed a national day care program and dedicated her energies to community initiatives in child support and family planning. From 1914 to 1951, Lenroot worked with the Children's Bureau, the United Nations, and UNICEF, serving on the latter's executive board.

Bibliography

Chafe, William. *The American Woman*. New York: Oxford University Press, 1972.

Alice Leopold (1909–)

Alice Leopold represented the town of Weston, Connecticut, in the state legislature's general assembly in 1949; she was then appointed secretary of state for Connecticut in 1950. In December 1953, Leopold was made director of the **Women's Bureau** of the United States Department of Labor, where she also became assistant in charge of women's affairs.

Bibliography

"New Head for Women's Bureau Takes Office." *Independent Woman* 37 (January 1954): 3.

Liberalism

Liberalism is a theory of the self, society, and the state, in which the freedom of the individual is the highest political value. Liberalism encapsulates a theory of individual moral psychology; concepts of liberty and equality; an understanding of individual rights, particularly private property rights; and a depiction of a limited state ruling under written laws. Although liberalism has many variants, they all share a set of core concepts.

Liberalism encompasses the supposition that the individual is the basic unit of political analysis. Thomas Hobbes' *Leviathan* started from this supposition, distinguishing liberalism from prior political theories that took the polis, class, estate, kingdom, or empire as the unit of political analysis. Starting from the individual, liberal thinkers proceed upon the moral claim that human beings are born free and essentially equal. This claim is best summed up in John Locke's *Second Treatise on Government*, in which he states that men are born in "a state of perfect freedom, to order their actions and dispose of their possessions, and persons, as they see fit . . . a state also of equality." Liberal freedom is conceived of as the ability to act according to one's desires where the law does not limit or proscribe those desires. Liberal equality is also typically seen in relationship to the law. A core meaning of liberal equality is being subject to the same laws, regardless of individual differences. Thus, for example, it has been argued that liberal equality dictates that men and women be treated the same by law.

Liberalism conceives the world as divided into different spheres: one of the primary distinctions within the liberal world view is that between civil society and the state. Civil society is conceived of as a natural domain free from the workings of the political power of the state. Individuals most clearly express themselves in civil society, where they acquire private property, make contracts with others, and form various subgroups.

Liberal thinkers see the state as the product of human ingenuity and as the sole site in which political power is at play. John Locke, for instance, depicted the origins of the state as a contract in which the members of a society define and limit the state's purposes and powers. The state's primary purpose is to protect its members and their property: "The only way whereby any one devests himself of his natural liberty, and puts on the bonds of civil society is by agreeing with other men to joyn and unite into a community, for their comfortable, safe, and peaceable living one amongst another, in a secure enjoyment of their properties, and a greater security against any that are not of it." Historically, liberals have held that the state has no higher purpose than the protection of its members; whenever the state undertakes other tasks, it calls its legitimacy into question. Liberal thinkers have been reluctant to ascribe other functions to the state, fearing the abuse of power. The liberal state is seen as both a reflection of human nature (as perceived by liberal thinkers) and as an amelioration of it. The Federalists, for instance, at the founding of the American Constitution, wrote: "But what is government itself but the greatest of all reflections on human nature? If men were angels, no government would be necessary." The answer to the dilemma as perceived by liberal thinkers such as the Federalists was to create a limited state in which laws, rather than self-interested people, ruled. The liberal state is thus a constitutional state, in which individuals are accorded rights to protect them from others and liberties to protect them from excess arrogation of power by the state. The state is thus a protector of and an ever-present threat to individual freedom.

These shared concepts distinguish liberalism from its two main ideological counterparts, **socialism** and **conservatism**. Typically, liberalism is placed between the two in a "mapping" of the three dominant political ideologies, to the right of socialism and to the left of conservatism. Liberalism may be distinguished from these two alternative ideologies by their differing depictions of the individual, society, and the state. Compared to socialism, in which there is an emphasis on communal cooperation and communal responsibility, the individual under liberalism is portrayed as far more responsible for his or her fate. The individual under liberalism exercises her or his freedom in society, where he or she is accorded rights to private property and freedom to make contracts. Socialist thinkers criticize liberal societies for the oppression they see lurking beneath rights to private property and contract, and for the resulting economic inequality. Most famous, perhaps, is Karl Marx's claim that "property is theft." The state, under liberal regimes, is given a much smaller role than in socialist regimes, where the state redistributes income to achieve a certain degree of economic equality. Historically, socialism as a political doctrine has had little success in the United States, attracting few supporters among either men or women.

Conservatives are far more cautious of change than are liberals and tend to defend tradition much more than liberals. Conservative thinkers such as Edmund Burke see individuals not as isolated beings, but as creatures embedded in families, religious institutions, and governments that should be maintained. Thus conservatives often have defended traditional forms of authority such as patriarchy or monarchy, whereas liberals have demanded that such institutions recognize individual rights. Conservatives also tend to emphasize the importance of some form of traditional moral consensus and may be willing to accord the state a role in preserving such a moral consensus. Liberals, on the other hand, are unwilling to allow political institutions to determine or to enforce values and goals for individuals. One of the distinctive attributes of liberalism is its refusal to grant power to the state to determine individual morality. John Locke's *Letter Concerning Toleration*, the First Amendment's principle of separation of church and state, and John Stuart Mill's *On Liberty* exemplify this viewpoint. Michael Sandel, a contemporary political theorist, in *Democracy's Discontent*, describes this attribute as the defining feature of liberalism:

> "Its central idea is that government should be neutral toward the moral and religious views its citizens espouse. Since people disagree about the best way to live, government should not affirm in law any particular vision of the good life. Instead, it should provide a framework of rights that respects persons as free and independent selves, capable of choosing their own values and ends."

Conservatism, unlike socialism, has achieved support within the United States, and variants of it serve as the main ideological alternative to liberalism for women as well as men.

Liberalism has been the dominant political discourse throughout United States history, although there have been contending voices. Key American political thinkers and documents affirm the centrality of liberalism. For example, Thomas Jefferson's Declaration of Independence starts from the "self-evident truths" that "all men are created equal" and are "endowed by their Creator with certain inalienable rights." The Constitution and the essays of James Madison, Alexander Hamilton, and John Jay, collectively known as *The Federalist Papers*, also display many of the central principles of liberal doctrine. The Constitution limits the power of the government by separating the functions of government and establishing a system of checks and balances that reflects a suspicion of political power. The First Amendment to the Constitution establishes the separation of church and state. In *Federalist Paper #10*, Madison explains that the "first object of Government . . . is the protection of different and unequal faculties of acquiring property" from which "the possession of different degrees and kinds of property immediately results."

Women have played a crucial role in American politics in that they have demanded that liberal practice live up to liberal ideals. In that regard, American women, along with African Americans, have been among the most eloquent and avid liberals, arguing for the importance of recognizing each individual, regardless of gender or race, as an equal being. However, not all women within American politics have embraced liberal doctrines; notable numbers of women espouse conservative views and have argued for conservative causes. Even some feminist theorists have challenged liberal assumptions, especially those regarding the portrayal of the individual and the boundaries between public and private life.

Many political efforts by women throughout United States history have focused on attempts to obtain political, legal, and economic equality—in essence, for the American polity to live up to its promise of liberal equality with regard to American women. American political history is replete with examples of women challenging the denial of their freedom and equality. These examples date all the way back to the seventeenth century, when **Anne Hutchinson** challenged the Puritan Commonwealth of Massachusetts by asserting her equal right to preach, and the eighteenth century, when **Abigail Adams** reminded her husband John, while he was attending the Second Continental Congress, to "remember the ladies." The "ladies," of course, would not receive the right to vote until 1920 and would suffer under numerous other political, legal, economic, and social inequalities throughout United States history.

Throughout the nineteenth century, as the American economy and the state expanded, liberal capitalism was ascendant. However the liberal principle that human beings were essentially equal and born with natural rights was limited in its application to white males (and, until the advent of Jacksonian Democracy in the 1830s to those who held property). Slavery stands as the central dilemma of American politics and American liberalism, and women played key roles in the **abolitionist** movement. Liberal political discourse provided ammunition for American women in their struggles for African-American, as well as their own, equality. A famous document in the history of the American women's rights movement, the **Declaration of Sentiments and Resolutions**, was ratified at the **Seneca Falls Convention** in 1848. It precisely mimics Jefferson's Declaration of Independence, substituting "man" for the king of Great Britain—the tyrant who "has never permitted her to exercise her inalienable right to the elective franchise," and includes a list of "repeated injuries and usurpations."

In the post–Civil War period through the early twentieth century, the primary goal of the American **women's movement** was winning the national right to vote. Many states granted women the right to vote before the national government did. When Wyoming became a state in 1890, it was the first to grant full **suffrage** to women. Other western states followed, but it was not until 1920 that the **Nineteenth Amendment** was ratified, guaranteeing women the right to vote. Through the nineteenth and early twentieth centuries, women also struggled against economic and social discrimination. Many states deprived married women of their property upon marriage. In 1873, the Supreme Court upheld the decision of the Illinois Bar Association to deny admission to women. As late as the 1930s, 26 of 48 states had legislation prohibiting the employment of married women.

Disappointment greeted those women who hoped that their ability to vote would dramatically change their status and national politics. Women did not vote as a bloc, and many of them did not vote at all. From 1920 until approximately 1960, women's political attitudes and voting behavior did not differ significantly from men's. The stratification of social roles may have encouraged women to be more concerned about family issues and to allow men to take responsibility for national and world affairs. As a result, most married women tended to mirror their husband's political attitudes, and most women at that time were married.

The 1960s marked the ascension of the women's movement and women's effects on American politics became much more pronounced. Inspired by the civil rights movement and struck by the discrimination women found as they entered the workforce in large numbers, American women formed a new set of organizations dedicated to equality in all spheres. The **National Organization for Women (NOW)**, the **Women's Equity Action League (WEAL)**, and the **National Women's Political Caucus (NWPC)** strove to combat the unequal treatment of women in the workplace and in schools; fought for **abortion** rights, maternity leave, and equal pay and opportunities; and promoted the election of female candidates. Liberal ideals certainly played a major role in the 1960s women's movement. A key document presented in 1967, the National Organization for Women's Bill of Rights, is modeled after the Bill of Rights. It argues for the equal treatment of women within the public sphere, emphasizing the importance of legal and political reform to enable women to fully participate in the economy. This may be labeled liberal **feminism** in its emphasis on equal rights and individualism. The underlying proposition is that women should be treated as autonomous beings and are entitled to the same rights as men were under Jefferson's Declaration—the right to "life, liberty, and the pursuit of happiness."

By the early 1970s, women had achieved notable successes in Congress and in the courts. The most dramatic, and possibly most significant for the women's movement, was the 1973 Supreme Court decision of ***Roe v. Wade*** legalizing abortion. Women's organizations next turned to the passage of an **Equal Rights Amendment (ERA)**, but here their momentum was stymied as the amendment fell three states short of the 38 needed for ratification.The failure of the ERA must be attributed partly to the emergence of a conservative backlash led by **Phyllis Schlafly** and the fact that not all American women were liberal feminists. Although the ERA failed, this did not mark the end of the liberal women's movement in the United States. A number of developments point to the continuing, if not accentuating, role of women within American politics.

First, in the 1980s women began to display distinctive voting patterns. The so-called **gender gap** was first noted in the presidential election of 1980, in which men voted in large numbers for the Republican Ronald Reagan and women split their votes between Reagan and Democrat Jimmy Carter. Since that election, gender differences have been evident in congressional and state elections as well. Women have tended to vote in larger numbers for Democratic candidates while men have been more likely to support Republican candidates. Underlying these party differences are ideological differences: more women than men take liberal positions on policy issues ranging from foreign policy to domestic issues. For instance, women are more likely than men to oppose violence in various forms, including the death penalty and new weapons systems. Women are also more likely than men to favor government programs that provide health care, aid for the homeless, and family services. Women are also more concerned than men about women's rights, enforcement of child support, sexual abuse and rape, unequal treatment of women in the workplace, the environment, peace, and **pornography**. The gender gap has, in turn, reinforced the ideological differences between the parties, making Republicans more conservative (in response to the majority of men's policy preferences), and the **Democratic Party** more liberal (in response to women's concerns). However, the gender gap does not mean that all women vote more liberally than all men. There are significant differences between the voting patterns of married women homemakers and single women. Single women tend to take the most liberal positions, while married women homemakers tend to vote like their husbands.

A second important development has been the increasing number of women political officials. Historically, the number of women elected to public office has been low; since 1917, fewer than 6 percent of representatives in the U.S. House have been women. However, in 1992, women doubled their numbers in the House and tripled them in the Senate, leading journalists to dub 1992 as "The Year of the Woman. " By 1996, women held 52 seats in the House and nine seats in the Senate, and over 20 percent of state legislators were women. While women in public office do not take uniformly liberal positions on policy issues, surveys do show that, on the whole, women in office are more supportive of women's rights, health care spending, and children's and family issues, representing a more typically "liberal agenda."

The third development pointing to the increasing significance of women in American politics has been the continuing prominence of policy issues of special concern to them. Before the women's movement of the 1960s, men tended to control the political agenda of the United States. Presently, however, issues such as reproductive rights, sexual harassment, **comparable worth**, maternity leave, and **child care** policies are central political issues. Thus, women have placed on the American political agenda issues of concern to them, many of which reflect a liberal bent.

Whether the vitality of liberalism within the American polity has been, on balance, healthy or unhealthy has been disputed. Critics of liberalism tend to criticize it not merely as a political system, but as a way of life. What is the liberal way of life? If there is what may be called a "liberal way of life," it is one with a central creed of, as Justice Louis Brandeis wrote in 1928 in *Olmstead v. United States*, "the right to be let alone." Brandeis referred to this right as "the most comprehensive of rights and the right most valued by civilized men." Critics of liberalism take issue with the liberal vision of the individual who lives by such a creed. Some contend the liberal vision encourages the creation of private, isolated, and acquisitive individuals, ones who are lonely and in need of communal ties. This criticism contends that the liberal portrayal of the individual is accurate but partly because liberal politics creates such an individual, and that the life led by such individuals is far from ideal. Others argue that the liberal vision is inaccurate; that in depicting individuals as autonomous, liberals fail to recognize that our identities are partly or wholly constituted by our familial and communal memberships. Others criticize liberalism for failing to perceive threats to freedom that do not originate in the state—that liberalism tends to be blind to the threats posed to individual freedom by corporate power. Finally, democrats (dating all the way back to Jean Jacques Rousseau) complain that liberalism is indifferent to democracy; that liberalism as a political doctrine underestimates the importance of political participation and substantive equality.

Feminist thinkers have raised a series of intriguing criticisms of liberalism as well. Although liberalism has served as a dominant discourse through which American women have argued for equality before the law; other feminist thinkers conceive of liberal political doctrines as a cause, rather than a correction, for their subordinate status in society and the state. Feminist thinkers claim that the depiction of the liberal individual is a particularly masculine construction. The autonomous individual who interacts with others through contractual exchanges in a social world divided between the private sphere of the family and the public sphere of the state and economy is a masculine being, they believe, but not necessarily a human being. Feminists challenge this depiction and argue that a nurturing, giving self is a more accurate depiction of women than an autonomous self, and that affiliative relationships rather than contractual ones are the norm for most women. Likewise, they claim that the liberal boundary between the private and the public is problematic both descriptively and prescriptively. Feminist thinkers point to the ways in which the liberal state determines what is considered private, and thus what forms of "private" life deserve public protection. State policies concerning child care, birth control, and marriage all have had a great impact on the family. (BAW) **See also** Abolition; Health Care Policy; Republican Party; Sex Discrimination; Voting Rights.

BIBLIOGRAPHY

Hamilton, Alexander, James Madison, and John Jay. *The Federalist Papers*. New York: New American Library, 1961.

Hartmann, Susan M. *From Margin to Mainstream*. New York: Alfred A. Knopf, 1989.

Hartz, Louis. *The Liberal Tradition in America*. New York: Harcourt, Brace, Jovanovich, 1955.

Hobbes, Thomas. *Leviathan*. Michael Oakeshott, ed. New York: Collier Books, 1962.

Hofstadter, Richard. *The American Political Tradition*. New York: Vintage Books, 1948.

Klein, Ethel. *Gender Politics*. Cambridge, MA: Harvard University Press, 1984.

Locke, John. *Second Treatise of Government*. Cambridge: Cambridge University Press, 1960.

Mill, J.S. *On Liberty*. Cambridge: Cambridge University Press, 1989.

Okin, Susan Moller. *Justice, Gender, and the Family*. New York: Basic Books, 1989.

Rawls, John. *A Theory of Justice*. Cambridge, MA: Harvard University Press, 1971.

Blanch Lambert Lincoln (1960–)

Blanch Lambert Lincoln was first elected to the U.S. House of Representatives from Arkansas in 1992 and re-elected in 1994. A moderate Democrat, she served on the Commerce Committee for her two terms. She chose not to stand for reelection in 1996. Prior to her tenure in Congress, Lincoln was a lobbyist from 1985 to 1991.

BIBLIOGRAPHY

Greenblatt, Alan. "Ex-Rep. Lincoln to Seek Bumpers' Senate Seat." *Congressional Quarterly Weekly Report* 55, no. 31 (August 2, 1997): 1887.

Greenblatt, Alan and Jonathan D. Salant. "Out with the Old and the New." *Congressional Quarterly Weekly Report* 54, no. 2 (January 13, 1996): 102.

Margolies-Mezvinsky, Marjorie. *A Woman's Place*. New York: Crown, 1994.

Mary Todd Lincoln (1818–1882)

Well-educated, impulsive, and interested in politics, Mary Todd Lincoln is perhaps the most misunderstood of the **first ladies**. Born December 13, 1818, Mary Todd Lincoln was raised in a prominent family in Lexington, Kentucky. She married Abraham Lincoln in 1842, encouraged his political career, and actively campaigned during his Senate bids. As first lady from 1861 to 1865, Mary Todd Lincoln freely expressed her opinions and attempted to influence patronage and appointments. Her lavish tastes raised controversy when she quickly overspent the White House redecorating budget. She was criticized also by her husband for the debts she incurred buying expensive clothing. Mary Lincoln became a target of public criticism during the Civil War because of her Confederate family ties, which strained her relationship with her husband and aggravated her mental instability. Throughout their marriage, Abraham Lincoln referred to Mary as his "child wife"; she suffered from nervousness and blinding headaches. Her condition worsened following her husband's assassination in 1865, and in 1875 her youngest son committed her to a mental asylum (her sister removed her two months later). Mary Todd Lincoln then returned to Springfield where she died of a stroke in 1882. (LvA)

BIBLIOGRAPHY

Baker, Jean H. *Mary Todd Lincoln: A Biography*. New York: W. W. Norton & Company, 1987.

Ross, Ishbel. *The President's Wife: Mary Todd Lincoln.* New York: Putnam, 1973.

Patricia Sullivan Lindh (1928–)

Patricia Lindh acted as special assistant to President Gerald Ford from 1974 to 1976. From 1976 to 1977, Lindh acted as assistant secretary of state for educational and cultural affairs for the Department of State. In 1985, she became a member of the Public Affairs Committee for the San Francisco World Affairs Council.

BIBLIOGRAPHY

Johnston, Laurie. "White House Assistant for Women's Affairs." *New York Times* (January 13, 1975): 42.

Shanahan, Eileen. "President Ford Signs Executive Order, January 9." *New York Times* (January 10, 1975): 15.

Marilyn Lloyd (1929–)

Tennessee Democrat Marilyn Lloyd served in the U.S. House of Representatives from 1974 until her retirement in 1994. She was elected chair of the Science Subcommittee on Energy during her last term in office. Lloyd's political career began when she campaigned for and won her late husband's vacated House seat. Her treatment for breast cancer made her an advocate for the Women's Health Equity Act. (JHT)

BIBLIOGRAPHY

Ehrenhalt, Alan, ed. *Politics in America, 1994.* Washington, DC: Congressional Quarterly Inc., 1993.

Gertzog, Irvin N. *Congressional Women: Their Recruitment, Integration, and Behavior.* 2nd ed. Westport, CT: Praeger, 1995.

Belva Ann Bennett McNall Lockwood (1830–1917)

In May 1873, Belva Lockwood completed courses at the National University Law School, a school that would not award diplomas to women. She protested the school's policy to President Ulysses S. Grant, a former dignitary of the school, and received her law degree. In 1876, Lockwood petitioned for admission to the United States Supreme Court. She was denied admission on the grounds of custom. She lobbied for the entitlement of women to pursue legal matters in all the nation's courts. Finally, on March 3, 1879, Lockwood became the first woman to practice law before the Supreme Court.

On March 3, 1879, Belva Lockwood became the first woman to be admitted to practice before the U.S. Supreme Court. Library of Congress, National American Woman Suffrage Association Collection.

Belva Lockwood was also a founder of the Universal Franchise Association in 1867 and became active in the **National Woman Suffrage Association (NWSA)** in the 1870s and early 1880s. In addition, she assisted in the passing of 1872 legislation granting women government workers equal pay. In 1884, Lockwood became one of the first women to run for president of the United States on the National Equal Rights Party ticket. She ran again in 1888. Lockwood finished her political career as a member of the Universal Peace Union in the late 1880s and the 1890s. **See also** Suffrage.

BIBLIOGRAPHY

Winner, Julia H. *Belva A. Lockwood.* Lockport, NY: Niagara County Historical Society, 1969.

Zoe Lofgren (1947–)

Zoe Lofgren, a Democrat, serves the 16th District of California in the U.S. House of Representatives. Elected in 1994 and re-elected in 1996, Lofgren gained notoriety by trying unsuccessfully to have her occupation on the ballot listed as "Mother/County Supervisor." Election officials said that California law forbids candidate descriptions based on status such as motherhood. Lofgren also served as Santa Clara County supervisor in California from 1981 until 1994. (MEK)

BIBLIOGRAPHY

Bingham, Clara. *Women on the Hill.* New York: Times Books, 1997.

Margolies-Mezvinsky, Marjorie. *A Woman's Place.* New York: Crown Publishers, 1994.

Catherine S. Long (1924–)

Catherine Long, a delegate to the 1980 and 1984 Democratic National Conventions, served as staff assistant to both U.S. Senator Wayne Morse and U.S. Representative James G. Polk during her political career. Long, who was also a member of the Louisiana State Democratic Finance Council, the State Central Committee, and the Democratic Leadership Council, served in the U.S. House of Representatives from March 30, 1985, to January 3, 1987, filling the vacancy created by the death of her husband Gillis Long. She did not run for re-election in 1988.

Bibliography

Women in Congress. Washington, DC: U.S. Government Printing Office, 1991.

Jill L. Long (1952–)

Democrat Jill Long won her first elected position in 1984 on the Valparaiso (Indiana) City Council. In 1986, she ran unsuccessfully for the United States Senate, and then in 1988 failed in an attempt at a seat in the U.S. House of Representatives from Indiana. Long finally won a seat on March 28, 1989, when she was elected in a special election to the U.S. House of Representatives. She lost her re-election bid in 1994. In 1995, she was appointed as an undersecretary of agriculture, a post she still holds.

Bibliography

"Elected, Jill Long." *Time* 133, no. 15 (April 10, 1989): 35.

Rose McConnell Long (1892–1970)

After the death of her husband, Senator Huey Pierce Long of Louisiana, Rose Long was named to the Senate to complete her husband's term. She served as a Democrat from January 31, 1936, until January 3, 1937. She chose not to stand for re-election in 1936 and retired from public life.

Bibliography

"Lady from Louisiana." *Time* 27 (February 10, 1936): 12.

"Women Senators." *Literary Digest* 121 (February 15, 1936): 34.

Katie Scofield Louchheim (1903–1991)

Katie Louchheim joined the Democratic National Committee during President Franklin D. Roosevelt's second presidential campaign in 1936. She also directed the women's activities for the committee from 1953 to 1956 and served as vice-chair from 1956 until 1960. During and after World War II, Louchheim was involved in relief and rehabilitation work with the U.S. government and the United Nations. In the early 1960s, she became assistant secretary of state for public affairs, and in the late 1960s she was appointed U.S. ambassador to UNESCO.

Bibliography

Louchheim, Katie. *By the Political Sea.* Garden City, NY: Doubleday, 1970.

———. "Vote Democratic." *Independent Woman* 35 (October 1956): 2–5, 35.

"What Women Do in Politics: C. B. Williams and Katie Louchheim." *U.S. News & World Report* 45 (December 12, 1958): 72–79.

Lowell Female Industrial Reform and Mutual Aid Society

Originally called the Lowell Female Labor Reform Association, the group was founded in 1844 by **Sarah Bagley**, who also served as the president. The labor union consisted of more than 600 members who worked in the Lowell, Massachusetts, textile mills. The Lowell Female Labor Reform Association won a number of early victories, including helping overturn a planned increase in the amount of work assigned to the mills' female weavers and overcoming "black list" threats made by mill owners. The group also collected 2,000 signatures on a petition asking for 10-hour work day legislation, which resulted in public hearings on the matter on February 13, 1845.

In January 1847, the Lowell Female Labor Reform Association changed its name to the Lowell Female Industrial Reform and Mutual Aid Society. Under this title, the group continued to petition the state legislature on work reform issues and began to provide financial and medical assistance to needy members. Some of the issues the organization fought after restructuring included factory health conditions, work hours, and pay scales. The organization's membership eroded as married New Englanders were replaced with nonmarried immigrant workers willing to work in worse conditions for less money. **See also** Lowell Mill Girls; *Lowell Offering; Voice of Industry.*

Bibliography

Dublin, Thomas. *Women at Work: The Transformation of Work and Community in Lowell, Massachusetts, 1826–1860.* New York: Columbia University Press, 1979.

Robinson, Harriet Hanson. *Loom and Spindle: or Life Among the Early Mill Girls.* New York: Crowell, 1898.

Lowell Mill Girls

The Lowell Mill Girls was the nickname for the group of female textile workers who were employed in the mills of Lowell, Massachusetts, during the mid-1800s. This group included a number of later known rights activists and other influential women, including Louisa M. Wells, Lucy Larcom, and **Harriet Farley**. The Lowell workers were often subjected to 13-hour work days and poor conditions; some of the conditions these women had to overcome included long hours, low wages, poor lighting and ventilation, and other health hazards. Even though these hardships seemed monumental, many of the women sought self-betterment, spending the evenings educating themselves by reading, writing, and attending lectures. Many of the female workers also contributed to the ***Lowell Offering***, a magazine published by fellow workers that printed poetry, short stories, or other pieces of interest; or the ***Voice of Industry***, a paper that took a proactive approach to the mill discrimination. Other workers participated in the **Lowell Female Industrial Reform and Mutual Aid Society**, a group established to gain better working conditions in the mills. In the late 1800s, after many of the obstacles that the Lowell Mill Girls faced were overcome, a monument was erected in the Lowell Cemetery to honor the women's achievements and remember their struggles.

BIBLIOGRAPHY

Eisler, Benita, ed. *The Lowell Offering: Writings by New England Mill Women (1840–1845).* Philadelphia: Lippincott, 1972.

Josephson, Hannah. *The Golden Threads, New England's Mill Girls and Magnates.* New York: Duell, Sloan and Pearce, 1949.

Wright, Helena. "The Uncommon Mill Girls of Lowell." *History Today* 23 (1973): 10–19.

Lowell Offering

The *Lowell Offering*, a literary magazine featuring poems, short stories, and articles written by the female workers of the Lowell mills in Massachusetts, began publication in 1840 under the editorial guidance of Reverend Abel Charles Thomas, pastor of the First Universalist Church. Thomas maintained his editorial duties from 1840 to 1842, helping the *Lowell Offering* merge with another literary newspaper called *Operatives Magazine* in August 1841. In 1842 **Harriet Farley**, one of the areas' mill workers, took over editorial duties of the magazine, serving in this capacity until 1845. During this time, Farley elevated the magazine to international appeal.

For years, the *Lowell Offering* focused on literary subjects and articles on women's societies and female achievement, neglecting to speak on issues the **Lowell Mill Girls** were subjected to, like low wages, poor conditions, and long work hours. This fact caused mixed reactions; some individuals like **Sarah Bagley**, a female labor organizer, denounced the magazine for rejecting critical articles while other people like poet Lucy Larcom felt the literary nature of the *Lowell Offering* provided an escape for the mill workers. The *Lowell Offering* eventually met direct opposition when Bagley began to produce another magazine, the ***Voice of Industry***, to provide a more critical and independent outlet for women's issues.

In 1845, the *Lowell Offering* ceased publication. The magazine remained in limbo until September of 1847, at which time Harriet Farley revived the magazine under a new title, the *New England Offering*. This revamped publication followed the philosophy of its predecessor, providing literary works to its audience. It also sought to expand its scope by accepting entries from individuals throughout the Northeast. In March 1850, this new magazine also ceased publication.

BIBLIOGRAPHY

Adickes, Sandra. "Mind Among the Spindles: An Examination of Some of the Journals, Newspapers and Memoirs of the Lowell Female Operatives." *Women's Studies* 1 (1973): 279–87.

Eisler, Benita, ed. *The Lowell Offering: Writings by New England Mill Women (1840–1845).* Philadelphia: Lippincott, 1997.

Nita M. Lowey (1937–)

Democrat Nita M. Lowey serves the 18th District of New York in the U.S. House of Representatives. She was first elected to the House in 1988. Perhaps best known for her engagement in a variety of women's issues, Lowey has served as the co-chair of the **Congressional Caucus for Women's Issues**. She has also chaired the House Pro-Choice Task Force since the 103rd Congress. In 1997, President Bill Clinton appointed her to the presidential **Glass Ceiling** Commission. By the time Lowey ran for office, she had spent many years as a Democratic activist, having once worked on a campaign for Governor Mario Cuomo. Lowey was also New York assistant secretary of state from 1985 until 1987. (MEK)

BIBLIOGRAPHY

Bingham, Clara. *Women on the Hill.* New York: Times Books, 1997.

Clare Boothe Luce (1903–1987)

Clare Luce, a Republican from Connecticut, served in the United States House of Representatives from 1943 until 1947. After declining an appointment by President Dwight D. Eisenhower as secretary of labor, she was appointed ambassador to Italy in 1953, a post she held until 1957. Luce was twice appointed to the President's Foreign Intelligence Advisory Board, serving from 1973 to 1977, and from 1982 to 1987.

BIBLIOGRAPHY

Luce, Clare Boothe. "Victory's a Woman." *Woman's Home Companion* 70 (November 1943): 34, 121–22.

Shadegg, Stephen C. *Clare Boothe Luce.* New York: Simon and Schuster, 1970.

Georgia Lee Witt Lusk (1893–1971)

Georgia Lusk began her political career in 1924 when she was elected as superintendent of Lea County (New Mexico) schools. From 1928 to 1956, she served six two-year terms as superintendent of public administration for New Mexico and served one term in Congress (1947–1949). A Democrat, Lusk lost her bid for re-election. From 1949 to 1953, she served on the War Claims Commission. She spent much of her later life directing the political career of her son, Eugene Lusk.

BIBLIOGRAPHY

Fraser, Alice. "Two New But Not Too New." *Independent Woman* (January 1947): 2–3, 27.

Hardaway, Roger D. "New Mexico Elects a Congresswoman." *Red Valley Historical Review* (Fall 1979).

M

Catharine A. MacKinnon (1946–)

In 1986, Catharine MacKinnon served as co-counsel for Mechelle Vinson in the landmark Supreme Court sexual harassment case, ***Meritor Savings Bank v. Vinson***. MacKinnon, a University of Michigan law professor, has written and lectured widely on feminist jurisprudence and **pornography** as a form of **sex discrimination**. (CKC) **See also** Andrea Dworkin.

BIBLIOGRAPHY

MacKinnon, Catherine A. *Feminism Unmodified: Discourses on Life and Law.* Cambridge, MA: Harvard University Press, 1986.

———. *Sexual Harassment of Working Women.* New Haven, CT: Yale University Press, 1979.

MacKinnon, Catherine A. and Andrea Dworkin. *Pornography and Civil Rights: A New Day for Woman's Equality.* Minneapolis, MN: Organizing Against Pornography, 1988.

Dolley Payne Todd Madison (1768–1849)

Dolley Madison, wife of America's fourth president James Madison, is widely recognized as one of the nation's favorite **first ladies**. She served as surrogate hostess during widower President Thomas Jefferson's two terms while her husband served as secretary of state, and then as "lady presidentress" during James Madison's own presidency. Dolley Madison effectively fulfilled and defined the role for 16 years. It was her frequent and widely attended parties, dinners, and receptions, as well as her exhaustive hospitality and graceful social skills, that have established her as American history's quintessential hostess. Dolley Madison tactfully used her ceremonial role as first lady to advance her husband's political career. Known for her imported French fashions, she single-handedly created a social life for the new capital and was even apt to invite her husband's enemies to dinner.

Dolley Madison served as the official White House hostess during the two terms of widower Thomas Jefferson as well as during her husband's two terms. Library of Congress.

Born to a Quaker family of nine children in North Carolina, Dolley Madison was raised in eastern Virginia, and later in Philadelphia, Pennsylvania. In 1790, she married a Quaker lawyer named John Todd with whom she had two sons, but soon lost her husband and youngest child to yellow fever. She was then courted by James Madison, who was 17 years her senior. (MBS)

BIBLIOGRAPHY

Means, Marianne. *The Women in the White House: The Lives, Times and Influence of Twelve Notable First Ladies.* New York: Random House, 1963.

Maher v. Roe (1976)

This case involved two women in Connecticut who were unable to gain a physician's certificate of medical necessity to obtain Medicaid funding for an **abortion**. In their suit, they claimed that the equal protection clause of the Fourteenth Amendment forbids excluding nontherapeutic abortions from a Medicaid program that generally subsidizes medical expenses of pregnancy and childbirth. This decision of the lower court was later overturned on appeal (*Maher v. Roe*, 432 U.S. 464 [1976]). The Supreme Court, citing its decision in ***Beal v. Doe***, ruled that the equal protection clause did not require states participating in the Medicaid program to pay for nontherapeutic abortions even if they paid for medical expenses of pregnancy and childbirth. **See also** *Roe v. Wade.*

BIBLIOGRAPHY

Murphy, Walter F. and C. Herman Pritchett. *Courts, Judges and Politics.* New York: Random House, 1979.

Ellen Malcolm (1947–)

Ellen Malcolm, founder and president of **EMILY's List**, was born in 1947 in Montclair, New Jersey. Her father, William Reighley, was the grandson of A. Ward Ford and co-founder of International Business Machines Corporation (IBM). Although Malcolm grew up Republican, she changed her political outlook as a student at Hollins College, campaigning for Senator Eugene McCarthy in 1968 and working for Common Cause in the early 1970s. She later served as press secretary for the

National Women's Political Caucus (NWPC), and in 1980 she joined President Jimmy Carter's White House staff as press secretary for **Esther Peterson**. In 1985, she formed EMILY's List, a political action committee (PAC) for Democratic, pro-choice women candidates, in response to the defeat of her friend Harriet Woods by 1 percent of the vote in the 1982 Missouri senate race. Malcolm then realized the need for a women's fund-raising network. EMILY's List, which stands for "Early Money Is Like Yeast—it makes dough rise" has since become the largest source of funds for national candidates, helping to elect 42 pro-choice Democratic women to the U.S. House of Representatives and three women as governors. (LvA)

BIBLIOGRAPHY

Friedman, Jon. "The Founding Mother." *The New York Times* (May 2, 1993): 50.

Carolyn Bosher Maloney (1948–)

Carolyn Maloney, a former staff member of the New York State Assembly Housing Committee from 1977 to 1979, served as director of special projects for state senate minority leader Manfred Ohrenstein. In 1979, Maloney became executive director of the Advisory Council on the Democracy. This position was followed by service on the New York City Council, where Maloney served as councilwoman from 1982 to 1993.

In 1992, Maloney, a Democrat, was elected into the United States House of Representatives. She also served in this capacity as a member of the Banking and Financial Services Committee on Capital Markets, Securities, and Government Sponsored Enterprise and was a member of the Financial Investments and Consumer Credit Committee.

BIBLIOGRAPHY

Bingham, Clara. *Women on the Hill.* New York: Times Books, 1997.

Margolies-Mezvinsky, Marjorie. *A Women's Place.* New York: Crow Publishers, 1994.

Wilma P. Mankiller (1945–)

Indian affairs activist Wilma P. Mankiller was born to Irene and Charlie Mankiller in Tahlequah, Oklahoma in 1945. In 1957, her family moved to San Francisco under the Bureau of Indian Affairs (BIA) relocation program. The Native American takeover of Alcatraz Island activated her involvement in Indian affairs. In the mid-1970s, she returned to Oklahoma and began working for the Cherokee Nation while earning a B.A. in social science from Flaming Rainbow University in Stilwell. In 1981, she founded and directed the Community Development Department of the Cherokee Nation, leading her to be Ross Swimmer's running mate for chief in the 1983 election. When Swimmer became director of the BIA, Wilma Mankiller was sworn in as principal chief, the first woman to hold the position. She served in that position until 1995. (AM)

BIBLIOGRAPHY

Mankiller, Wilma and Michael Wallis. *Mankiller: A Chief and Her People.* New York: St. Martin's Press, 1993.

Swartz, Melissa. *Wilma Mankiller: Principal Chief of the Cherokees.* New York: Chelsea House, 1994.

Helen Douglas Mankin (1894–1956)

Helen Mankin, a Democrat, served in the Georgia legislature from 1937 until 1946. In 1946, she resigned from the legislature to run for the unexpired term of U.S. Congressman Robert Ramspeck. She won the special election largely due to African-American support. She was defeated for re-election in 1946, and returned to private practice after an unsuccessful 1948 attempt to regain her congressional seat.

BIBLIOGRAPHY

Chamberlin, Hope. *A Minority of Members.* New York: Praeger, 1973.

Mansell v. Mansell (1988)

At issue in the case *Mansell v. Mansell*, 490 U.S. 581 (1988), was whether the Uniformed Services Former Spouses Protection Act (1982), making a veteran's retirement pay subject to alimony, should exempt that portion of the pension the veteran converts to disability benefits. The U.S. Supreme Court ruled 7-2 that the portion that was received as disability was exempt. Writing for the majority, Justice Thurgood Marshall conceded that the ruling of the Court "may inflict economic harm on many former spouses." However, he continued, "We decline to misread the statute . . . to reach a sympathetic result when such a reading requires us to do violence to the plain language . . . and ignore much of the legislative history." The Court acknowledged that it was common for veterans to convert part of their pensions into disability pay because the latter is tax-exempt, but that there was little that could be done to prevent a conversion as long as the veteran qualified for disability.

Justice **Sandra Day O'Connor** and Justice Harry Blackmun, the two dissenters, noted that the ability of a veteran to convert pension to disability payments would be to deny the spouse "a fair share."

BIBLIOGRAPHY

"Mansell v. Mansell." *Journal of Family Law* 30 (1991-1992): 97–110.

"Mansell v. Mansell." *The National Law Journal* (June 12, 1989): 25.

Pierre, John K. "The Divisibility of Military Retired Pay in Louisiana in Light of McCarty, Mansell and the Uniformed Former Spouses Protection Act." *Southern University Law Review* 17 (Fall 1990): 149–70.

Arabella "Belle" Mansfield (1846–1911)

Born August 23, 1846, Arabella "Belle" Mansfield was the first woman admitted to the American bar Association. In spite of her high Iowa bar exam score, Mansfield was initially denied admittance to the bar based on her gender. Iowa law stated that any white male person could become a lawyer. However, in 1869 a judge ruled in Mansfield's favor, reasoning that "an affirmative declaration for men is not a denial of the right of females." Mansfield never actually practiced law. (JW1)

BIBLIOGRAPHY

Haselmayer, Louis A. "Belle A. Mansfield." *Women Lawyers Journal* 55, no. 1 (Winter 1969): 46–54.

March for Women's Lives

On April 5, 1992, 700,000 women, men, and children gathered in Washington for a rally sponsored by the **National Organization for Women (NOW)** in response to limits on **abortion** rights. Republican President George Bush was admittedly anti-abortion, and the march was orchestrated to focus attention, in this presidential election year, on the voting power of the pro-choice movement. The frontrunning Democratic presidential candidate, Bill Clinton, had announced his pro-choice stance the previous year in an address to the **National Women's Political Caucus (NWPC)**. (EP)

BIBLIOGRAPHY

Allen, Charles F. and Jonathon Porter. *The Comeback Kid: The Life and Career of Bill Clinton.* New York: Birch Lane Press, 1992.

"The Talk of the Town." *The New Yorker* (April 27, 1992): 29-30.

Marjorie Margolies-Mezvinsky (1949–)

Marjorie Margolies-Mezvinsky, a Pennsylvania Democrat, was elected to the U.S. House of Representatives in 1992. The TV journalist and author won by capitalizing on anti-incumbency and using a large campaign fund drawn largely from out-of-state contributors. In 1994, she lost her re-election bid to her 1992 opponent Republican Jon D. Fox. Margolies-Mezvinsky wrote a study of the impact the new women had on Congress in *A Woman's Place*. She now heads the National Woman's Business Council and was a delegate to the United Nations 4th World Conference on Women.

BIBLIOGRAPHY

Margolies-Mezvinsky, Marjorie. *A Woman's Place*. New York: Crown, 1994.

McElwaine, Sandra. "What Makes Marjorie Win." *Good Housekeeping* 218, no. 1 (January 1994): 84.

Married Woman's Property Act (1848)

The Married Woman's Property Act passed by the New York State legislature in March 1848 set the stage for the historic meeting the following July in Seneca Falls that produced the **Declaration of Sentiments and Resolutions**.

The New York statute was the product of a petition drive that involved such important figures in the nascent women's rights movement as Ernestine Rose, **Elizabeth Cady Stanton**, and **Paulina Wright Davis**. The grassroots campaign that sparked the petition drive represented one of the first times in American history that women had organized to further their own political interests. The Married Woman's Property Act of 1848 was a milestone in the relationship between women and the law because it gave women limited control over real property that they had brought with them into marriage. Thus, it granted married women property rights that were traditionally denied to wives under **common law**.

The Married Woman's Property Act of 1848 was an example of the evolving legal status of nineteenth-century woman as changing economic, social, and political forces challenged legislatures to codify law and courts to interpret questions of equity. As such, the New York statute represented an important step on the road to sexual equality because it began the process of the legal recognition of women as autonomous subjects who retained separate rights to their property after marriage. Specifically, the Married Woman's Property Act of 1848 represented the codification of equity practices that protected a wife's real property from confiscation by her husband's creditors. In this respect, the statute disproportionately benefited the economic interests of upper and middle class women. The statute itself was conservative in nature, addressing the concerns of wealthy fathers who did not want to see their daughter's dowry or inheritance dissipated by her speculating husband.

While the Married Woman's Property Act of 1848 signaled a transformation in the legal status of married women in the United States, it would take further reforms in law and custom before wives could control their wages or enter contracts on their own behalf. Yet the New York statute was critical to the emerging movement for women's rights because it provided a model for the other Married Woman's Property Acts that were drafted by state legislatures throughout the nation in the 1850s. (WGC) **See also** Seneca Falls Convention.

BIBLIOGRAPHY

Glendon, Mary Ann. "Modern Marriage Law and its Underlying Assumptions: The New Marriage and the New Property." *Family Law Quarterly* (Winter 1980): 441–60.

Lynn Morley Martin (1939–)

Lynn Martin worked as a high school teacher before getting involved in local and state politics in the 1970s. She served in the Illinois legislature from 1976 to 1980. In 1980, she won the Republican nomination for the U.S. House of Representatives in the 16th District. She served in the House for 10 years and was the first woman to assume a position in the **Republican Party** leadership. Following her 1990 Senate race loss to Democrat Paul Simon, she was appointed secretary of labor by President George Bush and established the **Glass Ceiling** Commission to investigate the underrepresentation of women at higher levels of business. (CKC)

BIBLIOGRAPHY

Adams, Bob. "An Interview with Lynn Martin." *CQ Researcher.* 3 (October 29, 1993): 954.

Women in Congress, 1917–1990. Washington, DC: U.S. Government Printing Office, 1991.

Mary Matalin (1953–)

Known as a tough-talking, hard-nosed Republican political consultant, Mary Matalin ran President George Bush's failed 1992 campaign. She married James Carville, the political consultant to Democrat Bill Clinton in 1992, and the two wrote a book on the campaign. However, the marriage to Carville raised controversy among Republican ranks and forced her to leave the Bob Dole presidential campaign in 1996.

BIBLIOGRAPHY

Collins, Gail. "The Rise and Fall of Mary Matalin." *Working Woman* 19 (August 1994): 34–37.

Matalin, Mary. *Love, War and the Art of Politics*. New York: Random House, 1994.

Matalin, Mary and James Carville. *All's Fair*. New York: Simon and Schuster, 1995.

"Maude's Dilemma"

In the early 1970s, Beatrice Arthur played the title character in a CBS situation comedy called *Maude*. The show's creator, Norman Lear, designed Arthur's liberal feminist character as a comedic counterpart to Archie Bunker, the arch-conservative character in Lear's other popular television show, *All in the Family*. In 1972, two Maude espisodes entitled "Maude's Dilemma" dealt with the 47-year-old lead character's unplanned pregnancy. The episdoes showed Maude and her husband struggling with the situation and included discussions of both **abortion** and vasectomy. In the end, Maude decided to have an abortion. When the episodes were originally run in November 1972, only two states in the country refused to air them, but a tremendous amount of opposition arose when the episodes were scheduled for rebroadcast in August 1973. Anti-abortion groups and the Catholic Church accused Lear of advocating abortion and mounted a nationwide protest, threatening to boycott CBS if the episodes were televised again. Although the episodes aired as scheduled, many local sponsors and affiliates were convinced by the threat of boycott to withdraw their support or to refuse to televise the episodes. The "Maude's Dilemma" episodes were not purchased when the series went into syndication and have not been televised since 1973. (CKC)

BIBLIOGRAPHY

Harmetz, Aljean. "Maude Didn't Leave 'em All Laughing." *New York Times* (December 10, 1972): 3.

Krebs, Albin. "25 C.B.S. Affiliates Won't Show 'Maude' Episodes on Abortion." *New York Times* (August 14, 1973): 38.

Catherine Dean May (1914–)

In 1952, Catherine May, a Republican, was elected to the Washington State legislature, a position she held until 1958. While in the legislature, she served as vice-chair of the Governor's Statewide Committee on Television and on the Governor's Safety Council. In January 1959, May became the first woman from the state of Washington to serve in the U.S. House of Representatives, having been elected in 1958. She served in Congress until 1971. From 1971 to 1981, May worked for the U.S. International Trade Commission, and in 1982 she acted as a special consultant to the president on the 50 States Project.

BIBLIOGRAPHY

Bedell, Catherine May. *Oral History Interview, Former Member of Congress Association*. Washington, DC: Manuscript Division, Library of Congress, 1979.

May, Catherine Dean. "Every Man Should Have His Say." *Vital Speeches*. 31 (August 1, 1965): 622–624.

———. "Salute to Three Freshman." *National Business Woman* 38 (February 1959): 12.

Carolyn McCarthy (1944–)

First elected to Congress in 1996, New York Democrat Carolyn McCarthy entered politics as a result of personal tragedy. After her husband was killed and her son seriously injured in what became known as the Long Island Railroad Massacre, McCarthy learned that her representative would not support a ban on assault weapons. She then switched to the **Democratic Party** and ran for Congress. McCarthy writes a monthly column in *McCalls* and wrote the screenplay for a movie of her life produced by Barbra Streisand. In the 105th Congress, she served on the House Education and Welfare and the Small Business committees. (EP)

BIBLIOGRAPHY

Golden, Kristen. "From Personal Tragedy, A Run for Congress." *Ms.* (September-October 1996): 19.

Karen P. McCarthy (1947–)

In 1976, Karen McCarthy was elected to the Missouri House of Representatives. During her political career, she also served on the Energy Commission from 1978 to 1984 and the Federal Taxation, Trade and Economic Committee in 1986. In 1987, she became chair of the Budget and Taxation Committee, and in 1988 vice-chair of the state assembly. In 1994, McCarthy, a Democrat, was elected to the U.S. House of Representatives where she serves on the Commerce Committee, among others.

BIBLIOGRAPHY

Shafer, Ronald G. "Women Democrats Win More Influential Roles in the House." *The Wall Street Journal* (November 22, 1996): A1.

Kathryn O'Laughlin McCarthy (1894–1952)

Kathryn McCarthy served as a delegate to Kansas State Democratic Conventions in 1930, 1931, 1932, 1934, and 1936 and as a delegate to the 1940 and 1944 Democratic National Conventions. She served two terms in the state legislature in 1931 and 1932 before being elected to the U.S. House of Representatives in 1932. She was defeated in her re-election bid in 1934 and resumed her private law practice.

BIBLIOGRAPHY

Chamberlin, Hope. *A Minority of Members*. New York: Praeger, 1973.

McCarty v. McCarty (1981)

Two years prior to his retirement, an army colonel sought a divorce from his wife. During the divorce proceedings, a controversy arose as to whether the military pension was considered community or quasi-community property as defined by the state of California. The judge ruled that the retirement benefits were quasi-community property and ordered that upon dispersement the husband pay his wife 45 percent of the benefits. The husband appealed the ruling of the court claming that the funds were his alone because he had earned them and should be considered separate personal property. The California supreme court upheld the lower court's ruling.

On appeal to the U.S. Supreme Court, however, the decision of the lower court was overturned (*McCarty v. McCarty*, 453 U.S. 210 [1981]). The justices stated that dividing the military retirement was overstepping the intended rights of the retiree because retirement funds had been established as benefits for the work and dedication of the employee. The Court reasoned that a state dividing such benefits interfered with congressional goals of using retirement money as an inducement for enlistment, re-enlistment, and promotion. Further, in reviewing the language of the military retirement guidelines, there was no clause stipulating that these benefits were joint property and that dividing the funds overstepped a state's authority because jurisdiction over the funds was a federal matter. **See also** *Mansell v. Mansell.*

BIBLIOGRAPHY

Pierre, John K. "The Divisibility of Military Retired Pay in Louisiana in Light of McCarty, Mansell and the Uniformed Former Spouses Protection Act." *Southern University Law Review* 17 (Fall 1990): 149–70.

Quinn, J.B. "Housewives' Lot." *Newsweek* 98 (September 14, 1981): 79.

McCarvey v. Magee-Women's Hospital (1972)

In *McCarvey v. Magee-Women's Hospital*, 340 F. Supp. 751 (1972), a U.S. district court in Pennsylvania ruled that a fetus is not a "person" guaranteed rights under the Fourteenth Amendment or the Civil Rights Act. In *McCarvey*, Dr. Richard McCarvey brought suit against Magee-Women's Hospital as guardian ad litem on behalf of Baby Boy Doe and Baby Girl Roe and other members of "a class of conceived but unborn children," arguing that as persons they should be protected by the Fourteenth Amendment of the United States Constitution and the Civil Rights Act. The district court responded that neither the Supreme Court nor Congress had ever declared the fetus a "person" or a "citizen." Therefore, a fetus had no right to due process under the Fourteenth Amendment—nor did it have rights under the Civil Rights Act, which guaranteed "full and equal benefits of all laws and security of persons and property." Dr. McCarvey believed that **abortion** was murder, and he wanted the court to mandate an unspecified method of pre-abortion review. Before ***Roe v. Wade*** in 1973, Pennsylvania banned all abortions. In 1972, 14,232 Pennsylvania women left the state to obtain abortions elsewhere. (EP)

BIBLIOGRAPHY

Craig, Barbara Hinkson and David M. O'Brien. *Abortion and American Politics*. Chatham, NJ: Chatham House, 1993.

Faux, Marian. Roe v. Wade*: The Untold Story of the Landmark Supreme Court Decision That Made Abortion Legal.* New York: New American Library, 1988.

Ellen McCormack (1926–)

Ellen McCormack became a national figure in American politics when she entered the 1976 Democratic presidential primary over the issue of **abortion**. McCormack was pro-life and opposed to the U.S. Supreme Court ruling in ***Roe v. Wade***. Her presence in the first presidential election after *Roe* forced both parties to address the issue of abortion. She failed to win the **Democratic Party** nomination in 1976 (capturing 22 delegates) and was offered a position on the American Independent Party ticket, but declined. In 1978, she ran unsuccessfully for lieutenant governor of New York. In 1980, she again ran for president, but this time on the Right to Life Party ticket. **See also** Right-to-Life Movement.

BIBLIOGRAPHY

O'Connor, Karen. *No Neutral Ground?* Boulder, CO: Westview, 1996.

Spitzer, Robert J. *The Right to Life Movement and Third Party Politics*. Westport, CT: Greenwood, 1987.

Ruth Hanna McCormick (1880–1944)

Ruth Hanna McCormick came from a political family—her father was Marcus Alonzo Hanna, the driving force in Ohio Republican politics and a backer of President William McKinley in the 1890s. She served as her father's confidential secretary when he was in the U.S. Senate from 1897 until his death in 1904. Her husband, Medill McCormick, was both a U.S. Representative (1917–1919) and U.S. Senator (1919–1925) from Illinois.

At the 1924 Republican National Convention, Ruth McCormick was elected a national committee member and in 1928 ran successfully for the U.S. House of Representatives. She spent one term in the House and in 1930 defeated incumbent Senator Charles Deneen for the Republican nomination for U.S. senator from Illinois. She was defeated in the general election because of a growing scandal over the amount she had spent to win the primary ($250,000 to her rival's $25,000). She never ran for another elective office and adamantly refused any appointed ones. However, she did remain active in the **Republican Party** until her death.

BIBLIOGRAPHY

Chamberlin, Hope. *A Minority of Members*. New York: Praeger, 1973.

Women in Congress. Washington, DC: U.S. Government Printing Office, 1991.

Mary McGrory (1918–)

Mary McGrory, a long-time political news reporter, has gained a reputation of being one of the best in her field. From 1942 to 1947, McGrory was a reporter for the *Boston Herald Traveler*. From 1947 until 1954, she became a book reviewer for the *Washington Star*. From 1954 to 1981, she worked as a feature writer for the national staff and then as a syndicated columnist for the *Washington Post*. In 1981, she became a syndicated columnist for Universal Press Syndicate. In 1975, McGrory won the Pulitzer Prize for her commentary, which was critical recognition of her dedication, knowledge, and persuasiveness.

Bibliography

Freeman, Neal B. "The Potomac All-Stars." *National Review* 32 (March 7, 1980): 274.

"Post's McGrory, Dash Win RFK Journalism Awards; Columnist Honored for Lifetime Achievement, Reporter for Series Titled 'Rose Lee's Story'" *Washington Post* 118 (April 13, 1995): A15.

Margaret Anne McKenna (1945–)

Margaret McKenna began her federal governmental service as an attorney for the Department of Justice from 1971 until 1973. In 1973, she took a two-year position as a management consultant at the Department of Treasury. She was appointed a deputy counsel for President Jimmy Carter in 1976 and served in that post until 1979 when she served for the duration of the Carter administration as deputy for the Department of Education.

Bibliography

"The First Team." *American Education* 16 (May 1980): 20.

"Who's Who in the Carter Administration." *Washington Monthly* 12 (May 1980): 52.

Ida Saxton McKinley (1847–1907)

Ida Saxton McKinley was not a politically active first lady. As a young woman, however, McKinley broke with convention by working in her father's bank and may have become a manager there. Beset by illness and tragedy, McKinley's bad fortune began during her marriage to William McKinley when both her mother and two young daughters died. Later, McKinley suffered an undisclosed illness, possible epilepsy, which caused her to have seizures. Despite her illness, McKinley insisted upon center stage throughout her husband's career. She often publicly accompanied her husband and presided at official dinners. Surprisingly, because of her illness, newspapers of the day portrayed her as a model of docile femininity. Her husband was assassinated in 1901. (BN) **See also** First Ladies.

Ill throughout most of her marriage, Ida McKinley still served as White House hostess during her husband's presidency. Library of Congress.

Bibliography

Caroli, Betty Boyd. *First Ladies.* New York: Oxford University Press, 1995.

Truman, Margaret. *First Ladies.* New York: Random House, 1995.

Cynthia McKinney (1955–)

Georgia Democrat Cynthia McKinney is the first African-American woman to represent her state in the U.S. House of Representatives. A former political science instructor at Clark Atlanta University and a former staff member for Senator Herman Talmadge, McKinney's interest in politics developed early; her father is a long-time member of the Georgia legislature. Upon her own election to the Georgia assembly in 1988, the McKinneys were the only father-daughter team of legislators in the nation. While in the Georgia legislature, McKinney focused on legislative redistricting and ran for Congress in 1992 in one of Georgia's three newly created majority-minority districts. Once in Congress, McKinney became the freshman class secretary and headed the Women's Caucus Task Force on Children, Youth, and Families. Currently, she sits on the Banking and Financial Services and International Relations committees and has used her platform in Congress to champion the rights of poor women and minorities. For example, during a 1993 House debate on public funding for **abortion**, McKinney argued, "The real choice for low-income women becomes carrying their pregnancy to term or finding alternative funding—that is, for rent, food, or clothing, or money for unsafe and sometimes self-induced abortions." Reelected in 1994 and 1996, McKinney continues to be an outspoken member on women's issues. (ST)

Bibliography

Bingham, Clara. *Women on the Hill.* New York: Time Books, 1997.

Margolies-Mezvinsky, Marjorie. *A Women's Place.* New York: Crown Publishers, 1994.

Anne Dore McLaughlin (1941–)

In 1971, Anne McLaughlin served President Richard Nixon's Committee to Reelect the President as director of communications. In 1973, she was appointed director of public affairs for the Environmental Protection Agency, a position she held until Nixon's resignation in August 1974.

McLaughlin returned to national politics during the administration of President Ronald Reagan. From 1981 to 1984, she served as assistant secretary for public affairs at the Department of the Treasury. In 1984, she was appointed secretary of the interior serving until November 3, 1987, when President Reagan nominated McLaughlin as secretary of labor. As secretary of labor, she focused on **child care**, parental leave, employee polygraph testing, and worker education programs.

She served in this capacity until 1989, at which time she became chair of the President's Commission on Aviation Security and Terrorism until 1990.

BIBLIOGRAPHY

Barnes, Fred. "Baby Face-Off." *The New Republic* 198, no. 19 (1988): 8.

Polsgrove, Carol. "Feminine and Tough." *The Progressive* 52, no. 3 (March 1988): 34.

Wright, Robert. "Firing Lines." *The New Republic* 198, no. 18 (May 2, 1988): 18.

Clara Gooding McMillan (1894–1976)

Clara McMillan, a Democrat, served in the U.S. House of Representatives from November 7, 1939, to January 3, 1941, filling the vacancy left by her late husband, South Carolina Representative Thomas McMillan. In 1941, she served in the National Youth Administration and the Office of Governmental Reports for the Office of War Information. McMillan also worked as an information liaison officer for the Department of State, a post she held from January 1, 1946, to July 31, 1957.

BIBLIOGRAPHY

Chamberlin, Hope. *A Minority of Members.* New York: Praeger, 1973.

Margaret Mead (1901–1978)

Anthropologist and feminist Margaret Mead was curator of the American Museum of Natural History from 1964 to 1969 and an adjunct professor of anthropology at Columbia University from 1954. She won a worldwide reputation as a scholar and anthropologist for her studies of child-rearing, personality, and culture, mainly among the peoples of Oceania. Her field trips to Samoa, New Guinea, and Bali in the 1920s and 1930s resulted in some of the best known and most important works in American anthropology in the twentieth century, including *Coming of Age in Samoa* (1928), *Growing Up in New Guinea* (1930), and *Sex and Temperament in Three Primitive Societies* (1935). In her later career, Mead also became a popular and controversial writer and lecturer on social and political issues, including women's rights. In 1965, Mead was one of the editors of *American Women*, the report issued by the **President's Commission on the Status of Women (PCSW).** Mead also wrote the introduction and epilogue for the report, which focused on issues of equality in the workforce, such as equal pay and benefits for women. Mead's other works include *Male and Female* (1949), *New Lives for Old* (1956), *Culture and Commitment: A Study of the Generation Gap* (1970), and her autobiography *Blackberry Winter* (1972.

Scholar and feminist Margaret Mead is shown here attending the National Women's Conference in 1977. National Archives.

BIBLIOGRAPHY

Cassidy, Robert. *Margaret Mead: A Voice for the Century.* New York: Universe Books, 1982.

Howard, Jane. *Margaret Mead: A Life.* New York: Simon and Schuster, 1984.

Mead, Margaret. *Blackberry Winter: My Earlier Years.* New York: W. Morrow, 1972.

Medical Research and Funding

Partly due to **feminism**, a realization has occurred that women's bodies are fundamentally different than men's. This, together with the fact that until the 1980s women had largely been excluded from research trials, has prompted a tremendous increase in the number of initiatives, research dollars, and even approaches devoted to women's health issues. In the United States, medical research and funding for women's health problems is a biological, socio-political, ethical, legal, moral, medical, and economic issue. From the narrow scientific focus of the 1950s and 1960s, when women's health research centered around reproduction, women's health research in the 1990s has expanded to include nearly every conceivable issue of concern to women. Funding has increased 30 percent from 1993 to 1997, and this new focus includes reproductive technologies, HIV studies, mental health efforts, genetic and **domestic violence** research, environmental problems of particular interest to women, as well as standard biological inquiries. Sadly, women in other nations, particularly developing countries, have not benefited from this increased attention. Funding for research is in short supply and—though women's health and research is a stated concern of most leaders—cultural taboos, predispositions, and paternalistic attitudes have combined with the lack of money to relegate women's health research to the political back burner in developing nations.

In a 1995 expose on women's health and research, the journal *Science* noted that prior to the 1980s, women's research focused on reproductive issues. Pregnancy, neonatal concerns, and birth control were the primary investigative issues. A 1994 Institute of Medicine study noted that, until the 1980s research on women was protectionist, stemming from concerns for the unborn child. Women were generally excluded from disease research and drug trials. When women were occasionally included in research trials it is apparent that they were given inadequate information on which to base their decision to participate in such trials. When the **thalidomide** and diethylstilbestrol (DES) disasters were made public in the 1960s and 1970s, it was obvious that research abuses of women had occurred.

Thalidomide was a drug prescribed in Europe to prevent nausea during pregnancy and DES was given to prevent miscarriages. Diethylstilbestrol was given during the 1940s and 1950s, and thalidomide during the 1960s. Neither drug had been tested on women. Doctors noted that thalidomide was responsible for severe birth defects and that daughters of women who took DES were suffering from rare sex organ cancers.

These disasters amplified public sentiment about the need for protecting the unborn and women from research abuses. Buttressed by the 1949 Nuremberg Code requiring guidelines for humane research, the 1964 Helsinki Declaration of Human Rights and the realization that drugs for women's problems must be tested on women, concern for women's research became a top political priority. In 1974, the U.S. Department of Health, Education and Welfare established the "Institutional Review Board," which created guidelines for risk-benefit reviews of research involving human subjects. Also in 1974, the U.S. Congress passed the National Research Act, which extended the research guidelines to mandate limited inclusion of pregnant women into drug and disease research trials. In 1977, however, the Food and Drug Administration (FDA) recommended that no pregnant women be included in clinical drug research. A research dilemma was posed to the scientific community. Generally, wishing to avoid legal liability, most corporate and university researchers kept women out of their studies.

During the 1980s, a new health crisis was discovered that had the potential to kill millions. The advent of AIDS galvanized an activist socio-political movement that demanded more research and funding to fight the disease. Feminist activists, re-energized by AIDS activists, reignited their political movement to promote the cause of women's inclusion in research. Each group of activists fed off the other's political and economic successes, and the decade saw a tremendous increase in funding for each respective problem. Charging paternalism and discrimination over the exclusion of women in research trials and the generally poor financial incentives for researchers to investigate women's concerns, feminists and some concerned scientists demanded more attention from the government and corporate researchers.

The United States government listened. In 1985, a U.S. Public Health Service task force concluded that women had not been sufficiently included as research participants and led the National Institutes of Health (NIH), the nation's foremost health policy research agency, to mandate inclusion of women in all grant programs for research.

At about the same time, the Food and Drug Administration, perhaps feeling the political heat, called for a study to determine the proportions of men and women in various drug trials. The FDA reviews corporate drug development efforts in a three-stage process to determine a drug's operation in the body, its side effects, and its overall effectiveness against the disease or problem at which it is targeted. The last two phases of the three-stage trial include testing of the drug on up to 3,000 people. As of 1987, less than 43 percent of these studies had any gender-based information. The FDA could not accurately say how many women, if any, had been included in which studies.

By 1990, the General Accounting Office (GAO), the U.S. government's main watchdog agency, attacked the NIH and the FDA for their lack of comprehensive data concerning women in research. The GAO also noted that no women had been included in two of the biggest research studies in the history of medicine—the "Multiple Risk Factor Intervention Trial" and the "Physician's Health Study," both of which looked at factors contributing to heart disease, stroke, and cancer. Private researchers also noted that women were included in only 16 percent of the HIV studies despite the fact that women's infection rates were twice that of men's. A privately researched study of all non-gender-specific articles published by the *Journal of the American Medical Association* from 1990 to 1992 found that women were excluded from three-fourths of the studies, and the greatest disparity was found in the exclusion of older women.

Following these revelations, several female members of Congress sponsored legislation to correct the deficiencies, but these measures were vetoed by President George Bush because they contained amendments allowing fetal tissue research. Finally, in 1993, President Bill Clinton incorporated the congresswomen's proposals into what became the NIH Revitalization Act of 1993. In the act, the NIH acknowledged significant gaps in research involving women and mandated the inclusion of women in all NIH-sponsored research. That same year, the FDA also removed its ban on the inclusion of women in drug trials and announced it would require drug companies that had applied for FDA review to include women in their drug research.

Many critics of the new policy objected for numerous reasons. They claimed most diseases operated the same in men as in women, therefore their inclusion or exclusion may have no bearing on a study's validity. They also complained that including women may be prohibitively expensive, that forced inclusion was a denial of research freedom, and that the government was merely pandering to feminist political pressure. Researchers critical of the new policy cited other studies to show that women had been included in studies in proportionate numbers.

Much of the controversy, aside from feminist charges of discrimination and paternalism, stems from the medical fact that women have a different and variable hormonal pool that allows drugs to be metabolized differently in women's bodies than in men's bodies. It also means that drugs operate differently in an individual woman's body during the different stages of her menstrual cycle in response to changes in the levels of estrogen and progesterone. If women are excluded from disease and drug research, the drug's effectiveness and side effects on women will not be known because these results cannot simply be transferred from men to women. Therefore, women's exclusion from research becomes a biological, ethical, moral, and legal issue.

Government remains the predominant funding source, and is concerned about the biological, ethical, and moral issues surrounding the exclusion of women in research. Does disparate treatment in research result in disparate benefits in health? Are women being short-changed? More oversight and study is needed to ensure appropriate compliance with the law.

According to the provisions of the 1993 Revitalization Act, women may only be justifiably excluded from government sponsored research and inquiry for a compelling purpose. Obviously, where research concerns diseases and drugs of singular concern to men, such as prostate cancer, there is a compelling purpose to exclude women. But rarely is a medical issue so clearly delineated as to allow open exclusion of one group; and if women are being excluded in government sponsored trials, the question of equal protection of the law becomes paramount. All government research offices must provide equal protection of the law to all groups; and corporations, under government sponsorship, must do the same. Case law suggests that corporations that include women in research trials may face liability if the women suffer as a result, but the corporations may also be liable if women are excluded and suffer damages from subsequently taking the drugs or treatments. A legal minefield has been created.

The 1987 budget of the NIH indicated that 13 percent of grant money was directed toward women's issues. By 1996, medical research into women's issues expanded with the creation of offices devoted to women's problems in the Department of Health and Human Services, the Public Health Service, the NIH, and the Centers for Disease Control and Prevention (CDC). The Health and Human Services Department has focused increased resources and national attention on women's health. Funding is up $800 million (about 30 percent) since 1993. At the start of 1997, the NIH had 75 separate initiatives covering a wide range of women's health issues.

Research grants to female researchers have increased 34 percent from 1984 to 1994 and have decreased to men by 15 percent in the same period. Despite the increase, men still outnumber women in grant awards by a four to one ratio and are awarded an average of $240,000 compared to the average women's grant amount of $214,000. Grants cover studies on reproductive technology, better diagnostics, breast cancer genetics, workplace safety, domestic violence, and surgical techniques.

Feminist scholars and various government agencies recommend that more women enter scientific fields despite discriminatory treatment reported by women in science. More female researchers are needed to help remove any male bias in research perspectives and to promote appropriate gender representation in science, new avenues of inquiry, and updated ways of thinking about and doing research.

A similar, though less comprehensive, initiative on women's health research exists in most Western, industrialized nations. Unfortunately, in developing countries, paternalistic attitudes, traditions, cultural taboos, and corruption have stymied efforts at women's health research. In India, China, most sub-Saharan African nations, and southeast Asian nations there is an appalling lack of research or advancement in reproductive technologies, drugs, and disease on women. The World Health Organization (WHO), the CDC, and an international federation of doctors continue to push for more research dollars in countries where the ruling class or the military siphons off available money. These agencies have noted that little has changed since a health conference was held in Nairobi, Kenya, in 1985. International researchers are hopeful that the Women's Conference held in Beijing, China, in 1996 will reignite the push for the study of women's health. Research and health care are primitive, at best, in developing nations. In nations where female genital mutilation is still practiced as a cultural norm, pro-female research attitudes and action are not likely to develop quickly.

Research into women's health is important to all. Whether part of a developing nation's concern about population explosion or a thriving country's overall design, as women's health goes, so goes the health of future generations. (BLN) **See also** Abortion; Health Care Policy; Reproductive and Contraceptive Technologies for Women.

Bibliography

Bird, Chloe. "Women's Representation as Subjects in Clinical Studies: A Pilot Study of Research Published in JAMA." In Institute of Medicine. *Women and Health Research: Ethical, and Legal Issues of Including Women in Clinical Trials.* Washington, DC: National Academy of Sciences, 1994.

Charo, Alta. "Brief Overview of Constitutional Issues Raised by the Exclusion of Women from Clinical Trials." In Institute of Medicine. *Women and Health Research: Ethical and Legal Issues of Including Women in Clinical Trials.* Washington, DC: National Academy of Sciences, 1994.

Fee, Elizabeth and Nancy Krieger, eds. *Women's Health, Politics and Power: Essay in Sex/Gender Medicine and Public Health.* Amityville, NY: Baywood Publishers, 1994.

Meinert, Curtis L. "The Inclusion of Women in Clinical Trials." *Science* 269 (August 11, 1995): 795–96.

Mongella, Gertrude. "Global Approach to the Promotion of Women's Health." *Science* 269 (August 11, 1995): 780–90.

Morse, Mary. *Women Changing Science, Voices from a Field in Transition.* New York: Insight Books, 1995.

National Institutes of Health. "NIH Guidelines on the Inclusion of Women and Minorities as Subjects in Clinical Research." *NIH Guide* 123, no. 11 (March 18, 1994): 1–15.

Popkin, R. and L. Peddle. *Women's Health Today: Perspectives on Current Research and Clinical Practice.* New York: Parthenon Publishers, 1994.

———. "Women's Health Research Blossoms." *Science* 269 (August 11, 1995): 793–95.

Carrie Meek (1926–)

Carrie Meek, a Florida Democrat, was elected to the House of Representatives in 1992, the so-called Year of the woman. At age 66, Meek came to Congress with a strong background in public service, education, finance, and support for minorities, women, the elderly, and the poor. She previously served in the Florida state house from 1979 to 1982 and in the state senate from 1982 to 1993. The granddaughter of slaves and the daughter of sharecroppers, Meek was also a divorced mother.

In 1993, Meek supported the **Congressional Caucus for Women's Issues** in an ultimately unsuccessful fight with Illinois Republican Representative Henry Hyde over renewal of the **Hyde Amendment**, which banned the use of Medicaid funds for **abortions**. In the 105th Congress, Meek served on the Appropriations Committee. (EP)

BIBLIOGRAPHY

Bingham, Clara. *Women on the Hill: Challenging the Culture of Congress.* New York: Times Books, 1997.

Margolies-Mezvinsky, Marjorie. *A Woman's Place . . . The Freshmen Women Who Changed the Face of Congress.* New York: Crown Publishers, Inc., 1994.

Meritor Savings Bank v. Vinson (1986)

In *Meritor Savings Bank v. Vinson*, 477 U.S. 57 (1986), the U.S. Supreme Court ruled for the first time that sexual harassment was a form of **sex discrimination** prohibited by **Title VII of the Civil Rights Act of 1964**.

There are two types of sexual harassment in the workplace: quid pro quo and environmental harassment. The first occurs when a supervisor makes sexual demands on an employee with the threat of retaliation if refused. Environmental harassment occurs when a supervisor or fellow employee creates a hostile environment for the employee based on sexual comments or pictures.

The *Meritor* case began in 1980 when Mechelle Vinson filed suit in federal court, claiming that her supervisor made sexual advances to her, touched her inappropriately, and even assaulted her. The district court dismissed her case, saying she had not made a valid Title VII claim of sex discrimination. The appellate court, held that in situations where one employee subjects another to pervasive harassment in the workplace a hostile or offensive environment is created.

On appeal, the Supreme Court affirmed the appellate court, ruling that a hostile work environment created by sexual harassment violates Title VII. Speaking for a unanimous Court, Justice William Rehnquist defined harassment as "severe" and "pervasive" behavior. It was irrelevant, he said, whether the plaintiff voluntarily participated in the sexual relationship; the important issue was whether the sexual advances were "unwelcome."

Rehnquist said lower courts must examine the facts of each case to determine when employers are responsible for harassing behavior by supervisory personnel. Although a company could not escape responsibility merely by claiming it lacked notice of a supervisor's harassing behavior, by pointing to a nondiscrimination policy, or by showing that the victim did not use a company grievance procedure, the Court also did not believe that employers were automatically liable for sexual harassment by supervisors. In this case, the Court criticized the employer's grievance policy because it was a general policy against discrimination and did not specifically forbid harassment; it also required the employee to direct complaints to her supervisor, without any exceptions in cases where the supervisor was the harasser. (SM)

BIBLIOGRAPHY

MacKinnon, Catharine. *Sexual Harassment of Working Women.* New Haven, CT: Yale University Press, 1979.

Vermuelen, Joan. "Sexual Harassment." *Women and the Law.* New York: Clark Boardman, 1987.

Jan Meyers (1928–)

Jan Meyers, a Republican member of the U.S. House of Representatives from the 3rd District of Kansas, served from 1985 until 1996. She became chair of the Small Business Committee in 1995 after the Republican takeover of the House. There was talk of eliminating the Small Business Committee when the Republicans reorganized the committees. However, it was spared after it became apparent that Meyers was the only woman in line for chair of a major committee. Meyers was also a Kansas state senator from 1972 until 1984. (MEK)

BIBLIOGRAPHY

Jones, Joyce. "Setback for Small Business: But GAO Report Cites Little Reason to End SBA Program." *Black Enterprise* 26, no. 9 (April 1996): 20.

Worsham, James. "Same Gavels, New Hands." *Nation's Business* 83, no. 2 (February 1995): 42.

Helen Stevenson Meyner (1929–)

A foreign policy specialist and committed member of the **Congresswomen's Caucus**, Democrat Helen Meyner of New Jersey was first elected to the U.S. House of Representatives in 1974. She served two terms. The wife of a former state governor and a cousin of former Democratic presidential nominee Adlai Stevenson, Meyner worked in party and state politics, wrote a newspaper column, and conducted interviews on television. (JHT)

BIBLIOGRAPHY

Gertzog, Irvin N. *Congressional Women: Their Recruitment, Integration, and Behavior.* New York: Praeger, 1984.

Barbara Mikulski (1936–)

Barbara Mikulski is currently the senior woman in the U.S. Senate, having served as the senator from Maryland since 1987. She was the first Democratic woman to hold a seat in the Senate not previously held by her husband.

After her 1992 re-election, she was named the assistant floor leader, the first Senate leadership position held by a woman. Before the Republican takeover in 1995, she served as the chair of the Appropriations Subcommittee for the Veteran's Administration, the Department of Housing and Urban Development, and various independent agencies.

As a U.S. representative (1977–1987), Mikulski played a key role in the formation of the **Congresswomen's Caucus** in 1977, serving on the first Executive Committee of the organization as a member-at-large. She served as a link between outside interest groups and the congresswomen.

The one-time social worker was a member of the Baltimore City Council from 1971 to 1977; she gained prominence there in the feminist movement. She began her political career by organizing a move against a project that would have built a highway through her own historic Baltimore neighborhood and another neighborhood dominated by black homeowners. (MEK) **See also** Feminism.

BIBLIOGRAPHY

LeVeness, Frank P. and Jane P. Sweeney, eds. "Barbara Mikulski: Reporting the Neighborhood." *Woman Leaders in Contemporary U.S. Politics.* Boulder, CO: Lynne Rienner, 1987, 105–16.

Mikulski, Barbara. "How We Lost the Election but Won the Company." *Ms.* 4, no. 1 (July 1975): 59–61.

Seifer, Nancy. "Barbara Mikulski and the Blue-Collar Woman." *Ms.* 2, no. 5 (November 1973): 70–74.

Military Academies

On October 7, 1975, President Gerald Ford signed Public Law 94-106. It required the military services to admit women into their sacrosanct academies the following year in response to various demands in the political system, including calls for

Once all-male institutions, the military academies have all integrated to give greater military opportunities to women. Here a class at the Naval Academy celebrates graduation. Department of the Navy.

women's equality, the decline in the pool of males eligible for **military service**, and the replacement of the male draft in 1973 with an all volunteer military force.

Thus, the U.S. Military Academy at West Point, New York; the U.S. Naval Academy at Annapolis, Maryland; the Air Force Academy near Colorado Springs, Colorado; and the U.S. Coast Guard Academy in New London, Connecticut, admitted their first classes of women in 1976. Women were subjected to the same curricula as men except for some modifications in physical training to reflect the differences in men's and women's bodies. Women also were shielded from direct combat duty. The graduating classes of 1980 were the first coeducational classes in the history of the military academies.

More than a decade later, the battleground for women's admission into the military service shifted to the nation's remaining state-supported military academies, the Citadel in Charleston, South Carolina, and the Virginia Military Institute (VMI) in Lexington, Virginia. The courts forced both institutions to open their doors to women, the Citadel in 1995 and VMI in the fall of 1997. (CGM)

BIBLIOGRAPHY

Rustand, Richard. *Women in Khaki: The American Enlisted Woman.* New York: Praeger, 1982.

Wekesser, Carol. *Women in the Military.* San Diego : Greenhaven Press, 1991.

Military Service

Women have served with American military forces since the beginning of the nation. During the Revolutionary War they were, among other things, cooks, laundresses, military nurses, and espionage agents. Women were couriers, spies, and saboteurs during the Civil War, and performed duties such as laundering, cooking, and supplying ammunition on the battlefield. Some women also disguised themselves as men and fought in combat. Their major contribution, however, was in the field of health care. Approximately 6,000 female nurses served with the Union Army during the Civil War. During the Spanish-American War some 1,500 nurses served as civilian workers under contract to the Army and Navy. It was not until the early 1900s that Congress established the first nurse corps within the armed forces—the Army Nurse Corps in 1901 and the Navy Nurse Corps in 1908.

The first formal, organized military service by groups of nonmedical women came when the United States began to mobilize for World War I. Personnel shortages in some administrative skills led to the enrollment of approximately 12,500 Yeomenettes in the naval reserves and approximately 300 Marinettes in the Marine Corps reserves. There were requests from Army military leaders for the administrative skills and services of women in a military status, but they were disapproved by the secretary of war who was opposed to such status for women. Women who worked for the Army during World War I did so as civilian contract workers.

Faced with another global war in the early 1940s, a small military force that needed to expand quickly, and manpower shortages, the armed forces needed women as World War II began. Women's "line" (nonmedical) components were established in all branches of the service—the **Women's Army Corps (WAC)**, the Navy Women's Reserve (WAVES), the Marine Corps Women's Reserve, and the Coast Guard Women's Reserve (SPARS). The WAC, however, was the only women's corps established by law.

The Women's Army Auxiliary Corps (WAAC) was established on May 14, 1942. The following summer, Congress passed Public Law 78-110, which eliminated the auxiliary

Women have served the military needs of the nation since the Revolutionary War. Department of the Army.

status and established a Women's Army Corps (WAC) as a component of the Army. Although the WAAC bill specifically stipulated that women could only be noncombatants, there was no such wording in the WAC law. Legislators made it clear, however, during hearings on the bill, that they expected the noncombatant rule to still apply.

By the summer of 1945, there were 100,000 WACS, 86,000 WAVES, 18,000 women Marines, and 11,000 SPARS on active duty. Military women accounted for 2.3 percent of the total military strength during the war. They were deployed to all overseas theaters and proved that they could endure the hardships of field environments. They served in the traditional career fields of administration, personnel, and medical care as well as numerous nontraditional jobs such as parachute riggers, radio operators, and heavy equipment operators. The **Women's Airforce Service Pilots (WASPS)** also flew almost every airplane in the Army Air Corps inventory, including bombers, as they performed the demanding and often dangerous mission of ferrying aircraft overseas. Army nurses served close to the front lines and were exposed to danger with more than 200 becoming casualties. Fifty-four Army nurses survived the defeat of Bataan and Corregidor and were interned in the Japanese civilian camp of Santo Tomas in the Philippines for 33 months.

The strength of the women's components declined drastically following World War II with demobilization accompanied by efforts to disband them altogether. But proponents for women in the military prevailed, and in June 1948 the Women's Services Integration Act (Public Law 625) gave permanent status to women in the regular and reserve elements of all the armed forces, established a 2 percent ceiling on the proportion of women on duty in the regular forces, gave permanent status to the WAC as a separate organization within the Army (although no such organizational entities were established for the Navy, Marines, and Air Force), limited the services to one full line female colonel or Navy captain (which meant that women could not be promoted to general officer), and specifically precluded Navy and Air Force women from assignments to vessels and aircraft engaged in combat missions. Although no such legal restrictions were placed on Army women, Army policies were to comply with the "no combat" intent of the law.

The strength of the women's components remained low during both the Korean and Vietnam Wars because military personnel requirements were primarily being met by the draft. The total number of the women's components when the Korean War broke out was 22,000. It reached a high of 48,700 in October 1952 and dropped to approximately 35,000 by June 1955. Although there were 463,000 Americans in Vietnam by June 1967, the total number of military women who served there during the entire war was only 7,500 and the majority of these were nurses.

In the 1960s, military women constituted a small token force; the outlook for their programs was not positive, and recruiting remained difficult. The peacetime draft was operational, hence there was no pressure, need, or interest in using more women. The advancement potential for women in the military was also low during this time because of limited opportunities both in career fields and promotion. For example, there were 10 career management fields open to Army enlisted women in 1962, but 95 percent of the WACs were serving in only two—administration and medical care and treatment.

On November 8, 1967, Public Law 90-130 removed promotion restrictions on women officers and the 2 percent strength limitation on military women. The door was now opened for greater numbers of women in the military and for promotion of women to general officer rank, which occurred on June 11, 1970, when Anna Mae Hays, chief of the Army Nurse Corps, and Elizabeth Hoisington, director of the WAC, became the first women in U.S. history to be promoted to general officer.

With the establishment of the All Volunteer Force in 1973, the services could no longer rely upon the draft to provide their personnel needs and this led to an increase in the number of women in the military. The strength of women in the Army is a good example of the increases that occurred. From the dissolution of the draft in 1970 to 1981, the number of women in the Army increased from 17,865 to 73,778, or 9.4 percent of Army strength.

Women in the military were not immune to the feminist movement, which began to gain momentum in the late 1960s and early 1970s. Equal rights became a significant factor in the political environment and gender-based policies came under scrutiny and legal challenge in both the civilian and military sectors of society. Married military women began to receive the same family entitlements as married male service members, and women were no longer involuntarily separated for pregnancy. The increased numbers of women in the military brought about by the enactment of the All Volunteer Force, coupled with changing societal values regarding the role of women, created a climate of expanding occupational areas in general and led to new opportunities in nontraditional fields.

Women became naval aviators in 1973, Army aviators in 1974, and Air Force aviators by 1977. By the late 1970s, Navy women could be assigned to sea duty aboard noncombatant ships as well as to temporary duty (less than 180 days) aboard combatant ships. Assignments on combat logistics force ships were opened to women in December 1987, and the Navy selected its first woman to command a seagoing commissioned vessel in 1989. In the 1980s, the Marine Corps opened all occupational fields to women, except those involving combat, including overseas embassy guard duty assignments. Coast Guard vessels went to sea with mixed crews and women were given command of cutters. Coast Guard women led armed boarding parties on drug interdiction missions and piloted search and rescue aircraft.

Two other significant events for military women occurred during the 1970s—the admission of women to the all-male **military academies** and the disestablishment of the WAC. In 1975, Congress passed legislation (Public Law 94-106) admitting women to the academies. The first coed classes entered the U.S. Naval Academy, the U.S. Military Academy, and the U.S. Air Force Academy in the fall of 1976 and graduated in June 1980. Although the WAC was the only separate women's component required by law, all the services had established support structures for their women. As equality and integration moved forward, these support structures were abolished. The Navy, Marines, and Air Force accomplished this internally, and, in October 1978, Public Law 95-485 disestablished the WAC. Women officers in the Army could then be permanently assigned to all branches with the exception of the combat arms (infantry, armor, field artillery, and air defense artillery).

Military operations in the 1980s and early 1990s set the stage for removing the "no combat" policy for military women. The Army force that deployed to Grenada for Operation Urgent Fury in October 1983 included integrated units. The Coast Guard had women assigned to the crews of vessels patrolling the waters around Grenada, and the Air Force had women pilots, navigators, and enlisted crew members assigned to aircraft that were used to transport troops and equipment. In June 1987, when the destroyer tender the USS *Acadia* sailed to the Persian Gulf to repair the USS *Stark*, a frigate that had been damaged by Iraqi missiles, there were 248 women sailors (25 percent of the crew) aboard. Approximately 800 women deployed with U.S. forces to Panama in December 1989 for Operation Just Cause. Captain Linda L. Bray, the commander of the 988th Military Police Company, gained national attention when her unit's mission to seize a supposedly lightly defended objective turned into a successful infantry-style fire fight.

By 1990, there were approximately 223,000 military women on active duty, constituting almost 12 percent of the total active force. There were also 151,000 women in the reserves and guard accounting for over 13 percent of the reserve forces. Women were being used in almost all career fields except those involving combat or close proximity to combat, and as American troops mobilized and deployed for the **Persian Gulf War** it became evident that integrated male-female units were an essential part of the armed forces. The American public became aware of these integrated units as the media gave extensive publicity to military women in the field, side-by-side with their male counterparts in full desert battle gear, performing their duties, and enduring the same conditions and hardships. Approximately 41,000 military women (7 percent of U.S. forces) were deployed in the Persian Gulf theater of operations during Desert Shield and Desert Storm, and, according to **Jeanne Holm**, they performed almost all tasks except those associated with actual fighting. Thirteen women died in the war, including five Army women killed in action. Twenty-one were wounded in action, and two were taken as Prisoners of War (POWs).

The realities of modern warfare and the evolution of policies on women in the military were demonstrated during the Persian Gulf War. This crisis provided an "empirical demonstration" of the new image and role of military women—serving in the desert, on ships or planes, side-by-side with their male counterparts, being killed, wounded, and captured by the enemy. In 1991, Congress repealed the combat exclusion policy for military women aviators with the passage of Public Law 102-190. Two years later, in November 1993, Congress repealed the law that prohibited Navy and Marine Corps women from serving on combat vessels. The following year, the Department of Defense revised its policies to permit women to serve in all positions for which they are qualified, except those involving direct ground combat.

Military women constitute more than 12 percent of active duty forces and 14 percent of the reserves in the mid-1990s. The role of women in the military will continue to evolve and expand because all legal barriers to their use have been removed. Only defense policies restrict their participation in ground combat, and time will tell whether or not these policies will be challenged. (GG) **See also** *United States v. Virginia.*

Bibliography

Binkin, Martin. "The New Face of the American Military." *The Brookings Review* Summer 1991): 7–13.

Department of the Army, Office of the Deputy Chief of Staff for Personnel. *Women in the Army Policy Review.* Washington, DC: U. S. Government Printing Office, 1982.

Devilbiss, M.C. *Women in Military Service.* Maxwell Air Force Base, AL: Air University Press, 1990.

General Accounting Office. *Women in the Military: Deployment in the Persian Gulf War.* Washington, DC: U. S. Government Printing Office, 1993.

Holm, Jeanne M. *Women in the Military: An Unfinished Revolution.* rev. ed. Novato, CA: Presidio Press, 1992.

Morden, Bettie J. "The Women's Army Corps 1945–1978." *Army Historical Series.* Washington, DC: U. S. Government Printing Office, 1990.

Presidential Commission on the Assignment of Women in the Armed Forces. Washington, DC: U. S. Government Printing Office, 1992.

Rogan, Helen. *Mixed Company.* New York: Putnam's Sons, 1981.

Treadwell, Mattie E. *The Women's Army Corps.* Washington, DC: U. S. Government Printing Office, 1954.

Women's Research and Education Institute (WREI). *Women in the Military: Where They Stand.* Washington, DC: WREI, 1994.

Juanita Millender-McDonald (1938–)

Democrat Juanita Millender-McDonald was elected to the U.S. House of Representatives from California in 1996 in a special election and re-elected to a full term in November 1996. In Congress, she serves on the Transportation and Infrastructure and Small Business committees. Prior to her election to the House, she served in the California assembly from 1993 to 1996. She also served on the Carson City Council from 1990 to 1992 and as temporary mayor from 1991 to 1992.

Bibliography

Gill, LaVerne. *African American Women in Congress*. New Brunswick, NJ: Rutgers University Press, 1997.

Emma Guffey Miller (1874–1970)

Emma Miller, an active advocate of **suffrage**, was a delegate to the 1924 Democratic National Convention, the first of 12 conventions she attended. At the convention, she gave a secondary speech for Alfred E. Smith. She also served with the Women's Organization for National Prohibition Reform from 1929 to 1933 and gained an appointment to the Interstate Commerce Commission in 1933. Miller later won a seat as Democratic national committeewoman, serving from 1932 until her death. She worked closely with Mary Dawson and **Eleanor Roosevelt** on the New Deal policies to aid women. She chaired the **National Woman's Party (NWP)** from 1960 to 1965. Never running for public office, she actively campaigned for Democratic presidential nominees from Smith to Adlai Stevenson in 1952.

Bibliography

Miller, Emma. "Equal Rights: A Debate." *New York Times Magazine* (May 7, 1944): 14.
"Obituary." *New York Times*. (February 25, 1970): 51.

Frieda Segelke Miller (1890–1973)

Frieda Miller served as the director of the **Women's Bureau** of the United States Department of Labor from 1944 until 1953. Prior to this, she worked as the New York State commissioner of labor from 1938 until 1943 and helped found the Workers' Education Bureau of America.

Bibliography

"Frieda Miller Heads Women's Bureau." *Democratic Digest* 21, nos. 6–7 (June-July 1944): 31.

Kate Millet (1934–)

In 1970, Kate Millet published *Sexual Politics*, her doctoral dissertation, which analyzed various forms of victimization. The book resulted in her reputation as a forerunner in the **women's movement**. In the mid-1960s, she joined the Congress of Racial Equality and the **National Organization for Women (NOW)**. She served as chair of NOW's educational committee from 1965 to 1968. At a conference in 1970, Millet revealed her homosexuality, an action that helped unite lesbian rights with the women's movement.

On March 8, 1979, Millet traveled to Iran to speak at an **International Women's Day** rally; two weeks later, she was deported for making alleged provocations against the government, an issue she dealt with in her 1982 book *Going to Iran*. Her other works, *Flying* (1974) and *The Looney Bin Trip* (1980), focused on the plight of mentally abused individuals, helping to attract national political attention to the issue.

Bibliography

Myron, Nancy and Charlotte Bunch. *Lesbianism and the Women's Movement*. Baltimore: Diana Press, 1975.
Wandersee, Winifred D. *On the Move: American Women in the 1970s*. Boston: Twayne, 1988.

Minimum Wage/Maximum Hours Laws

Minimum wage and maximum hour laws are examples of **protective legislation** sought by the National Consumers' League and other progressive women's organizations to address the problems of working women at the turn of the century. Between 1867 and 1893, 13 states passed maximum hours laws for women as a means of improving working conditions. Most states set 10 hours as the maximum day's work, penalizing employers if they compelled women to work beyond legal maximums. Although the Illinois Supreme Court, in *Ritchie v. People* (1895), declared the hours limit unconstitutional on the grounds that it deprived women of the freedom to contract, the U.S. Supreme Court in ***Muller v. Oregon*** in 1908 upheld the right of states to enact 10-hour laws to protect the health of women workers. By 1917, 41 states had maximum-hour laws for women, with most limiting the work day to nine hours or the work week to 54 hours. Although some women benefited from the limitations on hours of work, in the absence of minimum wage laws many women found their incomes lowered and, given additional restrictions on night work and heavy work, found themselves at a disadvantage in competing with men for jobs.

Massachusetts enacted the first minimum wage for women in 1912, and by 1923, 17 states had such laws. In 1923, the Supreme Court ruled in ***Adkins v. Children's Hospital*** that minimum wage was unconstitutional and continued its opposition to legislation regulating work until the passage of the **Fair Labor Standards Act of 1938**, which set maximum hours and minimum pay standards for women and men. (AMD)

Bibliography

Kessler-Harris, Alice. *Out to Work: A History of Wage-Earning Women in the United States*. New York: Oxford University Press, 1982.

Patsy Takemoto Mink (1927–)

A liberal Democrat from Hawaii, Congresswoman Patsy Mink served in the U.S. House of Representatives from 1965 to 1977 and again from 1990 to present. As a member of the **Congressional Caucus for Women's Issues** and the Economic and Educational Opportunities Committee, Mink advocates gender equity in education and job training. As a mother who

Patsy Mink (at the podium), Democratic congresswoman from Hawaii, addresses the National Women's Conference in 1977. At the time, she was an official in the State Department. Photo by Pat Field. National Archives.

used diethylstilbestrol (DES) during pregnancy, she opposes efforts to limit product liability lawsuits and supports universal health insurance based upon the Hawaiian model.

Prior to entering Congress, Mink was a private practice attorney, state legislator, and a delegate to the 1960 Democratic Convention. In 1972, she entered the Oregon Democratic primary as a candidate for president. After leaving the House to run unsuccessfully for the Senate in 1976, Mink worked in the State Department under President Jimmy Carter. She also served as president of the Americans for Democratic Action and as a member of the Honolulu City Council. Mink lost primary contests for governor in 1986 and for mayor of Honolulu in 1988.

Reflecting on her own and her daughter's experiences with gender discrimination, Mink believes that as a female member of Congress she must "represent all the women who have no (female) representative here." (JHT)

Bibliography

Chamberlin, Hope. *A Minority of Members: Women in the U.S. Congress.* New York: Praeger, 1973.

Gertzog, Irvin N. *Congressional Women: Their Recruitment, Integration, and Behavior.* 2nd ed. Westport, CT: Praeger, 1995.

Mayer, Caroline E. "Getting Personal on Product Liability." *Washington Post* 118 (March 7, 1995): D1.

Virginia Louisa Minor (1824–1894)

In 1861, Virginia Minor joined the St. Louis Ladies Union Aid Society to help wounded soldiers and their families, a role she filled until the organization disbanded in 1865. Minor also worked closely with the Western Sanitary Commission in providing St. Louis hospitals with clothing, food, and medical supplies.

After a rejected petition to the legislature to allow women to vote, Minor went on to organize the Woman Suffrage Association of Missouri on May 8, 1867, serving in the group until 1871. From 1879 to 1890, she served as president of the St. Louis branch of the **National Women Suffrage Association (NWSA)**. She continued to fight for woman' **suffrage** until her death in 1894.

Bibliography

Minor, John B. *The Minor Family of Virginia.* Lynchburg, VA: J.P. Bell Co.,1923.

Morris, Monia Cook. "The History of Women Suffrage in Missouri, 1867–1901." *Missouri History Review* xxv (October 1930): 67-82.

Mississippi University for Women v. Hogan (1982)

In *Mississippi University for Women v. Hogan*, 458 U.S. 718 (1982), the U.S. Supreme Court ruled that the women-only admissions policy of Mississippi University for Women (MUW) violated the equal protection clause of the Fourteenth Amendment of the U.S. Constitution.

The case arose when a male was rejected by the nursing program at MUW because of his sex. Mississippi University for Women's School of Nursing only offered admission to women, although men were allowed to audit classes. When the case reached the Supreme Court, Mississippi argued that its admission policy was intended to compensate women for past discrimination against them. Speaking for a 5-4 majority, Justice **Sandra Day O'Connor** ruled that the nursing program must admit men. To justify the single-sex policy, O'Connor said, the state must establish an "exceedingly persuasive justification" with evidence of past discrimination. O'Connor indicated that MUW could only compensate women if it could show that they had been discriminated against by the university. There was no evidence, O'Connor said, that the nursing program had discriminated against women. The justice noted that Mississippi's policy helped maintain the stereotypical image of nursing as a female occupation. Additionally, the policy failed to serve its purpose; because men were admitted to the classroom as auditors and allowed to participate fully in class, MUW did not even provide women nursing students with a classroom to themselves.

In *Brown v. Board of Education* (1954), the Supreme Court had announced it was unconstitutional to separate public school students on the basis of race. In ***Vorchheimer v. Philadelphia*** (1977), the Court upheld separate public high schools for boys and girls. In *Hogan*, although the Court forced MUW to admit men, it refused to declare that "separate but equal" education on the basis of sex is unconstitutional. In ***U.S. v. Virginia*** (1996), the Supreme Court ruled that the Virginia Military Institute's policy of excluding women violated the equal protection clause of the Fourteenth Amendment. (SM) **See also** Sex Discrimination.

Bibliography

Brown v. Board of Education, 347 U.S. 483 (1954).

Gelb, Joyce and Marian Lief Palley. *Women and Public Policies.* 2d ed. Princeton, NJ: Princeton University Press, 1987.

Mezey, Susan Gluck. *In Pursuit of Equality: Women, Public Policy and the Federal Courts.* New York: St. Martin's Press, 1992.

United States v. Virginia, 116 S.Ct. 2264 (1996).

Martha "Bunny" Mitchell (1918–1976)

Martha Mitchell was married to John N. Mitchell, who served as attorney general in the Nixon administration before resigning to head Nixon's re-election campaign in 1972. She was a flamboyant and outspoken Washington insider who was one of the first to tell the press that President Nixon was involved in the Watergate cover-up. (CKC)

BIBLIOGRAPHY

Bernstein, Carl and Bob Woodward. *All The President's Men.* New York: Warner Books, 1974.

McQuiston, John T. "Martha Mitchell, 57, Dies of Bone-Marrow Cancer." *The New York Times Biographical Service* (June 1976): 885–86.

McLendon, Winzola. *Martha.* New York: Random House, 1979.

Rose Mofford (1922–)

Former Arizona governor Rose Mofford, a Democrat, worked in state government for nearly five decades. She served in the state treasurer's office (1941–1943), the Arizona State Tax Commission (1943–54), and the Arizona secretary of state's office (1954–1975). She was elected Arizona secretary of state in 1977 and served until 1988 when Republican Governor Evan Mecham was impeached and convicted by the Arizona legislature. As the highest ranking state official, Secretary Mofford succeeded him as governor, serving from 1988 to 1990. (AM)

BIBLIOGRAPHY

BPW Member: From Secretary to Governor. *National Business Woman* 69, no. 5 (October-November 1988): 41.

Susan Molinari (1958–)

Republican Susan Molinari was elected to the U.S. House of Representatives from New York in a special election in 1990, becoming the youngest member of Congress. She became an active force within the party and in national politics very quickly. She was an active and articulate defender of the "contract with America" and delivered the keynote address at the 1996 Republican National Convention. In Congress, she served as the Republican Conference vice-chair in a position that placed her in key legislative decision-making meetings. In August 1997, Molinari resigned from Congress to pursue a career in broadcasting as cohost of the CBS Saturday Morning News. Molinari resigned from the program in 1998 after only nine months on the air.

BIBLIOGRAPHY

Baker, Russ. "Molinari Family Values." *The Nation* (August 26, 1996): 20.

Bumiller, Elisabeth. "The Politics of Personality." *The New York Times Magazine* (November 2, 1997): 36.

Molinari, Susan. "Legacy of Hope and Opportunity." *Vital Speeches* 62, no. 22 (September 1, 1996): 681.

"Mommy Track." *See* Family Leave/Mommy Track

Elizabeth Kortright Monroe (c. 1763–1830)

Elizabeth Kortright Monroe, wife of President James Monroe, supported her husband in his political career as U.S. senator, minister to France, governor of Virginia, minister to Great Britain, secretary of state, and president of the United States. While James Monroe served as U.S. minister to France from 1794 to 1796, Elizabeth Monroe, known as "la belle Americaine," convinced the Committee of Public Safety in France to release Madame de Lafayette, the wife of an influential friend. While serving as first lady, she was active in managing the social affairs of the president. During President Monroe's second term, she played a small role because her health began to fail. **See also** First Ladies.

BIBLIOGRAPHY

Caroli, Betty Boyd. *First Ladies.* New York: Oxford University Press, 1987.

Montana State Federation of Negro Women's Clubs

The Montana State Federation of Negro Women's Clubs formed after individual regional groups from Kalispell, Butte, Helena, Anaconda, Billings, and Bozeman met from August 3 to August 5, 1921. The organization was established with the distinct purpose of unifying all of Montana's regional clubs to provide a more powerful base to their goals.

The Montana State Federation of Negro Women's Clubs set a number of goals, including college scholarship funds for black students, delegations to the National Convention of Negro Women's Clubs, and support for the Anti-Lynching League and the NAACP. In addition, the group was active with civil rights and in promoting pride in the African-American community by sponsoring the Frederick Douglass Day Program and donating books by African Americans to libraries. Working for racial unity and harmony, the group disbanded in the 1970s because of declining membership. **See also** Club Movement.

BIBLIOGRAPHY

Williams, Fannie Barrier. "The Club Movement Among Colored Women of America." In Booker T. Washington, Norman B. Wood, and Fannie B. Williams, eds. *A New Negro for a New Century.* New York: Arno Press, 1969.

Zinn, Maxine Baca and Bonnie Thornton, eds. *Women of Color in U.S. Society.* Philadelphia: Temple University, 1994.

Constance A. Morella (1931–)

Constance A. Morella, one of the most liberal Republicans in the U.S. House, has served the 8th District of Maryland since 1987. Examples of her liberal votes include seven votes against measures in the Republican "contract with America," which she signed. She cast three more negative votes against the contract than any other Republican. She was one of three Republicans who voted against the Gulf War resolution in 1991. She was also one of three Republicans who voted "present" for the close election of Newt Gingrich's second term as speaker of the House in January 1997. She is pro-choice and in favor of gun control. These votes and views have helped her continue to win elections in her primarily Democratic suburban Washington, D.C., district.

Despite her record, she was appointed chair of the high-profile Technology Subcommittee of the Science Committee. In becoming a voice for women's issues, Morella has served as the co-chair of the **Congressional Caucus for Women's Issues**, and in the 105th Congress, served on its Executive Committee.

She served in the Maryland House of Delegates from 1979 until 1986. (MEK)

BIBLIOGRAPHY

Bingham, Clara. *Women on the Hill.* New York: Times Books, 1997.

Carol Moseley-Braun (1947–)

In 1992, Illinois Democrat Carol Moseley-Braun became a symbol of change in the U.S. Congress when she was elected the first black woman in the Senate. She had served 10 years in the Illinois state legislature (1979–1988) where she became the first female assistant majority leader in the state house in 1983. She also served as Cook County recorder of deeds from 1988 through 1992. In the 1992 Senate race, her opposition to the Supreme Court nomination of Clarence Thomas helped propel her to an upset primary victory over incumbent Democrat Alan Dixon.

Moseley-Braun has become known as an energetic politician and eloquent spokesperson for women and African Americans. Early in her congressional career, this role was highlighted by a highly publicized threat to filibuster a vote on a controversial congressional design patent for the **United Daughters of the Confederacy**, which sparked a discussion of racism and slavery in American history on the Senate floor. Moseley-Braun has also led the charge against "dead-beat" dads, pursuing legislation to enforce child support payments. She has supported issues dealing with family and health, including women's reproductive rights. (MBS)

BIBLIOGRAPHY

Jelen, Ted G. "Carol Moseley-Braun: The Insider as Insurgent." In Elizabeth Adell Cook, Sue Thomas, and Clyde Wilcox, eds. *The Year of the Woman.* Boulder, CO: Westview, 1994, 71–86.

Moseley-Braun, Carol. "Student on the Extension of the Patent of the Insignia of the United Daughters of the Confederacy." *Vital Issues* 14, no. 1–2 (1992): 20–27.

Belle Lindner Israels Moskowitz (1877–1933)

From 1908 to 1910, Belle Moskowitz served on the staff of *The Survey*, a paper dedicated to the analysis of social problems. She also worked with the **Progressive Party** beginning in 1912, and served as secretary of the Mayor's Committee of Women on National Defense in New York during World War I. Moskowitz acted as consultant to New York Governor Alfred Smith from 1919 to 1921 and from 1923 to 1929, helping to formulate social reform policy.

BIBLIOGRAPHY

Moskowitz, Belle L. "Junior Politics and Politicians." *Saturday Evening Post* 203 (September 6, 1930): 6–7, 149–50.

Perry, Elisabeth Israels. *Belle Moskowitz: Feminine Politics and the Exercise of Power in the Age of Alfred E. Smith.* New York: Oxford University Press, 1987.

Lucretia Coffin Mott (1793–1880)

Lucretia Mott's faith as a Quaker led her to pursue an activist life, becoming a leader in both the abolitionist and the **suffrage** movements in the nineteenth century.

Born to a whaling family on Nantucket Island, Massachusetts, Lucretia Coffin was raised with a spirit of independence and a firm conviction in the equality of the sexes that was fostered by her family's religious beliefs. After her marriage to James Mott, she taught school in Philadelphia before being ordained as a Quaker minister of the Hicksite Sect. Thus commenced her public career as a speaker, first in the cause of anti-slavery and, later, in the name of woman suffrage.

Lucretia Mott founded the Female Anti-Slavery Society and her household was a stop on the underground railroad for fugitive slaves on their way to freedom in the north. It was her action on behalf of **abolition** that led her to London in 1840 for the World Anti-Slavery Convention. When the women delegates were denied entrance to the proceedings, Lucretia Mott and **Elizabeth Cady Stanton** resolved to convene a conference on women's rights upon their return to the United States.

Eight years later, Mott coauthored the **Declaration of Sentiments and Resolutions** with Stanton, marking the beginning of an organized **women's movement** at Seneca Falls, New York. Mott's influence on Stanton and **Susan B. Anthony** was profound. Her moral leadership helped to guide the **National Woman Suffrage Association (NWSA)**.

Like many of the leaders of the early women's movement, Lucretia Mott's activism extended beyond abolition and suffrage to include related social and political issues such as **temperance** and legislative reform of the laws governing marriage and divorce. It was the breadth of this reformist social agenda that led to the formation of a rival suffrage organization, the **American Woman Suffrage Association (AWSA)** led by **Lucy Stone** and **Julia Ward Howe**. Before her death in 1880, Lucretia Mott tried to bring these two organizations together to achieve the vote for women. (WGC) **See also** Seneca Falls Convention.

BIBLIOGRAPHY

Bacon, Margaret H. *Valiant Friend.* New York: Willer & Company, 1989.

Bryant, Jennifer. *Lucretia Mott.* Grand Rapids, MI: Eerdman's, 1996.

Farber, Doris. *Lucretia Mott.* Boston: Chelsea House, 1990.

Ms. Magazine

When *Ms.* magazine appeared in 1972 with **Gloria Steinem** as its first editor, it was designed to deliver the message of the revitalized **women's movement** and to promote passage of the **Equal Rights Amendment (ERA)**, which had been proposed but had not received the needed approval by 38 states. *Ms.* became so closely linked with the ERA that opponent **Phyllis Schlafly** charged that it was for **abortion** and against family and children. In a study conducted by E. Barbara Phillips, comparing *Ms.* with the more traditional *Family Circle*, it was revealed that women covered in *Ms.* were more likely to be in politics or public service and to come from racially diverse backgrounds.

Initially unable to convince backers that the concept of *Ms.* was viable, the editors won approval for only 300,000 sample copies, which sold out in eight days. Despite its eventual success, many feminists were offended by advertising they perceived as sexist. This criticism of its advertising continued to plague *Ms.*, and in 1990 the magazine shut down for seven months to recreate itself. The new version, appearing in July 1993, maintains vigilant control of its content amidst criticism that it exhibits a middle-class bias. Former editor Robin Morgan insists, however, that *Ms.* has received awards for multicultural inclusiveness, general excellence, content, and design. (EP) **See also** Feminism.

Bibliography

Deckard, Barbara Sinclair. *The Women's Movement: Political, Socioeconomic, and Psychological Issues.* New York: Harper and Row, 1983.

Phillips, E. Barbara. "Magazines' Heroines: Is *Ms.* Just Another Member of the *Family Circle?*" In Gaye Tuchman, ed. *Hearth and Home: Images of Women in the Mass Media.* New York: Oxford Books, 1978.

Muller v. Oregon (1908)

Muller v. Oregon, 208 U.S. 412 (1908), challenged an Oregon maximum hours statute that limited the work day for women in factories, laundries, and other "mechanical establishments" to 10 hours. The suit challenged the law by claiming that it violated the equal protection clause of the Fourteenth Amendment.

In a previous decision, *Lochner v. New York* (1905), the Supreme Court ruled that maximum hour legislation interfered with the individual's right to contract guaranteed by the Fourteenth Amendment. In light of this precedent, Oregon's attorney in the *Muller* case, Louis D. Brandeis, prepared over 100 pages of "statistical" information on the relationship between hours of labor and the health and morals of women.

The "Brandeis brief" convinced the Court to rule unanimously in favor of Oregon. In the Court's opinion, Justice Brewer wrote that the precedent of *Lochner* did not apply because the differences between the sexes justified a "different rule respecting a restriction of the hours of labor." Woman's "physical structure and a proper discharge of her maternal functions, having in view not merely her own health, but the well-being of the race, justify legislation to protect her from the greed as well as the passion of man." As far as a woman's right to contract, Brewer responded that "there is that in her disposition and habits of life which will operate against a full assertion of those rights . . . she is properly placed in a class by herself, and legislation designed for her protection may be sustained."

The decision in *Muller v. Oregon* and the rationale of the Court's opinion was used as precedent to uphold **protective legislation** barring women from employment and other opportunities for more than six decades. A standard of "ordinary scrutiny" was developed for deciding cases for sex-based classifications, under which only a "reasonable" connection between a law and the public interest need be demonstrated to sustain the classification. (MBS)

Bibliography

Goldstein, Leslie Friedman. *The Constitutional Rights of Women.* New York: Longman, 1979.

"Murphy Brown"

Murphy Brown, a fictional character on a popular situation comedy, became a political target when she dealt with an unplanned pregnancy by deciding to have the baby as a single mother. The episodes in this story line aired in the spring of 1992. Republican Vice President Dan Quayle was on the campaign trail when he attributed the 1992 Los Angeles riots to a "poverty of values," which he said was exemplified by "a character who supposedly epitomizes today's intelligent, highly-paid professional woman—mocking the importance of fathers, by bearing a child alone and calling it just another 'lifestyle choice.'" The attack triggered a national debate on "family values." The remarks caused trouble for the **Republican Party;** as one Republican woman commented, "You can't be strongly pro-life and then criticize single mothers." (CKC)

Bibliography

Clift, Eleanor and Clara Bingham. "The Murphy Brown Policy." *Newsweek* 119 (June 1, 1992): 46.

"Dan Quayle vs. Murphy Brown." *Time* 22 (June 1, 1992): 22.

Patty Murray (1950–)

In 1992, Patty Murray became the first woman elected to the U.S. Senate from Washington State. Murray previously served on her local school board and in the Washington State senate. She campaigned as the "mom in tennis shoes"—a moniker she had received as a volunteer fighting school funding cuts—to set her apart as an outsider and average mother concerned about community issues. In office, Murray, a Democrat, has fought for resources for **child care**, nutrition, health care, and education as part of a legislative package she calls "commitment to children." Other areas of activity for Murray have included environmental protection and international trade for her state, reproductive rights for women, veterans' affairs, and **sexual harassment** issues. (MBS)

Bibliography

Schroedel, Jean R. and Bruce Snyder. "Patty Murray: The Mom in Tennis Shoes Goes to the Senate." In Elizabeth Adell Cook, Sue Thomas, and Clyde Wilcox, eds. *The Year of the Woman.* Boulder, CO: Westview, 1994, 49–70.

Pauli Murray (1911–1985)

Pauli Murray, an African American, began her political career as a civil rights activist in 1940 when she began to fight segregation on interstate buses. In 1945, Murray became deputy attorney general of California. From 1956 to 1960, she returned to private practice. In the 1960s and 1970s, Murray served on the President's Commission for Civil Rights, the national board of the American Civil Liberties Union, and the **National Organization for Women (NOW)**. In 1977, Murray was ordained into the Episcopal priesthood, making her the first ordained woman of the church. Besides her active approach to reform, Murray also wrote on her views of government and equal rights in a number of her works, including *States' Law on Race and Color* (1951) and *Proud Shoes* (1956).

Bibliography

Murray, Pauli. "The Liberation of Black Women." In Mary L. Thompson, ed. *Voices of the New Feminism.* Boston: Beacon, 1976.

——. "The Negro Woman's Stake in the Equal Rights Amendment." *Harvard Civil Rights-Civil Liberation Law Review* 6 (March 1971): 253–59.

——. *Pauli Murray: The Autobiography of a Black Activist, Feminist, Lawyer, Priest, and Poet.* Knoxville: University of Tennessee Press, 1989.

Murray, Pauli and Mary O. Eastwood. "Jane Crow and the Law: Sex Discrimination and Title VII." *George Washington Law Review* 34 (December 1965): 232–56.

Betsy Myers (1960–)

Betsy Myers, deputy assistant to President Bill Clinton and director of Women's Initiatives and Outreach, serves as liaison between the president and women's organizations. In an interview with *Working Woman*, Myers pointed out that as a former business owner and as a previous assistant administrator, she understands women's business concerns. (EP)

Bibliography

Klely, Kathy. "Washington Watch." *Working Woman* (December 1995): 14.

Dee Dee Myers (1961–)

Dee Dee Myers served as White House press secretary in the Clinton administration from 1993 to 1994. The first woman to ever serve in that post, she did not enjoy the same salary and perks as previous press secretaries. Her relations with the press were also strained; she functioned more as a daily briefer than a policymaker because she was not a part of President Bill Clinton's inner circle. She finally gained some salary and status concessions just prior to her resignation. She is currently an editor at *Vanity Fair.* (JCS)

Bibliography

O'Brien, Patricia. "A Cautionary Tale." *Working Woman* 21 (January 1996): 48–51.

Sue Myrick (1941–)

Sue Myrick represents the 9th District of North Carolina in the U.S. House of Representatives, a position she won in 1994 after the retirement of Republican Representative Alex McMillian. A conservative Republican, she supported the "contract with America." Her Republican freshman colleagues elected her the freshman class liaison to the leadership, and Newt Gingrich named her to the 104th Congress Transition Team. In the 105th Congress, she continued to interact with the Republican leadership as the sophomore liaison to the leadership and held a position on the powerful Rules Committee.

Some argue Myrick's victory in 1994 was something of a political comeback for the former mayor of Charlotte, North Carolina (1987–1991). During her re-election campaign for mayor, Myrick feuded with religious activists, which tarnished her image and resulted in attacks on her personal life. This feud contributed to a loss in 1992 when she ran in the Senate primary against Lauch Faircloth. In 1994, Myrick benefited from redistricting in North Carolina. The creation of two majority black districts removed many of the district's black voters, creating a comfortable Republican seat. After winning a run-off primary in 1994, her victory was almost assured. Myrick also served on the Charlotte City Council from 1983 to 1985. (MEK)

Bibliography

Bowens, Gregory J. "Myrick Easily Wins GOP Runoff in 9th." *Congressional Quarterly Weekly Report* 52, no. 22 (June 4, 1994): 1458.

N

Nashville Gas Company v. Satty (1977)

In *Nashville Gas Company v. Satty*, 434 U.S. 136 (1977), Nora Satty sued her employer, Nashville Gas Company, for violating her rights under **Title VII of the Civil Rights Act of 1964**. At issue was the company's policy of requiring pregnant employees to take leave, but not allowing the employee to receive sick-leave pay or accumulate seniority while on leave although it allowed employees to do both when they were out for other reasons. The district court found in favor of Satty. On appeal, however, the U.S. Supreme Court separated the two issues of sick-leave pay and accumulation of seniority. On the issue of seniority, the Court found that the company's policy did discriminate against women because it imposed a burden. However, following its decision in ***General Electric Company v. Gilbert***, the Court found that the company was free to decide for itself whether to fund pregnancy under its sick-leave policy.

Bibliography

Flygare, Thomas. "Schools and the Law—A Legal Embarrassment." *Phi Delta Kappan* 59 (April 1978): 558–59.

Mezey, Susan. *In Pursuit of Equality*. New York: St. Martin's Press, 1992.

National American Woman Suffrage Association (NAWSA)

The National American Woman Suffrage Association resulted from the merger in 1890 of the **American Woman Suffrage Association (AWSA)** led by **Lucy Stone** and the **National Woman Suffrage Association** led by **Elizabeth Cady Stanton** and **Susan B. Anthony**. Stanton served as its first president for one year and then was succeeded by Anthony who served as president until 1900. However, **Carrie Chapman Catt** (president 1900–1904, 1916–1920) led the final successful campaign for **suffrage**. For decades, the NAWSA had separated its state and national campaigns for the franchise. It was not until 1916 when Catt took over the organization again with her "winning plan" of campaigning simultaneously on both the state and federal levels that success was achieved. Under her leadership, she converted members of Congress as well as President Woodrow Wilson to the cause, and on August 26, 1920, the **Nineteenth Amendment** became part of the United States Constitution. The passage of a suffrage amendment in New York State (1917) and the adoption of prohibition in the form of the **Eighteenth Amendment** (1919) were crucial to the success of the campaign. The NAWSA disbanded in 1920 but reformed shortly thereafter as the League of Women Voters whose honorary president was Carrie Chapman Catt until her death in 1947. (AM) **See also** National League of Women Voters.

Bibliography

Anthony, Susan B. and Ida Husted Harper, eds. *History of Woman Suffrage*. vol. IV. New York: Source Book Press, 1970.

Catt, Carrie Chapman and Nettie Rogers Shuler. *Woman Suffrage and Politics: the Inner Story of the Suffrage Movement*. Seattle: University of Washington Press, 1969.

National Association of Colored Women (NACW)

The National Association of Colored Women was founded in July 1896. The organization was created at a convention in Washington, D.C., when a number of regional colored women's clubs merged with the **National Federation of Afro-American Women (NFAAW)** to provide a more unified stand. Membership of the NACW consisted of women born both before and after slavery, including such historic figures as **Harriet Tubman**, **Ida Wells-Barnett**, President **Mary Church Terrell**, Vice Presidents Frances E. W. Harper, Josephine St. Pierre Ruffin, and Fanny J. Coppin, and Charlotte Foster Grimke. With the motto "Lifting As We Climb," the group actively supported various regional African-American women's clubs. The NACW also helped organize kindergartens, safe housing for young working women, and child and elderly care programs in various communities. Through the years, the group also supported whatever issues were relevant to the group and the particular period, including **temperance**, **suffrage**, and equal rights. **See also** Club Movement; Slavery and Woman.

Bibliography

Jones, Beverly Washington. "Mary Church Terrell and the National Association of Colored Women, 1896–1901." *Journal of Negro History* 67, no. 1 (1982): 20–33.

Shaw, Stephanie F. "Black Club Women and the Creation of the NACW." *Journal of American History* 78, no. 2 (September 1991): 559–90.

National Association of Women Business Owners

The National Association of Women Business Owners was founded in 1974 as the Association of Women Business Owners. This organization is dedicated to three main purposes that summarize its overall philosophy: providing mutual support in its collective membership, sharing relevant experiences and skills among its members, and broadening the amount of opportunities available to women in business. To achieve these goals, the group offers a number of workshops, seminars, and leadership training programs to its members. The organization also sponsors the Annual Economic Conference, a gathering of businesswomen from across the country, and provides representation before local, state, and national government bodies.

BIBLIOGRAPHY

Tan-Whelan, Linda. *The Women's Economic Justice Agenda: Ideas for the States.* Washington, DC: National Center for Policy Attention, 1994.

———. "Political Careers Appealing to More Women." *National Business Woman* 63, no. 1 (February-March 1982): 5–6.

National Black Women's Health Project (NBWHP)

The National Black Women's Health Project, a private, nonprofit organization headquartered in Washington, D.C., was created in 1981 as a self-help organization dedicated to improving the health status of African-American women, especially those of low income. This association operates several major programs in various regions of the country, holds national and regional conferences annually, and offers wellness education services in 42 states. Furthermore, it works to collect and disseminate useful information to health care providers and educators, helps shape workable prevention programs, and motivates African-American women to assume responsibility for their health.

Among the major programs operated by the NBWHP is The Center for Black Women's Wellness, located in the Atlanta Public Housing Community. This center provides an array of services, including a self-help program, preventative health screening and gynecological exams, social services, and educational and career opportunities for adult women and adolescents. Sister Reach is an international networking and self-help program of the NBWHP designed to include women's groups in West Africa, Central and South America, the Caribbean, and Canada. The Walking for Wellness Program organizes walkathons designed to promote health and wellness through fitness. It targets black women in the workplace who are underpaid and in sedentary jobs, and women who are at home and unable to afford membership in health clubs. The Public Policy and Education Program is another of its major undertakings, which researches, analyzes, and promotes public policies that will improve the health status of black women. (JDG)

BIBLIOGRAPHY

Office of Minority Health Resource Center Database Record. *National Black Women's Health Project* (July 11, 1997).

National Child Care Staffing Study

The National Child Care Staffing Study, conducted in 1989 as part of the Child Care Employee Project, explored the relationship between staff working conditions and the quality of center-based **child care**. Information was obtained through child assessments, interviews with teaching staff and center directors, and classroom observations in 227 centers in five metropolitan areas. The study's major findings indicate that the education level of the teaching staff and the organization of the adult work environment, particularly staff wages, strongly determine the caliber of services provided to children at care facilities.

In light of these findings, the study recommends an increase in child care teacher salaries, which fall substantially below wages earned by comparably educated individuals in other fields. This lack of adequate compensation, the study reports, contributes to the high turnover rate among child care providers and thus lowers the quality of care children receive. The study further recommends an increase in the number of child care teachers with formal and specialized education and calls for the adoption of state and national standards in regard to child-adult ratios and staff training, education, and compensation. Many specific suggestions as to how to carry out the recommendations are described, with the need for parental pressure on government and employers cited as key to catalyzing the necessary change. (AMR)

BIBLIOGRAPHY

Whitebook, Marcy. *Who Cares? Child Care Teachers and the Quality of Care in America. Final Report, National Child Care Staffing Study.* Berkeley, CA: Child Care Employee Project, 1989.

———. *Who Cares? Child Care Teachers and the Quality of Care in America. Executive Summary, National Child Care Staffing Study.* Berkeley, CA: Child Care Employee Project, 1989.

National Council of Negro Women (NCNW)

The National Council of Negro Women was founded in 1935 after many years work by **Mary MacLeod Bethune,** among others. The NCNW has been the most successful African-American women's group working in a host of areas, including labor rights, civil rights, jobs, education, and health care reform. The organization has also been dedicated to international peace and has had an official observer at the United Nations for decades. Bethune was the organization's first president and helped to establish it as a leading organization. The NCNW has benefited from strong presidents, including **Dorothy I. Height,** who helped to place the organization on a sound financial footing.

Bibliography

Giddings, Paula. *When and Where I Enter*. New York: Morrow, 1984.

National Federation of Afro-American Women (NFAAW)

The National Federation of Afro-American Women was founded in 1895 by Josephine St. Pierre Ruffin. The NFAAW was the first national organization for African-American women. The group was active in seeking social changes to improve the status of women and to preserve the contributions of African-American women to both American society and to each other. The organization chose Margaret Washington, wife of Booker T. Washington, as its first president. In 1896, however, the organization merged with the Colored Women's League to form the **National Association of Colored Women (NACW)**.

Bibliography

Davis, Elizabeth. *Lifting as They Climb*. Washington, DC: NACW, 1933.

National Federation of Business and Professional Women's Clubs, Inc., of the USA (BPW/USA)

The National Federation of Business and Professional Women's Clubs was founded in 1919 as an exclusive organization for women business workers. The group currently includes membership from both sexes and every age, religion, and social, economic, and political background. The BPW has expanded its original practices as a self-support foundation for its female business workers to include wider sweeping reforms in achieving equality in the workplace as well as educational and informational resources. The BPW provides professional development, networking, and career advancement opportunities for working women while also sponsoring and influencing elected officials on women's issues.

Bibliography

Lemons, J. Stanley. *The Woman Citizen*. Urbana: University of Illinois Press, 1973.

National League of Women Voters

The National League of Women Voters, called the League of Women Voters since 1946, formed in 1920 following ratification of the **Nineteenth Amendment** to the U.S. Constitution granting women the right to vote. The league is an offshoot of the now defunct **American Woman Suffrage Association (AWSA)**.

Educating women to the governmental process and socializing them to the importance of political participation became the League's main organizational goals. Further, the League advocated public policies that extended maternal and marital benefits to women as well as protect infants and children.

Maud Wood Park served as the first president of the National League of Women Voters, a nonpartisan civic organization open to all. Library of Congress.

The League has since broadened its approach and moved away from its feminist roots, now focusing its attention on political education and empowerment. Achieving this goal is accomplished in two ways. First, the organizational structure is grassroots in orientation. Each of the more than 1,200 state and local leagues is autonomous in its decision making. Second, the league does not take a partisan stand on any political issue, nor does it make donations to electoral campaigns or political parties. Its primary focus is to provide neutral information about issues and candidates, including their voting records, and to increase voter registration. The League also provides an effective training ground for women entering politics. The League has promoted its educational mission by sponsoring the 1976, 1980, and 1984 presidential and vice presidential debates through its education fund. In 1974, the League extended its membership to men. Current membership is approximately 120,000 and includes about 5,000 men. (TSF) **See also** Suffrage.

Bibliography

Black, Naomi. "The Politics of the League of Women Voters." *International Social Science Journal* 35, no. 4 (1983): 585–603.

Cain, Becky. "The League of Women Voters." *Social Education* 59, no. 5 (September 1995): 290–92.

Smith, Ethel M. *Toward Equal Rights for Man and Women*. Washington, DC: National League of Women Voters, 1929.

Stuart, Mrs. Robert J. "New Political Power of Women." *Ladies Home Journal* 81 (September 1964): 68.

Young, Louise M. *In the Public Interest: The League of Women Voters, 1920–1970*. New York: Greenwood, 1989.

National Organization for Women (NOW)

The National Organization for Women is the largest feminist organization in the country, with 600 chapters in all 50 states representing 250,000 members. The organization is dedicated to pushing for social change to achieve equality for women. Its activities include electoral mobilization, legislative lobbying, litigation, and other forms of political expression, including marches and demonstrations. In 1992, over 750,000 **abortion** rights supporters participated in NOW's "**March for Women's Lives**" in Washington, D.C., the largest protest ever in the U.S. capital. In addition to feminist issues of economic equality and abortion rights, and an **Equal Rights Amendment (ERA)** to the U.S. Constitution, NOW's agenda also includes gay and lesbian rights, opposition to racism, and prevention of violence against women.

The National Organization for Women is affiliated with a nonprofit education and litigation organization called NOW Foundation as well as two political action committees, NOW/PAC and NOW Equality PAC (NEP), which fund feminist candidates in national and state/local elections, respectively. The National Organization for Women/Political Action Committee's 1992 "Elect Women for a Change" campaign contributed greatly to that year's electoral victory for women and helping 1992 to become known as "The Year of the Woman."

The National Organization for Women, Inc., was founded in 1966 in Washington, D.C., by attendees of the **Third National Conference of State Commissions on the Status of Women**. The group's first president was **Betty Friedan**, author of ***The Feminine Mystique*** (1963). (MBS) **See also** Feminism; Women's Movement.

Bibliography

Friedan, Betty. "N.O.W. How it Began." *Woman Speaking* (April 1967).

Goldsmith, Judy B. "How to Win Friends and Influence Legislators." *Ms.* 2 (July-August 1990): 90.

Hanmel, Lisa. "NOW Organized." In June Sochen, ed. *The New Feminism in 20th Century America.* Lexington, MA: D.C. Heath, 1971, 173–78.

Ireland, Patricia. *What Women Want.* New York: E.P. Dutton, 1995.

Smeal, Eleanor. "Why I Support a New Party." *Ms.* 2 (January-February 1991): 72–73.

Wandersee, Winifred D. "Into the Mainstream: The National Organization for Women and Its National Constituency." *On the Move.* Boston: Twayne, 1988, 36–54.

National Woman Suffrage Association (NWSA)

The National Woman Suffrage Association was founded in 1869 by **Elizabeth Cady Stanton** and **Susan B. Anthony**, who were angered by the policies of the **Equal Rights Association (ERA)**. The ERA would not shift its focus from securing rights for the newly freed slaves and women to one that focused more on women. As a result, Stanton and Anthony founded the NWSA, which focused exclusively on the rights of women. The NWSA's goal was a national women's suffrage amendment to the U.S. Constitution while the **American Woman Suffrage Association (AWSA)**, the successor to the Equal Rights Association, took a state-by-state approach. The NWSA was also markedly more feminist in its approach and policies; for example, it barred men from holding office in the organization. The group also sent a delegation to disrupt the Centennial celebration being held at Philadelphia in 1876 when it presented its **Declaration of the Rights of Women**. The NWSA soon became the nation's leading **suffrage** organization. As the ideological differences between it and the AWSA narrowed, the two merged in 1890 to form the **National American Woman Suffrage Association (NAWSA). See also** Feminism; Women's Movement.

In this 1913 photo, two suffragists hold a banner reading "National Woman Suffrage Association." Library of Congress, National Woman Suffrage Association Collection.

Bibliography

Lutz, Alma. *Created Equal: A Biography of Elizabeth Cady Stanton, 1815-1902.* New York: Day, 1940.

———. *Susan B. Anthony*. Boston: Beacon, 1959.

Stanton, Elizabeth C., Susan B. Anthony, and Matilda J. Gage, eds. *History of Woman Suffrage*. Rochester, 1881–1922.

National Woman's Loyal League (NWLL)

The National Woman's Loyal League formed on May 14, 1863, to support the **abolition** of slavery and the passage of the Thirteenth Amendment. At its founding meeting in New York City, **Lucy Stone**, its president, **Elizabeth Cady Stanton**, **Susan B. Anthony**, and **Angelina Grimke**, the group's vice president, spoke to the gathering about the Civil War, the Emancipation Proclamation, and other abolition topics. After some debate, women's rights was added to the issues that the group supported, although some members still held that such an inclusion diverted their focus and energy from group's original purpose.

On February 9, 1864, the National Woman's Loyal League presented a massive petition in support of the proposed Thirteenth Amendment to Senator Charles Sumner, the amendment's sponsor. The petition contained more than 100,000 signatures. When Stone and other members of the group delivered the document to Congress, it was too heavy for the pages, usually young boys, to carry. Two free black men were found to present the petition. The group continued to gather petition signatures and later presented an additional 300,000 signatures to Congress. The Thirteenth Amendment was ratified on December 18, 1865, abolishing slavery in the United States. The NWLL disbanded soon thereafter. **See also** Slavery and Women.

BIBLIOGRAPHY

Flexinor, Eleanor. *Century of Struggle.* Cambridge, MA: Belknap Press, 1959.

Ken, Andrea. *Lucy Stone: Speaking Out for Equality.* New Brunswick, NJ: Rutgers University Press, 1992.

National Woman's Party (NWP)

Founded in 1916 as an outgrowth of the **Congressional Union**, the National Woman's Party is known for its militant suffragist tactics under the leadership of **Alice Paul**. Focused solely

Formed in 1916, the National Woman's Party used controversial tactics like this 1917 demonstration at the White House to draw attention to its goals. Library of Congress, National Woman's Party Collection.

on winning **suffrage** for women, the NWP's strategy included raising public awareness through demonstrations and holding the "pro-suffrage" **Democratic Party** accountable for its lack of progress by campaigning against Democratic candidates. Following ratification of the **Nineteenth Amendment** in 1920, the NWP devoted itself exclusively to passage of the **Equal Rights Amendment (ERA).** Although the party has declined in size and influence, it remains dedicated to the single issue of ratification of the ERA. (LvA)

BIBLIOGRAPHY

Lunardini, Christine A. *From Equal Suffrage to Equal Rights: Alice Paul and the National Woman's Party, 1910–1928.* New York: New York University Press, 1986.

———. "National Woman's Party." In Sarah Slavin, ed. *U.S. Women's Interest Groups: Institutional Profiles.* Westport, CT: Greenwood Press, 1995.

National Woman's Rights Convention

The National Woman's Rights Convention was held in 1850 in Worcester, Massachusetts, at Brinkley Hall. The event was organized by **Lucy Stone**, **Abby Kelley Foster**, and **Paulina Wright Davis**, some of the leading suffragists of the time. The convention also included a number of noted feminist leaders, including Ernestine Rose, **Angelina Grimke**, **Lucretia Mott**, and **Sojourner Truth**, as well as such other prominent figures as Wendell Philips, William H. Channing, Gerrit Smith, Bronson Alcott, and William Lloyd Garrison. Over 1,000 people attended the convention, making it one of the most widely attended equal rights conferences of the time. The 1850 convention also passed resolutions on legal, educational, and social rights for women, along with a number of other plans for equal civil rights. After 1850, conferences were held yearly from 1851 to 1856 and again from 1858 to 1860. **See also** Abolition; Suffrage.

BIBLIOGRAPHY

Anthony, Susan B. and Ida Husted Harper. "National Organizations of Women." In Susan B. Anthony and Ida Husted Harper, eds. *History of Woman Suffrage.* vol. 4. New York: Arno Press, 1969.

Ken, Andrea. *Lucy Stone: Speaking Out for Equality.* New Brunswick, NJ: Rutgers University Press, 1992.

National Women's Conference (1977)

The National Women's Conference was held from November 18 to November 21, 1977, in Houston, Texas, to meet the needs and concerns of women nationwide. The conference was organized by the National Commission on the Observance of **International Women's Year**, a group begun by President Gerald Ford on January 9, 1975. The committee overseeing the conference was chaired first by Jill Ruckelshaus and then by Elizabeth Athanasakos during Ford's administration. During President Jimmy Carter's administration, **Bella Abzug** served as chair.

Between 130,000 and 150,000 women participated in state conferences dedicated to devising a National Plan of Action to be voted on at the National Women's Conference; this plan included a number of issues that women believed government needed to address to make progress in achieving equality. On opening day, the final leg of a national torch relay from Seneca Falls, New York, the location of the first women's rights conference in 1848, to Houston was completed. During the four days, over 20,000 people attended the conference, mak-

Held in Houston from November 18 to 21, 1977, the National Women's Conference met to vote on proposals from the state conferences. Photo by Pat Field. National Archives.

ing it the largest women's conference to date. Topics covered by the National Plan of Action include policy changes regarding **child care**, employment, rape, education, battered women, the **Equal Rights Amendment (ERA)**, **abortion**, and lesbian and minority rights. There was some dissent over the Equal Rights Amendment, reproductive freedom resolutions, and homosexual protection. On March 22, 1978, President Carter received the National Plan of Action and the conference's report, the Spirit of Houston; however, few of the recommendations made by either ever went into practice and, in some cases, still await investigation **See also** Seneca Falls Convention.

BIBLIOGRAPHY

Rossi, Alice S. *Feminists in Politics: A Panel Analysis of the First National Women's Conference.* New York: Academic Press, 1982.

Steinem, Gloria. "The First National Women's Conference." In James David Barber and Barbara Kellerman, eds. *Women Leaders in American Politics.* Englewood Cliffs, NJ: Prentice Hall, 1982.

National Women's Political Caucus (NWPC)

Founded in 1971, the National Women's Political Caucus defines itself as "a national, grassroots organization dedicated to increasing the number of women in elected and appointed office at all levels of government, regardless of party affiliation." In 1997, there were approximately 300 local chapters and the Caucus estimates that 50,000 women participate in its activities each year.

The Caucus undertakes a number of activities to help place women in political leadership positions. For women seeking elective office, the national Caucus holds regional campaign skills workshops, endorses candidates, and provides technical assistance. Many of the local chapters also endorse state and local candidates, raise money, and provide volunteer assistance. For women seeking appointive office, the NWPC spearheaded the formation of the **Coalition for Women's Appointments (CWA)** in 1976. This organization brings together numerous groups to recommend qualified women to serve in presidential administrations. In 1993, the CWA forwarded the names of over 600 women to the Clinton administration.

The Caucus also collects and publishes information on women in politics. In addition to its quarterly newsletter, "The Women's Political Times," the NWPC biennially publishes a *Directory of Women Elected Officials* and a "Fact Sheet on Women's Political Progress." (JAD)

BIBLIOGRAPHY

Burrell, Barbara C. "A New Dimension on Political Participation: The Woman's Political Caucus." In Marianne Githens and Jewell Prestage, eds. *A Portrait of Marginality.* New York: McKay, 1977, 241–58.

Rogus, Mary Beth. *How to Be Effective.* Washington DC: National Women's Political Caucus, 1979.

Tillet, Rebecca. *Empower America: Your Campaign and Abortion Rights.* Washington DC: National Women's Political Caucus, 1989.

National Women's Trade Union League

Inspired by the apparent success of the British Women's Trade Union League, William Walling and Mary Kenney O'Sullivan in 1903 developed plans for a new organization to help women form unions or enter existing unions. Initially named the Women's National Trade Union League, the organization expected local women's unions to affiliate with national American Federation of Labor (AFL) unions, an action that was blocked repeatedly by the AFL. The first officers were nationally known women reformers and labor organizers. The league played an important role in assisting striking workers during the **Shirtwaist Workers' Strike of 1909**. The League disbanded in 1950 after most of its functions were absorbed by other unions. (AMD)

BIBLIOGRAPHY

Kenneally, James J. *Women and American Trade Unions.* Montreal: Eden Press Women's Publications, 1981.

Maurine Brown Neuberger (1907–)

Maurine Neuberger, a Democrat, served as a legislator at the state and national levels. She won election to the Oregon State House of Representatives from 1951 to 1955 and secured a seat for Oregon in the United States Senate from 1960 to 1967. An advocate of antismoking policies, she introduced important pieces of legislation and authored *Smoke Screen: Tobacco and the Public Welfare*. (MG)

BIBLIOGRAPHY

Fritschler, A. Lee and James M. Hoefler. *Smoking and Politics: Policy Making and the Federal Bureaucracy.* 5th ed. Upper Saddle River, NJ: Prentice Hall, 1996.

Neuberger, Maurine. *Smoke Screen: Tobacco and the Public Welfare.* Englewood Cliffs, NJ: Prentice Hall, 1963.

United States Congress. *Biographical Directory of the United States Congress, 1774–1989.* Bicentennial ed. Washington, DC: U.S. Government Printing Office, 1989.

New Century Guild for Working Women

The New Century Guild for Working Women evolved from low-cost evening classes started by the New Century Club in 1882, as well as from the leadership and initiative of the program's instructor, Eliza Sprat Turner. Membership in the guild included people from a variety of work backgrounds, such as dressmaking, sales, mill work, office work, and book binding. The group itself offered a number of services to improve members' working skills and social standing. The guild offered classes in cooking, shorthand, typing, stenography, and female hygiene and physiology; other services provided included a library, a cafeteria, and gymnasium facilities. In 1891, the group became so popular that it opened the School of Women's Trades, which offered full-time, certified day courses in dressmaking and millinery, making it one of the first institutions to offer day-time higher education opportunities to women. In 1897, the group began publishing its own magazine, *The Working Women's Journal*, which featured articles on women's issues; the magazine ceased publication as the guild lost momentum and influence in the early 1900s.

Bibliography

Stanislow, Gail. "Domestic Feminism in Wilmington: The New Century Club, 1889–1917." *Delaware History* 22, no. 3 (1987): 158–85.

New Era Club

The New Era Club began in 1893 as a group dedicated to helping the less fortunate and discriminated of the nation. In 1895, the group helped found another organization, the **National Federation of Afro-American Women (NFAAW)**, the country's first national black women's organization of clubs. In 1896, the National Federation of Afro-American Women merged with the Colored Women's League to create the **National Association of Colored Women (NACW)**. The New Era Club also provided a number of other services, including establishing relief organizations for the poor, sick, and elderly; publishing its own newspaper, the *Women's Era*, to spread its philosophy; and endorsing political and educational reforms. **See also** Club Movement.

Bibliography

Lerner, Gerda. "Early Community Work of Black Club Women." *Journal of Negro History* 59 (April 1974): 158–68.

News Media

Media coverage in American political campaigns has brought about many changes in candidates' election strategies and how campaigns are conducted. For example, the rise of political consultants has been linked to candidates' needs to provide sophisticated political ads and to compete for free media coverage. As women have made inroads into elective and appointive office, previously as a male domain, female candidates have also struggled with gaining positive coverage as a part of any successful political race or appointment to public office.

Studies have indicated that women have been and still are treated differently by the news media. The focus in many races is on the female candidate's hair and other physical features; women candidates have had to field such questions as who is minding the children while she is out campaigning. Female candidates have experienced difficulty in getting their messages across in the mass media; issues and positions may be ignored. Women generally have had difficulty establishing credibility and being taken seriously as viable candidates.

Research into how the media has covered the contemporary **women's movement** reveals evidence of gender stereotypes. When the **National Organization for Women (NOW)** was formed in 1966, the event was not considered to be hard news by the *Washington Post.* The *New York Times* reported the event, but the story appeared on the "Food, Fashion, Family and Furnishings" page. As David Broder explains the women's movement did not make the front pages of the *Post* or the *Times* until August 1970. This happened after **Betty Friedan**, a key figure in the women's movement and founder of NOW, organized a strike of women workers (housewives as well as office and factory workers) and protest marches in Washington, New York, and other cities throughout the United States. The strategy worked, the movement became hard news, and issues of concern (discrimination in pay and employment opportunities, passage of the **Equal Rights Amendment (ERA)**, provision of **child care** and **abortion** facilities) were finally debated.

Thirty years later, this media trend of stereotyping female candidates and office holders is still in existence. According to Clara Bingham in *Women on the Hill*, 40 female members of Congress met with **Hillary Rodham Clinton** in 1993 to discuss politics and policy. When the *Washington Post* published a story about the first meeting of the women's caucus with the first lady, the story ran on the front page of "Style," the newspaper's section devoted to lifestyle features and cultural happenings. However, when the first lady met several weeks before with members of the congressional black and Hispanic caucuses, the story appeared in the "A" section of the newspaper. In many cases, the messages sent by the mass media stereotype women and anything related to female issues as being separate from the rough-and-tumble world of American politics.

In another example, **Patty Murray** (D-WA), the woman who ran for the U.S. Senate in 1992 as the "mom in tennis shoes," won her bid for election and landed an assignment on the powerful Senate Appropriations Committee. The *Seattle Times* reported this committee assignment in the local pages instead of on the front page. The newspaper personnel downplayed this news item with their placement decision. Would the same "news" have been sent to inside pages if the Washington senator had been male?

As Maria Braden points out in *The Ladies Auxiliary Is Alive and Well*, "When the news media imply that women are anomalies in high public office, the public is likely to regard them as bench warmers rather than as an integral part of government....More women than ever hold high-level government positions, yet they are still portrayed by the media as novelties."

Perhaps the mass media's problem in dealing with the increasing role of the American woman in U.S. politics is best illustrated with the press's discomfort in covering First Lady Hillary Rodham Clinton. Writing in *Quill,* Junior Bridge points out that we often read such comments as "ambition is acceptable for males but disliked in females" and that coverage of **first ladies** is often couched in terms of their roles rather than their substance. Bridge goes on to suggest that it is difficult for the media to accept Hillary Rodham Clinton as a powerful and talented woman who gave up a lucrative career to serve the country as a "free hostess" and "national mommy." Katha Pollitt points out in *Nation* that journalists have generally attacked Hillary Rodham Clinton, despite the fact that she has, for the most part, been a popular first lady. Pollitt also argues that in women, power is always seen as sexual. As a consequence, the mass media have basically portrayed this perceived female power in Hillary Rodham Clinton in a negative manner.

The disparity in media coverage between men and women has been especially evident when one examines political races. Kim Fridkin Kahn in the *Journal of Politics and Public Opinion Quarterly* analyzed newspaper coverage in 47 statewide campaigns between 1982 and 1988. Her findings showed that the media differentiated between male and female candidates in their campaign coverage. The differences were found to be more dramatic in U.S. Senate races, but the distinctions were evident in gubernatorial contests as well. In senatorial races, women received less campaign coverage than their male counterparts; the coverage they received was more negative—emphasizing their unlikely chances of winning. In both senatorial and gubernatorial races, women received consistently less attention than their male counterparts. Also, the news media seemed more responsive to the messages sent by male candidates. The media's agenda more closely resembled the agenda issued by male candidates in their televised political advertisements.

On the other hand, Lynda Lee Kaid, Sandra L. Myers, Val Pipps, and Jan Hunter reported in *Women and Politics* some more positive findings. They used an experimental study to test reactions to both male and female candidates in each of six advertising settings. Two of these were settings traditionally associated with females, two were settings traditionally associated with males, and two were neutral settings. The researchers found that female candidates can be just as successful in television advertisements as male candidates, and that females are particularly successful when performing in male settings. In fact, the female candidate received her highest overall rating on the semantic differential scales when she appeared in a male setting, the hard hat spot. The authors suggest one possible reason is that the appearance of a female in such a role would be somewhat novel to the audience.

A 1994 study of statewide campaigns also indicates that portrayals of female candidates seem to have been more positive. Kevin B. Smith in his article "When All's Fair: Signs of Parity in Media Coverage of Female Candidates" in *Political Communication*, found much smaller coverage differences than in studies relying on pre-1990 data. Although systematic gender-based patterns are still detectable, they are not so glaring as reported in previous studies, and not always to the disadvantage of female candidates. This study indicates such a shift may be underway and that one could expect even more equal treatment of female candidates in the press in the future.

The nature of the news-making process dictates that reporters, journalists, editors, and publishers, by necessity, must make news decisions. Judgments as to what is news and what is not; decisions of how to "play" a story as far as importance; judgments regarding placement of news; the amount of coverage to be given a particular issue, event, or personality; and other internal decisions within the media organization will always be determined by institutional norms of what is and ought to be "news." Also, the nature of news reporting dictates that a complex message must be packaged in a condensed form. As Bernard Rubin points out in *When Information Counts*, the technology, format, economic costs, and journalistic presentation of the news product further lend themselves to stereotypes and myths. For example, it is much easier to package the "You've come a long way baby" new woman in a cigarette advertisement than it is to portray the so-called liberated woman in a documentary film or in-depth news story.

In addition, mass media professionals bring their own culture, social norms, and political views and preferences to the news-making procedure. It falls, then, to the American public to recognize media coverage for what it is and to work beyond the stereotypes that end up in the news. The role of women in all facets of American political life has changed significantly over the past four decades and is continuing to change. Clearly, these changes have been and are being reported by the mass media. Yet newspaper columns that subdue the opinions and stances of female politicians still exist, such as this one reported by Paula LaRocque in *Quill* in May 1996: "At 36, she's still a knockout, her clear English skin and sparkling blue eyes set off by auburn curls [column about a woman who had won political office]." (LD)

BIBLIOGRAPHY

Bingham, Clara. *Women on the Hill*. New York: Times Books, 1997.

Bridge, Junior. "The Media Mirror: Reading Between the (News) Lines." *Quill* (January-February 1994): 18–19.

———. "Media Remain Uncomfortable Covering Hillary." *Quill* (March 1995): 19.

Broder, David. *Behind the Front Page*. New York: Simon and Schuster, 1987.

Kahn, Kim Fridkin. "The Distorted Mirror: Press Coverage of Women Candidates for Statewide Office." *Journal of Politics* 56, no. 1 (February 1994): 154–73.

———. "Does Gender Make a Difference? An Experimental Examination of Sex Stereotypes and Press Patterns in Statewide Campaigns." *American Journal of Political Science* 38, no. 1 (February 1994): 162–95.

Kahn, Kim Fridkin and Edie N. Goldenberg. "Women Candidates in the News: An Examination of Gender Differences in U.S. Senate Campaign Coverage." *Public Opinion Quarterly* 55 (Summer 1991): 180–99.

Kaid, Lynda Lee, Sandra L. Myers, Val Pipps, and Jan Hunter. "Sex Role Perceptions and Televised Political Advertising: Comparing Male and Female Candidates." *Women and Politics* 4 (Winter 1985): 41–53.

LaRocque, Paula. "Political Correctness Has Its Roots in Cultural Condition." *Quill* 84, no. 4 (May 1996): 34.

Pollitt, Katha. "The Male Media's Hillary Problem." *Nation* 256, no. 19 (May 17, 1993): 657–60.

Rubin, Bernard. "Visualizing Stereotypes: Updating Walter Lippmann." Bernard Rubin, ed. *When Information Counts: Grading the Media*. Lexington, MA: D. C. Heath, 1985.

Smith, Kevin B. "When All's Fair: Signs of Parity in Media Coverage of Female Candidates." *Political Communication* 14 (1997): 71–82.

Nineteenth Amendment

The Nineteenth Amendment granting women the right to vote was ratified in 1920. This right was won by women following a 70-year struggle. Initial efforts to promote women's **voting**

A cartoon showing the woman of the house going out to vote while the children are left with their father. Library of Congress.

rights were addressed at the 1848 **Seneca Falls Convention**. Both women and men argued that the government should extend to women many of those rights already held by men.

The Seneca Falls experience was significant because it called on the government to address three critical arenas of women's lives: economic rights, **suffrage**, and legal sovereignty. The convention passed a resolution that called for women to achieve political empowerment with the vote (rather than holding actual positions in the government). However, the resolution was not enthusiastically endorsed; just over half the delegates (both female and male) supported the resolution. This weak endorsement foreshadowed a 70-year struggle as concerns associated with gender roles were tied to women's voting rights.

Following the convention, state efforts and the formation of pro-suffrage organizations ensued. For example, a Kansas referendum denied women voting rights in 1867 whereas Wyoming became the first state to enter the Union granting women full suffrage in 1890. Colorado granted women suffrage in 1893 and Utah and Idaho followed suit in 1896. Further, the **National Woman Suffrage Association (NWSA)** and the **American Woman Suffrage Association**, each formed in 1869, later merged to form the **National American Women's Suffrage Association (NAWSA)** in 1890.

The period following Seneca Falls demonstrated that lobbying for women's suffrage for the sake of achieving gender equality was not a worthwhile strategy. By the early twentieth century, suffragists changed their tactics by arguing that an emerging social reform agenda (including child labor reforms, consumer protection, and public health) was best achieved by granting women voting rights. These policy arenas were largely viewed as women's domain and expertise. This lobbying approach legitimized women's suffrage, which was won in 1920 in time for the November election.

Most women did not use this right until much later. Many women and men were hostile to women's voting rights in 1920. In 1972, in the midst of the **women's movement**, women began voting as often as men. Today, women comprise 53% of the electorate. (TSF)

Bibliography

Chafe, William H. *The American Woman: Her Changing Social, Economic, and Political Roles, 1920–1970.* New York: Oxford University Press, 1972.

Darcy, R., Susan Welch and Janet Clark. *Women Elections and Representation.* 2nd ed. Lincoln: University of Nebraska Press, 1994.

DuBois, Ellen Carol. *Feminism and Suffrage: The Emergence of an Independent Women's Movement in America, 1948–1869.* Ithaca, NY: Cornell University Press, 1978.

Thelma Catherine (Patricia) Ryan Nixon (1912–1993)

Patricia Ryan was teaching high school in Whittier, California, when she met and married young attorney Richard Nixon. In 1946, he began a political career that took them from Congress, to the Senate, to the vice presidency, and, on his second attempt, to the presidency in 1968.

Political life required much sacrifice from the independent and self-reliant Patricia Nixon. Less influence and increased scrutiny were trying parts of political prominence. She did not want her husband to run for the presidency in 1968 after his 1960 defeat. She was more a private than a public person. As the president's wife, she supported causes, such as volunteerism, but she was not a political activist. However, she did support the **Equal Rights Amendment (ERA)** and encouraged her husband to appoint a woman to the Supreme Court.

Even during the Watergate crisis, Pat Nixon remained a strong supporter of her husband. Library of Congress, Prints and Photographs Division

With the Watergate scandals and President Nixon's resignation in 1974, she confronted some of the most trying times ever faced by any president's wife. Privately angry at what she viewed as relentless and unfair attacks on the president, she carried out her public role within the constraints of the expanding political crisis. She worked to maintain the symbolic importance of the first lady as a unifying force at a time of great political divisiveness. (RRT) **See also** First Ladies.

Bibliography

Eisenhower, Julie Nixon. *Pat Nixon—the Untold Story.* New York: Simon and Schuster, 1986.

Nixon, Richard. *RN: The Memoirs of Richard Nixon.* New York: Grosset and Dunlap, 1978.

No-Fault Divorce

No-fault divorce legislation is based on the assumption that housewives who have been out of the job market for a period of time can become self-supporting upon legal divorce. In practice, however, **divorce** often results in a lower standard of living for both the ex-wife and the family's children. Therefore, legislation was adopted to assist divorced women to develop skills that would help them to enter the workforce and provide for themselves. The first no-fault divorce legislation was enacted in California in 1969; by the mid-1980s, all but two U.S. states had adopted some form of no-fault divorce.

BIBLIOGRAPHY

Freed, Doris Jonas and Henry H. Foster Jr. "Divorce in the Fifty States: An Overview." *Family Law Quarterly* 14 (Winter 1985): 229–83.

Kay, Herma Hill. "Equity and Difference: A Perspective on No-Fault Divorce and Its Aftermath." *University of Cincinnati Law Review* 56 (1987): 1–90.

Mae Ella Nolan (1886–1973)

After the death of her husband John I. Nolan, Mae Ella Nolan was appointed to the U.S. House of Representatives to fill the remainder of her husband's term from January 23, 1923 to March 3, 1925. A Republican from California, she chaired the Committee on Expenditures in the Post Office Department. After her term expired, Nolan retired from politics and returned to California.

BIBLIOGRAPHY

Chamberlin, Hope. *A Minority of Members.* New York: Praeger, 1973.

Peggy Noonan (1950–)

Peggy Noonan joined the Reagan administration as a speech writer in 1984. Renowned for her hot conservative rhetoric, she is credited with providing some of the most moving moments of President Ronald Reagan's speeches. She left the White House in 1986, but returned two years later as a speech writer in George Bush's 1988 presidential campaign. She is credited with coining Bush's "thousand points of light" theme. (JCS)

BIBLIOGRAPHY

Dowd, Maureen. "High Noonan." *Vogue* 179 (December 1989): 338–41.

Noonan, Peggy. *First 100 Days.* New York: Random House, 1996.

———. *Life, Liberty & the Pursuit of Happiness.* New York: Random House, 1994.

———. *What I Saw at the Revolution.* New York: Random House, 1990.

Catherine Doris Norell (1901–1981)

Catherine Norell was active in Washington political circles beginning in 1939 when her husband, Democrat W. F. Norell, was elected from Arkansas to the U.S. House of Representatives. She served as an active member of the Women's National Democratic Club and the Democratic Wives Forum and was president of the Congressional Club. Norell was elected to fill the vacancy created by the death of her husband in 1961. She served until January 3, 1963. From 1963 to 1965, Norell served as deputy assistant secretary of state. In 1965, she became director of the U.S. Department of State Reception Center in Hawaii, a post she held until 1969.

BIBLIOGRAPHY

Chamberlin, Hope. *A Minority of Members.* New York: Praeger, 1973.

Norplant

Norplant, a contraceptive administered by surgically inserting a time-released hormone into the bloodstream of a woman, became the center of a heated legal and civil rights debate in the 1980s. The saftey of the hormone was first questioned by **Planned Parenthood** and family rights groups. Questions of funding arose as some groups speculated that government funding and insurance coverage would not be provided for Norplant operations. However, Norplant gained acceptance as a standard procedure. Judges in child abuse and neglect cases have ordered some women to use Norplant to prevent them from reproducing. This controversial use of the contraceptive has raised the question of whether bearing children is a right or a privilege. Norplant will continue to be used as an effective means of contraceptive because it does not require its user to do anything once the devices are implanted. **See also** Reproductive and Contraceptive Technologies for Women.

BIBLIOGRAPHY

Gordon, Linda. *Women's Body, Women's Right.* New York: Penguin, 1983.

North Haven v. Bell (1982)

In *North Haven v. Bell*, 456 U.S. 512 (1982), the U.S. Supreme Court ruled that **Title IX of the Educational Amendments Act of 1972**, banning **sex discrimination** in "any education program or activity receiving Federal financial assistance," applies to employees of educational institutions as well as to students. The case arose in North Haven, Connecticut, when a tenured teacher was not rehired after a one-year maternity leave.

In a 6-3 vote with Justices Harry Blackmun, William Brennan, Byron White, Thurgood Marshall, John Paul Stevens, and **Sandra Day O'Connor** in the majority (and Justices Lewis Powell, William Rehnquist, and Warren Burger dissenting), the Court held that the ban on discrimination against any "person" in Title IX included rather than excluded employees. The Court felt that Congress had intended to bring employment practices within the reach of Title IX.

The Court also cited language in Title IX that restricted the government to terminating funds for noncompliance to the particular program guilty of the noncompliance. Although it did not define the word "program," the Court held that the federal government only had authority to enforce the ban on sex discrimination in the program receiving federal funds. The case was sent back to the lower court with instructions to find which program in the North Haven school system was federally funded. (SM)

Bibliography

Gelb, Joyce and Marian Lief Palley. *Women and Public Policies.* 2nd ed. Princeton, NJ: Princeton University Press, 1987.

Mezey, Susan Gluck. "Gender Equality in Education: A Study of Policymaking by the Burger Court." *Wake Forest Law Review* 20 (1984): 793–817.

Anne M. Northup (1948–)

Anne Northup, a Republican, began her political career in 1986 when she was elected to the Kentucky house. While in the state house, she sought to hold down taxes and regulatory burdens and was a vocal critic of tobacco in a major tobacco state. In 1996, she narrowly defeated incumbent Mike Ward by 1,299 votes to win a seat in the U.S. House of Representatives. A political conservative, Northup has been a vocal supporter of the House leadership, including Speaker Newt Gingrich. In Congress, she serves on the powerful Appropriations Committee.

Bibliography

Vilbig, Peter. "Freshman Rush." *Scholastic Update* 130, no. 1 (September 8, 1997): 2.

Eleanor Holmes Norton (1937–)

Eleanor Norton, a Democrat, has served in the U.S. House since 1991 as the District of Columbia delegate. She maneuvered the change in House rules to allow the five congressional delegates to vote in the Committee of the Whole, although the delegates lost that right in 1995 when the Republicans took over Congress. In the 105th Congress, she co-chaired the **Congressional Caucus for Women's Issues**. She also served on the New York City Human Rights Commission from 1971 through 1977 and chaired the federal **Equal Employment Opportunity Commission (EEOC)** under President Jimmy Carter from 1977 to 1981. (MEK)

Bibliography

Lamson, Peggy. "Eleanor Holmes Norton Reforms the Equal Employment Opportunity Commission." In James David Barber and Barbara Kellerman, eds. *Woman Leaders in American Politics.* Englewood, NJ: Prentice Hall, 1986, 340–42.

Lavin, Maud. "Waging War on Wages, Eleanor Holmes Norton." *New Woman* 25, no. 2 (1995): 126–29.

Mary Teresa Norton (1875–1959)

Mary Norton served in New Jersey as vice-chair of the State Democratic Committee from 1921 to 1931 and as chair from 1932 to 1935. She was also a delegate to the Democratic National Convention seven times between the years of 1924 and 1948. Norton served in Congress from March 4, 1925, until January 3, 1951, and was a consultant from 1951 to 1952 for the Women's Advisory Committee on Defense Manpower for the Department of Labor.

Bibliography

Anderson, Eleanor. "She Gets Her Way: Introducing Representative Norton, The First Woman State Chairman." *Today Magazine* 2, no. 19 (September 1, 1934): 5.

Norton, Mary T. "Women in Congress Should Raise Voice Against War." *Democratic Digest* 14, no. 1 (January 1937): 7.

O

Mary Rose Oaker (1940–)

Ohio Democrat Mary Rose Oaker was a member of the Cleveland City Council from 1973 to 1976. During this time she also served as Democratic state central committeewoman and as an alternate delegate to the 1976 Democratic National Convention. Elected to the U.S. House of Representatives in 1976, she became an effective legislator on liberal and women's issues. She was defeated for re-election in 1992 amidst the congressional check cashing scandal. In 1997, she negotiated a plea to the charges that included no jail time.

BIBLIOGRAPHY

Clarity, James. "The Fight for Equality Continues." *50 Plus* 24 (December 1984): 11.

Kempton, Beverly. "Just Call Me Mary Rose." *New Choices for the Best Years* 29, no. 12 (December 1989): 52.

Olin, Dirk. "Unequal Opportunities." *The New Republic* 188 (May 30, 1983): 12.

Simpson, Peggy and Helene Brooks. "The Ten Best Legislators." *50 Plus* 24 (March 1984): 20.

Oberlin College

Established in 1833 and located in Oberlin, Ohio, Oberlin College was the first coeducational college in the United States. Initially, 15 women were admitted to take a "ladies' course," but within four years women became part of the regular curriculum. Oberlin also admitted students regardless of race. Oberlin began as an evangelical experiment in Christian living and student life for women and was tightly regulated. In 1841, the first three women graduated from Oberlin, who were also the first female college graduates in the United States with bachelor's degrees. In 1862, Oberlin graduate Mary Jane Patterson became the first black woman to graduate from college in the United States. (SD)

BIBLIOGRAPHY

Lasser, Carol. *Educating Men and Women Together: Co-education in a Changing World.* Urbana: University of Illinois Press, 1987.

Sandra Day O'Connor (1930–)

Sandra Day O'Connor was the first woman appointed to the United States Supreme Court. Born in El Paso, Texas, on March 26, 1930, O'Connor graduated *magna cum laude* from Stanford University in 1950 and received her L.L.B. in 1952 after winning a place in the *Stanford Law Review*. Unable to obtain work in a private firm because of discrimination against women in the law profession, she worked in public service as a deputy county attorney in San Mateo, California. In 1965, she worked as assistant attorney general for Arizona and was appointed to a state senate seat in 1969 following the resignation of Isabel A. Burgess. In 1970, she campaigned on the Republican ticket for the same state senate seat and won, becoming the first woman senate majority leader in any state legislature. She was greatly admired for her "precise and concise mind" and developed a moderate to conservative voting record, although she did not always follow the party line. While not a strong feminist, O'Connor supported the revision of statutes that discriminated against women and developed model legislation allowing women to manage joint property held with their husbands. She also voted in favor of the **Equal Rights Amendment (ERA)**. She left politics in 1974 to return to the legal profession as a judge on the Maricopa County Superior Court. In 1978 Democratic Governor Bruce Babbit appointed her to the Arizona Court of Appeals and in 1981 President Ronald Reagan nominated O'Connor as an associate justice to the U.S. Supreme Court. She was confirmed by the Senate by a vote of 99-0. She built an exemplary record as a Supreme Court justice, and is often perceived as one of the most prolific members of the Court and one who is proficient at reconciling competing ideologies. (GVS)

BIBLIOGRAPHY

Henry, Christopher. *Sandra Day O'Connor.* Watts, 1994.

Huber, Peter. *Sandra Day O'Connor*. Chelsea House, 1990.

Caroline Love Goodwin O'Day (1875–1943)

Caroline O'Day was vice-chair of the New York Democratic State Committee from 1916 until 1920 and associate chair from 1923 until 1942. She was a delegate to four Democratic National Conventions between 1924 and 1936 and was elected commissioner of the State Board of Social Welfare, serving from 1923 to 1934. In 1935, O'Day was elected to the U.S. House of Representatives where she served until her death in 1943.

BIBLIOGRAPHY

Canning, Hazel. "She Represents New York." *Independent Woman* (December 1934).

Kate Richards O'Hare (1876–1948)

During the early part of the twentieth century, Kate O'Hare was a popular socialist organizer and speaker in the Plains states and the Southwest. A socialist agitator, she worked to organize exploited workers and tenant farmers. She was a staunch advocate of women's rights, worked to reform prisons, and sought an end to the arms race. In 1916, she was a candidate on the **Populist Party** ticket for the U.S. Senate from Missouri. In 1917, she was sentenced to prison under the Espionage Act for her anti-war activities. Ironically, in 1938 she became an assistant director in the prison system for the state of California.

BIBLIOGRAPHY

Basen, Neil K. "Kate Richards O'Hare: 'First Lady' of American Socialism." *Labor History* 21 (Spring 1980): 165–99.

Foner, Philip S. and Sally McMille, eds. *Kate Richards O'Hare: Selected Writings and Speeches*. Baton Rouge: Louisiana State University Press, 1982.

Ohio v. Akron Center for Reproductive Health (1990)

In *Ohio v. Akron Center for Reproductive Health*, 497 U.S. 502 (1990), the United States Supreme Court upheld an Ohio statute requiring physicians to notify or obtain written consent from one parent within 24 hours prior to performing an **abortion** on an unmarried or unemancipated minor. The requirements of the statute could be waived if both the minor and an adult sibling or relative certified that the minor feared physical, sexual, or severe emotional abuse from one of her parents. The statute also allowed a minor to seek a court order of approval. In a 6-3 decision, the Supreme Court reversed the decision of the Court of Appeals, ruling that the statute did not violate the **Fourteenth Amendment** on the grounds that it included a judicial bypass option. (LvA) **See also** Reproductive and Contraceptive Technologies for Women.

BIBLIOGRAPHY

Blank, Robert and Janna C. Merrick. *Human Reproduction, Emerging Technologies, and Conflicting Rights*. Washington, DC: Congressional Quarterly Press, 1995.

Shapiro, Ian, ed. *Abortion: The Supreme Court Decisions*. Indianapolis: Hackett Publishing Company, Inc., 1995.

Pearl Peden Oldfield (1876–1962)

Pearl Oldfield, a Democrat, was appointed to the U.S. House of Representatives on January 9, 1929, to fill the vacancy left by the death of her husband Arkansas Representative William Oldfield. She served in Congress until March 3, 1931, at which time she retired from politics. While in Congress, she served the needs of her district in a time of natural disasters. She secured flood-relief and the construction of several free bridges.

BIBLIOGRAPHY

"Representative Pearl Peden Oldfield." *Democratic Bulletin* 4, no. 4 (April 1929): 10.

Hazel O'Leary (1937–)

During Gerald Ford's administration, Hazel O'Leary was appointed to her first national political position as director of the Office of Consumer Affairs for the Federal Energy Administration. In 1977, O'Leary became deputy director and later director of the Economic Regulatory Administration for President Jimmy Carter. In this role, she enforced price controls on the oil, natural gas, and electric utilities industries in an attempt to deal with the energy crisis.

O'Leary left public life when Ronald Reagan assumed the presidency in 1981. However, after providing major contributions to the Minnesota **Democratic Party** during Bill Clinton's 1992 presidential campaign, O'Leary was appointed secretary of energy. She left office after Clinton's first term in 1997. O'Leary continues to be controversial because she is part of an ongoing investigation of influence peddling in the Clinton administration.

BIBLIOGRAPHY

Glick, Daniel. "Hazel O'Leary Had Better Be Tough." *Working Woman* 19 (December 1994): 42–47.

Jacqueline Lee Bouvier Kennedy Onassis (1929–1994)

The wife of President John F. Kennedy, Jacqueline Bouvier Kennedy was born in New York on July 28, 1929. Growing up among the most distinguished social circles of New York City, Jacqueline Bouvier made headlines from the time she was two years old. She attended Vassar and George Washington University and graduated with a bachelor's degree in journalism before starting a job with the *Times Herald* in 1952. As "the inquiring camera girl" columnist, she often had the opportunity to talk with the popular Massachusetts congressman, John F. Kennedy. They were married in a spectacular wedding in September 1953 and had two children, Caroline and John F. Kennedy, Jr., although Jacqueline Kennedy endured several miscarriages and the death of two-day-old baby named Patrick.

Perhaps the most popular American first lady, Jacqueline Kennedy tried to maintain privacy for her young family. Library of Congress, Prints and Photographs Division.

Although the Kennedys were extremely popular even before they entered the White House, Jacqueline Kennedy always treasured her privacy and that of her family. She did not enjoy the demands of political life and tried hard to shelter her children from the public eye. Still, she was extremely popular both at home and abroad. Every aspect of her life was followed closely by the press, and her charm and good taste made her a world fashion leader. During her tenure as first lady, she remodeled the White House with the advice of historians, museum directors, and art experts. However, she is most remembered for her stoic and courageous handling of her husband's funeral arrangements after his tragic death in Dallas in November 1963, when she led the nation through one of its darkest moments.

Even after leaving the White House, Jacqueline Kennedy's intelligence and charm enthralled the American public. In 1968, after the assassination of Robert Kennedy, she left the United States to marry Greek businessman Aristotle Onassis. During the last years of her life, she worked as an editor for Doubleday in New York City. Jacqueline Kennedy Onassis died of cancer in 1994. (GVS) **See also** First Ladies.

Bibliography

Anderson, Catherine C. *Jacqueline Kennedy Onassis: Woman of Courage.* New York: Lerner Group, 1995.

David, Lester. *Jacqueline Kennedy Onassis: The Woman She Has Become.* New York: Carol Publishing Group, 1994.

Davis, John H. *Jacqueline Bouvier: An Intimate Memoir.* New York: Wiley, 1996.

Lowe, Jacques. *Jacqueline Kennedy Onassis: The Making of a First Lady.* New York: General Public Group, 1996.

Operation Rescue

Operation Rescue was founded in 1984 by Randall Terry as a militant pro-life organization dedicated to the prevention of abortions. The group takes a proactive role in achieving its goal, holding large demonstrations outside **abortion** clinics, blockading facilities, and physically moving or surrounding women attempting to enter clinics. The group functions out of a number of major cities across the nation, including Atlanta, Baton Rouge, New Orleans, Buffalo, Boston, Charlotte, Chicago, Indianapolis, Little Rock, Los Angeles, Milwaukee, and New York City.

Over the years, the group has been faced with a number of legal issues. To date, over 10,000 members of Operation Rescue have been arrested for various actions. The Legal Defense and Education Fund of the **National Organization for Women (NOW)** has tried several times to put a legal end to Operation Rescue. In January 1993, in the case of ***Bray v. Alexandria Women's Clinic***, Operation Rescue was found not to have violated women's civil rights by their activities. However, in 1994 the **Freedom of Access to Clinic Entrances Act** was signed by President Bill Clinton. The act prevents organizations like Operation Rescue from stopping individuals from entering abortion clinics. **See also** Right-to-Life Movement.

Bibliography

Blanchard, Dallas A. *The Anti-Abortion Movement and the Rise of the Religious Right: From Polite to Fiery Protest.* New York: Maxwell, 1994.

Terry, Randall. *Operation Rescue.* Springdale, PA: Whitaker House, 1988.

Wills, Gary. "Save the Babies: Operation Rescue, A Case Study on Galvanizing the Antiabortion Movement." *Time* 135 (May 1, 1989): 26, 28.

Kay Orr (1939–)

Not only was Kay Orr the first female governor of Nebraska, she was also the first woman Republican governor in the United States. Her election in 1986 was also the first governor's race between two women. Orr was pitted against former Lincoln, Nebraska, mayor Helen Boosalis. Ironically, the race focused less on issues that traditionally interest women, such as **abortion** or the **Equal Rights Amendment (ERA)**, and more on issues such as agriculture. Orr lost her re-election bid in 1990 in a close race against Democratic lawyer Ben Nelson.

Orr has been a high-profile Republican, serving as a delegate to several national conventions. She also served as chair of the platform committee in 1984 and 1988. Kay Orr was appointed to the state treasurer's position in 1981, and subsequently won the position for herself in 1982. With that victory, she became the first woman elected to a statewide constitutional office in Nebraska. (MEK)

Bibliography

Barrette, John B. *Prairie Politics.* Media Publishing, 1987.

Orr v. Orr (1979)

At issue in *Orr v. Orr,* 440 U.S. 268 (1979), was the constitutionality of Alabama's statute under which husbands, but not wives, may be required to pay alimony. In this particular case, William Orr was ordered to pay alimony to his wife Lillian Orr. Initially William paid the alimony, but then fell behind. Lillian took him to court for failing to pay. At a hearing, William challenged the constitutionality of Alabama's law claiming that it violated the equal protection clause of the Fourteenth Amendment. The trial court ruled against him and ordered him to pay back alimony and lawyer's fees.

In a 6-3 decision, however, the U.S. Supreme Court reversed the lower courts by stating that a law based solely on gender was in fact a violation of the equal protection clause. The majority opinion, written by Justice William Brennan, stated that "classifications by gender must serve important governmental objectives, and must be substantially related to achievement of those objectives. . . . The statutes cannot be validated on the basis of the State's preference for an allocation of family responsibilities under which the wife plays a dependent role." The Court left the Alabama court to decide if William Orr's stipulation to pay alimony or any other Alabama laws require him to pay alimony.

Bibliography

Morganthau, T. and D. Camper. "Equalimony: Overturning Alabama Gender-Specific Statute." *Newsweek* 93 (March 19, 1979): 40.

Ruth Bryan Owen (Rohde) (1885–1954)

After the death of her husband, Major Reginald Altham Owen, in 1927, Ruth Owen became a popular lecturer and advocate of women in politics. She was a Democratic member of the U.S. House of Representatives from Florida, serving from 1929 to 1933. President Franklin D. Roosevelt appointed her United States minister to Denmark in 1933, a post she held until 1936. In 1949, she was appointed as an alternate U.S. delegate to the general assembly of the United Nations and served as chair of the executive committee of the Speakers Research Committee of the United Nations.

Bibliography

Hard, Anne. "Three Ruth's in Congress." *Ladies Home Journal* 46 (March 1929): 13.

Owen, Robert L. "Discussion of Equal Suffrage for Woman." *Annuals of the American Academy of Political and Social Science* 35 Supplement (May 1910): 6–9.

Owen, Ruth Bryan. "New Minister to Denmark." *Newsweek.* 1 (April 15, 1933): 18–19.

———. "Women in the House." *Woman's Home Companion* 58 (November 1931): 11–12.

P

Pacifism

Pacifism is a philosophy based on the belief that wars and other forms of violence are immoral and do not address the underlying causes of disputes. It is associated with women through various women's peace organizations that adhere to this belief.

The height of the women's peace movement came in the 1920s out of the devastation of World War I and the desire of former suffragists to remain politically active. Organizations formed during this time include The Women's International League for Peace and Freedom, the **Women's Peace Party**, and the Women's Peace Union.

The late 1960s saw a resurgence of women's pacifist groups in response to the Vietnam War. The best known group to emerge during this era is Women Strike for Peace. More recently, the ideas of feminist pacifism and the environmental movement have merged, resulting in the formation of several women's environmental peace groups like the Seneca Women's Peace Camp. This and several other women's peace groups sponsor the Women's Pentagon Action, an annual peace demonstration held in Washington, D.C. (SJW) **See also** Feminism; Suffrage.

Bibliography

Alonso, Harriet Hyman. *Peace as a Woman's Issue, A History of the U.S. Movement for World Peace and Women's Rights.* Syracuse, NY: Syracuse University Press, 1993.

Pierson, Ruth Roach, ed. *Women and Peace: Theoretical, Historical, and Practical Perspectives.* New York: Croom Helm, 1987.

Parent-Teacher Associations (PTA)

Parent-Teacher Associations began in 1897 to involve mothers in the public education system. The PTA was founded by Phoebe Apperson Hearst and Alice McLellan Birney and soon after dedicated itself to strengthening the relationship between parents and teachers to implement higher standards of education at home, at school, in the legal system, and in health care. The PTA also contributed to child-labor laws, mandatory school attendance legislation, and the development of school-lunch programs, and assisted other community programs, such as drug and child abuse programs, social issues monitoring, and other educational programs. The organization even spawned two satellite groups, the National Congress of Parents and Teachers, which was established in 1924, and the National Congress of Colored Parents and Teachers, created in 1927; these two groups merged in 1970 to more closely work with other Parent-Teacher Associations. Currently, there are local PTA organizations in almost every community in the nation.

The PTA has focused much of its energy on securing adequate funding for school programs. National Archives.

Bibliography

Birney, T.W. *Childhood.* New York: Frederick A. States, 1905.

_______. *Golden Jubilee History, 1897–1947.* Chicago: National Congress of Parents and Teachers, 1947.

Rosa Parks (1913–)

Despite her long career as a civil rights advocate, Rosa Parks is best remembered as the black woman who refused to surrender her seat to a white passenger on a Montgomery, Alabama, bus. This 1955 act sparked the civil rights movement. Parks' refusal was part of an NAACP-organized attempt to challenge segregation. Parks' association with the NAACP began in 1943 when she became the first woman member of its Montgomery chapter. She was its secretary from 1943 to 1956 and also assisted as its youth advisor. Parks participated in many civil and **voting rights** efforts and received formal activist training at the celebrated Highlander Folk School. Following her arrest in 1955, Parks helped organize the bus boycott, which lasted over a year, culminating in the U.S. Supreme Court's order to integrate the Montgomery bus system. Parks continued to advance civil rights by working in U.S. Representative John Conyers' district office from 1965 to 1988. Parks has received numerous citations, including the U.S. Medal of Honor. (BN)

Bibliography

Metcalf, George R. *Black Profiles.* New York: Manor Books, 1976.

Robinson, Jo Ann. *The Montgomery Bus Boycott and the Women Who Started It.* Knoxville: University of Tennessee Press, 1987.

Elizabeth J. Patterson (1939–)

Elizabeth Patterson, a recruiting officer for the **Peace Corps** from 1962 to 1964 and for VISTA from 1965 to 1967, was director for the Head Start Program from 1967 to 1968. She also worked as staff assistant for U.S. Representative James R. Mann from 1969 to 1970. From 1975 to 1976, she served on the Spartanburg, South Carolina, County Council. In 1979, she was elected to the South Carolina state senate as a Democrat. She served until 1986. Patterson was elected to the U.S. House of Representatives in 1988 and served from January 3, 1989, until January 3, 1993. She was defeated for re-election in 1992.

Bibliography

Rosenfeld, Megan. "Anatomy of a Defeat: How a Middle-of-the-Road Incumbent Got Run Over on Election Day." *Washington Post* (November 12, 1992): D1.

Alice Paul (1885–1977)

Alice Paul dedicated her life to the **suffrage** movement and passage of the **Equal Rights Amendment (ERA)**. Born to affluent Quaker parents in 1885, Paul graduated from Swarthmore College in 1905, earned a master's degree from the University of Pennsylvania in 1907, a Ph.D. in 1912, and three law degrees later in life. It was in graduate school in London, however, where she was introduced to the Pankhurst sisters and the British militant suffragist movement. Under their influence, she participated in demonstrations and was arrested, jailed, and force-fed through a nasal tube in her fight for suffrage.

Understanding that suffrage was not enough, Alice Paul began to work on the Equal Rights Amendment immediately after ratification of the Nineteenth Amendment in 1920. Library of Congress, National American Woman Suffrage Association Collection.

Returning to the United States in 1910, she helped reorganize the **National American Woman Suffrage Association (NAWSA)**, changing its focus from a state-by-state approach to a national constitutional amendment. Paul was appointed chair of the Congressional Committee through which she raised funds and recruited thousands of women to participate in demonstrations, including a march down Pennsylvania Avenue the day before Woodrow Wilson's inauguration in 1913. Paul escorted delegations to the White House, organized pickets, lobbied Congress, and campaigned against Democrats as the party in power. Paul's tactics were regarded as controversial.

In 1913, Paul and her followers broke away from NAWSA and formed the **Congressional Union**, renamed the **National Woman's Party (NWP)** in 1916. After the **Nineteenth Amendment** was ratified in 1920, Paul realized that suffrage was a necessary but insufficient guarantee of equal rights for women. Consequently, she drafted the Equal Rights Amendment and fought for its passage and for the rights of women worldwide until her death in 1977. (LvA)

Bibliography

Lunardini, Christine A. *From Equal Suffrage to Equal Rights: Alice Paul and the National Woman's Party, 1910–1928.* New York: New York University Press, 1986.

Peace Corps

The Peace Corps began as a bureau of the United States government in 1961. The group was established to help countries meet their needs for trained workers, promote American culture abroad, and create understanding of ethnic difference between people so the differences could be overcome. Volunteers of the organization had to be over 18 years of age, although no maximum age limit was ever established. Volunteers were to serve two years in other countries doing anything from teaching to construction work. The Peace Corps also steered away from sex biases found in other groups, seeking to equally enlist the aid of men and women.

Volunteerism in the group has varied over the years depending on social events occurring in the world; for example, a marked decrease in participation occurred in the late 1960s and early 1970s, mostly because of American involvement in Vietnam.

Bibliography

Adams, Velma. *The Peace Corps in Action.* Chicago: Follett, 1964.

Nancy Pelosi (1940–)

Nancy Pelosi served as chair of the California State **Democratic Party** from 1981 to 1983. In 1985, she served as the finance chair of the Democratic Senatorial Campaign Committee. On June 2, 1987, Pelosi was elected in a special election to the U.S. House of Representatives, and was re-elected for four succeeding terms. She is especially interested in issues involving China and funding for AIDS.

Bibliography

Sciolino, Elaine. "A Chinese Visitor Comes Between Longtime California Allies." *The New York Times* 147 (October 30, 1997): A13, A19.

———. "Should the House Approve the President's Resolution to Release Population Planning Funds?: Honorable Nancy Pelosi." *Congressional Digest* 76, no. 4 (April 1997): 112.

People v. Belous (1969)

Four years before the landmark case of ***Roe v. Wade*** was decided by the U.S. Supreme Court, the supreme court of California in *People v. Belous* (1969) overturned the state's restrictive **abortion** law and established the principle that marriage and reproductive rights should be free from state interference. In reaching its decision, the court established that a physician in consultation with a woman should determine whether an abortion or childbirth posed more risk. As a result, many early (first trimester) abortions were performed because abortions were far less risky than childbirth. The court's decision fueled the abortion rights movement and led to even more liberalized abortion laws in California.

BIBLIOGRAPHY

Abortion in California: 1968–1976. Sacramento: State of California, 1977.

Duffy, Edward A. *The Effect of Changes in the State Abortion Laws.* Washington, DC: U.S. Government Printing Office, 1971.

Reiterman, Carl, ed. *Abortion and the Unwanted Child. The California Committee on Therapeutic Abortion.* New York: Springer, 1971.

Frances Perkins (1882–1965)

The first female cabinet member in the history of the United States, Frances Perkins was instrumental in passing revolutionary labor laws during her tenure as secretary of labor under President Franklin D. Roosevelt. Born in Boston on April 10, 1880, Perkins graduated from Mount Holyoke College in 1902 with a bachelor's degree in physics and chemistry. Firmly committed to social justice at a young age, Perkins worked as a volunteer for the Congregational Church and briefly for **Jane Addams' Hull House** settlement before earning an M.A. in social economics from Columbia in 1910.

Appointed by Franklin Roosevelt as secretary of labor in 1933, Frances Perkins became the first woman cabinet member. This painting by Arthur Syzk was done in 1941. National Archives.

Perkins volunteered in the **suffrage** movement, and as executive secretary for the Consumers' League of New York, she lobbied for state legislation on factory safety standards, maximum hours, and minimum wages. In 1913, she married economist Paul Wilson, and they had a daughter in 1916. In 1918, after witnessing the **Triangle Shirtwaist Company Fire**, she served on the investigative committee that sought to prevent similar industrial abuses. Governor Al Smith appointed Perkins to the State Industrial Commission, and in 1926 Governor Franklin D. Roosevelt confirmed her as chair of the New York Commission. Four years later, when Roosevelt became president, he appointed Perkins secretary of labor, a decision that prompted much controversy.

For the following 12 years, Perkins displayed excellent administrative talent, which included drafting the Social Security Act (1935), the National Labor Relations Act (1935), the **Fair Labor Standards Act** (1938), and the Wages and Hours Act (1938). She published numerous articles and books, including *People at Work* (1934) and *The Roosevelt I Knew* (1946). She worked successfully with other Democratic women to open up party politics to the participation of women. She resigned from her position in 1945; however, shortly thereafter President Harry Truman appointed her to the Civil Service Commission, where she remained until 1952. She was appointed professor at the Cornell School of Industrial Relations in 1956. She died in New York City on May 14, 1965. **See also** Minimum Wage/Maximum Hours Laws. (GVS)

BIBLIOGRAPHY

Hinshaw, August W. "The Story of Frances Perkins." *Century* (September 1927): 596–605.

Jones, Inis W. "Frances Perkins, Industrial Crusader." *World's Work* (April 1930): 64–67.

Martin, George. *Madam Secretary: Frances Perkins.* Boston: Houghton Mifflin, 1976.

Young, Marguerite. "Frances Perkins, Liberal Politician." *American Mercury* (August 1934): 398–407.

Persian Gulf War

American women have served this country in time of war since the Revolutionary War. However, not until the Persian Gulf War in 1991 were women's roles expanded. Five of the 15 nations sent women as part of their contingents to the Gulf. While not technically assigned to combat divisions, women were active in the combat zone to a greater degree than ever before. Women constituted nearly 6 percent of the total forces. They served as pilots, mechanics, police officers, consultants, crew chiefs, and communication operators. Two women were taken prisoner and 11 killed in the line of duty. (EP)

BIBLIOGRAPHY

Cornum, Rhonda. *She Went to War: The Rhonda Cornum Story.* Novato, CA: Presidio, 1992.

Moore, Molly. *A Woman at War: Storming Kuwait with the U.S. Marines.* New York: Charles Scribner's Sons, 1993.

Personnel Administrator of the Commonwealth of Massachusetts v. Feeney (1977)

In *Personnel Administrator v. Feeney*, 429 U.S. 66 (1977), the U.S. Supreme Court decided that Massachusetts' veteran's preference statute did not violate **Title VII of the Civil Rights Act of 1964** or the Fourteenth Amendment. The case began in 1976 when Helen B. Feeney filed suit against the personnel director and other members of the Civil Service Commission claiming that the policy of giving preferences to veterans was discriminatory against women. Feeney had been passed over for a job despite her qualifications because of the veterans' preference statute. A federal district court ruled in favor of

Feeney and declared the veteran's preference law unconstitutional because it had a discriminatory effect. However, the Supreme Court overturned this decision because the intent of the law was not discriminatory.

BIBLIOGRAPHY

Goldstein, Leslie Friedman. *The Constitutional Rights of Women.* New York: Longman, 1979.

Lindgren, J. Ralph and Nadine Taub. *The Law of Sex Discrimination.* St. Paul, MN: West Publishing, 1988.

Esther Peterson (1906–)

Esther Peterson was director of the **Women's Bureau** in the Department of Labor and then assistant secretary of labor under Presidents John F. Kennedy and Lyndon B. Johnson during the 1960s. As a representative for labor unions, Peterson established a working relationship with Kennedy when he was in Congress. This enabled her to later play an influential role in his administration, especially regarding the establishment and work of the **President's Commission on the Status of Women**. In the 1960s and 1970s, she worked for the inclusion of a consumer's' office in the Executive Office of the President, an issue of concern to women at that time. (JMM)

BIBLIOGRAPHY

Martin, Janet M. *A Place in the Oval Office: Women and the American Presidency.* Ann Arbor: University of Michigan Press, forthcoming.

Shirley Pettis (1924–)

A congressional widow and charter member of the **Congresswomen's Caucus**, Republican Shirley Pettis of California served in the U.S. House of Representatives from 1975 until her retirement in 1979 when she became vice president of the Women's Research and Education Institute. Prior to her 1975 election, Pettis helped manage two family businesses in California, raised two children, and wrote a local newspaper column entitled, "From Your Congressman's Wife." (JHT)

BIBLIOGRAPHY

Gertzog, Irvin N. *Congressional Women: Their Recruitment, Integration, and Behavior.* New York: Praeger, 1984.

Gracie Bowers Pfost (1906–1965)

Former U.S. congresswoman, Gracie Bowers Pfost, an Idaho Democrat, was born to William Lafayette and Lilly Elizabeth Wood Bowers in Harrison, Arkansas. She married John Walter Pfost in 1923 and settled in Idaho. She served as Canyon County deputy county clerk (1929–1939) and county treasurer (1941–1950) until she ran for Congress in 1950. Defeated in her first race, she was elected in 1952 and became the first woman in Idaho history elected to the United States House of Representatives, serving from 1953 to 1963. (AM)

BIBLIOGRAPHY

Shelton, Isabelle. "Her Gracie Is Also Called Hell's Belle." *Democratic Digest* 1, no. 1 (August 1953): 73–75.

Philadelphia Female Anti-Slavery Society

After attempting to attend William Lloyd Garrison's founding meeting of the American Anti-Slavery Society in 1833 during which she was informed that women were not permitted to join, **Lucretia Coffin Mott** helped create the Philadelphia Female Anti-Slavery Society. Other female **abolition** societies soon began to form throughout the states, realizing that such independent groups were the only way women could support anti-slavery issues.

The Philadelphia Female Anti-Slavery Society met a number of roadblocks throughout its existence. On May 15, 1838, in Pennsylvania Hall, Philadelphia, the group sponsored the first Anti-Slavery Convention of American Women; in reaction, an angry mob burned the hall two days later. In 1840, Lucretia Mott and **Elizabeth Cady Stanton** traveled to London, England, to represent both the Philadelphia and Boston Female Anti-Slavery Societies at the World Anti-Slavery Convention. After being denied access, Mott and Stanton organized their own women's world abolition convention in 1848. This chain of events is considered by many the unofficial beginning of the American women's rights movement. **See also** Seneca Falls Convention; Women's Movement.

BIBLIOGRAPHY

Bacon, Margaret Hope. *Valiant Friend: The Life of Lucretia Mott.* New York: Walker, 1980.

Lerner, Gerda. *The Grimke Sisters from South Carolina: Pioneers for Women's Rights and Abolition.* New York: Schocken, 1971.

Phillips v. Martin Marietta Corp. (1971)

In *Phillips v. Martin Marietta Corp.*, 400 U.S. 542 (1971), the Supreme Court held that under **Title VII of the Civil Rights Act of 1964** an employer may not, in the absence of business necessity, refuse to hire women (or men) with school-aged children. This was a watershed case because it was the first time the Supreme Court began to implement the **sex discrimination** provisions of Title VII.

Phillips attempted to apply for a job with Martin Marietta but was told that the company did not accept applications from women with school-aged children. Phillips sued Martin under Title VII, arguing that she had been denied employment because of her sex. The district court ruled that there was no bias against women because 70–75 percent of the applicants for the position that Phillips sought were women, 75–80 percent of those hired for the position were women, and Martin did hire men with preschool-aged children. The Supreme Court unanimously disagreed, reaffirming that Title VII requires that persons of like qualifications be given employment opportunities irrespective of their sex. The Court discounted Martin's justification for the separate employment policies that conflicting family obligations were more relevant to job performance for a woman than a man. (RW)

BIBLIOGRAPHY

Baer, Judith A. *Women in American Law.* New York: Holmes and Meier, 1991.

Goldstein, Leslie Friedman. *The Constitutional Rights of Women.* Madison: University of Wisconsin Press, 1989.

Phyllis Schlafly Report

From 1967 until 1972, the monthly *Phyllis Schlafly Report* reflected Schlafly's conservative and anti-communist beliefs. Carol Felsenthal writes that Schlafly started the *Report* as a way to "communicate with stalwarts" after she lost her bid for presidency of the National Federation of Republican women." When the **Equal Rights Amendment (ERA)** passed Congress in 1972, Schlafly used the *Report* to organize a national anti-ERA movement. Each month, the *Report* detailed how ratification of the ERA would hurt women, reported on how women around the country were working against the ERA, and described successful fund-raising ideas. Although Schlafly claimed the *Report* was based on fact, much of its coverage inspired fear among its readers, many of whom were housewives. For instance, the November 1972 issue of the *Report* stated that the ERA "would abolish the husband's duty to support the wife." The December 1974 issue had banner headlines that read, "ERA Means **Abortion** and Population Shrinkage." Such proclamations helped galvanize women against the ERA and greatly contributed to its defeat in 1982 when it fell three states short of ratification. The *Phyllis Schlafly Report* is still being published today. (MP) **See also** Phyllis Schlafly.

Bibliography

Felsenthal, Carol. *The Sweetheart of the Silent Majority.* Garden City, NY: Doubleday, 1981.

Mansbridge, Jane. *Why We Lost the ERA.* Chicago: University of Chicago Press, 1986.

Jane Means Appleton Pierce (1806–1863)

Jane Appleton Pierce joins her husband, Franklin, as perhaps one of the least effective residents of the White House. Jane Pierce often opposed Franklin's political endeavors. Although Franklin was a U.S. congressman at the time of their marriage, Jane Pierce vocally lamented his increasing success. Prior to the presidential inauguration, the Pierces' son died in a train wreck. Distraught, Jane Pierce viewed the accident as divine punishment for her husband's ambition. This personal tragedy earned much sympathy for Jane Pierce, who took to her bed throughout much of her husband's presidency and rarely appeared publicly. (BN) **See also** First Ladies.

Jane Pierce was unhappy about her husband's election to the presidency and rarely appeared in public during his single term in office. Library of Congress.

Bibliography

Caroli, Betty Boyd. *First Ladies.* New York: Oxford University Press, 1995.

Truman, Margaret. *First Ladies.* New York: Random House, 1995.

Planned Parenthood Federation of America (PPFA)

Founded in 1921, the Planned Parenthood Federation of America (PPFA), headquartered in New York City, is linked historically to the American birth control movement and the activism of **Margaret Sanger** and **Mary Ware Dennett,** among others. Planned Parenthood Federation of America runs approximately 750 health clinics nationwide providing birth control information and care to both men and women. Planned Parenthood Federation of America clinics also provide legal **abortion** services. Based on the belief that each woman should choose for herself her reproductive options, PPFA tries to meet the needs of clients in a safe and effective way. The PPFA has an extensive public education mission and seeks to inform people about safe and effective birth control, how to avoid exposure to sexually transmitted diseases, and ways to teach teenagers about human sexuality with the hope of avoiding sexual abuse, pregnancy, and sexually transmitted diseases.

Planned Parenthood Federation of America has recently been in the forefront in several important legal battles over abortion policies at both the state and federal levels. The PPFA has been a direct party to litigation or has filed *amicus curiae* (friend of the court) briefs concerning restrictions on women's rights to choose for themselves whether or not to have an abortion and general restrictions on access to abortion choices.

Planned Parenthood Federation of America also participates in the general women's health movement on many issues related to women's reproductive health and birth control availability. The PPFA has an international affiliate that seeks to help women worldwide understand their bodies and become active agents in making the best reproductive decisions for their own spiritual and physical well-being. (LW) **See also** Health Care Policy; Reproductive and Contraceptive Technologies for Women.

Bibliography

Critchlow, Donald T., ed. *The Politics of Abortion and Birth Control in Historical Perspective.* University Park: The Pennsylvania State University Press, 1996.

Garrow, David J. *Liberty & Sexuality: The Right to Privacy and the Making of* Roe v. Wade. New York: MacMillan Publishing Co., 1994.

Luker, Kristin. *Abortion & The Politics of Motherhood.* Berkeley: University of California Press, 1984.

O'Connor, Karen. *No Neutral Ground: Abortion Politics in an Age of Absolutes.* Boulder, CO: Westview Press, 1996.

Planned Parenthood of Southeastern Pennsylvania v. Casey (1992)

In 1989, Pennsylvania enacted the **Abortion Control Act**, which included among its provisions compulsory anti-abortion counseling by doctors, a 24-hour waiting period after counseling, reporting requirements by doctors and clinics, spousal notification, and parental consent that required at least one parent to accompany the minor to the clinic or judicial approval. The law was immediately challenged by **Planned Parenthood** in district court. On appeal to the U.S. Supreme Court, Planned Parenthood was supported by more than 178 organizations, including the **National Organization for Women (NOW)** and the National Abortion Rights Action League. The administration of President George Bush weighed in on an amicus brief arguing that the Court should overrule ***Roe v. Wade*** in this case.

The decision of the case (*Planned Parenthood of Southeastern Pennsylvania v. Casey*, 505 U.S. 833 [1992]) was a mixed message for all parties involved. The Court was heavily divided into three camps. The result was that the decision turned around a three-justice plurality made up of Justices **Sandra Day O'Connor**, Anthony Kennedy, and David Souter. The 184-page decision specifically upheld the central tenet of *Roe*, i.e., a woman's right to have an **abortion**. The three-justice majority was joined by Justices John Paul Stevens and Harry Blackmun in its statement to reaffirm *Roe*. However, the decision also gave states greater ability to regulate abortions by upholding as constitutional all of the provisions of the Pennsylvania act with the exception of spousal notification. Four justices, including Chief Justice William Rehnquist and Justices Byron White, Antonin Scalia, and Clarence Thomas, wrote that they would have overturned *Roe* completely.

In the end, the Court's opinion established a modified principle of *Roe* by deciding that states could regulate abortions as long as the restrictions were not undue burdens. The result has been to push the abortion debate back to the state level.

BIBLIOGRAPHY

Ford, John Christopher. "The Casey Standard for Evaluating Facial Attacks on Abortion Statutes. *Michigan Law Review* 95 (March 1997): 1443–71.

O'Connor, Karen. *No Neutral Ground?* Boulder, CO: Westview, 1996.

"Salvaging the Undue Burden Standard." *Washington University Law Quarterly* 73 (Spring 1995): 295–332.

Pocahontas (c. 1595–1617)

The daughter of Powhatan, chief of the Powhatan Confederation of Tribes in eastern Virginia and North Carolina, Pocahontas was instrumental in saving the life of Captain John Smith who had been taken prisoner by her father and sentenced to be executed. Her actions helped to improve relations between the colonists and the Indians. However, after Smith left Jamestown in 1610, she was taken prisoner by the colonists and baptized a Christian with the given name, Rebecca. In 1614, she married John Rolfe and returned with him to England in 1616 where she died a year later. (AM)

BIBLIOGRAPHY

Mossiker, Frances. *Pocahontas; The Life and the Legend*. New York: Knopf, 1976.

Rountree, Helen C. *Pocahontas' People: The Powhatan Indians of Virginia Through Four Centuries.* Norman: University of Oklahoma Press, 1990.

Poelkner v. Doe (1977)

At issue in *Poelkner v. Doe*, 432 U.S. 519 (1977), was a St. Louis, Missouri, ordinance that barred nontheraputic **abortions** from being performed in public hospitals. By a 6-3 decision, the restriction was found to be constitutional by the U.S. Supreme Court. The Court had ruled in a series of public funding cases, including *Poelkner*, ***Beal v. Doe***, and ***Maher v. Roe,*** that while the state could not outlaw abortions, it could decide not to fund them even though it chose to fund childbirth. The dissenters argued that for many this placed the exercise of their abortion rights beyond their means.

BIBLIOGRAPHY

Baer, Judith A. *Women in American Law*. New York: Holmes & Meier, 1996.

Boumil, Marcia Mobilia and Stephen C. Hicks. *Women and the Law*. Littleton, CO: Fred B. Rothman & Co., 1992.

Political Participation

Women have always participated in American politics, although they have moved from the margins to the mainstream over the course of American history. From **Abigail Adams**'s solitary, and unheeded, plea to "remember the ladies" in 1776 to the collective voice of millions of women who re-elected Bill Clinton to the presidency of the United States in 1996, women's participation in American politics has evolved in many domains.

To illuminate the impact of women's political participation in the United States, four distinct areas of participation may be examined: (1) grass-roots political activities, (2) electoral politics, (3) **Republican Party** and **Democratic Party** politics, and (4) the participation of women as public officials.

The traditional notion that women and men inhabited separate spheres of influence, with men active in the public sphere and women restricted to the private sphere, resulted in women's marginal participation in politics during much of American political history. The women's rights advocates of the mid–nineteenth century focused their demands on improving the situation of women within their homes and families, rather then advocating a role outside the home. Women's isolation from public life led them to develop community ties to other women and began the tradition of grass-roots women's organizations to deal with the problems that faced women. **Harriet Tubman** and the Underground Railroad rescued slaves, **Jane Addams** established **Hull House**, **Florence Kelley** and others organized to provide health care services to mothers and children and to prevent the exploitation of child labor. Many women's organizations, such as the **Young Women's Christian Association (YWCA)** and the **American Association of University Women (AAUW)** were established before 1920 and continue to be active today in promoting women's issues. The tradition of grass-roots political participation continues to this day with countless women active in local **domestic violence** shelters and **Parent-Teacher Associations** and tackling other problems at the local level.

Although this form of activity had not traditionally been associated with political participation, the second-wave feminist maxim, "The personal is the political," has led many women to realize that local, community-based action to improve the situation of women and children is, indeed, political in nature.

In a more traditional form of political participation, electoral politics, women were late entrants to the political system. After battling for more than 75 years, women won the right to vote in 1920 with the passage of the **Nineteenth Amendment**. However, voting is a learned habit, and women did not immediately flock to the polls to exercise their franchise in large numbers. The first scientific polls of voting behavior in the 1950s and 1960s showed that women were significantly less likely to vote than men, by a margin of about 10 percent. Political scientists attributed this lower turnout among women to factors such as child-rearing responsibilities and lack of interest in politics. However, studies showed that in the 1970s women's turnout increased, perhaps as a result of the increasing labor force participation of women that brought many of them out of the private sphere to which they had been previously relegated. The **women's movement** of the late 1960s and the 1970s undoubtedly attributed to the increased political awareness of women and to their increased participation in electoral politics. In 1980, for the first time ever, women turned out to vote at a higher rate than did men. The gap in turnout between men and women has persisted throughout the elections of the 1980s and 1990s.

The difference in turnout rates would not have a significant impact on the outcome of elections if women and men voted in the same ways. But in 1980, a **gender gap** in voter choice also emerged. Women voters are significantly more likely than men to vote for the Democratic presidential candidate. When one combines the increasing turnout rate with the increased propensity of women to vote Democratic, it is easy to see the tremendous impact that women have on contemporary electoral politics. For the first time ever in 1996, women cast the determinative votes for president. Women voted for Bill Clinton over Bob Dole by a margin of 54 percent to 38 percent, while men voted for Bob Dole over Bill Clinton by a margin of 44 percent to 43 percent. Helped by their numerical superiority in the electorate, women played a large role in re-electing Bill Clinton.

Participation in party politics is another traditional avenue to achieving influence in the American political system. Women's participation as delegates at the national party conventions is important, not only because presidential candidates are selected, but because party platforms are also agreed upon that will determine the official party position on political issues. Historically, women were rare participants in party politics, but their representation in this area of participation, as in others, has increased markedly. Following the 1968 Democratic National Convention, the **Democratic Party** made a concerted effort to increase the representation of women and minorities among their delegates. In 1972, women made up almost 40 percent of the Democratic delegates and 30 percent of the Republican delegates. This is in marked contrast to the previous two decades in which women's representation varied between 10 and 17 percent. Since 1980, the Democratic Party has required that women comprise 50 percent of the delegates to their national convention, and the presence and support of female delegates helped assure the nomination of **Geraldine Ferraro** for the vice presidential spot on the 1984 Democratic ticket. In 1996, women comprised 57 percent of the delegates to the Democratic National Convention and 39 percent of the delegates at the Republican National Convention. The conventions of 1996 also marked the first time in history that both of the candidates' wives (**Hillary Rodham Clinton** and **Elizabeth Dole**) made major addresses to their respective parties at the nominating conventions. A 1990 study by Rapoport, Stone, and Abramowitz found that women party activists were more liberal on social and foreign policy issues and more supportive of women's issues than comparable male party activists in both the Republican and Democratic Parties. Their ideological distinctiveness combined with their increasing numerical representation suggests that women will continue to play an increasingly important role as partisan political participants in American politics.

The fourth area of political participation in which women have made great strides has been in the realm of running for and holding public office. Surprisingly, women served as public officials long before women earned the right to vote in national elections. In 1894, three Republican women were elected to the Colorado House of Representatives. The tradition of **coverture** contributed to the early, sporadic representation of women in the national legislature as well. Ten of the first 17 women to serve in the United States Senate were either appointed by their husbands to fill a vacancy or were appointed to succeed their husbands when they died in office. To date, only 25 women have ever served in the U.S. Senate. Coverture also contributed to a dearth of female candidates running on their own merits because women lacked the financial resources and legal status to run for political office. However, women candidates and office-holders have made modest strides in the level of representation that they enjoy in state and national government.

Figure 1 presents a bar graph that examines the level of female representation in state legislatures and the United States Congress from 1977 through 1997, with each set of bars representing a two-year interval. In 1977, women held only 10 percent of all state legislative seats. That level of representation has increased dramatically over two decades and in 1997 women held one of every four state legislative seats. Of course, the average obfuscates the extent of differences in women's representation among states. While 38.1 percent of the state legislators in Washington State are women, only 4.3 percent of Alabama state legislators are women. Southern states, including Alabama, Kentucky, Louisiana, Mississippi, South

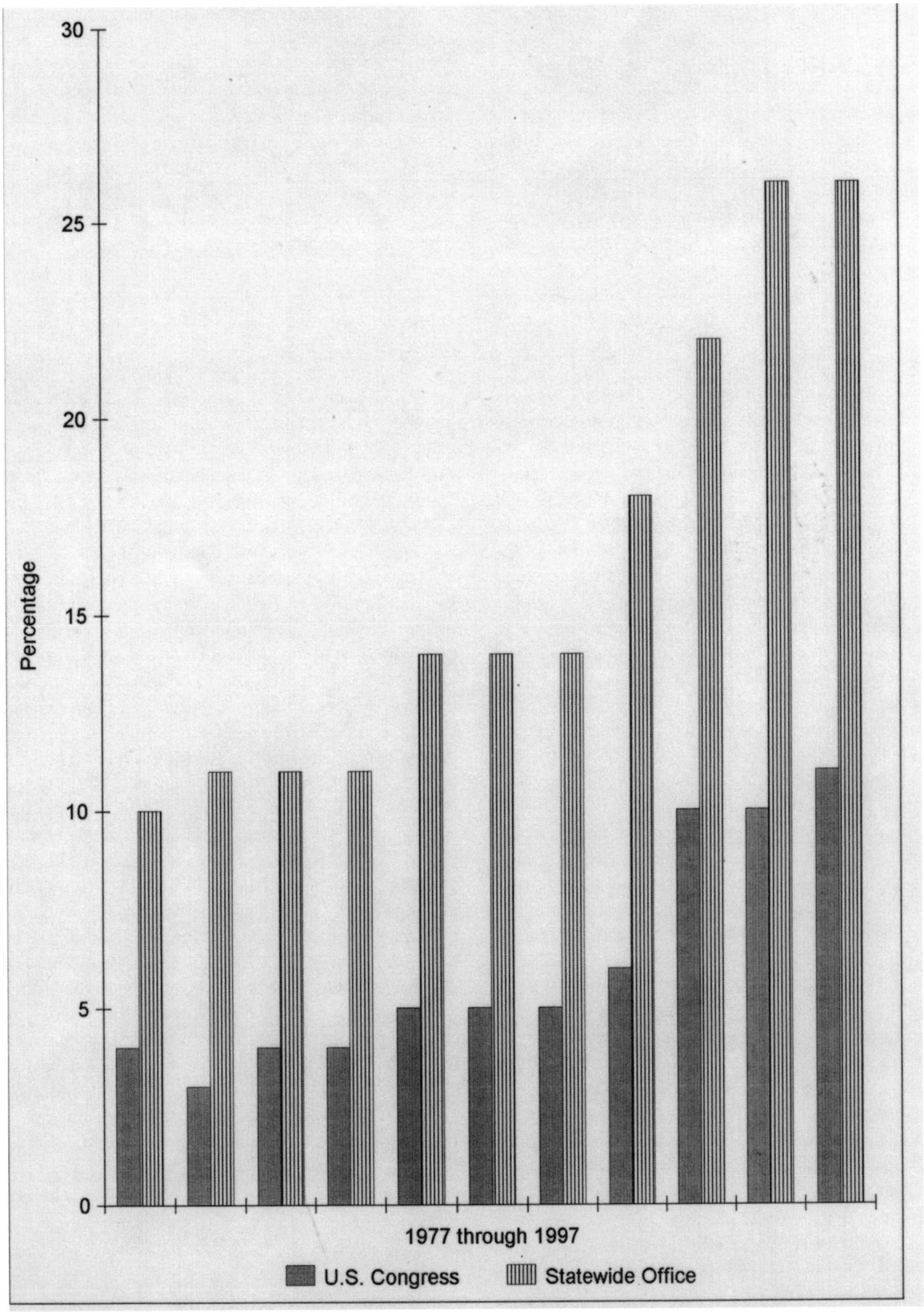

Women Elected at the State and National Levels

Figure 1

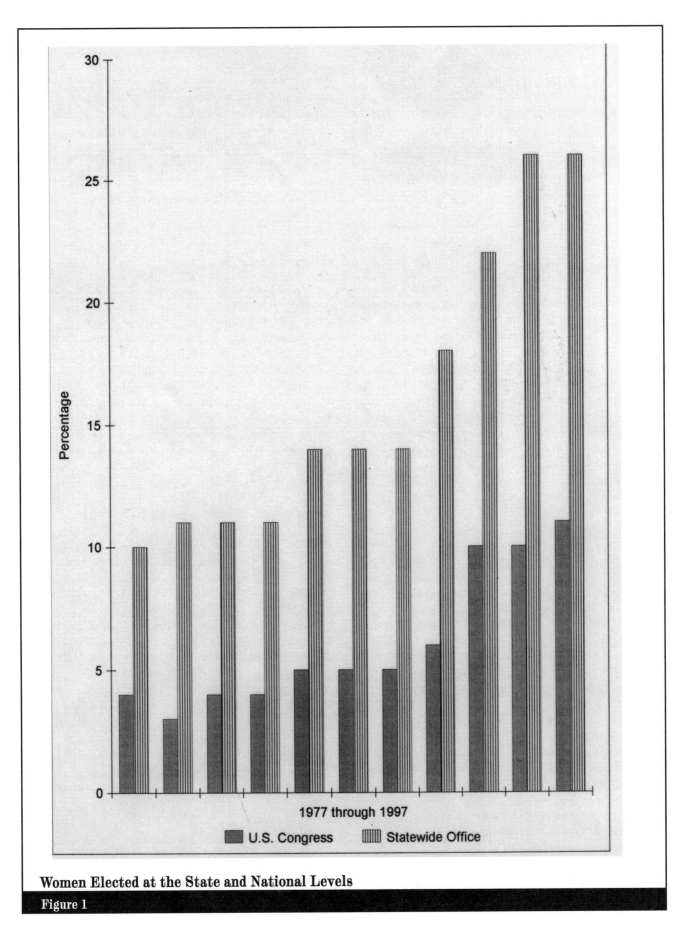

Carolina, and Tennessee, are overrepresented in the sample of the 10 states with the lowest percentage of women state legislators.

In the national legislature, progress has been slower, as women candidates contend with the difficulty of ousting incumbents, mounting expensive campaigns, and dealing with the family difficulties associated with holding public office. Women's responsibilities in the private sphere still hinder their pursuit of a public career in politics, especially at the national level. Women candidates at the national level are significantly older than male candidates and are less likely to have school-age children. And while women are generally able to raise as much money for campaigns as men, they are fighting against House and Senate incumbency return rates that are as high as 95 percent. The incumbency barrier to the increased participation of women in national governance was lowered somewhat in the elections of 1992, when reapportionment created new districts and scandal forced the retirement of many incumbents. The "**Year of the Woman**" saw a dramatic increase in women's representation in the House and Senate. However, progress since then has returned to an incremental pace. In 1997, women held 11.2 percent of the 535 seats in the 105th Congress. Thirty-five Democratic and 16 Republican women held seats in the House, while six Democratic and three Republican women were U.S. senators.

Once again, if women office holders are no different than their male counterparts, the level of political participation of women in public office would not have a substantive impact on American politics. However, extensive research has shown that women office holders are distinctive from their male counterparts at both the state and national levels of government.

A 1988 Center for the American Woman and Politics survey of state legislators revealed that women state legislators are more feminist and more liberal in their attitudes on issues and that they are more active on women's rights than men state legislators. The success of state legislation that affects women also depends on the level of female representation. In Washington State in 1993, women legislators took to wearing buttons proclaiming themselves members of the "Ladies Sewing Circle and Terrorist Society," when it appeared that a bill mandating insurance coverage of mammograms was in danger. The bill passed and was signed by the governor.

A recent study of the 103rd Congress (1993–1994) showed that women members often cast more liberal or more feminist votes than did their male counterparts. This study also revealed that women office holders feel a special responsibility to champion issues that affect women and children. Although women represented only about 10 percent of the 103rd Congress, their impact was evident in such landmark legislation as the **Family and Medical Leave Act**, the **Violence Against Women Act**, and the **Freedom of Access to Clinic Entrances Act (FACE).**

Women's political participation has moved from the periphery to the center of American politics in a relatively brief period of time. However, every successful social movement will create a powerful counter-movement, and the women's movement in the United States is no exception. Although it is clear that generally women are more liberal and more supportive of the feminist agenda than men, there is a vocal and active group of conservative women who oppose the feminist agenda and advocate a return of women to their "rightful place" in the home. Starting in the 1970s, antifeminist activists such as **Phyllis Schlafly** and Beverly LaHaye were instrumental in organizing women in opposition to the feminist agenda and they were remarkably successful in derailing the ratification of the **Equal Rights Amendment (ERA)**. It is ironic that the progress women have made in the American political system, from enfranchisement through office holding, has enabled antifeminists to pursue their political goals of returning women to the private sphere.

The future nature of women's political participation in the Untied States is likely to increasingly reflect the nontraditional, feminist, and liberal positions on issues that are already evident in the electorate. Research on the youngest of Americans has shown that the ideological gulf between young men and young women is larger than among any other group of men and women, with women significantly more likely to advocate feminist and liberal issue positions. As this group ages and becomes active in politics, it is likely that the gender gap—in turnout, vote choice, and issue positions—will be exacerbated rather then minimized. As for women's participation in holding office, structural barriers such as incumbency exist that will keep the pace of progress slow and steady as has been evident in the past 30 years. Certainly future political decisions could increase the level of women's representation dramatically. Term limits at the state level have already lowered the incumbency advantage in state electoral politics. However, the courts have not upheld the constitutionality of term limits at the national level and it is unlikely that members of Congress will pass a constitutional amendment to limit their own political livelihoods. There is even the possibility of a change in our electoral system from the single-member district to a proportional representation system, like the one that has contributed to the increased representation of women in countries such as Norway, Israel, and the Netherlands. However, this type of drastic change in the structure of American political competition is unlikely. Hence, it appears likely that women's political participation in electoral and party politics is the most likely vehicle for change in the American political system. (CKC) **See also** Antifeminism; Feminism.

Bibliography

Bookman, Ann and Sandra Morgan, eds. *Women and the Politics of Empowerment.* Philadelphia: Temple University Press, 1988.

Carroll, Susan J., Debra Dodson, and Ruth Mandel. *The Impact of Women in Public Office.* New Brunswick, NJ: Center for the American Woman and Politics, 1991.

Chaney, Carole and Barbara Sinclair. "Women in the 1992 House Elections." In Elizabeth Cook et al., eds. *The Year of the Woman: Myths and Realities.* Boulder, CO: Westview Press, 1994.

Cox, Elizabeth M. *Women in Modern American Politics: A Bibliography, 1990–1995.* Washington, DC: CQ Press, 1997.

Dodson, Debra L., Susan J. Carroll, Ruth B. Mandel, Katherine E. Kleeman, Ronnee Schreiber, and Debra Liebowitz. *Voice, Views and Votes: The Impact of Women in the 103rd Congress.* New Brunswick, NJ: Center for the American Woman and Politics, 1995.

Freeman, Jo. "Whom You Know versus Whom You Represent: Feminist Influence in the Democratic and Republican Parties." In Mary Fainsod Katzenstein and Carol McClug Mueller, eds. *The Women's Movements of the United States and Western Europe.* Philadelphia: Temple University Press, 1984.

George, Carol V. R. *Remember the Ladies: New Perspectives on Women in American History.* Syracuse, NY: Syracuse University Press, 1975.

Klein, Ethel. *Gender Politics.* Cambridge, MA: Harvard University Press, 1984.

McGlen, Nancy and Karen O'Connor. *Women, Politics, and American Society.* Englewood Cliffs, NJ: Prentice-Hall, 1995.

Rapoport, Ronald B., Walter J. Stone, and Alan I. Abramowitz. "Sex and the Caucus Participant: The Gender Gap and Presidential Nominating Conventions." *American Journal of Political Science* 34, no. 3 (1990): 725–40.

Sarah Childress Polk (1803–1891)

An astute political advisor and partner, Sarah Polk helped her husband into the U.S. presidency. Indeed, Sarah informed James Polk that she would not even marry him unless he won a seat in the Tennessee legislature. Through her lobbying and promotion of him, Sarah Polk was key to advancing James' career. Her centrality to his political ambitions is demonstrated by her role as political campaign boss in both his run for governor and his 1844 presidential campaign. While in the White House, Sarah Polk served as an advisor to the president by redrafting both his letters and speeches and marking news stories for his viewing. The consummate political partner, she looked out for her husband's interests by charming and lobbying powerful politicians. Although it is difficult to judge her influence on political issues, Vice President George Dallas remarked, "She is certainly mistress of herself and I suspect of somebody else also." Sarah Polk's ambitions and talents make her one of the most outspoken and politically involved U.S. **first ladies** of her time. (BN)

Sarah Polk was a driving force behind her husband's political career. Library of Congress, Prints and Photographs Division.

BIBLIOGRAPHY

Caroli, Betty Boyd. *First Ladies.* New York: Oxford University Press, 1995.

Sellers, Charles. *James K. Polk.* Princeton University Press, 1957.

Truman, Margaret. *First Ladies.* New York: Random House, 1995.

Populist Party of America

A radical third party founded in the 1890s, the Populist Party was one of the few parties that allowed women to be members. The party worked for both woman's **suffrage** and **temperance**. It achieved its greatest success in the western farming states of Kansas and Colorado. In Colorado, the party was successful in aiding the franchise of women in 1893. In both states, women achieved some electoral and appointed offices. Membership in the party began to decline in the 1890s. By 1896, the Populist Party endorsed Democratic candidate William Jennings Bryan.

BIBLIOGRAPHY

Jensen, Joan M. *With These Hands.* Old Westbury, NY: Feminist Press, 1981.

Pornography

While the regulation of sexually explicit materials has been an important issue in American politics for many years, the 1980s witnessed a unique approach to this topic. In a number of cities, an unusual coalition of social conservatives and feminists attempted to pass "anti-pornography statutes," which would effectively treat the production and dissemination of pornography as a civil rights violation. In the mid-1980s, the city councils of Indianapolis and Minneapolis passed such measures. The Indianapolis ordinance was struck down by a federal court on the grounds that the measure violated the First Amendment guarantee of free expression. The Minneapolis measure was twice vetoed by Mayor Fraser, again on First Amendment grounds.

The ordinances in question treated pornography as a violation of the equal protection rights of women. Indeed, the Indianapolis measure defines "pornography" as the sexually explicit subordination of women, graphically depicted (in pictures or in words) in the following ways:

1. Women presented as sexual objects who enjoy pain or humiliation.
2. Women presented as sexual objects who experience sexual pleasure in being raped.
3. Women presented as being penetrated by objects or animals.
4. Women presented as sexual objects for domination, conquest, violation, exploitation, possession, or use, or through postures or positions of servility or submission or display.

In this definition, it is not simply the manner of representation that triggers the ordinance; it is the depiction of women as sexually subordinate that forms the basis for regulation.

It is important to distinguish this analysis of pornography from more standard justifications for the regulation of "obscenity." Analyses of obscenity typically involve the assertion that the purpose of the First Amendment is to protect the free interplay of ideas thought to be necessary to self-governance. Free expression is thought to be desirable because such expression permits competition between different ideas and allows self-governing citizens the opportunity to choose among alternative ideas. Obscenity, as defined by the Supreme Court, is thought to be bereft of ideas, and is therefore not deserving of First Amendment protection. Typically, sexually explicit expressions have been constitutionally protected if they have made some contribution to the free exchange of ideas, although the precise definition of "redeeming social...value" has varied across court decisions over time. The essential point, however, is that obscenity is not considered speech, and is therefore not afforded constitutional protection.

By contrast, attempts to regulate pornography have been justified by the content of ideas contained in pornographic expression. Feminist accounts of pornography have emphasized that pornography is indeed political speech, and conveys (rather effectively) certain highly pernicious ideas. Among these ideas are the beliefs that women enjoy submission and humiliation, that violence against women is sexually enjoyable, and that women are objects whose main purpose is to provide physical pleasure to men. The problem, toward which recent attempts to regulate pornography have been directed, is not that pornography is devoid of ideas (as obscenity is regarded), but that pornography persuasively conveys certain important (if ultimately harmful) ideas.

It is the ideational content of pornography that has posed constitutional obstacles to its regulation. In recent years, standard accounts of the First Amendment have required government to be neutral between competing viewpoints. This is not the equivalent of asserting that government cannot regulate expression at all. The power of government may be invoked to enforce content-neutral restrictions on expression (e.g., a prohibition on loud talking during a theater performance), and government may also, on occasion, be permitted to enforce content-based, but viewpoint neutral, restrictions on free expression. For example, local governments routinely prohibit electioneering within a certain distance of a polling place. Such a restriction is typically regarded as permissible, as long as the prohibition applies to advocates of all candidates and parties. A much different constitutional issue would be raised were a government to ban electioneering selectively (e.g., only Republican advocates are allowed to perform in proximity to polling places).

What this last example illustrates is the principle that, under the First Amendment, government is generally required to be neutral between competing viewpoints or ideas. Because free expression is thought to play such an important role in the practice of democratic self-governance, the First Amendment rights of free speech, free press, and free association are regarded by some as occupying a "preferred position" in the American constitutional regime. That is, the right of free expression is typically granted a high level of constitutional protection, with apparent exceptions drawn narrowly. Typically, the Supreme Court has only permitted speech to be regulated under highly specific conditions, in which specific identifiable individuals are harmed in direct, identifiable ways. For example, the "clear and present danger exception" (which is often illustrated with the familiar example of shouting "fire" in a crowded theater) is typically applied to circumstances in which reasonable people would not have an opportunity to deliberate and that would result in immediate and tangible harms (such as being trampled by a crowd fleeing the imagined theater fire). Other apparent exceptions to the right of free speech, such as libel or sexual harassment, are generally justified by the fact that specific individuals are harmed by certain speech acts in concrete ways. At least since the 1969 case of *Brandenberg v. Ohio*, "bad tendency," or the possibility that speech may result in societal harm, has not been sufficient to justify the regulation of free expression. General societal harm resulting from the expression of harmful or pernicious ideas is not an adequate warrant for the regulation of free expression.

Such a broad view of the right of free expression is based on the belief that free citizens are capable of comparing the merits and demerits of competing ideas, and making reasonable, if informed, choices between them. The free exchange of ideas is thought to have an educative effect on citizens, which might render them more suited to the tasks associated with democratic self-governance. Moreover, were government permitted to distinguish between ideas that should and should not be expressed, public officials might well yield to the temptation to suppress ideas that are critical of government's performance or legitimacy. Many analysts have suggested that measures such as the anti-pornography ordinances would lead inevitably to a "slippery slope": once government is in the position of permitting or suppressing political speech, it is not clear where the distinction between protected and unprotected expression would be drawn. Since the First Amendment is intended to protect the expression of controversial or unpopular ideas, governments (especially democratically elected governments) are perhaps not to be trusted with making such distinctions.

The proponents of the legal regulation of pornography have developed responses to this perspective. One basic objection is that the theory on which a broad view of the right of free speech is based contains contradictory assumptions about human nature. On one hand, democratic citizens are deemed capable of making informed choice between ideas and even benefiting from exposure to any set of ideas (regardless of their apparent value to democratic politics). On the other, governments are regarded as incapable of making distinctions between controversial political ideas and "dirty" pictures. It may seem unreasonable to suppose that an enlightened citizenry (to which democratic governments are ultimately accountable) can be trusted to choose between competing conceptions of the public good and are not able to see the essential political difference between, for example, *The Communist Manifesto* and *Sluts in Space*.

Moreover, proponents of anti-pornography measures have suggested that the principle of value neutrality is itself open to question. By allowing apparent nondiscrimination between competing ideas, government essentially endorses the status quo but permits the contemporary configuration of power relations to prevail. "Neutrality" masks the fact that diverse interests have vastly unequal access to the means of communication, and that government inaction in this area preserves and maintains existing power inequalities. In other areas (e.g. property rights), government has intervened actively to preserve values such as economic competition. Further, it is argued that pornography itself intimidates women and prevents them from full participation in the public dialogue. The fact that some men act on the themes of pornographic ideas restricts women's mobility and assertiveness and thus may prevent women from exercising the full powers of democratic citizenship. Therefore, defending the rights of pornographers for the sake of a wide-ranging public debate in which multiple viewpoints are expressed and debated may ultimately be self-defeating, by limiting the access of certain ideas and advocates to the public arena.

It has been noted that the "preferred position" of the right of free expression is itself based on assumptions underlying liberal individualism. This perspective is the result of a particular political theory, which has been rendered controversial by the insights of modern psychology and sociology. It is not clear, for example, that self-governing citizens choose impartially between competing ideas, or that public and private discourse is not incorrigibly gendered. Thus, the principle of government neutrality between competing ideas may be genuinely paradoxical; the choice of such a value makes sense only from the standpoint of particular theories, which are not themselves value neutral.

Proponents and opponents of anti-pornography legislation differ to some extent over the nature of public discourse. How fundamental such differences are remains open to debate. Advocates of both positions have attempted to justify their positions (at least partially) in defense of First Amendment values. Proponents of the legal regulation of pornography are regarded by some as attempting to subvert the values underlying the principle of free expression, and by others as trying to actualize such values in the "real world" of political dialogue. (TGJ)

Bibliography

"Anti-Pornography Laws and First Amendment Values." *Harvard Law Review* (December 1984): 460.

Bollinger, Lee. *The Tolerant Society*. New York: Oxford University Press, 1986.

Dworkin, Andrea and Catharine A. MacKinnon. *Pornography and Civil Rights: A New Day for Women's Equality*. Minneapolis: Organization Against Pornography, 1988.

Downs, Donald Alexander. *The New Politics of Pornography*. Chicago: University of Chicago Press, 1989.

Elshtain, Jean Bethke, "The New Porn Wars." *The New Republic* (June 25, 1984): 15–20.

MacKinnon, Catharine A. *Only Words*. Cambridge, MA: Harvard University Press, 1993.

Sustain, Cass R. *Democracy and the Problem of Free Speech*. New York: The Free Press, 1993.

Poverty

Poverty is a state or condition that occurs when people do not have the means to support themselves and are unable to meet their own basic needs as human beings, such as food, clothing, and shelter. There are many causes of poverty, including job loss, divorce, death of a spouse, single parenthood, and the lack of an adequate education or job training. Poverty rates vary greatly according to demographic categories, including gender, race/ethnicity, and age. With respect to gender, more women tend to be poor than men, a phenomenon that has become known as the "feminization of poverty." The feminization of poverty has occurred not only in the United States, but worldwide. In addition to gender differences, poverty rates vary significantly between racial and ethnic groups. While whites make up the majority of the poor in the United States in terms of numbers, racial and ethnic minorities tend to be disproportionately represented in the poverty population. Age also significantly affects poverty rates. Children tend to be disproportionately represented among the poor, and statistics show that children, as well as the elderly, are less likely than nonelderly adults to escape poverty. Along with the economic concerns poverty presents, there are a host of social problems that often accompany poverty, including physical health problems, mental illness, developmental disabilities, **domestic violence**, and substance abuse.

In 1955, the United States Department of Agriculture conducted a survey of food consumption and determined that families of three or more people spent one-third of their after-tax income on food. In the late 1950s, this information was used to calculate federal poverty lines, or poverty thresholds. The government calculated these lines by multiplying the cost of the Department of Agriculture's least costly economic food plan by three. Hilda Scott, in *Working Your Way to the Bottom: The Feminization of Poverty*, notes that the food plan was multiplied by three because the government needed a baseline from which to operate but lacked adequate definitions and measures of nonfood items, such as housing, clothing, and furniture, that were necessary for living. Since food purchases represented one-third of after-tax expenditures, government officials inferred that three times those food expenditures was an adequate basis upon which to calculate poverty thresholds. Additionally, the government recognized that factors such as family size, householder age, and the number of children in the home under the age of 18 would influence a family's income and whether a family was considered poor. Therefore, the government established, and continues to establish, a number of poverty thresholds to account for the varying situations of families. For example, in 1996 the United States Census Bureau's Current Population Survey listed 45 different poverty lines based on the number of people in the family, the age of the householder (under 65 years of age or older), and the number of related children under 18 years of age in the household. These poverty lines ranged from a low of about $8,000 for a single person under the age of 65 to over $30,000 for a family of nine with between zero and six related children under 18. Because of the number of poverty lines calculated by the government, statistics on "the" poverty line generally will specify "for a family of three," "for a family of four," and the like. Each year, poverty thresholds are increased by a factor that is based on the change in the Consumer Price Index (CPI).

While the government has an established method of determining poverty lines, the number of persons classified as poor and the poverty rate vary with alternative definitions of income. Government assistance in the form of cash and noncash benefits, such as Temporary Assistance for Needy Families (TANF) funds, Medicaid, and food stamps, significantly affect poor people's incomes, and therefore, the poverty rate. In the Current Population Survey, the United States Census Bureau calculates poverty rates on the basis of as many as nine different definitions of low income, producing poverty rates for 1995 ranging from a low of 10.3 percent to a high of 22.1 percent.

According to the United States Census Bureau, the percentage of all persons in poverty has hovered between 13 and 15 percent since 1980, while the percentage of all families in poverty has ranged from approximately 11 to 14 percent since that time. These figures, however, mask significant variation among subpopulations of Americans. As noted, poverty rates vary widely by gender, marital status, age, and race/ethnicity.

The "feminization of poverty" phenomenon continues today, regardless of age or race/ethnicity. United States Census Bureau statistics reveal that, as of 1995, 57 percent of all poor persons were female. Moreover, among households maintained by women alone, one-third of the families had incomes that fell below the federal poverty line. In comparison, according to the United States Census Bureau's March 1996 Current Population Survey, the poverty rate for married couples was not quite 6 percent, while the poverty rate for male heads-of-household was 14 percent.

McLanahan, Sorenson, and Watson, in their article "Sex Differences in Poverty, 1950–1980," show that while poverty rates have decreased for both men and women overall since 1950, the poverty rate for men declined more quickly than the rate for women, producing a gap between women and men. The poverty rate for women has increased relative to the poverty rate for men over time. Much of this gap can be explained, according to McLanahan, Sorenson, and Watson, by examining changes in parental and family arrangements—that is, by the increase in single parenting.

According to the United States Census Bureau's "Highlights of the Population Profile," the number of single parents grew from under 4 million in 1970 to over 11 million in the mid-1990s. Single-parent families represent almost one-third of all United States families that have children under the age of 21 who have never been married. One factor that contributes to the problem of poverty in single-parent households is the failure of noncustodial parents to pay court-mandated child support. According to the Income Statistics Branch of the United States Census Bureau, approximately one-third of total child support payments due went unpaid in the early 1990s. There is little disagreement that payment of delinquent child support would assist single parents and their children. However, according to the Census Bureau, even full payment of overdue child support would be unlikely to lift a significant portion of female-headed families out of poverty. While male-headed single-parent households had a poverty rate of 13 percent in the early 1990s, female-headed single-parent households had a poverty rate of 35 percent; and women who maintained custody of their children were two-and-a-half times more likely to live in poverty than men who maintained custody of their children.

Children have a higher poverty rate than any other age group. While the national poverty rate has remained between 13 and 15 percent for a number of years, the poverty rate for children has been significantly higher, usually running over 20 percent. According to the National Center for Children in Poverty, the number of children in poverty who were under six years of age increased from 5 to 6 million from 1987 to 1992, and the poverty rate for these same children grew to 26 percent. Half of these children live in what is termed "extreme poverty," or less than half of the federal poverty threshold. With respect to race and ethnicity, while Hispanic and African-American children compose less than 30 percent of all children under the age of six in the United States, they represented over half of poor children under the age of six in 1992.

The outlook for poor children in the United States is not good. Poor children are more likely to experience health problems and to suffer from chronic illnesses and developmental disabilities than are other children, according to the National Center for Children in Poverty. Additionally, children who are poor have little chance of being lifted out of poverty by government benefits in the United States. The Children's Defense Fund, in *The State of America's Children*, shows that the United States has a lackluster record (8.5 percent) when it comes to lifting low income children out of poverty, compared to almost 41 percent in Canada, 45 percent in Australia, and over 70 percent in the United Kingdom, France, the Netherlands, and Sweden. Similarly, a study in *Child Poverty News and Issues*, "U.S. Doing Poorly — Compared to Others," reveals that children in the United States are worse off than children in 16 other industrialized countries in terms of poverty rates and income levels.

While children's poverty rates have increased in recent years, statistics on poverty among the elderly from the United States Department of Commerce reveal that the proportion of poor people 65 years of age and older has declined over the past 20 years. This change is due primarily to Social Security. Again, however, significant variation exists among subpopulations of the elderly. Elderly women are more likely to be poor than elderly men for a number of reasons. Women earn less as paid workers throughout their lives; they do a majority of the world's unpaid labor, such as house-cleaning and child-rearing. Widows receive only a portion of their husbands' Social Security benefits.

In addition to differences in poverty rates according to gender among the elderly, which holds across racial/ethnic categories and time, poverty rates among the elderly vary further by age and race/ ethnicity. People between the ages of 65 and 74 have a lower rate of poverty than those 75 and older. With respect to race/ethnicity, elderly Hispanics and elderly African Americans tend to have a poverty rate two-to-three times that of elderly whites, respectively.

African Americans and Hispanics have poverty rates of more than twice that of non-Hispanic whites, while Asian and Pacific Islanders' rates are closer to those of non-Hispanic whites.

What does the future look like for poor people in the United States? Many interested observers anticipate that the Personal Responsibility and Work Opportunity Reconciliation Act of 1996, which replaces the federal **Aid to Families with Dependent Children (AFDC)** program with the state-run Temporary Assistance for Needy Families (TANF) block grant program, will move poor people off welfare and out of poverty. However, this anticipation may ignore some realities of being poor in the United States. Statistics from *Child Poverty News and Issues* show that almost three out of five children under age 6 who live below the poverty line have parents who work in full- or part-time jobs. Moreover, according to the United States Census Bureau, in the early 1990s, half of poor households were employed. These families represent the "working poor"—families with householders who are employed but do not earn enough money to bring their families above the federal poverty line. Additionally, this focus on employment does not acknowledge the fact that many of the poor need assistance in combating such problems as substance abuse, mental illness, and domestic violence. Recent reports show that a disproportionate number of women on **welfare** have serious substance abuse problems, are currently or have been victims of family violence, or have experienced depression or other mental impairments. The federal welfare reform law does not mandate that states put funds towards programs that will address these problems. Therefore, it will be up to individual states to decide to what extent they will provide assistance in these areas, as well as in the areas of job training and development. (HNF) **See also** Social Security.

BIBLIOGRAPHY

Blank, Rebecca. "Welfare Recipients Aren't the Only Ones with Plenty of Hard Work Ahead." *Chicago Tribune* (January 12, 1997): Section Perspective, 1.

Children's Defense Fund. *The State of America's Children, 1994.* Washington, DC, 1994.

Economics and Statistics Administration, United States Department of Commerce. *Statistical Brief: Sixty-Five Plus in the United States.* Washington, DC: Government Printing Office, 1995.

McLanahan, Sara, Annemette Sorenson, and Dorothy Watson. "Sex Differences in Poverty, 1950–1980." *Signs: Journal of Women in Culture and Society* 15, no. 1 (Autumn 1989): 102–22.

National Center for Children in Poverty. "Number of Poor Children Under Six Increased from Five to Six Million 1987–1992." *Child Poverty News and Issues* 5, no. 1. (Winter 1995).

———. "Young Children Still live in Poverty — Despite Parental Employment." *Child Poverty News and Issues* 3, no. 1 (Winter/Spring 1993).

Rainwater, Lee and Timothy M. Smeeding. "U.S. Doing Poorly — Compared to Others: Policy Point of View." *Child Poverty News and Issues* 5, no. 3 (Fall 1995).

Scott Hilda. *Working Your Way to the Bottom: The Feminization of Poverty.* Boston: Pandora Press, 1984.

United States Bureau of the Census. *Highlights of the Population Profile*. Washington, DC: Government Printing Office, 1997.

———. *March Current Population Survey.* Washington, DC; Government Printing Office: 1996.

Eliza Jane Pratt (1902–1981)

Eliza Jane Pratt served as secretary to members of the House of Representatives from North Carolina's 8th Congressional District twice in her career, from 1924 to 1946 and from 1957 to 1962. In 1946, she became the first woman elected to the House of Representatives from North Carolina when she won the special election to fill the vacancy of Congressman William Burgin, who had died in April. A Democrat, Pratt served only until 1947. She was also employed in the Office of Alien Property from May 27, 1947, until February 2, 1951; with the Department of Agriculture from February 5, 1951, to April 12, 1954; and with the Library of Congress from April 13, 1954, to December 7, 1956.

BIBLIOGRAPHY

Chamberlin, Hope. *A Minority of Members.* New York: Praeger, 1973.

Ruth Stevens Baker Pratt (1887–1965)

Ruth Pratt served as chairwoman of the Woman's Liberty Loan Commission. During her political career, she was also a Republican member of the United States House of Representatives from New York, serving from 1929 until 1933. She was also a member of the Republican National Committee from 1924 until 1943.

BIBLIOGRAPHY

Pratt, Mrs. John T. "Plea for Party Partisanship." *The Woman Citizen* 10 (March 1926): 23.

Pratt, Ruth. "Lady or the Tiger." *Ladies Home Journal* 45 (May 1928): 8.

———. "Lady of the House." *Outlook* 152 (July 3, 1929): 377.

Pregnancy Discrimination Act (1978)

The Pregnancy Discrimination Act, passed October 31, 1978, amends **Title VII of the Civil Rights Act of 1964** to prohibit discrimination in the workplace on the basis of pregnancy, childbirth, or related medical conditions among employees who share a similar ability or inability to work. The act applies to all aspects of employment, including fringe benefits. It requires pregnancy to be treated the same as a short-term disability for insurance purposes. The act does not require, however, employers to provide health benefits for **abortion**.

While the prohibition against **sex discrimination** in employment contained in Title VII, as amended by the **Equal Employment Opportunity Act** of 1972, was originally interpreted to include pregnancy discrimination, the vague terminology led to inconsistent application of the law according to a House report. In ***General Electric Company v. Gilbert*** (1976), the Supreme Court ruled that General Electric's exclusion of coverage for pregnancy-related disabilities was condition- not gender-related and was thus in accordance with Title VII. Conversely, in ***Nashville Gas Company v. Satty*** (1977), the Court found that the denial of accumulated seniority due to childbirth-related absence was in violation of Title VII. To clear up such ambiguities and reaffirm the illegality of sex discrimination in all its forms, Congress passed this act. (AMR)

Bibliography

U.S. House Education and Labor Committee. *Pregnancy Discrimination Act* (H. Rpt. 95-948). Washington, DC: U.S. Government Printing Office, 1978.

President's Commission on the Status of Women (PCSW)

The President's Commission on the Status of Women was established on December 14, 1961, by President John F. Kennedy's **Executive Order 10980**. Chaired by **Eleanor Roosevelt**, with **Esther Peterson**, the executive vice-chair, the high-powered bipartisan commission had 26 members (15 women, 11 men), including five cabinet secretaries, two senators, two representatives, the chair of the U.S. Civil Service Commission, and leaders from academia, labor unions, and industry. The members of the PCSW facilitated action on the final recommendations of the commission.

The PCSW organized its work through a series of committees and subcommittees, the most important being in the following areas: civil and political rights, education, federal employment, home and community, private employment, social insurance and taxes, and protective labor legislation. The commission focused on the role of the federal government as an employer, and issues of equality in the workforce, including equal pay and benefits. The PCSW's final report, published as *American Women: Report of the President's Commission on the Status of Women*, was a lengthy document that served as a blueprint for federal policy considered or enacted over the next three decades.

Given its strong ties to the **Women's Bureau**, the commission focused on such political rights as jury service, property rights, and family relations and recommended that courts be used as a vehicle to test the Fourteenth Amendment as a way to gain and guarantee equal rights for women. However, members of the commission did not want to lose the **protective legislation** for women and children and therefore did not recommend passage of the **Equal Rights Amendment (ERA).** The failure of the commission to enforce the prohibitions against **sex discrimination** in the **Civil Rights Act of 1964** led women to form the **National Organization for Women (NOW).**

While many policy changes would take years to achieve, the work of the PCSW helped open up jobs in the civil service to women, move equal pay legislation forward, open up top-ranking officer slots for women in the **military service**, change the tax code concerning **child care** deductions, and equalize benefits for men and women in the workforce. The commission also reviewed means to increase **political participation** by women—including federal structures to systematically search for women for appointive posts, and the use of quotas to ensure a 50-50 split in participation of women as delegates to national conventions. (JMM)

Bibliography

Harrison, Cynthia. *On Account of Sex: The Politics of Women's Issues, 1945–1968.* Berkeley: University of California Press, 1988.

Martin, Janet M. *A Place in the Oval Office: Women and the American Presidency.* Ann Arbor: University of Michigan Press, forthcoming.

Price Waterhouse v. Hopkins (1988)

In 1982, Ann Hopkins, a senior manager at Price Waterhouse, was considered for a partnership in the firm. The partners decided at that time to neither offer nor deny her partnership, instead holding her candidacy for consideration in the next year. When the following year passed and the office's partners refused to consider her candidacy, Hopkins sued the firm claiming that she had been discriminated against by the partner's decisions on the basis of her gender in violation of **Title VII of the Civil Rights Act of 1964**. As evidence, Hopkins could show a host of remarks that described her in stereotypical terms from both opponents and proponents of her candidacy. The district court ruled in her favor and the court of appeals affirmed the decision.

In a 6-3 decision in *Price Waterhouse v. Hopkins*, 490 U.S. 228 (1988), the U.S. Supreme Court stated that the mere evidence of sex-biased remarks was not enough to show that illegal employment activity had taken place. Rather, a plaintiff had to prove that the employer used her sex as the basis of making its decision. With that, the case was remanded to district court for trial to give Price Waterhouse a chance to show that its decision was not based upon sex. Once again, the firm lost in district court and the decision was reaffirmed on appeal to the appellate court.

Bibliography

Boumil, Marcia Mobilia and Stephen C. Hicks. *Women and the Law.* Littleton, CO: Fred B. Rothman & Co., 1992.

"Despite the Smoke, There is No Gun: Direct Evidence Requirements in Mixed-motives Employment Law." *Stanford Law Review* 46 (April 1994): 959–86.

"Price Waterhouse Revisited." *Women's Rights Law Reporter* 15 (Fall 1993): 87–100.

Pro-Family Movement

The pro-family movement is a social movement among conservative Christians aimed at promoting policies that support traditional nuclear families, including organizations such as Focus on the Family, the Christian Coalition, and **Concerned**

Women for America (CWA). The agenda of pro-family groups is large and includes opposition to **abortion** and to the **Equal Rights Amendment (ERA),** opposition to policies that make it easier for women to enter the paid labor force (such as after-care programs in schools), opposition to sex education and psychological testing in the schools, and support for tax cuts that group leaders argue would allow women to stay at home with their children. Pro-family organizations oppose many policies that might help non-traditional families, including social welfare programs, and laws to prevent discrimination against gays and lesbians. The pro-family movement overlaps substantially with the Christian Right. (CW)

BIBLIOGRAPHY

Moen, Matthew. *The Transformation of the Christian Right.* Tuscaloosa: University of Alabama Press, 1992.

Wilcox, Clyde. *Onward Christian Soldiers: The Christian Right in American Politics.* Boulder, CO: Westview, 1996.

Progressive Movement

The Progressive movement was a reform movement of the early twentieth century that focused on control of big business for the benefit of the average citizen and ostensibly for the preservation of democracy. This movement was an attempt to address the many social problems emerging in the United States as a result of the combination of rapid industrialization, corporate growth, and dramatic rates of immigration. This social consciousness was combined with a concern for the needs of democracy as well as the requirements of economic opportunity. The movement spawned other social and political movements as a result of the attention it brought to a myriad of issues. Two examples with explicit reference to women in the United States include the **Settlement House movement** and the **suffrage** movement.

The **women's movement** began with the emergence of women's civic and department clubs from the Progressive movement. Many of these clubs organized to improve municipal services and to bring about government reform. Others promoted specific issues, such as abolition of child labor or improved conditions for working women. As members of these Progressive-type organizations, women were confronted with their inability to act on behalf of the disadvantaged because of their lack of legal standing. In this way, women recognized their inferior political status and their need for the ballot. (JEH) **See also** Club Movement.

BIBLIOGRAPHY

Addams, Jane. "My Experience as a Progressive Delegate." *McClune* 40 (November 1912): 12–14.

Allen, Davis. "Social Wonders and the Progressive Party, 1912–1916." *American Historical Review* 69, no. 3 (1964): 671–88.

Keating, Margaret. "The Progressives and Peace." *The Woman Citizen* 9 (November 1, 1924): 14.

Kendig, Isabelle. "Woman's Opportunity: The Progressive Movement." *The Nation* (November 19, 1924): 544.

Prostitution

Prostitution is the act of selling one's body for sexual purposes in exchange for money or monetary goods. Until recently, public awareness was limited to female prostitutes; however, recognition of male prostitution has increased in the last 25 years.

Unlike in many other countries, prostitution is a criminal act in the United States, with the exception of some 13 rural counties in Nevada. Until World War I, prostitution was not considered a criminal act. Prostitutes instead were punished under vagrancy or adultery regulations, or for being a "common nightwalker." Nightwalking had been outlawed in colonial times. Moral concerns drove much of the pressure against nightwalking in the North; in the South, many slaveholders forced their female slaves into having sex with them, thereby reducing the need for prostitutes. In the settlement of the West, men greatly outnumbered women and prostitution was tolerated to a degree by law enforcement.

Efforts to regulate legalized prostitution were approved by the New York legislature in the 1870s but were never signed into law. Some women's groups opposed the move, citing the failure of similar efforts in Europe to effectively implement the changes.

The majority of middle class feminists in the United States in the early nineteenth century viewed prostitution more as evidence of the lack of educational opportunities and low wages for women rather than as a lapse in morals. They backed the position that women had the right to work as prostitutes without being harassed by police. Economic justifications for prostitution were used less often, however, as feminist groups aligned themselves with moralistic organizations against the importation of foreign women as prostitutes and against child prostitution. The alliance lobbied for and won passage in 1910 of the Federal White Slave Act, known as the Mann Act, to prevent the transport of women and girls across state lines for prostitution. But this tenuous alliance began to break down as feminists became increasingly leery of the reactionary positions of the purity crusaders. Crusaders, such as the **Women's Christian Temperance Union (WCTU)** and Protestant religious leaders, played upon the fears brought on by industrialization and migration to U.S. urban areas in the early 1900s; this sparked a crackdown on prostitutes in many states. Ruth Rosen has argued that the hard line did not eliminate prostitution but only transformed it. Control of prostitution had previously been in the hands of the "madams" (female heads of prostitution houses) and prostitutes themselves, but it shifted to the "pimps" (men who organize and control prostitutes for a profit) and organized crime. Further, Rosen said prostitutes now faced violence from both the police and the pimps and organized crime factions. Officially, prostitutes were not prosecuted for prostitution until 1917 in Massachusetts.

Following World War I, the reform movement weakened and prohibition was repealed and prostitution became more tolerated, although it was still illegal. The tide changed again during World War II when fears concerning the spread of venereal disease heightened. In the post-World War II era, however, public attitudes regarding prostitution grew more tolerant. New York again moved to the forefront on prostitution reform efforts following Governor Nelson Rockefeller's efforts to study and reform many of the state's criminal laws. Soliciting for prostitution in New York was changed in 1964 from a criminal offense to a violation and punishment reduced from one year in jail to 15 days. Measures against the customers of prostitutes ("johns") were also added a year later. However, the reform was short-lived; during the 1968 presidential campaign increases in violent crime stirred fears, and in 1969 prostitution was again made a crime along with solicitation.

While prostitution remains illegal today in the United States, the enforcement and punishment vary according to the race and class of the prostitute. Studies have shown that streetwalkers (those prostitutes generally of a lower class background) comprise only 10 to 20 percent of all prostitutes but they make up 85 to 90 percent of prostitutes arrested. Further, women of color who account for approximately 40 percent of all street prostitutes comprise 55 percent of all those arrested and 85 percent of those jailed.

Thirteen rural Nevada counties have legalized prostitution but control it through strict local and county regulations. These regulations range from issuing work permits, to specifying how many businesses can operate in a town, and how many prostitutes can work in a given business as well as the hours of operation. Lawmakers have also seen fit to control the prostitutes themselves by forbidding them to be in town during the evening. This regulation is aimed at preventing "freelancing" as well as protecting a man from meeting a prostitute on the street that he may have "hired" in the past.

For long periods of human history, a woman was limited to three options for economic survival: she could marry, she could become a nun, or she could become a prostitute. In the United States, women's options have been somewhat more broad, particularly in the last century. Why then do women become prostitutes? In the case of young girls, one study found that half of all female juvenile prostitutes were incest survivors. Some studies suggest these girls might enter prostitution because they are somewhat accustomed to sexual exploitation and may receive some sense of control over the situation by receiving payment. **Kate Millett** and others have found that "turning a trick" (engaging in a sexual act with a customer) can be a young woman's first experience of controlling a situation. However, not all prostitutes were victims of sexual abuse.

Nannette Davis argues that the psychological conclusion that prostitutes are somehow sexual deviants overlooks the strong drive to survive, which street women, particularly those with children, possess.

Another possible cause for prostitution is drug addiction. Street prostitutes were found to be addicted at a rate of nearly four times that of "higher class" prostitutes, and half of all addicted prostitutes were addicted to drugs before "entering the life."

A former prostitute, recovering heroin addict, and drug rehabilitation program director explained the link between drugs and prostitution to Kate Millett in the "Prostitution Papers." "M" said she thought drug addiction drove many into prostitution. She added many women have told her they needed the anesthetizing high before and after "turning a trick" to be able to psychologically accept what they had done.

Some radical feminists describe prostitution as a reminder that all women are defined by their sexuality within a patriarchal (male-dominated) society wherein they survive by trading one commodity (their bodies) for a particular good (money or economic security). Other feminists view prostitution as evidence of an oppressive patriarchal system that dehumanizes women and reduces them to sexual objects. Others see prostitution as part of the wider social phenomenon of violence against women that occurs whether a society is at peace or at war. **Catharine MacKinnon** sees prostitution as illustrative of the sexual objectification of women within the larger social dynamic of gender inequality. **Andrea Dworkin** sees prostitution as one of many institutional mechanisms similar to marriage and **pornography** through which men control women's bodies in an imperialist fashion. Carol Pateman argues that the attitudes about prostitution held by society and some prostitutes are byproducts of the free enterprise system. She agrees with Dworkin in the existence of a male colonization of women and adds it is dependent upon a perception that the relationship between the "john" and the prostitute is a private business deal between a buyer and a seller.

Feminists from a variety of perspectives generally agree that prostitution and the laws surrounding it have been designed to favor the male participant in the relationship. Prostitute self-help movements have frequently called for decriminalization rather than legalization, arguing that legalization would lead to increased male control over women's bodies.

Prostitutes have organized themselves in a bid to secure their rights and press for decriminalization or abolition of laws against prostitution. By decriminalizing prostitution, the statutes and penalties would be removed, leaving regulation up to the civil code as with "straight" businesses. Legalization has been opposed by some prostitute self-help groups because the licensing process benefits the business owner and the customers but not the prostitutes.

Legalization in other countries and in Nevada has not resulted in more rights for prostitutes, such as the ability to choose one's customers or retain the bulk of one's earnings. Another argument for decriminalization pertains to the cost to local governments of arrest, prosecution, and incarceration of prostitutes, particularly when compared with the lack of funds used for prostitute rehabilitation efforts.

Additionally, prostitutes and, more recently, some law enforcement officers have cited the futility of prostitution arrests, which generally result in a fee payment or even case dismissal and a quick release from custody. A move to decriminalization, those proponents argue, would move the "business" relationship out of public sight and back into the private realm where they believe it belongs.

The most famous of the self-help organizations is COYOTE/NTFP or Call Off Your Old Tired Ethics/National Task Force on Prostitution. Call Off Your Old Tired Ethics was founded in 1978 in San Francisco by former prostitute Margo St. James to serve as a voice for prostitutes and a lobby for their rights.

The NTFP works for the repeal of all laws against prostitution, assists prostitutes in labor negotiations with their employers, enlightens the public about prostitution, dispels myths, and helps to end the discrimination against women's employment in the sex industry, as well as to educate the public about AIDS and sexually transmitted diseases.

United States Prostitution Collective (U.S. PROS) is a similar organization with somewhat different goals. The U.S. PROS is a national network of women working in the sex industry and their supporters. The group lobbies for the abolition of all prostitution laws so that women can act as independent business owners. They favor abolition over decriminalization (unlike COYOTE) because they believe decriminalization has been equated with legalization in the Nevada case and in some European cases.

Women Hurt in Systems of Prostitution, Engaged in Revolt (WHISPER) is a national newsletter created by and for survivor prostitutes and those wishing to leave "the life." Sarah Wynter is the founder and editor of the newsletter. Wynter argues that by viewing prostitution as an occupation, society validates the perception that men possess the need and have the right to buy and sell women's bodies. In a 1987 article, Wynter says the pervasiveness of the myth, perpetuated by men, that women enter prostitution in search of exciting and well-paying work obscures the structures that condemn women to unequal stature and sometimes force them into prostitution as a means of economic survival. WHISPER opposes existing attempts to decriminalize or legalize prostitution, which remove it from public view but allow it to continue. The goal of WHISPER is to end the sexual enslavement of women by men. (PS)

Bibliography

Davis, Nannette, ed. *Prostitution: An International Handbook on Trends, Problems, and Policies.* Westport, CT: Greenwood Press, 1993.

Delacosta, Frederique and Priscilla Alexander, eds. *Sex Work: Writings for Women in the Sex Industry.* Pittsburgh: Cleis Press, 1987.

Dworkin, Andrea. *Pornography: Men Possessing Women.* New York: E.P. Dutton, 1989.

Goldstein, Leslie Friedman. *The Constitutional Rights of Women.* New York: Longman, 1979.

James, Jennifer, Jean Withers, Marilyn Haft, and Sara Theiss. *Politics of Prostitution.* Seattle: Social Research Associates, 1975.

Millet, Kate. *The Prostitution Papers.* New York: Ballatine, 1973.

Pateman, Carol. *The Sexual Contract.* Cambridge, MA: Polity Press, 1989.

Rosen, Ruth. *The Lost Sisterhood: Prostitution in America 1900-1918.* Baltimore: John Hopkins University Press, 1982.

Scambler, Gerald and Annette Scambler, eds. *Rethinking Prostitution: Purchasing Sex in the 1990s.* London: Routledge, 1997.

Walkowitz, Judith R. *Prostitution and Victorian Society.* New York: Cambridge University Press, 1980.

Protective Legislation

Protective legislation provides legal exceptions for women to improve their working conditions and protect them from exploitation. The history of protective legislation illustrates that federal and state governments have passed laws limiting the number of hours women can work, establishing a minimum wage for female workers, and prohibiting certain types of work.

During the early 1900s, reformers achieved the passage of protective legislation by convincing the courts that the abilities of men and women workers were significantly different and that special provisions had to be made to protect a woman's reproductive health. The Supreme Court placed women in a class separate from men in 1908 with the landmark decision in ***Muller v. Oregon***. Since the 1908 decision, the courts have played a central role in the debate over protective legislation.

Many female reformers proposed and supported protective legislation that sheltered women from harsh labor conditions, yet women also spoke out against the protective laws. Among the first women to voice discontent were those who worked in male-dominated trades, such as printing, polishing, and streetcar conducting. These women opposed protective legislation because they had lost their jobs because of the new laws.

Feminists in the **National Woman's Party (NWP)** also argued that protective legislation was harmful to women's interests. They asserted that gender-specific legislation reinforces the perceptions that women are different from men, costs women jobs, leads to reduced wages, and further segregates the labor market.

The deep divisions over protective legislation became increasingly evident after the passage of the **Civil Rights Act of 1964**. **Title VII,** of the act banned employment discrimination based on sex, thus making the status of protective legislation unclear. With the enactment of Title VII, feminists sought legal equality for women and called for the removal of protective legislation.

Over half the states enforced some form of protective legislation laws at the time Title VII, became law. The **Equal Employment Opportunity Commission (EEOC)** took on the responsibility of deciding how to enforce the non-sex discrimination provision of Title VII in light of the protective laws that still existed.

The work of the EEOC to date further emphasizes the vital role the courts play in the protective legislation issue. Women continue to challenge the legal status of protective laws and seek to improve their position in the workplace. (MG)

Bibliography

Kenney, Sally J. *For Whose Protection?: Reproductive Hazards and Exclusionary Policies in the United States and Britain.* Ann Arbor: University of Michigan Press, 1992.

Lehrer, Susan. *Origins of Protective Labor Legislation for Women 1905–1925.* Albany: State University of New York Press, 1987.
Maschke, Karen J. *Litigation, Courts and Women Workers.* New York: Praeger, 1983.

Deborah D. Pryce (1951–)

Deborah Pryce, a member of the **Republican Party**, was elected in 1992 from Ohio to the U.S. House of Representatives. While in Congress, Pryce has served on a number of influential committees, including banking and government operations. She was re-elected to Congress in 1994 and 1996, helping the Republicans to win and maintain a majority.

BIBLIOGRAPHY

Bingham, Clara. *Women on the Hill.* New York: Time Books, 1997.
Margolies-Mezvinsky, Marjorie. *A Women's Place.* New York: Crow Publishers, 1994.

Public Health Service Act, Title VII

The Public Health Service Act of 1975 was one of many pieces of education legislation passed by Congress in the 1970s that prohibited **sex discrimination**. Title VII of the Public Health Service Act of 1975 establishes federal guidelines for federally funded programs for the training of physician assistants. Included in these guidelines is a prohibition against sex discrimination. This provision explicitly identifies which institutions of medical training are covered under the legislation and stipulates that these institutions must demonstrate that their admissions procedures do not discriminate on the basis of sex.

The legislation allowed some institutions, with the approval of the secretary of health and human services, to continue to receive federal assistance until June 30, 1979, at which time they had to be in full compliance with the legislation to continue their federal assistance. Although the Public Health Service Act was amended in both 1991 and 1993, this provision remains intact. (JEH)

BIBLIOGRAPHY

Morgan, Sandra. "Into Our Own Hands." Myna Marx Ferree and Patricia Yancey Muntin, eds. *Feminist Organizations.* Philadelphia: Temple University Press, 1995.

Public Health Service Act, Title VIII

The Public Health Service Act of 1975 was one of many legislative efforts directed at eliminating **sex discrimination** in education. Title VIII of the Public Health Service Act of 1975 establishes federal guidelines for the funding of nurse education. According to this title, institutions providing continuing and specialized education of nurses may receive federal funding if programs meet certain requirements. The title includes a provision requiring programs to demonstrate that their admission requirements do not discriminate on the basis of sex. If an institution applying for federal assistance such as a grant, loan guarantee, or subsidy payment fails to demonstrate that it does not discriminate on the basis of sex, federal support will be denied. The Public Health Service Act was amended in both 1991 and 1993, however, the prohibition against sex discrimination in nurse education remains intact. (JEH)

BIBLIOGRAPHY

Ruzek, Sheryl. *The Women's Health Movement.* New York: Praeger, 1978.

Public Health Service Act, Title X

The Public Health Service Act of 1975 was one of many pieces of education legislation passed by Congress in the 1970s that made **sex discrimination** illegal. The act created the Public Health Service, a government agency charged with the oversight of the public health. The Public Health Service is headed by the surgeon general and falls under the jurisdiction of the Department of Health and Human Services.

Title X of the Public Health Service Act establishes guidelines for federal funding of population research and voluntary family planning programs. Federal attention to this issue had long been a key goal of members of the equal rights movement. With the inclusion of Title X, women's right activists felt an important step had been achieved toward increasing access for all women (and men) to family planning services. Title X, established federal funding for a full range of family planning methods and services. The legislation requires that such services remain voluntary. Finally, the title stipulates that institutions using **abortion** as a method of family planning are ineligible for federal assistance under this legislation. (JEH)

BIBLIOGRAPHY

Ruzek, Sheryl. *The Women's Health Movement.* New York: Praeger, 1978.

Pure Food Act of 1906

The Pure Food Act was one of the first legislative victories that owed its passage in large measure to the efforts of women. The act prevented the manufacture, sale, or distribution of adultered, misbranded, poisonous, or deleterious foods, drugs, medicines, and liquors.

Women played a critical role in the passage of the law through their lobbying and educational efforts. In the 1890s, the Food Consumers' League under the leadership of Alice Lakey sought to increase the public's awareness of hazardous additives to food. This information campaign gained strength when the National Consumer League under the leadership of **Florence Kelley** began inspections of factory conditions in 1899. The movement even included the **Women's Christian Temperance Union (WCTU)** because many medicines contained large amounts of alcoholic fillers.

Support for the act grew with the publication of Sinclair Lewis' *The Jungle*—which described the conditions in the meat-packing industry—in 1905 and the concerted efforts of women's groups. In 1906, representatives in both houses of Congress passed the first laws regulating the purity of food.

Bibliography

May, Charles Paul. *Warning! Your Health Is at Stake*. New York: Hawthorn Books, 1975.

"Report of the Pure Food Committee of the General Federation of Women's Clubs." *Annals of the American Academy of Political and Social Science* 28 (September 1906): 296–301.

Gladys Pyle (1890–1989)

Gladys Pyle's first elected post was to the South Dakota legislature in 1922, where she served two terms. She served as secretary of state in 1922 and won the Republican nomination for governor in 1930. In 1938, she won a special election to serve in the U.S. Senate. However, her entire tenure from November 9, 1938, until January 3, 1939, was during a congressional recess. Although she failed to win renomination by the party for the 1938 general election, she remained active in politics. In 1940, she served as a delegate to the Republican National Convention and as a member of the State Board of Charities and Corrections from 1943 until 1957.

Bibliography

"In-Between Senators." *Time* 32 (December 19, 1938): 10.

Kinyon, Jeannette. *Incredible Gladys Pyle.* Vermillion, SD: Dakota Press, 1985.

R

Jeannette Pickering Rankin (1880–1973)

A suffragist, politician, lobbyist, and activist, Jeannette Rankin was best known as the first woman to be elected to Congress. Born in Missoula, Montana, and educated at Montana University and the New York School of Philanthropy, Rankin moved in 1909 to Seattle, where she became a social worker. Her first foray into politics came in 1910 when she joined the woman's **suffrage** campaign in Washington State. Later, she formed the Equal Franchise Society in Montana to press for female enfranchisement in her home state. She worked in the suffrage campaigns of New York and California before becoming a legislative secretary for the **National American Woman Suffrage Association (NAWSA)** in 1914.

In 1917, Rankin entered the House of Representatives as a Republican from Montana, becoming the first woman ever elected to Congress. During her first term (1917–1919), she worked for passage of the **Nineteenth Amendment** (1920) to the Constitution, which allowed women to vote, and for laws protecting children and female workers. She was one of 56 representatives who voted against the U.S. entry into World War I in 1917. Her opposition to the war cost Rankin her 1919 bid to become the first female senator.

Throughout the 1920s and 1930s, Rankin worked for peace and women's rights as a lobbyist and activist for several organizations, including the Women's International League for Peace and Freedom, the Women's Peace Union, the National Council for the Prevention of War, and the National Consumers League. She was also a vice president of the American Civil Liberties Union.

Rankin won a second term in the House in 1940, becoming the only member of Congress to vote against U.S. entry into World War II in December 1941. Rankin thereby earned the distinction of being the only member of Congress to have voted against American entry into both World Wars. Her vote against war again cost Rankin her congressional seat, and she left office in 1943.

Rankin re-entered public life in 1968 as the leader of the Jeannette Rankin Brigade in the Women Strike for Peace March on Washington to protest the Vietnam War; she spent the last five years of her life actively protesting the war. In 1971, Rankin became the **National Organization for Women's (NOW)** first inductee into the Susan B. Anthony Hall of Fame. (SJW) **See also** Susan B. Anthony; Pacifism.

BIBLIOGRAPHY

Harris, Ted Carlton. "Jeannette Rankin: Suffragist, First Woman Elected to Congress, and Pacifist." Unpublished Ph.D. dissertation, University of Georgia, 1972.

Josephson, Hannah. *Jeannette Rankin, First Lady in Congress: A Biography.* New York: Bobbs Merrill, 1974.

Carol Hampton Rasco (1948–)

Carol Hampton Rasco is a domestic policy advisor to President Bill Clinton. From 1983 to 1985, Rasco served Arkansas Governor Clinton as liaison to human services and health agencies. From 1985 to 1991, she was Clinton's executive assistant for governmental operations, and acted as his senior executive assistant from 1991 to 1992. She served as liaison to the National Governors Association from 1985 to 1992. When he assumed the presidency in January 1993, Clinton appointed Rasco to be a presidential assistant for domestic policy. In this position, which she still holds in 1998, Rasco has been credited with keeping President Clinton focused on education and health care reform issues.

BIBLIOGRAPHY

DeParle, Jason. "She's the Advocate She Once Needed." *New York Times* (June 17, 1993): C1.

Nichols, Bill. "Behind-the-Scenes Player in Front on Domestic Policy." *USA Today* (February 10, 1993): A7.

Radcliffe, Donnie. "Clinton's Window on the Home Front." *Washington Post* (August 24, 1993): D1.

Dixy Lee Ray (1914–1994)

Dixy Lee Ray, a Democrat, was governor of Washington from 1977 until 1981. She failed to win re-election in 1980 in large part because of increased taxation that she spearheaded. From 1972 to 1975, she was a member of the United States Atomic Energy Commission, serving as chair from 1973 to 1975. During her career, Ray served as assistant secretary of state overseeing the Bureau of Oceans, International Environment, and Scientific Affairs, and she often spoke in favor of the nuclear industry and in opposition to those environmentalists she viewed as alarmists.

BIBLIOGRAPHY
Ray, Dixy L. and Louis R. Guzzo. *Environmental Overkill.* New York: Harper Collins, 1994.
———. *Trusting the Planet.* New York: Harper Collins, 1992.

Nancy Davis Reagan (1923–)

Nancy Davis Reagan is the wife of former President Ronald Reagan and a noted advocate of volunteerism. Born in New York on July 6, 1923, Nancy Davis majored in theater at Smith College and became a professional actress. She performed in many films, including *Hellcats of the Navy,* in which she played opposite Ronald Reagan. Married in 1952, the couple had two children, Patricia Ann and Ronald Prescott Reagan. During her husband's' years as governor of California (1967-1973), Nancy Reagan was a devoted political wife, dedicating herself to the support of volunteer and charitable groups. She visited veterans, emotionally and physically handicapped people, and the elderly; she also became increasingly interested in fighting drug and alcohol abuse among young people. As first lady from 1981 to 1989, Nancy Reagan strongly promoted the performing arts through the PBS program, *In Performance at the White House,* and took the lead in combatting drug use with her "Just Say No" [to drugs] campaign. In 1985, she held a conference for **first ladies** from 17 different nations to focus international attention on the drug problem. She also directed the renovation of the second and third floors of the White House. As first lady, Nancy Reagan was a devoted and protective wife, exerting firm control over her husband's political affairs; she was even known to have consulted astrologers to organize the president's schedule. She also had a strong influence on policy and personnel matters and was believed to be influential in the dismissal of Chief of Staff Donald Regan in 1987. Since leaving the White House in 1989, Nancy Reagan has continued campaigning against drug abuse. She has published two books, *To Love a Child* (1982), which focused on the Foster Grandparent Program, and *My Turn* (1989), in which she discussed her White House years from her own perspective. She has continued to protect the image and privacy of Ronald Reagan since the onset of his Alzheimer's. (GVS)

While first lady, Nancy Reagan waged an effective anti-drug campaign called "Just Say No." Library of Congress, Prints and Photographs Division.

BIBLIOGRAPHY
Kelly, Kitty. *Nancy Reagan: An Unauthorized Biography.* Boston: G.K. Hall, 1992.
Wheeler, Jill and Judith A. Stone. *Nancy D. Reagan.* New York: Abdo & Daughters, 1991.

Louise Goff Reece (1898–1970)

Louise Goff Reece, a Republican, won a special election to the United States House of Representatives on May 16, 1961, filling the vacancy left by the death of her husband Brazilla Carroll Reece. She represented the 1st District of Tennessee in Congress until January 3, 1963. Declining to run for reelection, Louise Reece remained active in state and national politics until her death in 1970.

BIBLIOGRAPHY
Chamberlin, Hope. *A Minority of Members.* New York: Praeger, 1973.

Reed v. Reed (1971)

In the landmark case of *Reed v. Reed*, 404 U.S. 71 (1971), the Supreme Court, for the first time, used the equal protection clause of the Fourteenth Amendment to strike down a gender-based classification. Prior to *Reed*, the Court had upheld differential treatment of men and women as constitutional as long as there was a rational basis for it. For example, the Court had upheld bans on the practice of law by women (*Bradwell v. Illinois,* 1873), prohibitions on women tending bar (*Goesaert v. Cleary,* 1948), and blanket exclusions of women from jury service (*Hoyt v. Florida*, 1961). With *Reed*, the Court broke with this long line of precedents and began to interpret the equal protection clause more vigorously in regard to the rights of women.

In the *Reed* case, Mr. and Mrs. Reed, who were separated, were competing for legal appointment as administrator of their deceased son's estate. Idaho law provided that males be prefered to females in the administration of a decedent's estate. Idaho argued that this law was administratively convenient because it helped avoid intrafamily conflict and reduced the workload on probate courts by eliminating one class of contests. The Supreme Court unanimously found that Idaho's legitimate objectives were being advanced on the basis of arbitrary criteria wholly unrelated to the objectives of the statute. Mandating the choice of administrator solely on the basis of sex was therefore ruled unreasonable, discriminatory, and unconstitutional. (RW)

BIBLIOGRAPHY
Baer, Judith A. *Women in American Law.* New York: Holmes and Meier, 1991.
Goldstein, Leslie Friedman. *The Constitutional Rights of Women.* Madison: University of Wisconsin Press, 1989.

Charlotte Thompson Reid (1913–)

From January 3, 1963, to October 7, 1971, Charlotte Thompson Reid served in the United States House of Representatives as a Republican from Illinois. In 1968, she also served as an advisor to Richard Nixon and Spiro Agnew's presidential election campaign and sat on Senator John Tower's (R-TX) Key Issues Committee. President Nixon named Reid to the Federal Communications Commission (FCC) in October 1971.

The Commission's first female member, Reid served on the FCC until July 1976. After a brief respite from public life, Reid served on the President's Task Force on International Private Enterprise from 1983 to 1985.

BIBLIOGRAPHY
Chamberlin, Hope. *A Minority of Members.* New York: Praeger, 1973.

Janet W. Reno (1938–)

In 1993, President Bill Clinton appointed Janet Reno the first woman attorney general of the United States. Reno was Clinton's third nominee for the post. His first two, Zoe E. Baird and Kimba Woods, were withdrawn from consideration because of failure to pay social security taxes on domestic employees. Reno vowed to use her position to defend **abortion** rights, but her first days in office were occupied with the standoff at Waco, Texas, between the FBI and the Branch Davidian cult. Her tough and business-like approach has consistently made her one of the more politically popular Clinton cabinet members. However, the growing scandals surrounding the Clinton administration have required her to appoint several special prosecutors and have often placed her in a precarious position between congressional Republicans and the Democratic administration. Reno gained most of her legal experience in various positions with the Florida state government in the 1970s. Known as a staunch upholder of defendants' rights and a tough enforcer of child-support laws, Reno was elected state attorney for Dade County, Florida, in 1978. She was reelected to that post five times. (JCS)

BIBLIOGRAPHY
Anderson, Paul. *Janet Reno.* New York: John Wiley & Sons, 1994.
Drew, Elizabeth. *On the Edge: The Clinton Presidency.* New York: Simon and Schuster, 1994.
Meachum, Virgina. *Janet Reno.* Springfield, NJ: Enslow Publishers, 1995.
Reno, Janet W. *The Hell with Politics.* Atlanta: Peachtree Publishers, 1994.

Reproductive and Contraceptive Technologies for Women

The United States government plays an active role in the development and cultivation of reproductive and contraceptive technologies. Numerous social phenomena have contributed to the demand for such technologies. Each branch of government has addressed concerns associated with these technologies through judicial decisions, regulations, and legislation.

The demand for female reproductive and contraceptive technologies has been largely tied to significant political, social, and economic shifts that have occurred since 1960. Unlike condoms, which were available to males before the 1960s, female contraceptive and reproductive technologies have largely been devised in the last four decades.

The desire to develop reproductive opportunities and contraceptives for women through technology is largely attributable to lifestyle changes among women born since 1945. Women of the "baby boom" generation (born 1945–1964) have shown a propensity to delay attempts at conception until they have completed post-secondary education or been employed in a career for a minimum period of time. Younger women, those born since 1965 ("baby busters"), have a higher tendency to engage in premarital sexual relations than older women, and have a greater likelihood of attending college and pursuing careers in male-dominated majors and professions, thereby increasing their social interaction with heterosexual men.

Public attitudes toward extramarital sexual relations, raising a child as a single parent, and bearing children later in life have also relaxed. The social stigmas attached to these phenomena have reduced. Coupling technological advances that facilitate increased reliability, safety, and accessibility with increased social acceptance has led to greater use of contraceptive and reproductive technologies since 1960. Although a recent conservative ideological shift, coupled with fear of contracting sexually transmitted diseases, has altered some attitudes, reported extramarital sexual activity is still far greater now than in the past.

Increased use and access has placed greater demands on the political system to provide research, regulation, consumer safety, and availability to the appropriate constituent populations. Public views toward **abortion** and extramarital sex have also played roles in determining accessibility to new reproductive technologies. In many instances, conflicting demands exist regarding whether, and to what extent, such technologies should be available and to whom. In other cases, questions have arisen about whether such technologies should be used in an unintended manner, such as a punishment for crimes or as a condition for receiving public assistance.

Public demands on access to contraceptive and reproductive technology among baby boomer women is largely a result of the **women's movement** and its associated implications. Efforts to secure greater control over their lives (including reproduction) as well as to broaden educational and occupational opportunities compelled women to push for anti-discrimination legislation (passed with **Title VII of the Civil Rights Act of 1964** and **Title IX of the Educational Amendments Act of 1972**). Partaking of these new opportunities, coupled with changing sexual mores, meant that baby boomer women sought to delay childbearing until their educational goals had been achieved or until their careers were established.

Female contraceptives developed since 1960 take many forms. For example, some manipulate hormone levels and some place physical barriers between sperm and ova. Certain forms provide long-term contraception, whereas others are short-term in their contraceptive efficacy.

Several technologies that manipulate hormone levels and ovulation to achieve contraception have been developed. Oral contraceptives, for instance, are intended to prevent ovulation when taken on a daily basis. The percent of women taking oral contraceptives has increased significantly since the development of such contraceptives. Hormones that achieve contraception are also available in a different form. **Norplant** (its trade name) consists of tubes surgically implanted in a woman's arms. The effects of the timed release formula last for up to five years. Surgery is required to have the tubes removed. Norplant earned Food and Drug Administration (FDA) approval in 1990.

One technology not available to American women is a hormonal treatment that causes a miscarriage in the first days of pregnancy. Also called "the morning after pill," **RU-486** (its trade name) requires that large doses of specific hormones be taken soon after sexual intercourse. This treatment causes a miscarriage if conception occurs. Abortion foes have successfully prevented RU-486 from being imported into the United States. The FDA must test and approve drugs before they are marketed to the general public. The successful lobbying efforts aimed at Congress have prevented RU-486 from coming into the United States, thereby preventing its testing and approval for public distribution.

Four other technologies create physical barriers to conception. Intra-uterine devices (IUDs) create a chemical imbalance in the uterus that prevents conception. The diaphragm forms a physical barrier around the cervix that prevents sperm from entering the uterus. Female condoms create a physical barrier around the cervix as well as line the vagina with a latex barrier similar to male condoms. The Dalkon shield rendered the uterus physically incapable of implantation by an embryo. The Dalkon shield is no longer manufactured or prescribed because it was found to create short-term and permanent damage to women's reproductive organs.

Finally, spermicides have also been developed in the form of foam, gel, and vaginal suppositories. Often, spermicides are used in addition to other contraceptives, such as with a diaphragm. Each of these technologies has given women greater control over their reproductive lives.

Baby boomer women also constitute a substantial proportion of those seeking access to reproductive technologies. A significant increase in the number of women pursuing advanced degrees and career opportunities has led to higher proportions of women postponing childbearing. Further, many women experience physiological and social difficulty once the decision to bear a child is reached, thereby placing greater demands on reproductive opportunities.

Physiological concerns are associated with women's hormonal changes over time. Ovulation rates decline as women age. During late teens, women tend to be their most fertile. Ovulation declines to the point of complete cessation of menstruation (menopause) by the time most women reach their early 50s. This process means that an increasing percentage of women seeking to bear children are doing so as their ovulation rates decline. Further, the risks of tubal pregnancies and endometriosis increase as women age. These conditions prevent an embryo from uterine implantation or prevent conception by obstructing fallopian tubes so that sperm are unable to reach ova.

The divorce and never-married rate is also much higher than earlier generations. Further, the women's movement has supported women without partners (as well as lesbian couples) seeking to parent children. These social changes, women delaying conception or having difficulty conceiving, and women pursuing conception opportunities without male partners have meant increasing demands for new reproductive technologies.

There are numerous reasons why reproductive technology has received so much attention. The issues surrounding these demands are not necessarily those borne out of medical necessity because the technologies developed do not have life-saving properties or indications. Rather, many argue that the population seeking such conception opportunities has the economic and political resources to lobby for the development, testing, approval, and regulation of such technologies. Additionally, this population is not seeking other parenting opportunities (such as adoption or foster care) with similar enthusiasm.

Several reproductive technologies have been developed that address these concerns. One, in-vitro fertilization, involves bringing sperm and ova together outside the womb for conception and then being implanted in the biological mother's uterus or that of a surrogate. Often called "test tube" babies, the number of children fertilized through in-vitro fertilization has increased significantly over the last 15 years. This process is one that seeks to offset the effects of endometriosis and the risks of tubal pregnancy because the fallopian tubes are not required for fertilization. Further, fertility drugs have been developed that increase the number of eggs released from woman's ovaries. Such fertility drugs have been used to offset declining ovulation or to increase the number of eggs that are taken for in-vitro fertilization procedures. Further, drugs have been developed that cause the uterine lining to thicken. The likelihood that a fertilized egg will become implanted in the uterine wall is increased by such efforts.

Two significant conflicts resulting from in-vitro fertilization and artificial insemination have been addressed in the political arena. Each issue arose from conflicts regarding the identification and responsibility of biological and surrogate parents. In one case, Mary Sue Davis and Junior Davis had seven eggs fertilized and cryogenically preserved for later uterine implantation after Mary Sue Davis experienced several tubal pregnancies. While there was no question regarding who were the biological parents of the "frozen embryos," conflict arose regarding the disposition of the embryos once the couple decided to divorce. Mary Sue Davis wanted control (as custody) of the frozen embryos so that she could retain the option to have them implanted, whereas Junior Davis wanted the embryos to remain in their frozen state (as property) until he decided whether he wanted to become a father. The court decided that the wishes of the biological father should prevail over that of the biological mother. This case demonstrates the far-reaching implications of two concomitant social phenomena: the increase in the percentage of couples who use available reproductive technologies and the increase in the divorce rate.

In another case, the Calverts contracted a surrogacy agreement with Anna Johnson. An embryo conceived from the Calverts' sperm and egg was implanted in Ms. Johnson's uterus. She agreed to bring the baby to term in exchange for $10,000. At the seventh month of gestation, Ms. Johnson changed her mind and sought to break the contract with the Calverts. The court ruled against Ms. Johnson, arguing that biological parenthood outweighed gestational motherhood.

Biological mothers have also served as surrogate mothers. Conflicts have arisen regarding custody when the biological parents do not plan to raise the child as a couple. William and Elizabeth Stern desired biological children although a case of multiple sclerosis prevented Ms. Stern from bearing a child. Mary Beth Whitehead contracted a surrogacy agreement with William and Elizabeth Stern for $10,000. Ms. Whitehead would be artificially inseminated with Mr. Stern's sperm and would forfeit parental rights giving Elizabeth Stern the opportunity to adopt the baby after birth. Ms. Whitehead changed her mind after giving birth to the baby girl on March 27, 1986. A protracted custody battle ensued. In the end, the Sterns were granted custody of the baby girl in 1988. The court reasoned that the surrogacy contract was invalid and Mr. Stern was a more fit parent for the baby than was Ms. Whitehead.

These three cases demonstrate how policy decisions stemming from the implementation of reproductive technology are often tied to gender roles and expectations. Both Ms. Johnson and Ms. Whitehead were deemed unfit parents while Ms. Davis's desire to be a biological mother did not prevail over her ex-husband's desire not to be a biological father.

One last concern associated with contraceptive technology involves recent efforts aimed at requiring women to use contraception as a condition of probation or as an incentive to receive **Aid to Families with Dependent Children (AFDC)** (welfare) benefits beyond those specified. The surgical insertion of Norplant has been addressed at the state legislative and superior court levels in these ways. These efforts have generally failed, but have raised questions regarding whether, and to what extent, the judicial and legislative process perceives the legitimacy of reproductive control over women who lack political resources and influence.

The implications of developments in reproductive technologies demonstrate that the political system has become involved regarding conflicts over the results of such technologies, including situations stemming from divorce, canceled contracts, criminal activity, and receipt of public assistance. (TSF) **See also** Medical Research and Funding.

Bibliography

Bonnicksen, Andrea L. *In Vitro Fertilization: Building Policy from Laboratories to Legislatures*. New York: Columbia University Press, 1989.

Cohen, Sherrill and Nadine Taub, eds. *Reproductive Laws for the 1990's*. Clifton, NJ: Humana Press, 1989.

Conway, M. Margaret, David W. Ahern, and Gertrude A. Steuernagel. *Women and Public Policy: A Revolution in Progress*. Washington, DC: Congressional Quarterly Press, 1995.

Lindgren, J. Ralph and Nadine Taub. *The Law of Sex Discrimination*. 2nd ed. Minneapolis: West Publishing Company, 1994.

Overall, Christine. *Human Reproduction: Principles, Practices, Policies*. Toronto: Oxford University Press, 1993.

Sen, Gita and Rachel C. Snow. *Power and Decisions: The Social Control of Reproduction*. Boston: Harvard School of Public Health, 1994.

Stetson, Dorothy McBride. *Women's Rights in the USA*. Pacific Grove, CA: Brooks/Cole, 1991.

Tong, Rosemarie. *Feminine and Feminist Ethics*. Belmont, CA: Wadsworth Publishing Company, 1993.

Reproductive Freedom Project (RFP)

The Reproductive Freedom Project (RFP) is a special litigating group formed in 1974 by the American Civil Liberties Union (ACLU) to protect reproductive rights as established by the Supreme Court in ***Roe v. Wade*** (1973). Established to ensure compliance with the Court's decision, the RPF, in response to later trends, also fought against fetal protection laws and the criminal prosecution of pregnant women for conduct that might cause harm to a fetus.

The RFP has been involved in virtually every **abortion** rights case that has come before the Supreme Court, and has acted as a coordinator for the many pro-choice groups involved in litigation and as an information clearinghouse for the pro-choice movement. The RFP has often directly represented individuals in test cases, and has joined other cases indirectly through *amicus curiae* briefs, which allow the RFP to explain its position on a case even though not a direct participant in it.

The Reproductive Freedom Project, one of the best funded of the ACLU's special projects, concentrated its resources on litigation until the early 1990s. During the Reagan and Bush administrations (1981–1993), the ACLU decided to shift its attention away from the courts and litigation and towards influencing public opinion and joining legislative battles in Congress and the states. The ACLU reasoned that the courts were increasingly hostile to the extension of reproductive rights and judges were turning the issue over to the elected branches and the states.

This change in tactics caused a major rift between the parent ACLU and the Reproductive Freedom Project, whose staff wanted to continue emphasizing litigation. The entire staff of the RFP left the ACLU in 1992 to form the Center for Reproductive Law and Policy. The new center soon announced two other departures from the policies of the American Civil Liberties Union. First, the center wanted to expand its concerns with reproductive rights to the international level. The ACLU charter specifically forbids international activity. Second, the Center for Reproductive Law and Policy wanted to change its emphasis from the ACLU's civil libertarianism to a more feminist orientation. Since the original staff's departure, the ACLU has reconstituted the Reproductive Freedom Project and has declared its inteniton to continue fighting for abortion rights. (RLP) **See also** Feminism.

BIBLIOGRAPHY
Epstein. Lee and Joseph Kobylka. *The Supreme Court and Legal Change: Abortion and the Death Penalty.* Chapel Hill: University of North Carolina Press, 1992.
Walker, Samuel. *In Defense of American Liberties: A History of the ACLU.* New York: Oxford University Press, 1990.

Republican Party

Although women's movements differ on a number of perspectives, certain political issues, such as **suffrage**, equal rights, and reproductive rights, have been dominant concerns of all these movements. Although women hold differing views on these questions, all these concerns have been marked out as "women's issues" in American political discourse. Over the past 150 years, support for these issues has shifted from one major party to the other. Republican-controlled state legislatures were active in promoting women's **voting rights** in the late nineteenth and early twentieth centuries, while the **Democratic Party** was initially opposed to women's suffrage. However, in the second half of the twentieth century, the Republican Party has drifted further away from support of women's movements, eventually coming out against both the **Equal Rights Amendment (ERA)** and **abortion** rights. At the same time, the Democratic Party began pushing anti-discrimination policies and supporting equal rights and reproductive rights. Although Republican administrations put some of the first women in top government positions, and a number of prominent female politicians are Republicans, women's movements typically do not look to Republicans for support on their positions.

Movements for women's rights, which began in the mid-nineteenth century among abolitionists and crusaders for social justice, initially displayed a great variety of causes, from voting rights to sexual liberation to freedom from the tyranny of pregnancy, family, and male domination. The one issue around which most women's movements could rally was universal and equal suffrage. Because the suffrage movement had a broader appeal than the other women's movements of the time, it early gained the patronage of the Republican Party. Although women were not granted the vote by the United States until the **Nineteenth Amendment** was passed in 1920, the suffrage movement had been active in the U.S. since the demand for the enfranchisement of American women was first seriously formulated at the 1848 **Seneca Falls Convention**. Agitation by women for the ballot became increasingly vociferous after the Civil War. In 1869, a rift developed among feminists over the proposed Fifteenth Amendment, which gave the vote to black men. **Susan B. Anthony, Elizabeth Cady Stanton**, and others refused to endorse the amendment because it did not give women the ballot. Other suffragists, including **Lucy Stone** and **Julia Ward Howe**, argued that once the black man was enfranchised, women would achieve their goal.

During the Reconstruction Period (1865–1877), the Republican Party first came to support women's voting rights. In 1872, when Susan B. Anthony went to the polls and asked to be registered, the two Republican members of the board accepted her claim that the Fourteenth Amendment's privileges and immunities clause granted women the right to vote (a claim later rejected by the Supreme Court, which declared that voting was not a privilege of citizenship) and agreed to receive her name, against the advice of their Democratic colleague and a United States supervisor. Anthony and 13 other women were arrested when they voted, but Republican President Ulysses S. Grant unconditionally pardoned them. In 1878, Anthony wrote and submitted to Congress a proposed right-to-vote amendment that later became the Nineteenth Amendment to the U.S. Constitution.

In 1896, the Republican Party officially sanctioned the women's suffrage movement, becoming the first major party to do so. Starting that year, Republican-controlled state legislatures began granting women the right to vote in state and local elections, and by the time the federal amendment was passed, 12 states, all with Republican-controlled legislatures, had enfranchised women. Also in 1896, Republican Senator A. A. Sargent of California introduced into Congress a proposed constitutional amendment that would grant women the right to vote. The proposal was defeated four times in the Democratic-controlled Senate, but when the Republican Party regained control of Congress, the Equal Suffrage Amendment, with the original language drafted by Anthony, finally passed the House by a vote of 304-88—only 16 of the 88 opposing votes were cast by Republicans. When the amendment was submitted to the states, 26 of the 36 ratifying states had Republican-controlled legislatures, and of the states voting against ratification, only one was controlled by Republicans.

Despite the fervor surrounding the passage of the Nineteenth Amendment, women did not go to the polls in great numbers during the 1920s; however, the women who did cast ballots voted overwhelmingly Republican, thereby strengthening the Republican domination of both the presidency and Congress throughout that decade. During the next several decades, the women's movement was relatively inactive, and the Republican Party, although instrumental in securing the vote for women, did not continue to promote women's causes or make women's rights central—or even peripheral—to its party platform. By the 1960s, when feminist activism revived interest in women's rights through the proposed Equal Rights Amendment (ERA), the Republican Party was no longer as supportive of women's movements as it had once been.

Originally drafted by the **National Woman's Party (NWP)** and introduced in Congress in 1923, the ERA stated that "equality of rights under the law shall not be denied or abridged by the United States nor by any State on account of sex." For decades, the ERA was ignored by Republicans and Democrats alike, until the formation of the **National Organization for Women (NOW)** in 1966 heightened awareness of women's issues and forced politicians to take notice of the ERA. The ERA was approved by the House of Representatives in 1971 and by the Senate in 1972. Despite being endorsed by Republican presidents Richard Nixon and Gerald Ford,

The Republican Party gave early endorsement to woman suffrage. Here the National Woman Suffrage Association meets at the Republican National Convention in 1856. National Archives.

the controversial amendment was strongly opposed by conservative Republican majorities in various state legislatures. Republican nominee Ronald Reagan also opposed the ERA, and he forced the party to drop support for the ERA from its 1980 platform. Although national polls indicated that a majority of Americans favored passage of the ERA, the anti-ERA movement, with the aid of newly elected President Reagan, managed to quash what support remained for the amendment.

The Republican stance on abortion underwent a similar drift away from support for women's rights toward stalwart opposition. Originally outlawed by most states in the mid-nineteenth century, abortion was made legal nationwide in 1973 when the Supreme Court ruling in ***Roe v. Wade*** overturned a Texas anti-abortion law. The *Roe* Court was dominated by the unlikely mix of Republican-appointed left-leaning justices whose tendency had been to extend the sphere of protected liberties, often by direct judicial intervention. The *Roe* decision (made by a 7 to 2 margin, with five Republican justices joining the majority) found abortion to be a matter of "privacy," which early Republican-dominated Supreme Courts had ruled was implied by the "penumbra" of protections found in the First, Third, Fourth, Fifth, and Ninth Amendments. The Court found that despite the fact that the Constitution makes no explicit mention of a right to privacy, and certainly no mention of a right to abortion, such rights are implicitly contained in the Bill of Rights.

Although personally opposed to abortion, Republican presidents Richard Nixon and Gerald Ford were hesitant to directly attack *Roe v. Wade*, but, just as he had done with the ERA, President Ronald Reagan forged a new official Republican Party stance on abortion, turning support—or at least, acceptance—into vigorous opposition. The 1980 Republican platform supported a constitutional amendment and other congressional legislation aimed at overturning *Roe v. Wade*. More important, Reagan's Department of Justice scrutinized potential appointees to the federal bench, screening out those deemed potentially supportive of pro-choice positions. Reagan also sought to curtail abortion through restrictive regulations that could only be challenged in federal courts packed with Reagan judges. Reagan also made executive branch appointments in line with his anti-abortion policy. Surgeon General C. Everett Koop publicly attacked abortion, and Reagan's secretary of Health and Human Services, **Margaret Heckler**, was an outspoken supporter of the anti-abortion movement, lobbying Congress to ban funding for abortions and counseling on abortion while at the same time pushing for funding of religious organizations. In 1988, George Bush, Reagan's vice president and the party's presidential candidate for that year, called for the "criminalization of abortion."

By the late 1980s, the liberal majority on the Court had been significantly undermined, as the original justices from *Roe* retired and were replaced by Reagan's anti-abortion appointees. The two original dissenters in *Roe*, William Rehnquist and Byron White, were reinforced by three Reagan appointees—two of whom were avowedly anti-abortion, while the third, Justice **Sandra Day O'Connor**, leaned toward the pro-life position. With the Court's new make-up, the string of rulings in support of abortion was interrupted in 1989 in ***Webster v. Reproductive Health Services,*** where the Court ruled 5 to 4 that some state-imposed restrictions on abortion were constitutionally permissible. Were it not for Democratic President Bill Clinton's liberal and moderate appointments to the Court after 1993, many Court-watchers thought that a Court dominated by Reagan and Bush appointees might actually overturn *Roe*, leaving it once again up to the states whether or not to outlaw abortion.

Although in many ways opposed to the causes supported by women's movements, the Reagan administration did take steps to further the position of women in important government positions, including the appointment of the first female Supreme Court justice (Sandra Day O'Connor), the first female secretary of transportation (**Elizabeth Dole**), and the first female representative to the United Nations (**Jeane Kirkpatrick**). However, Reagan never had more than three women in his cabinet at the same time, indicating that Republican efforts at gender-equality were limited. In both its opposition to abortion and its emphasis on traditional family values, the post-Reagan Republican Party continued to align itself against the rights and interests espoused by the **women's movement**. In 1994, the Republican Contract with America not only came out against abortion but aimed at cutting **welfare** spending for single, working mothers. The Republican economic agenda was based on the nuclear family, which has often been the target of women's movements. Although some internal opposition has arisen to the party's stance on women's issues (e.g., in 1992 and 1996, a group of Republican women attempted to alter the platform's opposition to abortion), it is unlikely that Republicans will soon shift to supporting women's movements in their political battles. (JW2) **See also** Abolition.

BIBLIOGRAPHY

Barone, Michael, et al. *Almanac of American Politics*. Washington, DC: National Journal, 1996.

Brown, Dorothy M. *Setting a Course: American Women in the 1920s*. Boston: Twayne Publishers, 1987.

Clark, Judith Freeman. *Almanac of American Women in the 20th Century*. New York: Prentice Hall, 1987.

Hecker, Eugene A. *A Short History of Women's Rights*. Westport, CT: Greenwood Press, 1971.

Langley, Winston E. and Vivian C. Fox, eds. *Women's Rights in the United States: A Documentary History*. Westport, CT: Greenwood Press, 1994.

Le Veness, Frank P. and Jane P. Sweeney, eds. *Women Leaders in Contemporary U.S. Politics*. Boulder, CO: Lynne Rienner Publishers, 1987.

Patterson, James T. *America in the Twentieth Century*. New York: Harcourt, Brace, Jovanovich, 1983.

Ann W. Richards (1933–)

Ann Richards, the former governor of Texas, is known for her wit and political savvy. After a career as a junior high school teacher, Richards served six years as a county commissioner and eight as state treasurer. Richards first came to national prominence when she was selected to deliver her now famous keynote address at the 1988 Democratic Convention. In that speech, she referred to George Bush, the 1988 Republican presidential candidate and a fellow Texan, as having been born "with a silver foot in his mouth."

Elected governor in 1990, Richards earned a reputation as a maverick for tackling stereotypically "unfeminine" issues, such as the state's economy and insurance regulation, and for imposing much-needed ethics reform on lobbyists and special interests. However, Richards also placed women and minorities in more than half of her political appointments.

As governor, Richards was generally popular and much appreciated for her direct communication style, which was characterized by colloquialisms and stories of her youth in Waco, Texas. However, in the Republican sweep of 1994, George W. Bush, son of the former president, defeated Richards's bid for a second term. (MBS)

BIBLIOGRAPHY

Richards, Ann W. "What's Gender Got to Do with It?" *Redbook* 182 (November 1993): 99.

Tolleson-Rinehart, Sue and Jeanie R. Stanley. *Claytie and the Lady: Ann Richards, Gender, and Politics in Texas*. Austin: University of Texas, 1994.

Winegarten, Ruth, ed. *Governor Ann Richards and Other Texas Women: A Pictorial History*. Austin: Eakin Press, 1986.

Right-to-Life Movement

In 1973, when the U.S. Supreme Court struck down state laws restricting **abortion** in ***Roe v. Wade***, an anti-abortion movement quickly mobilized. Movement leaders chose the "pro-life" label to put forward a positive image, and to focus attention on their core argument—that abortion amounts to taking the life of an unborn child. Like all social movements, the pro-life movement is decentralized, characterized by competing organizations and leaders, and by diverse arguments and rationales. The Catholic bishops organized first, recommending in 1973 that the U.S. Catholic Conference adopt a coordinated response to the Court's ruling, and providing key resources to the National Committee for a **human life amendment**, which sought to amend the Constitution to ban abortion. In the late 1970s and 1980s, many fundamentalist, pentecostal, and evangelical Protestant churches issued official pronouncements against abortion, and the movement was soon characterized by a wide array of groups appealing to different religious communities with different rationales.

American Catholics, for example, have generally supported the "seamless garment of life" principle, which maintains that life is sacred and therefore proscribes nuclear war and the death penalty as well as abortion. In contrast, Protestants have often linked their opposition to legal abortion to the broader issue of controlling extra-marital sexuality, but not to the death penalty or other issues. As a consequence, most but not all pro-life organizations take no official position on any issue—not even contraception.

The pro-life movement is also divided over strategy. Most activists have given up on an effort to amend the U.S. Constitution to protect fetal life, although several groups continue to pursue this end. A sizable majority of pro-life groups work within the **Republican Party,** hoping to influence the selection of Supreme Court justices and to nominate and elect more Republicans to enact whatever legislation the Court will permit. Since 1980, when pro-life activists gained control of the Republican platform committee, Republican platforms have called for a human life amendment. Yet, a sizable minority of pro-life groups and activists are otherwise liberal on political and social issues. Within the Catholic community, the "seamless garment network" of organizations opposes abortion, military spending, and the death penalty, and pushes for social justice on economic issues. A similar network among "peace-church" evangelicals pursues similar goals. Feminists for Life seeks to promote feminist policies on all issues except abortion. These organizations often work at the local level to counsel pregnant women on alternatives to abortion, and seek to support progressive pro-life candidates.

Some pro-life groups and activists endorse more confrontational tactics. **Operation Rescue** promotes the blockading of abortion clinics, and some activists have resorted to violence, firebombing clinics and even murdering abortion providers. In the 1990s, as it became obvious that the Court would not overturn *Roe v. Wade*, such violence became more common on the fringes of the movement. (CW) **See also** Feminism; Women's Movement.

BIBLIOGRAPHY

Blanchard, Dallas A. *The Anti-Abortion Movement and the Rise of the Religious Right.* New York: Twayne, 1994.

Cook, Elizabeth Adell, Ted G. Jelen, and Clyde Wilcox. *Between Two Absolutes: Public Opinion and the Politics of Abortion.* Boulder, CO: Westview, 1992.

Granberg, Donald. "The Abortion Activists." *Family Planning Perspectives* 13 (1981): 158-61.

Luker, Kristin. *Abortion and the Politics of Motherhood.* Berkeley: University of California Press, 1984.

Maxwell, Carol. "Denomination, Meaning, and Persistence: Difference in Individual Motivation to Obstruct Abortion Practice." Presented at the annual meeting of the Society for the Scientific Study of Religion, 1992.

Corinne Boyd Riley (1893–1979)

Corinne Riley, a lifelong Democrat, was a field representative for the South Carolina State Textbook Commission from 1938 to 1942, helping manage state educational standards. From 1942 to 1944, she worked in the Personnel Office at Shaw Air Force Base, where she continued to amass political contacts. On April 10, 1962, she won a special election to the U.S. House of Representatives, filling the vacancy left by her deceased husband, John J. Riley. She served in Congress until January 3, 1963.

BIBLIOGRAPHY

Chamberlin, Hope. *A Minority of Members.* New York: Praeger, 1973.

Lynn N. Rivers (1956–)

After serving as a member of the Ann Arbor, Michigan, City Council from 1984 to 1992, Lynn Rivers was elected in 1992 to the Michigan House of Representatives, where she served until 1994. A Democrat, Rivers now serves in the U.S. House of Representatives, to which she was elected in 1994.

BIBLIOGRAPHY

Bingham. Clara. *Women on the Hill.* New York: Time Books, 1997.

Alice Rivlin (1931–)

The first director (1975–1983) of the Congressional Budget Office, Alice Rivlin became director of the Office of Management and Budget (OMB) in June 1994. She had served as deputy director of the OMB from the beginning of the Clinton administration in 1993, and was known for her pro-deficit reduction position. In 1996, she was confirmed by the Senate as vice chair of the Federal Reserve Board. (JCS)

BIBLIOGRAPHY

Drew, Elizabeth. *On the Edge: The Clinton Presidency.* New York: Simon and Schuster, 1994.

Wilke, John. "Senate Easily Confirms Fed's Greenspan to 3rd Term, and Rivlin Wins Close Vote." *Wall Street Journal* (June 21, 1996): A2.

Barbara Roberts (1936–)

In 1990, Barbara Roberts, a Democrat, became the first women elected to serve as governor of Oregon. During her tenure, Roberts worked unsuccessfully for the passage of a state sales tax to counteract property tax reductions. Falling tax revenues forced the Roberts administration to make some unpopular belt-tightening decisions. She did not stand for re-election in 1994 because of failing health and the recent death of her husband. Prior to her election as governor, Roberts served as Oregon's secretary of state from 1985 to 1990. From 1981 to 1985, she sat in the state house of representatives, serving as majority leader in 1983–1984.

BIBLIOGRAPHY

Dowling, Carrie. "Meet the USA's New Governors and Senators." *USA Today* (November 10, 1994): 12A.

Knickerbocker, Brad. "Belt-Tightening in Oregon as Voters Reject Sales Tax." *The Christian Science Monitor* (November 12, 1993): 2.

Alice Mary Robertson (1854–1931)

Alice Robertson was government supervisor of Creek Indian Schools from 1900 to 1905. In 1920, she was elected to the U.S. House of Representatives as a Republican from Oklahoma. She served only one term, leaving office in 1923. In May 1923, President Warren G. Harding appointed Robertson to be a welfare worker for Muskagee's Veterans' Hospital.

Congresswoman Alice Robertson, an Oklahoma Republican (left), stands on the Capitol steps in 1923 with her Republican colleagues Mae Ella Norton of California and Winifred Huck of Illinois. The arrival of the three marked the first time so many women had served in the U.S. House of Representatives. Library of Congress.

Robertson finished her life in public service at the Oklahoma State Historical Society, where she provided historical research on Native Americans.

BIBLIOGRAPHY

"Congresswomen Elected with West Ads." *Current Opinion* 70 (January 1921): 41-44.

Morgan, Tom P. "Miss Alice of Muskagee." *Ladies Home Journal* 38 (March 1921): 21.

Morris, Cheryl. "Alice M. Robertson: Friend or Foe of the American Soldier?" *Journal of the West* 12, no. 12 (April 1973): 307–16.

Josephine Aspinwall Roche (1886–1976)

Although Josephine Roche, a Democrat, lost her 1934 bid for the governorship of Colorado, President Franklin D. Roosevelt appointed her assistant secretary of the Treasury in charge of the United States Public Health Service, a post she held from 1934 to 1937. She later served as the first director of the United Mine Workers Welfare and Retirement Fund, as well as president of the National Consumers League.

BIBLIOGRAPHY

Essary, Helen. "Josephine Roche, Candidate for Governor of Colorado." *Democratic Digest* 11, no. 7 (July 1934): 11–12.

Roe v. Wade (1973)

Roe v. Wade, 410 U.S. 113 (1973), is a landmark United States Supreme Court decision handed down in 1973 by a vote of 7-2. The case evolved from years of effort by groups within the birth control and **abortion** reform movements to liberalize American abortion laws. The majority opinion, authored by Justice Harry A. Blackmun, struck down a Texas criminal abortion statute, and all similar state statutes, for violating the constitutional right to privacy that covers a woman's decision, in consultation with her doctor, to terminate a pregnancy. The Court noted, however, that this right to privacy is not absolute. The state, through its police powers, has an interest both in potential human life and in insuring the woman's health. The majority opinion reasoned that because pregnancy is divided into three trimesters based on the gestational age of the fetus and its potential for living outside the womb, the state's interest in the abortion decision heightens as the trimesters progress. During the first trimester, the fetus is not viable, and the woman's privacy rights, in consultation with her doctor, are determinative. During the second trimester, the state may regulate the abortion so as to insure the woman's health. During the third trimester, the state may strictly regulate or prohibit abortions, except when necessary to save maternal life or health, because the fetus might be viable and because abortions are more difficult for women at these later stages.

The minority opinion asserted that the proper domain for abortion policymaking was the state legislatures, not the federal courts. The dissenters also stated that with the majority opinion the Court had created a right not specifically found in the U.S. Constitution.

Roe v. Wade overturned existing abortion laws in all but four states and established a national precedent for a woman's right to a legal, safe abortion based on constitutional privacy doctrines. This 1973 decision unleashed a storm of protest from many quarters, particularly the Roman Catholic Church. Subsequent Supreme Court decisions have established the constitutionality of restrictive abortion regulations, including viability testing, 24-hour waiting periods, parental notification for minors, and mandatory informative lectures about the development of the fetus.

The medically based definition of fetal viability has caused further litigation about the boundaries of abortion choices for women and the proper role of the state. As medical technology has made it possible for some premature babies to live, questions arise about the trimester standard for viability. Medical advances also make it safer for most women to have an abortion well into the third trimester. These issues are hotly debated in modern abortion politics. For some pro-life groups, however, viability and trimesters are not the point; they believe that human life begins at the moment of conception, and any and all abortions are murder. Some pro-life advocates, though not all, make exceptions for pregnancies that result from rape or incest. Although the *Roe v. Wade* decision has been attacked on many sides, the legal right to an abortion that it established still exists. (LW) **See also** Human Life Amendment; Right-to-Life Movement; *Webster v. Reproductive Health Services.*

BIBLIOGRAPHY

Faux, Marian. *Roe v. Wade: The Untold Story of the Landmark Supreme Court Decision that Made Abortion Legal.* New York: Penguin Books, 1988.

Garrow, David J. *Liberty & Sexuality: The Right to Privacy and the Making of* Roe v. Wade. New York: Macmillan, 1994.

Luker, Kristin. *Abortion & the Politics of Motherhood.* Berkeley: University of California Press, 1984.

Mohr, James C. *Abortion in America: The Origins and Evolution of National Policy.* New York: Oxford University Press, 1978.

O'Connor, Karen. *No Neutral Ground: Abortion Politics in an Age of Absolutes.* Boulder, CO: Westview Press. 1996.

Petchesky, Rosalind Pollack. *Abortion and Woman's Choice: The State, Sexuality, & Reproductive Freedom.* Boston: Northeastern University Press, 1990.

Edith Nourse Rogers (1881–1960)

Edith N. Rogers, a Republican from Massachusetts, was elected to the United States House of Representatives in 1924. She was reelected 17 times, serving in the House from 1925 until shortly before her death in 1960. At the time, Rogers's term of congressional service was the longest of any woman.

BIBLIOGRAPHY

Rogers, Edith Nourse. "Women's New Place in Politics." *Nation's Business* 18 (August 1930): 39-41, 120, 124.

Anna Eleanor Roosevelt (1884–1962)

Eleanor Roosevelt was one of the most prominent and influential women of the twentieth century. In 1905, Eleanor married her distant cousin Franklin Roosevelt, who was elected president of the United States four times between 1932 and his death in 1945. During her husband's presidency, which spanned the Great Depression and World War II, Eleanor established an important activist role as first lady. As American representative to the United Nations from 1946 to 1952, she was a strong advocate for global human rights.

Eleanor Roosevelt's early years were hard. Her parents died before she was 10. Raised by a strict grandmother, she was shy and lacked confidence. Thus, Eleanor Roosevelt was a traditional mother and wife as her husband's political career began to rise. Two great shocks forced her to find her own identity. In 1918, she discovered her husband's' affair with another woman, and, in 1921, Franklin Roosevelt was paralyzed by polio. Eleanor Roosevelt's subsequent emergence in the wake of these crises enabled her to rebuild her marriage as a partnership, to help her husband continue his political career, and to strike out on her own. She was important to Franklin's successful campaign for governor of New York in 1930 and for president in 1932. Eleanor Roosevelt became an active, involved presidential wife. For the first time, a first lady became as well known as her husband. She was the first to hold regular press conferences, she gave lectures and radio broadcasts, and she wrote a syndicated newspaper column entitled "My Day." She was Franklin Roosevelt's "eyes and ears." Although her activities were a source of some controversy, she continued to work in a determined and diligent way for the rights of women, blacks, workers, and the poor. Franklin Roosevelt depended on his wife's information, and others depended on her influence with the president.

Eleanor Roosevelt, the wife of President Franklin D. Roosevelt, was one of the most influential women of the twentieth century. Library of Congress.

After her husband's death, Eleanor Roosevelt continued her public service. As a delegate to the United Nations from 1946 to 1952, she became known as the "Woman of the World." She played a key role in the adoption of the Universal Declaration of Human Rights in 1948. Eleanor Roosevelt encouraged others to meet adversity "with courage and with the best that you have to give." She published her autobiography in 1962, the year of her death. (RRT) **See also** First Ladies.

Bibliography

Goodwin, Doris Kearns. *No Ordinary Time.* New York: Simon and Schuster, 1994.

Lash, Joseph. *Eleanor and Franklin.* New York: Norton, 1971.

Roosevelt, Eleanor. *This I Remember.* New York: Harper and Row, 1949.

Wiesen, Blanche Cook. *Eleanor Roosevelt.* Vol. 1, 1884–1933. New York: Viking, 1992.

Edith Carow Roosevelt (1861–1948)

Edith Roosevelt, the second wife of U.S. President Theodore Roosevelt, was key in promoting the modern institutionalization of the role of U.S. first lady. During her husband's presidency (1901–1909), Edith Roosevelt brought both six children (the most to reside there) and order to the White House. She recognized the demands of the press and made special efforts to provide newspeople with time and photos of the first family. She additionally spearheaded the re-design of the White House to separate the family section from the public and administration areas. Edith Roosevelt also drew her husband's attention to issues she deemed important by marking news stories for him. To meet the public demands placed on political wives, she hired the first White House social secretary and met to coordinate calendars and responsibilities with wives of cabinet members. Viewing entertaining as part of her political job, Edith Roosevelt hired professionals to assist in this task. As an honor to those she followed, Roosevelt established the **first ladies** gallery in the White House. In 1932, Edith Roosevelt, whose husband had been a Republican, endorsed the candidacy of Republican Herbert Hoover over Democrat Franklin D. Roosevelt, a distant cousin of her husband. Her Republican stance against a Democratic relative made the front page of newspapers, especially after she appeared at rallies on Hoover's behalf. (BN)

To meet the demands of her duties, Edith Roosevelt, wife of President Theodore Roosevelt, became the first presidential wife to hire a press secretary. Library of Congress, Prints and Photographs Division.

Bibliography

Caroli, Betty Boyd. *First Ladies.* New York: Oxford University Press, 1995.

Truman, Margaret. *First Ladies.* New York: Random House, 1995.

Rosenfeld v. Southern Pacific Corporation (1971)

In *Rosenfeld v. Southern Pacific Corporation,* 444 F. 2d 1219 (9th Cir. 1971), the Ninth Circuit Court of Appeals ruled that a company policy of denying all women certain jobs violated **Title VII of the Civil Rights Act of 1964**. The case arose when Leah Rosenfeld was denied a transfer to the job of agent-telegrapher because company policy excluded women from these jobs. The company's defense was that (1) the jobs were unsuitable for women and (2) California law restricted maximum working hours and weight lifting for women employees.

The company relied on a provision of Title VII that allowed employers to hire employees of one sex only when sex was a "bona fide occupational qualification" (BFOQ) for the position. The BFOQ was included in Title VII because members of Congress were concerned that the ban on **sex discrimination** would prevent employers from hiring on the basis of sex for any reason—even when sex was relevant to the job performance. The BFOQ defense permitted employers charged with sex discrimination to argue that it was "necessary" to their business to make hiring decisions on the basis of sex.

California was one of many states with laws restricting women from entering certain occupations or regulating the conditions under which they could work. Such laws, called **protective legislation**, were enacted in most states during the late nineteenth and early twentieth centuries. Although defended on the grounds that they protected women from harm in the workplace, these statutes kept women out of better-paying jobs and occupations. Passage of Title VII raised questions about whether such laws violated the ban on sex discrimination or whether they constituted a valid BFOQ, allowing employers to hire on the basis of sex.

The court rejected the company's BFOQ defense, ruling that relying on the California protective legislation would allow employers to evade Congress's intention of preventing them from basing employment decisions on group characteristics instead of on individual qualifications. The court ruled that Title VII does not permit employers to make assumptions about the physical characteristics of a group as a whole in forming the basis of employment decisions; Title VII did not permit a company to characterize all women as being incapable of performing certain jobs. (SM)

BIBLIOGRAPHY

Brown, Barbara, Ann Freedman, Harriet Katz, and Alice Price. *Women's Rights and the Law.* New York: Praeger Publishers, 1977.

Maschke, Karen. *Litigation, Courts, and Women Workers.* New York: Praeger Publishers, 1989.

Rosie the Riveter

Rosie the Riveter was a World War II symbol for women who worked in manufacturing and defense industries. She was part of a recruitment drive to bring women into the labor force to replace the men who were away at war. By 1947, more than 18 million women were at work in the United States; because many of them were married or over 35, the nature of the workplace changed. Alhough entering the workforce in greater numbers, women still faced discrimination, especially in terms of wages. What's more, society expected them to leave the workforce after the war when the men returned. (SD)

During World War II, women entered the workforce in large numbers to support the war effort. Many did not leave when the war ended. Pictured here is Geraldine Donna Blair, a riveter at the Douglas Aircraft plant in Long Beach, California, in 1942. National Archives.

BIBLIOGRAPHY

Honey, Maureen. *Creating Rosie the Riveter: Class, Gender, and Propaganda during World War II.* Amherst: University of Massachusetts Press, 1984.

Ileana Ros-Lehtinen (1952-)

In 1989, Ileana Ros-Lehtinen, a Cuban-born Republican from Miami, Florida, became the first Cuban-American elected to Congress. Known for her careful attention to the interests of her heavily Cuban-American district, she has worked to precipitate the downfall of Cuban dictator Fidel Castro. Ros-Lehtinen has on several occasions broken rank with her party, for example, over the "motor voter" registration bill, which promised to help enfranchise more minority voters in her district. In the 105th Congress (1997–1999), she served on both the Government Reform and Oversight Committee and on the International Relations Committee. From 1983 to 1989, Ros-Lehtinen served in both the Florida house and senate. (MEK)

BIBLIOGRAPHY

Fernandez, Mayia. *Ileana Ros-Lehtinen, Lawmaker.* Columbus, OH: Modern Curriculum, 1994.

Nellie Tayloe Ross (1876–1977)

Nellie Tayloe Ross became the first woman governor in the United States in 1925 when she was elected governor of Wyoming to complete the unexpired term of her late husband William Bradford Ross. A Democrat, Ross served almost two years before being narrowly defeated for re-election in 1926. In 1928, Ross served as vice-chair at the Democratic National Convention, where she seconded the nomination of Al Smith. After 1928, she actively organized women for the **Democratic Party**, and in 1932 directed women's activities for Franklin D. Roosevelt's presidential campaign. In 1933, she became the first women to direct the U.S. Mint, where she served until 1953.

BIBLIOGRAPHY

"Nellie Tayloe Ross." *Business Week* (February 24, 1940): 24.

"Nellie Tayloe Ross." *Current Biography* (1940): 697-99.

Rostker v. Goldberg (1981)

At issue in *Rostker v. Goldberg,* 448 U.S. 1306 (1981), was the Military Selective Service Act enacted by Congress in 1979 at the request of President Jimmy Carter, a Democrat. Carter asked Congress to reactivate military draft registration after the Soviet Union invaded Afghanistan. Because Congress provided funds for the registration of males only, several young men filed suit claiming the law violated the due process clause of the Fifth Amendment and asked that the registration be suspended. The Court of Appeals agreed that the law was invalid, but reinstated the procedures for registration pending review. The U.S. Supreme Court, in a 6-3 vote, reversed the decision of the lower court. In the majority opinion, Justice William Rehnquist deferred to congressional authority in military affairs. He also argued that a distinction in law could be made between men and women because the two were not similarly situated—women were excluded from combat, but draft registration was being reinstated to fill the potential need for combat troops.

Bibliography

Baer, Judith A. *Women in American Law*. New York: Holmes & Meier, 1996.

Boumil, Marcia Mobilia and Stephen C. Hicks. *Women and the Law*. Littleton, CO: Fred B. Rothman & Company, 1992.

"Constitutional Law—Gender-based Discrimination—Separation of Powers—The Total Exclusion of Women from the Military Selective Service Act Does Not Violate Due Process." *Villanova Law Review* 27 (November 1981): 182-97.

Marge Roukema (1929–)

Marge Roukema, a Republican, has represented the 5th District of New Jersey in the U.S. House of Representatives since 1980, when she was swept into office as part of the Reagan landslide. In the 105th Congress (1997–1999), Roukema was the senior Republican woman in the House, serving as chair of the Banking Committee's Financial Institutions and Consumer Credit Subcommittee, one of the most influential subcommittees in the House. Roukema was the lead Republican sponsor of the **Family and Medical Leave Act**, which was enacted into law in 1993. Although she worked eight years for enactment of this law, and has supported other "women's" issues, Roukema has not joined the **Congressional Caucus for Women's Issues**. Roukema has broken with her party on numerous occasions, and is a part of the more liberal northern wing of the **Republican Party**, the so-called "gypsy moths." However, on fiscal matters, she is known as a conservative, voting in favor of the balanced budget amendment and reduction in spending on big ticket items. The former high school government and history teacher also served on her local board of education from 1970 until 1973. (MEK)

Bibliography

Bingham, Clara. *Women on the Hill*. New York: Time Books, 1997.

Lucille Roybal-Allard (1941–)

Lucille Roybal-Allard became the first Mexican-American woman in Congress when she was elected by California's 33rd Congressional District in 1992. Easily re-elected in 1994 and 1996, Roybal-Allard was also selected to chair the California Democratic Congressional Delegation; the first woman and Latina to head the 29-member delegation. In the 105th Congress (1997–1999), she served on the Budget Committee and on the Banking and Finance Committee. Prior to serving in Congress, Roybal-Allard served three terms in the California State Assembly. A strong advocate of women's issues, she was recognized by the California National Organization for Women as Legislator of the Year in 1991.

Bibliography

"The Decade of Hispanic." *Hispanic* 10, no. 12 (December 1997): 53.

Margolies-Mezvinsky, Marjorie. *A Woman's Place*. New York: Crown, 1994.

RU-486

RU-486 is an anti-progestin drug that results in **abortion** when ingested early in pregnancy. Developed by a French company, Roussel-Uclaf (hence the occasional designation of RU-486 as "the French abortion pill"), the drug has been used in France and found to be safe and effective. RU-486 treatment consists of two or three visits to the doctor, with the woman taking different stages of the pills (the anti-progestin combined with a small dose of prostaglandin). The abortion occurs without surgical or any bodily intrusion by medical personnel. Medical supervision is required to monitor the health of a woman using RU-486. The woman may choose to stay at the doctor's office until the abortion is complete, or go home.

RU-486 is politically controversial in the United States. Calling the drug "chemical murder," right-to-life groups have threatened to boycott the manufacturer of RU-486 and any affiliate companies if the drug is introduced in this country. Pro-choice groups have sought to have the drug licensed for use by American women. In 1992, Leona Benten, a 29-year-old pregnanat woman, was arrested in John F. Kennedy Airport in New York for attempting to bring RU-486 into the United States from France. The arrest was coordinated by Lawrence Lader of the Abortion Rights Mobilization (ARM), who chose Benten as a test case to challenge the ban on use of RU-486 in the United States. When the Supreme Court ruled 7-2 in *Benten v. Kessler* (1992) against returning the pills to Benten, Food and Drug Administration testing and possible licensing of RU-486 were delayed. After taking office in 1993, President Bill Clinton, a Democrat, encouraged Food and Drug Administration (FDA) testing and clinical trials of the drug. The company that held the patent for RU-486 sold American licensing rights to the non-profit Population Council to avoid further political turmoil. RU-486 has the potential to change abortion practices and politics because its use need not be restricted to easily identifiable clinics that pro-life groups could target for blockades and demonstrations. Because RU-486 could make abortion more accessible to more women, the drug is a highly emotional issue for both sides in the abortion debate. **See also** Reproductive and Contraceptive Technologies for Women; Right-to-Life Movement. (LW)

Bibliography

Craig, Barbara Hinkson and David M. O'Brien. *Abortion and American Politics*. Chatham, NJ: Chatham House, 1993.

Garrow, David J. *Liberty & Sexuality: The Right to Privacy and the Making of* Roe v. Wade. New York: Macmillan, 1994.

O'Connor, Karen. *No Neutral Ground: Abortion Politics in an Age of Absolutes.* Boulder, CO: Westview Press, 1996.

Mary Harriman Rumsey (1881–1934)

During World War I, Mary Rumsey supported and worked for various community councils organized in conjunction with the U.S. Council of National Defense. In the late 1920s and early 1930s, Rumsey worked with the Emergency Exchange Association. In June 1933, President Franklin Roosevelt appointed Rumsey chair of the Consumers' Advisory Board of the National Recovery Administration, a post she held until her death.

BIBLIOGRAPHY

Woolf, J.S. "Mary Harriman Rumsey." *New York Times* (August 6, 1933): 6.

"Obituary." *New York Times* (December 19, 1934).

Rust v. Sullivan (1991)

Title X of the **Public Health Service Act** barred the use of federal funds for family-planning services that included **abortion**. In 1988, Louis Sullivan, the secretary of Health and Human Services in the Republican Reagan administration, clarified the provision through the promulgation of regulations that stated that no program receiving funds under Title X could engage in counseling concerning abortions, provide referrals for abortion services, or sponsor activities that advocated abortion as a method of family planning. All Title X projects were required to maintain separate facilities, personnel, and accounting records from any institution that advocated or used abortion as a form of family planning. The regulations were challenged in court on several grounds, including that the specific regulations promulgated by the secretary were not inherently contained in the act. Additionally, the plaintiffs challenged the regulations as violating the First and Fifth Amendment rights of the patient. In *Rust v. Sullivan*, 500 U.S. 173 (1991), the U.S. Supreme Court upheld the lower court's ruling that the regulations were a reasonable interpretation of the act, although by no means the only possible one. The Court rejected the First Amendment argument because the regulations, while not providing certain information, did not prevent individuals from obtaining this information from other sources. The Court also determined that the Fifth Amendment claim of due process was not violated because the woman's ability to have an abortion was not prevented by the secretary's clarification.

BIBLIOGRAPHY

Baer, Judith A. *Women in American Law*. New York: Holmes & Meier, 1996.

Boumil, Marcia Mobilia and Stephen C. Hicks. *Women and the Law*. Littleton, CO: Fred B. Rothman & Company, 1992.

"Rust Corrodes: The First Amendment Implications." *Stanford Law Review*. 45 (November 1992): 185-227.

S

Sacajawea (c.1786–1812?)

Sacajawea (also, Sacagawea, Sakakawea) was born about 1786 in present-day Idaho. A member of the Lemhi band of the Shoshoni tribe, she was captured and enslaved by the Hidatsa (or Minnetaree) tribe about 1800. In 1804, her husband, Toussaint Charbonneau, a French-Canadian trapper, was hired as a guide by the Lewis and Clark Expedition. Sacajawea and the couple's son, Jean Baptiste Charbonneau, also accompanied the expedition in its journey westward. A happenstance meeting with Sacajawea's brother, chief of the Lemhi Shoshoni, provided the expedition with horses and guides over the continental divide. After the expedition returned to St. Louis, Sacajawea fell into obscurity. Unverified reports of her death place it as early as 1812 and as late as 1884 on the Wind River Reservation in Wyoming. (AM)

Bibliography

Kessler, Donna J. *The Making of Sacajawea: A Euro-American Legend*. Tuscaloosa: University of Alabama Press, 1996.

Madsen, Brigham. *The Lemhi: Sacajawea's People*. Caldwell, ID: Caxton Printers, 1979.

Patricia Fukuda Saiki (1930–)

Patricia Saiki was born in Hilo, Hawaii, on May 28, 1930. She served in the Hawaii legislature from 1968 to 1978. In 1986, Saiki became the first Republican ever to represent Hawaii in the U.S. House of Representatives. From 1991 to 1993, following an unsuccessful bid for the U.S. Senate, Saiki served as the administrator of the Small Business Administration, where she oversaw reforms to streamline procedures. In 1994, Saiki ran unsuccessfully for the governorship of Hawaii. (CKC)

Bibliography

"Hawaii's Patricia Saiki Sworn in as Chief of SBA." *Wall Street Journal* (April 11, 1991): B2.

"Republicans Select Woman in Hawaii." *New York Times* (September 20, 1994): A19.

Richards, Rhonda. "Small Business Administration Chief Noted for Agency Reform." *USA Today* (December 3, 1992): B4.

Wood, Daniel B. "GOP Has Rare Shot in Hawaii Governor Race." *Christian Science Monitor* (September 23, 1994): 7:1.

Katharine Price Collier St. George (1896–1983)

In 1942, Katharine St. George became the first woman in New York State to become chair of a county campaign committee. A Republican, she supported Governor Thomas Dewey's election over the re-election of her Democratic cousin, President Franklin D. Roosevelt, in the 1944 presidential campaign. St. George served in the U.S. House of Representatives from New York from 1946 until 1964. In 1962, she became the first woman to serve on the powerful House Rules Committee. After leaving Congress, she remained active in national and state politics until 1981.

Bibliography

Lockett, Edward B. "FDR's Republican Cousin in Congress." *Colliers* 126 (August 19, 1950): 26-27, 40-41.

St. George, Katharine Price Collier. *Oral History Interview, Former Member of Congress Association.* Washington, DC: Manuscript Division, Library of Congress, 1979.

Deborah Gannett Sampson (1760–1827)

Deborah Sampson was the only woman to have served in the American Revolutionary War. She enlisted in the Fourth Massachusetts Regiment under the name Robert Shutleff/Shirtliff in May 1781. Her true sex was discovered only after she was hospitalized for a wound received at Tarrytown. General Henry Knox discharged her on October 25, 1783, and sent her back to Massachusetts. The state awarded her a pension for her service in the war, but her church, the First Baptist Church in Middleborough, Massachusetts, expelled her from the congregation when her enlistment became known.

Bibliography

Wright, Richardson. *Forgotten Ladies*. Philadelphia: Lippencott, 1928.

Loretta Sanchez (1960–)

Loretta Sanchez, a Democrat, was elected to the U.S. House of Representatives in 1996, defeating the long-term and ultra-conservative Republican incumbent, Robert K. Dornan. Sanchez's election was close; fewer than 1,000 votes separated the candidates. Her victory was marred somewhat by election irregularities, including more than 800 documented ineligible voters and an ongoing investigation that lasted until February 1998. Prior to her election, Sanchez was a business consultant and community activist.

BIBLIOGRAPHY

Gugliotta, Guy. "Dornan Challenge to Sanchez Rejected." *Washington Post* (February 5, 1998): A4.

Yang, John E. "Democrat Sanchez Claims Victory Over Rep. Dornan." *Washington Post* (November 14, 1996): A4.

Margaret Sanger (1879–1966)

Margaret Sanger was the sixth of 11 surviving children; Anna Higgins, her mother, endured 18 pregnancies before succumbing to tuberculosis. Sanger was a visiting nurse to New York's poor, pioneering the provision of birth control information and services to women. In 1914, after traveling to France to do research, Sanger published *The Woman Rebel*, a newspaper dedicated to "the prevention of conception." Prosecuted under the **Comstock Act** for illegally distributing information about contraception through the mail, Sanger fled to England and continued her research into European birth control methods.

In 1916, Sanger opened the first birth control clinic in the nation in the Brownsville District of Brooklyn, New York. She was promptly arrested and jailed for violating the Comstock Act. Upon her release, she continued to defy the law and went on to establish the **American Birth Control League** and the International Planned Parenthood Federation. When asked what she wanted to be remembered for, Sanger responded that she hoped she would be "remembered for helping women, because women are the strength of the future." **See also** Planned Parenthood Federation of America (PPFA). (CKC)

BIBLIOGRAPHY

Chesler, Ellen. *Woman of Valor: Margaret Sanger and the Birth Control Movement in America.* New York: Simon and Schuster, 1992.

Sanger, Margaret. *Margaret Sanger: An Autobiography.* New York: W.W. Norton, 1938.

Lynn Schenk (1945–)

Lynn Schenk, a Democrat, was elected to the U.S. House of Representatives from California in 1992 in a close election in which she outspent her opponent nearly 3–1. While in Congress, Schenk served on both the Energy and Commerce Committee and the Merchant Marine and Fisheries Committee. She was not re-elected in 1994. Prior to serving in Congress, Schenk served on the San Diego Unified Port Commission from 1990 to 1993. She also served in the cabinet of Democratic California Governor Edmund G. "Jerry" Brown, Jr., as secretary of business, transportation, and housing from 1980 to 1983.

BIBLIOGRAPHY

Mintz, John. "Pentagon Assailed on Merger Aid." *Washington Post* (July 28, 1994): D9.

Saffir, Barbara. "Life After the House." *Washington Post* (May 31, 1995): A17.

Phyllis Schlafly (1924–)

Anti-feminist, author, and politician, Phyllis Schlafly is a crusader for conservative causes. Born in St. Louis, Missouri, on August 15,1924, Schlafly was educated at the Convent of the Sacred Heart. She graduated from Washington University in 1944, earned a master's degree from Radcliffe in 1945, and received a law degree from Washington University in 1978. Before marrying John Schlafly, Jr., in 1949, she managed a successful Republican congressional campaign and edited a bank newsletter. After having six children, Schlafly, although maintaining an active professional life, declared that raising a family is the most important career for women. Schlafly ran unsuccessfully for Congress in 1952 and 1970 and served as a delegate to the Republican National Convention in 1956. She became an ardent opponent of the **Equal Rights Amendment (ERA)**, founding **STOP ERA** in 1972. A master of grassroots mobilization, Schlafly led the battle against ratification of the ERA at the state level, while proponents of the amendment focused on the national level. Schlafly also organized the Eagle Forum in 1975 to represent conservative women on a broad variety of issues. As editor of the ***Phyllis Schlafly Report*** and the *Eagle Forum Newsletter*, Schlafly attacked the ERA as a vehicle for the appearance of unisex toilets and establishment of a female draft. Schlafly was instrumental in defeating the ERA by dividing women into homemakers and career-oriented feminists, and by using her public criticism of the Supreme Court's ***Roe v. Wade*** (1973) decision to create a link between the ERA and **abortion**. The ERA fell short of ratification by three states in 1982. The symbol of the anti-ERA movement, Schlafly has continued to champion **conservatism** throughout her adult life. She is the president of the Eagle Forum and the author of nine books, including *An Echo, Not a Choice*, in which she promoted the presidential candidacy of Republican Senator Barry Goldwater in 1964. (LvA)

BIBLIOGRAPHY

Hoff-Wilson, Joan, ed. *Rights of Passage: The Past and Future of the ERA*. Bloomington: Indiana University Press, 1986.

Mansbridge, Jane. *Why We Lost the ERA*. Chicago: University of Chicago Press, 1986.

Claudine Schneider (1947–)

In 1980, following a career as a television talk-show host, Claudine Schneider won election to the U.S. House of Representatives, the first Republican to be sent to Congress by the state of Rhode Island in 40 years. She served five terms in the House, resigning in 1990 to pursue an unsuccessful bid for the U.S. Senate seat held by incumbent Democrat Claiborne Pell.

BIBLIOGRAPHY

Women in Congress, 1917–1990. Washington, DC: United States Government Printing Office, 1991.

Rose Schneiderman (1882–1972)

Rose Schneiderman helped organize the **National Women's Trade Union League** and became its first elected president in 1928. From 1933 to 1935, she was the only woman member of the Labor Advisory Board to the National Industrial Recovery Administration, and from 1937 to 1944 served as the secretary of the New York State Labor Department. When the New York Woman's Trade Union League closed in 1955, Schneiderman returned to politics and the labor movement.

BIBLIOGRAPHY

Endelman, Gary E. *Solidarity Forever.* North Stratford, NH: Ayer Company, 1981.

Schneiderman, Rose. *All for One.* New York: P.S. Erikson, 1967.

Patricia Scott Schroeder (1940–)

Congresswoman Patricia Schroeder, a Democrat from Colorado, served in the United States House of Representatives from 1972 until her retirement in 1996. A Harvard Law School graduate, wife, and mother, she was one of the most well-known and most respected members of the modern Congress. A leader for women's rights and the first woman on the powerful House National Security Committee, Schroeder was widely known for her wit, including coining the phrase "teflon president" to describe Republican President Ronald Reagan's seeming ability to avoid being stuck with the blame for anything bad that happened during his administration. Schroeder was instrumental in achieving many positive reforms for military families and children, including better base housing, day care, health care, schools, and living allowances. In 1985, she succeeded in passing the Military Family Act and the Women's Health Initiative, one part of which increased funding for breast cancer research. Schroeder is a staunch defender of a woman's right to choose a safe and legal **abortion**. Schroeder was also a keen budget watchdog for military waste and mismanagement. She briefly campaigned for the 1988 Democratic presidential nomination, but withdrew from the race in September 1987. (LW)

BIBLIOGRAPHY

Barone, Michael and Grant Ujifusa. *The Almanac of American Politics, 1996.* Washington, DC: The National Journal, 1995.

Burrell, Barbara C. *A Woman's Place Is in the House: Campaigning for Congress in the Feminist Era.* Ann Arbor: University of Michigan Press, 1994.

Witt, Linda, Karen M. Paget, and Glenna Matthews. *Running As a Woman: Gender Power in American Politics.* New York: The Free Press, 1994.

Seaman, Elizabeth Cochrane. *See* Bly, Nellie.

Andrea H. Seastrand (1941–)

In 1994, Andrea Seastrand was elected to the U.S. House seat from California vacated by Republican Michael Huffington. Also a conservative Republican, Seastrand was narrowly elected. In Congress, she served on the Transportation and Infrastructure Committee and on the Science Committee. She was defeated for re-election in 1996 by Democrat Walter Capps, her 1994 opponent.

BIBLIOGRAPHY

Greenblatt, Alan. "GOP Wants Brown to Fall, 2nd Term for Seastrand." *Congressional Quarterly Weekly Reporter* 54, no. 34 (August 24, 1996): 2367.

Kiely, Kathy. "The New(t) Women in Congress." *Working Women* 20, no. 4 (April 1995): 12.

Rosin, Hanna. "Invasion of the Church Ladies." *The New Republic* 212, no. 17 (April 24, 1995): 20.

Seidenberg v. McSorleys' Old Ale House (1970)

The Supreme Court decision in *Seidenberg v. McSorleys' Old Ale House* (1970) was indicative of the changing social climate created by the **women's movement**. Faith Seidenberg and Karen De Crow, members of the **National Organization for Women (NOW),** entered McSorleys' Old Ale House in New York City, a bar that had a 115-year history of refusing to admit women. After being asked to leave, the women sued, arguing that McSorleys' actions were "illegal, discriminatory, and unconstitutional." The Court decided in favor of the plaintiffs, agreeing that denying them admission to the bar was in violation of the equal protection clause of the Fourteenth Amendment because McSorleys' was a public bar and its liquor license was regulated by the state of New York.

A second aspect of *Seidenberg v. McSorleys' Old Ale House,* 317 F. Supp. 593 (1970), dealt with whether or not the presence of women in bars gives rise to moral and social problems. In *Goesaert v. Cleary* (1948), the Supreme Court found that the state had a legitimate interest in combating the moral and social problems that arose from bartending by women. In *McSorleys'*, however, the court concluded that "social mores have not stood still," and that most bars catered to both sexes and no longer believed that women were "peculiarly delicate and impressionable." The decision led to an article in the conservative *National Review* that bemoaned the end of a sacred tradition. (EP)

BIBLIOGRAPHY

Coyne, John R., Jr. "Ale, Cheese, Onions, and Woman." *National Review* (September 22, 1970): 997.

Grossman, Joel B. and Richard S. Wells. *Constitutional Law and Judicial Policy Making.* New York: Longman, 1988.

Selective Service Act

The Selective Service and Training Act of September 1940 provided for the first peacetime draft in American history; it required all men from 21 to 35 years of age to register for compulsory military training and service. Changes in the age and period of service were made constantly during World War II. This authority to induct men ended in March 1947. However, in the summer of 1948, Congress approved the new Selective Service Act which, as later amended and extended, constituted the basic law that drafted men between the ages of 19 and 26 and subjected them to compulsory service for not

While exempt from the draft, many women, like the one pictured here in her civil defense flight suit, served their country well. National Archives.

more than 21 months. The provisions of the Selective Service Act of 1948 were incorporated in the 1951 Universal Military Training and Service Act that extended the draft to 1955. This act was renewed quadrennially in 1955, 1959, and 1963.

During the Vietnam War, compulsory **military service** became highly controversial. The Military Selective Service Act of 1967 required the president to establish national criteria for the draft and, to the extent consistent with national interest, require the criteria to be administered uniformly by local boards. Women were to be accepted as members of local boards and service on those boards was limited to 25 years or to retirement at age 75. Draft cases were to be given scheduling preference in federal court dockets. The act prohibited the induction of undergraduate students until they completed their baccalaureate degrees, reached age 24, or lost good standing, unless the president found the needs of the armed forces required their induction. (CGM)

BIBLIOGRAPHY

Jacobs, Clyde, and John F. Gallagher. *The Selective Service Act: A Case Study of the Governmental Process.* New York: Dodd, Mead, and Company, 1968.

Marmion, Harry A. *Selective Service: Conflict and Compromise.* New York: John Wiley and Sons, Inc., 1968.

Wamsley, Gary. *Selective Service and a Changing America.* Columbus, OH: Charles Merrill Publishing Company, 1969.

Seneca Falls Convention (1848)

The Seneca Falls Convention, held in Seneca Falls, New York, July 19-20, 1848, was the first women's rights convention. As advertised by **Elizabeth Cady Stanton** and **Lucretia Mott** in the *Seneca County Courier*, the purpose of the convention was to discuss "the social, civil, and religious rights of women." Stanton and Mott had met in 1840 at the World Anti-Slavery Convention in London, England, which they attended with their husbands. Expecting to participate in the meeting, Stanton and Mott were shocked when they were restricted to the balcony. They realized then that the status of women in society was no greater than that of the slaves they were working to free. After discussing their ideas as they walked the streets of London, the two women vowed to organize a women's rights convention upon their return to the United States. As both women had families to raise, the convention was postponed until 1848 when they gathered at Seneca Falls. Approximately 300 people attended the meeting, including at least 40 men. James Mott, Lucretia Mott's husband, presided over the convention. Both Lucretia Mott and Elizabeth Cady Stanton gave speeches at the convention, as did Frederick Douglass, a former slave who had become a well-known abolitionist orator. Stanton largely drafted the convention's **Declaration of Sentiments and Resolutions**, which was signed by 68 women and 32 men, including Charlotte Woodward, the only woman at the Seneca Falls Convention who lived long enough to exercise her right to vote. Modeled after the Declaration of Independence, the Seneca Declaration of Sentiments and Resolutions proclaims, "We hold these truths to be self-evident: that all men and women are created equal. . . ." The document listed 18 "repeated injuries and usurpations on the part of man toward woman, having in direct object the establishment of an absolute tyranny over her." These injuries included the lack of woman **suffrage**, the laws of **coverture** that rendered a woman civilly dead upon marriage, the inavailability of higher education for women, and the exclusion of women from the ministry, the law, and medicine. All the resolutions in the Declaration of Sentiments and Resolutions were supported unanimously by the convention participants, with the exception of woman suffrage, which passed by a close margin. Even Lucretia Mott did not support the suffrage resolution, in fear of the ridicule it might invoke. Although the convention attracted little public attention at the time, and

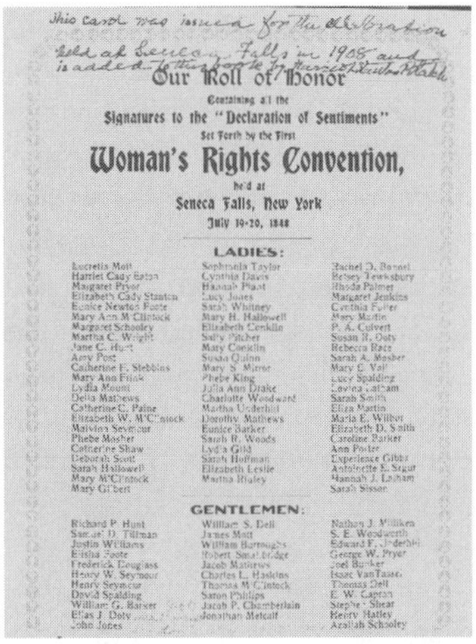

This card was issued for the celebration held at Seneca Falls in 1908 and is added to this

Our Roll of Honor

Containing all the

Signatures to the "Declaration of Sentiments"

Set Forth by the First

Woman's Rights Convention,

held at

Seneca Falls, New York

July 19-20, 1848

LADIES:

Lucretia Mott	Sophronia Taylor	Rachel D. Bonnel
Harriet Cady Eaton	Cynthia Davis	Betsey Tewksbury
Margaret Pryor	Hannah Plant	Rhoda Palmer
Elizabeth Cady Stanton	Lucy Jones	Margaret Jenkins
Eunice Newton Foote	Sarah Whitney	Cynthia Fuller
Mary Ann M'Clintock	Mary H. Hallowell	Mary Martin
Margaret Schooley	Elizabeth Conklin	P. A. Culvert
Martha C. Wright	Sally Pitcher	Susan R. Doty
Jane C. Hunt	Mary Conklin	Rebecca Race
Amy Post	Susan Quinn	Sarah A. Mosher
Catherine F. Stebbins	Mary S. Mirror	Mary E. Vail
Mary Ann Frink	Phebe King	Lucy Spalding
Lydia Mount	Julia Ann Drake	Lovina Latham
Delia Mathews	Charlotte Woodward	Sarah Smith
Catherine C. Paine	Martha Underhill	Eliza Martin
Elizabeth W. M'Clintock	Dorothy Mathews	Maria E. Wilbur
Malvina Seymour	Eunice Barker	Elizabeth D. Smith
Phebe Mosher	Sarah R. Woods	Caroline Barker
Catherine Shaw	Lydia Gild	Ann Porter
Deborah Scott	Sarah Hoffman	Experience Gibbs
Sarah Hallowell	Elizabeth Leslie	Antoinette E. Segur
Mary M'Clintock	Martha Ridley	Hannah J. Latham
Mary Gilbert		Sarah Sisson

GENTLEMEN:

Richard P. Hunt	William S. Dell	Nathan J. Milliken
Samuel D. Tillman	James Mott	S. E. Woodworth
Justin Williams	William Burroughs	Edward F. Underhill
Elisha Foote	Robert Smalldridge	George W. Pryer
Frederick Douglass	Jacob Mathews	Joel Bunker
Henry W. Seymour	Charles L. Hoskins	Isaac VanTassel
Henry Seymour	Thomas M'Clintock	Thomas Dell
David Spalding	Saron Phillips	E. W. Capron
William G. Barker	Jacob P. Chamberlain	Stephen Shear
Elias J. Doty	Jonathan Metcalf	Henry Hatley
John Jones		Azaliah Schooley

Pictured here is a commemorative listing of those who signed the Declaration of Rights and Sentiments issued at the first women's rights convention held at Seneca Falls, New York, in 1848. Library of Congress.

many of those who signed the document later withdrew their names, the Declaration of Sentiments and Resolutions adopted at the Seneca Falls Convention became the focus of women's movements for decades to come. The right of women to vote became law in 1920 with ratification of the **Nineteenth Amendment**; complaints about property rights and divorce law under the laws of **coverture** were largely remedied by the 1920s as well; but equality in educational and occupational opportunities continue to be issues that concern women's rights activists today. The Seneca Falls Convention is recognized as the birth of the **women's movement**; the Declaration of Sentiments and Resolutions articulated the concerns of the women activists and focused their efforts. The success of the convention also encouraged them to continue to fight for women's rights. A 150th anniversary convention was held in Seneca Falls in July 1998 to celebrate the original gathering. (LvA) **See also** Abolition.

Bibliography

Burko, Miriam. *The Ladies of Seneca Falls: The Birth of the Woman's Rights Movement.* New York: Schocken Books, 1974.

Flexner, Eleanor and Ellen Fitzpatrick. *Century of Struggle: The Woman's Rights Movement in the United States.* Cambridge, MA: Harvard University Press, 1996.

Griffith, Elisabeth. *In Her Own Right: The Life of Elizabeth Cady Stanton.* New York: Oxford University Press, 1984.

Settlement House Movement

The Settlement House movement began in England where social reformers created centers to aid the urban poor. In the United States, the Settlement House movement was founded in 1887 by **Jane Addams** and Ellen Starr, wealthy middle-class women who had toured London's Toynbee Hall, the first settlement house. Upon their return to the United States in 1889, Addams and Starr purchased **Hull House** in Chicago and founded the American settlement movement, which focused on helping immigrants adjust to living in a new country.

Hull House served the needs of the poor by providing such basic services as food, health care, clothing, and **child care** together with such more advanced needs as education, job placement, and citizenship training. For Addams, the settlement movement provided an outlet for her personal frustrations with the limited roles society allowed women at the time. Addams saw the settlement movement as a way to open new opportunites to women. Working to help the poor would give women something useful to do that conformed with both society's and their own moral expectations. Settlement houses allowed well-educated women to live independently, forming friendships and contacts helpful to later careers. Eventually the Settlement House movement spread throughout the eastern and midwestern United States, numbering some 400 establishments by 1910. The settlement movement helped the poor while simultaneously increasing the involvement of women in society. It also had the side effect of making women aware of their own limited social and political powers. Settlement houses declined during the 1920s, in part because of quota laws restricting immigration and in part because of increasing opportunities for women in newly formed progressive organizations. (JEH)

Bibliography

Chambers, Charles A. *Seedtime of Reform.* Minneapolis: University of Minnesota Press, 1963.

Davis, Allen F. *American Heroine: The Life and Legend of Jane Addams.* New York: Oxford University Press, 1973.

Seven Sisters Colleges

The "Seven Sisters" colleges are Mount Holyoke (South Hadley, MA), Vassar (Poughkeepsie, NY), Wellesley (Wellesley, MA), Smith (Northampton, MA), Radcliffe (Cambridge, MA), Bryn Mawr (Bryn Mawr, PA), and Barnard (New York, NY). These private northeastern colleges for women were known for their high educational standards and their social ties to the

This turn-of-the-century photo pictures a group of women attending Mount Holyoke College, one of the "seven sisters" colleges. Library of Congress.

seven male Ivy League colleges. The oldest, Mount Holyoke, was founded in 1837 by Mary Lyon; the youngest, Barnard, was established in 1889. Smith College was the first college to be endowed by a woman, Sophia Smith. (SD)

Bibliography

Soloman, Barbara Miller. *In the Company of Educated Women: A History of Women and Higher Education in America.* New Haven, CT: Yale University Press, 1985.

Sex Discrimination

Sex discrimination, the practice of treating men and women differently, is a familiar concept in American law. For example, **Title VII of the Civil Rights Act of 1964** forbids most employment discrimination "because of sex." The Supreme Court refers to "classifications by gender." Long before sex discrimination became a legal term, it was a reality that American society took for granted. Laws denied women the vote, excluded them from occupations, or gave husbands control of their wives' property. But the aftermath of the Civil War and the rise of the women's **suffrage** movement brought sex discrimination onto the political agenda. During Reconstruction (1865–1877), the suffragists urged Congress to protect women's rights along with those of the ex-slaves—or at least the male ex-slaves. Congress refused, but left the door open for change. The Fourteenth Amendment forbids states to deny to "any person" the "equal protection of the laws." The constitutional language is not limited to any particular kind of discrimination. After the amendment was ratified in 1868, the courts had to decide what kinds of discrimination the equal protection clause does and does not allow—including sex discrimination.

The Supreme Court's first major sex discrimination ruling came 40 years after the Fourteenth Amendment was ratified. ***Muller v. Oregon*** (1908) upheld a law that prevented employers from requiring women to work more than 10 hours a day. Whether this decision was a victory or a defeat for women's rights was a moot point. Two interest groups supported this type of so-called "**protective legislation**" for different reasons. "Social feminist" reformers like **Jane Addams** and **Florence Kelley** attacked the long hours, low pay, and dangerous conditions endured by women workers during the Industrial Revolution. But labor unions sought to protect male workers from replacement by women. In *Muller*, the Court saw the issue as the social feminists framed it. "Woman's physical structure and the performance of child-bearing functions" justified "legislation designed for her protection. . . even when like legislation is not necessary for men." Courts followed *Muller* long after it had become clear that the effect of most women's labor laws was to reserve good blue-collar jobs for men. "Sex is a valid basis for classification" became the binding principle to uphold virtually any type of sex discrimination.

The **Nineteenth Amendment**, ratified in 1920, gave women the vote, but this hard-won victory lulled the feminist movement instead of invigorating it. In the first half of the twentieth century, most Americans accepted traditional sex roles and most laws reflected this acceptance. The 1960s brought changes in these attitudes, as in so much else. The publication of **Betty Friedan**'s ***The Feminine Mystique***, President John F. Kennedy's appointment of a Presidential Commission on the Status of Women, and two new anti-discrimination laws drew attention to women's rights. Friedan's book was a bold feminist statement for its time. But the other developments did not live up to the expectations of many women. The Commission's report glorified women's role in the family, opposed the **Equal Rights Amendment (ERA)**, and supported protective legislation. The **Equal Pay Act of 1963** applied only to men and women in the same jobs, not to the female "job ghetto" where the majority of women worked. And the inclusion of sex in the Civil Rights Act of 1964 resulted from an effort by Southern Democrats and conservative Republicans to ridicule the bill to death. The bill's supporters refused the bait, but the final version of the law included a big enough loophole to render most of Title VII useless. It allowed discrimination in cases where sex, religion, or national origin (but not race) was a "bona fide occupational qualification" (BFOQ.) Observers called the inclusion of sex a "joke," while the administrator in charge of enforcing Title VII called it a "fluke." But the resurgence of the feminist movement in the late 1960s turned Title VII into a powerful weapon against legalized sexism and changed the law of sex discrimination forever.

Title VII gave individuals the right to bring complaints to the **Equal Employment Opportunity Commission (EEOC)** and to sue the employer if the EEOC could not resolve the complaint. The federal courts that heard the first cases acted on the assumption that Congress had meant what it said, whether it had or not. Within five years, protective legislation was history. In ***Weeks v. Southern Bell*** (1969), a federal appeals court ruled that a Georgia law prohibiting women from lifting more than 30 pounds at work did not create a BFOQ. Lorena Weeks could not be rejected outright for a telephone switchman's job because "Title VII rejects just this type of romantic paternalism as unduly Victorian and instead vests the individual woman with the power to decide whether or not to take on unromantic tasks." Later that year, the EEOC ruled that Title VII pre-empted all contradictory state laws. Sometimes the BFOQ defense works—for example, the Supreme Court sustained Alabama's same-sex rule for prison guards and prisoners—but outright sex discrimination rarely survives a Title VII challenge. This law has helped women of every socioeconomic status, race, ethnic background, and education level leave the job ghetto.

The federal government did not stop with Title VII. Congress has increased the powers of federal agencies, limited sex discrimination in areas other than employment, and negated decisions by an increasingly conservative Supreme Court. The EEOC issued guidelines in 1980 defining sexual harassment as a type of sex discrimination. **Title IX of the Educational Amendments Act of 1972**, which forbade sex discrimination in any educational program receiving federal funds, has been one of the most effective civil rights laws. Public discussion about Title IX has centered around its application to athletic programs and the reluctance of colleges and universities to spend as much money and effort on women's sports as on men's. The controversy over sports has obscured the effect of Title IX in academic programs. Here, the compliance has been uneventful and the results dramatic. For example, the proportion of women law students in the U.S. tripled between 1971 and 1974. Since lawyers are more likely than the average American to become legislators, it is probably no accident that the number of women elected to offices at the state and national levels has increased.

Constitutional law has also changed. The ERA was not ratified, but the Supreme Court revisited the equal protection issue. The Court has compromised between the old "blank check" and treating sex discrimination as presumptively unconstitutional, like race discrimination. Instead, "classifications by gender must serve important governmental objectives and be substantially related to these objectives" (***Craig v. Boren***, 1976). Men have benefitted at least as much as women from the *Craig* rule. ***Orr v. Orr*** (1979), for instance, overturned a men-only alimony law, while ***Mississippi University for Women v. Hogan*** (1982) ordered a nursing school to admit men. But the most recent ruling, ***U.S. v. Virginia*** (1996), was an important victory for women's rights. It rejected the Virginia Military Institute's (VMI) argument that "inherent differences" between the sexes justified its men-only admissions policy. Justice **Ruth Bader Ginsburg** found these differences "cause for celebration, but not for denigration of either sex or for artificial constraints on an individual's opportunity."

Changes in the law have loosened many of these constraints. However, civil rights laws have not eliminated sex segregation in the labor force or made women welcome at VMI. Women's earnings still lag behind men's. Part of the problem lies in the inherent limitations of the legal system. To get laws enforced, people have to bring cases; the time, money, and energy required to do this are powerful disincentives to litigation. Two formidable constraints on women's opportunities still exist: the conflicts between job and family and indirect discrimination against women workers.

The working world has yet to accommodate so-called "maternal functions." Mandatory maternity leaves and employee benefits plans that excluded pregnancy and childbirth remained commonplace years after passage of Title VII. The Supreme Court has yet to discover any sex discrimination in these rules. ***General Electric Company v. Gilbert*** (1976) found no conflict between Title VII and the exclusion of pregnancy-related conditions from G.E.'s benefits plan because the plan actually paid out as much on the average to women employees as to men. This ruling bewildered the dissenters, the public, and Congress, which reversed it with the **Pregnancy Discrimination Act** of 1978 (PDA). But the PDA did not resolve the pregnancy issue. ***California Federal Savings and Loan v. Guerra*** (1987) presented a conflict between the PDA and a state law requiring employers to grant maternity leaves. When Lillian Garland tried to return to her job, California Federal insisted the PDA pre-empted the law and refused to put her back on the payroll. Garland's case was no simpler for feminists than the old protective laws had been. The **National Organization for Women (NOW)** argued that guaranteed maternity leaves would discourage employers from hiring women of childbearing age, even though Title VII forbade this—an implicit omission that civil rights laws are hard to enforce. But other feminists insisted that such leaves were necessary accommodations to women's responsibilities. The Court found California's law compatible with the purpose of the PDA: "to guarantee women the right to participate fully and equally in the workforce, without denying them the fundamental right to full participation in family life." The **Family and Medical Leave Act** of 1993 gives male and female workers the right to 12 weeks of unpaid leave to care for family members. In a political climate increasingly hostile toward government control of business, this may be as far as the law will go toward helping women reconcile job and family responsibilities.

Some employment policies are gender-neutral on their face but have a disparate impact on men and women. A minimum height requirement, for example, will exclude more women than men because women tend to be shorter. Veteran's preferences in civil service jobs will have a similar effect, since the vast majority of veterans are male. The fate of policy rules like these depends on whether the cases involve statutes or constitutional provisions. The Supreme Court sustained a Massachusetts veterans' preference rule in 1979 even though it virtually excluded women the age of World War II veterans from all but clerical civil service jobs. The Court cited precedents which held that facially neutral rules with a disparate impact are constitutional unless they are arbitrary or were intended to discriminate by race or sex. But height requirements for police officers fell under Title VII. As amended in 1991, the law stipulates that indirectly discriminatory rules are illegal unless the employer can show that the rule is a business necessity.

Disparate impact can be more subtle than these examples. Employers' standards may be imprecise. Decisions to grant tenure to a professor or to make a lawyer a partner in a firm, for instance, often involve criteria like "originality" or "excellence." These criteria are not like being 5'6" tall; the judgments are subjective. Personnel decisions couched in such neutral terms may be perfectly honest—or they may be rationalizations for discrimination. Women who sue employers in these cases usually lose. Judges tend to accept facially neutral explanations from fellow professionals. Some plaintiffs and government officials have argued that sex discrimination exists if the proportion of women in a given occupation is smaller than their proportion in the available labor pool. *EEOC v. Sears, Roebuck* (1986) categorically rejected this position. The Court agreed with Sears that the scarcity of women commissioned salespeople reflected the women's own choices.

Since the 1970s, any institution receiving federal funds must provide evidence of efforts to hire and promote qualified women, racial minorities, disabled people, and Vietnam veterans. State and local governments and private companies also have **affirmative action** plans. Affirmative action is designed to counterbalance any remaining employer prejudice, overt or covert. These programs have become increasingly unpopular in the 1990s, struck down by courts and voter initiatives and attacked by the Republican majority in Congress. But these were race-based programs, and race discrimination is judged by tougher standards than sex discrimination. ***Johnson v. Transportation Agency of Santa Clara County, California*** (1987) sustained a city's decision to "consider sex as one factor" in its hiring.

Maternity leaves and affirmative action confront lawmakers with a double bind. Rules that favor women may be necessary to assure sexual equality in fact as well as on paper. But these legal remedies do constitute sex discrimination. Therefore, they may violate the laws that were passed to promote equality. American law does not distinguish between discrimination in favor of a disadvantaged group and discrimination against it. The carefully neutral term "sex discrimination" reflects a choice about how to construct and interpret the social world. The neutrality obscures the fact that most "sex discrimination" has been instituted by men to limit women. Constitutional doctrine has enabled men to reinforce their privileged position. And, from *Muller* to *Guerra*, disagreement has always existed about who, exactly, is helped or hurt by certain laws. The law cannot eradicate sex discrimination from American society by itself. But the law has given women tools to remedy their disadvantages. (JAB)

Bibliography

Baer, Judith A. *The Chains of Protection: The Judicial Response to Women's Labor Legislation*. Westport, CT: Greenwood Press, 1978.

———. *Women in American Law*. 2nd ed. New York: Holmes & Meier Publishers, Inc., 1996.

Harrison, Cynthia E. *On Account of Sex: The Politics of Women's Issues, 1945-68*. Berkeley: University of California Press, 1988.

Hoff, Joan. *Law, Gender, and Injustice: A Legal History of U.S. Women*. New York: New York University Press, 1991.

Kanowitz, Leo. *Women and the Law: The Unfinished Revolution*. 2nd ed. Albuquerque: University of New Mexico Press, 1969.

Lemons, J. Stanley. *The Woman Citizen: Social Feminism in the 1920s*. Urbana: University of Illinois Press, 1973.

Mezey, Susan Gluck. *In Pursuit of Equality: Women, Public Policy, and the Federal Courts*. New York: St. Martin's Press, 1992.

Rupp, Leila J. and Verta Taylor. *Survival in the Doldrums: The American Women's Rights Movement, 1945 to the 1960s*. New York: Oxford University Press, 1987.

Jeanne Shaheen (1947–)

In 1996, Jeanne Shaheen, a Democrat, became the first woman to be elected governor of the state of New Hampshire. Governor Shaheen has pursued a fiscally conservative approach to state spending while championing such causes as public kindergarten and increased tobacco taxes. Shaheen is seen as a rising star in the **Democratic Party**. Prior to being elected governor, Shaheen served in the New Hampshire state senate.

Bibliography

Ghioto, Gary. "Torr, Shaheen Trading Barbs and Stands on Issues." *Boston Globe 1990* (October 7, 1990): 10.

Maiona, Justin G. "The Consummate Politician: Jeanne Shaheen Is Doing to the Republican Majority in New Hampshire What Bill Clinton Is Doing in Washington." *National Review* 49, no. 16 (September 1, 1997): 24.

Donna Edna Shalala (1941–)

Donna Shalala assumed responsibility for leading the United States Department of Health and Human Services on January 22, 1993, as a member of the Clinton cabinet. During her tenure, Shalala has had to preside over a profound change in national **welfare** policy. The federal government has given the states broad powers to administer their own welfare policies, placed limitations on benefits, and required that recipients find employment within two years, all actions marking a distinct break with the past 60 years of welfare policy. Before becoming secretary of health and human services, Shalala served as chancellor of the University of Wisconsin—Madison from 1988 to 1993, the first woman to run a Big Ten university. She was president of Hunter College at the City University of New York from 1980 until 1988. Her prior government service was in the Carter administration as an assistant secretary in the Department of Housing and Urban Development. Shalala's academic research is on the political economy of state and local governments. She served in the **Peace Corps** (1962–1964) following graduation from the Western College for Women, and received her Ph.D. from the Maxwell School of Citizenship and Public Affairs at Syracuse University in 1970. (KM)

Bibliography

Kopkind, Andrew. "It's Lonely Out There on the Left." *The Nation* (February 22, 1993): 217, 221, 237.

Toobin, Jeffrey R. "The Shalala Strategy." *New Yorker* (April 26, 1993): 53-59, 62.

Anna Howard Shaw (1847–1919)

In October 1880, Anna Shaw became the first woman minister of the Methodist Church. A lecturer and organizer for the Massachusetts Woman Suffrage Association from 1885 to

Active in both the temperance and suffrage movements, Anna Shaw was the first woman minister of the Methodist Church. Library of Congress, National American Woman Suffrage Association Collection.

1887, Shaw was superintendent of the Franchise Department of the National Woman's Christian Temperance Union from 1888 to 1892. Shaw also served as vice-president of the **National American Woman Suffrage Association (NAWSA)** from 1892 until 1904 and as president from 1904 to 1915. During World War I, she worked as chair of the Woman's Committee of the United States Council of National Defense. **See also** Suffrage; Women's Christian Temperance Union.

BIBLIOGRAPHY

Fonn, Barbara R. "Anna Howard Shaw and Woman's Work." *Frontiers* 4, no. 3 (1979): 21-25.

Shaw, Anna Howard. "Equal Suffrage—A Problem of Political Justice." *Annuals of the American Academy of Political and Social Science* 56 (November 1914): 93-98.

Spencer, Ralph W. "Anna Howard Shaw." *Methodist History* 13, no. 2 (1975): 33-51.

Sheppard-Towner Maternity and Infancy Protection Act (1921)

In 1921, Congress enacted the Sheppard-Towner Act, providing $1,250,000 in federal matching funds to the states for the development of the first national public health program targeting poor pregnant women, mothers, and children. The **Children's Bureau** administered the program and provided the mechanism for cooperation between the states and the federal government. Despite high levels of congressional support, opponents were able to limit the program primarily to health education rather than the direct provision of medical services. Opposition came from two sources—the American Medical Association, which opposed having the Children's Bureau administer medical services, and social conservatives, who opposed all government social welfare programs. Although the program succeeded in meeting its goal, opponents managed to eliminate it in 1929.

Despite its short duration, the Sheppard-Towner Act established two important precedents. First, its passage represented a fundamental shift toward greater governmental responsibility for the health and well-being of citizens. As the first federally funded and administered social welfare program, Sheppard-Towner served as a model and precursor for the Social Security Act of 1935 and other New Deal programs. Second, its passage also was a milestone in the history of women's involvement in politics. Prior to the 1920 passage of the **Nineteenth Amendment** granting woman **suffrage**, legislators had tended to ignore women's issues and to dismiss lobbying by women's groups. The Sheppard-Towner bill was the first significant post-Nineteenth Amendment legislation that had strong support from women. Female social workers, women administrators from the Children's Bureau, and representatives from the newly formed League of Women Voters lobbied on behalf of the bill, and its passage marked the first time that members of Congress had consciously tried to appeal to women voters by enacting legislation that women supported. When politicians discovered in subsequent elections that the newly enfranchised women voters did not vote as a unified block, they stopped worrying about appealing specifically to women voters and opponents of the act were able to muster enough votes to repeal it. Yet, by the 1930s, the federal government was playing a large role in the crafting and funding of a wide range of social welfare policies of the Sheppard-Towner model, and women administrators, who had grained valuable experience in the act's administration, were central to the creation of these new programs. **See also** National League of Women Voters. (NL; JS)

BIBLIOGRAPHY

Kerber, Linda K., Alice Kessler-Harris, and Kathryn Kish Sklar. *U.S. History as Women's History: New Feminist Essays.* Chapel Hill: The University of North Carolina Press, 1995.

Gordon, Linda. *Pitied But Not Entitled.* Cambridge, MA: Harvard University Press, 1994.

Gordon, Linda, ed. *Women, the State, and Welfare.* Madison: The University of Wisconsin Press, 1990.

Graham, Sara Hunter. *Woman's Suffrage and the New Democracy.* New Haven, CT: Yale University Press, 1996.

Laurie Shields (1932–1989)

With **Tish Sommers**, Laurie Shields cofounded the Alliance for Displaced Homemakers in 1974. Shields continued her affiliation with the organization until her death in 1989. The Alliance has twice changed its name since its founding—to The National Displaced Homemakers Network for Women's Employment in 1978 and to Women Work! The National Network for Women's Employment in 1993. Shields and Sommers also founded the Older Women's League Educational Fund in 1978, and Shields remained with the organization until after it was renamed the Older Women's League in 1980. Throughout her career, Shields worked for legislation to combat **poverty** among elderly women, for homemakers' rights, and for other women's programs.

BIBLIOGRAPHY

Shields, Laurie. *Displaced Homemakers.* New York: McGraw-Hill, 1980.

Sommers, Tish and Laurie Shields. *Women Take Care.* Denver: Triad Publishing, 1987.

Shirtwaist Workers' Strike of 1909

On November 24, 1909, more than 20,000 waistmakers in Manhattan and Brooklyn, New York, went on strike. The workers, organized by the **International Ladies' Garment Workers Union**, demanded an immediate 10 percent wage increase, improvements in working conditions, and union recognition. The public sympathized with the strikers, mostly women, who were violently harassed by police and private guards. Although strikers quickly reached agreements with those employers most hurt by the strike, other firms simply increased production in Philadelphia facilities. In February 1910, the union reached agreements on wages and working conditions with 400 firms, but did not gain industry-wide union recognition. Without recognition, many of the union's gains proved fleeting. (AMD)

Bibliography

Foner, Philip Sheldon. *Women and the American Labor Movement.* New York: Free Press, 1982.

Edna Oakes Simpson (1891–1979)

Edna Simpson was elected to the U.S. House of Representatives from Illinois in November 1958, nine days after the death of her husband, eight-term congressman Sidney Simpson. She served one term from January 3, 1959, to January 3, 1961. She never spoke on the floor of the House during her term. A Republican, Simpson decided not to seek re-election in 1960 and retired from national politics.

Bibliography

"Salute to Three Freshman." *National Business Woman* 38 (February 1959): 12.

Louise M. Slaughter (1929–)

Louise Slaughter, a Democrat, began her political career by serving in the Monroe County (NY) legislature from 1976 to 1979; during this time, she was also the regional coordinator for the New York Department of State. In 1979, she was appointed regional coordinator for the office of Lieutenant Governor Mario Cuomo. From 1982 to 1986, she served in the New York state assembly. In 1986, Slaughter was elected to the U.S. House of Representatives, and has been re-elected to each successive Congress. She serves on the powerful House Rules Committee, and has been an important advocate for women's health care issues.

Bibliography

Barr, Stephen. "'Forging' Alleged." *The Washington Post* 118 (October 19, 1995): A4.

Slavery and Women

Slavery began in England's American colonies in the seventeenth century, with slave ships constantly replenishing the number of African slaves. Unsuccessful attempts were made to end slavery with the Declaration of Independence in 1776 and the United States Constitution in 1787, but slavery opponents only achieved a ban on the importation of slaves after 1808. This ban was achieved because slave owners had discovered that slave women could be bred to produce new slaves. Each year as many as one-fifth of all slave women of childbearing age delivered a child. Many of these children were the product of rape. Health complications were common, and maternal and infant mortality was high, as was the incidence of what is now known as Sudden Infant Death Syndrome (SIDS).

The documentation of the lives of slave women comes in large part from diaries and word-of-mouth stories. Two of the most prominent former slaves who helped to document this history were **Sojourner Truth** and **Harriet Tubman**. Truth traveled the country advocating **abolition** and women's rights. Tubman, best known for her role as a conductor on the Underground Railroad, also worked for the Union army. Other indications of the lot of slave women come from abolitionist and statesman Frederick Douglass, a former slave, who explained that he never knew his own mother, and from Linda Brent, a slave who hid in a concealed garret for almost seven years to escape what she called the "mortifications" of being a slave woman. (EP)

Bibliography

Brent, Linda. "From Incidents in the Life of A Slave Girl." In Sandra M. Gilbert and Susan Gubar, eds. *The Norton Anthology of Literature by Women.* New York: W.W. Norton, 1985.

White, Deborah Gray. "The Nature of Female Slavery." In Linda K. Kerber and Jane Sherron DeHart, eds. *Women's America: Refocusing the Past.* New York: Oxford University Press, 1991.

Eleanor Smeal (1939–)

A woman's rights activist and author, Eleanor Smeal is a former three-term president of the **National Organization for Women (NOW)**. Before becoming national president, she headed the state NOW organization in her native Pennsylvania. Smeal served two consecutive terms as NOW president from 1977 to 1982. She led the organization through some of its most tumultuous times, including the battle over the ratification of the **Equal Rights Amendment (ERA)**. During Smeal's first two terms as NOW president, the organization more than doubled in size and gained political clout and prestige. However, controversy also marked her terms; Smeal was often criticized for being too confrontational.

In 1984, she published *Why and How Women Will Elect the Next President*, a call to women to become more actively engaged in politics. She was elected to a third term as NOW president in 1985 but left in 1987 to engage in a "feminization of power" tour to recruit and campaign for women candidates in the 1988 elections. Smeal is also a cofounder of the Feminist Majority Foundation, an organization that seeks to empower women by supporting research and distributing information. (SJW)

Bibliography

Doan, Michael and Patricia A. Avery. "Warrior for Women's Rights." *U.S.News and World Report* 100 (March 24, 1986): 11.

Koeppel, Barbara. "Eleanor Smeal." *The Progressive* 59, no. 3 (March 1995): 32-34.

Abby Hadassah Smith (1797–1878)

In 1873, Abby Smith attended the first meeting of the Association of the Advancement of Women and soon after began speaking in public for woman **suffrage** with her sister, **Julia Evelina Smith**. The sisters became involved in court hearings from 1874 to 1876, successfully using the Revolutionary cry of "no taxation without representation" to secure local suffrage for women.

Bibliography

Hale, Addie Stancliffe. "Those Five Amazing Smith Sisters." *Hartford Courant* (May 15, 1932).

Julia Evelina Smith (1792–1886)

In 1869, Julia Smith attended a woman **suffrage** meeting in Hartford, Connecticut, and soon began speaking on the issue with her sister, **Abby Hadassah Smith**. Between 1874 and 1876, the sisters became involved in court hearings that tested the right of a state or locality to impose taxes on land owned by citizens (i.e., women) who were not allowed to vote. The Smiths eventually prevailed in their argument that it was unlawful to tax the land if its women owners were not permitted to vote on the taxes. Continuing to speak on woman suffrage issues, Julia Smith appeared at a January 1878 hearing before the Senate Committee on Privileges and Elections arguing for women's suffrage.

Bibliography

Hale, Addie Stancliffe. "Those Five Amazing Smith Sisters." *Hartford Courant* (May 15, 1932).

Linda A. Smith (1950–)

Linda Smith, a Republican, served in the lower house of the Washington legislature from 1983 to 1986 before moving to the Washington state senate in 1987. During her career in Washington State, she managed seven tax preparation offices and served on committees for resources and small businesses, and on the Endangered Species Act Task Force. In 1994, Smith declined to stand for re-election to the state senate and was instead elected to the U.S. House of Representatives. In the 105th Congress, Smith served as vice-chair for the Subcommittee on Tax, Finance and Exports.

Bibliography

Bowermaster, David. "She Just Wants to 'Clean Congress'." *U.S. News & World Report* 120, no. 13 (April 1, 1996): 20.

Greenblatt, Alan. "Rep. Smith Becomes First to Challenge Murray." *Congressional Quarterly Weekly Report* 55, no. 20 (May 17, 1997): 1153.

Leiter, Lisa. "Congress: Campaign Finance—Members Play Hardball with Some Soft Money." *Insight on the News* 12, no. 32 (August 26, 1996): 15.

Rosin, Hanna. "Invasion of the Church Ladies: The GOP Bid to Close the Gender Gap." *The New Republic* 212, no. 17 (April 24, 1995): 20.

Margaret Chase Smith (1897–1995)

Margaret Chase Smith of Maine served as a Republican in the United States Senate from 1949 until 1973. Early in her first Senate term, on June 1, 1950, Smith delivered a speech on the floor of the Senate that became famous as the "Declaration of Conscience." In it, she denounced Wisconsin Republican Senator Joseph R. McCarthy, who in February 1950 had made unsubstantiated accusations that communists had infiltrated the State Department. Smith stated that she did "not want to see the party ride to political victory on the four horsemen of calumny—fear, ignorance, bigotry and smear." She also called for national unity in the face of McCarthy's vilifying tactics. Smith was the first woman elected to the Senate in her own right, the first woman to seek the presidential nomination of her party (in 1964), the first woman elected to a leadership post in the Senate, and the first woman to serve in both chambers of Congress. Smith initially came to Congress as secretary to her husband, Clyde H. Smith. After he died in office, she was elected to his seat in the House of Representatives on June 3, 1940. She served in the House until moving to the Senate on January 3, 1949. In the House, Smith maneuvered the Women's Armed Services Integration Act of 1948 out of the Armed Services Committee, where there was substantial opposition, to the floor of the House, where there was strong support. Passage of the act insured regular status, instead of limited reserve status, for women in the armed services. Smith was defeated for re-election in 1972 in part because of her unwillingness to engage in contemporary campaign tactics; she did not hire campaign staff, did not advertise, and refused to campaign in Maine during weekdays while the Senate was in session. (KM)

Bibliography

Schmidt, Patricia L. *Margaret Chase Smith: Beyond Convention.* Orono: University of Maine Press, 1996.

Smith, Margaret Chase. *Declaration of Conscience.* Edited by William C. Lewis, Jr. New York: Doubleday, 1972.

Mary Louise Smith (1914–1997)

Mary Smith was the first woman to head the Republican National Committee when she served as chair from 1974 until 1977. A dedicated party member, Smith began her involvement with the **Republican Party** in the 1950s. She served on the national committee from 1964 until 1984 and the executive board from 1969 to 1984. Smith also served on the U.S. Commission on Civil Rights in 1982 and 1983, but was forced off the commission by the Reagan administration for her more liberal views. Pro-choice and a committed feminist who listed **Betty Friedan**'s ***The Feminine Mystique*** as one of the most important books she had read, Smith's more liberal Eisenhower Republicanism was out of step with many in the more conservative Republican Party of the 1980s.

Bibliography

Cranberg, Gilbert. "Too Moderate for Today's GOP." *The Washington Post* (September 4, 1997): A19.

Mann, Judy. "GOP Women." *The Washington Post* (February 15, 1984): B1.

Virginia Smith (1911–)

Virginia Smith of Nebraska was first elected to the U.S. House of Representatives in 1975. A Republican, she was re-elected every term until her retirement in 1991. Smith maintained a career-long interest in the agricultural programs of Congress that directly affected her rural farming district. By the time of her retirement, she was the dean of Republican women in the House as well as a member of the powerful Appropriations Committee.

Bibliography

Bovard, James. "Lock the Barn! The Farm Bill's Coming." *The Washington Post* (January 21, 1990): B5.

Havemann, Judith. "Two in GOP Try to Block Pay Raise for Congress." *The Washington Post* (January 7, 1987): A14.
Women in Congress. Washington, DC: Government Printing Office, 1991.

Smith-Hughes Act of 1917

The Smith-Hughes Act of 1917 was a victory for those who favored specific trade training for specific jobs. The act's primary intent was to foster vocational education among youth age 14 or over, for the purpose of useful employment in areas such as agriculture, home economics, trade, and industry. Matching federal funds could be used to pay the salaries of teachers in the occupations named in the act and to train vocational teachers. The act also established a Federal Board for Vocational Education (FBVE) to administer the program and monitor the use of federal funds.

The Smith-Hughes Act helped legitimize the idea that preparation for work was a primary function of public schooling, and, by assuming that job training in school required federal support, constituted a major step in the evolution of the use of education as a tool of federal social and economic policy. However, critics of the program contended that the act established a bifurcated system whereby high school girls who had previously taken college-prep courses were now encouraged to take vocational classes to better prepare them as future wives and mothers, or to obtain positions in a sex-segregated job market. (JJK)

Bibliography

Daniel, Robert L. *American Women in the 20th Century: The Festival of Life*. Orlando, FL: Harcourt Brace Jovanovich Publishers, 1987.
Kantor, Harvey A. *Learning to Earn*. Madison: University of Wisconsin Press, 1988.

Smith-Lever Act of 1914

In 1914, Democratic President Woodrow Wilson called the Smith-Lever Act "one of the most significant and far-reaching measures for the education of adults ever adopted by any government." The Smith-Lever Act was intended to improve life for both men and women who lived on American farms. The act provided farmers with instructional services in how to better grow, process, and market their crops. Additionally, the act provided federal financing for home economics curricula in coeducational land-grant colleges and universities established by the Morrill Act of 1862.

While proponents contend that the Smith-Lever Act had a positive impact in stimulating the establishment of agricultural extension education, not only in farm practices, but also in child rearing, health and nutrition, and many cultural activities, the program also had its critics. Home economics programs developed under Smith-Lever pervaded curriculums not only at the high school level, but also at the college level. Although both men and women were being educated in larger numbers in the 1920s, the home economics training provided under Smith-Lever was steering the two sexes along different paths after graduation. Unlike education during the previous generation, colleges in the 1920s were encouraging women to follow more traditional gender roles, producing housewives, rather than leaders in the academic or business communities. (JJK)

Bibliography

Cubberly, Ellwood P. *Public Education in the United States*. New York: Houghton Mifflin, 1934.
Good, Harry G. and James D. Teller. *A History of American Education, Third Edition*. New York: Macmillan, 1973.
Woloch, Nancy. *Women and the American Experience*. New York: Knopf, 1984.

Olympia Jean Snowe (1947–)

Republican Olympia Snowe, the senior senator from Maine, is the first Greek-American woman to serve in Congress. After serving Maine's 2nd District in the U.S. House of Representatives since 1979, Snowe ran in 1994 for the Senate seat vacated by the retirement of Democratic Majority Leader George Mitchell. Senator Snowe, a moderate Republican, votes with conservatives on economic issues but takes more liberal positions on social issues, particularly those affecting women. Snowe championed child support enforcement in the Senate and was an outspoken supporter of **abortion** rights at the Republican National Convention in 1996. Before her election to Congress, Snowe served in both chambers of the Maine legislature. She was elected in 1973 to fill the vacancy in the Maine House of Representatives left by the death of her husband, Peter Snowe. After serving for two terms in the state house, she was elected to the Maine senate in 1976, serving one term. Senator Snowe married former Maine Governor John R. McKernan, Jr., in 1989. **See also** Child Support Enforcement Amendment of 1984. (KM)

Bibliography

Bingham, Clara. *Women on the Hill*. New York: Time Books, 1997.

Social Security

Declining birth rates, increased life expectancy, and the baby boom generation have all contributed to transforming the elderly into a significant portion of the current population. There are in the late 1990s over 10 times as many people age 65 and older than there were at the turn of the century. Hidden within this phenomenal growth is the fact that women continue to outlive men. Coupling a woman's life expectancy of 79.6 years with a trend towards early retirement, many women will spend a considerable number of years in retirement. And because many of these women do not have adequate investments and pensions, or sufficient Social Security income (Old Age and Survivor's Insurance [OASI]) to support them during their retirement years, financial hardship has become a serious problem among older women.

We are indeed witnessing the "graying of America." Until the twentieth century, high birth rates balanced high death rates and kept the United States a youthful nation. Yet, with the progress made during this century in the areas of nutrition, sanitation, and vaccinations, mortality rates have decreased and life expectancy has increased. In addition, the "baby boomers," those persons born during a period of high birth rates (1946–1964), are themselves beginning to enter middle and late adulthood. For the first time in our history there are more people age 65 and over than there are teenagers. Still, among this aging population the mortality rate for women has been declining much more rapidly than that for men. Women at any age are less likely to die than men, and continue to outlive men on the average of seven to nine years. This has then produced an imbalance within the aging population, creating a situation where there are now more women than there are men over the age of 65.

While there is no mandatory retirement age for most people in the United States, few people continue working past the age of 65. In fact, nearly 90 percent of Americans age 65 and older are retired, even though many are intellectually and physically capable of working. No doubt retirement has some advantages for the larger society, such as allowing younger workers to fill the positions left vacant by those who retire. But there are serious personal disadvantages. Retirement means facing a new life in a society that views an individual's worth partly in terms of their occupational status. Work is one of the most important aspects of our lives, as our lifestyle and our life chances are directly affected by both the work we do and the income earned through our work. Thus, retirement can not only diminish an individual's self-worth, but can negatively impact an individual's chances for a productive and satisfying life. Surprisingly, attitudes about retirement are generally favorable. Those who do not evaluate their lives in retirement positively are mostly those persons who are entering retirement, or expect to live in retirement, with fewer economic resources. Attitudes toward retirement are positively related to financial security.

One of the most pressing problems an individual faces during retirement is a decrease in annual income. Social Security (OASI), the nation's basic method of providing income to the elderly, was not intended to be an individual's only source of income during the retirement years. In fact, Social Security was designed to supplement an individual's pension, personal savings, and investments. Today, however, Social Security has become a primary source of income for persons aged 62 and older, and the only source of income for many. As such, three immediate problems arise when Social Security and women are considered: (1) not all women are covered by Social Security; (2) Social Security benefits are dependent upon the amount of income one has been paid; and (3) Social Security benefits are dependent upon the length of time one has paid into the program.

First, because Social Security is funded through a proportional tax on earnings in occupations not excluded from coverage, a woman who has worked as a homemaker all her life receives no financial credit for the work she has done. If she is married and her husband is employed and has paid into the system, she is then entitled to share what her husband receives. If, however, she is divorced, for her to be eligible to declare any entitlement upon her ex-spouse's benefits, she must have been married to him for a minimum of 10 years. Thus, some women, such as unmarried women not working outside the home or unemployed women divorced within a few years of marriage, are left unprotected.

Second, because women are almost always paid less than men and have more interruptions during their careers, women receive lower monthly Social Security benefits. Historically, women and men have been concentrated in occupations considered to be appropriate for each sex. Men, for example, are concentrated in such occupations as skilled crafts, operative jobs, and labor, while women are concentrated in clerical, sales, and other service occupations. One of the most serious consequences of this dual labor market is the lack of economic equity: full-time female workers earn only about 74.6 percent of what male workers earn. In fact women with college degrees can expect to earn just slightly more than male high school dropouts, but less than men with high school diplomas. Just as women often turn to part-time employment to accommodate flexible scheduling for housework and caregiving responsibilities, many women leave the paid labor force, temporarily or permanently. Leaving the paid labor force on a short-term basis can indeed have long-term consequences resulting from loss of professional contacts or professional skills. Women on the average spend more than 10 years out of the paid labor force to provide care for family members, whereas men generally spend a little over a year out for the same reasons. Again, these years without earnings result in lower Social Security benefits.

As a result of a decrease in income, one of the most serious problems women face during their retirement years is the prospect of **poverty**. Although the U.S. government has greatly improved the economic conditions of the elderly population, income security for women in their later years continues to lag. In fact, elderly women constitute one of the poorest segments of our society. According to government studies, despite Social Security, at the beginning of this decade, 42 percent of older separated women, 24 percent of older divorced women, and 19 percent of older widows lived in poverty. The situation is even worse for women of color, as poverty rates are three times as high for African-American women as for white women. Because women live longer and have not paid as much in Social Security, older women are many times more likely than older men to live in poverty.

Poverty refers to a condition in which people do not have enough money to maintain a standard of living that includes the basic necessities of life, including adequate food, clothing, and shelter. Yet, in the later years of life, a lack of financial resources can have an impact far beyond food, clothing, and shelter. With the natural process of aging comes increasing physical limitations which then lead to a need for additional services. For example, after age 75, tasks such as hanging drapes, washing windows, and heavy yard work are more likely to be hired out rather than done by the older adult. Because of this, lack of income can severely impact the maintenance of a home and send many elderly women into a situation of living in substandard housing. In addition, physical changes may affect the ability of some older adults to drive, making paid transportation vital for such tasks as grocery shopping. A lack of finances will also directly affect health care needs, which, for the elderly, are greater than those of the young. Generally speaking, if an older woman lacks the resources to remain financially solvent, her aging process will be less successful than that of someone who can afford to live a lifestyle that includes the basic necessities.

Poverty among elderly women has often been investigated, and the United States has made progress in combating poverty among the elderly. Social Security benefits have increased and are now protected from inflation; Medicare provides the elderly with a national health insurance; Supplemental Security Income provides a guaranteed minimum income for those in need, and the Older Americans Act supports services for the elderly. As a consequence, the poverty rate has declined. Still, to combat the problems that aging women face, many have proposed a re-evaluation of the current Social Security system. Some critics have argued for a flat benefit for all persons who reach age 62 that would provide a satisfactory standard of living for both women and men; or for subjecting couples to earnings sharing, which would improve the situation of divorced women, widows, and women who earned few dollars while employed. Earnings sharing would raise the typically lower Social Security payments of elderly woman. Others have argued that penalizing a woman for leaving the labor force to care for a family member is unfair. One proposal is to either reimburse wages lost during the years women spend caring for a family member or to calculate a minimum wage standard to replace lost wages resulting from caregiving.

Because financial difficulties have been identified as problematic for aging women, retirement and Social Security policies likely will continue to undergo development, revision, and implementation to ensure that members of the fastest growing segment of our population can live their older lives without the fear of impoverishment. (NJM) **See also** Economic Equity Act (1986).

Bibliography

Atchley, Robert C. *Social Forces and Aging*. Belmont, CA: Wadsworth Publishing Co., 1994.

Barrow, Georgia M. *Aging, the Individual, and Society*. Minneapolis: West Publishing Co, 1992.

Eitzen, D. Stanley and Maxine Baca Zinn. *Social Problems*. Boston: Allyn and Bacon, 1997.

Hochschild, Arlene. *The Second Shift*. New York: Viking, 1989.

Kingson, Eric R. and Regina O'Grady-LeShane. "The Effects of Caregiving on Women's Social Security Benefits." *The Gerontologist* 33 (1993): 230-39.

Lamanna, Mary Ann and Agnes Riedmann. *Marriages and Families: Making Choices in a Diverse Society*. Belmont, CA: Wadsworth Publishing Co, 1997.

Meyer, Madonna Hanington. "Making Claims as Worker or Wives: The Distribution of Social Security Benefits." *American Sociological Review* 61 (June 1996): 449-65.

Olson, Laura Katz. "Women and Social Security: A Progressive Approach." *Journal of Aging and Social Policy* 61 (1994): 43-56.

Renzetti, Claire M. and Daniel J. Curran. *Women, Men, and Society*. Boston: Allyn and Bacon, 1995.

Sullivan, Thomas J. *Introduction to Social Problems*. Boston: Allyn and Bacon, 1997.

Socialism

Socialism is a set of political ideas that focuses on human economic, social, and political relationships within capitalism, particularly in relation to the institution of private property. Specifically, socialism advocates collective or governmental ownership of property. Feminist socialism is a school of thought focusing on the special oppressive condition of women under capitalism and also under the system of patriarchy (i.e., systemic male domination) found in some religious sects.

The tension between the two philosophies has been both theoretical and historical. American socialists, like their European predecessors, pondered "the Woman Question" for decades. Was it possible to emancipate women from the oppression of the institution of private property or was a separate but connected movement required?

A number of American women, such as **Kate Richards O'Hare** and Mary Wood Simons, attempted to liberate women through their efforts in the Socialist Party of America (SP) in the late 1800s and early 1900s. Meta Burger became the first socialist woman elected to a public post as a member of the Milwaukee school board. Despite forming the Women's National Socialist Union (1904) and *Socialist Woman* magazine (1907), SP women found their political opportunities limited by the traditional stereotypes held by many male party members. (PS)

Bibliography

Miller, Sally, ed. *Flawed Liberation: Socialism and Feminism*. Contributions in Women's Studies, no. 19. London: Greenwood Press, 1981.

Sargent, Lydia, ed. *Woman and Revolution: A Discussion of the Unhappy Marriage Between Marxism and Feminism*. Boston: South End Press, 1981.

Tish Sommers (1924–1985)

Along with **Laurie Shields,** Tish Sommers founded the Alliance for Displaced Homemakers in California in 1974. The group became the National Displaced Homemakers Network for Women's Employment in 1978 and Women Work! The National Network for Women's Employment in 1983. Sommers also assisted Shields in creating the Older Women's League Educational Fund in 1978, which in 1980 became the Older Women's League. During her career, Sommers worked for a number of women's causes, including homemaker's rights and an end to the **poverty** of elderly women.

Bibliography

Huckle, Patricia. *Tish Sommers, Activist: The Founding of the Older Women's League*. Nashville: University of Tennessee, 1991.

Sommers, Tish. "A Free-Lance Agitator Confronts the Establishment." In Ronald Gross, Beatrice Gross, and Sylvia Sideman, eds. *The New Old: Struggling for Decent Aging.* Garden City, NY: Anchor, 1978.

Gladys Noon Spellman (1918–1988)

The first woman elected president of the National Association of Counties, Maryland Democratic Congresswoman Gladys Spellman served in the U.S. House of Representatives from 1974 to 1980. A leader in the **Congresswomen's Caucus**, Spellman was a regional party whip and a member of the Democratic Steering and Policy Committee. When a heart attack put her into a coma in 1980, her husband became the first man to seek his wife's congressional seat. (JHT)

BIBLIOGRAPHY

Gertzog, Irvin N. *Congressional Women: Their Recruitment, Integration, and Behavior.* New York: Praeger, 1984.

Anna Carpenter Garlin Spencer (1851–1931)

Anna Spencer served as a member of the board of control of the New York State Home and School for Dependent Children from 1891 to 1897 and as associate director of the New York School of Philanthropy from 1903 to 1907. She remained as a lecturer at the latter institution until 1912. Beginning in 1908, Spencer wrote articles on women and family issues for a number of magazines, including *The American Journal of Sociology*, *The Ladies' Home Journal*, and *Harper's*. From 1915, Spencer was also active with the **Women's Peace Party**.

BIBLIOGRAPHY

Spencer, Anna G. *The Family and Its Members.* Westport, CT: Hyperion, 1976.

———. *Woman's Share in Social Culture.* Stratford, NH: Ayer Company, 1974.

Debbie Stabenow (1950–)

In 1975, moderate Democrat Debbie Stabenow was elected to the Ingham County (MI) Commission. In 1979, she was elected to the Michigan state house of representatives and in 1991 to the Michigan state senate, where she served until failing to win re-election in 1994. In 1996, she defeated one-term incumbent Dick Chrysler for a seat in the U.S. House of Representatives, where Stabenow serves on the Agriculture and Science committees.

BIBLIOGRAPHY

Groppe, Maureen. "It's the 'Year of the Incumbent' as 3 Women Lose Narrowly." *Congressional Quarterly Weekly* 52, no. 31 (August 6, 1994): 2276.

Winifred Claire Stanley (1909–)

Republican Winifred Stanley was the first woman to serve as assistant district attorney of Erie County, New York, a post she held from 1938 to 1943. In 1942, she was elected to one of New York's two at-large congressional districts. In the 78th Congress, she worked for post-war readjustment. She also advocated amendments to the National Labor Relations Act that would make it illegal to discriminate on the basis of sex. From January 1, 1945, to April 1, 1955, she worked for the New York State Employees' Retirement System. In 1955, Stanley was appointed assistant attorney general for the New York State Law Department, a position she held until 1979.

BIBLIOGRAPHY

Chamberlin, Hope. *A Minority of Members.* New York: Praeger, 1973.

Elizabeth Cady Stanton (1815–1902)

Elizabeth Cady Stanton holds a preeminent place in the history of women's political activism in the United States. Her lifelong campaign for women's rights changed the nature of citizenship and the character of the nation. Elizabeth Cady was born into a socially prominent family in New York State. Her father, Daniel Cady, was a judge, and her mother, Margaret Livingston, bore 10 children. Stanton's autobiography, *Eighty Years and More*, published in 1898, chronicled the development of an ardent **feminism** that began in her girlhood. After the loss of her only brother, she was forced to contend with her father's lament that she should have been born a boy. Elizabeth Cady responded by excelling at her studies, learning Greek and Latin to make her father proud. Her formal instruction began in a co-educational academy in her hometown and concluded at **Emma Willard**'s famed school. In 1840, she married the abolitionist leader, Henry B. Stanton, and combined raising a family with anti-slavery work. In July 1848, Stanton called for the first women's rights convention to meet at Seneca Falls, New York, and she coauthored the **Declaration of Sentiments and Resolutions** passed at the convention with her mentor, **Lucretia Mott**. She joined forces with **Susan B. Anthony** in 1850, beginning a partnership that would transform the lives of their sex. Together they took on such political issues as securing a wife's property in marriage, reforming divorce laws, and extending the franchise to women. In 1869, they founded the **National Woman Suffrage Association (NWSA)**. As the first elected president of this organization, Stanton tirelessly wrote and lectured, passing on the lessons of the movement in her multi-volume *History of Woman Suffrage*. At the end of her life, she focused her attention on the relationship of theology and womanhood, and in 1896 published the controversial *Women's Bible*. Until her death in 1902, Elizabeth Cady Stanton continued to write and lecture on women's issues, capping her lifelong efforts with a European tour that brought international attention to the rights of woman. (WGC) **See also** Abolition; Seneca Falls Convention; Suffrage; Women's Movement.

BIBLIOGRAPHY

DuBois, Ellen Carol, ed. *The Elizabeth Cady Stanton-Susan B. Anthony Reader.* Boston: Northeastern University Press, 1992.

Griffith, Elizabeth. *In Her Own Right. The Life of Elizabeth Cady Stanton.* New York: Oxford University Press, 1984.

Lutz, Alma. *Created Equal: A Biography of Elizabeth Cady Stanton, 1815–1902.* New York: John Day, 1940.

State Status of Women Commissions

President John F. Kennedy's creation of the **President's Commission on the Status of Women** in 1961 led to the formation of state commissions on the status of women. Michigan became the first state to establish a commission in 1962, and by 1967 all 50 states had their own commissions. Because the validity of the state commissions varied greatly, often operating according to the political whims of individual governors, the overall conclusion was that state commissions did not work.

But members of various state commissions came together to form the **National Organization for Women**, better known as NOW, because they believed that discrimination should end *now*, and they dedicated themselves to fighting sexual discrimination. In 1987, NOW published *The State-by-State Guide to Women's Rights*, which examined the status of women in five areas: the legal process, home and family, education, employment, and the community. NOW subsequently ranked each state based on a point system in each of the specific fields within the five general areas. Washington State led the country, South Carolina, where marital rape was not considered a crime and collection of back child support was low, trailed the other 49 states and the District of Columbia. After NOW's report, the various state commissions responded to governors and legislatures and remedial legislation was frequently enacted. (EP)

Klein, Ethel. *Gender Politics.* Cambridge, MA: Harvard University Press, 1984.

NOW Legal Defense Fund and Dr. Renee Cherow-O'Leary. *The State-by-State Guide to Women's Rights.* New York: McGraw-Hill, 1987.

Gloria Steinem (1934–)

A leader of the United States feminist movement, writer, editor, and lecturer Gloria Steinem was born on March 25, 1934, in Toledo, Ohio. She graduated *magna cum laude* with a B.A. from Smith College in 1956. In the 1960s, she moved to New York and became well-known nationally as a free-lance writer. In 1968, she became a contributing editor of *New York Magazine* and in 1971 she cofounded the **National Women's Political Caucus** and the Women's Action Alliance with **Bella Abzug** and **Shirley Chisholm**. In 1972, she founded ***Ms. Magazine*,** the first American feminist magazine for mass distribution. She was also a founding member of the Coalition of Labor Union Women in 1974. She has written several books, including *Outrageous Acts and Everyday Rebellions* (1983), *Marilyn: Norma Jean* (1986), and *Revolution from Within: A Book of Self-Esteem* (1992), in which she summarizes the journey of her life. In *Revolution from Within*, Steinem argues for a redistribution of family power, less violence against women, and equal pay for comparable work. In the 1990s, Steinem continues to be a leading activist for the modern **women's movement.** (GVS) **See also** Feminism.

A leader of the feminist movement, Gloria Steinem founded *Ms.* Magazine in 1972. Photo by Pat Field. National Archives.

BIBLIOGRAPHY

Carmody, Diedre. "Power to the Readers: *Ms.* Thrives without Ads." *New York Times* (July 22, 1991): D6.

Henry, Sondra and Emily Taitz. *One Woman's Power: A Biography of Gloria Steinem.* Minneapolis: Dillon Press, 1987.

Lucy Stone (1818–1893)

Abolitionist and **suffrage** leader Lucy Stone grew up in a family that enforced different roles for boys and girls. Determined to improve her status, Stone entered Mount Holyoke Female Seminary in 1839; at her graduation in 1847, she became the first female college graduate in Massachusetts. A popular lecturer for the American Anti-Slavery Society, Stone spoke as often for women's rights as for **abolition**. In 1850, she helped convene the first National Women's Rights Convention at Worcester, Massachusetts, and her conference speech was reprinted internationally. She married Henry Blackwell in 1855; the ceremony included a protest against marital law and Stone kept her maiden name. She supported the Loyal League during the Civil War, and later campaigned for woman suffrage in Kansas. Stone also served as president of the New Jersey Woman Suffrage Association and on the executive committe of the American **Equal Rights Association**. In 1869, she split with suffrage leaders **Elizabeth Cady Stanton** and **Susan B. Anthony** over supporting the Fifteenth Amendment, and she founded, with **Julia Ward Howe**, the **American Woman Suffrage Association (AWSA).** She also founded, financed, and eventually edited the ***Woman's Journal***. In 1890, she joined with Stanton and Anthony to reunite the suffrage movement into the **National American**

Under the leadership of Lucy Stone, the American Woman Suffrage Association focused its efforts at the state level. Library of Congress, National American Woman Suffrage Association Collection.

Woman Suffrage Association (NAWSA). She died in 1893, becoming the first person to be cremated in New England. (AM)

BIBLIOGRAPHY

Blackwell, Alice Stone. *Lucy Stone, Pioneer of Woman's Rights*. Boston: Little, Brown, 1930.

Kerr, Andrea Moor. *Lucy Stone: Speaking Out for Equality*. New Brunswick, NJ: Rutgers University Press, 1992.

STOP ERA

Phyllis Schlafly founded STOP ERA in 1972 to defeat the **Equal Rights Amendment (ERA)** to the Constitution. STOP ERA and her later group, Eagle Forum, organized quickly and effectively in states where legislators were due to consider ratification of the amendment. Schlafly, herself a Catholic, mobilized Protestant fundamentalist and Catholic women to lobby state legislators. Many of these women were new to politics and were unlikely activists because they had little or no college education and few financial resources. Yet STOP ERA proved effective, as conservative Christian women pinned roses in the buttonholes of male legislators while they made their arguments heard. STOP ERA argued that the ERA would damage American families by altering the balance of power between men and women and by encouraging women to abandon their roles as mothers for positions in the paid workforce. STOP ERA supporters argued that the proposed amendment devalued motherhood and would lead to the drafting of women, unisex toilets, the end of alimony and child support, and the end of a woman's ability to collect her husband's pension. Such arguments were especially effective with middle-aged and elderly women, and among highly religious conservative Christians. STOP ERA never won the battle for public opinion; a majority of Americans supported the ERA throughout the ratification battle. But the ERA was ultimately defeated, falling three states short of the 38 needed for ratification when the ratification deadline expired on June 30, 1982. (CW)

STOP ERA was an effective lobbying group that helped defeat the Equal Rights Amendment. Photo by Marcia Fram. National Archives.

BIBLIOGRAPHY

Mansbridge, Jane. *Why We Lost the ERA*. Chicago: University of Chicago Press, 1986.

Mathews, Donald G. and Jane Sherron DeHart. *Sex, Gender, and the Politics of the ERA*. New York: Oxford University Press, 1990.

Melich, Tanya. *The Republican War Against Women*. New York: Bantam, 1996.

Harriet Beecher Stowe (1811–1896)

Harriet Beecher Stowe is best remembered as the author of *Uncle Tom's Cabin*, a controversial 1852 novel that helped fuel the **abolition** movement. The book was an international bestseller with more than 300,000 copies sold in the first year. When Stowe met President Abraham Lincoln at the White House in 1863 to urge him to do something for the slaves who had fled to the North, Lincoln greeted her as "the little woman who wrote the book that made this great war." Stowe wrote several other works, including *Dred* (1856), *The Minister's Wooing* (1859), and *Old Town Folks* (1869). In later life, Stowe became an outspoken activist for **temperance** and women's **suffrage**.

Harriet Beecher Stowe, pictured here in Alanson Fisher's 1853 portrait, was best known as the author of *Uncle Tom's Cabin*, but was also active in the temperance and suffrage movements. Library of Congress.

BIBLIOGRAPHY

Adams, John R. *Harriet Beecher Stowe*. New York: Twayne, 1963.

Crozier, Alice C. *The Novels of Harriet Beecher Stowe*. New York: Oxford University Press, 1969.

Wilson, Forrest. *Crusader in Crinoline: The Life of Harriet Beecher Stowe*. Philadelphia: Lippincott, 1941.

Suffrage

Historically, suffrage, or the right to vote, has expanded only gradually in the United States. Initially, suffrage was limited to landholding white males, then it was expanded to include all adult white males, black males, women, and citizens 18 years of age. Suffrage for women was initially proposed at the first women's rights convention held at Seneca Falls, New York, in 1848. The **Nineteenth Amendment** to the Constitution guaranteeing women the right to vote was passed three-quarters of a century later in 1920.

The early **women's movement** was broadly concerned with women's rights, not just suffrage. Thus, when slavery became the dominant political issue for the nation in the mid-nineteenth century, women's rights activists agreed that they should focus their attention on the abolitionist movement. As a result, the battle for women's suffrage did not become a concentrated effort until after the Civil War and passage of the Fifteenth Amendment to the Constitution. The Fifteenth Amendment extended suffrage to black males and represented the first time the word "male" was used in the Constitution. This legalization of discrimination on the basis of sex mobilized many women's rights activists to focus their efforts on achieving women's suffrage. Moreover, with the end of the

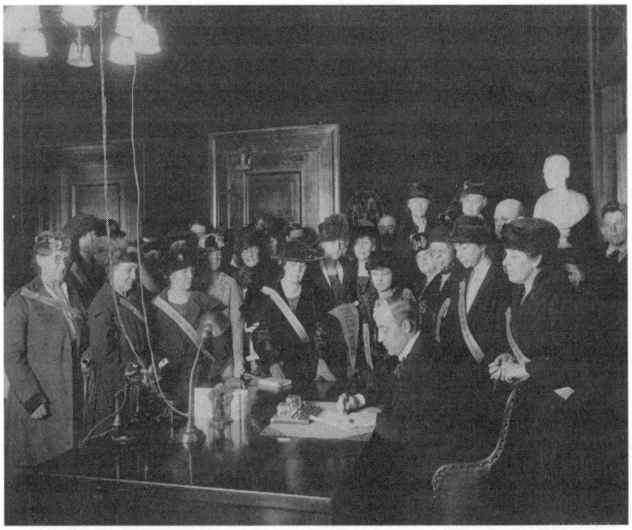

On January 6, 1920, Governor Edwin P. Morrow signed the Anthony Amendment, making Kentucky the 24th state to ratify the Nineteenth Amendment to the Constitution granting women the vote. Library of Congress, National American Woman Suffrage Association Collection.

Civil War in 1865, women returned to previous concerns, among them such social issues as serving the poor, helping immigrants, or addressing labor inequities. Women became active in the **Progressive movement**, the **Settlement House movement**, the **temperance movement**, and other social efforts. Through their efforts on behalf of others, women realized that their inability to effect social and political change was rooted in their lack of political and legal rights. In fact, women had no more political power than the people or causes they sought to aid.

At this point, a deep rift in the women's movement occurred, largely as a result of the passage of the Fifteenth Amendment. Suffragists had lobbied to have women included in this amendment, but abolitionists, fearing failure, refused to support them. Women's rights activists felt betrayed by the very people they had worked closely with, and for whom they had postponed their suffrage goals during the Civil War. In 1869, the split was formalized when **Elizabeth Cady Stanton** and **Susan B. Anthony** secretly formed the **National Woman Suffrage Association (NWSA)**. Excluded members of the movement formed a counter organization, the **American Woman Suffrage Association (AWSA).** The split lasted 23 years and organized itself along differing viewpoints on how to achieve women's suffrage, with the AWSA focusing exclusively on suffrage and the NWSA adopting a general women's rights approach with suffrage as an important element.

From 1890 on, the effort to win suffrage for women intensified. However, despite the efforts of women's rights groups, the movement was unsuccessful until it became mass based. Suffrage for women emerged as a mass movement in 1915 after national attention to the issue was achieved through the efforts of **Alice Paul** and others. Social changes played an enormous role in ensuring the success of the amendment. Since the Industrial Revolution, women increasingly worked outside the home and were organized in the workforce. Increasingly, the vote was viewed as a mainstream issue as opposed to a radical position. The emergence of this kind of support culminated in the ratification of the Nineteenth Amendment in 1920. (JEH) **See also** Abolition; Seneca Falls Convention; Voting Rights.

Bibliography

Flexnor, Eleanor. *Century of Struggle.* Cambridge, MA: Belknap Press, 1959.

Kraditor, Aileen S. *The Ideas of the Woman Suffrage Movement, 1890–1920.* New York: Columbia University Press, 1965.

Scott, Anne Finor and Andrew M. Scott. *One Half the People: The Fight for Woman Suffrage.* Philadelphia: Lippincott, 1975.

Leonore Kretzer Sullivan (1902–1988)

Leonore Sullivan, a Democrat from Missouri, served in the U.S. House of Representatives from 1952 until 1977. She was the first woman ever elected to Congress from Missouri. While in office, Sullivan supported the preservation of environmental resources, consumer protection laws for food and drugs, and improved conditions of employment, as well as helping to draft the 1954 legislation that created the food stamp program.

Bibliography

Sullivan, Leonore K. "Luck of Leadership in Washington." *Vital Speeches* 23 (June 1, 1957): 489-92.

Sussman, Robert. *Leonore K. Sullivan, Democratic Representative from Missouri.* Washington, DC: Grossman Publishers, 1972.

Jessie Sumner (1898–1994)

Jessie Sumner, a Republican from Illinois, served in the U.S. House of Representatives from 1939 to 1947. In Congress, Sumner opposed Franklin Roosevelt's New Deal reform legislation and his World War II efforts, especially his support of Soviet leader Josef Stalin. Sumner retired from national politics on January 3, 1947, returning to Illinois and her career in law and banking.

Bibliography

Chamberlin, Hope. *A Minority of Members.* New York: Praeger, 1973.

T

Helen Herron Taft (1861–1943)

First lady of the United States from 1909 to1913, Helen "Nellie" Taft grew up with an enthusiasm for music and an unbridled determination to find a challenging and exciting life beyond southern Ohio, where she was born in 1861. At 17, she had visited President Rutherford B. and **Lucy Hayes** in the White House and became fascinated by the prospects of a political life. In 1886, she married William Howard Taft, whose political career, culminating with election to the presidency in 1908, appears to have been driven, in part, by his wife's ambition, Taft himself being more interested in a Supreme Court appointment than in the White House. On the day of her husband's inauguration, Nellie Taft broke precedent by riding with the new president back to the White House. She involved herself in every detail of White House management and openly included herself in important political discussions, although the impact of her involvement was limited by a debilitating stroke that she suffered two months after the inauguration. As first lady, Nellie Taft refused to take a public stand in favor of woman's **suffrage** or other reforms, although in her diaries she recorded her own frustrations with the limits on the rights of women in her time. Although William Howard Taft was defeated for re-election in 1912, Nellie Taft's public role in Washington continued when her husband was appointed chief justice of the United States Supreme Court in 1921. She resided in Washington until her death in 1943. (LvA) **See also** First Ladies.

As first lady, Helen Taft refrained from taking public stands on issues like suffrage. Library of Congress, Prints and Photographs Division.

BIBLIOGRAPHY

Caroli, Betty Boyd. *First Ladies.* New York: Oxford University Press, 1993.

Gould, Lewis L., ed. *American First Ladies: Their Lives and Their Legacy.* New York: Garland Publishers, 1996.

Tailhook Scandal (1991)

The Tailhook Scandal occurred at the annual Tailhook Association convention held in Las Vegas in 1991. At the convention, more than 26 women were assaulted by scores of drunken naval and marine officers. In the hallway of the hotel, the women—14 of them officers—were forced to walk down a gauntlet of pawing male officers who molested them as they passed.

When the Navy failed to investigate the incident properly, Navy Lt. Paula Coughlin went public with her complaints. In a matter of hours, President George Bush announced the resignation of Navy Secretary H. Lawrence Garrett III. Although responsible for investigating the incident, Garrett might actually have been a participant in the harassment. Congress also took steps by freezing more than 4,500 promotions, retirements, and changes of command until the assailants were identified and punished. The accusations of mishandling the investigation and the congressional and presidential actions deeply damaged the Navy. While many officers where justly punished, others were falsely accused by investigators seeking a more sensational story.

The Tailhook Association—named after the hook that grabs planes as they land on carrier decks—had been holding conventions for more than 30 years. Reports indicate that by the 1990s the convention, originally begun as an event to network and discuss advances in aviation, had turned into an uncontrollable fraternity party. The Association still holds an annual convention.

BIBLIOGRAPHY

Donnelly, Elaine. "The Tailhook Scandal." *National Review* 46, no. 4 (March 7, 1994): 59.

Kanner, Gideon. "Sailor, Curse No More." *The Weekly Standard* 1, no. 10 (November 20, 1995): 15.

Salholz, Eloise and Douglas Waller. "Tailhook: Scandal Time." Newsweek (July 6, 1992): 40.

"Sticking Together." *The New Republic* 209, no. 18 (November 1, 1993): 9.

Take Our Daughters to Work Day

Take Our Daughters to Work Day (TODWD) originated in April 1992 as a public education campaign of the Ms. Foundation for Women. The foundation urged parents to take their daughters, ages 9 through 15, to work with them for one day to expose the girls to career opportunities and to encourage them to formulate and pursue their career goals. The campaign was prompted by research by Carol Gilligan, which showed that girls were more likely than boys to lack self-confidence and self-esteem during the adolescent years when educational and training decisions that influence future career options are made. Over one million girls participated in the 1992 event, which was so successful that TODWD has become an annual event, attracting the participation of over 16.6 million girls in 1997.

Almost immediately following the initiation of the program, a backlash occurred against the annual event because it did not include boys. Some firms renamed the day, "Take Your Child to Work Day." Yet a Roper poll in 1996 showed that 71 percent of Americans were aware of TODWD and that 93 percent of that number believed that the program was beneficial to girls. (CKC)

BIBLIOGRAPHY

Baron, Talila. "Daughters Learn About Careers on Work Day." *Business Journal Serving San Jose and Silicon Valley* 12, no.7 (May 30, 1994): 3.

Ms. Foundation for Women Web Page at <http://www.ms/foundation.org>.

Pogrebin, Letty. "The Stolen Spotlight Syndrome." *Ms. Magazine* 4 (November-December 1993): 96.

Ellen O. Tauscher (1951–)

When Ellen Tauscher was active in San Francisco area politics, she raised funds for Democratic Senator **Dianne Feinstein**. However, being more moderate than Senator Feinstein, Tauscher has, since her election to the House of Representatives in 1996, been aligned with the Blue Dogs, the group of conservative Democrats also known as the Coalition, and the moderate New Democratic Coalition rather than with the more liberal wing of the **Democratic Party**. Tauscher is an advocate of gun control and tough environmental restriction, but supports the welfare reforms of 1996 and the death penalty.

BIBLIOGRAPHY

Beinart, Peter. "Why the Center Can't Hold: The New Democrats Bite the Hand That Feeds Them." *Time* (November 24, 1997): 52.

"For Better or Worse." *Los Angeles Times* (July 23, 1997): A5.

Snieder, Daniel. "Two California Races Show Why Democrats Are Upbeat." *Christian Science Monitor* (September 17, 1996): 1.

Margaret Mackall Smith Taylor (1788–1852)

Margaret Taylor, wife of President Zachary Taylor, spent most of her married life from 1810 to 1845 traveling with her husband to his various military posts. During that time, she coordinated social activities for him and managed hospitality. In 1848, Margaret Taylor opposed Whig efforts to have her husband run for president. Taking office in 1849 and dying while in office in July 1850, Zachary Taylor's term was brief, and Margaret Taylor took little part in White House activities during that time. She relegated official hostess duties to her daughter Mary Elizabeth. **See also** First Ladies.

BIBLIOGRAPHY

Caroli, Betty Boyd. *First Ladies*. New York: Oxford University Press, 1987.

Temperance Movement

Throughout the nineteenth century and into the early twentieth century, temperance reformers attempted to control alcohol consumption in American society. Women played a significant role in every phase of the campaign because, from the inception of the movement, women perceived temperance as a woman's issue. Under the laws of **coverture**, a married woman had no legal recourse against a drunken husband who abused her or squandered the family's income. Thus, involvement in the temperance crusade allowed women to address serious domestic problems. Moreover, by participating in the temperance movement, women acquired a medium for political and social action.

The battle for temperance was waged at both the national and state levels. Here workers in the Capitol count the prohibition vote. Library of Congress.

During the early nineteenth century, women joined and created voluntary temperance associations, yet they lacked leadership positions and the same standing as male temperance reformers. Denied the opportunity to fully participate in the 1852 Sons of Temperance Conference, **Elizabeth Cady Stanton**, **Susan B. Anthony**, and **Amelia Bloomer** walked out and subsequently formed the Woman's New York State Temperance Society. The organization added **suffrage** and women's equality to its prohibition message.

After the Civil War, women ascended to prominent positions within the temperance movement. The creation of the **Women's Christian Temperance Union (WCTU)** in 1874 launched the first women's mass movement. Feminists gradually began to perceive the negative effect of the temperance movement on their efforts to obtain suffrage. When the Prohibition Party was created in 1882, the liquor industry financed much of the opposition to the **Nineteenth Amendment**, fearing that support for prohibition would increase with the women's vote. With the passage in 1919 of the **Eighteenth Amendment** banning the production, sale, and consumption of alcohol. both women and men violated the new national Prohibition, and women reformers realized that they needed to focus on equal rights and divorce reform rather than on maintaining the prohibition of alcohol. (MG)

Bibliography

Blocker, Jack S. *American Temperance Movements: Cycles of Reform.* Boston: Twayne Publishers, 1989.

Bordin, Ruth. *Women and Temperance: The Quest for Power and Liberty, 1873–1900.* Philadelphia: Temple University Press, 1981.

Mary Church Terrell (1863–1954)

Mary Terrell, an early club woman civil rights leader, and educator, was largely responsible for the founding of the **National Association of Colored Women (NACW)**. In addition to serving as the NACW's first president, Terrell was also active in the founding of the Women's International League for Peace and Freedom. An advocate of woman's rights, Terrell was active in the **National Woman's Party (NWP)** and lobbied for reforms through her lifelong membership in the **Republican Party**. A leader in the National Association for the Advancement of Colored People (NAACP), she fought the segregationist policies of fellow woman's groups like the **American Association of University Women (AAUW). See also** Club Movement.

Active in the suffrage movement, Mary Church Terrell was also a leader in the civil rights movement. Library of Congress, National American Woman Suffrage Association Collection.

Bibliography

"Mary Terrell" *Journal of Negro History* 39 (October 1954): 385-88.

Terrell, Mary. *Colored Woman in a White World.* Washington, DC: Ransdell, 1940.

Thalidomide

Thalidomide was prescribed as a sleeping pill in Europe in the early 1960s. The drug was pending Food and Drug Administration (FDA) approval for consumption in the United States when reports of severe fetal deformities linked to its use by pregnant women began to surface in Europe. The issue was widely publicized when **Sherri Finkbine** of Phoenix, Arizona, and host of a popular children's show, discovered she had taken the drug while pregnant with her fifth child. Finkbine requested a therapeutic **abortion**, which triggered controversial debate over American abortion laws and practices. Another consequence of the thalidomide experience was increased public support in the United States for stricter drug regulation that aided passage of the Kefauver-Harris Drug Amendment in 1962. (LW)

Bibliography

Garrow, David J. *Liberty & Sexuality: The Right to Privacy and the Making of* Roe v. Wade. New York: Macmillan, 1994.

Luker, Kristin. *Abortion & the Politics of Motherhood.* Berkeley: University of California Press, 1984.

O'Connor, Karen. *No Neutral Ground: Abortion Politics in an Age of Absolutes.* Boulder, CO: Westview Press, 1996.

Thelma and Louise

Thelma and Louise is a 1991 film produced by Ridley Scott. The title characters are two working-class women who become fugitives from the law after killing a rapist. Callie Khouri, a first time screenwriter, wrote this feminist parable, which inspired a national debate on the meaning of **feminism**. The film inspired such headlines as "Killer Bimbos," "Toxic Feminism on the Big Screen," and "Women Who Kill Too Much." Khouri was accused by some of glorifying violence and promoting male-bashing, and praised by others for accurately depicting the reality of patriarchal society and the damaging effects it has on women. (CKC)

Bibliography

Boozer, Jack. "Seduction and Betrayal in the Heartland: Thelma and Louise." *Literature Film Quarterly* 23, no. 3 (1995): 188.

Greenberg, H. R. and C. J. Clover, et al. "The Many Faces of Thelma and Louise." *Film Quarterly* 45 (Winter 1991–1992): 20.

Rapping, Elayne. "Gender Politics on the Big Screen." *Progressive* 56 (October 1992): 36.

Third National Conference of State Commissions on the Status of Women (1966)

The Third National Conference of State Commissions on the Status of Women, which was held in Washington, D.C., in 1966, is recognized as the birthplace of the **National Organization for Women (NOW)**. After President John F. Kennedy signed an executive order in 1961 establishing a Presidential Commission on the Status of Women, the 50 states followed suit and set up **state status of women commissions**. Devoted to conducting research on the status of women in their states, these commissions met once a year at a national conference. When delegates from these commissions convened in Washington in 1966 for the Third National Conference, a small group suggested that the conference adopt a resolution calling on the **Equal Employment Opportunity Commission (EEOC)** to begin treating sex discrimination in employment as seriously as race discrimination. Although **Title VII of the Civil Rights Act of 1964** mandated that the EEOC enforce laws barring discrimination on the basis of sex or race, few thought the agency was serious about the sex provision. When it became clear that the National Conference of State Commissions would not take a stand against the EEOC, a number of women agreed to form the National Organization for Women "to bring women into full participation in the mainstream of American society."

BIBLIOGRAPHY

Freeman, Jo. *The Politics of Women's Liberation.* New York: David McKay Company, Inc., 1975.

Helen Thomas (1920–)

Helen Thomas is the first female member of the Gridiron Club, the first woman to be named president of the White House Correspondent's Association, and United Press International (UPI) bureau chief at the White House, a post she has held since 1974. She is best known for her press coverage of every president since John F. Kennedy and her front row seat as UPI White House correspondent at presidential news conferences. She has won numerous awards for her journalistic talents, including the National Press Club's 4th Estate Award, the William Allen White Journalism Award, and Woman of the Year in Communication for the *Ladies Home Journal* in 1975. (SD)

BIBLIOGRAPHY

Fitzwater, Marlin. *Call the Briefing: Bush and Reagan, Sam and Helen: A Decade with Presidents and the Press.* New York: Times Books, 1995.

Thomas, Helen. *Dateline: White House.* New York: Macmillan, 1975.

Lera Millard Thomas (1900–1993)

Democrat Lera Thomas, a member of the Houston League of Voters, was nominated to fill the vacancy in the United States Congress left by the death of her husband, Texas Representative Albert Thomas. She served in Congress from March 26, 1966, until January 3, 1967, at which time she retired from national politics.

BIBLIOGRAPHY

Chamberlin, Hope. *A Minority of Members.* New York: Praeger, 1973.

Martha Carey Thomas (1857–1935)

Martha Carey Thomas helped found Bryn Mawr College for women in 1885, serving as its president from 1894 to 1922. In 1906, Thomas worked for the College Equal Suffrage League and began lecturing on **suffrage** and education. In 1908, she became the first president of the national College Women's Equal Suffrage League, which led to her participation with the **National American Woman Suffrage Association (NAWSA)**. Thomas joined the Bull Moose Progressive Party in 1912, and backed the League to Enforce Peace in 1914. In 1920, she began working for the **National Woman's Party (NWP).**

BIBLIOGRAPHY

Dobkin, Marjorie Houspian. *The Making of a Feminist: Early Journals and Letters of M. Carey Thomas.* Kent, OH: Kent State University, 1979.

Thomas Confirmation Hearings

In 1991, when long-time liberal Supreme Court Justice Thurgood Marshall, the first African-American justice, retired from the United States Supreme Court, Republican President George Bush nominated conservative African-American jurist Clarence Thomas to take Marshall's seat on the Court. Women's rights groups opposed the nomination, fearing that Thomas would provide the fifth vote needed to overturn ***Roe v. Wade*** (1973). In the course of Thomas' confirmation hearings before the Senate Judiciary Committee, word was leaked to the press that the committee had been informed that Thomas was accused of sexually harassing one of his former employees at the **Equal Employment Opportunity Commission (EEOC)** in the early 1980s. Yet, the committee had decided not to investigate the charges and to continue the confirmation process.

Public outrage, especially on the part of women, led to a publicly televised hearing in which the Senate Judiciary Committee interrogated and attempted to discredit law professor **Anita Hill**, Thomas' African-American accuser. The television pictures of the all-white and all-male committee attacking Anita Hill galvanized the women's movement. The Hill-Thomas hearings became symbolic of the lack of representation of women in higher office and of the consequential lack of influence that women had on the political system. The hearings and the subsequent confirmation of Thomas by a 52-48 Senate vote stimulated unprecedented contributions to women candidates. Many of the women who ran for the Senate in 1992 claimed to be doing so in response to the Thomas hearings. (CKC)

BIBLIOGRAPHY

Danforth, John C. *Resurrection: The Confirmation of Clarence Thomas.* New York: Viking Press, 1994.

Mayer, Jane and Jill Abramson. *Strange Justice: The Selling of Clarence Thomas.* Boston: Houghton Mifflin, 1994.

Miller, Anita, ed. *The Complete Transcripts of the Clarence Thomas-Anita Hill Hearings.* Chicago: Academy Chicago Publishers, 1994.

Ruth Thompson (1887–1970)

Ruth Thompson, a Republican, had a long political career before winning election to the U.S. House of Representatives from Michigan's 9th District in 1950. From 1939 to 1941, she was a legislator in the Michigan house. She held posts with the Social Security Board from 1941 to 1943, the Labor Department in 1942, and the Adjutant General's Office from 1942 to 1945. Thompson chaired the State Prison Commission for Women from 1946 until her election in 1950. Re-elected to Congress in 1952 and 1954, she was narrowly defeated in 1956.

BIBLIOGRAPHY

Chamberlin, Hope. *A Minority of Members.* New York: Praeger, 1973.

Thornburgh v. American College of Obstetricians and Gynecologists (1986)

In 1982, Pennsylvania enacted the **Abortion Control Act**, which sought to limit the number of **abortion**s by including among its restrictions a second-trimester hospitalization, a 24-hour waiting period, a ban on public funds for abortions, and parental consent for minors. The U.S. Supreme Court heard the case on appeal from a lower court that had granted an enjoinment of the act based upon the U.S. Supreme Court's decision in ***Akron v. Akron Center for Reproductive Health,*** among others.

In *Thornburgh v. American College of Obstetricians and Gynecologists*, 476 U.S. 747 (1986), the Supreme Court limited its ruling to the three provisions of the act covering informed consent, physician's duty of care, and reporting. The five-justice majority struck down the procedure that required women to read or be read information about abortion alternatives like adoption and the growth stages of the fetus before giving consent. Justice Harry Blackmun wrote that the requirement was "nothing less than an outright attempt to edge the Commonwealth's message discouraging abortion into the privacy of the informed-consent dialogue between the woman and her physician." The majority concluded that the purpose of the informed consent provisions was to discourage abortion rather than to aid the woman in making a choice.

The Court also found a constitutional problem with the physician's duty clause that required doctors to file a report on a number of factors, including the viability of the fetus, even though the woman's name was not part of the report. In addition, if viability were possible, a second doctor had to be ready to attempt to preserve the child's life. While the provision was similar to one upheld in *Planned Parenthood Association of Kansas City v. Ashcroft*, the Court struck down the Pennsylvania provision because it did not have an exemption for emergencies.

The dissenters on the Court were outraged by how far the majority had gone to preserve an almost unlimited right to abortion. The justices argued that the majority had gone far beyond ***Roe v. Wade*** and had decided that there were almost no compelling state interests in limiting abortion.

BIBLIOGRAPHY

Baer, Judith A. *Women in American Law*. New York: Holmes & Meier, 1996.

Boumil, Marcia Mobilia and Stephen C. Hicks. *Women and the Law*. Littleton, CO: Fred B. Rothman & Company, 1992.

Mezey, Susan. *In Pursuit of Equality*. New York: St. Martin's Press, 1992.

Richards, David A. "Constitutional Legitimacy and Constitutional Privacy." *New York University Law Review* 61 (November 1986): 60-62.

Karen L. Thurman (1951-)

Karen Thurman was a member of the Dunnellon City Council (Florida) from 1974 to 1982. Thurman also served as mayor of Dunnellon from 1979 to 1981 and as a member of the Florida state senate from 1982 to 1992. In 1992, she was elected as a Democrat to the U.S. House of Representatives. In the 105th Congress, she served on the House Ways and Means Committee. Thurman has also served as a delegate to both the Florida Democratic Convention and the National Democratic Convention.

BIBLIOGRAPHY

Shafer, Ronald G. "Women Democrats Win More Influential Roles in the House." *The Wall Street Journal* (November 22, 1996): A1.

Title IX of the Educational Amendments Act of 1972

Title IX of the Educational Amendments Act of 1972 bans **sex discrimination** in "any education program or activity receiving Federal financial assistance." The provision applies to three major areas: admissions, treatment of students, and hiring practices. It covers admissions policy in vocational, professional, graduate, and most public undergraduate schools; single sex admissions remain legal in private institutions.

Title IX also forbids educational institutions from discriminating against employees on the basis of sex. Courts have interpreted it to bar sexual harassment of students in elementary and high school by other students as well as by teachers and administrators.

Although a number of federal agencies monitor compliance with Title IX, the Office of Civil Rights of the Department of Education is the federal government's lead agency in Title IX enforcement.

Title IX requires gender equity in athletic programs in institutions receiving financial aid—whether the aid is directly targeted at the athletic program or not. As a result of Title IX, colleges and universities have increased funding for women's athletic programs by adding women's sports teams, increasing the number and amount of scholarships for women, and providing better equipment and training. Because of Title IX, women have become more involved in athletics and were able to compete more successfully in the 1996 Olympics in both individual and team sports. (SM)

BIBLIOGRAPHY

Fishel, Andrew and Janice Pottker. *National Politics and Sex Discrimination in Education.* Lexington, MA: Lexington Books, 1977.

Gelb, Joyce and Marian Lief Palley. *Women and Public Policies.* 2nd ed. Princeton: Princeton University Press, 1987.

Mezey, Susan Gluck. *In Pursuit of Equality: Women, Public Policy and the Federal Courts.* New York: St. Martin's Press, 1992.

Salomone, Rosemary. *Equal Education Under Law.* New York: St. Martin's Press, 1986.

Title VII of the Civil Rights Act of 1964

Title VII of the **Civil Rights Act of 1964** bans employment discrimination in hiring, firing, privileges, or compensation on the basis of sex, race, color, national origin, and religion. Title VII can be used in wage discrimination as well as sexual harassment suits.

In 1972, Title VII was expanded to cover private employers or unions with 15 or more employees, as well as employees of federal, state, and local governments, and of educational institutions. Title VII established the **Equal Employment Opportunity Commission (EEOC),** although initially giving it little enforcement authority. In 1972, Congress authorized the EEOC to sue employers directly, and in 1974 the agency was empowered to bring discrimination suits against entire industries.

Title VII applies to intentional and unintentional discrimination. The first, called disparate treatment, occurs when an employer's employment policy or practice is motivated by discriminatory intent. Unintentional discrimination, known as disparate impact, occurs when employers use ostensibly objective criteria, such as test scores or height and weight requirements, to hire or promote employees; such facially neutral criteria can restrict job opportunities for women and minorities.

The **Civil Rights Act of 1991** broadened the protections of Title VII, reversing several Supreme Court rulings from 1988 and 1989. The act made it easier for plaintiffs to prove discrimination, allowed workers to collect money damages in cases of intentional discrimination, and permitted jury trials. (SM)

BIBLIOGRAPHY

Maschke, Karen. *Litigation, Courts and Women Workers.* New York: Praeger Publishers, 1989.

Mezey, Susan Gluck. *In Pursuit of Equality: Women, Public Policy and the Federal Courts.* New York: St. Martin's Press, 1992.

Samuels, Suzanne Uttaro. *Fetal Rights, Women's Rights: Gender Equality in the Workplace.* Madison: University of Wisconsin Press, 1995.

Trammel v. United States (1979)

On March 10, 1976, Otis Trammel was indicted along with Edwin Lee Roberts and Joseph Freeman for importing heroin from Thailand and the Philippines. The indictment named six co-conspirators, including Trammel's wife Elizabeth, who were not indicted in the proceeding. Trammel and his wife transported the heroin from Asia and then the other two defendants distributed the drugs in the United States. The couple had been arrested on a routine customs search in Hawaii.

Elizabeth Trammel agreed to cooperate with the government in exchange for favorable treatment. Her cooperation included testifying against her husband. Otis Trammel objected to his wife testifying against him because it violated spousal privilege as defined in *Hawkins v. United States* (358 U.S. 74 [1958]), which declared that both parties had to waive privilege for one spouse to testify against the other.

The trial court ruled that Elizabeth Trammel could only testify to those things said by her husband in the presence of a third party, but that any communications between just the two of them was privileged. Elizabeth Trammel testified against her husband and he was convicted.

Otis Trammel challenged the trial court's ruling to the U.S. Supreme Court, which ruled in *Trammel v. United States*, 445 U.S. 40 (1979), that the third party statements were admissible and that as long as one spouse waived privilege all statements could be entered. The Court stated that "the existing rule should be modified so that the witness-spouse alone has a privilege to refuse to testify adversely."

BIBLIOGRAPHY

"Mate v. Mate." *Time* 115 (March 10, 1980): 49.

"Supreme Court Review." *Journal of Criminal Justice and Criminology* 71 (Winter 1980): 593-600.

Triangle Shirtwaist Company Fire

The Triangle Shirtwaist Company in New York City, occupying the three upper floors of a 10-story building with only one fire escape, caught fire on March 25, 1911. Within moments, the entire eighth floor of the building was in flames. Escaping women and girls leaped to their deaths, were crushed when the fire escape collapsed, or were burned at their workbenches. Most of the 145 women who died were immigrants. The owners of the Triangle Factory, Isaac Harris and Max Blanck, were tried for manslaughter but found not guilty. The fire renewed interest in issues of factory safety and health, leading many northern and western states to define specific safety regulations. (AMD)

BIBLIOGRAPHY

Foner, Philip Sheldon. *Women and the American Labor Movement.* New York: Free Press, 1982.

Elizabeth Virginia Wallace Truman (1885–1982)

Wife of President Harry Truman, Elizabeth Wallace Truman was born on February 13, 1885. "Bess" or "The Boss" as the president called her, was only five when she first met her future husband. They grew up together, and attended the same schools from fifth grade through high school. They were married in 1919, when Harry returned from World War I, and their only daughter, Mary Margaret, was born in 1924. When Truman was elected to the Senate as a Democrat from Missouri in 1934, they moved to Washington, and Bess was hired as his secretary, a decision he defended by saying that "she earned every cent she was paid." After President Franklin Roosevelt's death on April 12, 1945, the Trumans moved to the White House, and Elizabeth Truman reluctantly took up the duties of first lady. She preferred the privacy of her family and disliked the political obligations that campaigns and her husband's position imposed upon her. Still, she dutifully and admirably fulfilled her social responsibilities throughout a second term. Elizabeth Truman was

Affectionately referred to as "the Boss" by her husband, Bess Truman shunned the public spotlight of the White House. Library of Congress, Prints and Photographs Division.

happy to return to Independence, Missouri, in 1953. She died in 1982. (GVS) **See also** First Ladies.

BIBLIOGRAPHY

Truman, Margaret. *Souvenir: Margaret Truman's Own Story.* New York: McGraw-Hill, 1955.

Sojourner Truth (c.1779–1883)

Sojourner Truth was the name taken by a former slave named Isabella in response to what she believed to be divine revelation. After New York State freed its slaves in 1827, Truth traveled the country speaking at **abolition** and women's **suffrage** meetings. She is best remembered for her appearance at an Akron, Ohio, women's rights convention in 1851. Truth addressed the assemblage of white men and women and simply yet eloquently spoke of the twin injustices visited upon her as a black woman. Her "Ain't I a Woman" speech had a profound effect on the hostile crowd, and Truth became a living symbol of the link between blacks' and women's rights in the Civil War era. (CKC) **See also** Slavery and Women.

Sojourner Truth, shown here with President Abraham Lincoln in 1864, asked an 1851 women's rights convention in Akron, Ohio, "Ain't I a Woman?" Library of Congress, Prints and Photographs Division.

BIBLIOGRAPHY

Mabee, Carleton. *Sojourner Truth: Slave, Prophet, Legend.* New York: New York University Press, 1993.

Painter, Nell Irvin. *Sojourner Truth: A Life, A Symbol.* New York: W. W. Norton & Company, 1996.

Harriet Ross Tubman (c.1820–1913)

Harriet Tubman was born a slave in Maryland. She escaped from slavery to Pennsylvania with the help of the Underground Railroad in 1849. Tubman became a "conductor" on the railroad and made 19 trips back into the South and personally brought out 300 slaves between 1850 and 1860. She was active throughout her life on behalf of women's **suffrage** and civil rights. She was also an active member of the **National Association of Colored Women (NACW)**, which she helped organize in 1896. She also frequently addressed and attended suffrage conventions. (CKC) **See also** Abolition; Slavery and Women.

BIBLIOGRAPHY

Hymowitz, Carol and Michaele Weissman. *A History of Women in America.* Toronto: Bantam Books, 1978.

Woloch, Nancy. *Early American Women, A Documentary History: 1600–1900.* New York: McGraw-Hill, 1997.

Julia Gardiner Tyler (1820–1889)

Julia Tyler, the second wife of Whig President John Tyler, served as an important political advisor to her husband. The daughter of a U.S. Senator from New York, Julia Tyler was long interested in politics, and was something of a rebel for her time, as illustrated by her shocking appearance as a model in a bonnet ad. While first lady, she visited the House gallery often and frequently lobbied congressmen on issues of interest to her. Her efforts on behalf of the Tyler administration's proposed annexation of Texas helped garner support for the bill. In addition to her personal lobbying on the issue, Julia Tyler used her role as first lady to hold an official ball to which only those politicians wavering on the Texas issue were invited. As a testament to her importance to the bill's passage, she received the pen with which the president signed the legislation into law. She was also interested in shaping the public's perception of her. Toward this end, she hired a press agent to encourage positive coverage. In her effort to promote her image of the presidency, Julia Tyler initiated the playing of "Hail to the Chief" and greeted guests from her seat on a raised platform. (BN) **See also** First Ladies.

BIBLIOGRAPHY

Caroli, Betty Boyd. *First Ladies.* New York: Oxford University Press, 1995.

Truman, Margaret. *First Ladies.* New York: Random House, 1995.

Letitia Christian Tyler (1790–1842)

In 1839, two years before her husband, John Tyler, ascended from the vice presidency to the White House on the death of President William Henry Harrison, Letitia Christian Tyler suffered a stroke that left her crippled. As first lady, Letitia delegated the role of hostess to her daughter, Priscilla. She publicly left the family quarters only once for her daughter's wedding in 1842. She became the first president's wife to die in the White House. (BN) **See also** First Ladies.

BIBLIOGRAPHY

Caroli, Betty Boyd. *First Ladies.* New York: Oxford University Press, 1995.

Truman, Margaret. *First Ladies.* New York: Random House, 1995.

Laura D'Andrea Tyson (1947–)

Laura Tyson served as chairwoman of the Council of Economic Advisors and, later, as head of the National Economic Policy Council in the Democratic administration of President Bill Clinton. She met with some criticism because she does not fully embrace free trade. Rather, she supports what she has termed "cautious actuism" when dealing with foreign nations. Noted for her views on government support in trade issues, which she outlined in her 1992 book *Who's Bashing*

Whom?, she left Washington in December 1996 to return to an academic position at the University of California at Berkeley. (JCS)

BIBLIOGRAPHY

Drew, Elizabeth. *On the Edge: The Clinton Presidency.* New York: Simon and Schuster, 1994.

"Tyson Set to Join Ameritech Board." *New York Times* (February 13, 1997): D20.

U

UAW v. Johnson Controls, Inc. (1991)

In *UAW v. Johnson Controls, Inc.*, 111 S.Ct. (1991), employees of a battery factory and their union, the United Automobile Workers, challenged the fetal protection policy of their employer, Johnson Controls, Inc. The policy prohibited fertile women from holding jobs that required exposure to lead because of concern for their unborn children. The workers claimed that the policy violated **Title VII of the Civil Rights Act of 1964**, which makes it unlawful for an employer to discriminate on the basis of sex except where it can be shown that such discrimination is a "bona fide occupational qualification reasonably necessary to the normal operation of that particular business," an exception otherwise known as a BFOQ.

Challenges to fetal protection policies began to emerge in the early 1980s, but the courts had previously modified their interpretation of Title VII to uphold the policies and only required employers to show a risk to a fetus existed to exclude fertile women.

In *UAW v. Johnson Controls*, the Supreme Court unanimously ruled that the practice of limiting the employment of fertile women in jobs posing reproductive health hazards constituted **sex discrimination** because the policy, requiring infertility, did not satisfy the BFOQ. The Court's opinion asserted that "decisions about the welfare of future children must be left to the parents who conceive . . . them rather than to the employers who hire those parents." (MBS)

Bibliography

Giacomini, Mita K. and James C. Robinson. "A Reallocation of Rights in Industries with Reproductive Health Hazards." *The Milbank Quarterly* 70, no. 4 (1992): 587-603.

Una

The *Una* was a Boston monthly that was "devoted to the elevation of woman." It was the first **suffrage** paper and was edited by **Paulina Wright Davis**. Founded in 1853, the paper was a vocal advocate of women's rights. Davis consciously challenged what a woman's magazine ought to be. She was disappointed in the nation's most widespread women's publication, ***Godey's Lady's Book***. The *Una* took a more feminist and proactive stand on issues from education and economic equality to marriage reform and suffrage. The paper ceased publication in 1855. **See also** Feminism.

Paulina Wright Davis was the publisher of the *Una*, one of the first women's rights journals. Library of Congress.

Bibliography

The Una. Vols 1-3. Boston: Sayles, Miller & Simons, 1853-55.

United Daughters of the Confederacy (UDC)

The United Daughters of the Confederacy (UDC), originally founded in 1894, is a national organization of women descendants of Confederate Veterans of the American Civil War. The group focuses on the Civil War years of 1861 to 1865, specifically in terms of educational, historical, memorial, and patriotic activities. The UDC also studies, examines, and shares literature and poetry by southern writers, especially writers of the Civil War period; sponsors community activities; and often works in conjunction with the Children of the Confederacy, an organization with similar beliefs. The group holds an annual meeting every November in cities across the nation and publishes the *United Daughters of the Confederacy Magazine.*

Bibliography

Foster, Gaines M. *Ghosts of the Confederacy: Defeat, the Lost Cause, and the Emergence of the New South.* New York: Oxford University Press, 1987.

Poppenheim, Mary B., et al. *The History of the United Daughters of the Confederacy.* Raleigh, NC: Edwards & Broughton, 1956.

United Nations Decade for Women

As a result of the **International Women's Year** Conference held in Mexico City in the summer of 1975, the General Assembly of the United Nations on December 15, 1975, approved a resolution proclaiming the period from 1976 to 1985 as the United Nations Decade for Women: Equality, Development and Peace. The declaration was a conscious attempt by the United Nations to call upon its members to examine and implement the World Plan of Action adopted at the first International Women's Year Conference. A second conference of governments met in Copenhagen in 1980 to approve a "World Program of Action." A third conference convened in Nairobi, Kenya, in 1985 to review and appraise progress achieved and to approve the "Forward Looking Strategies to the Year 2000." The fourth UN-sponsored women's conference was held in Beijing, China, in 1995. (CGM)

Bibliography

The United Nations and the Advancement of Women (1945–1996). New York: Department of Public Information, United Nations, 1996.

Winslow, Anne. *Women, Politics, and the United Nations.* Westport, CT: Greenwood Press, 1995.

United States Children's Bureau

The United States Children's Bureau was created in 1912 through the efforts of individuals like **Florence Kelley** and **Lillian Ward**. **Julia Lathrop** was the bureau's first director and sought to use its regulating powers to influence reforms in children's rights and education. Some of the group's earliest functions included conducting studies in maternal mortality, juvenile delinquency, mental illness, child labor, and mother's pensions. The results of these studies caused a number of governmental and legal changes.

In 1917, **Grace Abbott** began working with the Children's Bureau, eventually becoming its director in 1921. Along with **Katherine Lenroot**, who began her association with the group in 1914, and **Clara Beyer**, Abbott helped revitalize the bureau under the jurisdiction of President Franklin Roosevelt's New Deal reform programs. Abbott served as director until 1934, at which time Lenroot took the position, a role she filled until 1951. Over the years, the United States Children's Bureau continued to champion minor's rights, taking up such platforms as child labor laws, prevention of child abuse, and education reform.

Bibliography

Addams, Jane. *My Friend, Julia Lathrop.* New York: Macmillan, 1935.

Ladd-Taylor, May Madeleine and Molly Taylor. "Hull House Goes to Washington: Women and the Children's Bureau." In Noralee Frankel and Nancy S. Dye, eds. *Gender, Class, Race and Reform: The Progressive Era.* Lexington: University Press of Kentucky, 1991.

United States v. Virginia, et. al. (1996)

In 1990, the U.S. Justice Department sued state-supported Virginia Military Institute (VMI) on the grounds that its exclusively male admissions policy violated the equal protection clause of the Fourteenth Amendment. Founded in 1839, VMI was the only single-sex public institution of higher learning in Virginia. Using an "adversative method" of training not available elsewhere in Virginia, the school's mission is to produce "citizen soldiers," which Virginia argued was appropriate for males, but not for females. Virginia also defended VMI on the grounds that it added diversity to the state's otherwise co-educational system. Although the District Court ruled in favor of VMI, the Fourth Circuit Court of Appeals ordered Virginia to remedy the constitutional violation by either admitting females to VMI, providing an equal alternative for women, or allowing VMI to revert to a private institution. Virginia responded by establishing the Virginia Women's Institute of Leadership (VWIL), a four-year, all-female parallel program at Mary Baldwin College. In contrast to VMI's emphasis on military training, VMIL embraced "a cooperative method which reinforces self-esteem," designed to address the specific developmental needs of women. The District Court upheld the VWIL program as a constitutional alternative to VMI and the Fourth Circuit Court agreed. The Supreme Court reviewed both issues at stake, whether the exclusion of females from VMI violated the Fourteenth Amendment, and whether the VWIL program was a constitutional remedy. In a 7 to 1 opinion in *U.S. v. Virginia, et al.*, 116 S.Ct. 2264 (1996), with Chief Justice William Rehnquist concurring, the Court ruled that VWIL did not provide an equal opportunity for women. (Justice Clarence Thomas did not participate in the decision.) Writing for the majority, Justice **Ruth Bader Ginsburg** stated that "the Commonwealth has created a VWIL program fairly appraised as a 'pale shadow' of VMI in terms of the range of curricular choices and faculty stature, funding, prestige, alumni support and influence." The Court also failed to use the VMI decision to raise the standard of review for gender discrimination to strict scrutiny. Although the state of Virginia at least temporarily continued funding for the VWIL program, VMI opened its doors to women beginning in September 1997, when 30 females enrolled. VWIL admitted an additional 45 women, raising the total enrollment in the program to over 100. In a similar case, The Citadel in South Carolina was forced to admit women in 1994, leaving many observers to question the future of single-sex education. (LvA)

Bibliography

Frost-Knappman, Elizabeth. *Women's Rights on Trial: 101 Historic Trials from Anne Hutchinson to the Virginia Military Institute Cadets.* Detroit: Gale, 1997.

United States v. Virginia, et al., 116 S. Ct. 2264 (1996).

Jolene Unsoeld (1931–)

Jolene Unsoeld was an experienced Capitol Hill lobbyist before she ran for the Washington legislature in 1985. She also served on the Democratic National Committee from 1980 to 1988. In 1988 she was elected to the 101st Congress, but defeated for re-election in 1994.

Bibliography

Kamen, Al. "Interior's Ramspeck Relocators." *The Washington Post* 118 (February 1, 1995): A17.

V

Nydia M. Velazquez (1953–)

Nydia Velazquez began her national political career in 1983 when she became a special assistant to Congressman Ed Towns. From 1984 to 1986, Velazquez served as a member of the New York City Council. In 1986, she became the director of the Migration Division Office for the Department of Labor and Human Resources of Puerto Rico, a role she filled until 1989. From 1989 to 1992, Velazquez worked as director of the Department of Puerto Rican Community Affairs in the United States. On November 3, 1992, Nydia Velazquez was elected to the U.S. House of Representatives as a Democrat from New York. She was re-elected in 1994 and 1996.

BIBLIOGRAPHY

Bingham, Clara. *Women on the Hill.* New York: Time Books, 1997.

Margolies-Mezvinsky, Marjorie. *A Women's Place.* New York: Crow Publishers, 1994.

Violence Against Women Act (1994)

This Violence Against Women Act became law when President Bill Clinton signed it on September 13, 1994, as part of an omnibus crime bill. It is a wide-ranging act that addresses many areas of concern regarding violence against women by providing a better and more uniform response by the criminal justice system. The act includes provisions that allow women to sue their abusers for civil rights violations, battered immigrant spouses to apply for legal resident status, federal penalties for persons who cross state lines with the intent of harming a spouse, increased funding for battered women's shelters and a national **domestic violence** hotline, and for the education of judges and prosecutors about violent crimes committed against women. (SJW)

BIBLIOGRAPHY

Hirshman, Linda. "Making Safety a Civil Right." *Ms.* 4, no. 5 (September/October 1994): 44-47.

Symons, Joanne L. "Legislation for Women: The End of Gridlock?" *Executive Female* (May/June 1993): 51.

Voice of Industry

The *Voice of Industry*, which became known as the most widely read labor newspaper of the mid-to-late 1840s, began publication on May 19, 1845, in Fitchburg, Massachusetts. The paper was edited by William F. Young, who used the publication as an outlet for challenging labor standards and for seeking labor reform.

On July 3, 1845, Young and the *Voice of Industry* directly challenged another labor newspaper, the ***Lowell Offering***, for ignoring the plights of workers in the Lowell mills while focusing on literary material instead of reform issues. In October 1845, the *Voice of Industry* merged with two other publications and relocated to Lowell, Massachusetts. **Sarah Bagley**, a leading labor activist, served on the publication committee.

In May 1846, the Lowell Female Reform Association purchased the *Voice of Industry* and named Bagley its new chief editor. Under Bagley's guidance, the paper began to carry poetry, stories, and advice along with attacks on a number of labor abuses, including the factory system and long workdays. In 1848, the *Voice of Industry* ceased publication. **See also** Lowell Mill Girls.

BIBLIOGRAPHY

Cantor, Milton, ed. *American Working Class Culture: Exploration in American Labor and Social History.* Westport, CT: Greenwood, 1979.

Voluntary Parenthood League

After noted birth control reformer **Margaret Sanger** moved to Europe in 1915 to avoid American court proceedings, **Mary Coffin Ware Dennett**, took control of Sanger's organization, the National Birth Control League. Dennett changed the group's name to the Voluntary Parenthood League, which moved from Sanger's militant tactics to more mainstream tactics like lectures and lobbying Congress.

Under Dennett's leadership, the group sought an amendment of existing birth control restrictions and the distribution of public information on these topics. It also supported the distribution through the mail of the 1918 essay, "The Sex Side of Life," a piece eventually declared obscene by the postmaster general. Dennett and the Voluntary Parenthood League continued to mail the essay, which led to Dennett's arrest. All charges against her, however, were later dropped as a result of the case *United States v. Dennett.* In 1925, the Voluntary Parenthood League merged with the **American Birth Control League**, an organization begun by Margaret Sanger after her return from London. This united group, which kept the Voluntary Parenthood League title, pursued the establishment of legalized birth control freedom under the jurisdiction of the medical community. It also sponsored its own newspaper, *The Birth Control Herald*, from 1922 to 1925.

BIBLIOGRAPHY

Chesler, Ellen. *Women of Valor. Margaret Sanger and the Birth Control Movement.* New York: Simon and Schuster, 1992.

Sanger, Margaret. *My Fight for Birth Control.* New York: Fanar, Reinhart, 1931.

Vorchheimer v. Philadelphia (1976)

In *Vorchheimer v. Philadelphia*, 532 F. 2d 880 (3d Cir. 1976), the Third Circuit Court of Appeals ruled that Philadelphia had not violated Susan Lynn Vorchheimer's constitutional rights by denying her admission to all-male Central High School. Philadelphia only had two "academic" high schools with exclusively college preparatory classes: Central High for boys and Girls High. When Vorchheimer applied to Central High because its science classes were reputed to be superior, she was denied admission because of her sex.

The district court ruled that the separate school policy was unconstitutional because it was not substantially related to the city's educational objectives. The Court of Appeals for the Third Circuit reversed that decision, ruling that under some circumstances sex differences may be legally justified. The appellate court held that the two sexes were equally affected by the sex-segregated school system. And because there was evidence that single-sex high schools offered advantages to males and females, the city could maintain separate high schools.

One of the appellate judges disagreed, arguing that the concept of "separate but equal," no longer acceptable for racial classifications, should not be tolerated for classifications based on sex. In 1977, the U.S. Supreme Court voted 4-4 (Justice William Rehnquist did not vote) to affirm the lower court's decision; a tie vote in the Supreme Court upholds the appellate court decision. (SM)

BIBLIOGRAPHY

Mezey, Susan Gluck. *In Pursuit of Equality: Women, Public Policy and the Federal Courts.* New York: St. Martin's Press, 1992.

Vorchheimer v. Philadelphia, 430 U.S. 703 (1977).

Voting Rights

It took a powerful social movement for voting rights to be expanded to women in the United States. Before the American Revolution, some colonies included women landowners in the electorate. Ironically, with the passage of the U.S. Constitution and new state constitutions, female **suffrage** was explicitly barred in the move to near universal male suffrage. Despite the beginnings of the woman's movement at Seneca Falls, New York, in 1848, voting rights activists set aside their interests in favor of supporting **abolition**. Much to their chagrin, their efforts were rewarded with the passage of the Fourteenth Amendment, which officially limited suffrage to males, and the Fifteenth Amendment, which barred the denial of voting rights based on "race, color, or previous condition of servitude" but not on sex. In response to this exclusion, **Elizabeth Cady Stanton** and **Susan B. Anthony** formed the **National Women's Suffrage Association (NWSA)** in 1869. Later that year, **Lucy Stone** founded the **American Woman Suffrage Association (AWSA).** Litigating for the vote, NWSA brought a test case, *Minor v. Happersett* (1875), to the U.S. Supreme Court. The Court unanimously rejected the claim that denying women voting rights was a violation of the Fourteenth Amendment's privileges or immunities clause. Despite the failure of women to gain suffrage protection through the federal courts, individual states began at this time to enfranchise women in local elections. Kansas, for example, allowed women to vote in school board elections (1859), and other states, including Massachusetts in 1879, soon followed. The NWSA and the AWSA joined forces in 1890 to press exclusively for suffrage. Their goals were achieved in 1920 with the passage of the **Nineteenth Amendment** forbidding denial of suffrage on account of sex. However, even after passage of the Nineteenth Amendment, minority women's right to vote continued to be hampered by violence, intimidation, racist registration procedures, and English-only ballots. Many of these barriers were removed with the passage of the Voting Rights Act of 1965 and its subsequent amendments. Today, women have emerged as a powerful factor at the ballot box. Because their voting rates are generally higher than those of men, women's votes have the potential to determine election outcomes. **See also** Seneca Falls Convention. (BN)

Women exercising the right to vote in New York in 1917. Library of Congress.

BIBLIOGRAPHY

Davidson, Chandler and Bernard Grofman, eds. *Quiet Revolution in the South.* Princeton: Princeton University Press, 1994.

Kraditor, Eileen. *The Ideas of the Woman Suffrage Movement 1890–1920.* New York: Norton, 1981.

McGlen, Nancy E. and Karen O'Connor. *Women's Rights: The Struggle for Equality in the Nineteenth and Twentieth Centuries.* New York: Praeger, 1983.

Barbara Farrell Vucanovich (1921–)

Barbara Vucanovich served as staff assistant for Nevada Republican Senator Paul Laxalt from 1974 to 1982, and as a delegate to a number of Nevada State Republican Conventions between 1952 and 1980. She was also a delegate to the 1976 and 1980 Republican National Conventions. In 1982, she was elected to the U.S. House of Representatives as a Republican from Nevada. She was re-elected to six succeeding Congresses, choosing not to run again in 1996. She was active in obtaining increased funding for breast cancer research and prevention.

BIBLIOGRAPHY

Cassata, Donna. "Quality of Life is Top Priority." *Congressional Quarterly Weekly Report* 53, no. 20 (May 20, 1995): 1380.

Gruenwald Juliana and Alan Greenblatt. "Three House Veterans Join Departure List." *Congressional Quarterly Weekly Report* 53, no. 48 (December 9, 1995): 3759.

W

Enid Greene Waldholtz (1958–)

Republican Enid Greene Waldholtz was elected to the U.S. House of Representatives from Utah in 1994, defeating incumbent Democrat Karen Shepherd. The election was a rematch of the 1992 congressional contest. Enid Waldholtz and her husband Joe Waldholtz, a former Utah Republican executive director, were accused of a series of financial misdeeds, including failure to pay thousands of dollars in state and federal taxes, failure to file a joint 1994 federal tax return, and failure to account properly for $1.5 million of campaign funds. Representative Waldholtz blamed the acts on her husband, who disappeared when the scandal broke. Representative Waldholtz did not stand for re-election in 1996, although she did manage to forestall a resignation.

BIBLIOGRAPHY

Carlson, Margaret. "The Answer Lady." *Time* 146, no. 26 (December 25, 1995): 136.

Cloud, David S. "Waldholtz Admits Problems But Blames Husband." *Congressional Quarterly Weekly Report* 53, no. 49 (December 16, 1995): 3786.

Eddings, Jerelyn. "He Flees and She Stumbles." *US News and World Report* 119, no. 21 (November 27, 1995): 17.

Gruenwald, Juliana. "Utah." *Congressional Quarterly Weekly Report* 54, no. 8 (February 24, 1996): 495.

Rosin, Hanna. "TRB: The Crying Game." *The New Republic* 214, no. 22 (May 27, 1996): 4.

Mary Edwards Walker (1832–1919)

Mary Walker served as an assistant surgeon for the United States Army during the Civil War, earning the rank of first lieutenant. Walker was the first woman commissioned to serve on a surgical staff for any American military force in time of war. Later in life, Walker became active in the **suffrage** movement.

BIBLIOGRAPHY

Leonard, Elizabeth D. *Yankee Women.* New York: W.W. Norton, 1994.

Snyder, Charles M. *Dr. Mary Walker.* Stratford, NH: Ayer Company, 1977.

Lurleen Burns Wallace (1926–1968)

In 1966, Lurleen Wallace was elected governor of Alabama, continuing the administration of her husband George C. Wallace, who was prevented by state law from succeeding himself. Lurleen Wallace was inaugurated on January 16, 1967, becoming Alabama's first woman governor. Her husband stayed on as an official senior advisor, a position he used to circumvent Alabama's law against consecutive terms for governors. Her term as governor served as an extension of her husband's terms.

BIBLIOGRAPHY

"Pa and Ma Wallace as a Dynasty." *Life* 60 (March 11, 1966): 4.

Wards Cove Packing Company v. Antonio (1989)

In *Wards Cove Packing Company v. Antonio*, 490 U.S. 642 (1989), the U.S. Supreme Court held that cannery employees had failed to prove their employer violated **Title VII of the Civil Rights Act of 1964**. The case arose when nonwhite workers sued two Alaskan canneries for discriminating against them on the basis of race in hiring and promotion policies and working conditions. The plaintiffs' statistics showed a higher percentage of minority workers in lower-paid cannery jobs and a lower percentage of minority workers in higher-paid noncannery jobs. The plaintiffs cited *Griggs v. Duke Power Company* (1971), in which the Supreme Court held that Title VII forbids employment practices with a disproportionate impact on minorities.

The Court ruled that plaintiffs cannot simply count the number of minority workers in the better jobs; they must instead compare the racial composition of qualified persons in the labor market with the racial composition of persons holding the better paying jobs. Moreover, workers had to point to specific employment practices that were leading to the unequal distribution of jobs. Finally, the Court announced that the burden of proving discrimination was always on the employee. (SM)

BIBLIOGRAPHY

Griggs v. Duke Power Company, 401 U.S. 424 (1971).

Mezey, Susan Gluck. *In Pursuit of Equality: Women, Public Policy and the Federal Courts.* New York: St. Martin's Press, 1992.

Washerwoman's Strike of 1881

The Washerwoman's Strike was an attempt by laundresses, cooks, and other domestic servants in Atlanta, Georgia, to obtain higher wages. The strike was timed to interfere with the Cotton States Exposition that was taking place in Atlanta in the summer of 1881. Inspired by local ministers, both men and women went on strike for higher wages and encouraged others to participate in the strike. Ultimately, the strike failed to achieve its goals; striking workers were forced back to work because landlords raised rents to break the strike. Although the strike failed to garner higher wages, it is often cited as a turning point in Southern labor relations because it became a symbol of the labor movement.

BIBLIOGRAPHY

Rabinowitz, Howard. *Race Relations in the Urban South, 1865–1900.* New York: Oxford University Press, 1978.

Martha Dandridge Custis Washington (1731–1802)

As the first American presidential spouse, Martha Washington, the wife of President George Washington, set important precedents for the position. Martha Washington's actions as first lady indicated the public role the wife of the president would be expected to play. The public nature of her position was evident even before she entered New York City, the nation's first capital; she made this journey on a government barge rather than through private means. Once her husband entered office in 1789, Martha Washington promoted both her country and her husband's interests, setting the tone for future **first ladies**. She used entertaining as a way to lend both accessibility and dignity to the presidency. She held Friday drawing room receptions for meeting guests and personally returned the calls of all visitors within three days. Martha Washington was seen as a surrogate for the president, receiving official receptions on her private outings. She was also the first presidential wife to lament the confines of her unelected position. Writing to a friend, Martha Washington explained, "I have not had one half hour to myself since the day of my arrival." (BN)

As the first presidential wife, Martha Washington, shown here in a painting by Gilbert Stuart, helped define the role of the first lady. Library of Congress.

BIBLIOGRAPHY

Caroli, Betty Boyd. *First Ladies.* New York: Oxford University Press, 1995.

Truman, Margaret. *First Ladies.* New York: Random House, 1995.

Maxine Waters (1938–)

United States Representative Maxine Waters, a Democrat, rose from a St. Louis **welfare** family of 13 children to become a leading California legislator. Serving first as a member of the California state assembly, Waters made history as the first African-American woman to become majority whip, chair of the Democratic Caucus, chair of the Rules Committee, and chair of a Budget Conference Committee. During her 14-year stint in the California legislature, Waters created set-aside programs for minorities and women and the first public school in a public housing project. She also successfully battled to prohibit the investment of state funds in apartheid-era South Africa.

Since her election to Congress in 1991, Waters has served as the chair of the Congressional Black Caucus and on the committees on Veterans Affairs, Small Business, Banking and Finance, Urban Affairs, and the Judiciary. In Congress, Maxine Waters has continued to ceaselessly champion the causes of youth, the poor, minorities, and women. Among other achievements, she initiated and gained passage for the Gang Prevention and Youth Recreation Act, the Job and Life Skills Improvement Act, and the act creating the Center for Women Veterans within the Department of Veterans Affairs. (ST)

BIBLIOGRAPHY

California Women Speak. Davis, CA: Alta Vista Press, 1994.

Webster v. Reproductive Health Services (1989)

Webster v. Reproductive Health Services, 492 U.S. 490 (1989), was a highly visible United States Supreme Court decision that upheld certain Missouri state restrictions on **abortion**. With the extensive media coverage it generated, the case became a high stakes political and legal showdown over the continuation of the ***Roe v. Wade*** (1973) precedent. A record number of interest groups participated in 81 *amicus curiae* (friend of the court) briefs submitted to the Court regarding this case. The solicitor general of the United States for the Bush Administration Justice Department, in an important and controversial amicus brief, requested that *Roe v. Wade* be overturned, the first time a solicitor general had ever made such a request in abortion law. The split decision by the Court in *Webster* left the *Roe* precedent weakened but standing. Four justices seemed willing to overturn *Roe*, but the necessary fifth vote was lacking. Justice **Sandra Day O'Connor**, the first woman on the U.S. Supreme Court, and at the time the only one, refused to join her four colleagues in overturning *Roe*. She did, however, vote to uphold all the Missouri restrictions, reasoning that they did not pose an "undue burden" on women's abortion rights, and were within a state's police powers (reserved under the Tenth Amendment) to protect and regulate public health. The Missouri statute stated that human life began at conception and barred the use of public funds for abortions, prohibiting abortions in public hospitals and requiring viability testing after 19 weeks. O'Connor's unwillingness to overturn *Roe v. Wade* was criticized by Justice Antonin Scalia in his written opinion. The other four justices voted to uphold *Roe* and strike down some of the restrictions and regulations in the Missouri legislation. The unusual 4–1-4 decision had O'Connor in the middle agreeing in part with each block of four votes.

The *Webster* decision permits state restrictions on abortion as long as they do not impose an "undue burden" on the woman's privacy-based right to a legal abortion. The criteria for what constitutes an "undue burden" is unclear and has led to further litigation over other states' abortion restrictions and regulations. *Webster* signaled a willingness on the part of the Court to permit state restrictions on *Roe's* privacy and viability criteria. The votes on the Court displayed how narrowly the *Roe* precedent survived, and how divided the Court was on this issue. In the 1992 presidential election, the vulnerability of *Roe* was a factor in the vote, with both pro-life and pro-choice adherents noting the importance of future Supreme Court nominations for the future of abortion jurisprudence. The 1992 presidential candidates, Republican George Bush and Democrat Bill Clinton were clear opposites on abortion—Bush was pro-life and Clinton pro-choice. (LW) **See also** Human Life Amendment.

BIBLIOGRAPHY

Garrow, David J. *Liberty & Sexuality: The Right to Privacy and the Making of* Roe v. Wade. New York: Macmillan, 1994.

O'Connor, Karen. *No Neutral Ground: Abortion Politics in an Age of Absolutes*. Boulder, CO: Westview Press, 1996.

Petchesky, Rosalind Pollack. *Abortion and Woman's Choice: The State, Sexuality, & Reproductive Freedom*. Boston, MA: Northeastern University Press, 1990.

Woliver, Laura R. "Rhetoric and Symbols in American Abortion Politics." In Marian Githens and Dorothy McBride Stetson, eds. *Abortion Politics: Public Policy in Cross-Cultural Perspective.* New York: Routledge, 1996.

Sarah Ragle Weddington (1945–)

Sarah Weddington, a Democrat, began her political career as a member of the Texas House of Representatives, where she served from 1973 to 1977. Weddington stepped into the national political spotlight in 1977 when she was appointed as general counsel to the Department of Agriculture by President Jimmy Carter. She served as a presidential assistant from 1979 to 1980. Weddington also served on a number of boards, committees, and councils during her political career. From 1978 to 1981, she was acting chair of the Interdepartmental Task Force on Women and in 1981 a member of the President's Commission on Executive Exchange. Weddington returned to private life in 1981 after the Carter administration left office. In 1992, she wrote *A Question of Choice*, a book that illustrates her political and moral views on government and society.

BIBLIOGRAPHY

Crawford, Ann Fears and Crystal Sasse Ragsdale. "Advisor to the President, Sarah Ragle Weddington." In *Women in Texas*. Austin, TX: State House Press, 1992.

Stern, Lynn. "Sarah Weddington: Advocate with Clout." *Working Women* 5 (February 1981): 35-37.

Weddington, Sarah. "Carter Women: Where Will They Go Now?" *Glamour* 79 (April 1981): 106, 110.

——. *A Question of Choice*. New York: Grosset-Putnam, 1992.

Weeks v. Southern Bell Telephone and Telegraph (1969)

In 1968, in *Weeks v. Southern Bell Telephone and Telegraph*, 408 F. 2d 228 (5th Cir., 1969), Lorena Weeks sued Southern Bell when she was denied a job because it required lifting more than 30 pounds. Southern Bell claimed it was acting in accordance with the Georgia state labor commission rule that prohibited women, for safety reasons, from holding jobs requiring the lifting of more than 30 pounds. This case raised the question of whether such **protective legislation** was a bona fide occupational qualification (i.e., a necessary rule that could be relied upon in hiring decisions). The district court agreed with the company and its bona fide occupational qualification (BFOQ) claim. However, before the case reached the appellate court, the state of Georgia repealed the 30-pound rule. On appeal, Weeks claimed that the company's policy violated **Title VII of the Civil Rights Act of 1964** because Southern Bell could not prove that gender had anything to do with the job requirements. The Fifth Circuit agreed with Weeks, shifting the burden of proof to Southern Bell to show that the restriction was a BFOQ. The company had no evidence to that effect, having relied upon the Georgia protective legislation.

BIBLIOGRAPHY

Baer, Judith A. *Women in American Law*. New York: Holmes & Meier, 1996.

Boumil, Marcia Mobilia and Stephen C. Hicks. *Women and the Law*. Littleton, CO: Fred B. Rothman & Company, 1992.

Weinberger v. Wiesenfeld (1975)

Under the Social Security Act, only widows were entitled to survivor's benefits. In 1972, a widower challenged the distinction as a violation of the equal protection and due process clauses of the Fifth Amendment because the law unfairly denied benefits to men based upon their gender. In *Weinburger v. Wiesenfeld*, 420 U.S. 636 (1975), the U.S. Supreme Court ruled that the Social Security Act's survivors regulations were unconstitutional. The Court relied heavily on its decision in ***Frontiero v. Richardson*** (1973). At the heart of the case, the Court found that the government made no reasonable distinction between men and women that justified limiting benefits to one gender. **See also** Social Security.

BIBLIOGRAPHY

Boumil, Marcia Mobilia and Stephen C. Hicks. *Women and the Law*. Littleton, CO: Fred B. Rothman & Company, 1992.

Mezey, Susan. *In Pursuit of Equality*. New York: St. Martin's Press, 1992.

Jessica McCullough "Judy" Weis (1901–1963)

Jessica Weis was vice-chair of the Monroe County Republican Committee in New York from 1937 until 1952. She also served as president of the National Federation of Republican Women in 1940 and 1941. Weis was a member of the Republican National Committee from 1944 to 1963, as well as a delegate at the Republican National Conventions in 1940, 1944, 1948, 1952, and 1956. In 1953, President Dwight D.

Eisenhower appointed Weis to the National Civil Defense Advisory Council, to which she was reappointed in 1956 and 1960. In 1958, Weis was elected to the U.S. House of Representatives from New York; she served there until her death in 1963.

Bibliography

Weis, Jessica McCullough. "Organizing the Women." In James Cannon, ed. *Politics U.S.A.: A Political Guide to the Winning of Public Office.* New York: Doubleday, 1960.

Welfare

The **Aid to Families with Dependent Children (AFDC)** Program provided financial assistance to poor women and children from 1935 to 1996, representing one of the nation's most important public welfare assistance programs. On August 22, 1996, President Bill Clinton signed the Personal Responsibility and Work Opportunity Reconciliation Act of 1996 (Public Law 104–193), ending the AFDC program and creating a new welfare policy for the poor. The new law transferred almost all decision-making power over welfare policy for the poor to state governments, giving the states responsibility for creating their own welfare programs. Federal funds will now be transferred to the states in lump-sum payments called block grants.

Until 1935, U.S. welfare policy was left to state and local governments. In the early twentieth century, many states created Mothers' Pensions programs as a substitute for the Poor Laws, which required women and, often, children in poor families to work or be sent to poorhouses or orphanages. The Mothers' Pensions programs provided limited aid to poor widows to allow them to remain at home with their children.

In the 1930s, in reaction to the widespread **poverty** that characterized the Great Depression, the federal government began to take a more active interest in the plight of poor women and their children. As part of President Franklin Roosevelt's efforts to counter the effects of the Depression, the federal government created the Aid to Dependent Children program (ADC), later renamed Aid to Families with Dependent Children (AFDC), as part of the Social Security Act of 1935.

The 1935 act created two social insurance programs, Old Age/Retirement Insurance and Unemployment Insurance, and three public assistance programs, Old Age Assistance (for needy persons over 65), Aid to the Blind (for the needy adult blind), and Aid to Dependent Children (for needy children). The Social Security Disability Insurance program, enacted in 1956, provided benefits for totally and permanently disabled workers no longer capable of working. In 1972, Congress established the means-tested Supplemental Security Income (SSI) program, combining the Old Age Assistance and Aid to the Blind programs; it also included assistance for the disabled poor.

The public assistance programs, commonly known as welfare, comprise varying degrees of federal-state involvement; they are funded by both state and federal taxes and administered by state and local governments. The ADC program was created with divided responsibilities for policymaking between states and the federal government, with states exercising a great deal of autonomy over the rules of eligibility and the allocation of benefits. For the most part, the decisions over benefits and eligibility, especially in the South, led to the exclusion of many minority group members from the program. For the first 30 years of its existence, the ADC program primarily served white widows and their children.

In the 1960s, as the nation began to pay more attention to the problems of race and poverty, welfare reformers made increasing efforts to expand the welfare rolls to minority families. As welfare rolls expanded, state officials tried to reduce the number of recipients and the amount of benefits available to them. Welfare recipients turned to the federal courts for help and, as a result of this litigation, the federal courts began to play an important role in national welfare policymaking.

Welfare reformers hoped the courts would accept their claim that the U.S. Constitution guaranteed a "right to live," and that the courts would be willing to use their authority to expand welfare rights. At first it appeared that the U.S. Supreme Court was receptive to their argument that governmental resources should be distributed more equitably. The Court's rulings in *King v. Smith* (1968), *Shapiro v. Thompson* (1969), and *Goldberg v. Kelly* (1970) signaled that it might be willing to place limits on the state's control of AFDC eligibility policy. But after their initial successes in *King, Shapiro*, and *Kelly*, followed by a few victories in later years, welfare reformers were disappointed by the Court's refusal to use its constitutional authority to force states to raise benefit levels.

In 1967, government officials tried to lower the welfare rolls by creating a Work Incentive Program (WIN) that required AFDC beneficiaries to accept jobs or enroll in work-training programs; the 1971 Talmadge Amendments, or WIN II, attempted to make these work requirements more stringent by emphasizing placement in entry-level jobs rather than education and training.

Debate over welfare policy continued throughout the 1970s. The welfare initiative begun by President Richard Nixon, called the Family Assistance Plan (FAP), was designed to provide a guaranteed annual income for poor families with dependent children. Also termed a "negative income tax," the plan called for the federal government to provide cash assistance to bring people up to the poverty line. For a variety of reasons, the FAP never succeeded in gaining enough support in Congress.

In 1975, a version of the negative income tax, the Earned Income Tax Credit (EITC), was added to the Internal Revenue Code to offset a raise in the Social Security payroll tax. The EITC is a refundable tax credit, that is, a family gets money from the government if the tax the family owes is less than the amount of the credit. It is designed to increase the earnings of low income working families by giving them a specified amount of dollars based on their earnings. The EITC was significantly expanded during the Clinton administration.

During the 1970s, the federal government also attempted to reduce the welfare rolls by increasing state efforts at child support enforcement. In 1974, Congress passed legislation requiring states to develop programs to shift the child support burden from public AFDC funds to absent parents who failed to meet their child support obligations. The law was precipitated by congressional concern over the rising costs of public assistance and congressional belief that the states were insufficiently committed to enforcing child support obligations to reduce AFDC expenses.

The legislation specified that state agencies had to prove the paternity of children born to unmarried mothers and establish and enforce child support obligations; states were also required to set up services to locate absent parents. Additionally, the law also attempted to lower AFDC expenses by requiring AFDC mothers to assign their child support payments to the state so that the father would pay the child support award directly to the state, and the child would receive AFDC benefits instead of the child support award. AFDC mothers were forced to identify and help locate the fathers of their children as a condition of AFDC eligibility; unmarried mothers were also required to assist in establishing paternity unless they could prove they had "good cause" not to cooperate.

Beginning in 1981, the Republican administration of President Ronald Reagan tried to trim the welfare rolls by tightening rules of eligibility and instituting new procedures for determining family income. The Reagan administration also attempted to persuade states to establish experimental work programs in which AFDC recipients might be required to work in public sector jobs in exchange for their benefits.

In 1988, Congress passed the **Family Support Act (FSA)** offering job training, education, and support services, while emphasizing work activity for recipients. The FSA required states to create job opportunities and teach basic skills to assist women on welfare in finding jobs. It also provided **child care** and medical benefits.

Congress also attempted to strengthen efforts at child support enforcement in Title I of the FSA. Proclaiming the lack of child support from absent parents as one of the leading causes of poverty among female-headed households, Title I created federal standards for establishing paternity and provided up to 90 percent of the cost of paternity tests. The FSA also aimed at coordinating the child support enforcement system with the AFDC system.

Since one of the goals of the FSA was to emphasize work, education, and training, welfare recipients were also given child care assistance to enable them to work or participate in education or training programs. Additionally, the FSA recognized that parents who left welfare for work would continue to need child care subsidies to allow them to remain off welfare.

Beginning in the 1980s, states, with the encouragement of the Reagan administration, began to experiment with welfare demonstration projects. Because such projects often conflicted with federal law, states were required to obtain "waivers" from the federal government. Although waivers had been available to states since 1962, President Reagan created a faster approval process. For the most part, these policies attempted to alter recipients' behavior with penalties, rewards, and, sometimes, better services. Among the more well-known experimental projects were those in California, Wisconsin, Ohio, New Jersey, and Maryland. Some states imposed "family caps," in which mothers were denied benefits for children born or conceived while they were on welfare, required unmarried minor mothers to live at home with their parents to receive benefits, and raised the maximum income recipients were allowed to earn as well as the value of the resources they could have. These state experiments eventually helped pave the way for a more comprehensive change in welfare policy.

President Bill Clinton's 1992 campaign promise to "end welfare as we know it" led to renewed attempts by government officials to change the rules of eligibility for welfare recipients. These efforts were primarily directed at limiting the amount of time welfare beneficiaries could continue to receive benefits. Although the Clinton White House introduced a package of welfare reforms, Congress never voted on it. Interest in changing welfare policy revived when the Republicans gained control of the Senate and House of Representatives in 1994. The result was a major overhaul of the welfare system in 1996.

The Personal Responsibility and Work Opportunity Reconciliation Act of 1996 resulted in part from recommendations from such governors as Wisconsin's Tommy Thompson and Michigan's John Engler, who had argued for more state control over welfare programs. The heart of the new welfare law, entitled Block Grants to States for Temporary Assistance for Needy Families (TANF), articulated three goals: to provide assistance to needy families, to end welfare dependency by promoting "job preparation, work and marriage" to "prevent and reduce" out of wedlock births, and to encourage two-parent families."

TANF mandates that after two years of receiving cash assistance a recipient has to go to work to continue receiving benefits. It imposes on recipients a lifetime limit of five years for receipt of cash assistance; states may shorten this time limit if they choose. A state may exempt up to 20 percent of its recipients from these time limits for undefined "hardship." The act also requires states to meet certain work participation rates; failure to meet these rates leads to reduced federal funds. Additionally, TANF allows states to impose "family caps" and deny assistance to unwed parents under 18; it also permits states to limit newly arrived residents to the benefits they would have received in their former states for up to 12 months.

The 1996 welfare bill also revises existing child care policy, consolidating all existing child care programs for low and middle income families into a new Child Care and Development Block Grant, with federal funds going to states to match their child care expenditures. However, with increasing numbers of welfare recipients required to work under TANF, states might be faced with the possibility of having insufficient funds to provide aid for all TANF recipients who need child care assistance. (SM) **See also** Child Custody and Support; Child Support Enforcement Amendment of 1984; Social Security.

BIBLIOGRAPHY

Garfinkel, Irwin and Sara S. McLanahan. *Single Mothers and Their Children: A New American Dilemma*. Washington, DC: Urban Institute Press, 1986.

Handler, Joel F. *The Poverty of Welfare Reform*. New Haven, CT: Yale University Press, 1995.

Kamerman, Sheila B. and Alfred J. Kahn. *Mothers Alone: Strategies for a Time of Change*. Dover, MA: Auburn House Publishing, 1988.

Katz, Michael. *In the Shadow of the Poorhouse: A Social History of Welfare in America*. New York: Basic Books, 1986.

———. *The Undeserving Poor: From the War on Poverty to the War on Welfare*. New York: Pantheon Books, 1989.

Marmor, Theodore, Jerry Mashaw, and Philip L. Harvey. *America's Misunderstood Welfare State*. New York: Basic Books, 1990.

Melnick, R. Shep. *Between the Lines: Interpreting Welfare Rights*. Washington, DC: Brookings Institute, 1994.

Sidel, Ruth. *Women & Children Last: The Plight of Poor Women in Affluent America*. New York: Penguin Books, 1986.

Welfare Rights Movement

In the 1960s, as the **welfare** rolls increased, welfare recipients began to organize for better distribution of benefits and more expansive rules of eligibility in the **Aid to Families with Dependent Children (AFDC)** program, created as part of the Social Security Act of 1935. One organization that was part of the welfare rights movement was the National Welfare Rights Organization (NWRO), a group that sought to expand the welfare rolls and increase welfare benefits. Composed primarily of African-American welfare recipients, the NWRO was headed by Executive Director George Wiley, an anti-**poverty** activist. The goals of the movement, adopted at its conference in August 1967, were to improve the lives of the poor through justice and dignity, as well as to provide an adequate income for indigent people. The NWRO adopted a strategy of trying to provoke a crisis in the welfare system by increasing benefits and expanding the welfare rolls until the system was overloaded and Congress was forced to change it. The organization assisted welfare applicants in applying for benefits, helped recipients apply for special needs grants, and fought attempts to diminish the welfare rolls. The NWRO's efforts on behalf of the poor also included sponsoring street demonstrations, lobbying members of legislatures, and litigating in the federal courts. (SM) **See also** Social Security.

BIBLIOGRAPHY

Davis, Martha F. *Brutal Need: Lawyers and the Welfare Rights Movement, 1960–1973*. New Haven: Yale University Press, 1993.

Lawrence, Susan E. *The Poor in the Court*. Princeton: Princeton University Press, 1990.

Ida Bell Wells (1862–1931)

A journalist and social reformer who led an anti-lynching crusade in the United States and promoted economic rights for women and blacks, Ida Bell Wells (also known as Ida Wells-Barnett after her marriage to Ferdinand Barnett in 1895) was born a slave in Holly Springs, Mississippi, on July 16, 1862. After attending Rust College, she worked as a teacher. In 1883, she moved to Memphis where she became editor and part owner of the *Memphis Free Speech*. She began a life-long mission of speaking out against the ill treatment of blacks in 1884, when she sued a railroad company for not providing her with suitable accommodations. Although awarded damages by the circuit court, she lost her case on appeal in the Tennessee Supreme Court. Barnett became well-known as a crusading journalist who wrote a column carried by black newspapers throughout the country. Earning the nickname "Princess of the Press," Wells called for militant activism by blacks against lynching and discrimination. She was forced to leave Memphis in 1892 when her denunciation of the lynching of three black grocers by their white competitors led to threats against her life and the sacking of her newspaper. In 1893, she moved to Chicago, where she founded the city's first black newspaper, *The Chicago Conservator*. Wells organized national and international campaigns against lynching, and lectured against discrimination throughout the United States and Great Britain. In 1895, she published *The Red Record*, a statistical study of lynching. She was the first president of the Negro Fellowship in Chicago and helped organize the National Association for the Advancement of Colored People (NAACP). She also served on the NAACP executive committee. In 1913, she served as a probation officer and organized legal aid for victims of racial discrimination. She was a strong advocate of women's **suffrage** and organized the first black suffrage association, the Alpha Suffrage Club of Chicago, and helped integrate the suffrage movement. (GVS) **See also** Association of Southern Women for the Prevention of Lynching (ASWPL).

BIBLIOGRAPHY

Boyd, Melba Joyce. "Review Essay: Canon Configuration for Ida B. Wells-Barnett." *Black Scholar* 24, no. 1 (Winter 1994): 8–13.

Duster, Alfreda M., ed. *Crusader for Justice, the Autobiography of Ida B. Wells*. Chicago: University of Chicago Press, 1970.

Sterling, Dorothy. *Black Foremothers: Three Lives*. Old Westbury, NY: Feminist Press, 1979.

Townes, E. M. "Ida B. Wells-Barnett: An Afro-American Prophet." *Christian Century* (March 15, 1989): 285-86.

Western New York Anti-Slavery Society (WNYASS)

In 1835 and 1836, as many as five anti-slavery societies were formed in Rochester, New York. The groups were split along racial and class lines, but united in their desire to end slavery. Some groups, such as the all-female Rochester Ladies' Anti-Slavery Sewing Society and the Union Anti-Slavery Sewing Society, faded quickly. The most successful of the groups was the fully integrated Western New York Anti-Slavery Society (WNYASS), which was formed by a small group of Quakers under the leadership of **Abby Kelley Foster**. The WNYASS was active in drawing attention to the plight of slaves and was a financial supporter of Frederick Douglass's paper, *North Star*.

In 1848, the group helped sponsor the woman's rights convention at Seneca Falls, New York, that successfully launched the **women's movement**. **See also** Abolition; Seneca Falls Convention; Slavery and Women.

BIBLIOGRAPHY

Hewitt, Nancy A. *Women's Activism and Social Change: Rochester, New York, 1822–1872*. Ithaca, NY: Cornell University Press, 1984.

Anne Wexler (1930–)

Anne Wexler succeeded **Midge Costanza** as chief of the Office of Public Liaison during the second half of the Carter administration. Known as an ambitious and skilled political operator, Wexler gained most of her experience in state and local politics in Connecticut before making a name for herself in the 1972 presidential campaign of Democrat George McGovern. She maintained her contact with the **Democratic Party** after leaving the government, serving as a top advisor to the 1984 vice presidential campaign of **Geraldine Ferraro**. (JCS)

BIBLIOGRAPHY

Cifelli, Anna. "At Home on Both Sides of the Street." *Fortune* 110 (September 17, 1984): 142.

Glad, Betty. *Jimmy Carter: In Search of the Great White House*. New York: W.W. Norton, 1980: 423.

Margita Eklund White (1937–)

In 1960, Margita White became assistant press secretary for Richard Nixon's presidential campaign. In 1963, she became minority news secretary for the Hawaii House of Representatives, and in 1963-64 she served as a research assistant to Senator Barry Goldwater and the Republican National Committee. From 1969 to 1973, she also served as assistant to Herbert Klein, White House director of communications. In 1975 ,White was named assistant press secretary to President Gerald Ford, as well as director of the White House Office of Communications, serving in this position from 1975 to 1976. In 1976, she was appointed to a two-year term as a commissioner on the Federal Communications Commission (FCC). White left government service in 1979 for the private sector. She is currently president of the Association for Maximum Service TV.

BIBLIOGRAPHY

Johnston, Laurie. "White House Press Secretary." *New York Times* (January 22, 1975): 86.

White, Margita E. "Senate Commerce Approves." *New York Times* (September 9, 1976): 24.

———. "TV Upgrades to Digital Depends on Government." *Miami Herald* (January 25, 1996): A20.

Sue Shelton White (1887–1943)

Sue White chaired industrial registration for the Tennessee Division of the Woman's Committee of the United States Council of National Defense during World War I. In 1918, she served as executive secretary of the Tennessee Commission for the Blind. In June 1918, White, a **suffrage** advocate, accepted the post of president of the state branch of the more militant **National Woman's Party (NWP)** because she believed that the **National American Woman Suffrage Association (NAWSA)** was going to ignore southern states in its push for the **Nineteenth Amendment**. She was one of 26 protesters in Washington who were imprisoned for five days for burning President Woodrow Wilson in effigy. After her release, she toured the country speaking on woman's suffrage. During Franklin Roosevelt's New Deal, White served in several agencies, including the Consumers' Advisory Board of the National Recovery Administration and the Social Security Board.

BIBLIOGRAPHY

Louis, James P. "Sue Shelton White and the Woman Suffrage Movement in Tenn., 1913–1920" *Tennessee History* Quarterly 22 (June 1963). 170-90.

Stevens, Doris. *Jailed for Freedom*. New York: Schocken, 1976.

Christine Todd Whitman (1946–)

Currently one of the most prominent woman in the **Republican Party**, Christine Todd Whitman is the first modern challenger to defeat an incumbent governor of New Jersey and the first woman governor of New Jersey. Born in New York City on September 26, 1946, Whitman grew up in a wealthy, politically active family. Both her grandfathers were New Jersey Republican finance chairmen; her grandmother was a Republican national committeewoman; her father was chairman of the New Jersey Republican Party; and her mother was national vice-chairman of the Republican Party. Whitman started attending National Republican Party Conventions in 1956 at the age of nine. After graduating from Wheaton College with a degree in government in 1968, Whitman worked in Washington in the U.S. Office of Economic Opportunity and became involved with the Republican National Committee. In 1983, she was elected to the Somerset County Board of Freeholders and served two terms. Appointed president of the state Board of Public Utilities by Governor Tom Kean in 1988, she resigned in 1990 to run for the U.S. Senate. She came within three percentage points of defeating her Democratic opponent, incumbent Senator Bill Bradley. Whitman spent the next three years campaigning; she established a political action committee, wrote a newspaper column, hosted a radio talk show, and won endorsements across the state from party leaders. She won the Republican gubernatorial primary in 1993 and defeated incumbent Governor Jim Florio 49 percent to 48 percent in the general election. As governor, Whitman has cut taxes, enacted a "three strikes and you're out" policy for repeat criminal offenders, and reformed **welfare** programs in the state. A rising figure in national politics, Whitman gave the Republican response to President Bill Clinton's 1995 State of the Union Address. Whitman was suggested as a possible vice presidential candidate in 1996 and has been mentioned as a presidential candidate in 2000, although her support of **abortion** rights is a controversial issue among Republican party leaders. She won re-election as governor of New Jersey in 1997. (LvA)

BIBLIOGRAPHY

Beard, Patricia. *Growing Up Republican: Christie Whitman: The Politics of Character*. New York: HarperCollins Publishers, 1996.

Sheila Evans Widnall (1938–)

In 1993, President Bill Clinton appointed Sheila Widnall secretary of the Air Force. Her tenure as secretary has been controversial—not for her actions—but for scandals that have plagued the service. Prior to her service as secretary, she was a professor of aeronautics and astronautics at institutes like M.I.T. She also served on the Carnegie Commission on Science, Technology and Government.

BIBLIOGRAPHY

Carlin, Peter Ames. "Air Force One: Secretary Sheila Widnall Navigates Stormy Skies." *People Weekly* 48, no. 14 (October 6, 1997): 143.

Perl, Peter. "Affairs of State." *Working Woman* 21, no. 11 (November-December 1996): 32.

———. "Shaping Our Boundless Future." *Aviation Week & Space Technology* 146, no. 16 (April 16, 1997): 23.

Emma Hart Willard (1787–1870)

One of the first three women elected to the Women's Hall of Fame in Seneca Falls, New York, Emma Hart Willard was influential in expanding educational opportunities for women from finishing schools to colleges comparable to male institutions. Born to Samuel and Lydia Hinsdale Hart, Willard enrolled in the Berlin Academy in 1802 and began teaching there in 1804. Two years later, she managed the institution during its winter term. She married Dr. John Willard, who was 28 years her senior, in 1809 and bore him a son, John Hart Willard, one year later. In 1814, she opened Middlebury Female Seminary, teaching "nonornamental" subjects such as math, philosophy, and science. Initially unsuccessful, she moved the school to Waterford, New York, and then to Troy, New York. After she lost an appeal to the New York legislature for funding, residents of Troy raised $4000 to build her a female academy. The Troy Female Seminary (1821) was the first school in the United States to offer women a college curriculum. Willard operated the seminary until 1838 when she turned its operation over to her son. In 1895, the institution was renamed the Emma Willard School in commemoration of her work. (AM)

BIBLIOGRAPHY

Lutz, Alma. *Emma Willard: Pioneer Educator of American Women*. Westport, CT: Greenwood Press, 1983.

Willard, Emma. *Mrs. Emma Willard's Life*. Marietta, GA: Larlin Corporation, 1987.

———. *A Plan for Improving Female Education by Emma Willard*. Marietta, GA: Larlin Corporation, 1987.

———. *Work in Middlebury*. Marietta, GA: Larlin Corporation, 1987.

Frances Elizabeth Caroline Willard (1839–1898)

An early leader in the **Women's Christian Temperance Union (WCTU),** feminist Frances Elizabeth Caroline Willard was born in Churchville, New York, to Mary Thompson Hill Willard and Josiah Flint Willard. After graduation from North Western Female College in 1859, she taught school, and in 1871 she became president of Evanston College for Ladies until it was absorbed by Northwestern University, which then appointed Willard dean of women. In 1873, she cofounded the Association for the Advancement of Women and served as vice president. She left academics in 1874 and became active in the **temperance movement**, and in 1879 became president of the WCTU, where she served until her death in 1898. She organized the "Home Protection" Party (1882), which merged with the Prohibition Party and managed to get the latter to adopt a woman **suffrage** plank. An exceptional organizer, Willard networked with other women's groups, lobbied both state legislatures and Congress in support of suffrage, and actively campaigned for candidates who supported her cause. In 1891, she expanded the WCTU internationally and served as president of the World's WCTU when it met in Boston. (AM)

An effective political organizer, Frances Willard served as president of the Women's Christian Temperance Union (WCTU) from 1879 to 1898. Library of Congress, National American Woman Suffrage Association Collection

BIBLIOGRAPHY

Bordin, Ruth. *Frances Willard, a Biography*. Chapel Hill: University of North Carolina, 1986.

Willard, Frances Elizabeth. *Women and Temperance; or the Work and Workers of the Woman's Christian Temperance Union*. New York: Arno Press, 1972.

Edith Bolling Galt Wilson (1872–1961)

As the second wife of President Woodrow Wilson, Edith Wilson perhaps exercised more political power than any other American woman. Married to a sitting president, Edith Wilson was an indispensable political helpmate and advisor. When President Wilson suffered a stroke in October 1919, Edith Wilson kept him highly isolated and became his liaison to Congress and the nation. She submitted documents to him, at times reading them aloud if he appeared too weak to read them independently. Edith Wilson also translated the president's official response. She even signed memos from

President Woodrow Wilson's second wife, Edith Wilson, became the president's chief advisor and personal secretary after his stroke in 1919. Library of Congress.

the president with her name. Throughout her life, Edith Wilson contended that her role during her husband's illness was no more than that of secretary. However, how much influence she had over presidential decision-making continues to be debated. Edith Wilson admitted that she tried to persuade her husband to accept amendments to the League of Nations Treaty that would have limited American responsibilities. When Woodrow Wilson refused her suggestions, the Treaty was defeated in the U.S. Senate by those who shared Edith Wilson's concerns. (BN) **See also** First Ladies.

BIBLIOGRAPHY

Caroli, Betty Boyd. *First Ladies.* New York: Oxford University Press, 1995.

Truman, Margaret. *First Ladies.* New York: Random House, 1995.

Ellen Axson Wilson (1860–1914)

Using the White House as her forum, Ellen Wilson was an early crusader for housing reform. The first wife of President Woodrow Wilson, she served as a political advisor to the president by critiquing his speeches and discussing pending legislation. At a time when the interests of racial minorities received little attention from powerful politicians, Wilson was an advocate for improved city housing. Her focus on the issue allowed her to use her celebrity to promote her agenda. To promote model housing for urban minorities, she became a stockholder in the Sanitary Housing Company. She actively lobbied congressmen for passage of a slum clearance bill, and worked to improve the working conditions of women and blacks. While suffering from Bright's disease, Wilson continued to pressure Congress for the passage of the alley bill, which cleaned the alleys of Washington, DC. The bill was adopted immediately prior to her death. (BN) **See also** First Ladies.

An advocate of housing reform, Ellen Wilson, President Woodrow Wilson's first wife, effectively lobbied Congress on the issue. Library of Congress, Prints and Photographs Division.

BIBLIOGRAPHY

Caroli, Betty Boyd. *First Ladies.* New York: Oxford University Press, 1995.

Truman, Margaret. *First Ladies.* New York: Random House, 1995.

Effiegene Wingo (1883–1962)

Effiegene Wingo was the second woman from Arkansas to be elected to the 72nd Congress, the first being fellow Democrat **Pearl Oldfield**. Elected to fill the unexpired term of her late husband, Otis T. Wingo, Effiegene Wingo served from November 1930 to March 1933. An active legislator on behalf of her district, she declined to stand for re-election in 1932 on the advice of her doctor. In 1934, she cofounded the national Institute of Public Affairs which provided on-the-job training for college-age youths interested in civil service.

BIBLIOGRAPHY

Chamberlin, Hope. *A Minority of Members.* New York: Praeger, 1973.

WISH List

WISH List (an acronym for "Women in the Senate and House"), founded by Glenda Greenwald in 1991, is a political donor network that uses the **EMILY's List** strategy to assist Republican pro-choice female candidates. WISH List endorses candidates based on their ability to win. Members select at least two candidates from the roster of endorsed candidates and write checks for $100 or more to the candidates. WISH List then bundles the checks to maximize the organization's impact while still giving credit to the individual donors. WISH List has grown from 25 members in 1991 to approximately 3,000 members today. Fund raising continues to be the primary focus of the organization. (LvA)

BIBLIOGRAPHY

Burrell, Barbara C. *A Woman's Place Is in the House.* Ann Arbor: The University of Michigan Press, 1994.

Witt, Linda, Karen M. Paget, and Glenna Matthews. *Running as a Woman: Gender and Power in American Politics.* New York: The Free Press, 1995.

Woman Suffrage Party

On October 29, 1909, the Woman Suffrage Party was organized by women in New York, which was considered the key state in the national campaign for a constitutional amendment on woman **suffrage**. Eight hundred women delegates and 203 alternates attended the party's first convention at Carnegie Hall. With 2,127 election districts in New York City's five boroughs, the party's strategy included parades and quick response efforts to attacks by the anti-suffrage forces. The party membership rapidly expanded from 20,000 in 1910 to 500,000 in 1917, when New York State voted for the state woman suffrage amendment, creating the momentum for the final victory of the **Nineteenth Amendment** in 1920. (AM)

BIBLIOGRAPHY

Anthony, Susan B. and Ida Husted Harper. "National Organizations of Women." In Susan B. Anthony and Ida Husted Harper, eds. *History of Woman Suffrage, Volume 4.* New York: Arno Press, 1969.

Kraditor, Aileen S. *The Ideas of the Woman Suffrage Movement, 1890–1920.* New York: Columbia University Press, 1965.

Woman's Journal

The *Woman's Journal*—the official publication of the **American Woman Suffrage Association (AWSA)**—was a weekly **suffrage** magazine edited by **Lucy Stone** and Henry Blackwell. Begun in 1870, the publication focused its efforts on spreading information about conferences and on reprinting speeches and national and international news about women's issues. The *Woman's Journal* also contained more traditional women's magazine items, such as poetry, stories, and book reviews. The magazine continued publication as the official organ of the **National American Woman Suffrage Association (NAWSA)** when the AWSA merged with the **National Woman Suffrage Association (NWSA)** in 1890. After the death of Stone in 1893, the duties of editor passed to her daughter Alice Stone, who continued as editor until the journal merged with several smaller publications in 1917 to become the *Woman Citizen*.

BIBLIOGRAPHY

Hays, Elinor Rice. *Morning Star: A Biography of Lucy Stone, 1810–1893.* New York: Harcourt, Brace & World, 1961.

Women Accepted for Volunteer Emergency Service (WAVES)

The Women's Reserve of the Navy, under the jurisdiction of Commander Mildred McAfee, founded the first WAVES organization in June 1942, the acronym standing for Women Accepted for Volunteer Emergency Service. During World War II, over 100,000 members served with the armed forces overseas and on the American homefront. In October 1944, President Franklin D. Roosevelt declared that racial integration should be allowed within the WAVES, a decision that subsequently helped bolster the organization's ranks and influence. During these years, the WAVES members served in a number of positions, including as air-traffic controllers, parachute riggers, pilot instructors, clerical workers, record keepers, and aircraft mechanics. The group worked with the military until 1978, at which time all separate female units were integrated into the armed forces.

In 1979, the WAVES organization was re-established as an entity related to yet separate from the United States military. This new group comprised women who currently or previously served as members of the U.S. Navy, Naval Reserve, Navy Nurse Corps, Women Marines, or Coast Guard, and who, during their service, performed honorably. The group focused on the principles of naval service, specifically patriotism and loyalty to God, country, and family. The WAVES also began providing networking services to establish communication and support among members and to inform members of any benefits or policy changes that might affect them. The group currently publishes a bi-monthly newsletter, *White Caps*, and holds a biennial convention.

BIBLIOGRAPHY

Binkin, Martin and Shirley J. Buch. *Women and the Military.* Washington, DC: Brookings Institution, 1977.

Women's Action Coalition (WAC)

The Women's Action Coalition (WAC) was founded in New York City in January 1992 as a result of **Anita Hill**'s testimony at the 1991 Supreme Court confirmation hearings of Judge Clarence Thomas. The group soon dedicated itself to focusing on dealing with women's rights issues and other topics relevant to American women. WAC supports ratification of the **Equal Rights Amendment (ERA)**; equal economic representation and opportunities for women; continued positive development in women's health care and reproductive freedom; an end to racism, religious prejudice, homophobia, and other discrimination against women; and the abolition of violence against women. Some WAC' activities include protests, demonstrations, and other forms of public resistance, as well as active petitioning for government and legislative reform. The group currently has branches in the United States, Canada, and Europe. **See also** Thomas Confirmation Hearings.

BIBLIOGRAPHY

Palley, Marian Lief and Howard A. Palley. "The Thomas Appointment: Defeats and Victories for Women." *PS* 25, no. 3 (September 1992): 473-76.

Richardson, Laurel and Verta Taylor, eds. *Feminist Frontiers: Rethinking Sex, Gender and Society.* Reading, MA: Addison-Wesley, 1993.

Women's Airforce Service Pilots (WASPS)

Following orders by General Henry "Hap" Arnold, chief of the Air Corps, the Women's Auxiliary Ferrying Squadron (WAFS), founded by Nancy Harkness Love in September 1942, and the Women's Airforce Service Pilots (WASPS), founded by Jacquelin Cochran around the same time, were unified into one organization. On August 5, 1943, the newly reformed and expanded WASPs officially began, with Cochran as first director.

The members of the Women's Airforce Service Pilots served in a variety of noncombat roles; WASP members flew military aircraft from factories to bases, tested new planes, repaired aircraft and Air Force equipment, towed weapon targets for cadets, and taught Air Force students gunnery and flight. Because the group consisted of civilian units, it was initially unable to receive veterans' benefits, a situation changed in 1977 under the guidance of Congress and the initiative of Arizona Republican Senator Barry Goldwater. The WASP organization was abolished in 1978 when all female units were fully integrated into the United States military.

BIBLIOGRAPHY

Chun, Victor K. "The Origins of the WASPs." *American Aviator Historical Society Journal* 14 (Winter 1969): 259-62.

Cochran, Jacqueline. *The Stars at Noon.* Boston: Little Brown, 1954.

Women's Army Corps (WACS)

The Women's Army Corps (WACS) was founded on May 14, 1942, as the Women's Army Auxiliary Corps (WAAC). Massachusetts Representative **Edith Nourse Rogers** assisted in creating the organization and helped secure the appointment of Major **Oveta Culp Hobby** as director. Culp served in this position until July 1945. On July 1, 1943, the WAAC officially became the Women's Army Corps after being integrated into the regular army.

During World War II, 140,000 members served with the WACS, a number that included 17,000 women stationed abroad. These members worked in a number of jobs, including as electricians, radio operators, weather forecasters, cartographers, photographers, sheet metal workers, parachute packers, and chemists. The group remained a separate unit until 1978, when it was fully integrated into the armed forces.

Bibliography

Binkin, Martin and Shirley J. Bach. *Women and the Military.* Washington, DC: Brookings Institution, 1977.

Treadwell, Mattie E. *The Women's Army Corps. The United States Army in World War II.* Vol. VIII. Washington, DC: Department of the Army, 1954.

Women's Bureau

The Women's Bureau, formed in 1920, is a division within the federal Department of Labor. Interest groups and reform advocates argued that poor working conditions affected women's ability to properly nurture their children. The Women's Bureau was charged with "formulating standards and policies to promote the welfare of wage earning women." At the time, women's representation in the paid workforce was increasing, particularly in the garment and other light industries, but women were facing multiple difficulties in the workplace, including wage discrimination, poor and unsafe working conditions, and long hours.

Today, the Women's Bureau focuses on promoting employment opportunities for women in nontraditional occupations through skills development and education. The Women's Bureau is also concerned with the particular needs of displaced homemakers, older women, working mothers, and women veterans. The director now serves as an assistant secretary of labor and is appointed to her position. Ten regional offices staffed by fewer than 100 employees carry out the Bureau's responsibilities. (TSF)

Bibliography

Conway, M. Margaret, David W. Ahern, and Gertrude A. Steuernagel. *Women and Public Policy: A Revolution in Progress.* Washington, DC: Congressional Quarterly Press, 1995.

Koontz, Elizabeth Duncan. "Women's Bureau Looks to the Future." *Monthly Labor Review* 93 (June 1970): 3-9.

Sealander, Judith. *As Minority Becomes Majority.* Westport, CT: Greenwood, 1983.

———. "In the Shadow of Good Neighbor Diplomacy: The Women's Bureau and Latin America." *Prologue* 11, no. 4 (1979): 236-50.

Wunder, Suzanne A. "Woman's Bureau Celebrates 25th Anniversary." *Independent Woman* 22 (July 1943): 200, 217.

Women's Campaign Fund (WCF)

Founded in 1974, the Women's Campaign Fund (WCF) defines itself as "the first national, non-partisan political committee founded in America dedicated to providing the first contributions to progressive women running at all levels of government." Headquartered in Washington, the WCF received much attention in 1992 for its assistance in electing a historic number of women to the U.S. Congress. The WCF is also committed to building a base of future national leaders at the state and local levels. To do so, the WCF devotes 30 percent of its contributions to candidates running in state and local elections and helps these candidates identify available resources if they eventually decide to run for Congress. The WCF also provides campaign advice and technical assistance to its candidates, often helping them to network with other progressive political action committees in Washington.

Since 1974, the WCF has contributed to over 1,500 women candidates. In the 1996 election cycle, it supported 200 candidates with nearly $1 million in financial and technical assistance. The WCF is not a membership organization and does not engage in any lobbying activities. (JEH)

Bibliography

Nelson, Candice J. "Women's PAC's in the Year of the Woman." In Elizabeth Adell Cook, Sue Thomas, and Clyde Wilcox, eds. *The Year of the Woman.* Boulder, CO: Westview, 1994.

"Shaking the Money Tree." *Campaigns and Elections* 15, no. 9 (September 1994): 30–31.

Women's Christian Temperance Union (WCTU)

Founded in 1874, the Women's Christian Temperance Union (WCTU) became the the largest women's organization of the late nineteenth century, with a peak membership of 176,000. The Woman's Christian Temperance Union successfully restricted the sale of liquor in many communities, and across the entire country between the passage in 1919 and the repeal

While the Women's Christian Temperance Union (WCTU) was the largest temperance organization, many women formed local temperance groups, like the Keeley League of Illinois, pictured here in 1893, to work for prohibition at the local and state levels. Library of Congress.

in 1933 of the **Eighteenth Amendment**. The WCTU organized women, providing a training ground for future **suffrage** leaders. Women linked **temperance** to family issues, although the WCTU did not endorse suffrage until **Frances E. Willard** became president in 1879. Willard further expanded the role of the WCTU to include social reform, ranging from divorce and property rights, to prison reform and education. After Willard's death in 1898, the WCTU returned to its central focus on temperance. The WCTU is still active today in worldwide campaigns against alcohol, tobacco, and drugs. (AM)

Bibliography

Bordin, Ruth. *Woman and Temperance: The Quest for Power and Liberty, 1873–1900.* Philadelphia: Temple University Press, 1981.

Hays, Agnes Dubbs. *Heritage of Dedication: One Hundred Years of the National Woman's Christian Temperance Union, 1874–1974.* Evanston, IL: Signal Press, 1973.

Stanley, Edith Kirkendall. *Ten Decades of White Ribbon Service, 1883–1983: A Historical Review of a Service of the World's Woman's Christian Temperance Unions.* Cincinnati: Revivalist Press, 1983.

Women's Educational Equity Act (1974)

The Women's Educational Equity Act is a piece of legislation enacted in 1974 to address the discrimination against women in education. Gender equity in education implies equal education, free of discrimination on the basis of sex. It means helping students free themselves from limiting, rigid, sex-role stereotypes and sex biases. Some manifestations of inequity are girls starting school academically ahead of boys but finishing academically behind, self-esteem in females falling by high school, males outperforming females in ACT (American College Testing) and SAT (Scholastic Aptitude Test) test scores, and math and science fields dominated by males.

Several pieces of legislation have made gender equity a legal requirement. The basis of this legislation is **Title IX of the Educational Amendments Act of 1972**, which prohibits discrimination based on sex in education programs that receive federal funding. Academic institutions are required under the law to provide equitable programs for men and women if they are to continue receiving federal funding.

In 1974, two years after Congress passed the Education Amendments Act, which included the assurances of Title IX, it enacted the Women's Educational Equity Act (WEEA) to help remedy the discrimination against women and girls in education. The Women's Educational Equity Act is a funding program under which grants and contracts are awarded annually for the development, demonstration, and dissemination of model products and programs for achieving gender equity in education. However, the funding for WEEA was eliminated in 1995 as part of the Republican reductions in bureaucracy and spending. Women congressional leaders have been successful in revitalizing parts of it. (CGM) **See also** Equal Educational Opportunities Act of 1972.

Bibliography

Goodland, John and Pamela Keating, eds. *Access to Knowledge: The Continuing Agenda for Our Nation's Schools.* New York: College Entrance Examination Board, 1994.

Women's Equity Action League (WEAL)

The Women's Equity Action League (WEAL) was founded in 1968 to protest the pro-**abortion** stand of the **National Organization for Women (NOW)** and to provide a more "conservative" approach to women's rights, largely emphasizing the attainment of equality through lobbying and litigation. By 1972, the group was advocating reproductive choice and other relatively controversial positions. The Women's Equity Action League grew from a voluntary endeavor in the 1970s to a large staff and a membership of 7,000 by the 1980s. It specialized in combatting Title IX and academic discrimination against women and emphasized action for economic equity and against discrimination of women in **military service**. The Women's Equity Action League ceased to exist in 1989, due to financial problems. (JG) **See also** Economic Equity Act; Sex Discrimination; Title IX of Educational Amendments Act of 1972.

Bibliography

Daniels, Arlene. "W.E.A.L.: The Growth of a Feminist Organization." In Bernice Cummings, ed. *Women Organizing: An Anthology.* Metuchen, NJ: Scarecrow Press, 1979.

Sandler, Bernice. "A Little Help for Our Government: WEAL and Contract Compliance." In Alice Rossi and Anne Calderwood, eds. *Academic Women on the Move.* New York: Russell Sage Foundation, 1973.

Women's Liberation

Although many people associate women's liberation with the 1960s and 1970s, women have fought in an organized fashion for their rights since the early nineteenth century. At that time, most white, middle class women's lives were circumscribed by the feminine characteristics of piety, domesticity, submissiveness, and purity. These characteristics, which supposedly consigned women to the private sphere, gave women a belief in their own moral superiority and led them to become public activists in the **temperance** and abolitionist movements. To fully participate in the anti-slavery struggle, women challenged social norms that disapproved of their political activity and male abolitionists who relegated them to secondary positions. In the process, they realized the need to fight for their rights as women. The watershed event for them was the first meeting for women's rights, the **Seneca Falls Convention** of 1848. Organized by **Elizabeth Cady Stanton** and **Lucretia Mott**, the convention called for women's full political, legal, and social equality and issued the first public demand for women's **suffrage**.

During these same years, most African-American women were enslaved. As slaves, these women were denied their most basic human rights and subjected to physical abuse, forced separation from their families, difficult and unpaid labor, rape, and forced breeding. In their struggle to end slavery, many also fought to end their oppression as women. **Sojourner**

Truth, a former slave, embodied these multiple challenges to white and male supremacy when, in a women's rights convention in Akron, Ohio, in 1851, she asked, "And ain't I a woman?," simultaneously challenging existing conceptions of womanhood and race.

Under the leadership of **Carrie Chapman Catt**, the **National American Woman Suffrage Association (NAWSA)** intensified the drive for women's suffrage in the 1920s by increasing pressure on elected officials. Injecting militant direct action into the movement, **Alice Paul** and the Woman's Party began to picket the White House daily and, when they were arrested, declared themselves political prisoners and went on a hunger strike. Although these two groups did not always approve of each other, their combined efforts secured the passage of the **Nineteenth Amendment**, which gave women the right to vote in 1920.

The apparent period of quiescence that began after this victory ended in the 1960s. The civil rights movement shattered the surface tranquility of the 1950s, and with it women's supposed acceptance of their roles as mother and housewife. In 1963, **Betty Friedan** wrote ***The Feminine Mystique***, a powerful bestseller that effectively expressed the profound dissatisfaction many middle class white women felt in their lives. In 1966, Friedan, along with other women, founded the **National Organization for Women (NOW)**. Still in existence, NOW has led the drive for **abortion** rights, the passage of the **Equal Rights Amendment (ERA)**, and full equality for women.

Many women joined the civil rights and the anti-Vietnam War movements only to discover that most of the men in the struggles regarded them as inferior and limited their opportunities to contribute to the cause. Their awareness of this unfair treatment, their political commitment to social justice, and their participation in **consciousness raising** groups, informal meetings held among women who shared their feelings and experiences, led a number of women to form women's organizations that explicitly demanded the liberation of women. Instead of focusing on equality within the existing system, these women demanded an end to male supremacy and the abolition of gender-prescribed roles.

In combination, and sometimes in opposition, these two strands of the women's liberation movement have achieved some notable successes and some outstanding failures. In its 1973 ***Roe v. Wade*** decision, the Supreme Court approved a woman's right to first trimester abortion without state intervention. Although a powerful anti-abortion movement has succeeded in chipping away at this decision, women still have the legal right to abort a pregnancy. In 1972, the U.S. Congress passed the ERA, which generated spirited campaigns both for its ratification and its rejection. In 1982, the deadline for ratification elapsed without the ERA being adopted by the requisite number of states.

For women of color, the struggle for women's liberation is tied to their battle against racism. They have frequently charged that the women's liberation movement is dominated by white women who define goals based on their own experiences and needs, ignoring those of women of color. National polls show that African-American women are usually the sector of women most supportive of calls for economic and social equality because they tend to bear disproportionate responsibility for their families' finances. Building a women's liberation movement that truly reflects the ideas and demands of all women remains an ongoing challenge.

Although most women refuse to define themselves as feminists, many women support the key demands of the women's liberation movement. These specific demands include equal pay for equal work, shared responsibility for the household work and childcare, and an end to violence against women, as well as greater female political representation, abortion rights, the right to choose one's sexual orientation, and an end to sexual harassment in the workplace. (MP) **See also** Abolition; Feminism; Slavery and Women; Women's Movement.

BIBLIOGRAPHY

Evans, Sara. *Personal Politics. The Roots of Women's Liberation in the Civil Rights Movement and the New Left.* New York: Alfred A. Knopf, 1979.

Freeman, Jo. *The Politics of Women's Liberation. A Case Study of an Emerging Social Movement and Its Relation to the Policy Process.* New York: David McKay Company, 1975.

Kerber, Linda K. and Jane Sherron de Hart. *Women's American. Refocusing the Past.* New York: Oxford University Press, 1991.

Morgan, Robin. *Sisterhood Is Powerful. An Anthology of Writings from the Women's Liberation Movement.* New York: Vintage Books, 1970.

Women's Movement

The Women's movement has existed in the United States as an active social movement since the late nineteenth century. It did not exist earlier because women enjoyed more equal footing with men as sex roles remained indistinct until the promulgation of federal and state constitutions and the onset of the Industrial Revolution. The founding of the United States as a nation and new pressure for women to stay home as a result of the economic successes of the Industrial Revolution combined to reduce women's political and social status.

Pictured here is a suffrage parade down 5th Avenue in New York City in 1912. Library of Congress.

Women began to view themselves as politically and socially repressed as a result of their participation in the **Progressive, abolition,** and **temperance movements**. The U.S. women's movement formally emerged at the **Seneca Falls Convention** of 1848. During this conference, the **Declaration of Sentiments and Resolutions**, modeled after the Declaration of Independence, was promulgated. The conference marked not only the beginning of the women's movement but also the first three phases of the movement.

The first phase of the women's movement was characterized by the push to extend civil rights to women. Early women's rights advocates were concerned that women's lack of rights systematically diminished their ability to function in society independent of either fathers or husbands. As a result of their participation in the abolitionist movement, women recognized that they lacked basic protections under law that were guaranteed largely to men. Some activists began to compare the legal bondage of women to the bondage experienced by African slaves. This particular position succeeded in creating an enduring rift between the previously allied abolitionists and women's rights activists. This division had the effect of weakening the women's rights movement and limiting its effectiveness. The focus of this phase concerned a broad range of civil rights issues for women, but the movement was largely ignored by society. Eventually, the anti-slavery movement became a national issue that gained prominence as the Civil War approached. This prominence limited attention to the women's movement and augmented its status as a non-issue. These factors compounded the problems of the internally divided movement, resulting in continued ineffectiveness and failure. The first phase of the women's movement ended in the late 1870s, having made few gains for women's rights.

After the Civil War, a renewed concern for social issues again reminded women of their inferior political and social status as citizens of the United States. Women became active in the Progressive, **Settlement House**, and temperance movements. Through this participation, they again became aware that they were not able to effect social policy because they had no political power. Thus, in the second phase of the women's movement activists focused their energies on **suffrage**. The suffrage movement emerged from other reform movements when women, as members of these movements, recognized that suffrage was the political tool necessary for the achievement of their goals. At the same time (1880s and 1890s), the number of women's clubs and charitable organizations expanded. Women began to dedicate themselves to self-improvement or charitable organizations. Again, women often found in the course of working to improve the conditions of others that they had no more rights than those they were attempting to aid. Having realized their inferior political position relative to men, women soon understood that the solution was suffrage. Although women's rights groups worked to achieve suffrage from 1890 on, they were unsuccessful until the movement became mass based. Suffrage for women emerged as a mass movement in 1915 after national attention to the issue was achieved through the efforts of **Alice Paul** and others. This support led to the ratification of the **Nineteenth Amendment** in 1920.

After ratification of the Nineteenth Amendment, the women's movement maintained a low profile until the 1960s, when the third and current phase began. This phase is characterized by two distinct components, which can be described as an older branch that focuses on eliminating discrimination against women and a newer branch consisting of smaller radical or socialist feminist groups interested in achieving significant social change in the political, social, and economic systems of the United States. Again the women's movement was motivated to become active by the efforts of other social movements. The older branch was motivated by the civil rights movement and the new branch was influenced by the black power, student, and anti-war movements of the 1960s and 1970s. Politically prominent issues facing the women's movement during this stage have been the **Equal Rights Amendment (ERA),** which failed of ratification on June 30, 1982, and the **abortion** rights debate, which continues to be an important challenge for activists. (JEH) **See also** Club Movement; Feminism; Slavery and Women; Women's Liberation.

Bibliography

McGlen, Nancy and Karen O'Connor. *Women. Politics, and American Society.* Englewood Cliffs, NJ: Prentice Hall, 1995.

Women's Peace Party

The Women's Peace Party was established in 1915 by prominent suffragists **Jane Addams**, **Carrie Chapman Catt**, and Crystal Eastman out of frustration with the lack of response from male-led peace groups to the outbreak of World War I in Europe. The organization was based on the belief that women are the custodians of life and, as such, have a moral obligation to oppose war. The organization's most notable success was its coordination of a public opinion campaign that forced President Woodrow Wilson to withdraw his request from Congress to send troops to occupy northern Mexico in 1916 as the result of a border dispute. After World War I, the organization merged with other groups to form the Women's International League for Peace and Freedom. (SJW)

Bibliography

Addams, Jane. *Peace and Bread in Time of War.* Silver Springs, MD: National Association of Social Workers, 1983.

Woloch, Nancy. *Women and the American Experience*. New York: Alfred A. Knopf, 1984.

Women's Political Union

The Women's Political Union was the brainchild of **Harriot Stanton Blatch**, daughter of **Elizabeth Cady Stanton** and a veteran of the British suffragette campaign. Blatch witnessed the successes of Emmeline Pankhurst's Social and Political

Union and its violent tactics in attracting public sympathy. In January 1907, Blatch organized working class women into the Equality League of Self-Supporting Women, later called the Women's Political Union. Although never large or influential, the organization held the first **suffrage** parade in 1910; this popular tactic was quickly adopted by the staid **National American Woman Suffrage Association (NAWSA)**. The Women's Political Union later merged with the **Congressional Union**, which had been founded in 1915 by **Alice Paul** and Lucy Burns. (AM)

BIBLIOGRAPHY

Blatch, Harriot Stanton. "Women Suffrage in New York." *National Weekly* 6 (1914): 80.

Blatch, Harriot Stanton and Alena Lutz. *Challenging Years, The Memoirs of Harriot Stanton Blatch.* New York: G. P. Putnam's Sons, 1940.

DuBois, Ellen Carol. "Working Women, Class Relations, and Suffrage Militance, Harriot Stanton Blatch and the New York Woman Suffrage Movement, 1894–1909." *Journal of American History* 74 (June 1987): 34-58.

Women's Rights Conventions

The women's rights movement formally commenced with a series of conventions aimed at organizing and eventually sustaining and molding the direction of the movement. The first of these conventions, held in 1848 at Seneca Falls, New York, marked the official beginning of the women's rights movement. The convention was organized by **Lucretia Mott**, Jane Hunt, Martha Coffin Wright, Mary Ann McClintock, and **Elizabeth Cady Stanton**. At the convention, the **Declaration of Sentiments and Resolutions**, authored by Stanton, was presented as a call for the extension of the natural rights of men to women. In October 1850, the first **National Women's Rights Convention** was held at Worcester, Massachusetts. At this convention, the women's rights movement achieved additional definition from activist **Paulina Wright Davis**, who defined the movement as being radical, universal, and just in that it sought to significantly improve the condition of the majority of the world's population.

Women have used conventions to set agendas, energize supporters, and draw attention to issues that concern them. National Archives.

During the following three years, women's rights conventions were held in Akron, Ohio; Syracuse, New York; and New York City. Each of these conventions marked important points in the movement as a whole. In 1851, at the Akron, Ohio, convention, **Sojourner Truth** delivered her now famous "Ain't I a Woman?" speech. Truth used her status as a black woman and freed slave to point out the flaws in men's arguments that women were the weaker sex. The 1852 convention held in Syracuse was notable because religious teachings that women should be subordinate to men were the major topic of discussion. The last of the early conventions was held in 1853 in New York. At this convention women looked back at the impact of the movement to date and attempted to evaluate their successes and failures. Activists such as **Lucy Stone** felt that women had made progress as demonstrated by their higher public profiles and entrance into various professions. Others felt little had been achieved as women remained excluded from participation with the true source of power in society. Moreover, the church, state, and press were active in the anti-suffrage movement.

The conventions have long been a source of direction for the movement as a whole. The first convention marked the emergence of the movement because it was the first organized manifestation of women's complaints. Today, women's rights conventions continue to provide a unifying force allowing members of the **women's movement** to unite to share experiences and ideas about the continued direction of the movement. (JEH) **See also** Seneca Falls Convention.

BIBLIOGRAPHY

Flexner, Eleanor. *Century of Struggle.* Cambridge, MA: Belknap Press, 1959.

Langley, Winston E. and Vivian C. Fox, eds. *Women's Rights in the United States, A Documentary History.* Westport, CT: Greenwood, 1994.

Women's Rights Project (WRP)

The Women's Rights Project (WRP) is a legal arm of the American Civil Liberties Union that is dedicated to attacking gender discrimination. The ACLU established the Women's Rights Project (WRP) in 1971 to work toward establishing sex equality through litigation. The WRP had its initial success in the Supreme Court's ***Reed v. Reed*** (1971) decision, the first major gender discrimination case. The decision paved the way for a systematic and strategic program of women's rights litigation.

Current Supreme Court Justice **Ruth Bader Ginsburg** was an organizer of the WRP and its first executive director. The success and expertise of the ACLU in other areas gave the WRP instant credibility. The WRP was the dominant organization in the women's rights movement, entering approximately two-thirds of its Supreme Court cases as the moving party or as *amicus curiae*. The Women's Rights Project had a great deal of success in the Supreme Court, structuring the development of precedent in gender discrimination policy. The WRP used a strategy of focusing on narrowly defined problems that would create self-enforcing victories. In addition, the WRP took a leading role in coordinating the litigation efforts of other groups interested in women's rights. More recently, the ACLU has left leadership to the legal arm of the **National Organization for Women (NOW)**, concentrating its resources on other issue areas. (RLP) **See also** Sex Discrimination.

BIBLIOGRAPHY

Cowan, Ruth. "Women's Rights Through Litigation: An Examination of the American Civil Liberties Union Women's Rights Project." *Columbia Human Rights Law Review* 8, no. 1 (1977): 373-412.

O'Connor, Karen. *Women's Organizations' Use of the Courts.* Lexington, MA: Lexington Books, 1980.

Chase Going Woodhouse (1890–1984)

Economist Chase Going Woodhouse, a Democrat, was elected to the U.S. House of Representatives from Connecticut's 2nd District in 1944. A liberal in line with the policies of the New Deal, she worked to secure low- and middle-income housing and the use of federal funds to revitalize city slums. She lost re-election in 1946, but regained her seat in 1948. In 1951, after her losing re-election again, she was appointed by President Harry Truman to the Office of Price Stablization. From 1952 until 1980, she headed the Service Bureau for Women's Organization in Hartford, Connecticut.

BIBLIOGRAPHY

Chamberlin, Hope. *A Minority of Members.* New York: Praeger, 1973.

"Good Governor and Fighting Lady." *Time* 48 (August 26, 1946): 19-20.

Woodhouse, Chase Going. "The Status of Women." *American Journal of Sociology* 35 (May 1930): 1091–1100.

——-. *Oral History interview, Former Member of Congress Association.* Washington, DC: Manuscript Division, Library of Congress, 1979.

Victoria Claflin Woodhull (1838–1927)

Victoria Woodhull was a successful businesswoman, reformer, and controversial advocate of equal rights for women. Born in Ohio in 1838, Woodhull grew up working in her family's traveling medicine show. She married Dr. Canning Woodhull at the age of 15, but divorced in 1866 to marry Colonel James Blood. In 1868, Woodhull and her sister, Tennessee, traveled to New York, where they charmed multimillionaire Cornelius Vanderbilt and with his backing opened a successful investment company. Using her financial success to promote her politics, Woodhull, on April 2, 1870, declared herself a candidate for the U.S. presidency, endorsing Pantarchy in her platform—a perfect world in which women have sexual freedom and property and children are raised communally. Woodhull also campaigned for **suffrage** and was the first to testify before the House Judiciary Committee in favor of adding women to the Fifteenth Amendment. Woodhull's advocacy of free love and legalized **prostitution** gave her a controversial reputation and **Susan B. Anthony** ultimately disassociated the suffrage movement from Woodhull. Woodhull, her sister, and her daughter Zula later moved to England where Woodhull continued lecturing until her death in 1927. (LvA)

Victoria Woodhull addresses the Judiciary Committee of the U.S. House of Representatives, arguing that voting rights be extended to women as well as to black men. National Archives.

BIBLIOGRAPHY

Johnson, Johanna. *Mrs. Satan: The Incredible Saga of Victoria C. Woodhull.* New York: Putnam, 1967.

Sachs, Emanie. *The Terrible Siren: Victoria Woodhull.* New York: Knopf, 1976.

Ellen Sullivan Woodward (1887–1971)

Ellen Woodward succeeded her husband Albert Woodward in the Mississippi legislature, serving from February 1925 until 1926. In 1926, she was a member of the Mississippi State Board of Development, serving as director from 1929 through 1933. A Mississippi Democratic Committeewoman from 1932 to 1934, Woodward was appointed to the Works Progress Administration in 1933. In 1938, she was appointed to the Social Security Board. In 1946, Woodward became director of the Office of Inter-Agency and International Relations of the Federal Security Administration, where she served until her retirement in 1954.

BIBLIOGRAPHY

Swain, Martha H. "Eleanor Roosevelt and Ellen Woodward: A Partnership for Woman's Work." In Joan Hoff-Wilson, ed. *Without Precedent.* Bloomington: Indiana University Press, 1984.

——-. *Ellen S. Woodward: New Deal Advocate for Women.* Jackson: University of Mississippi, 1995.

Lynn C. Woolsey (1937–)

In 1966, Lynn Woolsey was a suburban stay-at-home mom with a stockbroker husband and three children. A divorce in 1967 left her jobless and with a family to raise on her own.

She found a low-paying secretarial job but went on **welfare** to help make ends meet. Woolsey recalls, "I wasn't the least bit embarrassed, because I was doing it for my children . . . but I hated it." Woolsey worked her way out of **poverty** and off of welfare in three years, but she never forgot the experience.

Woolsey went on to become a successful businesswoman and, after serving on the Petaluma, California, city council from 1984 to 1992, was elected to the U.S. House of Representatives. Woolsey has drawn upon her life experiences to contribute to the debate on welfare reform and other issues. She is a liberal Democrat who supports increased funding for poor women and their children, a federal system for collecting child support payments, universal healthcare coverage, and **abortion** rights. She also supports gay rights and has lobbied Congress with her gay stepson, Michael, on the issue of gays in the military. (CKC)

BIBLIOGRAPHY

Gordon, Meryl and Kim France. "Lynn Woolsey's Incredible Journey from Welfare to Washington." *Elle* 9 (July 1994): 45.

"Lynn Woolsey." *Congressional Quarterly Weekly Report* 51 (January 16, 1993): 45.

"Trying to Put Certainty into Child Support." *CQ Researcher* 5 (January 13, 1995): 39.

Frances Wright (1795–1852)

In 1825, Frances Wright, an early abolitionist, published a pamphlet asking Congress to set aside land for slaves to work to earn money for their emancipation. When her appeal received little attention, she purchased 640 acres in Tennessee to implement her plan. In addition to her activism on behalf of slaves, she wrote articles advocating equal education and rights for women and the end of capital punishment. **See also** Abolition.

BIBLIOGRAPHY

Kissel, Susan S. *In Common Cause.* Bowling Green, Ohio: Popular Press, 1995.

Perkins, A.J.G. and Theresa Wolfson. *Frances Wright, Free Enquirer.* Philadelphia: Porcupine Press, 1972.

Waterman, William. *Frances Wright.* New York: AMS Press.

Y

Molly Yard (1912–)

After becoming national organization secretary and eventual chair of the American Student Union in the 1930s, Molly Yard met First Lady **Eleanor Roosevelt**, a meeting that helped shape Yard's political views and career. Soon after the meeting, Yard became active in **Democratic Party** politics, serving a number of causes for the party in the 1940s. Yard also worked on **Helen Douglas**'s 1950 California Senate race against Richard Nixon, Joseph Clark's 1956 and 1962 senatorial campaigns, and John F. Kennedy's 1960 presidential campaign.

While working on civil rights campaigns and marches across the nation, Yard made an unsuccessful run for the Pennsylvania legislature in 1964. She went on to serve on the **National Organization for Women's (NOW)** Political Action Committee from 1978 to 1984 and acted as the group's political director from 1985 to 1987. In July 1987, Yard was elected to a three-year term as president of NOW.

Bibliography

McMurray, Kristan. "Septuagenarian Molly Yard May Not Be Unsinkable, But She's Just the Thing for NOW." *People's Weekly* 28 (October 12, 1987): 38-39.

"A New Battlefield for NOW's Fearless Leader." *Newsweek* 110 (July 20, 1987): 30-31.

Year of the Woman

1992 was hailed as the "Year of the Woman" in response to the record numbers of women who ran for elected office at all levels of government. At the national level, women's representation in Congress increased from 6 percent to 10 percent. Women gained three seats in the Senate for a total of seven; in the House, women gained 19 seats for a total of 48. California became the first state to elect two female U.S. Senators, **Barbara Boxer** and **Dianne Feinstein**, both Democrats. At the state level, women increased from 18 percent to 20 percent of both statewide elected executive offices and state legislatures. Several factors contributed to the mobilization of women in 1992, including the confirmation hearings for Supreme Court Justice Clarence Thomas, during which many women were angered by scenes of an all-white, male Senate Judiciary Committee questioning Oklahoma University law professor **Anita Hill** about charges of sexual harassment that they had initially disregarded. In the wake of the hearings, groups such as the **National Organization for Women (NOW)** and **EMILY's List** reported record levels of new memberships and contributions. These and other feminist groups engaged in active recruitment of women to run for office in 1992. For example, the Feminist Majority launched its Feminization of Power Campaign. Another contributing factor was the large number of open seats, due in part to the 1990 redistricting as well as to congressional scandals that led many incumbents to retire rather than risk defeat at the polls. Viewed as "outsiders," women benefited from the public's anti-incumbency mood. Women likewise had an advantage on issue positions as the nation shifted from a Cold War to a domestic agenda. Polls indicated that voters considered women more trustworthy with finances and more likely to promote education and healthcare. Finally, the Supreme Court's decision in ***Planned Parenthood of Southeastern Pennsylvania v. Casey*** (1992), which upheld restrictive regulations on **abortion**, motivated pro-choice women to become active to protect their reproductive rights. All 48 women elected to the U.S. House of Representatives in 1992 were pro-choice. 1992 appeared to be a year in which women held an advantage over men. Although the rate of increase in women's representation experienced during the Year of the Woman has not been sustained, women continue to make progress toward reaching equality in elective office. NOW. (LvA) **See also** Feminism; Thomas Confirmation Hearings.

Bibliography

Thomas, Sue, and Clyde Wilcox, eds. *The Year of the Woman.* Boulder, CO: Westview Press, 1994.

Witt, Linda, Karen M. Paget, and Glenna Matthews. *Running as a Woman: Gender and Power in American Politics.* New York: The Free Press, 1995.

Young Feminist Summit

Sponsored by the National Organization for Women Foundation, the first national Young Feminist Summit was held in Washington, D.C., in 1995. Designed to promote awareness and activism among high school and college age women, the Summit's mission was "to unify a diverse group of young feminists to empower themselves with the skills and strategies to affect change in their communities." The second Young Feminist Summit, "New Voices, New Visions: Young Women Taking Action for the Twenty First Century" was held in 1997 in

Washington, D.C., and had approximately 1,200 participants. The three-day conference focused on issues that directly affect young women's lives, from sexual harassment and violence against women to reproductive rights and **Title IX of the Education Amendments Act of 1972**. Participants attended informational sessions and skill-building workshops, and the Summit concluded with a march in front of the White House. (JW1) **See also** Abortion; Feminism; National Organization for Women (NOW); Sex Discrimination.

BIBLIOGRAPHY

Mann, Judy. "Young, Focused and NOW." *Washington Post* (November 22, 1995): E11.

Wukas, Mark. "NOW Sponsors Youth Meeting." *Chicago Tribune* (April 6, 1997): 3.

Z

Zbaraz v. Hartigan (1985)

In *Zbaraz v. Hartigan*, 763 F. 2d 1532 (7th Cir., 1985), the Seventh Circuit Court of Appeals ruled on the Illinois Parental Notice of Abortion Act of 1983, which required a minor seeking an **abortion** to notify her parents, or seek a court order instead, and wait 24 hours before having the abortion.

The Illinois federal district court found both provisions of the act unconstitutional. On appeal, the Seventh Circuit agreed that the waiting period was unconstitutional, citing several cases in which courts had struck down similar waiting periods. The court noted that the U.S. Supreme Court had never ruled in a case involving a waiting period for minors only. Also, citing opinions handed down by other courts, the appellate court found the parental notification requirement constitutional. However, the court delayed enforcement of the act until the Illinois Supreme Court could create rules assuring that the names of minors who sought court orders rather than notify their parents would be kept confidential. In *Hartigan v. Zbaraz* (1987), the U.S. Supreme Court voted to uphold the appellate court in a 4-4 vote; a tie vote in the Supreme Court affirms the lower court opinion. (SM)

BIBLIOGRAPHY

"Abortion." *Journal of Family Law* 24 (1985-86): 699-706.
Hartigan v. Zbaraz, 484 U.S. 171 (1987).

Appendices

1

Speeches and Documents

1. Nineteenth Amendment to the U.S. Constitution

(Ratified 1920)

Section 1. The right of citizens of the United States to vote shall not be denied or abridged by the United States or by any state on account of sex.

Section 2. Congress shall have power to enforce this article by appropriate legislation.

2. Sojourner Truth's "Ain't I a Woman?" Speech (1851)

Delivered in 1851 at the Women's Convention in Akron, Ohio.

Well, children, where there is so much racket there must be something out of kilter. I think that 'twixt the negroes of the South and the women at the North, all talking about rights, the white men will be in a fix pretty soon. But what's all this here talking about?

That man over there says that women need to be helped into carriages, and lifted over ditches, and to have the best place everywhere. Nobody ever helps me into carriages, or over mudpuddles, or gives me any best place! And ain't I a woman? Look at me! Look at my arm! I have ploughed and planted, and gathered into barns, and no man could head me! And ain't I a woman? I could work as much and eat as much as a man—when I could get it—and bear the lash as well! And ain't I a woman? I have borne 13 children, and seen most all sold off to slavery, and when I cried out with my mother's grief, none but Jesus heard me! And ain't I a woman?

Then they talk about this thing in the head; what's this they call it? [member of audience whispers, "intellect"] That's it, honey. What's that got to do with women's rights or negroes' rights? If my cup won't hold but a pint, and yours holds a quart, wouldn't you be mean not to let me have my little half measure full?

Then that little man in black there, he says women can't have as much rights as men, 'cause Christ wasn't a woman! Where did your Christ come from? Where did your Christ come from? From God and a woman! Man had nothing to do with Him.

If the first woman God ever made was strong enough to turn the world upside down all alone, these women together ought to be able to turn it back, and get it right side up again! And now they is asking to do it, the men better let them.

Obliged to you for hearing me, and now old Sojourner ain't got nothing more to say.

3. Declaration of Sentiments and Resolutions

Prepared by Elizabeth Cady Stanton and submitted to the Seneca Falls (New York) Convention in 1848.

When, in the course of human events, it becomes necessary for one portion of the family of man to assume among the people of the earth a position different from that which they have hitherto occupied, but one to which the laws of nature and of nature's God entitle them, a decent respect to the opinions of mankind requires that they should declare the causes that impel them to such a course.

We hold these truths to be self-evident: that all men and women are created equal; that they are endowed by their Creator with certain inalienable rights; that among these are life, liberty, and the pursuit of happiness; that to secure these rights governments are instituted, deriving their just powers from the consent of the governed. Whenever any form of government becomes destructive of these ends, it is the right of those who suffer from it to refuse allegiance to it, and to insist upon the institution of a new government, laying its foundation on such principles, and organizing its powers in such form, as to them shall seem most likely to effect their safety and happiness. Prudence indeed will dictate that governments long established should not be changed for light and transient causes and accordingly all experience hath shown that mankind are more disposed to suffer, while evils are sufferable, than to right themselves by abolishing the forms to which they were accustomed. But when a long train of abuses and usurpations, pursuing invariably the same object evinces a design to reduce them under absolute despotism, it is their duty to throw off such government, and to provide new guards for their future security. Such has been the patient sufferance of the women under this government, and such is now the necessity which constrains them to demand the equal station to which they are entitled.

The history of mankind is a history of repeated injuries and usurpations on the part of man toward woman, having in direct object the establishment of an absolute tyranny over her. To prove this, let facts be submitted to a candid world.

He has never permitted her to exercise her inalienable right to the elective franchise.

He has compelled her to submit to laws, in the formation of which she had no voice.

He has withheld from her rights which are given to the most ignorant and degraded men—both natives and foreigners.

Having deprived her of this first right of a citizen, the elective franchise, thereby leaving her without representation in the halls of legislation, he has oppressed her on all sides.

He has made her, if married, in the eye of the law, civilly dead.

He has taken from her all right in property, even to the wages she earns.

He has made her, morally, an irresponsible being, as she can commit many crimes with impunity, provided they be done in the presence of her husband. In the covenant of marriage, she is compelled to promise obedience to her husband, he becoming, to all intents and purposes, her master—the law giving him power to deprive her of her liberty, and to administer chastisement.

He has so framed the laws of divorce, as to what shall be the proper causes, and in case of separation, to whom the guardianship of the children shall be given, as to be wholly regardless of the happiness of women—the law, in all cases, going upon a false supposition of the supremacy of man, and giving all power into his hands.

After depriving her of all rights as a married woman, if single, and the owner of property, he has taxed her to support a government which recognizes her only when her property can be profitable to it.

He has monopolized nearly all the profitable employments, and from those she is permitted to follow, she receives but a scanty remuneration. He closes against her all the avenues to wealth and distinction which he considers most honorable to himself. As a teacher of theology, medicine, or law, she is not known.

He has denied her the facilities for obtaining a thorough education, all colleges being closed against her.

He allows her in Church, as well as State, but a subordinate position, claiming Apostolic authority for her exclusion from the ministry, and, with some exceptions, from any public participation in the affairs of the Church.

He has created a false public sentiment by giving to the world a different code of morals for men and women, by which moral delinquencies which exclude women from society, are not only tolerated, but deemed of little account in man.

He has usurped the prerogative of Jehovah himself, claiming it as his right to assign for a sphere of action, when that belongs to conscience and to her God.

He has endeavored, in every way that he could, to destroy her confidence in her own powers, to lessen her self-respect, and to make her willing to lead a dependent and abject life. Now, in view of this entire disfranchisement of one-half the people of this country, their social and religious degradation—in view of the unjust laws above mentioned, and because women do feel themselves aggrieved, oppressed, and fraudulently deprived of their most sacred rights, we insist that they have immediate admission to all the rights and privileges which belong to them as citizens of the United States.

In entering upon the great work before us, we anticipate no small amount of misconception, misrepresentation, and ridicule; but we shall use every instrumentality within our power to effect our object. We shall employ agents, circulate tracts, petition the State and National legislatures, and endeavor to enlist the pulpit and the press in our behalf. We hope this Convention will be followed by a series of Conventions embracing every part of the country.

(Lucretia Mott, Thomas and Mary Ann McClintock, Amy Post, Catharine A. F. Stebbins, and others, discussed these resolutions, which were later adopted.)

WHEREAS, The great precept of nature is conceded to be, that "man shall pursue his own true and substantial happiness." Blackstone in his Commentaries [*Commentaries on the Laws of England*] remarks, that this law of Nature being coeval with mankind, and dictated by God himself, is of course superior in obligation to any other. It is binding over all the globe, in all countries and at all times; no human laws are of any validity if contrary to this, and such of them as are valid, derive all their force, and all their validity, and all their authority, mediately and immediately, from this original; therefore,

Resolved, That such laws as conflict, in any way, with the true and substantial happiness of woman, are contrary to the great precept of nature and of no validity, for this is "superior in obligation to any other."

Resolved, That all laws which prevent woman from occupying such a station in society as her conscience shall dictate, or which place her in a position inferior to that of man, are contrary to the great precept of nature, and therefore of no force or authority.

Resolved, That woman is man's equal—was intended to be so by the Creator, and the highest good of the race demands that she should be recognized as such.

Resolved, That the women of this country ought to be enlightened in regard to the laws under which they live, that they may no longer publish their degradation by declaring themselves satisfied with their present position, nor their ignorance, by asserting that they have all the rights they want.

Resolved, That inasmuch as man, while claiming for himself intellectual superiority, does accord to woman moral superiority, it is pre-eminently his duty to encourage her to speak and teach, as she has an opportunity, in all religious assemblies .

Resolved, That the same amount of virtue, delicacy, and refinement of behavior that is required of woman in the social state, should also be required of man, and the same transgressions should be visited with equal severity on both man and woman.

Resolved, That the objection of indelicacy and impropriety, which is so often brought against woman when she addresses a public audience, comes with a very ill-grace from those who encourage, by their attendance, her appearance on the stage, in the concert, or in feats of the circus.

Resolved, That woman has too long rested satisfied in the circumscribed limits which corrupt customs and a perverted application of the scriptures have marked out for her, and that it is time she should move in the enlarged sphere which her great Creator has assigned her.

Resolved, That it is the duty of the women of this country to secure to themselves their sacred right to the elective franchise.

Resolved, That the equality of human rights results necessarily from the fact of the identity of the race in capabilities and responsibilities.

Resolved, therefore, That, being invested by the Creator with the same capabilities, and the same consciousness of responsibility for their exercise, it is demonstrably the right and duty of woman, equally with man, to promote every righteous cause by every righteous means, and especially in regard to the great subjects of morals and religion, it is self-evidently her right to participate with her brother in teaching them, both in private and in public, by writing and by speaking, by any instrumentalities proper to be used, and any assemblies proper to be held; and this being a self-evident truth growing out of the divinely implanted principles of human nature, any custom or authority adverse to it, whether modern or wearing the hoary sanction of antiquity, is to be regarded as a self-evident falsehood, and at war with mankind

Resolved, That the speedy success of our cause depends upon the zealous and untiring efforts of both men and women, for the overthrow of the monopoly of the pulpit, and for the securing to woman an equal participation with men in the various trades, professions, and commerce.

4. Elizabeth Cady Stanton's "Address to the New York State Legislature" (1860)

You who have read the history of nations, from Moses down to our last election, where have you ever seen one class looking after the interests of another? Any of you can readily see the defects in other governments, and pronounce sentence against those who have sacrificed the masses to themselves; but when we come to our own case, we are blinded by custom and self-interest. Some of you who have no capital can see the injustice which the laborer suffers; some of you who have no slaves, can see the cruelty of his oppression; but who of you appreciate the galling humiliation, the refinements of degradation, to which women (the mothers, wives, sisters, and daughters of freemen) are subject, in this the last half of the nineteenth century? How many of you have ever read even the laws concerning them that now disgrace your statute-books? In cruelty and tyranny, they are not surpassed by any slaveholding code in the Southern States; in fact they are worse, by just so far as woman, from her social position, refinement, and education, is on a more equal ground with the oppressor.

Allow me just here to call the attention of that party now so much interested in the slave of the Carolinas, to the similarity in his condition and that of the mothers, wives, and daughters of the Empire State. The negro has no name. He is Cuffy Douglas or Cuffy Brooks, just whose Cuffy he may chance to be. The woman has no name. She is Mrs. Richard Doe or Mrs. John Doe, just whose Mrs. she may chance to be. Cuffy has no right to earnings; he can not buy or sell, or lay up anything that he can call his own. Mrs. Roe has no right to her earnings; she can neither buy nor sell, make contracts, nor lay up anything that she can call her own. Cuffy has no right to his children; they can be sold from him at any time. Mrs. Roe has no right to her children; they may be bound out to cancel a father's debts of honor. The unborn child, even, by the last will of the father, may be placed under the guardianship of a stranger and a foreigner. Cuffy has no legal existence; he is subject to restraint and moderate chastisement. Mrs. Roe has no legal existence; she has not the best right to her own person. The husband has the power to restrain, and administer moderate chastisement.

Blackstone [author of *Commentaries on the Laws of England*] declares that the husband and wife are one, and learned commentators have decided that that one is the husband. In all civil codes, you will find them classified as one. Certain rights and immunities, such and such privileges are to be secured to white male citizens. What have women and negroes to do with rights? What know they of government, war, or glory?

The prejudice against color, of which we hear so much, is no stronger than that against sex. It is produced by the same cause, and manifested very much in the same way. The negro's skin and the woman's sex are both *prima facie* evidence that they were intended to be in subjection to the white Saxon man. The few social privileges which the man gives the woman, he makes up to the negro in civil rights. The woman may sit at the same table and eat with the white man; the free negro may hold property and vote. The woman may sit in the same pew with the white man in church; the free negro may enter the pulpit and preach. Now, with the black man's right to suffrage, the right is evidence that the prejudice against sex is more deeply rooted and more reasonably maintained than that against color. . . .

Just imagine an inhabitant of another planet entertaining himself some pleasant evening in searching over our great national compact, our Declaration of Independence, our Constitutions, or some of our statute-books; what would he think of those "Women and negroes" that must be so fenced in, so guarded against? Why, he would certainly suppose we were monsters, like those fabulous giants or Brobdingnagians of olden times, so dangerous to civilized man, from our size, ferocity, and power. Then let him take up our poets, from Pope down to Dana; let him listen to our Fourth of July toasts, and some of the sentimental adultations of social life, and no logic could convince him that this creature of the law, and this angel of the family alter, could be one and the same being. Man is in such a labyrinth of contradictions with his marital and property rights; he is so befogged on the whole question of maidens, wives, and mothers, that from pure benevolence we should relieve him from this troublesome branch of legislation. We should vote, and make laws for ourselves. Do not be alarmed, dear ladies! You need spend no time reading Grotius, Coke, Puffendorf, Blackstone, Bentham, Kent, and Story to find out what you need. We may safely trust the shrewd selfishness of the white man, and consent to live under the same broad code where he has so comfortably ensconced himself. Any legislation that will do for man, we may abide by most cheerfully. . . .

Now do not think, gentlemen, we wish to do a great many troublesome things for us. We do not ask our legislators to spend a whole session in fixing up a code of laws to satisfy a class of most unreasonable women. We ask no more than the poor devils in the Scripture asked, "Let us alone." In mercy, let us take care of ourselves, our property, our children, and our homes. True, we are not so strong, so wise, so crafty as you are, but if any kind of friend leaves us a little money, or we can by great industry earn fifty cents a day, we would rather buy bread and clothes for our children than cigars and champagne for our legal protectors. There has been a great deal written and said about protection. We, as a class, are tired of one kind of protection, that which leaves us everything to do, to dare, and to suffer, and strips us of all means for its accomplishment. We would not tax man to take care of us. No, the Great Father has endowed all his creatures with the necessary powers for self-support, self-defense, and protection. We do not ask man to represent us; it is hard enough in times like these for man to carry backbone enough to represent himself. So long as the mass of men spend most of their time on the fence, not knowing which way to jump, they are surely in no condition to tell us where we had better stand. In pity for man, we would no longer hang like a mill-stone round his neck. Undo what man did for us in the dark ages, and strikeout all special legislation for us; strike the words "white male" from all your constitutions, and then, with fair sailing, let us sink or swim, live or die, survive or perish together.

5. Carrie Chapman Catt's Speech on "The World Movement for Woman Suffrage 1904–1911: Is Woman Suffrage Progressing?" (1911)

In a debate upon the Woman Suffrage Bill in the Swedish Parliament a few weeks ago, a University Professor said, in a tone of eloquent finality: "The Woman Suffrage movement has reached and passed its climax; the suffrage wave is now rapidly receding." To those who heard the tone of voice and saw the manner with which he spoke, there was no room for doubt that he believed what he said. . . .

Long centuries before the birth of Darwin an old-time Hindoo wrote: "I stand on a river's bank. I know not from whence the waters come or whither they go. So deep and silent is its current that I know not whether it flows north or south; all is a mystery to me; but when I climb yon summit the river becomes a silver thread weaving its length in and out among the hills and over the plains. I see it all from its source in yonder mountains to its outlet in yonder sea. There is no more mystery." So these university professors buried in school books, these near-sighted politicians, fail to note the meaning of passing events. To them, the woman movement is an inexplicable mystery, an irritating excrescence upon the harmonious development of society. But to us, standing upon the summit of international union, where we may observe every manifestation of this movement in all parts of the world, there is no mystery. From its source, . . .we clearly trace the course of this movement through the centuries, moving slowly but majestically onward, gathering momentum with each century, each generation; until just before us lies the golden sea of woman's full liberty. Others may theorise about the woman movement but to us has been vouchsafed positive knowledge. Once, this movement represented the scattered and disconnected protests of individual women. In that period women as a whole were blinded by ignorance, because society denied them education; they were compelled to silence, for society forbade them to speak. They struggled against their wrongs singly and alone, for society forbade them to organise; they dwelt in poverty, for the law denied them the control of property and even the collection of wages. Under such conditions of sexual serfdom, what wonder that their cries for justice were stiffled, and that their protests never reached the ears of the men who wrote the history of those times? Happily those days are past; and out of that incoherent and seemingly futile agitation, which extended over many centuries, there has emerged a present-day movement possessing a clear understanding and a definite, positive purpose. . . .

To follow up the advantages already won, there is today an army of women, united, patient, invincible. In every land there are trained pens in the hands of women, eloquence and wit on women's lips to defend their common cause. More, there is an allied army of broad-minded, fearless, unyielding men who champion our reform. The powers of opposition, armed as they are with outworn tradition and sickly sentiment *only*, are as certain to surrender to these irresistible forces as is the sun to rise tomorrow.

These are the things *we know*. That others may share the faith that is ours, permit me to repeat a few familiar facts. A call for the first International Conference was issued nine years ago, and it was held in the City of Washington. At that time the Woman Suffrage agitation had resulted in nationally organised movements in five countries only. In chronological order of organisation these were: The United States, Great Britain, Australia, Norway, the Netherlands. Two years later, in 1904, the organisation of the Alliance was completed in Berlin, and associations in Canada, Germany, Denmark, and Sweden were ready to join. . . . Today, seven years later, however, our Alliance counts 24 auxiliary national associations, and correspondence groups in two additional countries. Are these evidences of a wave rapidly receding? . . .

Those familiar with our work may ask, what does this great body of men and women do? They do everything which human ingenuity can devise and human endurance carry out, to set this big, indifferent world to thinking. I believe more money has been contributed, more workers enlisted, more meetings held, more demonstrations made in Great Britain alone in behalf of Woman Suffrage than in the entire world's movement for man suffrage. Certainly the man suffrage movement never brought forth such originality of campaign methods, such superb organisation, such masterly alertness. Yet it is said in all countries that women do not want to vote. It is to be devoutly hoped that the obstinacy of no other Government will drive women to such waste of time, energy, and money, to such sacrifice and suffering, as has that of Great Britain.

Nor are demonstrations and unusual activities confined to Great Britain, Two thousand women swarmed to the Parliament of Canada last winter, thousands flocked to the Legislatures of the various capitals in the United States. A procession of the best womanhood in New York a few weeks ago marched through the city's streets in protest against legislative treatment. Sweden has filled the great Circus building in Stockholm to overflowing. Hungary, Germany, France "demonstrate," and in my opinion no campaign is moved by more self-sacrificing devotion, more passionate fervour, than that in Bohemia. . . . In our combined countries many thousands upon thousands of meetings are held every year, and millions of pages of leaflets are distributed, carrying our plea for justice into the remotest corners of the globe.

There are doubtless hard encounters ahead, but there are now educated women's brains ready to solve every campaign problem. There are hands willing to undertake every wearisome task; yea, and women's lives ready for any sacrifice. It is because they know the unanswerable logic behind our demands and the irresistible force of our growing army that Suffragists throughout the world repeat in unison those thrilling words of the American leader, Susan B. Anthony, "Failure is impossible." . . .

As all the world knows, an obstinate and recalcitrant Government alone stands between the women of Great Britain and their enfranchisement. A campaign which will always be conspicuous among the world's movements for human rights for its surpassing fervour, sacrifice, and originality has been maintained without a pause. . . . The Government evidently nurses a forlorn hope that by delay it may tire out the workers and destroy the force of the campaign. It little comprehends the virility of the movement. When a just cause reaches its flood-tide, as ours has done in that country, whatever stands in the way must fall before its overwhelming power. Political parties, governments, constitutions must yield to the inevitable or take the consequences of ruin. Which horn of the dilemma the English Government will choose is the only question remaining. Woman Suffrage in Great Britain is inevitable. . . .

Some may ask why we are not now content to wait for the processes of reason and evolution to bring the result we want. Why do we disturb ourselves to hasten progress? I answer, because we refuse to sit idly by while other women endure hideous wrongs. Women have suffered enough of martyrdom through the false position they have been forced to occupy for centuries past. We make our protest now hotly and impatiently, perhaps, for we would bequeath to those who come after us a fair chance in life. Modern economic conditions are pushing hundreds of thousands of women out of their homes into the labour market. Crowded into unskilled employments for want of proper training, they are buffeted about like a cork upon a sea. Everywhere paid less than men for equal work, everywhere discriminated against, they are utterly at the mercy of forces over which they have no control. Law-making bodies, understanding neither women nor the meaning of this woman's invasion of modern industry, are attempting to regulate the wages, the hours, the conditions under which they shall work. Already serious wrong has been done many women because of this ill-advised legislation. Overwhelmed by the odds against them in this struggle for existence, thousands are driven to the streets. There they swell that horrid, unspeakably unclean peril of civilisation, prostitution—augmented by the White Slave Traffic and by the machinations of the male parasites who live upon the earnings of women in vice. . . . We must be merciful, for they are the natural and inevitable consequence of centuries of false reasoning concerning women's place in the world. . . . Upon these women we have no right to turn our backs. Their wrongs are our wrongs. Their existence is part of our problem. They have been created by the very injustices against which we protest.

It is the helpless cry of these lost women who are the victims of centuries of wrong; it is the unspoken plea of thousands of women now standing on the brink of similar ruin; it is the silent appeal of the army of women in all lands who in shops and factories are demanding fair living and working conditions; it is the need to turn the energies of more fervoured women to public service; it is the demand for a complete revision of women's legal, social, educational, and industrial status all along the line, which permits us no delay, no hesitation. The belief that we are defending the highest good of the mothers of our race and the ultimate welfare of society makes every sacrifice seem trivial, every duty a pleasure. The pressing need spurs us on, the certainty of victory gives us daily inspiration.

We have come upon a new time, which has brought new and strange problems. Old problems have assumed new significance. In the adjustment of the new order of things we women demand an equal voice; we shall accept nothing less.

6. Lucy Stone's "Disappointment Is the Lot of Women" Speech (1855)

The last speaker alluded to this movement as being that of a few disappointed women. From the first years to which my memory stretches, I have been a disappointed woman. When, with my brothers, I reached forth after the sources of knowledge, I was reproved with "It isn't fit for you; it doesn't belong to women." Then there was but one college in the world where women were admitted, and that was in Brazil. I would have found my way there, but by the time I was prepared to go, one was opened in the young State of Ohio—the first in the United States where women and negroes could enjoy opportunities with white men. I was disappointed when I came to seek a profession worthy an immortal being—every employment was closed to me, except those of the teacher, the seamstress, and the housekeeper. In education, in marriage, in religion, in everything, disappointment is the lot of women. It shall be the business of my life to deepen this disappointment in every woman's heart until she bows down to it no longer, I wish that women, instead of being walking show-cases, instead of begging of their fathers and brothers the latest and gayest new bonnet, would ask them their rights.

The question of Woman's Rights is a practical one. The notion has prevailed that it was only an ephemeral idea; that it was but women claiming the right to smoke cigars in the streets, and to frequent bar-rooms. Others have supposed it a question of comparative intellect; others still, of sphere. Too much has already been said and written about woman's sphere. Trace all the doctrines to their source and they will be found to have no basis except in the usages and prejudices of the age. This is seen in the fact that what is tolerated in woman in one country is not tolerated in another. In this country women may hold prayer-meetings, etc., but in Mohammedan countries it is written upon their mosques, "Women and dogs, and other impure animals, are not permitted to enter." Wendell Phillips says, "The best and greatest thing one is capable of doing, that is his sphere." I have confidence in the Father to believe that when He gives us the capacity to do anything He does not make a blunder. Leave women, then, to find their sphere. And do not tell us before we are born even, that our province is to cook dinners, darn stockings, and sew on buttons. We are told woman has all the rights she wants; and even women, I am ashamed to say, tell us so. They mistake the politeness of men for rights—seats while men stand in this hall tonight, and their adultations; but these are mere courtesies. We want rights. The flour-merchant, the housebuilder, and the postman charge us no less on account of our sex; but when we endeavor to earn money to pay all these, then, indeed, we find the difference. Man, if he have energy, may hew out for himself a path where no mortal has ever trod, held back by nothing but what is in himself; the world is all before him, where to choose; and we are glad for you, brothers, men, that it is so. But the same society that drives forth the young man, keeps woman at home—a dependent—working little cats on worsted, and little dogs on punctured paper; but if she goes heartily and bravely to give herself to some worthy purpose, she is out of her sphere and she loses caste. Women working in tailor-shops are paid one-third as much as men. Someone in Philadelphia has stated that women make fine shirts for twelve and a half cents apiece; that no woman can make more than nine a week, and the sum thus earned, after deducting rent, fuel, etc., leaves her just three and a half cents a day for bread. Is it a wonder that women are driven to prostitution? Female teachers in New York are paid fifty dollars a year, and for every such situation there are five hundred applications. I know not what you believe of God, but I believe He gave yearnings and longings to be filled, and that he did not mean all our tie should be devoted to feeding and clothing the body. The present condition of woman causes a horrible perversion of the marriage relation. It is asked of a lady, "Has she married well?" "Oh, yes, her husband is rich." Woman must marry for a home, and you men are the sufferers by this; for a woman who loathes you may marry you because you have the means to get money which she can not have. But when woman can enter the lists with you and make money for herself, she will marry you only for deep and earnest affection.

I am detaining you too long, many of you standing, that I ought to apologize, but women have been wronged so long that I may wrong you a little. . . . I have seen a woman at manual labor turning out chair-legs in a cabinet-shop, with a dress short enough not to drag in the shavings. I wish other women would imitate her in this. It made her hands harder and broader, it is true, but I think a hand with a dollar and a quarter a day in it, better than one with a crossed ninepiece. . . . The widening of woman's sphere is to improve her lot. Let us do it, and if the world scoff, let it scoff—if it sneer, let it sneer—but we will go on emulating the example of the sisters Grimke and Abby Kelley. When they first lectured against slavery they were not listened to as respectfully as you listen to us. So the first female physician meets many difficulties, but to the next the path will be made easy.

Lucretia Mott has been a preacher for years; her right to do so is not questioned among Friends. But when Antoinette Brown felt that she was commanded to preach, and to arrest the progress of thousands that were on the road to hell; why, when she applied for ordination they acted as though they had rather the whole world should go to hell, than that Antoinette Brown should be allowed to tell them how to keep out of it.

7. Convention on the Elimination of All Forms of Discrimination Against Women

United Nations General Assembly Resolution 34\180 of December 1979.

The States Parties to the present Convention,

Noting that the Charter of the United Nations reaffirms faith in fundamental human rights, in the dignity and worth of the human person and in the equal rights of men and women,

Noting that the Universal Declaration of Human Rights affirms the principle of the inadmissibility of discrimination and proclaims that all human beings are born free and equal in dignity and rights and that everyone is entitled to all the rights and freedoms set forth therein, without distinction of any kind, including distinction based on sex,

Noting that the States Parties to the International Covenants on Human Rights have the obligation to ensure the equal right of men and women to enjoy all economic, social, cultural, civil and political rights,

Considering the international conventions concluded under the auspices of the United Nations and the specialized agencies promoting equality of rights of men and women,

Noting also the resolutions, declarations and recommendations adopted by the United Nations and the specialized agencies promoting equality of rights of men and women,

Concerned, however, that despite these various instruments extensive discrimination against women continues to exist,

Recalling that discrimination against women violates the principle of equality of rights and respect for human dignity, is an obstacle to the participation of women, on equal terms with men, in the political, social, economic and cultural life of their countries, hampers the growth of the prosperity of society and the family and makes more difficult the full development of the potentialities of women in the service of their countries and of humanity,

Concerned that in situations of poverty women have the least access to food, health, education, training and opportunities for employment and other needs,

Convinced that the establishment of the new international economic order based on equity and justice will contribute significantly towards the promotion of equality between men and women,

Emphasizing that the eradication of *apartheid*, all forms of racism, racial discrimination, colonialism, neo-colonialism, aggression, foreign occupation and domination and interference in the internal affairs of States is essential to the full enjoyment of the rights of men and women,

Affirming that the strengthening of international peace and security, the relaxation of international tension, mutual co-operation among all States irrespective of their social and economic systems, general and complete disarmament, in particular nuclear disarmament under strict and effective international control, the affirmation of the principles of justice, equality and mutual benefit in relations among countries and the realization of the right of peoples under alien and colonial domination and foreign occupation to self-determination and independence, as well as respect for national sovereignty and territorial integrity, will promote social progress and development and as a consequence will contribute to the attainment of full equality between men and women,

Convinced that the full and complete development of a country, the welfare of the world and the cause of peace require the maximum participation of women on equal terms with men in all fields,

Bearing in mind the great contribution of women to the welfare of the family and to the development of society, so far not fully recognized, the social significance of maternity and the role of both parents in the family and in the upbringing of children, and aware that the role of women in procreation should be a basis for discrimination but that the upbringing of children requires a sharing of responsibility between men and women and society as a whole,

Aware that a change in the traditional role of men as well as the role of women in society and in the family is needed to achieve full equality between men and women,

Determined to implement the principles set forth in the Declaration on the Elimination of Discrimination Against Women and, for that purpose, to adopt the measures required for the elimination of such discrimination in all forms and manifestations,

Have agreed on the following:

Part I

Article 1

For the purposes of the present Convention, the term "discrimination against women" shall mean any distinction, exclusion or restriction made on the basis of sex which has the effect or purpose of impairing or nullifying the recognition, enjoyment or exercise of women, irrespective of their marital status, on a basis of equality of men and women, of human rights and fundamental freedoms in the political, economic, social, cultural, civil or any other field.

Article 2

States Parties condemn discrimination against women in all its forms, agree to pursue by all appropriate means and without delay a policy of eliminating discrimination against women and, to this end undertake:

(a) To embody the principle of the equality of men and women in their national constitutions or other appropriate legislation if not yet incorporated therein and to ensure, through law and other appropriate means, the practical realization of this principle;

(b) To adopt appropriate legislative and other measures, including sanctions where appropriate, prohibiting all discrimination against women;

(c) To establish legal protection of the rights of women on an equal basis with men and to ensure through competent national tribunals and other public institutions the effective protection of women against any act of discrimination;

(d) To refrain from engaging in any act or practice of discrimination against women and to ensure that public authorities and institutions shall act in conformity with this obligation;

(e) To take all appropriate measures to eliminate discrimination against women by any person, organization or enterprise;

(f) To take all appropriate measures, including legislation, to modify or abolish existing laws, regulations, customs and practices which constitute discrimination against women;

(g) To repeal all national penal provisions which constitute discrimination against women.

Article 3

States Parties shall take all fields, in particular in the political, social, economic and cultural fields, all appropriate measures, including legislation, to ensure the full development and advancement of women, for the purpose of guaranteeing them the exercise and enjoyment of human rights and fundamental freedoms on a basis of equality with men.

Article 4

1. Adoption by States Parties of temporary special measures aimed at accelerating *de facto* equality between men and women shall not be considered discrimination as defined in the present Convention, but shall in no way entail as a consequence the maintenance of unequal or separate standards; these measures shall be discontinued when the objectives of equality of opportunity and treatment have been achieved.

2. Adoption by States Parties of special measures, including those measures contained in the present Convention, aimed at protecting maternity shall not be considered discriminatory.

Article 5

States Parties shall take all appropriate measures:

(a) To modify the social and cultural patterns of conduct of men and women, with a view of achieving the elimination of prejudices and customary and all other practices which are based on the idea of the inferiority or the superiority of either of the sexes or on stereotyped roles for men and women;

(b) To ensure that family education includes a proper understanding of maternity as a social function and the recognition of the common responsibility of men and women in the upbringing and development of their children, it being understood that the interest of the children is the primordial consideration in all cases.

Article 6

States Parties shall take all appropriate measures including legislation, to suppress all forms of traffic in women and exploitation of prostitution of women.

Part II

Article 7

States Parties shall take all appropriate measures to eliminate discrimination against women in the political and public life of the country and, in particular, shall ensure to women, on equal terms with men, the right:

(a) To vote in all elections and public referenda and to be eligible for election to all publicly elected bodies;

(b) To participate in the formulation of government policy and the implementation thereof and to hold public office and perform all public functions at all levels of government;

(c) To participate in non-governmental organizations and associations concerned with the public and political life of the country.

Article 8

States Parties shall take all appropriate measures to ensure to women, on equal terms with men and without any discrimination, the opportunity to represent their Governments at the international level and to participate in the work of international organizations.

Article 9

1. States Parties shall grant women equal rights with men to acquire, change or retain their nationality. They shall ensure in particular that neither marriage to an alien nor change of nationality by the husband during marriage shall automatically change the nationality of the wife, render her stateless or force upon her the nationality of the husband.

2. States Parties shall grant women equal rights with men with respect to the nationality of their children.

Part III

Article 10

States Parties shall take all appropriate measures to eliminate discrimination against women in order to ensure to them equal rights with men in the field of education and in particular to ensure, on a basis of equality of men and women:

(a) The same conditions for career and vocational guidance, for access to studies and for the achievement of diploma in educational establishments of all categories in rural as well as in urban areas; this equality shall be ensured in pre-school, general, technical, professional and higher technical education, as well as in all types of vocational training;

(b) Access to the same curricula, the same examinations, teaching staff with qualifications of the same standard and school premises and equipment of the same quality;

(c) The elimination of any stereotyped concept of the roles of men and women at all levels and in all forms of education by encouraging coeducation and other types of education which will help to achieve this aim and, in particular, by the revision of textbooks and school programmes and the adaptation of teaching methods;

(d) The same opportunities to benefit from scholarships and other study grants;

(e) The same opportunities for access to programmes of continuing education, including adult and functional literacy programmes, particularly those aimed at reducing at the earliest possible time, any gap in education existing between men and women;

(f) The reduction of female student drop-out rates and the organization of programmes for girls and women who have left school prematurely;

(g) The same opportunities to participate actively in sports and physical education;

(h) Access to specific educational information to help to ensure the health and well-being of families, including information and advice on family planning.

Article 11

1. States Parties shall take all appropriate measures to eliminate discrimination against women in the field of employment in order to ensure, on a basis of equality of men and women, the same rights, in particular:

(a) The right to work as an inalienable right of all human beings;

(b) The right to the same employment opportunities, including the application of the same criteria for selection in matters of employment;

(c) The rights to free choice of profession and employment, the right to promotion, job security and all benefits and conditions of service and the right to receive vocational training and retraining, including apprenticeships, advanced vocational training and recurrent training;

(d) The right to equal remuneration, including benefits and to equal treatment in respect of work of equal value, as well as equality of treatment in the evaluation of the quality of work;

(e) The right to equal social security; particularly in cases of retirement, unemployment, sickness, invalidity and old age and other incapacity to work, as well as the right to paid leave;

(f) The right to protection of health and to safety in working conditions, including the safeguarding of the function of reproduction.

2. In order to prevent discrimination against women on the grounds of marriage or maternity and to ensure their effective right to work, States Parties shall take appropriate measures:

(a) To prohibit, subject to the imposition of sanctions, dismissal on the grounds of pregnancy or of maternity leave and discrimination in dismissals on the basis of marital status;

(b) To introduce maternity leave with pay or with comparable social benefits without loss of former employment, seniority or social allowance;

(c) To encourage the provisions of the necessary supporting social services to enable parents to combine family obligations with work responsibilities and participation in public life, in particular through promoting the establishment and development of a network of child-care facilities;

(d) To provide special protection to women during pregnancy in types of work proved to be harmful to them.

3. Protective legislation relating to matters covered in this article shall be reviewed periodically in the light of scientific and technological knowledge and shall be revised, repealed or extended as necessary.

Article 12

1. States Parties shall take all appropriate measures to eliminate discrimination against women in the field of health care in order to ensure, on a basis of equality of men and women, access to health care services, including those related to family planning.

2. Notwithstanding the provisions of paragraph 1 of this Article, States Parties shall ensure to women appropriate services in connexion with pregnancy, confinement and the postnatal period, granting free services where necessary, as well as adequate nutrition during pregnancy and lactation.

Article 13

States Parties shall take all appropriate measures to eliminate discrimination against women in other areas of economic and social life in order to ensure, on a basis of equality of men and women, the same rights, in particular:

(a) The right to family benefits;

(b) The right to bank loans, mortgages and other forms of financial credit;

(c) The right to participate in recreational activities, sports and all aspects of cultural life.

Article 14

1. States Parties shall take into account particular problems faced by rural women and the significant roles which rural women play in the economic survival of their families, including their work in the non-monetized sectors of the economy, and shall take all appropriate measures to ensure the application of the provisions of the present Convention to women in rural areas.

2. States Parties shall take all appropriate measures to eliminate discrimination against women in rural areas in order to ensure, on a basis of equality of men and women, that they participate in and benefit from rural development and, in particular, shall ensure to such women the right:

(a) To participate in the elaboration and implementation of planning at all levels;

(b) To have access to adequate health care facilities, including information, counselling and services in family planning;

(c) To benefit directly from social security programmes;

(d) To obtain all types of training and education, formal and non-formal, including that relating to functional literacy, as well as *inter alia*, the benefit of all community and extension services, in order to increase their technical proficiency;

(e) To organize self-help groups and co-operatives in order to obtain equal access to economic opportunities through employment or self-employment;

(f) To participate in all community activities;

(g) To have access to agricultural credit and loans, marketing facilities, appropriate technology and equal treatment in land and agrarian reform as well as in land resettlement schemes;

(h) To enjoy adequate living conditions, particularly in relation to housing, sanitation, electricity and water supply, transport and communications.

Part IV

Article 15

1. States Parties shall accord to women equality with men before the law.

2. States Parties shall accord to women, in civil matters, a legal capacity identical to that of men and the same opportunities to exercise that capacity. In particular, they shall give women equal rights to conclude contracts and to administer property and shall treat them equally in all stages of procedure in courts and tribunals.

3. States Parties agree that all contracts and all other private instruments of any kind with a legal effect which is directed at restricting the legal capacity of women shall be deemed null and void.

4. States Parties shall accord to men and women the same rights with regard to the law relating to the movement of persons and the freedom to choose their residence and domicile.

Article 16

1. States Parties shall take all appropriate measures to eliminate discrimination against women in all matters relating to marriage and family relations and in particular shall ensure, on a basis of equality of men and women:

(a) The same right to enter into marriage;

(b) The same right freely to choose a spouse and to enter into marriage only with their free and full consent;

(c) The same rights and responsibilities during marriage and at its dissolution;

(d) The same rights and responsibilities as parents, irrespective of their marital status, in matters relating to their children; in all cases the interests of the children shall be paramount;

(e) The same rights to decide freely and responsibly on the number and spacing of their children and to have access to information, education and means to enable them to exercise these rights;

(f) The same rights and responsibilities with regard to guardianship, wardship, trusteeship and adoption of children, or similar institutions where these concepts exist in national legislation; in all cases the interests of the children shall be paramount;

(g) The same personal rights as husband and wife, including the right to choose a family name, a profession and an occupation;

(h) The same rights for both spouses in respect of the ownership, acquisition, management, administration enjoyment and disposition of property, whether free of charge or for a valuable consideration.

2. The betrothal and the marriage of a child shall have no legal effect, and all necessary action, including legislation, shall be taken to specify a minimum age for marriage and to make the registration of marriages in an official registry compulsory.

Part V

Article 17

1. For the purpose of considering the progress made in the implementation of the present Convention, there shall be established a Committee on the Elimination of Discrimination Against Women (hereinafter referred to as the Committee) consisting, at the time of entry into force by the Convention, of eighteen and after ratification of or accession to the Convention by the thirty-fifth State Party, of twenty-three experts of high moral standing and competence in the field covered by the convention. The experts shall be elected by States Parties from among their nationals and shall serve in their personal capacity, consideration being given to equitable geographical distribution and to the representation of the different forms of civilization as well as the principal legal systems.

2. The members of the Committee shall be elected by secret ballot from a list of persons nominated by States Parties. Each State Party may nominate one person from among its own nationals.

3. The initial election shall be held six months after the date of the entry into force of the present Convention. At least three months before the date of each election the Secretary-General of the United Nations shall address a letter to the States Parties inviting them to submit their nominations within two months. The Secretary-General shall prepare a list in alphabetical order of all persons thus nominated, indicating the States Parties which have nominated them, and shall submit it to the States Parties.

4. Elections of the members of the Committee shall be held at a meeting of States Parties convened by the Secretary-General at United Nations Headquarters. At that meeting, for which two-thirds of the States Parties shall constitute a quorum, the persons elected to the Committee shall be those nominees who obtain the largest number of votes and an absolute majority of these votes of the representatives of States Parties present and voting.

5. The members of the Committee shall be elected for a term of four years. However, the terms of nine of the members elected at the first election shall expire at the end of two years; immediately after the first election the names of these nine members shall be chosen by lot by the Chairman of the Committee.

8. Margaret Sanger's "Woman and the New Race" Speech (1920)

The most far-reaching social development of modern times is the revolt of woman against sex servitude. The most important force in the remaking of the world is a free mother–hood. . . .

Only in recent years has woman's position as the gentler and weaker half of the human family been emphatically and generally questioned. Men assumed that this was woman's place; woman herself accepted it. It seldom occurred to anyone to ask whether she would go on occupying it forever.

Upon the mere surface of woman's organized protests there were no indications that she was desirous of achieving a fundamental change in her position. She claimed the right of suffrage and legislative regulation of her working hours, and asked that her property rights be equal to those of the man. None of these demands, however, affected directly the most vital factors of her existence. Whether she won her point or failed to win it, she remained a dominated weakling in a society controlled by men.

Woman's acceptance of her inferior status was the more real because it was unconscious. She had chained herself to her place in society and the family through the maternal functions of her nature, and only chains thus strong could have bound her to her lot as a brood animal for the masculine civilizations of the world. In accepting her role as the "weaker and gentler half," she accepted that function. In turn, the acceptance of that function fixed the more firmly her rank as an inferior.

Caught in this "vicious circle," woman has, through her reproductive ability, founded and perpetuated the tyrannies of the Earth. Whether it was the tyranny of a monarchy, an oligarchy or a republic, the one indispensable factor of its existence was, as it is now, hordes of human beings—human beings so plentiful as to be cheap, and so cheap that ignorance was their natural lot. Upon the rock of an unenlightened, submissive maternity have these been founded; upon the product of such a maternity have they flourished. . . .

Today, however, woman is rising in fundamental revolt. . . .Millions of women are asserting their right to voluntary motherhood. They are determined to decide for themselves whether they shall become mothers, under what condition and when. This is the fundamental revolt referred to. It is for woman the key to the temple of liberty.

Even as birth control is the means by which woman attains basic freedom, so it is the means by which she must and will uproot the evil she has wrought through her submission.

As she has unconsciously and ignorantly brought about social disaster, so must and will she consciously and intelligently *undo* that disaster and create a new and better order. . . .

Two chief obstacles hinder the discharge of this tremendous obligation. The first and the lesser is the legal barrier. Dark-Age laws would still deny to her the knowledge of her reproductive nature. Such knowledge is indispensable to intelligent motherhood and she must achieve it, despite absurd statutes and equally absurd moral canons.

The second and more serious barrier is her own ignorance of the extent and effect of her submission. Until she knows the evil her subjection has wrought to herself, to her progeny and to the world at large, she cannot wipe out that evil. . . .

Most women who belong to the workers' families have no accurate or reliable knowledge of contraceptives, and are, therefore, bringing children into the world so rapidly that they, their families and their class are overwhelmed with numbers. Out of these numbers . . .have grown many of the burdens with which society in general is weighted; out of them have come, also, the want, disease, hard living conditions and general misery of the workers.

The women of this class are the greatest suffers of all. Not only do they bear the material hardships and deprivations in common with the rest of the family, but in the case of the mother, these are intensified. It is the man and the child who have the first call upon the insufficient amount of food. It is the man and the child who get the recreation, if there is any to be had, for the man's hours of labor are usually limited by law or by his labor union.

It is the woman who suffers first from hunger, the woman whose clothing is least adequate, the woman who must work all hours, even though she is not compelled, as in the case of millions, to go into a factory to add to her husband's scanty income. It is she, too, whose health breaks first and most hopelessly, under the long hours of work, the drain of frequent childbearing, and often almost constant nursing of babies. There are no eight-hour laws to protect the mother against ill health and the diseases of pregnancy and reproduction. In fact there has been almost no thought or consideration given for the protection of the mother in the home of the workingman.

There are no general health statistics to tell the full story of the physical ills suffered by women as a result of too great reproductivity. But we get some light upon conditions through the statistics on maternal mortality, compiled by Dr. Grace L. Meigs, for the Children's Bureau of the United States Department of Labor. These figures do not include the deaths of women suffering from disease complicated by pregnancy.

"In 1913, in this country at least 15,000 women, it is estimated, died from conditions caused by childbirth; about 7,000 of these died from childbed fever and the remaining 8,000 from diseases now known to be a great extent preventable or curable," says Dr. Meigs in her summary. "Physicians and statisticians agree that these figures are a *great underestimate*."

Think of it — the needless deaths of 15,000 women a "great underestimate"! Yet even this number means that virtually every hour of the day and night two women die as the result of childbirth in the healthiest and supposedly the most progressive country in the world.

It is apparent that Dr Meigs leaves out of consideration the many thousands of deaths each year of women who become pregnant while suffering from tuberculosis. . . . Nor were syphilis, various kidney and heart disorders and other diseases, often rendered fatal by pregnancy, taken into account by Dr. Meigs' survey. . . .

From what sort of homes come these deaths from childbirth? Most of them occur in overcrowded dwellings, where food, care, sanitation, nursing and medical attention are inadequate. Where do we find most of the tuberculosis and much of the other disease which is aggravated by pregnancy? In the same sort of home.

The deadly chain of misery is all too plain to anyone who takes the trouble to observe it. A woman of the working class marries and with her husband lives in a degree of comfort upon his earnings. Her household duties are not beyond her strength. Then the children begin to come—one, two, three, four, possibly five or more. The earnings of the husband do not increase as rapidly as the family does. Food, clothing and general comfort in the home grow less as the numbers of the family increase. The woman's work grows heavier, and her strength is less with each child. Possibly — probably — she has to go into a factory to add to her husband's earnings. There she toils, doing her housework at night. Her health goes, and the crowded conditions and lack of necessities in the home help to bring about disease—especially tuberculosis. Under the circumstances, the woman's chances of recovering from each succeeding childbirth grow less. Less too are the chances of the child's surviving. . . .

Women who have a knowledge of contraceptives are not compelled to make the choice between a maternal experience and a marred love life; they are not forced to balance motherhood against social and spiritual activities. Motherhood is for them to choose, as it should be for every woman to choose. Choosing to become mothers, they do not thereby shut themselves away from thorough companionship with their husbands, from friends, from culture, from all those manifold experiences which are necessary to the completeness and the joy of life.

For mothers of the race are these, the courted comrades of the men they choose, rather than the "slaves of slaves." For theirs is the magic power — the power of limiting their families to such numbers as will permit them to live full-rounded lives. Such lives are the expression of the feminine spirit which is woman *and all of her* — not merely part, nor professional skill, nor intellect — but all that woman is, or may achieve. . . .

Thousands of well-intentioned people who agree that there are times and conditions under which it is woman's highest duty to avoid having children advocate continence as the one permissible means of birth control. . . .

Loathing, disgust or indifference to the sex relationship nearly always lies behind the advocacy to continence. . . .

Much of the responsibility for this feeling upon the part of many thousands of women must be laid to two thousand years of Christian teaching that all sex expression is unclean. Part of it, too, must be laid to the dominant male's habit of violating the love rights of his mate.

The habit referred to grows out of the assumed and legalized right of the husband to have sexual satisfaction at any time he desires, regardless of the woman's repugnance for it. The law of the state upholds him in this regard. A husband need not support his wife if she refuses to comply with his sexual demands. . . .

When I have had the confidence of women indifferent to physical union, I have found the fault usually lay with the husband. His idea of marriage is too often that of providing a home for a female who would in turn provide for his physical needs, including sexual satisfaction. Such a husband usually excludes such satisfaction from the category of the wife's needs, physical or spiritual.

This man is not concerned with his wife's sex urge, save as it responds to his own at times of his choosing. Man's code has taught woman to be quite ashamed of such desires. Usually she speaks of indifference without regret; often proudly. She seems to regard herself as more chaste and highly endowed in purity than other women who confess to feeling physical attraction toward their husbands. She also secretly considers herself far superior to the husband who makes no concealment of his desire toward her. Nevertheless, because of this desire upon the husband's part, she goes on "pretending" to mutual interest in the relationship. . . .

As a means of birth control, continence is as impracticable for most people as it is undesirable. . .

Despite the unreliability of some methods and the harmfulness of some others, there *are* methods which are both harmless and certain. This much the woman who is seeking means of limiting her family may be told here. . . .

More and more perfect means of preventing conception will be developed as women insist upon them. Every woman should make it plain to her physician that she expects him to be informed upon this subject. She should refuse to accept evasive answers. An increasing demand upon physicians will inevitably result in laboratory researches and experimentation. Such investigation is indeed already beginning and we may expect great progress in contraceptive methods in the near future. We may also expect more authoritative opinions upon preventive methods and devices. When women confidently and insistently demand them, they will have access to contraceptives which are both certain and harmless. . . .

Sneers and jests at birth control are giving way to a reverent understanding of the needs of woman. They who today deny the right of a woman to control her own body speak with the hardihood of invincible ignorance or with the folly of those blind ones who in all ages have opposed the light of progress. . . .

As far back as 1900, I began to inquire of my associates among the nurses what one could tell these worried women who asked constantly: "What can I do?" It is the voice of the elemental urge of woman—it has always been there; and whether we have heeded it or neglected it, we have always heard it. Out of this cry came the birth control movement.

Economic conditions have naturally made this elemental need plain; sometimes they have lent a more desperate voice to woman's cry for freedom. . . . But the birth control movement of that unceasing cry of the socially repressed, spiritually stifled woman who is constantly demanding: "What can I do to avoid more children?" . . .

After a year's study in foreign countries for the purpose of supplementing the knowledge gained in my fourteen years as a nurse, I came back to the United States determined to open a clinic. I had decided that there could be no better way of demonstrating to the public the necessity of birth control and the welcome it would receive than by taking the knowledge of contraceptive methods directly to those who most needed it.

A clinic was opened in Brooklyn. There 480 women received information before the police closed the consulting rooms and arrested Ethel Byrne, a registered nurse, Fania Mindell, a translator, and myself. The purpose of this clinic was to demonstrate to the public the practicability and the necessity of such institutions. All women who came seeking information were workingmen's wives. All had children. No unmarried girls came at all. Men came whose wives had nursing children and could not come. Women came from the farther parts of Long Island, from cities in Massachusetts and Connecticut and even more distant places. Mothers brought their married daughters. Some whose ages were from 25 to 35 looked 50, but the clinic gave them new hope to face years ahead. These women invariably expressed their love for children, but voiced a common plea for means to avoid others, in order that they might give sufficient care to those already born. . . .

For ten days the two rooms of this clinic were crowded to their utmost. Then came the police. We were hauled off to jail and eventually convicted of a "crime."

Ethel Byrne instituted a hunger strike for eleven days, which attracted attention throughout the nation. It brought to public notice the fact that women were ready to die for the principle of voluntary motherhood. So strong was the sentiment evoked that Governor Whitman pardoned Mrs. Byrne.

No single act of self-sacrifice in the history of the birth control movement has done more to awaken the conscience of the public or to arouse the courage of women, than did Ethel Byrne's deed of uncompromising resentment at the outrage of jailing women who were attempting to disseminate knowledge which would emancipate the motherhood of America.

Courage like hers and like that of others who have undergone arrest and imprisonment, or who night after night and day after day have faced street crowds to speak or to sell literature — the faith and the untiring labors of still others who have not come into public notice — have given the movement its dauntless character and assure the final victory.

One dismal fact had become clear long before the Brownsville clinic was opened. The medical profession as a whole had ignored the tragic cry of womanhood for relief from forced maternity. The private practitioners, one after another, shook their heads and replied: "It cannot be dome. It is against the law," and the same answer came from clinics and public hospitals. . . . One of the chief results of the Brownsville clinic was that of establishing for physicians a [legal] right which they neglected to establish for themselves but which they are bound, in the very nature of things, to exercise to an increasing degree. Similar tests by women in other states would doubtless establish the right elsewhere in America.

We know of some thirty-five arrests of women and men who have dared entrenched prejudice and the law to further the cause of birth control. . . . Each of these arrests brought added publicity. Each became a center of local agitation. Each brought a part of the public, at least, face to face with the issue between the women in America and this barbarous law. . . .

Voluntary motherhood implies a new morality — a vigorous, constructive, liberated morality. That morality will, first of all, prevent the submergence of womanhood into motherhood.

9. Married Women's Property Act, New York State (1848)

The People of the State of New York, represented in Senate and Assembly, do enact as follows:

I. The real and personal property of any female who may hereafter marry, and which she shall own at the time of her marriage, and the rents, issues and profits thereof, shall not be subject to the disposal of her husband nor be liable for his debts and shall continue her sole and separate property as if she were a single female.

II . The real and personal property and the rents, issues and profits thereof of any female now married shall not be subject to the disposal of her husband; but shall be her sole and separate property as if she were a single female except so far as the same may be liable for the debts of her husband heretofore contracted.

III. It shall be lawful for any married female to receive by gift, grant device or bequest, from any person other than her husband and to hold to her sole and separate use, as if she were a single female, real and personal property and the rents, issues and profits thereof, and the same shall not be subject to the disposal of her husband, nor be liable for his debts.

IV. All contracts made between persons in contemplation of marriage shall remain in full force after such marriage takes place.

10. President's Commission on the Status of Women (1963)

Recommendations

Education and Counseling

Means of acquiring or continuing education must be available to every adult at whatever point he or she broke off traditional formal schooling. The structure of adult education must be drastically revised. It must provide practicable and accessible opportunities, developed with regard for the needs of women, to complete elementary and secondary school and to continue education beyond high school. Vocational training, adapted to the nation's growing requirement for skilled and highly educated manpower, should be included at all these educational levels. Where needed and appropriate, financial support should be provided by local, state, and federal governments and by private groups and foundations.

In a democracy offering broad and everchanging choices, where ultimate decisions are made by individuals, skilled counseling is an essential part of education. Public and private agencies should join in strengthening counseling resources. States and school districts should raise their standards for state employment service counselors and school guidance counselors. Institutions offering counseling education should provide both course content and ample supervised experience in the counseling of females as well as males, adults as well as adolescents.

The education of girls and women for their responsibilities in home and community should be thoroughly re-examined with a view to discovering more effective approaches, with experimentation in content and timing, and under auspices including school systems, private organizations, and the mass media.

Home and Community

For the benefit of children, mothers, and society, child-care services should be available for children of families at all economic levels. Proper standards of child care must be maintained, whether services are in homes or in centers. Costs should be met by fees scaled to parents' ability to pay, contributions from voluntary agencies, and public appropriations.

Tax deductions for child-care expenses of working mothers should be kept commensurate with the median income of couples when both husband and wife are engaged in substantial employment. The present limitation on their joint income, above which deductions are not allowable, should be raised. Additional deductions, of lesser amounts, should be allowed for children beyond the first. The 11-year age limit for child-care deductions should be raised.

Family services under public and private auspices to help families avoid or overcome breakdown or dependency and establish a soundly based homelife, and professionally supervised homemaker services to meet emergency or other special needs should be strengthened, extended, or established where lacking.

Community programs under public and private auspices should make comprehensive provisions for health and rehabilitation services, including easily accessible maternal and child health services, accompanied by education to encourage their use.

Volunteers' services should be made more effective through coordinated and imaginative planning among agencies and organizations for recruitment, training, placement, and supervision, and their numbers augmented through tapping the large reservoir of additional potential among youth, retired people, members of minority groups, and women not now in volunteer activities.

Women in Employment

Equal opportunity for women in hiring, training, and promotion should be the governing principle in private employment. An Executive Order should state this principle and advance its application to work done under federal contracts.

At present, federal systems of manpower utilization discourage part-time employment. Many able women, including highly trained professionals, who are not free for full-time employment, can work part time. The Civil Service Commission and the Bureau of the Budget should facilitate the imaginative and prudent use of such personnel throughout the government service.

Labor Standards

The federal Fair Labor Standards Act, including premium pay for overtime, should be extended to employment subject to federal jurisdiction but now uncovered, such as work in hotels, motels, restaurants, and laundries, in additional retail establishments, in agriculture, and in nonprofit organizations.

State legislation, applicable to both men and women, should be enacted, or strengthened and extended to all types of employment, to provide minimum-wage levels approximating the minimum under federal law and to require premium pay at the rate of at least time and a half for overtime.

The normal workday and workweek at this moment of history should be not more that 8 hours a day and 40 hours a week. The best way to discourage excessive hours for all workers is by broad and effective minimum-wage coverage, both federal and state, providing overtime of at least time and a half the regular rate for all hours in excess of 8 a day or 40 a week.

Until such time as this goal is attained, state legislation limiting maximum hours of work for women should be maintained, strengthened, and expanded. Provisions for flexibility under proper safeguards should allow additional hours of work when there is a demonstrated need. During this interim period, efforts should continuously and simultaneously be made to require premium rates of pay for all hours in excess of 8 a day or 40 a week.

State laws should establish the principle of equal pay for comparable work.

State laws should protect the right of all workers to join unions of their own choosing and to bargain collectively.

Security of Basic Income

A widow's benefit under the federal old-age insurance system should be equal to the amount that her husband would have received at the same age had he lived. This objective should be approached as rapidly as may be financially feasible.

The coverage of the unemployment-insurance system should be extended. Small establishments and nonprofit organizations should be covered now through federal action, and state and local government employees through state action. Practicable means of covering at least some household workers and agricultural workers should be actively explored.

Paid maternity leave or comparable insurance benefits should be provided for women workers; employers, unions, and governments should explore the best means of accomplishing this purpose.

Women Under the Law

Early and definitive court pronouncement, particularly by the United States Supreme Court, is urgently needed with regard to the validity under the Fifth and Fourteenth Amendments of laws and official practices discriminating against women, to the end that the principle of equality becomes firmly established in constitutional doctrine.

Accordingly, interested groups should give high priority to bringing under court review cases involving laws and practices which discriminate against women.

The United States should assert leadership, particularly in the United Nations, in securing equality of rights for women as part of the effort to define and assure human rights; should participate actively in the formulation of international declarations, principles, and conventions to improve the status of women throughout the world; and should demonstrate its sincere concern for women's equal rights by becoming a party to appropriate conventions.

Appropriate action, including enactment of legislation where necessary, should be taken to achieve equal jury service in the states.

State legislatures, and other groups concerned with the improvement of state statutes affecting family law and personal and property rights of married women, including the National Conference of Commissioners on Uniform State Law Institute, and state Commissions on the Status of Women, should move to eliminate laws which impose legal disabilities on women.

Women as Citizens

Women should be encouraged to seek elective and appointive posts at local, state, and national levels and in all three branches of government.

Public office should be held according to ability, experience, and effort, without special preferences or discriminations based on sex. Increasing consideration should continually be given to the appointment of women of demonstrated ability and political sensitivity to policy-making positions.

Continuing Leadership

To further the objectives in this report, an Executive Order should:

1. Designate a Cabinet officer to be responsible for assuring that the resources and activities of the federal government bearing upon the Commission's recommendations are directed to carrying them out, and for making periodic progress reports to the President.

2. Designate the heads of other agencies involved in those activities to serve, under the chairmanship of the designated Cabinet officer, as an interdepartmental committee to assure proper coordination and action.

3. Establish a citizens committee, advisory to the interdepartmental committee and with its secretariat from the designated Cabinet officer, to meet periodically to evaluate progress made, provide counsel, and serve as a means for suggesting and stimulating action.

Members of the Commission

The names of the men and women appointed to the Commission, and the posts they occupied at the time of their appointment, were:

Eleanor Roosevelt, *Chairman*

Esther Peterson, *Executive Vice Chairman*, Assistant Secretary of Labor

Dr. Richard A. Lester, *Vice Chairman*, Chairman, Department of Economics, Princeton University

The Attorney General, Honorable Robert F. Kennedy

The Secretary of Agriculture, Honorable Orville L. Freeman

The Secretary of Commerce, Honorable Luther H. Hodges

The Secretary of Labor, Honorable Arthur J. Goldberg, Honorable W. Willard Wirtz

The Secretary of Health, Education, and Welfare, Honorable Abraham A. Ribicoff, Honorable Anthony L. Celebrezze

Honorable George D. Aiken, United States Senate

Honorable Maurine B. Neuberger, United States Senate

Honorable Edith Green, United States House of Representatives

Honorable Jessica M. Weis, United States House of Representatives

The Chairman of the Civil Service Commission, Honorable John W. Macy, Jr.

Macon Boddy, Henrietta, Tex.

Dr. Mary I. Bunting, President, Radcliffe College

Mary E. Callahan, Member, Executive Board, International Union of Electrical, Radio and Machine Workers

Dr. Henry David, President, New School for Social Research

Dorothy Height, President, National Council of Negro Women, Inc.

Margaret Hickey, Public Affairs Editor, *Ladies Home Journal*

Viola H. Hymes, President, National Council of Jewish Women, Inc.

Margaret J. Mealey, Executive Director, National Council of Catholic Women

Norman E. Nicholson, Administrative Assistant, Kaiser Industries Corp., Oakland, Calif.

Marguerite Rawalt, Attorney; past president: Federal Bar Association, National Association of Women Lawyers, National Federation of Business and Professional Women's Clubs, Inc.

William F. Schnitzler, Secretary-Treasurer, American Federation of Labor and Congress of Industrial Organizations

Dr. Caroline F. Ware, Vienna, Va.

Dr. Cynthia C. Wedel, Assistant General Secretary for Program, National Council of the Churches of Christ in the United States of America

11. Susan B. Anthony's "Woman Wants Bread, Not the Ballot" Speech (1870)

Wherever, on the face of the globe or on the page of history, you show me a disfranchised class, I will show you a degraded class of labor. Disfranchisement means inability to make, shape or control one's own circumstances. The disfranchised must always do the work, accept the wages, occupy the position the enfranchised assign to them. The disfranchised are in the position of the pauper. You remember the old adage, "Beggars must not be choosers;" they must take what they can get or nothing! That is exactly the position of women in the world of work today; they can not choose. If they could, do you for a moment believe they would take the subordinate places and the inferior pay? Nor is it a "new thing under the sun" for the disfranchised, the inferior classes weighed down with wrongs, to declare they "do not want to vote." The rank and file are not philosophers, they are not educated to think for themselves, but simply to accept, unquestioned, whatever comes.

Years ago in England when the workingmen, starving in the mines and factories, gathered in mobs and took bread wherever they could get it, their friends tried to educate them into a knowledge of the causes of their poverty and degradation. At one of these "Monster bread meetings," held in Manchester, John Bright said to them, "Workingmen, what you need to bring to you cheap bread and plenty of it, is the franchise;" but those ignorant men shouted back to Mr. Bright, precisely as the women of America do to us today, "It is not the vote we want, it is bread." . . .

But at length, through the persistent demands of a little handful of reformers, there was introduced into the British Parliament the "household suffrage" bill of 1867 . . . . the opposition was championed by Robert Lowe, who presented all the stock objections to the extension of the franchise to "those ignorant, degraded working men," as he called them, that ever were presented in this country against giving the ballot to the negroes, and that are today being urged against the enfranchisement of women. . . . But notwithstanding Mr. Lowe's persistent opposition, the bill became a law; and before the session closed, that same individual moved that Parliament, having enfranchised these men, should now make an appropriation for the establishment and support of schools for the education of them and their sons. Now, mark you his reason why! "Unless they are educated," said he, "they will be the means of overturning the throne of England." So long as these poor men in the mines and factories had not the right to vote, the power to make and unmake the laws and lawmakers, to help or hurt the government, no measure ever had been proposed for their benefit although they were ground under the heel of the capitalist to a condition of abject slavery. But the moment this power is placed in their hands, before they have used it even once, this bitterest enemy to their possessing it is the first man to spring to his feet and make this motion for the most beneficient measure possible in their behalf — public schools for the education of themselves and their children. . . .

The great distinctive advantage possessed by the workingmen of the republic is that the son of the humblest citizen, black or white, has equal chances with the son of the richest in the land if he take advantage of the public schools, the colleges and the many opportunities freely offered. It is this equality of rights which makes our nation a home for the oppressed of all the monarchies of the old world.

And yet, notwithstanding the declaration of our Revolutionary fathers, "all men created equal," "governments derive their just powers from the consent of the governed," "taxation and representation inseparable" — notwithstanding all these grand enunciations, our government was founded upon the blood and bones of half a million human beings, bought and sold as chattels in the market. Nearly all the original thirteen States had property qualifications which disfranchised poor white men as well as women and negroes. . . .

It is said women do not need the ballot for their protection because they are supported by men. Statistics show that there are 3,000,000 women in this nation supporting themselves. In the crowded cities of the East they are compelled to work in shops, stores and factories for the merest pittance. In New York alone, there are over 50,000 of these women receiving less than fifty cents a day. Women wage-earners in different occupations have organized themselves into trades unions, from time to time, and made their strikes to get justice at the hands of their employers just as men have done, but I have yet to learn of a successful strike of any body of women. The best organized one I ever knew was that of the collar laundry women of the city of Troy, N.Y., the great emporium for the manufacture of shirts, collars and cuffs. They formed a trades union of several hundred members and demanded an increase in wages. It was refused. So one May morning in 1867, each woman threw her scissors and her needle, her starch-pan and flat-iron, and for three long months not one returned to the factories. At the end of that time they were literally starved out, and the majority of them were compelled to go back, but not at their old wages, for their employers cut them down to even a lower figure.

In the winter following I met the president of this union, a bright young Irish girl, and asked her, "Do you not think if you had been 500 carpenters or 500 masons, you would have succeeded?" "Certainly," she said, and then she told me of 200 bricklayers who had the year before been on strike and gained every point with their employers. "What could have made the difference? Their 200 were but a fraction of that trade, while your 500 absolutely controlled yours." Finally she said, "It was because the editors ridiculed and denounced us." "Did they ridicule and denounce the bricklayers?" "No," "What did they say about you?" "Why, that our wages were good enough now, better than those of any other workingwomen except teachers; and if we weren't satisfied, we had better go and get married. . . . It must have been because our employers bribed the editors." . . . in the case of the bricklayers, no editor, either

Democrat or Republican, would have accepted the proffer of a bribe, because he would have known that if he denounced or ridiculed those men, not only they but all the trades union men of the city at the next election would vote solidly against the nominees advocated by the editor. If those collar laundry women had been voters, they would have held, in that little city of Troy, the "balance of political power". . . .

There are many women equally well qualified with men for principals and superintendents of schools, and yet, while three-fourths of the teachers are women, nearly all of them are relegated to subordinate positions on half or at most two-thirds the salaries paid to men . . . . sex alone settles the question. . . .

And then again you say, "Capital, not the vote, regulates labor." Granted, for the sake of the argument, that capital does control the labor of women . . . but no one with eyes to see and ears to hear will concede for a moment that capital absolutely dominates the work and wages of the free and franchised men of this republic. It is in order to lift the millions of our wage-earning women into a position of as much power over their own labor as men possess that they should be invested with the franchise. This ought to be done not only for the sake of justice to the women, but to the men with whom they compete; for, just so long as there is a degraded class of labor in the market, it always will be used by the capitalists to checkmate and undermine the superior classes.

Now that as a result of the agitation for equality of chances, and through the invention of machinery, there has come a great revolution in the world of economics, so that wherever a man may go to earn an honest dollar a woman may go also, there is no escape from the conclusion that she must be clothed with equal power to protect herself. That power is the ballot, the symbol of freedom and equality, without which no citizen is sure of keeping even that which he hath, much less of getting that which he hath not.

12. Title VII of the Civil Rights Act of 1964

Sec. 703. (a) It shall be unlawful employment practice for an employer —

(1) to fail or refuse to hire or to discharge any individual, or otherwise to discriminate against any individual with respect to his compensation, terms, conditions, or privileges of employment, because of such individual's race, color, religion, sex, or national origin; or

(2) to limit, segregate, or classify his employees in any way which would deprive or tend to deprive any individual of employment opportunities or otherwise adversely affect his status as an employee, because of such individual's race, color, religion, sex, or national origin.

(b) It shall be an unlawful employment practice for an employment agency to fail or refuse to refer for employment, or otherwise to discriminate against, any individual because of his race, color, religion, sex, or national origin, or to classify or refer for employment any individual on the basis of his race, color, religion, sex, or national origin.

(c) It shall be an unlawful employment practice for a labor organization —

(1) to exclude or to expel from its membership, or otherwise to discriminate against, any individual because of his race, color, religion, sex, or national origin;

(2) to limit, segregate, or classify its membership, or to classify or fail or refuse to refer for employment any individual, in any way which would deprive or tend to deprive any individual of employment opportunities, or would limit such employment opportunities or otherwise adversely affect his status as an employee or as an applicant for employment, because of such individual's race, color, religion, sex, or national origin; or

(3) to cause or attempt to cause an employer to discriminate against an individual in violation of this section. . . .

(e) Notwithstanding any other provision of this title, (1) it shall not be an unlawful employment practice for an employer to hire and employ employees, for an employment agency to classify, or refer for employment any individual, for a labor organization to classify its membership or to classify or refer for employment any individual, or for an employer, labor organization, or joint labor-management committee controlling apprenticeship or other training or retraining programs to admit or employ any individual in any such program, on the basis of his religion, sex, or national origin in those certain instances where religion, sex, or national origin is a bona fide occupational qualification reasonably necessary to the normal operation of that particular business or enterprise. . . .

Sec. 705. (a) There is hereby created a Commission to be known as the Equal Employment Opportunity Commission, which shall be composed of five members, not more than three of whom shall be members of the same political party, who shall be appointed by the President by and with the advice and consent of the Senate. . . .

(g) The Commission shall have power —

(1) to cooperate with and, with their consent, utilize regional, State, local, and other agencies, both public and private, and individuals; . . .

(3) to furnish to persons subject to this title such technical assistance as they may request to further their compliance with this title or an order issued thereunder;

(4) upon the request of (i) any employer, whose employees or some of them, or (ii) any labor organization members or some of them, refuse or threaten to refuse to cooperate in

effectuating the provisions of this title, to assist in such effectuation by conciliation or such remedial action as is provided by this title;

(5) to make such technical studies as are appropriate to effectuate the purposes and policies of this title and to make the results of such studies available to the public;

(6) to refer matters to the Attorney General which recommendations for intervention in a civil action brought by an aggrieved party under section 706, or for the institution of a civil action by the Attorney General under section 707, and to advise, consult, and assist the Attorney General on such matters. . . .

13. Proposed Equal Rights Amendment to the U.S. Constitution

Section 1. Equality of rights under the law shall not be denied or abridged by the United States or any state on account of sex.

Section 2. The Congress shall have the power to enforce, by appropriate legislation, the provisions of this article.

Section 3. This amendment shall take effect two years after the date of ratification.

The Equal Rights Amendment was written in 1921 by suffragist Alice Paul. It has been introduced in Congress every session since 1923. It passed Congress in 1972, but failed to be ratified by the necessary 38 states by the July 1982 deadline. It was ratified by 35 states.

14. The National Organization for Women's 1966 Statement of Purpose

Adopted at NOW's first National Conference in Washington, D.C., on October 29, 1966.

We, men and women who hereby constitute ourselves as the National Organization for Women, believe that the time has come for a new movement toward true equality for all women in America, and toward a fully-equal partnership of the sexes, as part of the worldwide revolution of human rights now taking place within and beyond our national borders.

The purpose of NOW is to take action to bring women into full participation in the mainstream of American society now, exercising all the privileges and responsibilities thereof in truly equal partnership with men.

We believe the time has come to move beyond the abstract argument, discussion and symposia over the status and special nature of women which has raged in America in recent years; the time has come to confront, with concrete action, the conditions that now prevent women from enjoying the equality of opportunity and freedom of choice which is their right, as individual Americans, and as human beings.

NOW is dedicated to the proposition that women, first and foremost, are human beings, who, like all other people in our society, must have the chance to develop their fullest human potential. We believe that women can achieve such equality only by accepting to the full the challenges and responsibilities they share with all other people in our society, as part of the decision-making mainstream of American political, economic, and social life.

We organize to initiate or support action, nationally, or in any part of this nation, by individuals or organizations, to break through the silken curtain of prejudice and discrimination against women in government, industry, the professions, the churches, the political parties, the judiciary, the labor unions, in education, science, medicine, law, religion, and every other field of importance in American society.

Enormous changes taking place in our society make it both possible and urgently necessary to advance the unfinished revolution of women toward true equality, now. With a life span lengthened to nearly 75 years it is no longer either necessary or possible for women to devote the greater part of their lives to childrearing; yet childbearing and rearing, which continues to be a most important part of most women's lives—still is used to justify barring women from equal professional and economic participation and advance.

Today's technology has reduced most of the productive chores which women once performed in the home and in mass-production industries based upon routine unskilled labor. This same technology has virtually eliminated the quality of muscular strength as a criterion for filling most jobs, while intensifying American industry's need for creative intelligence. In view of this new industrial revolution created by automation in the mid-twentieth century, women can and must participate in old and new fields of society in full equality—or become permanent outsiders.

Despite all the talk about the status of American women in recent years, the actual position of women in the United States has declined, and is declining, to an alarming degree throughout the 1950s and 60s. Although 46.4 percent of all American women between the ages of 18 and 65 now work outside the home, the overwhelming majority—75 percent—are in routine clerical, sales, or factory jobs, or they are household workers, cleaning women, hospital attendants. About two-thirds of Negro women workers are in the lowest paid service occupations. Working women are becoming increasingly—not less—concentrated on the bottom of the job ladder. As a consequence, full-time women workers today earn on the average only 60 percent of what men earn, and that wage gap has been increasing over the past 25 years in every major industry group. In 1964, of all women with a yearly income, 89 percent earned under $5,000 a year; half of all full-time year round women workers earned less than $3,690; only 1.4 percent of full-time year round women workers had an annual income of $10,000 or more.

Further, with higher education increasingly essential in today's society, too few women are entering and finishing college or going on to graduate or professional school. Today, women earn only one in three of the B.A. s and M.A. s granted, and one in ten of the Ph.D. s.

In all the professions considered of importance to society, and in the executive ranks of industry and government, women are losing ground. Where they are present it is only a token handful. Women comprise less than 1 percent of federal judges; less than 4 percent of all lawyers; 7 percent of doctors. Yet women represent 51 percent of the U.S. population. And, increasingly, men are replacing women in the top positions in secondary and elementary schools, in social work, and in libraries—once thought to be women's fields.

Official pronouncements of the advance in the status of women hide not only the reality of this dangerous decline, but the fact that nothing is being done to stop it. The excellent reports of the President's Commission on the Status of Women and of the state commissions have not been fully implemented. Such commissions have power only to advise. They have no power to enforce their recommendation; nor have they the freedom to organize American women and men to press for action on them. The reports of these commissions have, however, created a basis upon which it is now possible to build. Discrimination in employment on the basis of sex is now prohibited by federal law, in Title VII of the Civil Rights Act of 1964. But although nearly one-third of the cases brought before the Equal Employment Opportunity Commission during the first year dealt with sex discrimination and the proportion is increasing dramatically, the commission has not made clear its intention to enforce the law with the same seriousness on behalf of women as of other victims of discrimination. Many of these cases were Negro women, who are the victims of double discrimination of race and sex. Until now, too few women's organizations and official spokesmen have been willing to speak out against these dangers facing women. Too many women have been restrained by the fear of being called "feminist." There is no civil rights movement to speak for women, as there has been for Negroes and other victims of discrimination. The National Organization for Women must therefore begin to speak.

WE BELIEVE that the power of American law, and the protection guaranteed by the U.S. Constitution to the civil rights of all individuals, must be effectively applied and enforced to isolate and remove patterns of sex discrimination, to ensure equality of opportunity in employment and education, and equality of civil and political rights and responsibilities on behalf of women, as well as for Negroes and other deprived groups.

We realize that women's problems are linked to many broader questions of social justice; their solution will require concerted action by many groups. Therefore, convinced that human rights for all are indivisible, we expect to give active support to the common cause of equal rights for all those who suffer discrimination and deprivation, and we call upon other organizations committed to such goals to support our efforts toward equality for women.

WE DO NOT ACCEPT the token appointment of a few women to high-level positions in government and industry as a substitute for serious continuing effort to recruit and advance women according to their individual abilities. To this end, we urge American government and industry to mobilize the same resources of ingenuity and command with which they have solved problems of far greater difficulty than those now impeding the progress of women.

WE BELIEVE that this nation has a capacity at least as great as other nations, to innovate new social institutions which will enable women to enjoy the true equality of opportunity and responsibility in society, without conflict with their responsibilities as mothers and homemakers. In such innovations, America does not lead the Western world, but lags by decades behind many European countries. We do not accept the traditional assumption that a woman has to choose between marriage and motherhood, on the one hand, and serious participation in industry or the professions on the other. We question the present expectation that all normal women will retire from job or profession for 10 or 15 years, to devote their full time to raising children, only to reenter the job market at a relatively minor level. This, in itself, is a deterrent to the aspirations of women, to their acceptance into management or professional training courses, and to the very possibility of equality of opportunity or real choice, for all but a few women. Above all, we reject the assumption that these problems are the unique responsibility of each individual woman, rather than a basic social dilemma which society must solve. True equality of opportunity and freedom of choice for women requires such practical and possible innovations as a nationwide network of child-care centers, which will make it unnecessary for women to retire completely from society until their children are grown, and national programs to provide retraining for women who have chosen to care for their children fulltime.

WE BELIEVE that it is as essential for every girl to be educated to her full potential of human ability as it is for every boy—with the knowledge that such education is the key to effective participation in today's economy and that, for a girl as for a boy, education can only be serious where there is expectation that it will be used in society. We believe that American educators are capable of devising means of imparting such expectations to girl students. Moreover, we consider the decline in the proportion of women receiving higher and professional education to be evidence of discrimination. This discrimination may take the form of quotas against the admission of women to colleges, and professional schools; lack of encouragement by parents, counselors and educators; denial of loans or fellowships; or the traditional or arbitrary procedures in graduate and professional training geared in terms of men, which inadvertently discriminate against women. We believe that the same serious attention must be given to high school dropouts who are girls as to boys.

WE REJECT the current assumptions that a man must carry the sole burden of supporting himself, his wife, and family, and that a woman is automatically entitled to lifelong support by a man upon her marriage, or that marriage, home, and family are primarily woman's world and responsibility—hers, to dominate—his to support. We believe that a true partnership between the sexes demands a different concept of marriage, an equitable sharing of the responsibilities of home and children and of the economic burdens of their support. We believe that proper recognition should be given to the economic and social value of homemaking and childcare. To these ends, we will seek to open a reexamination of laws and mores governing marriage and divorce, for we believe that the current state of "half-equity" between the sexes discriminates against both men and women, and is the cause of much unnecessary hostility between the sexes.

WE BELIEVE that women must now exercise their political rights and responsibilities as American citizens. They must refuse to be segregated on the basis of sex into separate-and-not-equal ladies' auxiliaries in the political parties, and they must demand representation according to their numbers in the regularly constituted party committees—at local, state, and national levels—and in the informal power structure, participating fully in the selection of candidates and political decision-making, and running for office themselves.

IN THE INTERESTS OF THE HUMAN DIGNITY OF WOMEN, we will protest, and endeavor to change, the false image of women now prevalent in the mass media, and in the texts, ceremonies, laws, and practices of our major social institutions. Such images perpetuate contempt for women by society and by women for themselves. We are similarly opposed to all policies and practices—in church, state, college, factory, or office—which, in the guise of protectiveness, not only deny opportunities but also foster in women self-denigration, dependence, and evasion of responsibility, undermine their confidence in their own abilities, and foster contempt for women.

NOW WILL HOLD ITSELF INDEPENDENT OF ANY POLITICAL PARTY in order to mobilize the political power of all women and men intent on our goals. We will strive to ensure that no party, candidate, president, senator, governor, congressman, or any public official who betrays or ignores the principle of full equality between the sexes is elected or appointed to office. If it is necessary to mobilize the votes of men and women who believe in our cause in order to win for women the final right to be fully free and equal human beings, we so commit ourselves.

WE BELIEVE THAT women will do most to create a new image of women by acting now, and by speaking out in behalf of their own equality, freedom, and human dignity—not in pleas for special privilege, nor in enmity toward men, who are also victims of the current, half-equality between the sexes—but in an active, self-respecting partnership with men. By so doing, women will develop confidence in their own ability to determine actively, in partnership with men, the conditions of their life, their choices, their future and their society.

This Statement of Purpose was coauthored by Betty Friedan, author of The Feminine Mystique, *and Dr. Pauli Murray, an African-American Episcopal minister*

2 Tables

Number of Women Members of Congress (1789-1997*)

Congress	Senate	House
1st-64th (1789-1917)	0	0
65th (1917-1919)	0	1 (1D, 0R)
66th (1919-1921)	0	0
67th (1921-1923)	1 (1D, 0R)	3 (0D, 3R)
68th (1923-1925)	0	1 (0D, 1R)
69th (1925-1927)	0	3 (1D, 2R)
70th (1927-1929)	0	5 (2D, 3R)
71st (1929-1931)	0	9 (5D, 4R)
72nd (1931-1933)	1 (1D, 0R)	7 (5D, 2R)
73rd (1933-1935)	1 (1D, 0R)	7 (4D, 3R)
74th (1935-1937)	2 (2D, 0R)	6 (4D, 2R)
75th (1937-1939)	3 (2D, 1R)	6 (5D, 1R)
76th (1939-1941)	1 (1D, 0R)	8 (4D, 4R)
77th (1941-1943)	1 (1D, 0R)	9 (4D, 5R)
78th (1943-1945)	1 (1D, 0R)	8 (2D, 6R)
79th (1945-1947)	0	11 (6D, 5R)
80th (1947-1949)	1 (0D, 1R)	7 (3D, 4R)
81st (1949-1951)	1 (0D, 1R)	9 (5D, 4R)
82nd (1951-1953)	1 (0D, 1R)	10 (4D, 6R)
83rd (1953-1955)	2 (0D, 2R)	12 (5D, 7R)
84th (1955-1957)	1 (0D, 1R)	17 (9D, 8R)
85th (1957-1959)	1 (0D, 1R)	15 (9D, 6R)
86th (1959-1961)	2 (1D, 1R)	17 (9D, 8R)
87th (1961-1963)	2 (1D, 1R)	18 (11D, 7R)
88th (1963-1965)	2 (1D, 1R)	12 (6D, 6R)
89th (1965-1967)	2 (1D, 1R)	11 (7D, 4R)
90th (1967-1969)	1 (0D, 1R)	11 (6D, 5R)
91st (1969-1971)	1 (0D, 1R)	10 (6D, 4R)
92nd (1971-1973)	2 (1D, 1R)	13 (10D, 3R)
93rd (1973-1975)	0	16 (14D, 2R)
94th (1975-1977)	0	19 (14D, 5R)
95th (1977-1979)	2 (2D, 0R)	18 (13D, 5R)
96th (1979-1981)	1 (0D, 1R)	16 (11D, 5R)
97th (1981-1983)	2 (0D, 2R)	21 (11D, 10R)
98th (1983-1985)	2 (0D, 2R)	24 (13D, 11R)
99th (1985-1987)	2 (0D, 2R)	23 (12D, 11R)
100th (1987-1989)	2 (1D, 1R)	23 (12D, 11R)
101st (1989-1991)	2 (1D, 1R)	29 (16D, 13R)
102nd (1991-1993)	4 (3D, 1R)	29 (20D, 9 R)
103rd (1993-1995)	7 (5D, 2R)	48 (36D, 12 R)
104th (1995-1997)	9 (5D, 4R)	49 (32D, 17 R)
105th (1997-1999)	9 (6D, 3R)	53 (36D, 17R)

*The table lists by Congress the number of women members of the Senate and House. These figures include women who were appointed and elected to the positions as well as nonvoting delegates.

Women in the U.S. House of Representatives

Name	State	Party	Dates
Abzug, Bella S.	New York	Democrat	1971-1977
Andrews, Elizabeth B.	Alabama	Democrat	1972-1973
Ashbrook, Jean	Ohio	Republican	1982-1983
Baker, Irene B.	Tennessee	Republican	1964-1965
Bentley, Helen Dedich	Maryland	Republican	1985-1995
Blitch, Iris F.	Georgia	Democrat	1955-1963
Boggs, Corinne C.	Louisiana	Democrat	1973-1991
Boland, Veronica G.	Pennsylvania	Democrat	1942-1943
Bolton, Frances P.	Ohio	Republican	1940-1969
Bono, Mary	California	Republican	1998-
Bosone, Reva Z.B.	Utah	Democrat	1949-1953
Boxer, Barbara	California	Democrat	1983-1993
Brown, Corrine	Florida	Democrat	1993-
Buchanan, Vera D.	Pennsylvania	Democrat	1951-1955
Burke, Yvonne B.	California	Democrat	1973-1979
Burton, Sala	California	Democrat	1983-1987
Byrne, Leslie L.	Virginia	Democrat	1993-1995
Byron, Beverly	Maryland	Democrat	1979-1995
Byron, Katherine E.	Maryland	Democrat	1941-1943
Capps, Lois	California	Democrat	1998-
Carson, Julia	Indiana	Democrat	1997-
Cartwell, Maria	Washington	Democrat	1993-1995
Chenoweth, Helen	Idaho	Republican	1995-
Chisholm, Shirley	New York	Democrat	1969-1983
Christian-Green, Donna M. (Del.)	Virgin Islands	Democrat	1997-
Church, Marguerite S.	Illinois	Republican	1951-1963
Clarke, Marian W.	New York	Republican	1933-1935
Clayton, Eva M.	North Carolina	Democrat	1993-
Collins, Barbara-Rose	Michigan	Democrat	1991-1997
Collins, Cardiss R.	Illinois	Democrat	1973-1997
Cubin, Barbara	Wyoming	Republican	1995-
Danner, Pat	Missouri	Democrat	1993-
Degette, Diana L.	Colorado	Democrat	1997-
DeLauro, Rosa	Connecticut	Democrat	1991-
Douglas, Emily T.	Illinois	Democrat	1945-1947
Douglas, Helen G.	California	Democrat	1945-1951
Dunn, Jennifer	Washington	Republican	1993-
Dwyer, Florence P.	New Jersey	Republican	1957-1973
Emerson, Jo Ann	Missouri	Republican	1997-
English, Karan	Arizona	Democrat	1993-1995
Eshoo, Anna G.	California	Democrat	1993-
Eslick, Willa M.B.	Tennessee	Democrat	1932-1933
Farrington, Mary E. (Del.)	Hawaii	Republican	1954-1957
Fenwick, Millicent	New Jersey	Republican	1975-1983
Ferraro, Geraldine	New York	Democrat	1979-1985
Fiedler, Bobbi	California	Republican	1981-1987
Fowler, Tillie K.	Florida	Republican	1993-
Fulmer, Willa L.	South Carolina	Democrat	1944-1945
Furse, Elizabeth	Orgeon	Democrat	1993-
Gasque, Elizabeth H.	South Carolina	Democrat	1938-1939
Gibbs, Florence R.	Georgia	Democrat	1940-1941
Granahan, Kathryn E.	Pennsylvania	Democrat	1956-1963
Granger, Kay	Texas	Republican	1997-
Grasso, Ella T.	Connecticut	Democrat	1971-1975

Women in the U.S. House of Representatives (continued)

Name	State	Party	Dates
Green, Edith	Oregon	Democrat	1955-1975
Greenway, Isabella S.	Arizona	Democrat	1933-1937
Griffiths, Martha W.	Michigan	Democrat	1955-1974
Hall, Katie	Indiana	Democrat	1982-1985
Hansen, Julia B.	Washington	Democrat	1960-1974
Harden, Cecil M.	Indiana	Republican	1949-1959
Harman, Jane	California	Democrat	1993-
Heckler, Margaret M.	Massachusetts	Republican	1967-1983
Hicks, Louise Day	Massachusetts	Democrat	1971-1973
Holt, Marjorie S.	Maryland	Republican	1973-1987
Holtzman, Elizabeth	New York	Democrat	1973-1981
Honeyman, Nan W.	Oregon	Democrat	1937-1939
Hooley, Darlene	Oregon	Democrat	1997-
Horn, Joan Kelly	Missouri	Democrat	1991-1993
Huck, Winnifred S.M.	Illinois	Republican	1922-1923
Jenckes, Virginia E.	Indiana	Democrat	1933-1939
Johnson, Eddie Bernice	Texas	Democrat	1993-
Johnson, Nancy L.	Connecticut	Republican	1983-
Jordan, Barbara C.	Texas	Democrat	1973-1979
Kahn, Florence P.	California	Republican	1925-1927
Kaptur, Marcy	Ohio	Democrat	1983-
Kee, Maude E.	West Virginia	Democrat	1951-1965
Kelly, Edna F.	New York	Democrat	1949-1969
Kelly, Sue W.	New York	Republican	1995-
Kennelly, Barbara B.	Connecticut	Democrat	1982-
Keys, Martha E.	Kansas	Democrat	1975-1979
Kilpatrick, Carolyn C.	Michigan	Democrat	1997-
Knutson, Cova G.	Minnesota	Democrat	1955-1959
Langley, Katherine G.	Kentucky	Republican	1927-1931
Lee, Barbara	California	Democrat	1998-
Lee, Sheila Jackson	Texas	Democrat	1995-
Lincoln, Blanch Lambert	Arkansas	Democrat	1993-1997
Lloyd, Marilyn	Tennessee	Democrat	1975-1995
Lofgren, Zoe	California	Democrat	1995-
Long, Cathy	Louisiana	Democrat	1985-1987
Long, Jill	Indiana	Democrat	1989-1993
Lowey, Nita M.	New York	Democrat	1989-
Luce, Clare Boothe	Connecticut	Republican	1943-1947
Lusk, Georgia L.	New Mexico	Democrat	1947-1949
Maloney, Carolyn B.	New York	Democrat	1993-
Mankin, Helen D.	Georgia	Democrat	1946-1947
Margolies-Mezvinsky, Marjorie	Pennsylvania	Democrat	1993-1995
Martin, Lynn M.	Illinois	Republican	1981-1991
May, Catherine D.	Washington	Republican	1959-1971
McCarthy, Carolyn	New York	Democrat	1997-
McCarthy, Karan	Missouri	Democrat	1995-
McCarthy, Kathryn O'Laughlin	Kansas	Democrat	1933-1935
McCormick, Ruth H.	Illinois	Republican	1929-1931
McKinney, Cynthia A.	Georgia	Democrat	1993-
McMillan, Clara G.	South Carolina	Democrat	1939-1941
Meek, Carrie P.	Florida	Democrat	1993-
Meyers, Jan	Kansas	Republican	1985-1997
Meyner, Helen S.	New Jersey	Democrat	1975-1979
Mikulski, Barbara A.	Maryland	Democrat	1977-1987
Millender-McDonald, Juanita	California	Democrat	1996-
Mink, Patsy T.	Hawaii	Democrat	1965-1997; 1990-
Molinari, Susan	New York	Republican	1990-1997
Morella, Constance A.	Maryland	Republican	1987-

Women in the U.S. House of Representatives (continued)

Name	State	Party	Dates
Myrick, Sue	North Carolina	Republican	1995-
Nolan, Mae E.	California	Republican	1923-1925
Norrell, Catherine D.	Arkansas	Democrat	1961-1963
Northrup, Anne Meagher	Kentucky	Republican	1997-
Norton, Eleanor Holmes (Del.)	District of Columbia	Democrat	1991-
Norton, Mary T.	New Jersey	Democrat	1925-1951
O'Day, Caroline L.G.	New York	Democrat	1935-1943
Oakar, Mary Rose	Ohio	Democrat	1977-1995
Oldfield, Pearl P.	Arkansas	Democrat	1929-1931
Owen, Ruth B.	Florida	Democrat	1929-1933
Patterson, Elizabeth J.	South Carolina	Democrat	1987-1993
Pelosi, Nancy	California	Democrat	1989-
Pettis, Shirley N.	California	Republican	1975-1979
Pfost, Gracie B.	Idaho	Democrat	1953-1963
Pratt, Eliza J.	North Carolina	Democrat	1946-1947
Pratt, Ruth S.B.	New York	Republican	1929-1933
Pryce, Deborah	Ohio	Republican	1993-
Rankin, Jeanette	Montana	Republican	1917-1919; 1941-1943
Reece, Louise G.	Tennessee	Republican	1961-1963
Reid, Charlotte T.	Illinois	Republican	1963-1971
Riley, Corinne B.	South Carolina	Democrat	1962-1963
Rivers, Lynn N.	Michigan	Democrat	1995-
Robertson, Alice M.	Oklahoma	Republican	1921-1923
Rogers, Edith N.	Massachusetts	Republican	1925-1960
Ros-Lehtinen, Ileana	Florida	Republican	1989-
Roukema, Marge	New Jersey	Republican	1981-
Roybal-Allard, Lucille	California	Democrat	1993-
Saiki, Patricia	Hawaii	Republican	1987-1991
Sanchez, Loretta	California	Democrat	1997-
Schenk, Lynn	California	Democrat	1993-1995
Schneider, Claudine	Rhode Island	Republican	1981-1991
Schroeder, Patricia	Colorado	Democrat	1973-1997
Seastrand, Andrea H.	California	Republican	1995-1997
Simpson, Edna O.	Illinois	Republican	1959-1961
Slaughter, Louise M.	New York	Democrat	1987-
Smith, Linda	Washington	Republican	1995-
Smith, Margaret Chase	Maine	Republican	1940-1949
Smith, Virginia	Nebraska	Republican	1975-1991
Snowe, Olympia	Maine	Republican	1979-1995
Spellman, Gladys Noon	Maryland	Democrat	1975-1981
St. George, Katherine P.C.	New York	Republican	1947-1965
Stabenow, Deborah	Michigan	Democrat	1997-
Stanley, Winifred C.	New York	Republican	1943-1945
Sullivan, Leonore K.	Missouri	Democrat	1953-1977
Sumner, Jessie	Illinois	Republican	1939-1947
Tausher, Ellen	Califronia	Democrat	1997-
Thomas, Lera M.	Texas	Democrat	1966-1967
Thompson, Ruth	Michigan	Republican	1951-1957
Thurman, Karen	Florida	Democrat	1992-
Unsoeld, Jolene	Washington	Democrat	1989-1993
Velazquez, Nydia M.	New York	Democrat	1993-
Vucanovich, Barbara	Nevada	Republican	1983-1997
Waldholtz, Enid	Utah	Republican	1995-1997
Waters, Maxine	California	Democrat	1991-
Weis, Jessica McCullough	New York	Republican	1959-1963
Wingo, Effiegene	Arkansas	Democrat	1930-1933
Woodhouse, Chase G.	Connecticut	Democrat	1945-1947; 1949-1951
Woolsey, Lynn C.	California	Democrat	1993-

Women in the U.S. Senate

Name	State	Party	Years
Abel, Hazel H.	Nebraska	Republican	1954
Allen, Maryon Pittman	Alabama	Democrat	1978
Bowring, Eva K.	Nebraska	Republican	1954
Boxer, Barbara	California	Democrat	1993-
Bushfield, Vera C.	South Dakota	Republican	1948
Caraway, Hattie W.	Arkansas	Democrat	1931-1945
Collins, Susan	Maine	Republican	1997-
Edwards, Elaine S.	Louisiana	Democrat	1972
Feinstein, Diane	California	Democrat	1993-
Felton, Rebecca L.	Georgia	Democrat	1922
Frahm, Sheila	Kansas	Republican	1996
Graves, Dixie Bibb	Alabama	Democrat	1937-1938
Hawkins, Paula	Florida	Republican	1981-1987
Humphrey, Muriel Buck	Minnesota	Democrat	1978
Hutchison, Kay Bailey	Texas	Republican	1993-
Kassebaum, Nancy Landon	Kansas	Republican	1978-1997
Landrieu, Mary	Louisiana	Democrat	1997-
Long, Rose McConnell	Louisiana	Democrat	1936-1937
Mikulski, Barbara	Maryland	Democrat	1987-
Moseley-Braun, Carol	Illinois	Democrat	1993-
Murray, Patty	Washington	Democrat	1993-
Neuberger, Maurine B.	Oregon	Democrat	1960-1967
Pyle, Gladys	South Dakota	Republican	1938-1939
Smith, Margaret Chase	Maine	Republican	1949-1973
Snowe, Olympia	Maine	Republican	1995-

Women Governors

Name	State	Party	Years
Collins, Martha Layne	Kentucky	Democrat	1984-1987
Ferguson, Miriam "Ma"	Texas	Democrat	1925-1927, 1933-1935
Finney, Joan	Kansas	Democrat	1991-1995
Grasso, Ella	Connecticut	Democrat	1975-1980
Hull, Jane Dee	Arizona	Republican	1997-
Kunin, Madeleine	Vermont	Democrat	1985-1991
Mofford, Rose	Arizona	Democrat	1988-1991
Orr, Kay	Nebraska	Republican	1987-1991
Ray, Dixy Lee	Washington	Democrat	1977-1981
Richards, Ann	Texas	Democrat	1991-1995
Roberts, Barbara	Oregon	Democrat	1991-1995
Ross, Nellie Tayloe	Wyoming	Democrat	1925-1927
Shaheen, Jeanne	New Hampshire	Democrat	1997-
Wallace, Lurleen	Alabama	Democrat	1967-1968
Whitman, Christine Todd	New Jersey	Republican	1994-

First Ladies and Presidential Wives*

Name (Life Dates)	Year Married	Husband (Term of Office)
Martha Washington (1731-1802)	1759	George Washington (1789-1797)
Abigail Adams (1744-1818)	1764	John Adams (1797-1801)
Martha Jefferson (1749-1782)	1772	Thomas Jefferson (1801-1809)
Dolley Madison (1768-1849)	1794	James Madison (1809-1817)
Elizabeth Monroe (1768-1830)	1786	James Monroe (1817-1825)
Louisa Catherine Adams (1775-1852)	1797	John Quincy Adams (1825-1829)
Rachel Jackson (1767-1828)	1791	Andrew Jackson (1829-1837)
Hannah Van Buren (1783-1819)	1807	Martin Van Buren (1837-1841)
Anna Harrison (1775-1864)	1795	William Henry Harrison (1841)
Letitia Christian Tyler (1790-1842)	1813	John Tyler (1841-1845)
Julia Gardiner Tyler (1820-1889)	1844	John Tyler (1841-1845)
Sarah Childress Polk (1803-1891)	1824	James K. Polk (1845-1849)
Margaret Taylor (1788-1854)	1810	Zachary Taylor (1849-1850)
Abigail Fillmore (1799-1853)	1826	Millard Fillmore (1850-1853)
Jane Pierce (1806-1863)	1834	Franklin Pierce (1853-1857)
Mary Todd Lincoln (1818-1882)	1842	Abraham Lincoln (1861-1865)
Eliza Johnson (1810-1876)	1827	Andrew Johnson (1865-1869)
Julia Dent Grant (1826-1902)	1848	Ulysses S. Grant (1869-1877)
Lucy Webb Hayes (1831-1889)	1852	Rutherford B. Hayes (1877-1881)
Lucretia Garfield (1832-1918)	1858	James A. Garfield (1881)
Ellen Herndon Arthur (1837-1880)	1859	Chester A. Arthur (1881-1885)
Frances Folsom Cleveland (1864-1947)	1886	Grover Cleveland (1885-1889, 1893-1897)
Caroline Harrison (1832-1892)	1853	Benjamin Harrison (1889-1893)
Ida Saxton McKinley (1847-1907)	1871	William McKinley (1897-1901)
Alice Lee Roosevelt (1861-1884)	1880	Theodore Roosevelt (1901-1909)
Edith Kermit Roosevelt (1861-1948)	1886	Theodore Roosevelt (1901-1909)
Helen Herron Taft(1861-1943)	1886	William Howard Taft (1909-1913)
Ellen Axson Wilson (1860-1914)	1885	Woodrow Wilson (1913-1921)
Edith Bolling Wilson (1872-1961)	1915	Woodrow Wilson (1913-1921)
Florence Kling Harding (1860-1924)	1891	Warren G. Harding (1921-1923)
Grace Coolidge (1879-1957)	1906	Calvin Coolidge (1923-1929)
Lou Henry Hoover (1874-1944)	1899	Herbert Hoover (1929-1933)
Eleanor Roosevelt (1884-1962)	1905	Franklin D. Roosevelt (1933-1945)
Bess Truman (1885-1982)	1919	Harry S. Truman (1945-1953)
Mamie Doud Eisenhower (1896-1979)	1916	Dwight D. Eisenhower (1953-1961)
Jacqueline Bouvier Kennedy (1929-1994)	1953	John F. Kennedy (1961-1963)
Claudia "Lady Bird" Johnson (1912-)	1934	Lyndon B. Johnson (1963-1969)
Pat Nixon (1913-1993)	1940	Richard M. Nixon (1969-1974)
Betty Ford (1918-)	1948	Gerald R. Ford (1974-1977)
Rosalynn Carter (1927-)	1946	Jimmy Carter (1977-1981)
Nancy Reagan (1923-)	1952	Ronald Reagan (1981-1989)
Barbara Bush (1925-)	1946	George Bush (1989-1993)
Hillary Rodham Clinton (1947-)	1975	Bill Clinton (1993-)

*Names in **boldface** denote presidential wives who actually functioned in the role of First Lady and who have separate entries in the *Encyclopedia*. Names not in boldface denote wives who died before their husbands took office as president.

Women Cabinet Members

Appointee	Position[1]	Appointed By	Dates
Frances Perkins	Secretary of Labor	Roosevelt (D)	1933-1945
Oveta Culp Hobby	Secretary of Health, Educ. & Welfare	Eisenhower (R)	1953-1955
Carla Anderson Hills	Secretary of Housing & Urban Develop.	Ford (R)	1975-1977
Juanita A. Kreps	Secretary of Commerce	Carter (D)	1977-1979
Patricia R. Harris	Secretary of Housing & Urban Develop.	Carter (D)	1977-1979
Patricia R. Harris	Secretary of Health and Human Services	Carter (D)	1979-1981
Shirley M. Hufstedler	Secretary of Education	Carter (D)	1979-1981
Jeane J. Kirkpatrick	UN. Ambassador[2]	Reagan (R)	1981-1985
Margaret M. Heckler	Secretary of Health and Human Services	Reagan (R)	1983-1985
Elizabeth Hanford Dole	Secretary of Transportation	Reagan (R)	1983-1987
Ann Dore McLaughlin	Secretary of Labor	Reagan (R)	1987-1989
Elizabeth Hanford Dole	Secretary of Labor	Bush (R)	1989-1991
Carla Anderson Hills	Special Trade Representative[3]	Bush (R)	1989-1993
Lynn Morley Martin	Secretary of Labor	Bush (R)	1991-1993
Barbara H. Franklin	Secretary of Commerce	Bush (R)	1992-1993
Madeleine K. Albright	U. N. Ambassador[2]	Clinton (D)	1993-1997
Hazel R. O'Leary	Secretary of Energy	Clinton (D)	1993-1997
Alice M. Rivlin	Director, Office of Management & Budget	Clinton (D)	1994-1996
Laura D'Andrea Tyson	Chair, National Economic Council[4]	Clinton (D)	1995-1997
Carol M. Browner	Administrator, Envir. Protection Agency[5]	Clinton (D)	1993-present
Janet Reno	Attorney General	Clinton (D)	1993-present
Donna E. Shalala	Secretary of Health and Human Services	Clinton (D)	1993-present
Madeleine K. Albright	Secretary of State	Clinton (D)	1997-present
Aida Alvarez	Ádministrator, Small Business Admin[6]	Clinton (D)	1997-present
Charlene Barshefsky	U.S. Trade Representative[3]	Clinton (D)	1997-present
Alexis Herman	Secretary of Labor	Clinton (D)	1997-present

[1]Because each president defines Cabinet-level differently, a combined figure for Cabinet and Cabinet-level positions is unavailable.
[2]The position of U.N. Ambassador was considered Cabinet-level during the Reagan and Clinton administrations.
[3]The position of Special Trade Representative was considered Cabinet-level during the Bush Administration, as is the U.S. Trade Representative in the Clinton administration.
[4]The position of Chair of the National Economic Council is a Cabinet-level position in the Clinton administration.
[5]The position of Administrator of the Environmental Protection Agency is a Cabinet-level position in the Clinton administration.
[6]The position of Administrator of the Small Business Administration is a Cabinet-level position in the Clinton administration.

Source: Center for the American Woman and Politics (CAWP), National Information Bank on Women in Public Office, Eagleton Institute of Politics, Rutgers University.

3
Organizations

Women's Political Organizations

Abortion Rights Mobilization (ARM)
175 5th Avenue, Suite 814
New York, NY 10010
(212) 673-2040
(212) 460-8359 (fax)
President: Lawrence Lader

ARM seeks to protect the legal right to abortion through its lobbying activities.

Ad Hoc Committee in Defense of Life
1187 National Press Building
Washington, DC 20045
(202) 347-8686
(203) 347-3245 (fax)
Bureau Chief: Doug Scott

Founded in 1974, the Committee seeks to have *Roe v. Wade* overturned. It also actively opposes euthanasia through its lobbying efforts.

ALA Social Responsibilities Round Table Feminist Task Force
50 East Huron Street
Chicago, IL 60611
(312) 944-6780
(800) 545-2433
(312) 280-3256 (fax)
Coordinator: Veronda Pitchford
Web site: http://www.jessamyn.com/srrt/

Affiliated with the American Library Association, the Round Table was founded in 1971 for members of the ALA who were interested in women's issues. The group publishes a quarterly newsletter, *Women in Libraries*.

Always Causing Legal Unrest (ACLU)
PO Box 2085
Rancho Cordova, CA 95741
Contact: Nikki Craft
Web site: http://www.igc.apc.prg.nemesis/aclu/porn

Founded in 1990, ACLU is a membership organization of more than 500 feminists who are antipornography activists. The group lobbies corporations to put women's rights above property rights and profit motives. In addition, ACLU advocates that women learn self-defense and how to use firearms. The group also publishes *Nemesis: Justice Is a Woman with a Sword*.

American Association of University Women (AAUW)
1111 16th Street NW
Washington, DC 20036
(202) 785-7700
(202) 872-1425 (fax)
Executive Director: Janice Weinman
Web site: http://www.aauw.org

Founded in 1881, AAUW promotes equal educational opportunity for women. The group engages in both research and lobbying on a wide spectrum of women's issues. The organization is open to all graduates of accredited colleges and universities and currently has more than 150,000 members. The AAUW publishes a number of brochures and magazines, including *AAUW Outlook* (a bimonthly magazine), and *American Association of University Women—Action Alert* (a monthly newsletter).

Americans United for Life
343 S. Dearborn Street, Suite 1804
Chicago, IL 60604
(312) 786-9494
(312) 341-2656 (fax)
President: Clarke D. Forsythe

Founded in 1971, Americans United for Life is the oldest anti-abortion group in the country. It conducts legal research and litigation in addition to its educational and lobbying efforts.

Association of Junior Leagues International (AJLI)
660 1st Avenue
New York, NY 10016-3241
(212) 683-1515
(212) 481-7196 (fax)
Executive Director: Holly Sloan

Founded in 1921, the Junior League is active in development of women as volunteers in their communities. The organization provides leadership, networking, and educational programs. The Junior League publishes several items, including a newsletter (*What Works*) and various manuals.

Association of Libertarian Feminists
PO Box 20252 London Terrace
New York, NY 10011
National Coordinator: Joan Kennedy Taylor

The Association seeks to help women achieve self-sufficiency. It opposes government interference in any aspect of life, including reproductive rights. The group seeks libertarian alternatives to problems. In addition to various discussion papers, the group publishes a quarterly newsletter, *ALF News*.

Black, Indian, Hispanic, and Asian Women in Action (BIHA)
122 W. Franklin Avenue, Suite 306
Minneapolis, MN 55404
(612) 870-1193
(612) 870-0855 (fax)
Executive Director: Alice O. Lynch

Founded in 1983, BIHA is an empowerment organization offering educational programs and advocacy on women's issues as they pertain to women of color. It publishes a quarterly newsletter, *Unison*. The organization also grants the Women of Color Recognition Award for community involvement.

Black Women's Agenda
208 Auburn Avenue NE
Atlanta, GA 30303
(404) 524-8279
(404) 524-0778 (fax)
Vice President: Ruth A. Sykes

The Black Women's Agenda is dedicated to the protection and advancement of black women and their rights. The organization conducts research, lobbies on issues, and offers educational programs.

Capitol Hill Women's Political Caucus (CHWPC)
Longworth House Office Building
PO Box 599
Washington, DC 20515
(202) 986-0994
Co-Chair: Valerie Holford

Founded in 1971 as a chapter of the National Women's Political Caucus, the group is dedicated to increasing the election, appointment, and participation of women in local, state, and national governments. The group seeks to end inequities in the employment and salaries of women on Capitol Hill. The CHWPC also acts as a clearinghouse on legislative information. It publishes several newsletters, including *Capitol Hill Report* (monthly) and *Equal Times* (bimonthly), as well as an annual directory.

Catholics for a Free Choice (CFFC)
1436 U Street NW, Suite 301
Washington, DC 20009
(202) 986-6093
(202) 332-7995 (fax)
President: Frances Kissling

Founded in 1973, CFFC is an organization of Catholics that supports reproductive rights, including abortion. The group advocates social and economic programs for women, families, and children. It publishes and distributes a number of brochures and pamphlets.

Center for the American Woman and Politics (CAWP)
Eagleton Institute of Politics
Rutgers University
90 Clifton Avenue
New Brunswick, NJ 08901
(732) 932-9384
(732) 932-6778 (fax)
Acting Director: Debbie Walsh
Web site: http://www.rci.rutgers.edu/~cawp/

Founded in 1971, CAWP is the leading research and education center for women in American politics. It maintains extensive databases and other information for researchers. It publishes a number of reports, newsletters, and books.

Center for Women in Government
State University of New York
135 Western Avenue
Albany, NY 12222
(518) 442-3900
(fax) (518) 442-5768
Executive Director: Judith Saidel
Web site: http://www.albany.edu/~cwgweb

Founded in 1978, the center conducts and disseminates policy research, works to identify and remove barriers to women's employment equity, and develops women's and girls' public policy leadership. In addition, the center serves as a resource for government officials, union and business leaders, public employees, researchers, and members of advocacy and professional organizations.

Center for Women Policy Studies (CWPS)
1211 Connecticut Avenue NW, Suite 312
Washington, DC 20036
(202) 872-1770
(202) 296-8962 (fax)
President: Leslie R. Wolfe

Founded in 1972 as an independent feminist policy research and advocacy group, CWPS carries out research programs on a wide range of women's issues, including educational equity, economic equity, family law, health and medical funding, and reproductive rights. The center sponsors leadership development courses for women and has policy internships in many of its areas of research. It has an active publishing program with numerous reports and monographs.

Clare Booth Luce Policy Institute
112 Elden Street, Suite P
Herndon, VA 20170
(888) 891-4288
President: Michelle Easton

Founded in 1993, the Institute advocates free market principles and opposes communism. The group grants scholarships, conducts seminars, maintains a speakers' bureau, and publishes a newsletter.

Clearinghouse on Women's Issues (CWI)
PO Box 70603
Friendship Heights, MD 20813
(202) 362-3789
(202) 362-3789 (fax)
President: Ruth G. Nadel

Founded in 1972 as a nonpartisan clearinghouse for national, state, and local women's rights organization, CWI has more than 400 members dedicated to exchanging information on the economic, social, and educational status of women. The group publishes the *CWI Newsletter*.

Coalition for Women's Appointments (CWA)
c/o National Women's Political Caucus
1211 Connecticut Avenue NW, Suite 425
Washington, DC 20036
(202) 785-1100
(202) 785-3605 (fax)
President: Anita Perez Ferguson
Web site: http://feminist.com/nwpc.htm

Founded in 1976, CWA promotes the appointment of women to high-ranking governmental positions in all three branches of government. The group conducts research and evaluations of appointments and how they impact women and women's issues.

Coalition of Labor Union Women (CLUW)
1126 16th Street NW
Washington, DC 20036
(202) 466-4610
(202) 776-0537 (fax)
Executive Director: Chrystl Lindo-Bridgeforth

Founded in 1974, CLUW works to address common problems that face women members of unions. It promotes an aggressive recruitment of women into unions and disseminates information on equal opportunity and sexual discrimination in the workplace. In addition to its workplace initiatives, CLUW helps union members become active in the political process through lobbying and running for elected office. The group publishes a number of pamphlets and newsletters.

Commission for Women's Equality (CWE)
c/o American Jewish Congress
15 E. 84th Street
New York, NY 10028
(212) 360-1561
(212) 249-3672 (fax)
Contact: Lois Waldman
Web site: http://ajcongress.org/women/cweindex.htm

Founded in 1984, CWE, a commission of the American Jewish Congress, seeks to promote feminism that is compatible with Judaism. The group advocates reproductive freedom, economic and religious equity, and the empowerment of women in Judaism and public life. CWE publishes several brochures, a monthly newsletter, and the *International Jewish Feminist Directory*.

Commission on the Status of Women (CSW)
Division for the Advancement of Women/DPCSD
United Nations, Room DC2-1220
PO Box 20
New York, NY 10017
(212) 963-5086
(212) 963-3463 (fax)
Assistant Secretary General: Angela King
Web site: http://www.un.org

Founded in 1946, CSW is a coalition of representatives to the UN that promotes women's rights in all fields, including political, economic, social, and educational areas. The group helps coordinate the efforts on women's issues of other UN organs and is the body responsible for the world conference on women.

Committee of 200 (C200)
625 N. Michigan Avenue, Suite 500
Chicago, IL 60611-3108
(312) 751-3477
(312) 943-9401 (fax)
President: Anna K. Lloyd

Originally founded in 1982 for the 200 leading women in business, the group has now expanded to more than 350 members. C200 provides a forum for women to network with other top business women as well as to exchange educational information and ideas on economic, social and business opportunities for women. The group publishes a monthly newsletter, *Network*, and a semiannual newsletter, *Update*.

Concerned Women for America (CWA)
370 L'Enfant Promenade SW, Suite 800
Washington, DC 20024
(202) 488-7000
(202) 488-0806 (fax)
President: Beverly LaHaye
Web site: http://www.cwfa.org

Founded in 1979, the group is a conservative women's organization that seeks to defend traditional Christian-American values. With more than 600,000 members, it is one of the largest women's groups. It provides grants and scholarships, conducts research, and produces TV and radio shows.

Congressional Caucus for Women's Issues (CCWI)
1424 Longworth House Office Building
Washington, DC 20515
(202) 225-8050
(fax) (202) 225-4476
Democratic Co-Chair: Eleanor Holmes Norton

Originally founded in 1977 as the Congresswomen's Caucus, the bipartisan organization changed its name in 1982. CCWI, whose membership is open to those serving in the U.S. House of Representatives, seeks to improve women's status by focusing on legislative issues important to women, including Social Security, health care research and funding, and child support enforcement. The group also works to eliminate discrimination from federal programs and policies.

Congressional Club (CC)
2001 New Hampshire Avenue, NW
Washington, DC 20009
(202) 332-1155
(202) 797-0698 (fax)
President: Mary Clement

Founded in 1908, the organization is open to the wives of present and former U.S. representatives, senators, cabinet members, and Supreme Court justices. CC performs a number of community services and also maintains a museum.

Coordinating Council for Women in History
1500 N. Verdugo Road
Glendale, CA 91208
(818) 240-1000
(818) 549-9436 (fax)
Executive Director: Peggy Renner

Founded in 1969, the Council is active in promoting the teaching of women's history. It encourages research and graduate study of women's history; attempts to increase the number of women in the field of history; and fights discrimination in job opportunities and course offerings. The group publishes courses and job opportunities, the *CCWH Newsletter,* and several other reports.

Council of Presidents (COP)
c/o Susan Bianchi-Sand, Chair
National Committee on Pay Equity
1126 16th Street NW, Suite 411
Washington, DC 20036
(202) 331-7343
(202) 331-7406 (fax)

COP consists of more than 75 presidents of national women's organizations who unite to achieve common goals, including testifying before Congress, passage of the Equal Rights Amendment, and such other women's issues as health care, medical funding, educational opportunities, and reproductive rights.

Daughters of the American Revolution (DAR)
1776 D Street NW
Washington, DC 20006-5392
(202) 628-1776
(fax) (202) 879-3252
President General: Mrs. Charles K. Kemper
Web site: http://www.dar.org

Founded in 1890, DAR is an organization of women descendants of Revolutionary War patriots that conducts historical and educational programs, and maintains a museum and document collection. With more than 175,000 members in over 3,000 local chapters, DAR is active in a host of activities throughout the year. Additionally, the group offers a number of scholarships and publishes numerous brochures, manuals, and *Daughters of the American Revolution Magazine*.

Eagle Forum
PO Box 618
Alton, IL 62002
(618) 462-5415
President: Phyllis Schlafly
Web site: http://www.eagleforum.org

Founded in 1972 as Stop ERA, Eagle Forum is the leading conservative antifeminist organization in the country. It conducts lobbying, organizes grassroots campaigns, and holds conferences on a variety of topics, including pro-life, opposition to U.S. military participation in UN missions, and other conservative positions. The group publishes a number of brochures, pamphlets, and reports, including a monthly newsletter, *The Phyllis Schlafly Report*.

EMILY's List
805 15th Street NW, Suite. 400
Washington, DC 20005
(202) 326-1400
(202) 326-1415 (fax)
President: Ellen Malcolm
Web site: http://www.emilyslist.org

Founded in 1985, EMILY's List, which stands for Early Money Is Like Yeast, is a pro-choice Democratic women's political action committee. Since its inception, it has grown into one of the largest PACs in the nation.

Federation of Feminist Women's Health Centers (FFWHC)
633 E. 11th Avenue
Eugene, OR 97401
(541) 344-0966
(541) 344-1993 (fax)
President: Jude Hanzo

Founded in 1975, the group maintains a network of health centers that seek to secure reproductive rights and improve overall health care of women. The organization publishes several books on women's health.

Feminist.com
(212) 396-0262
President: Marianne Schall
Web site: http://www.feminist.com

Feminist.com is an Internet provider, consultant, and designer for feminist organizations. This site hosts a number of other organization's sites. It provides useful links on issues as well as its own information.

Feminist Majority Foundation
1600 Wilson Boulevard, Suite 801
Arlington, VA 22209
(703) 522-2214
(703) 522-2219 (fax)
President:: Eleanor Smeal
Web site: http://www.feminist.org

Founded in 1987 under the leadership of former NOW president Eleanor Smeal, the Feminist Majority Foundation seeks to increase the number of women in leadership positions in business, education, media, law, medicine, and government. The organization conducts leadership seminars, offers internships, and maintains a speakers' bureau. The foundation publishes a quarterly newsletter, *Feminist Majority Report*.

Feminists for Life of America (FFL)
733 15th Street NW, Suite 1100
Washington, DC 20005
(202) 737-3352
(202) 737-0414 (fax)
Executive Director: Serrin M. Foster
Web site: http://www.serve.com/fem4life

Founded in 1972, FFL has more than 4,000 members who are politically active in protecting all human life. The group supports both the Equal Rights Amendment and the Human Life Amendment, and conducts workshops, and sponsors speakers and research of current literature on abortion and feminism. FFL publishes several booklets and position papers in addition to its quarterly, *The American Feminist*.

Formerly Employed Mothers at the Leading Edge (FEMALE)
PO Box 31
Elmhurst, IL 60126
(630) 941-3553
(630) 941-3551 (fax)
Co-Director: Debbie Sawicki

Founded in 1987, this organization promotes respect for stay-at-home mothers. The group, with more than 3,000 members, also advocates improved child-care resources, family leave, and other workplace related issues including flextime and job sharing. The organization publishes a monthly newsletter, *FEMALE Forum*, and a quarterly, *The Leader's Edge*.

General Commission on the Status and Role of Women (GCSRW)
1200 Davis Street
Evanston, IL 60201
(708) 869-7330
(708) 869-1466 (fax)
General Secretariat: Stephanie Anna Hixon

Founded in 1972 as an organ of the United Methodist Church, GCSRW is dedicated to achieving full and equal participation of women in the church. The commission works as an advocate of women and women's issues. The group conducts leadership and educational seminars as well as other programs to raise awareness of sexual harassment and discrimination. The GCSRW publishes a number of brochures and reports in addition to its quarterly newsletter, *The Flyer*.

General Federation of Women's Clubs (GFWC)
1734 N Street NW
Washington, DC 20036-2990
(202) 347-3168
(800) 443-GFWC
(202) 835-0246 (fax)
International President: Faye Dissinger
Web site: http://www.gfwc.org

Founded in 1890, GFWC is one of the largest women's organizations with more than 275,000 members in over 7,500 local chapters. The group is an international volunteer service that provides community service in a wide range of areas, including the arts, education, public affairs, and international affairs. It maintains the Women's History and Resource Center, containing more than 1,000 photographs and audiovisuals. It publishes a quarterly magazine, *GFWC Clubwoman*.

Girl Scouts of the USA
420 5th Avenue
New York, NY 10018-2702
(212) 852-8000
(212) 852-6517 (fax)
Executive Director: Mary Rose Main
Web site: http://www.girlscouts.org

Founded in 1912, the Girl Scouts have more than 3.5 million members. The group's goals are to aid in the development of girls as active members of their communities. Girl Scouts provide opportunities to serve, develop core values, and interact with others. The group offers leadership and educational programs, international exchanges, and a host of conferences and seminars. The Girl Scouts also publish numerous books, brochures, reports, and newsletters.

Girls Nation
American Legion Auxiliary National Headquarters
777 N. Meridian Street
Indianapolis, IN 46204
(317) 635-6291
(317) 636-5590 (fax)
National Secretary: Peggy Sappenfield
Web site: http://www.legion-aux.org/program.htm

Founded in 1947, Girls Nation is a citizenship program conducted annually by the American Legion Auxiliary for high school juniors. The program is a simulation that offers practical experience in the processes of government. Forty-nine states hold Girls State programs at which two girls are selected to participate in Girls Nation. At both Girls State and Girls Nation, the participants run candidates, hold elections, enact legislation, and conduct other political endeavors.

Global Fund for Women
425 Sherman Avenue, Suite 300
Palo Alto, CA 94306
(415) 853-8305
(415) 328-0384 (fax)
President: Kavita N. Ramdas
Web site: http://www.globalfundforwomen.org

Founded in 1987, Global Fund makes grants to support overseas groups and projects working on female human rights. In addition to its grants, the fund publishes a number of brochures as well as a quarterly newsletter, *Network News*.

Human Life Foundation
150 E. 35th Street
New York, NY 10016
(212) 679-7330
Secretary: Faith A. McFadden

Founded in 1974, the Foundation works to end abortion. It makes grants to local organizations and publishes the *Human Life Review*, a scholarly quarterly.

Independent Woman's Forum (IWF)
2111 Wilson Boulevard, Suite 550
Arlington, VA 22201
(703) 243-8989
(800) 224-6000
(703) 243-9230 (fax)
Executive Director: Barbara Ledeen
Web site: http://www.iwf.org

Founded in 1992, IWF is an antifeminist organization dedicated to individual freedom and personal responsibility. It is a nonpartisan group that advocates strong families and less government. The group conducts research, disseminates information by testifying at legislative hearings, and maintains a speakers' bureau. IWF publishes *The Women's Quarterly*, a scholarly journal, and a quarterly newsletter, *Ex Femina*.

Institute for Republican Women
PO Box 6530
Washington, DC 20035
(202) 862-2604
(202) 466-8554 (fax)
President: Carolyn S. Parlato

The Institute conducts a number of conferences and seminars on a host of issues and does not focus on narrowly defined "women's issues." The group publishes a number of studies and a quarterly newsletter, *Forum*.

Institute for Research on Women's Health
1616 18th Street NW, Suite 109B
Washington, DC 20009
(202) 483-8643
(301) 949-8745 (fax)
Director: Dr. Margaret Jensvold

Founded in 1984, the Institute conducts scholarly research on health issues related to women.

Institute for Women's Policy Research
1400 20th Street NW, Suite 104
Washington, DC 20036
(202) 785-5100
(202) 833-4362 (fax)
Director: Heidi Hartmann
Web site: http://www.lwpr.org

Founded in 1987, the Institute works toward economic and social justice for women. It conducts research to help shape public policy on such issues as pay equity, family and medical leave, childcare, and equal opportunity. In addition to research reports, the group also publishes a monthly newsletter, *Research News Reporter*.

International Institute for Women's Political Leadership (IIWPL)
1101 14th Street NW, Suite 200
Washington, DC 20005
(202) 842-1523
Program Director: Anna Martin

Founded in 1988, IIWPL seeks to increase women's political participation to achieve significant impact on public policy. The organization offers workshops, leadership training, networking, and other programs to build political skills.

International Women's Forum
1826 Jefferson Place NW, Suite A
Washington, DC 20036
(202) 775-8917
(202) 429-0271 (fax)
President: Fran Streets

Founded in 1980, International Women's Forum is a network of domestic and international women's groups that share information, ideas, and resources on women's issues.

League of Women Voters Education Fund (LWVEF)
1730 M Street NW, Suite 1000
Washington, DC 20036
(202) 429-1965
(202) 429-0854 (fax)
Executive Director: Judith A. Conover

Founded in 1957, the Education Fund conducts research on a wide range of policy issues, including those related to women. The group publishes a number of reports on such subjects as nuclear waste, presidential debates, and drinking water.

Lesbian Herstory Educational Foundation (LHEF)
PO Box 1258
New York, NY 10116
(718) 768-3953
(718) 768-4663 (fax)

Founded in 1974, LHEF collects and shares information on lesbians and lesbianism throughout the world. The group has a large collection of materials and also makes speakers available. LHEF publishes a periodic newsletter, *Lesbian Herstory Archives Newsletter*.

MANA, A National Latina Organization
1725 K Street NW, Suite 501
Washington, DC 20006
(202) 833-0060
(202) 496-0588 (fax)
President: Elisa Sanchez

Founded in 1974, MANA is a leadership group that works to promote economic and educational opportunities for Mexican-Americans and other Latinas. In addition to running the Hermanitas Project—an annual conference for high school girls—MANA offers annual scholarships. An advocate on such issues as pay equity, teenage pregnancy, and poverty, the organization publishes a quarterly newsletter, *Issue Updates*.

March for Life Fund
PO Box 90300
Washington, DC 20090
(202) 543-3377
(202) 543-8202 (fax)
President: Nellie J. Gray

Founded in 1974, the group sponsors the annual March for Life on January 22, in Washington, DC. The organization seeks the adoption of the Human Life Amendment to the U.S. Constitution. March for Life engages in lobbying, runs seminars, and sponsors a speakers' bureau. It publishes a number of brochures and periodic reports.

Media Watch (MW)
PO Box 618
Santa Cruz, CA 95061
(408) 423-6355
(800) 631-6355
(408) 423-6355 (fax)
Director: Ann Simonton
Web site: http://www.mediawatch.org

Founded in 1984, MW seeks to improve the portrayal of women by the media. The group is concerned that the majority of images of women in the media are sexist, racist, and violent, and that these images promote low self-esteem. Media Watch conducts workshops and seminars, sponsors boycotts and letter-writing campaigns, and maintains both a speakers' bureau and archives. The group has produced a number of videos—*Don't Be a TV: Television Victim* and *The Media May Be Hazardous to Your Health*—and publishes a quarterly newsletter, *Media Watch*.

Ms. Foundation for Women (MFW)
120 Wall Street, 33rd Floor
New York, NY 10005
(212) 742-2300
(212) 742-1653 (fax)
President: Marie C. Wilson
Web site: http://www.ms.foundation.org

Founded in 1972, the Foundation supports a number of efforts including the annual Take Our Daughters to Work Day that seeks to expand girls' career goals. An active advocate for change in both law and social norms, the group funds projects that seek to remove impediments based on race, class, age, disability, culture, and sexual orientation. It annually grants the Gloria Steinem Women of Vision Awards.

Mujeres Activas en Letras Y Cambio Social (MALCS)
c/o Ethnic Studies Program
Santa Clara University
Santa Clara, CA 95053
(408) 554-4511
(408) 554-4189 (fax)
Chair: Dr. Alma Garcia

Founded in 1982, MALCS is a group that fosters greater research and writing on Latinas. Additionally, the group is active in seeking to end discrimination in higher education. MALCS has a speakers' bureau as well as a placement service that provides information on jobs and grants for Latinas and Latina studies. The group publishes a directory of scholars, a newsletter (*Noticiera de MALCS*), and an annual review of research in the field (*Trabajos Monográficos*).

National Abortion and Reproductive Action League (NARAL)
1156 15th Street NW, Suite 700
Washington, DC 20005
(202) 973-3000
(202) 973-3096 (fax)
President: Kate Michelman
Web site: http://www.naral.org

Founded in 1969, NARAL is the largest pro-choice organization in the country. It is active in maintaining and expanding reproductive rights for all women. NARAL engages in a host of activities, including lobbying and testifying before Congress, organizing political support, and supporting pro-choice candidates for office. The organization also publishes a quarterly newsletter, *NARAL Newsletter*.

National Action for Former Military Wives (NAFMW)
2090 N. Atlantic Avenue, Suite PH2
Cocoa Beach, FL 32931-5010
(407) 783-2101
(407) 783-3709 (fax)
President: Jeanne Buchan

Founded in 1979, NAFMW lobbies for federal legislation that would provide retroactive, pro rata shares of military benefits, including pensions and survivors benefits.

National Association of Commissions for Women (NACW)
c/o DC Commission for Women
Reeves Center, Room N-354
2000 14th Street NW
Washington, DC 20009
(202) 839-8083
(202) 939-8763 (fax)
Executive Director: Carrolena Key

Founded in 1970, NACW is the national body for state, city, and county commissions that focus on the status of women. The commission helps to coordinate efforts, exchange information, and share ideas in procuring equality for women in all aspects of life, including educational, workplace, political, and social. NACW conducts leadership workshops, disseminates information, and conducts research on a variety of issues. The group publishes a number of periodicals, brochures, and research reports.

National Association for Female Executives (NAFE)
127 West 24th Street
New York, NY 10001
(202) 289-8538
(202) 289-3743 (fax)
Washington Representative: Joanne Symons
Web site: http://www.nafe.org

NAFE is the largest professional women's organization with more than 250,000 members. It is dedicated to advancing women's careers through education, networking, and public policy. The group lobbies Congress, conducts research, runs educational and networking programs, and maintains a speakers' bureau.

National Association of Negro Business and Professional Women's Clubs
1806 New Hampshire Avenue NW
Washington, DC 20009
(202) 483-4206
(202) 462-7253 (fax)
Executive Director: Sheila Quarles
Web site: http://www.nanbpw.org

Founded in 1935, the Association encourages the networking of business professionals through its programs of service. Its activities include sponsoring educational assistance programs, maintaining a speakers' bureau, and advocating programs for prison reform and consumer education. The group seeks to raise the self-esteem, self-respect, and self-reliance of the members of its communities. The Association grants the Sojourner Truth Award, which recognizes community service. The group also publishes a number of periodicals, including a monthly and a bimonthly newsletter, and a quarterly, *Responsibility*.

National Association of University Women (NAUW)
1001 E Street SE
Washington, DC 20003-2847
President: Phyllis J. Eggleston

Founded in 1923, NAUW pursues activities that reinforce its theme: Women of Action: Reaching, Risking, Responding. The group seeks to improve education and educational opportunities for women. It offers tutoring services, youth development programs, and scholarships. The group is affiliated with the Leadership Conference on Civil Rights and the United Negro College Fund.

National Association of Women in Chambers of Commerce (NAWCC)
PO Box 4552
Grand Junction, CO 81502-4552
(970) 242-0075
(970) 242-0075 Fax
Corporate Secretary-Treasurer: Marie Davis Sope

Founded in 1985, NAWCC is a membership organization for women who belong to the chamber of commerce. The group seeks to aid the networking of professional women by providing educational and management information. In addition to a membership directory, the group publishes a quarterly newsletter and brochure.

National Association of Women Judges (NAWJ)
815 15th Street NW, Suite 601
Washington, DC 20005
(202) 393-0222
(202) 393-0125 (fax)
Executive Director: Esther K. Ochsman

Founded in 1979, NAWJ is an organization for women who hold judicial or quasi-judicial positions. The group seeks to increase opportunities for women as judges, conducts research into the role of women in the judiciary, and provides educational programming.

National Association of Women Lawyers (NAWL)
750 N. Lake Shore Drive
Chicago, IL 60611
(312) 988-6186
Executive Director: Peggy L. Golden

Founded in 1911, NAWL is a network of women in the legal profession. The group presents several awards each year for service and to outstanding law students. NAWL publishes a quarterly newsletter and a quarterly magazine, *Women Lawyer's Journal*.

National Association of Women's Centers (NAWC)
PO Box 18
Summer, ME 04292-0018
(207) 388-2098
National Coordinating Center Staff: Mary Ann Hasten

Founded in 1986, NAWC is committed to the empowerment of women in all aspects of their lives and seeks to end all forms of oppression and discrimination.

National Black Women's Political Leadership Caucus
3005 Bladensburg Road NE, Suite 217
Washington, DC 20018
(202) 529-2806
Director: Juanita Kennedy Morgan

Founded in 1971, the Caucus aids women interested in understanding the role they can play in politics and policy making. The group conducts programs aimed at educating women about the different functions of city, state, and federal governments. It conducts workshops on public speaking and research on issues important to African-American women.

National Chamber of Commerce for Women (NCCW)
10 Waterside Plaza, Suite 6H
New York, NY 10010
(212) 685-3454
Executive Director: R. Wright

Founded in 1977, NCCW seeks economic equity for women. The group publishes a bimonthly newsletter, *Enrich!*

National Commission on Working Women (NCWW)
1325 G Street NW, Lower Level
Washington, DC 20005
(202) 737-5764
(202) 638-4885 (fax)
Director: Cynthia Marano

Founded in 1977, NCWW is a commission of Wider Opportunities for Women that acts as an advocate for low wage-earning women. The group sponsors educational forums on such issues as pay equity, childcare, and the media's portrayal of women.

National Committee on Pay Equity (NCPE)
1126 16th Street NW, Room 411
Washington, DC 20036
(202) 331-7343
(202) 331-7406 (fax)
Executive Director: Susan Blanch-Sand
Web site: http://www.feminist.com/fairpay.htm

Founded in 1979, NCPE seeks to eradicate pay inequality. The group sponsors educational programs, maintains a speakers' bureau, and acts as a clearinghouse for information on pay equity. The group publishes a number of books and manuals in addition to its quarterly newsletter, *Newsnotes.*

National Council of Negro Women (NCNW)
633 Pennsylvania Avenue NW
Washington, DC 20004-2605
(202) 628-0015
(202) 785-8733 (fax)
President: Dorothy I. Height
Web site: http://www.ncnw.org

Founded in 1935, NCNW helps to develop women leaders. The group runs the Women's Center for Education and Career Advancement in New York City, which conducts programs to aid minority women pursuing nontraditional careers. NCNW also maintains the Mary McLeod Bethune Museum and Archives for Black Women's History. It publishes a quarterly, *Sisters Magazine.*

National Displaced Homemakers Network
1625 K Street NW, Suite 300
Washington, DC 20006
(202) 467-6346
(202) 467-5366 (fax)
Executive Director: Jill Miller

The Network empowers displaced homemakers by assisting them to achieve economic self-sufficiency. The group lobbies on public policy issues, conducts educational programs, collects information, and acts as a clearinghouse for more than 1,000 programs, agencies, and educational institutions that provide services to displaced homemakers.

National Federation of Business and Professional Women's Clubs (BPW)
2012 Massachusetts Avenue NW
Washington, DC 20036
(202) 293-1100
(202) 861-0298 (fax)
Acting Executive Director: Cynthia Gady

Founded in 1919, BPW has over 70,000 members in more than 3,500 local groups. The group seeks workplace equity for women through its advocacy and educational programs. It is active in grassroots advocacy, seeking to influence elected officials. BPW sponsors National Business Women's Week during the third week of October. The group also publishes a number of materials, including a quarterly newspaper, *National Business Woman.*

National Federation of Democratic Women (NFDW)
5422 2nd Street NW
Washington, DC 20011
(202) 723-8182
President: Annette C. Jones

Founded in 1972, NFDW is an organization that promotes women as leaders in party management and as elected candidates. Affiliated with the Democratic National Committee, the Federation offers internships, conducts research, and offers educational programs. In addition to a directory, the group publishes a quarterly, *The Communicator.*

National Federation of Republican Women (NFRW)
124 N. Alfred Street
Alexandria, VA 22314
(703) 548-9688
(703) 548-9836 (fax)
President: Marilyn Thayer
Web site: http://www.nfrw.org

Founded in 1938, NFRW sponsors a host of activities, including distributing educational materials, recruiting and supporting women candidates for both public office and party positions, fund raising, and conducting the Campaign Management School. The Federation publishes a number of books on running for office as well as a quarterly magazine, *The Republican Woman.*

National Organization for Women (NOW)
1000 16th Street NW, Suite 700
Washington, DC 20036
(202) 331-0066
(202) 785-8576 (fax)
President: Patricia Ireland
Web site: http://www.now.org

Founded in 1966, NOW, with more than 275,000 members in all 50 states, advocates equality of women in all aspects of life. The group lobbies on behalf of the Equal Rights Amendment and the enactment of legislation to end discrimination in the workplace and in society. NOW is active in promoting women to run for office. The group also publishes a bimonthly newspaper, *National NOW Times*.

NOW Legal Defense and Education Fund (NOW LDEF)
99 Hudson Street, 12th Floor
New York, NY 10013
(212) 925-6635
(212) 226-1066 (fax)
Executive Director: Kathryn J. Rodgers
Web site: http://www.nowldef.org

Founded in 1970, NOW LDEF has a staff of more than 20 and an annual budget of over $2.5 million. The fund litigates to end sex-based discrimination. It sponsors the National Judicial Education Program to Promote Equality for Women and Men in the Courts, and legal internships. It publishes a quarterly newsletter, *In Brief*, and offers legal resource kits on a host of topics, including divorce, lesbian rights, and sexual harassment.

National Organization of Black Elected Legislative Women (NOBEL Women)
4401 Crenshaw Boulevard, Suite 300
Los Angeles, CA 90043
(213) 295-6655
President: Diane E. Watson

Founded in 1985, the purpose of NOBEL Women is to improve the lives of African-American women by increasing the number of them elected and appointed to local, state, and national offices. The group sponsors educational programs, and speakers, and testifies at public hearings. Each year, the organization focuses on one issue to maximize its effectiveness in the public policy arena.

National Pro-Life Democrats (NPLD)
4249 Nicollet Avenue
Minneapolis, MN 55409-2014
Executive Director: Mary Jo Cooley

The NPLD promotes the participation of pro-life Democrats in the party. It conducts workshops and develops educational materials.

National Right to Life Committee (NRLC)
419 7th Street NW, Suite 500
Washington, DC 20004
(202) 626-8800
President: Wanda Franz
Web site: http://www.nrlc.org

Founded in 1973, NRLC is a grassroots pro-life organization that seeks to protect all human life. The group sponsors educational programs, seeks legislation to protect the unborn, and conducts research on social, political, and medical issues related to abortion. NRLC is active in lobbying Congress, maintains a speakers' bureau, and issues statements for the press. The committee also publishes a number of books and pamphlets in addition to its newspaper, *National Right to Life News*.

National Women and Media Collection
Western Historical Manuscript Collection
23 Ellis Library
Columbia, MO 65211
(573) 882-6028
(573) 884-4735 (fax)
Assistant Director: Nancy Langford
Web site: http://www.system.missouri.edu/whmc/womedia.htm

Founded in 1987, the group maintains an extensive collection on women in the media and the media's portrayal of women.

National Women's Conference (NWC)
University of Wisconsin-Eau Claire
Eau Claire, WI 54701
(715) 836-5717
(715) 836-5019 (fax)
Co-Chair: Mal Johnson
Web site: http://www.speakeasy.org/awr

Founded in 1977 by a mandate at the first National Women's Conference in Houston, Texas, NWC continues the move for women's equity. It is responsible for carrying out the National Plan of Action and participating in the United Nations' World Conference. The conference sponsors speakers and workshops on women's issues, and also publishes a number of works, including a quarterly, *NWC Newsletter—The Network Exchange*.

National Women's Conference Center
46 Waterford Circle, Suite 202
Madison, WI 53719
(608) 273-9760
(954) 389-1879
(608) 273-9760 (fax)
President: Gene Boyer

Founded in 1980, the Center advocates equality of women in all aspects of life. The organization collects and disseminates information, and works to establish partnerships with educational institutions, government agencies, and the private sector. It publishes a newsletter, *Network Exchange*.

National Women's Hall of Fame
Washington Office
406 Slyhill Road
Alexandria, VA 22314
(703) 370-3334
(703) 370-6762 (fax)
Executive Director: Susan Lowell Butler

Founded in 1968 in Seneca Falls, New York, the Hall is a national membership organization that honors and celebrates the achievements of extraordinary American women. Each year, distinguished women are inducted into the Hall's permanent exhibit. The Hall also conducts other educational programs in conjunction with its maintenance of the exhibits in Seneca Falls.

National Women's Health Network (NWHN)
514 10th Street NW, Suite 400
Washington, DC 20004
(202) 347-1140
(202) 347-1162 (fax)
Executive Director: Cynthia Pearson

Founded in 1976, NWHN is an active advocate on issues of women's health. The group testifies before Congress, monitors legislation, and supports feminist health programs. NWHN also sponsors the Women's Health Clearinghouse and a speakers' bureau. It publishes a bimonthly newsletter, *National Women's Health Network—Network News*, in addition to a number of brochures and booklets.

National Women's History Project (NWHP)
7738 Bell Road
Windsor, CA 95492-8518
(707) 838-6000
(800) 691-8888
(707) 838-0478 (fax)
Executive Director: Molly MacGregor
Web site: http://www.nwhp.org

Founded in 1977, NWHP is a publisher of a semiannual catalog of materials on the history of American women. In addition to the catalog, the group develops training sessions and curricula for the adoption of women's history. It sponsors the annual National Women's History Month. NWHP maintains a large archive of more than 6,000 books, clippings, photographs, and other materials related to women in American history. The group has an active publishing program that includes directories, lesson plans, catalogs, and a quarterly, *Women's History Network News*.

National Women's Law Center (NWLC)
11 Dupont Circle NW, Suite 800
Washington, DC 20036
(202) 588-5180
(202) 588-5185 (fax)
Co-President: Nancy Duff Campbell

Founded in 1972, NWLC is active in litigation to secure women's rights in a wide area of interests, including employment, education, child support, and reproductive rights. The center also conducts research on current and proposed policies to evaluate their impact on women's rights. The group publishes a number of resources, including fact sheets, reports, books, and a quarterly newsletter, *Update*.

National Woman's Party (NWP)
Sewall-Belmont House
144 Constitution Avenue NE
Washington, DC 20002
(202) 546-1210
(202) 546-3997 (fax)
President: Dorothy Ferrell

Founded in 1913 to promote the adoption of woman's suffrage, NWP has continued to be on the political forefront of women's issues, especially the Equal Rights Amendment. The party maintains a museum and suffrage art gallery in its historic locale, Sewall-Belmont House. It publishes a quarterly newsletter, *Equal Rights*.

National Women's Political Caucus (NWPC)
1275 K Street NW, Suite 750
Washington, DC 20005
(202) 898-1100
(202) 898-0458 (fax)
Executive Director: Jody Newman
Web site: http://www.feminist.com/nwpc.htm

Founded in 1971, NWPC is a multipartisan caucus that promotes the political influence of women at all levels of government. The group supports women candidates, raises women's issues in elections, and seeks nominations for women to appointive posts. NWPC lobbies legislatures to ensure reproductive rights, affirmative action, and comparable worth. The Caucus publishes a number of guides and a quarterly newsletter, *Women's Political Times*.

National Women's Studies Association (NWSA)
7100 Baltimore Avenue, Suite 301
College Park, MD 20740
(301) 403-0525
(301) 403-0524
(301) 403-4137 (fax)
Manager: Loretta Younger
Web site: http://www.feminist.com/nwsa.htm

Founded in 1977, NWSA is a network of teachers, students, and community activists that works to expand women's studies programs. The group lobbies for the inclusion of educational materials as part of the curriculum at all levels of education. It administers graduate scholarships, organizes conferences, and distributes information. The group sponsors a number of awards for writing, and publishes a wide range of books, directories, and reports, including its newsletter, *NWSAction*.

9 to 5, National Association of Working Women
231 W. Wisconsin Avenue, Suite 900
Milwaukee, WI 53203
(216) 566-9308
(414) 274-0925
(414) 272-2870 (fax)
Executive Director: Ellen Bravo
Web site: http://www.feminist.com/9to5.htm

Founded in 1973, 9 to 5 is a network of office worker chapters that seeks to improve work conditions, increase opportunities for advancement, and end sex discrimination. With more than 13,000 members, the organization is active in research and policy formation, including family and medical leave and stress. Its publications include *The 9 to 5 Guide to Combating Sexual Harassment* and *9 to 5: Working Women's Guide to Office Survival*. The association also publishes a newsletter.

Older Women's League (OWL)
666 11th Street NW, Suite 700
Washington, DC 20001
(202) 783-6686
(202) 638-2356 (fax)
Executive Director: Joan Kuriansky

OWL is a national advocacy group that seeks to secure social and economic equity for older women. The organization focuses on health care, retirement income, employment, and housing issues. It conducts research, issues reports, and acts as an advocate to national and state bodies.

Organization of Pan Asian Women
PO Box 39128
Washington, DC 20016
(202) 659-9370
President: Nguyen Minh Chau

Founded in 1976, the Organization seeks full participation of Asian and Pacific-American women in all aspects of American society. The group focuses on refugee and immigrant women and aids them in gaining the necessary skills, including language proficiency, to participate fully.

Operation Rescue (OR)
PO Box 740066
Dallas, TX 75374
(214) 348-8866
(214) 348-7172 (fax)
National Director: Flip Benham
Web site: http://www.orn.org

Founded in 1987, Operation Rescue organizes sit-ins and other forms of protest in the hope of preventing women from having abortions. Since it began its activities, the group has had more than 50,000 members arrested and has prevented over 1,000 abortions from occurring.

Peace Links
729 8th Street SE, Suite 300
Washington, DC 20003
(202) 544-0805
(202) 544-0809 (fax)
President: Betty Bumpers

Founded in 1982, Peace Links seeks to end violence at the family, community, and international levels. The group encourages political activity on a wide range of issues, from domestic violence to nuclear war. It sponsors debates, administers a pen pal program between American and Russian people, maintains a speakers' bureau, and promotes the annual celebration of Peace Month in October. The group also publishes information packets, an annual newsletter, *The Connection*, and a legislative update, *Action Alert*.

Planned Parenthood Federation of America
810 7th Avenue
New York, NY 10019
(212) 541-7800
(212) 247-6342 (fax)
Contact: Jane M. Johnson
Web site: http://www.plannedparenthood.org

Planned Parenthood is the largest pro-choice organization in the U.S. It runs more than 900 clinics and distributes information on reproductive rights and other women's health issues. The organization conducts seminars, lobbies for legislation, and pursues litigation. It has an extensive publishing program with dozens of pamphlets, brochures, and books, including a bimonthly newsletter, *Planned Parenthood Women's Health Letter*.

Pro-Life Action League (PLAL)
6160 N. Cicero, Suite 600
Chicago, IL 60646
(312) 777-2900
(312) 777-3061 (fax)
Executive Director: Joseph M. Scheidler

Founded in 1990, PLAL is a pro-life organization of doctors, lawyers, students, and business leaders. It seeks to end abortion on demand through nonviolent methods. It advocates a constitutional amendment outlawing abortion, conducts demonstrations at abortion clinics, and makes use of radio and television to get its message out. The organization trains volunteers to counsel on alternatives to abortion and maintains a lecture service for student groups. In addition to a number of videos and brochures, PLAL publishes two quarterlies, *Action News* and *Pro-Life Action News*.

Pro-Life Alliance of Gays and Lesbians
PO Box 33292
Washington, DC 20033
(202) 223-6697
(202) 265-9737 (fax)
President: Philip Arcidi

Founded in 1990, the alliance seeks human rights for all, including the unborn. The group publishes a monthly newsletter, *PLAGAL Memorandum*.

Radical Women (RW)
1908 Mission Street
San Francisco, CA 94103
(415) 864-1278
(415) 864-0778 (fax)
Organizer: Nancy Reiko Kato

Founded in 1967 to combat conservative antifeminist groups, Radical Women is a socialist-feminist political group that is interested in women's issues, including reproductive rights, affirmative action, rape, lesbianism, and police brutality.

Republican Network to Elect Women (RENEW)
1555 King Street
Alexandria, VA 22313-0507
(709) 836-2255
Co-Director: Karen Roberts
Web site: http://www.users.aol.com/gorenew/

The network seeks to increase the number of Republican women elected to local, state, and national office. The group espouses a belief in individual responsibility and free market principles.

Republicans for Choice (RFC)
2760 Eisenhower Avenue, Suite 260
Alexandria, VA 22314-5223
(703) 836-8907
(703) 960-9882
(703) 519-8843 (fax)
Chair: Ann Stone

Founded in1990, RFC is an organization for Republican Party members who are pro-choice. The group supports pro-choice candidates for office and seeks to change the national party's position on abortion.

Social Justice for Women
59 Temple Place, Suite 307
Boston, MA 02111
(617) 482-0747
(617) 695-2891 (fax)
Executive Director: Phyllis Buccio-Notaro

Founded in 1986, Social Justice for Women provides services to nonviolent female offenders, including substance abuse programs, health education, and community reintegration. The group publishes a quarterly, *Social Justice for Women Newsletter*.

United Daughters of the Confederacy (UDC)
328 N Boulevard
Richmond, VA 23220-4057
(804) 355-1636
(804) 359-1325 (fax)
Executive Secretary: Marion Giannasi
Web site: http://www.itd.nps.gov/cwss/udc.html

Founded in 1894, UDC is a women's organization for descendants of Confederate veterans of the Civil War. The group promotes service to community, knowledge of the Civil War, and pride in Southern culture and literature. It publishes a monthly, *United Daughters of the Confederacy Magazine*.

University Faculty for Life (UFL)
120 New North
Georgetown University
Washington, DC 20057
(202) 687-6101
(202) 687-8000 (fax)
President: Fr. Thomas M. King, S.J.

Founded in 1989, UFL is an organization of pro-life professors that conducts dialogue and promotes research on pro-life issues. The group is involved in political activities, disseminates scholarly studies, and maintains a speakers' bureau. UFL also publishes a newsletter, *Pro Vita*.

Victims of Choice (VOC)
PO Box 815
Naperville, IL 60566
(630) 378-1680
Executive Director: Elizabeth Verchio

Founded in 1983, VOC is a pro-life organization that offers counseling, referrals, and education activities to those who have had abortions or those who are considering one. The groups publishes a number of brochures as well as a newsletter, *VOC Journal*.

WAND Education Fund (WAND EF)
691 Massachusetts Avenue
Arlington, MA 02174
(617) 643-4880
(617) 643-6744 (fax)
Executive Director: Susan Shaer
Web site: http://www.wand.org

Founded in 1982, WAND EF sponsors lectures on nuclear disarmament, national security, and other military topics. Affiliated with the Women's Action for New Directions, the group also seeks to restore Mother's Day to a day of women calling for world peace. It publishes a number of manuals, brochures, and fact sheets.

WAVES National (WN)
PO Box 246
Mogadore, OH 44260-0246
(330) 628-3437
(fax)(330) 628-3295
President: Dorothy Budacki

Founded in 1979, WAVES (Women Accepted for Voluntary Emergency Service) National is a veterans' group for women who have served in the Navy, Naval Reserves, Navy Nursing Corps, Marines, or Coast Guard. The group encourages patriotism as well as opportunities for women in the military. The group also serves as a network for former WAVES to remain in communication with each other. It publishes a bimonthly newsletter, *White Caps*.

We Are AWARE
PO Box 242
Bedford, MA 01730-0242
(617) 893-0500
President: Nancy Bittle
Web site: http://www.aware.org

Founded in 1990, We Are AWARE (Arming Women Against Rape and Endangerment and Advancing Women's Armed Rights through Education) works to reduce violence against women. The group teaches self-defense, including the use of firearms, and maintains a speakers' bureau. It publishes a quarterly newsletter.

Wider Opportunities for Women (WOW)
1325 G Street NW
Washington, DC 20005
(202) 638-3143
(202) 638-4885 (fax)
President Cynthia Marano

WOW is a national organization that works to achieve economic independence and equal opportunity for women. The group sponsors education and job training programs and acts as an advocate for workplace reform and public policy issues.

The Woman Activist (TWA)
2310 Barbour Road
Falls Church, VA 22043-2940
(703) 573-8716
(703) 573-8716 (fax)
President: Flora Crater

Founded in 1975, TWA is a nonprofit consulting firm that provides political consulting, including issue analysis, report writing, and program development. The group also rates members of Congress on women's issues.

Women Against Pornography (WAP)
PO Box 845, Times Square Station
New York, NY 10108-0845
Contact: Dorchen Leidholdt

Founded in 1979, WAP is a feminist organization that seeks to end pornography which it believes is a form of prostitution. The group conducts a Times Square tour to expose people to the sexual exploitation and brutalization of women in the pornography industry. In addition to the tours, WAP conducts educational programs and maintains a speakers' bureau. It publishes a quarterly news report, *Women Against Pornography*.

Women Exploited by Abortion (WEBA)
PO Box 278
Dawson, TX 76639-0278
(817) 578-1681
(817) 578-1681 (fax)
President: Kathy Walker

Founded in 1982, WEBA is a Christian-oriented group of women who have had abortions and now regret having done so. It provides counseling and support services to women and men who suffer from physical as well as emotional problems associated with abortions. The group also engages in pro-life activities, including sponsoring speakers, collecting and disseminating statistics on abortion, and pro-life alternative counseling. WEBA has an extensive publishing program that includes books, brochures, pamphlets, and reports in addition to its bimonthly newsletter, *Reconciler*.

Women in Defense (WD)
2101 Wilson Boulevard, Suite 400
Arlington, VA 22201-3061
(703) 247-2552
(703) 522-1885 (fax)
President: Carol Sue Coupland

Founded in 1985, Women in Defense is a group whose members are employed in defense industries or government agencies involved in defense. WD seeks to promote opportunities for women in the defense profession. The organization conducts educational programs, maintains a speakers' bureau, and awards Horizons Foundation scholarships.

Women for Racial and Economic Equality (WREE)
198 Broadway, Room 606
New York, NY 10038
(212) 385-1103
Chair: Rudean Leinaeng

Founded in 1975, WREE is a working class organization that seeks to end racial and sexual discrimination in both the workplace and educational environments. The group promotes peace and passage of the Women's Bill of Rights. It conducts a number of programs, including leadership training, community education, and action campaigns. The group publishes a number of books, including collections of poetry, and a quarterly newspaper, *WREE-View of Women*.

Women in Municipal Government (WIMG)
National League of Cities
1301 Pennsylvania Avenue NW
Washington, DC 20004
(202) 626-3000
(202) 626-3169
(800) 658-8872
(202) 626-3043 (fax)
Manager: Mary France Gordon
Web site: http://www.nlc.org

Founded in 1974, WIMG is an organization of women mayors, council members, and commissioners. The group provides a network for the exchange of ideas and information as well as a voice to promote women's issues in local government. WIMG publishes a quarterly newsletter, *Constituency and Member Group Report*.

Women Work! The National Network for Women's Employment
1625 K Street NW, Suite 300
Washington, DC 20006
(202) 467-6346
(800) 235-2732
(202) 467-5366 (fax)
Co-Executive Director: Jill Miller
Web site: http://www.womenwork.org

Founded in 1978, Women Work! is an organization of displaced homemakers that provides training services and other programs for women re-entering the workforce. The group also acts as a clearinghouse of legislative information and research. Women Work! publishes a number of books and reports in addition to its quarterly newsletter, *Network News*.

Women's Action Alliance (WAA)
370 Lexington Avenue, Suite 603
New York, NY 10017
(212) 532-8330
(212) 779-2846 (fax)
Executive Director: Karel R. Amaranth

Founded in 1971, WAA seeks self-determination for women by sponsoring programs on self-esteem, health care, domestic violence, sexual harassment, and other issues that women face. The group provides resources to other organizations and acts as an advocate to the media, government, and the business community. WAA has an extensive publishing program that includes books, journals, directories, research reports, and several newsletters.

Women's Action for New Directions (WAND)
691 Massachusetts Avenue
Arlington, MA 02174
(617) 643-4880
(617) 643-6744 (fax)
Executive Director: Marjorie Smith
Web site: http://www.wand.org

WAND works to empower women to reduce violence and military expenditures. It is a grassroots organization that develops materials for education and lobbies Congress to enact its public policy goals.

Women's Agenda for the 90s
3133 Constitution Avenue NW, Suite 427
Washington, DC 20008
(202) 322-5494
(202) 232-4612 (fax)
Contact: Kristina Kiehl and Robin Wright

The Women's Agenda publishes an informational newsletter on political candidacies, coalition efforts, ballot initiatives, research and polling projects, conferences, and other information of interest to women's groups.

Women's Alliance for Job Equity (WAJE)
1422 Chestnut Street, Suite 1100
Philadelphia, PA 19102
(215) 561-1873
(215) 561-7112 (fax)
Executive Director: Maureen Cowley

Founded in 1979, WAJE works on economic and workplace issues for women in the Delaware Valley. The group publishes a bimonthly newsletter, *WAJE-Earner Notes*.

Women's Campaign Fund (WCF)
734 15th Street NW, Suite 500
Washington, DC 20005
(202) 393-8164
(202) 393-0649 (fax)
President: Marjorie Margolies-Mezvinsky
Web site: http://www.womenscampaignfund.org
Founded in 1974, WCF supports the election of progressive women to public office. The group accomplishes this goal by making contributions to candidates' campaigns, endorsing candidates in elections, and providing campaign consulting services. WCF publishes a quarterly newsletter, *Winning Choice*.

Women's Christian Temperance Union (WCTU)
1730 Chicago Avenue
Evanston, IL 60201-4585
(708) 864-1396
(708) 864-1397
(708) 864-9497 (fax)
President: Sarah F. Ward
Web site: http://www.uctu.org

Founded in 1874, WCTU is a nonpartisan, interdenominational Christian women's group dedicated to educating people about the dangers of alcohol, narcotic drugs, and tobacco on the human body and American society. It conducts a number of educational activities, including essay, picture, and speech contests. The group publishes and disseminates information on temperance. WCTU maintains an extensive library and museum at the Frances E. Willard Home. In addition to its numerous pamphlets and reports, the group also publishes two quarterlies, *Promoter* and *The Union Signal*.

Women's Education and Leadership Forum (WELF)
1390 Chainbridge Road, Suite 9600
McLean, VA 22101
(703) 237-2070
(703) 237-2073 (fax)
Executive Officer: Patricia Brockbank

Founded in 1986, WELF advocates self-sufficiency and self-esteem as a means to achieving empowerment. The organization sponsors conferences that assist in woman-to-woman networking.

Women's Funding Network (WFN)
332 Minnesota Street, Suite E-840
St. Paul, MN 55101-2830
(612) 227-1911
(612) 227-2213 (fax)
Executive Officer: Carol Mollner

Founded in 1985, WFN seeks to increase the funds available to programs and organizations that benefit women. The group publicizes the percentages that large funding organizations make available to women and serves as a clearinghouse of information about funds.

Women's Health Action and Mobilization (WHAM!)
PO Box 733
New York, NY 10009
(212) 560-7177

Founded in 1989, WHAM! is dedicated to securing complete reproductive freedom and quality health care for women. The group organizes political events and maintains a speakers' bureau. It publishes a weekly, *Contact Sheet*, and a quarterly, *Frontlines*.

Women's History Network (WHN)
7738 Bell Road
Windsor, CA 95492-8518
(707) 838-6000
(707) 838-0478 (fax)
Projects Director: Mary Ruthsdotter
Web site: http://www.nwhp.org

Founded in 1983, WHN is a project of the National Women's History Project that provides information and materials to celebrate women's contributions to American history. The network maintains an archive of more than 6,000 photographs, documents, and other materials as well as a women's history performers' bureau. The group publishes a quarterly newsletter, *Network News*.

Women's Information Exchange (WIE)
PO Box 68
Jenner, CA 95450
(707) 632-5763
(707) 632-5589 (fax)
Executive Officer: Jill Lippitt
Web site: http://www.electrapages.com

Founded in 1980, WIE is a group of feminist women computer specialists that uses computer technology to support the efforts of women's organizations. It provides information technology through its educational programs and speakers' bureau. The group publishes a directory of more than 10,000 women's organizations.

The Women's Institute Press (TWI)
PO Box 6005
Silver Spring, MD 20916
(301) 871-6106
(703) 356-0299
(301) 871-6106 (fax)
Managing Editor: Daisy B. Fields

Founded in 1975, TWI is a publisher of books, monographs, and articles on women's studies.

Women's International League for Peace and Freedom (WILPF)
1213 Race Street
Philadelphia, PA 19107
(215) 563-7110
(215) 864-2022 (fax)
President: Mary Zepernick
Web site: http://www.wilpf.org

WILPF has been working for international peace and justice for more than 80 years. The group maintains consultative status with the United Nations and is involved in grassroots efforts to end violence, racism, sexism, and other forms of oppression. The organization has an active publishing program, including *The Women's Budget*.

Women's Legal Defense Fund (WLDF)
1875 Connecticut Avenue NW, Suite 710
Washington, DC 20009
(202) 986-2600
(202) 986-2539 (fax)
President: Judith Lichtman

Founded in 1971, WLDF is an organization of attorneys, administrators, publicists, and secretaries that seeks equal rights for women through its advocacy and education programs. The group is particularly active in the areas of family law, employment, and health. It publishes a number of handbooks, manuals, and brochures in addition to its semiannual newsletter, *WLDF News*.

Women's Project
2224 Main Street
Little Rock, AR 72206
(501) 372-5113
(501) 372-0009 (fax)
Director: Janet Perkins

Founded in 1981, the Women's Project seeks to eliminate all forms of racism and sexism. It is particularly interested in issues of domestic violence and poverty. The project has published several books as well as a quarterly newsletter, *Transformation*.

Women's Rights Committee (WRC)
c/o American Federation of Teachers
Human Rights Department
555 New Jersey Avenue NW
Washington, DC 20001
(202) 879-4400
(202) 879-4502 (fax)
Director: Barbara Van Blake
Web site: http://www.aft.org

Founded in 1970, WRC implements women's rights policy decisions of the American Federation of Teachers. The Committee conducts research and educational programs and also maintains a speakers' bureau.

Women's Rights Project (WRP)
c/o American Civil Liberties Union
125 Broad Street
New York, NY 10004
(212) 549-2500
(212) 549-2642 (fax)
Web site: http://www.aclu.org/issues/women/hmwo.html

Founded in 1971, the Women's Rights Project of the ACLU works to end discrimination through litigation.

Young Women's Christian Association (YWCA)
726 Broadway
New York, NY 10003
(212) 614-2700
(212) 677-9716 (fax)
Executive Director: Dr. Prema Matillai
Web site: http://www.ywca.org

Founded in 1858, YWCA conducts recreational, developmental, self-improvement, and employment programs for women and girls. The group is also an active advocate for human rights and world peace. YWCA publishes a number of books, newsletters, manuals, and brochures.

Young Women's Project (YWP)
1511 K Street NW
Washington, DC 20005
(202) 393-0461
Executive Director: Nadia Moritz

Founded in 1989, YWP seeks to recognize and develop young women's leadership and to encourage political participation by providing an intergenerational and multicultural network of women ages 15 to 35.

Women's PACs and Donor Networks

Ain't I A Woman Network/PAC
PO Box 34484
Philadelphia, PA 19101

Alabama Solution
PO Box 370821
Birmingham, AL 35237
(205) 250-0205
(205) 995-1990 (fax)

American Nurses' Association, Inc. (ANA-PAC)
600 Maryland Avenue SW, Suite 100W
Washington, DC 20024-2571
(202) 651-7095
(202) 554-0189 (fax)

Arkansas Women's Action Fund
1100 North University, Suite 109
Little Rock, AR 72707
(501) 663-1202
(501) 663-1218 (fax)

Committee of 21
PO Box 19287
New Orleans, LA 70179
(504) 827-0112

Democratic Activists for Women Now (DAWN)
PO Box 6614
San Jose, CA 95150

Eleanor Roosevelt Fund of California
1001-158 Evelyn Terrace
East Sunnyvale, CA 94086
(408) 773-9791

EMILY's List
805 15th Street, Suite 400
Washington, DC 20005
(202) 326-1400
(202) 326-1415 (fax)

EMMA's List
PO Box 64
Louisville, KY 40201-0646

First Ladies of Oklahoma
8364 S. Urbana Avenue
Tulsa, OK 74137

Focus 2020
PO Box 660
Huntsville, AL 35804-0660

GROW (Greater Roles & Opportunities for Women, Inc.)
29 Emmons Drive Building F, Suite 4
Princeton, NJ 08540
(609) 989-7300

GWEN's List
4410 Flagler Street
Miami Beach, FL 33130
(305) 374-0521

Harriet's List
PO Box 16361
Baltimore, MD 21210
(410) 377-5709
(410) 377-2842 (fax)

The Hope Chest
4921 Dierker Road
Columbus, OH 43220
(614) 236-4268
(614) 236-2449 (fax)

HOPE-PAC
3220 E. 26th Street
Los Angeles, CA 90023
(213) 267-5845
(213) 262-1348 (fax)

Independent Women's Organization
13834 Octvia St.
New Orleans, LA 70125
(504) 525-2256

Indiana Women's Network for Political Action
PO Box 88271
Indianapolis, IN 46208-0271
(317) 283-2066

Latina PAC
915 L Street, Suite C222
Sacramento, CA 95814
(916) 395-7915

The Leader PAC
PO Box 7001
Fairfax Station, VA 22039-7001

Los Angeles African American Women's PAC
4102 Olympiad Drive
Los Angeles, CA 90043
(213) 295-2382

Los Angeles Women's Campaign Fund
c/o Kreff & Rosenbaum
1410 Ventura Boulevard, Suite 402
Sherman Oaks, CA 91423
(818) 990-7377
(818) 990-1840 (fax)

Make Women Count
PO Box 677
Richmond, VA 23218-0677
(804) 644-7450
(804) 643-1466 (fax)

Marin County Women's PAC
3310 Paradise Drive
Tiburon, CA 94920
(415) 435-2504

Michigan Women's Campaign Fund
PO Box 71626
Madison Heights, MI 48071
(810) 932-3540
(810) 932-1734 (fax)

Minnesota Women's Campaign Fund
550 Rice Street, Suite 106
St. Paul, MN 55103
(612) 904-6723
(612) 292-9417 (fax)

Missouri Women's Action Fund
1108 Hillside Drive
St. Louis, MO 63117
(314) 516-6622

National Federation of Business & Professional Women's Clubs (BPW/PAC)
2012 Massachusetts Avenue NW
Washington, DC 20036
(202) 293-1100, ext. 555

National Organization for Women PAC
1000 16th Street NW, Suite 700
Washington, DC 20036-5705
(202) 331-0066
(202) 785-8576 (fax)

National Women's Political Caucus
1211 Connecticut Avenue NW, Suite 425
Washington, DC 20036
(202) 785-1100
(202) 785-3605 (fax)

PAM's List
PO Box 3311
Cherry Hill, NJ 08034

Pennsylvania Women's Campaign Fund
PO Box 767
Hazleton, PA 18201

RENEW
1555 King Street, Suite 200
PO Box 507
Alexandria, VA 22313-0507
(703) 836-2255

Republican Women of the 90s
2 Hartford Drive
Tinton Falls, NJ 07724
(732) 530-8927

Republican Women's PAC of Illinois
223 W. Jackson Boulevard, Suite 100
Chicago, IL 60606
(312) 939-7300
(312) 939-7220 (fax)

Sacramento Women's Campaign Fund
PO Box 162212
Sacramento, CA 95816
(916) 443-8421
(916) 443-8440 (fax)

Santa Barbara Women's Political Committee
PO Box 90618
Santa Barbara, CA 93190-0618
(805) 682-6769

The Seneca Network
2035 Rough Gold Court
Gold River, CA 95670
(916) 638-8995
(916) 638-8996 (fax)

The Susan B. Anthony List
919 Prince Street
Alexandria, VA
(703) 683-5558
(703) 549-5588 (fax)

Task Force 2000 PAC
PO Box 36183
Houston, TX 77236
(713) 495-7539
(281) 495-0594 (fax)

VOW (Voices of Oklahoma Women)
6002 S. Atlanta Court
Tulsa, OK 74105
(405) 749-5629

Wednesday Committee
1531 Purdue
Los Angeles, CA 90025
(310) 477-8081

WIN PAC (Women's Pro-Israel National PAC)
2020 Pennsylvania Avenue NW
Washington, DC 20006
(202) 296-2946

WISH List
3205 N Street NW
Washington, DC 20007
(202) 342-9111
(202) 342-9190 (fax)

Women For
8913 West Olympic Boulevard, Suite 103
Beverly Hills, CA 90211-3552
(310) 657-7411
(310) 289-0719 (fax)

Women For: Orange County
PO Box 5402
Irvine, CA 92716
(714) 854-8024

Women in Psychology for Legislative Action
13 Ashfield Street
Roslindale, MA 02131
(617) 327-8015

Women in the Nineties (WIN)
1215 7th Avenue
PO Box 50452
Nashville, TN 37208
(615) 298-1250
(615) 298-9858 (fax)

Women Organizing Women PAC (WOW PAC)
233 Everit
New Haven, CT 06511

Women's Campaign Fund
734 15th Street NW, Suite 500
Washington, DC 20002
(202) 393-8164
(202) 544-4517 (fax)

Women's Council of the Democratic Senatorial Campaign Committee
430 South Capitol Street SE
Washington, DC 20003
(202) 224-2447
(202) 485-3120 (fax)

Women's Democratic Club of Delaware
402 West Clearview Avenue
Wilmington, DE 19809
(302) 798-2028
(302) 798-3153 (fax)
wdcofde@aol.com

Women's Democratic Club of Delaware PAC
18 Grist Mill Court
Wilmington, DE 19803
(302) 764-7831

Women's Investment Network (WIN-PAC)
3333 SW Arnold
Portland, OR 97219
(503) 246-6022

Women's Political Action Committee of New Jersey
PO Box 170
Edison, NJ 08818
(908) 638-6784

Women's Political Committee
2740 Club Drive
Los Angeles, CA 90064
(310) 558-8114

Women's Political Fund
PO Box 421811
San Francisco, CA 94142-1811
(415) 861-5168

Women's Political Summit
1531 Purdue
Los Angeles, CA 90025
(310) 477-8081

The Women's TAP Fund
64 Tudor Place
Buffalo, NY 14222
(716) 881-3241

4

Timeline

Date	Women's History	United States History	World History
1848	More than 300 people attend the Seneca Falls (NY) Convention on women's rights.	Treaty of Guadalupe Hidalgo ends Mexican-American War.	Karl Marx and Friedrich Engels publish the *Communist Manifesto*
1849	Elizabeth Blackwell, first woman physician, graduates from Geneva (NY) Medical College.	With its population swollen by the gold rush, California calls a convention to adopt a constitution.	Under Guiseppe Mazzini, Rome is declared a republic.
1850	First National Woman's Rights Convention held in Worcester, Massachusetts.	Compromise of 1850 attempts to settle the slave question in the territories.	Taiping Rebellion begins in China; Hung Hiu-tsuen proclaims himself emperor.
1851	Sojourner Truth delivers her "Ain't I a Woman?" speech at an Akron, Ohio, woman's rights convention.	The *New York Times* begins publication.	Cuba declares its independence from Spain.
1852	Susan B. Anthony forms the New York Woman's Temperance Society with Elizabeth Cady Stanton.	A reluctant Franklin Pierce of New Hampshire is elected president as a compromise candidate as the controversy between slave and free states grows.	Louis Napoleon, president of France, proclaims himself Emperor Napoleon III and establishes the Second Empire.
1853	Antoinette Louisa Brown Blackwell becomes the first women to be ordained a minister.	Gadsden Purchase from Mexico brings portions of southern Arizona and New Mexico to the U.S. for $10 million.	The Crimean War begins.

Date	Women's History	United States History	World History
1854	Elizabeth Cady Stanton becomes the first woman to address the New York State Senate.	Bleeding Kansas—slave and free forces clash over the admission of Kansas to Union.	Pope Pius IX declares the Immaculate Conception of the Blessed Virgin Mary an article of Catholic faith.
1855	*Woman's Advocate*—which focuses on blue-coller women—begins publication as the first entirely woman-run newspaper.	Conflict continues in Kansas as both free and slave state governments are formed.	Taiping Rebellion comes to an end in China.
1856	South Carolina court rules that a woman can change her name without the consent of her husband.	Republican Party holds its first convention and nominates John C. Fremont for president.	South African Republic organized under the leadership of Mathinius Pretorius.
1857	Elizabeth and Emily Blackwell found the New York Infirmary for Indigent Women and Children.	Speculation in U.S. railroad equities causes a financial and economic crisis in Europe.	Czar Alexander II begins emancipation of Russian serfs.
1858	When Lucy Stone refuses to pay taxes on her property because she is not allowed to vote, her belongings are auctioned off and bought by a neighbor who returns them to Stone.	The Lecompton Constitution is again rejected by Kansas voters; statehood for Kansas is delayed until 1861.	Control of British India is transferred from the East India Company to the British Crown.
1859		Abolitionist John Brown leads a raid on the federal arsenal at Harper's Ferry, Virginia.	German National Association is formed to unite Germany under Prussian rule.
1860	Olympia Brown becomes the first woman to study theology with men when she enters the Theological School of St. Lawrence University.	South Carolina secedes from the Union after Abraham Lincoln's election to the presidency.	Giuseppe Garibaldi proclaims Victor Emmanuel II king of Italy.
1861	Dorothea L. Dix organizes the Army Nursing Corps.	Confederates capture Fort Sumter and the Civil War begins.	Warsaw Massacre—Russian military opens fire on demonstrators protesting Russian rule in Poland.

Date	Women's History	United States History	World History
1862	U.S. law bans polygamy.	Union forces are defeated at the second Battle of Bull Run.	Otto I of Greece is forced to resign after a military coup.
1863	The National Woman's Loyalty League is formed to promote the abolition of slavery and the passage of the Thirteenth Amendment.	Abraham Lincoln issues Emancipation Proclamation; Union wins three-day battle at Gettysburg.	French capture Mexico City and proclaim Archduke Maximilian of Austria emperor of Mexico.
1864	Congress sets maximum wage for women government clerks at $600 per year; men earn $1800 per year.	Union General William T. Sherman marches to Atlanta and occupies Savannah.	First International Workingmen's Association is founded by Karl Marx.
1865	Clara Barton begins four years of work finding missing soldiers; she locates 22,000 men and indentifies nearly 15,000 who died at the Confederate prison camp at Andersonville.	Abraham Lincoln is assassinated and Vice President Andrew Johnson becomes president.	In South Africa, the Boers (descendants of Dutch settlers) of the Orange Free State and Basutos declare war on each other.
1866	American Equal Rights Association is formed at the 11th National Woman's Rights Convention; the ERA seeks the franchise for women and African Americans.	Fourteenth Amendment to the U.S. Constitution, which prohibits voting discrimination against African-American males, is ratified.	The sultan of Turkey grants the right of primogeniture (inheritance passes intact to eldest son) to Ismail, Khedive of Egypt.
1867	Kansas ballot question on woman's suffrage is defeated.	Russia sells Alaska to U.S. for $7.2 million.	Giuseppe Garibaldi's March on Rome ends with his defeat by French and papal forces at Mentana.
1868	Federal women's suffrage amendment is introduced in Congress by Senator S.C. Pomeroy of Kansas	President Andrew Johnson is impeached for violating the Tenure of Office Act, but is acquitted by the Senate.	The last shogun of Japan, Kekei, abdicates and the Meiji Dynasty is restored to power.
1869	National Woman Suffrage Association (NWSA) is formed by Susan B. Anthony and Elizabeth Cady Stanton.	National Prohibition Party is formed in Chicago.	Red River Rebellion begins in Canada.

Date	Women's History	United States History	World History
1870	Victoria C. Woodhull runs for president endorsing Pantarchy—a world of female sexual freedom, common property, and children raised in common.	Standard Oil is founded by John D. Rockefeller.	After a revolt in Paris, the French Third Republic is proclaimed.
1871	Massachusetts and Alabama become the first states to outlaw wife beating.	Treaty of Washington settles disputes between U.S. and Great Britain.	France cedes Alsace-Lorraine to Germany and pays 5-billion-franc indemnity to end Franco-Prussian War.
1872	Susan B. Anthony is found guilty of voting in Rochester, New York; she never serves any jail time.	U.S. General Amnesty Act pardons most ex-Confederates.	Three Emperors League comprising Germany, Russia, and Austria-Hungary is formed in Berlin.
1873	Comstock Act bans distribution through the mail of pornography and abortion/contraceptive information and devices.	Financial panic hits New York.	Republic proclaimed in Spain.
1874	Women's Christian Temperance Union (WCTU) is founded.	First zoo in U.S. opens in Philadelphia.	Fiji Islands become British possession.
1875	Smith and Wellesley Colleges are founded.	William Marcy "Boss" Tweed escapes from jail and flees to Cuba.	Political unrest begins in Bosnia and Herzegovina against Turkish rule.
1876	Susan B. Anthony and Matilda Joslyn Gage disrupt Centennial celebration at Independence Hall in Philadelphia by delivering a "Declaration of Rights for Women" to the vice president.	General George Custer is massacred with his troops at the Battle of Little Big Horn in Montana.	Korea becomes independent nation.
1877	The American Committee for the Prevention of Legalizing Prostitution is founded.	Electoral Commission decides 1876 presidential election in favor of Republican Rutherford B. Hayes, even though Democrat Samuel Tilden won a majority of the popular vote.	Queen Victoria is proclaimed empress of India.

Date	Women's History	United States History	World History
1878	Federal women's suffrage amendment is introduced in Congress by Senator A.A. Sargent of California.	District of Columbia's government is reorganized to a presidential commission in which the residents have no vote.	Treaty of Berlin temporarily settles the Eastern Question—the fate of Ottoman Turkey.
1879	Belva Ann Bennett Lockwood becomes the first woman attorney to practice before the U.S. Supreme Court.	Federal treasury reinstitutes specie payments after 18-year suspension.	The British Zulu War comes to an end.
1880	Women's National Indian Association is founded under the leadership of Mary Bonney and Amelia Quinton.	U.S. Supreme Court rules that African Americans cannot be excluded from juries.	Chile declares war on Bolivia and Peru.
1881	The American Association of University Women (AAUW), which seeks equal educational opportunity for women, is founded	President James Garfield is assassinated; Chester Arthur becomes president.	In South Africa, British recognize independent Transvaal Republic in the Treaty of Pretoria.
1882	The New Century Guild for Working Women offers low-cost evening courses to improve skills of working women.	U.S. bans Chinese immigrants for 10 years.	Hague Convention sets a three-mile limit for territorial waters.
1883	Women's Relief Corp becomes an auxillary to the Grand Army of the Republic.	The Northern Pacific Railroad line is completed.	The last male member of the French royal house of Bourbon, the Comte de Chambord, dies.
1884	Belva Ann Bennett Lockwood becomes the first woman to receive votes in a presidential election with 4,000 votes from six different states.	Mugwumps, members of an independent faction of the Republican Party, walk out of the Republican National Convention when James Blaine is nominated for president.	Berlin Conference on African Affairs opens with representatives from 14 nations in attendance.

Date	Women's History	United States History	World History
1885	Bryn Mawr College for women is founded under the leadership of Martha Carey Thomas.	Fencing of public lands in the West is prohibited.	Belgium, Germany, and Great Britain extend their territorial control in Africa.
1886	*Chicago Law Times* is founded by Catherine Waite.	The American Federation of Labor (AFL) is founded.	Bonaparte and Orleans families are banished from France.
1887	Utah repeals woman suffrage.	Dawes Severalty Act replaces reservation system with parcels given to individual Native Americans.	Queen Victoria celebrates her Golden Jubilee.
1888	National Council of Women—a clearinghouse for women's organizations—is founded.	The first secret ballot is used in Louisville, Kentucky.	Jack the Ripper murders six women in London.
1889	Jane Addams and Ellen Gates Starr found Hull House in Chicago.	Oklahoma is opened to non-Indian settlers.	Cecil Rhodes's British South Africa Company is granted a royal charter.
1890	Wyoming enters the Union becoming the first state to grant women full franchise since New Jersey (1776-1807).	Samoan Treaty gives joint control of Somoa to Germany, Great Britain, and the U.S.	Swiss government adopts social insurance for its citizens.
1891	Josephine Shaw Lowell founds New York Consumer League.	A mob in Valparaiso, Chile, attacks American sailors from the USS *Baltimore*; war is narrowly adverted.	The Triple Alliance of Germany, Austria, and Italy is renewed for 12 years.
1892	Susan B. Anthony, Elizabeth Cady Stanton, Ida Hauper, and Matilda Gage compile the first four volumes of the six-volume *A History of Woman Suffrage.*	Iron and steel workers strike over wages and working conditions.	Belgian forces defeat Arab slave traders in the upper Congo region of central Africa.
1893	Women win the vote in Colorado.	Hawaii is annexed and then released by the U.S.	In Great Britain, the second Irish Home Rule Bill is passed by the House of Commons but rejected by the House of Lords.

Date	Women's History	United States History	World History
1894		Coxey's Army of the unemployed marches from Massilon, Ohio, to Washington, D.C.	Chinese defeated at Port Arthur by Korean and Japanese troops.
1895	National Federation of Afro-American Women—the forerunner of the National Association of Colored Women—is founded by Josphine St. Pierre Ruffin.	U.S. is almost drawn into war with Great Britain over a border dispute between British Guiana and Venezuela.	Rhodesia is formed from British South Africa Company territory south of Zambezi River.
1896	Utah and Idaho enter Union with woman suffrage.	U.S. Supreme Court upholds the separate-but-equal doctrine in *Plessy v. Ferguson.*	Armenians are massacred in the Turkish city of Constantinople (Istanbul).
1897	"Mother Jones" organizes mine workers in West Virginia.	The first shipment of Klondike gold reaches San Francisco.	Peace of Constantinople settles war between Turkey and Greece over Crete.
1898	Charlotte Perkins Gilman publishes *Women and Economics.*	In Treaty of Paris ending Spanish-American War, Spain cedes Cuba, Puerto Rico, Guam, and Philippines to U.S. for $20 million.	Emile Zola is imprisoned for his open letter (*J'Accuse*) to the French president on the Dreyfus Affair.
1899	Women Lawyers Club is founded in New York City to promote women as lawyers.	Philippines demand independence from U.S.	Dreyfus Affair comes to an end when French president pardons Alfred Dreyfus.
1900	The International Ladies' Garment Workers Union (ILGWU) is founded to improve working conditions and pay of textile workers.	U.S. population is 76 million at the start of the new century.	Beginning of Boxer Rebellion against European influence in China.
1901	Carrie Nation leads a temperance army on a rampage in Topeka, Kansas.	President William McKinley is assassinated; Vice President Theodore Roosevelt becomes president.	The First Nobel Peace Prize is awarded to Henri Dunant and Frederic Passy.

Date	Women's History	United States History	World History
1902	Martha Washington becomes the first woman on a postage stamp.	U.S. gains control over Panama Canal.	National bankruptcy declared by Portugal.
1903	The Women's Trade Union League is founded under the leadership of Mary Morton Kehew.	U.S. Marines land in Panama to support its independence from Colombia.	The Russian Social Democratic Party splits between the Mensheviks and the Bolsheviks at the London Congress.
1904	Ida Husted Harper argues for women's suffrage to offset the "negro" influence.	American troops end occupation of Cuba.	Russo-Japanese War begins.
1905	International Workers of the World is founded and actively seeks women as members.	Despite efforts to limit immigration, over one million enter the U.S.	Norwegian Parliament decides to separate from Sweden and elects Prince Charles of Denmark to be King Haakon VII of Norway.
1906	The Pure Food and Drug Act is passed in large measure through the efforts of women.	U.S. troops occupy Cuba after failed Liberal revolt.	All India Moslem League founded by Aga Khan.
1907		J.P. Morgan stops bank panic by importing $100 million in gold from Europe.	Open Door Policy on access to China is adopted by France and Japan.
1908	The "Brandeis Brief" convinces the U.S. Supreme Court to uphold maximum hours legislation in the case of *Muller v. Oregon.*	First Model T (Tin Lizzie) rolls off an assembly line in Detroit.	Under Czar Ferdinand I, Bulgaria declares its independence from Ottoman Turkey.
1909	New York City police break-up a lecture being given by self-professed anarchist Emma Goldman.	Violence erupts at the Pressed Steel Car Company during a strike; five strikers are killed.	Civil war in Honduras.
1910	Mann Act, an attempt to end the white slave trade in immigrants, prohibits the interstate transport of women for immoral purposes.	Powerful Speaker of the House "Uncle" Joe Cannon is stripped of the power to appoint committee members.	China abolishes slavery.

Date	Women's History	United States History	World History
1911	California grants women's suffrage in close (3,587 votes) election.	U.S. signs commercial treaties with Japan.	Winston Churchill is appointed First Lord of the British Admiralty.
1912	Women mill workers in Lawrence, Massachusetts, strike over pay and working conditions.	Arizona and New Mexico enter the Union.	Turkey closes Dardanelles to shipping.
1913	Alice Paul and Lucy Burns found the Congressional Union to lobby for passage of a federal suffrage amendment; Paul also founds the National Woman's Party.	Sixteenth Amendment to the U.S. Constitution is ratified establishing a federal income tax.	First and Second Balkan Wars show instability of the region and foreshadow the outbreak of World War I.
1914	Montana and Nevada adopt woman suffrage.	U.S. Marines are detained in Mexico when they stop for supplies; the incident leads to the resignation of Mexican President Victoriano Huerta.	World War I begins with assassination of Austrian Archduke Francis Ferdinand in Sarajevo.
1915	Women's Peace Party is founded by Jane Addams and Carrie Chapman Catt.	Cornell University German instructor Erich Muenter blows up the reception room of the U.S. Senate, shoots J. Pierpont Morgan, Jr., and then commits suicide.	Germany sinks the ocean liner *Lusitania*.
1916	Jeannette Rankin (R-MT) is the first women elected to the U.S. House of Representatives.	Pancho Villa, Mexican revolutionary general, crosses U.S. border and raids Columbus, New Mexico.	Irish Easter Rebellion against British rule is led by Sinn Fein.
1917	New York adopts woman suffrage	Literacy Test for U.S. citizenship is passed over President Woodrow Wilson's veto.	French execute Mata Hari as a German spy; Russian Revolution begins.
1918	Michigan, Oklahoma, and South Dakota adopt woman suffrage	Eugene V. Debs, leader of the Socialist Party, is sentenced to a 10-year prison term for violating the espionage and sedition law.	Armistice ending World War I is signed by the Allies and Germany.

Date	Women's History	United States History	World History
1919	League of Women Voters is founded at the National Victory Convention of the National American Woman Suffrage Association (NAWSA) in Chicago.	Eighteenth Amendment to the U.S. Constitution—prohibiting the sale and consumption of alcohol—is ratified	In the Russian Civil War, the Red Army takes Ufa, marking the beginning of the end for the pro-Czarist White forces.
1920	Nineteenth Amendment, the wording of which was drafted by Susan B. Anthony in 1878, is ratified, thereby granting women the vote.	U.S. Senate votes against joining the League of Nations.	The International Court of Justice is established in The Hague, Netherlands.
1921	Planned Parenthood Federation of America is founded to distribute birth control information and services.	President Warren G. Harding commutes Eugene Debs' 10-year prison sentence.	Reza Khan leads coup d'etat in Teheran, Iran.
1922	Rebecca Latimer Felton becomes the first woman to serve in the U.S. Senate; her term lasts only one day.	A revitalized Ku Klux Klan gains political strength in the South and Midwest.	U.S.S.R. is officially formed.
1923	U.S. Supreme Court strikes down minimum wage law for women in *Adkins v. Children's Hospital*.	Teapot Dome Oil scandal breaks in Washington.	Adolf Hitler's Beer Hall Putsch fails to win him power in Germany.
1924	Miriam A. (Ma) Ferguson is elected governor of Texas.	J. Edgar Hoover is appointed director of the Bureau of Investigation, renamed the Federal Bureau of Investigation in 1935.	Fascist Benito Mussolini wins Italian elections.
1925	Nellie Tayloe Ross becomes governor of Montana.	John Scopes goes on trial in Tennessee for teaching evolution in violation of state law.	Japan grants universal suffrage to men.
1926	Federal Industrial Institute for Women—the first federal prison for women—is opened in West Virginia with Dr. Mary B. Harris as director.	President Calvin Coolidge pledges non-intervention in dispute between the Mexican government and Church.	Turkey enacts reforms that end polygamy and modernize female attire.

Date	Women's History	United States History	World History
1927	Women's groups unite in protest over restrictive immigration policies.	Massachusetts executes the anarchists Nicola Sacco and Bartolomeo Vanzetti for murder.	German economy collapses.
1928	Mabel Willebrandt becomes the first woman to chair a committee of the Republican National Committee.	More Marines are sent to Nicaragua to fight guerillas.	Kellogg-Briand Pact outlawing war is signed by 65 nations.
1929	Pauline Sabin establishes the Women's Organization for National Prohibition Reform.	Albert B. Fall, secretary of the interior in the Harding administration, is convicted of accepting bribes in the Teapot Dome scandal.	Unrest between Arabs and Jews in Palestine over Jewish use of the Wailing Wall.
1930	The Association of Southern Women for the Prevention of Lynching is formed by Jesse Daniel Ames.	Protectionist Smoot-Hawley tariff is enacted with President Herbert Hoover's support.	Revolutions in Brazil and Argentina bring new governments.
1931	Jane Addams becomes the first woman to win the Nobel Peace Prize for her dedication to peace and social justice.	President Herbert Hoover calls for a one-year moratorium on payment of European reparations and war debts to the U.S.	Austrian Credit-Anstalt collapses and causes a financial crisis in Central Europe.
1932	Hattie Wyatt Caraway (D-AR) becomes the first woman elected to serve in the U.S. Senate.	Troops under General Douglas MacArthur are summoned to disperse ex-serviceman who are rallying in Washington for payment of their military bonuses.	Mohandas Gandhi is arrested as Indian Congress is declared illegal by British.
1933	Frances Perkins is appointed secretary of labor by President Franklin D. Roosevelt, becoming the first woman to serve in the Cabinet.	U.S. Congress passes independence bill for Philippines.	Adolf Hitler is granted dictatorial powers in Germany by the passage of the Enabling Law.
1934	Florence Ellinwood Allen becomes the first woman appointed to the federal court (6th District Court of Appeals).	Congress grants President Franklin Roosevelt the power to reduce tariffs.	Soviet Union is admitted to the League of Nations.

Date	Women's History	United States History	World History
1935	National Council of Negro Women is founded by activist Mary McLeod Bethune.	Political demagogue Huey Long is assassinated by Dr. Carl Weiss in the Louisiana Capitol Building.	Italy invades Abyssinia (Ethiopia) despite League of Nation's condemnation and sanctions.
1936	Eleanor Roosevelt begins her "My Day" column.	Bruno Richard Hauptmann is convicted of kidnapping and killing Charles Lindbergh's baby.	German troops occupy the Rhineland; Spanish Civil War begins.
1937	U.S. Supreme Court upholds minimum wage law for women.	Violence erupts at Republic Steel strike in Chicago; 4 killed and 84 injured.	British royal commission on Palestine recommends the establisment of separate Arab and Jewish states.
1938	The Pure Food and Drug Act of 1906 is strengthened with the passage of the Wheeler-Lea Act.	The House Un-American Activities Committee is formed and chaired by Martin Dies (D-TX).	Japan continues its aggression in China.
1939	Dorothy Schiff becomes the first woman newspaper publisher in New York when she gains controlling interest in the *New York Post*.	Sitdown strikes are ruled illegal by the U.S. Supreme Court.	Great Britain, France, and the U.S. recognize General Francisco Franco's government in Spain.
1940	Republican Party becomes the first major party to endorse the Equal Rights Amendment.	President Franklin D. Roosevelt is re-elected to an unprecedented third term.	The German bombings of London ("the Blitz") begin; France falls to the Germans.
1941	Jeanette Rankin is the only member of Congress to vote against U.S. entry into World War II.	U.S. Naval base at Pearl Harbor, Hawaii, is attacked by Japan; U.S. declares war the next day (December 8).	Germany invades Soviet Union.
1942	Major Oveta Culp Hobby is appointed director of the newly formed Women's Army Corps.	Office of Price Administration freezes rents and begins rationing of staples like sugar, coffee, and gasoline.	American and Philippine prisoners of war are led on a forced march in which many die (Bataan Death March).
1943	Women on the home front adopt the motto "Use it up, Wear it out, Make it do, or Do without" in regard to rationing and shortages.	War Relations Board orders government takeover of coal mines when 500,000 miners strike.	Italy surrenders unconditionally to Allies.

Date	Women's History	United States History	World History
1944	Clare Boothe Luce is the keynote speaker at the Republican National Convention.	Sky-rocketing inflation (30%) raises the cost of living.	Allies land in Normandy, France, on D-Day (June 6).
1945	Eleanor Roosevelt is appointed delegate to the United Nations.	U.S. drops atomic bomb on Hiroshima and Nagasaki; Japan surrenders five days later.	Hitler commits suicide (April 30) and one week later the war ends in Europe (V.E. Day).
1946	Emily Greene Blatch receives the Nobel Peace Prize for her efforts on behalf of international peace.	New York is made the permanent home for the United Nations	Nuremberg trials come to an end with 12 sentenced to death, 2 to life in prison, and 2 acquitted.
1947	The Army-Navy Nurse Act enables the permanent commissioning of military nurses.	Taft-Hartley Act restricting the power of labor unions is passed over President Harry Truman's veto.	India wins its independence from Great Britain and is divided into India and Pakistan.
1948	Pauline Frederick becomes the first woman broadcaster to cover a national political convention.	Marshall Plan—$17 billion in aid for Europe—is passed by Congress.	Indian leader Mohandas Gandhi is assassinated.
1949	Eugenie Moore Anderson is appointed as the first female ambassador (Denmark).	North Atlantic Treaty Organization (NATO) is founded under U.S. leadership.	Mao Tse-tung leads a successful communist revolution in China.
1950	Maine Senator Margaret Chase Smith delivers "Declaration of Conscience" Speech in Senate denouncing Wisconsin Senator Joseph McCarthy and his tactics.	Alger Hiss is sentenced for perjury.	North Korea invades South Korea.
1951	Elizabeth Gurly Flynn is convicted of sedition under the Smith Act.	Julius and Ethel Rosenberg are sentenced to death for espionage.	Conservatives regain control of the British Parliament and Winston Churchill again becomes prime minister.
1952	Charlotta Bass becomes the first African-American woman to run for vice president on a party's ticket (Progressive Party).	Dwight D. Eisenhower resigns as supreme commander in Europe and is elected president.	Great Britain produces an atomic bomb.

Date	Women's History	United States History	World History
1953	Dr. Fae Margaret Adams becomes first woman doctor to receive a regular commission in the U.S. Army.	Department of Health, Education and Welfare is created.	Marshal Josip Tito is elected president of Yugoslavia under the country's new constitution.
1954	Eleanor Roosevelt and Lorena Hickok write *Ladies of Courage*, a tribute to women in American politics.	U.S. Supreme Court rules that segregated public schools are unconstitutional in *Brown v. Board of Education of Topeka, Kansas.*	Gamal Abdel Nasser seizes power in Egypt.
1955	Rosa Parks refuses to give up her seat on a Montgomery, Alabama, bus to a white passenger.	A.F.L. and C.I.O. labor unions merge under the leadership of George Meany.	The Vienna Treaty restores Austria's independence.
1956	Women constitute 32.3% of the total workforce.	Victor Riesel, labor columnist, is blinded by acid thrown by a gangster.	Soviet troops crush unrest in Hungary.
1957	Anne W. Wheaton becomes the first woman presidential spokesperson.	President Dwight Eisenhower issues "Eisenhower Doctrine" pledging protection of the Middle East from communist aggression and expansion.	The Rome Treaty is signed by France, Germany, Italy, Belgium, Holland, and Luxembourg, marking the beginning of the Common Market.
1958	Mildred Edie Brady—consumer activist—becomes senior editor of *Consumer Reports.*	Alaska becomes the 49th state in the Union.	Syria and Egypt form the United Arab Republic under the leadership of Gamal Abdel Nasser.
1959	Hawaii passes a law that requires women to take the last name of their husbands.	Hawaii becomes the 50th state in the Union	Fidel Castro successfully overthrows Cuban President Fulgencio Batista.
1960	Esther Peterson heads a coalition to prevent the Democratic Party platform from endorsing the ERA.	U-2 pilot Gary Powers is shot down over the U.S.S.R. and captured.	Adolf Eichmann, fomer chief of the Nazi Gestapo, is arrested and sent to Israel to stand trail.
1961	President John F. Kennedy issues Executive Order 10980, which establishes the Presidential Commission on the Status of Women.	American-supported Bay of Pigs invasion of Cuba is a failure.	Berlin Wall is constructed across the former German capital by the Soviets.

Date	Women's History	United States History	World History
1962	Sherri Finkbine, popular host of the "Romper Room" children's TV show, goes to Sweden to have a theraputic abortion after discovering she has taken thalidomide during her pregnancy.	Cuban Missile crisis heats up the Cold War.	Pope John XXIII opens the 21st Ecumenical Council (Vatican II).
1963	Equal Pay Act prohibits discrimination in compensation.	President John F. Kennedy is assassinated by Lee Harvey Oswald; Vice President Lyndon B. Johnson becomes president.	Buddhist priests and nuns in South Vietnam immolate themselves to protest the American-backed Diem regime.
1964	Title VII of the Civil Rights Act outlaws sexual discrimination.	Twenty-fourth Amendment to the U.S. Constitution—barring poll taxes—is ratified	China announces it has the atomic bomb.
1965	U.S. Supreme Court in *Griswold v. Connecticut* strikes down law banning the distribution of contraceptives to married couples.	25,000 march in civil rights demonstration in Selma, Alabama.	Rhodesia declares independence from Great Britain.
1966	Third National Conference of State Commissions on the Status of Women ends with call to form the National Organization for Women (NOW).	Supreme Court limits police interrogation powers in *Miranda v. Arizona*.	Mao Tse-tung launches the Cultural Revolution in China.
1967	Phyllis Schlafly, an anti-feminist activist, begins publication of *The Phyllis Schlafly Report*.	Massive anti-Vietnam War demonstrations in Washington, D.C.	Six-Day War between Israel and Arab nations.
1968	Women's Equity Action League is founded to protest pro-abortion stand of NOW and to take more conservative approaches to achieving women's equality.	Civil rights leader Martin Luther King, Jr., is assassinated in Memphis.	Soviet Union invades Czechoslovakia.
1969	First no-fault divorce legislation is enacted in California.	The Chicago Seven are indicted for violation of the anti-riot clause of the Civil Rights Act.	Yassir Arafat is elected chairman of the Palestine Liberation Organization (PLO); first moon landing.

Date	Women's History	United States History	World History
1970	NOW's Legal Defense and Education Fund is incorporated.	Four student protesters of the Vietnam War are killed by National Guardsmen at Kent State University (Ohio).	Civil war ends in Nigeria.
1971	U.S. Supreme Court in *Reed v. Reed* uses the equal protection clause of the Fourteenth Amendment for the first time to strike down a gender-based classification.	Ratification of the Twenty-sixth Amendment to the U.S. Constitution, which lowers the voting age to 18.	Women are granted the right to vote in Switzerland.
1972	Title IX of the Education Amendments eliminates discrimination in many aspects of higher education.	Democratic vice presidential candidate, Senator Thomas Eagleton of Missouri resigns from the party's presidential ticket when it is learned he had a history of mental depression.	Arab terrorists take nine hostages and kill two Israeli athletes during Munich Olympics; the hostages are killed in a shoot-out with West German police and soldiers.
1973	U.S. Supreme Court overturns anti-abortion laws with its decision in *Roe v. Wade.*	Watergate scandal deepens and begins to threaten Richard Nixon's presidency.	Ireland, Great Britain, and Denmark become full members of the European Economic Community.
1974	Equal Credit Opportunity Act prohibits discrimination on the basis of sex and marital status.	Richard Nixon resigns presidency under threat of impeachment; Gerald Ford becomes president.	Constantine Caramanlis returns from exile to resume premiership of Greece after military government resigns.
1975	United Nations declares 1976-1985 the "Decade for Women."	Vietnam War comes to an end.	Suez Canal reopens after 8 years of being closed.
1976	U.S. Supreme Court in *GE v. Gilbert* rules that employers can exclude pregnancy from sick and accident policies without violating sex discrimination.	Patty Hearst, former hostage of the Symbionese Liberation Army, is found guilty of armed robbery.	Israeli commandos successfully raid the Entebbe Airport in Uganda to free 105 hostages being held by pro-Palestinian hijackers.
1977	National Woman's Conference meets in Houston as part of the United Nation's International Woman's Year.	Trans-Alaskan oil pipeline opens.	Adolfo Suarez is victorious in Spain's first democratic elections in 41 years.

Date	Women's History	United States History	World History
1978	Pregnancy Discrimination Act prohibits discrimination on the basis of pregnancy, child birth, or related medical condition.	Proposition 13 is adopted by California voters and begins the taxpayers' revolt.	John Paul II, a Pole, becomes the first non-Italian in 455 years to be elected pope.
1979	U.S. Supreme Court strikes down a Pennsylvania law requiring doctors to choose the abortion technique most likely to enable the fetus to live in *Caulloti v. Franklin.*	U.S. embassy in Iran is seized by supporters of the Ayatollah Khomeini, who hold members of the embassy staff hostage.	Conservative Party leader Margaret Thatcher becomes the first woman prime minister of Great Britain.
1980	Mary Crisp, co-chair of the Republican National Convention, withdraws because of party's opposition to the ERA.	Eight members of Congress are indicted in an FBI investigation dubbed Abscam.	Polish government recognizes Solidarity labor union under the leadership of Lech Walesa.
1981	Sandra Day O'Connor becomes the first woman appointed to the U.S. Supreme Court.	First space shuttle flight.	President Anwar Sadat is murdered by Egyptian military officers.
1982	Proposed Equal Rights Amendment (ERA) ratification time expires; the amendment is three states short of adoption.	Nearly 1 million anti-nuke demonstrators rally in New York City.	Argentina and Great Britain go to war over the Falkland Islands.
1983	Proposed anti-abortion amendment to the U. S. Constitution (the Hatch Amendment) is defeated in the Senate.	216 Marines are killed in a Beirut bombing.	Benigno Aquino, Philippine President Ferdinand Marcos's chief rival, is assassinated at the Manilla airport.
1984	Geraldine Ferraro (D-NY) becomes the first woman vice presidential candidate of either major party.	U.S. Commission on Civil Rights votes to discontinue use of quotas.	Indian Army crushes Sikh uprising in Punjab region.
1985	Ellen Malcolm founds EMILY's List PAC for Democratic, pro-choice women.	John Walker and Jonathon Jay Pollard are arrested for spying—Walker for the Russians and Pollard for the Israelis.	Racial violence erupts in South Africa.

Date	Women's History	United States History	World History
1986	For the first time, U.S. Supreme Court rules in *Meritor Savings Bank v. Vinson* that sexual harassment is a form of sex discrimination prohibited by Title VII of the Civil Rights Act of 1964.	U.S. military bombs Libyan targets.	Jean-Claude Duvalier, self-proclaimed president for life, flees Haiti.
1987	Fund for Feminist Majority is founded by Eleanor Smeal.	The Dow falls 508 points to 1738.74 on "Black Friday."	Mikhail Gorbachev implements glasnost and perestroika reforms in Soviet Union.
1988	Under Title X of the Public Health Service Act, the Reagan administration issues a "gag rule" that prohibits abortion counseling in clinics that receive federal funds.	Four indicted in the Reagan administration's Iran-Contra scandal.	Benazir Bhutto of Pakistan becomes the first woman to head a Muslim nation.
1989	Associate Justice Sandra Day O'Connor provides the crucial fifth vote upholding many abortion restrictions in *Webster v. Reproductive Health Services.*	U.S. invades Panama and arrests Panamanian dictator Manuel Noriega.	Berlin Wall comes down.
1990	U.S. Supreme Court upholds parent notification law by a 6-3 vote in *Ohio v. Akron Center for Reproductive Health.*	Savings and Loan crisis deepens with the allegations against the "Keating Five" senators.	Iraqi army invades Kuwait.
1991	Senate Confirmation Hearings of Supreme Court nominee Clarence Thomas become controversial when Anita Hill, a former subordinate of Thomas's at the EEOC, charges that she was sexually harassed by Thomas.	U.S. leads Gulf War coalition against Iraq under the command of Chief of Staff General Colin Powell and General Norman Schwarzkopf.	The U.S.S.R. offically comes to an end when Boris Yeltsin assumes the presidency of Russia.

Date	Women's History	United States History	World History
1992	"Year of the Woman" is proclaimed when congressional elections return the largest number of women ever elected to Congress.	The acquittal of the Los Angeles police officers charged with beating Rodney King leads to rioting in Los Angeles.	War rages in Bosnia-Herzegovina.
1993	Janet Reno becomes the first woman attorney general after the failed nominations of Kimba Wood and Zoe Baird.	A terrorist bomb explodes at the World Trade Center in New York City killing six; Muslim fundamentalists are suspected.	Israel and the PLO sign a treaty that would establish Palestinian self-rule.
1994	Freedom to Access of Clinic Entrances Act prohibits obstruction of abortion clinics by protestors.	For the first time in 40 years, Congress comes under Republican control in the November elections.	Nelson Mandela, former political prisoner, is elected the first black president of South Africa.
1995	Senator Bob Packwood (R-OR) resigns under charges of sexual harassment.	A budget dispute between Democratic President Bill Clinton and the Republican-controlled Congress shuts down the government for 21 days.	India continues economic reforms by privatizing previously government-owned companies.
1996	U.S. Supreme Court rules in *U.S. v. Virginia* that the Virginia Military Institute must admit women.	The Unabomber, Theodore Kaczynski, is arrested after 16 bombs and 17 years.	An IRA bomb explodes near South Quays Station, London, ending a 17-month cease-fire.
1997	Madeleine Albright becomes the first woman secretary of state.	Oklahoma City bombing trials of Timothy McVeigh and Terry Nichols end in convictions.	Hong Kong is returned to China.
1998	President Bill Clinton, facing an investigation into the charge that he committed perjury and obstructed justice in the Paula Jones sexual harassment suit, admits to an "inappropriate relationship" with White House intern Monica Lewinsky.	First balanced budget in over 30 years is submitted to Congress.	Economic crisis rocks Asian economies.

Index

by Kay Banning

Page references to *Encyclopedia* entries are in **bold face.**

Index

Adkins, Bertha, **8**
Adkins v. Children's Hospital (1923), **8**, 147
Adolescent Family Life Act (1981), **8**
Adoption, 9
Advisory Committee on Trade and Policy Negations, 86
Advisory Committee on Women in the Service, 108
Advisory Council on the Democracy, 13
AERA (American Equal Rights Association), xv
AFDC. *See* Aid to Families with Dependent Children (AFDC)
Affirmative action, **9**
  antifeminism and, 15
  changes in, 10–11
  Congressional Caucus for Women's Issues and Women's Policy, Inc., 43
  definition of, 9
  Democratic National Committee and, 66
  Executive Order 11375 and, 71
  glass ceiling and, 96
  Ella Grasso and, 98
  Sheila Lee and, 126
  The New York Times and, 24
  origins of, 9
  sex discrimination and, 208, 209
  Supreme Court decisions and, 9–10, 37
  Title VII of the Civil Rights Act of 1964 and, 9, 37
Afghanistan, 199
AFL (American Federation of Labor), 126, 158
Africa, 142
African Americans
  abortion and, 5
  Jane Addams and, 8
  affirmative action and, 9
  Marian Anderson's concert and, 14
  Association of Southern Women for the Prevention of Lynching and, 16
  Corrine Boggs and, 22
  Sophonisba Breckinridge and, 25
  California Eagle and, 18
  Shirley Chisholm and, 36
  Frances Cleveland and, 39
  disenfranchisement of, xviii
  education and, 19, 48
  Equal Division Rule and, 66
  Equal Rights Association and, 69
  feminism and, 80–81
  Fifteenth Amendment and, 193
  glass ceiling and, 96
  health care and, 154
  Dorothy Height and, 108
  Barbara Jordan and, 119
  liberalism and, 128, 129
  Helen Mankin and, 135
  men's suffrage and, 69, 218
  Montana State Federation of Negro Women's Clubs and, 149
  Carol Moseley-Braun and, 150
  National Welfare Rights Organization and, 239
  poverty and, 180, 181, 214
  Roosevelt administration and, 19
  Eleanor Roosevelt and, 198
  suffrage and, 218
  Sojourner Truth and, 226
  Ida B. Wells and, 239
  Ellen Wilson and, 242
  women in appointive positions and, xxvi
  women's liberation movement and, 246
  women's rights movement and, 38
Age Discrimination Act of 1975, 38
Aging. *See* Elderly
Agnew, Spiro T., 19, 85, 189
Agriculture, 213
Agriculture Committee, 32, 36, 65, 108, 124, 216
Agriculture Department, 132, 179, 181, 236
Ahmed, Fukhruddin Ali, 30
Aid to Dependent Children (ADC), 11, 237
Aid to Families with Dependent Children (AFDC), **11**
  child support and, 238
  contraception and, 192
  improvements in, 78
  poverty and, 181
  purpose of, 11
  Franklin Roosevelt and, 237
  welfare reform and, 57, 237
  welfare rights movement and, 239
Aid to the Blind, 237
AIDS, 141, 169, 185
Ain't I a Woman Network/PAC, 299
"Ain't I a Woman" (Truth), 226, 246, 248, 257
Air Force Personnel Council, 110
AJLI (Association of Junior Leagues International), 285
Akron v. Akron Center for Reproductive Health (1983), **11**, 224
ALA Social Responsibilities Round Table Feminist Task Force, 285
Alabama, 10, 58–59, 166, 174, 207
Alabama Federation of Women's Clubs, 98
Alabama Solution, 299
Alaska, 33
Albright, Madeleine, xxiv, xxvii, **12**, 54
Alcatraz Island, 135
Alcohol abuse, 189
Alcott, Bronson, 88, 157
Alexander, Charles, 97
Alexander v. Yale University (1980), **12**
Alice Doesn't Day Strike (October 29, 1975), **12**
Alice Doesn't Live Here Anymore, 12
Alimony, 135, 166, 208, 218
All in the Family, 137
All Volunteer Force, 145
Allen, Emanuel, 122
Allen, Florence Ellinwood, **12**
Allen, James B., 13
Allen, Maryon Pittman, **13**
Alliance for Displaced Homemakers, 210, 215
Alpha Suffrage Club, 81
Alpha Suffrage Club of Chicago, 239
Always Causing Legal Unrest (ACLU), 285
AMA (American Medical Association), 106, 210
AMA (American Missionary Association), 61
Amalgamated Clothing and Textile Workers' Union, 115
American Anti-Slavery Society, xv, 69, 86, 217
American Association of University Women (AAUW), xxii, **13**, 62, 121, 173, 222, 285
American Bemberg Plant, 64
American Birth Control League, **13**, 203, 231
American Civil Liberties Union (ACLU), 8, 85, 95, 152, 188, 192–93, 248–49
American Enterprise Institute, 32, 123
American Equal Rights Association (AERA), xv
American Farm Bureau, 68
American Federation of Labor (AFL), 126, 158
American Glazstoff Rayon Plant, 64
American Independent Party, 138
The American Journal of Sociology, 216
American Ladies Magazine, 97, 101
American Medical Association (AMA), 106, 210
American Missionary Association (AMA), 61
American Museum of Natural History, 140
American Nurses' Association, Inc. (ANA-PAC), 299
American Political Science Association, 68
American Red Cross, 18, 56
American Society of Biological Chemists, 118
American Student Union, 251
American Unitarian Association, 59
American Woman Suffrage Association (AWSA), **13**
  Myra Colby Bradwell and, 24
  Equal Rights Association and, 69, 156
  founding of, 13, 219
  Matilda Gage and, 90
  Lucretia Mott and, 150
  National American Woman Suffrage Association and, 13, 14–15, 20, 153, 161
  National League of Women Voters and, 155
  Lucy Stone and, xv, 13, 217, 232
  Woman's Journal and, 243
American Women: Report of the President's Commission on the Status of Women, 140, 182
Americans for Democratic Action, 148
Americans for Indian Opportunity, 102
Americans United for Life, 285
Ames, Jessie Daniel, **13**, 16
ANA-PAC (American Nurses' Association, Inc.), 299
Anderson, Eugenie Moore, **14**
Anderson, Marian, **14**
Andrews, Elizabeth Bullock, **14**
Andrews, George W., 14
Annual Economic Conference, 154
Anthony, Susan Brownell, **14**
  abolition and, xiv, 38
  accomplishments of, 14–15
  Harriot Blatch and, 21
  Carrie Chapman Catt and, 31
  Daughters of Temperance and, 50
  Declaration of the Rights of Women and, 51

Flynn, Elizabeth Gurley, 42, **85**, 126
FMLA. *See* Family and Medical Leave Act
Focus 2020, 299
Focus on the Family, 45, 182
Folson, Oscar, 39
Fonda, Jane, **85**
Food and Drug Administration (FDA), 141, 191, 200, 222
Food and drug safety, 108
Food Consumers' League, 186
Food stamps, 180, 219
Ford, A. Ward, 134
Ford, Elizabeth "Betty," 69, 84, **85**, 125
Ford, Gerald
  abortion and, 194
  appointments of, 13, 20, 109, 165
  Liz Carpenter and, 30
  Citizen's Advisory Council on the Status of Women and, 70
  Equal Rights Amendment and, 193
  Betty Ford and, 85
  International Women's Year and, 157
  Patricia Lindh and, 131
  military academies and, 144
  President's Commission on the Status of Women and, 53
  Margita White and, 240
Ford-Carter presidential transition, 124
Foreign affairs, 121, 123, 129
Foreign Affairs Committee, 29, 59
Foreign Intelligence Advisory Board, 133
Foreign policy, 44, 45, 46, 143, 174
Forklift Systems, 103
Formerly Employed Mothers at the Leading Edge (FEMALE), 288
Foster, Abigail Kelley, **86**, 157, 239
Foster Grandparent Program, 189
Fourteenth Amendment
  abortion and, 55, 110, 134, 138, 165
  African American men and, 69
  as Civil War Constitutional Amendment, 38
  divorce laws and, 166
  Due Process Clause of, 39, 47
  Equal Protection Clause of, 18, 47, 64, 207
  Equal Rights Amendment and, 53
  gender-based classification and, 189
  Hyde Amendment and, 103
  jury service and, 112
  minimum wage/maximum hour laws, 151
  President's Commission on the Status of Women and, 182
  same-sex marriages and, 75
  sex discrimination and, 47, 148, 204, 207, 229
  suffrage and, xv–xvi, 193
  Unemployment Compensation Disability Fund and, 91
  veterans' preference statute and, 170–71
  voting rights and, 232
4th Estate Award, 223
Fourth Amendment, 194
Fowler, Tillie, **86**
Fox, Jon D., 136
Fox, Mary Frank, 118
Frahm, Sheila, **86**
France
  Lucille Curtis and, 48
  family leave and, 76
  Pamela Harriman and, 102
  Elizabeth Monroe and, 149
  poverty and, 180
  RU-486 and, 200
  Margaret Sanger and, 203
Franco-Prussian War, 18
Franklin, Barbara Hackman, **86**
Franklin, Benjamin, 125
Fraser, Mayor, 177
Frederick Douglass Day Program, 149
Freedom of Access to Clinic Entrances Act (FACE), **86**, 166, 176
Freedom of Choice Act, 4, **87**
Freeman, Jo, **87**
Freeman, Joseph, 225
Freshman Republican Task Force on Reform, 86
Frick, Henry Clay, 97
Friedan, Betty, **87**
  achievements of, 87–88
  feminine mystique and, 79
  feminism and, 207
  National Organization for Women and, 81, 156
  National Women's Political Caucus and, xix, 6
  news media and, 159
  Mary Louise Smith and, 212
  women's liberation movement and, 246
Friedan, Carl, 87
Frontiero, Sharron, 88
Frontiero v. Richardson (1973), **88**, 236
FSA (Family Support Act of 1988), 11, 35, 78, 238
Full Employment and Balanced Growth Act of 1978 (Humphrey-Hawkins Act), **88**, 113
Fuller, Margaret, **88**
Fullilove v. Klutznick (1980), 10
Fulmer, Hampton P., 89
Fulmer, Willa Lybrand, **89**
The Fun of It (Earhart), 61
FUND, 57
Furness, Betty, **89**
Furse, Elizabeth, **89**

Gag rule, **90**
Gage, Henry H., 90
Gage, Matilda Joslyn, 51, **90**
Gang Prevention and Youth Recreation Act, 235
Gardner, Helen Hamilton, **90**
Garfield, James A., 90, 91
Garfield, Lucretia Rudolph, **90**
Garland, Lillian, 208
Garrett, H. Lawrence, III, 220
Garrison, William Lloyd, 99, 157, 171
Gasque, Allard H., 91
Gasque, Elizabeth Hawley, **91**
Gay/lesbian rights
  Rita Mae Brown and, 26
  child custody and support, 34
  Midge Costanza and, 46
  Daughters of Blithis and, 49–50
  Family and Medical Leave Act and, 77
  Sheila Lee and, 126
  Kate Millet and, 147
  National Organization for Women and, 155
  National Women's Conference and, 158
  privacy rights and, 23–24, 100
  pro-family movement and, 183
  same-sex marriage and, 73, 74–75
  spousal benefits and, 45
  Women's Action Coalition and, 243
  women's liberation movement and, 246
  Lynn C. Woolsey and, 250
GCSRW (General Commission on the Status and Role of Women), 288–89
Geduldig v. Aiello (1974), **91**, 94
Gender bias, 62
Gender discrimination. *See* Sex discrimination
Gender gap, **91**
  abortion and, 5
  Bella Abzug and, 6
  conservatism and, 44, 45, 46
  Jennifer Dunn and, 59
  Geraldine Ferraro and, 83
  party identification and, xxii, 92
  political participation and, 174, 176
  in presidential elections, xxi, xxvii
  voter turnout by sex, 92
  voting patterns and, 91–94, 129
Gender politics, 3
General Accounting Office, 107, 141
General Commission on the Status and Role of Women (GCSRW), 288–89
General Electric Company v. Gilbert (1976), **94**, 153, 182, 208
General Federation of Women's Clubs (GFWC), xvi, **94**, 105, 111, 289
Genetics, 140
Georgia, xxii, 23, 55, 207, 236
Gephardt, Dick, 5
"Get Out the Vote," xxiii
"Get the Facts" alerts, xxii
GFWC (General Federation of Women's Clubs), D, 94–95, 105, 111, 289
Ghana, 20
Gibbs, Florence Reville, **95**
Gibbs, William Benjamin, 95
Giles County Council of National Defense, 70
Gilligan, Carol, 94, 221
Gilman, Charlotte Perkins, **95**
Gingrich, Newt, 149, 152, 163
Ginsburg, Ruth Bader, **95**
  abortion and, 4
  achievements of, 95
  Bill Clinton and, 54
  sex discrimination and, 47, 208, 229, 248
Girl Scouts of the United States, **95**, 289
The Girls in the Balcony (Robertson), 24
Girls Nation, 289
Glass ceiling, xxvii, 38, 76, **95**
Glass Ceiling Act, 96
Glass Ceiling Commission, 38, 96, 133, 136
Global Fund for Women, 289
God and Man at Yale (Buckley), 44

International Union of Electrical, Radio and Machine Workers (IUE), 115
International Union of Electrical, Radio and Machine Workers v. Westinghouse Electric (1980), **115**
International Woman Suffrage Alliance, 31
International Women's Day, **116**, 147
International Women's Forum, 290
International Women's League for Peace and Freedom, 8
International Women's Year (IWY), 24, 108, **116**, 157, 229
International Workers of the World, 42, 85
Interparliamentary Conference, 98
Interparliamentary Union, 117
Interstate Commerce Commission, 147
In-vitro fertilization, 191
Iowa, xvii, 43
Iowa Woman Suffrage Association, 31
IPL (Immigrant Protective League), 3, 115
Iran, 147
Ireland, 108
Ireland, Patricia, **116**
Is This Your Son, My Lord (Gardner), 90
Israel, 176
It Takes a Village (Clinton), 40
Italy, 30, 133
IUE (International Union of Electrical, Radio and Machine Workers), 115
IWF (Independent Woman's Forum), 289
IWY (International Women's Year), 24, 108, 116, 157, 229

J.S. Mill Liberal League, 41
Jackson, George, 50
Jackson, Jesse, 5, 36
Jackson, Jonathan, 50
Jackson Hole Group, 107
Jacksonian Democracy, 129
Jacob, Herbert, 74
Jane Club, 113
Jay, John, 128
Jeannette Rankin Brigade, 188
Jefferson, Martha Wayles, 125
Jefferson, Thomas, xiii, 51, 125, 128, 129, 134
Jenckes, Virginia Ellis, **117**
Jenkins, Louis "Woody," 125
Jenks, Anias, 22
Jenks, Lucy Webb, 22
Jepson, Roger W., 104
Jews, 5
Jim Crow laws, 81
Job and Life Skills Improvement Act, 235
Job Corps training, 98
Job Opportunities and Basic Skills (JOBS) Training Programs, 78
Job training programs
  Family Support Act and, 238
  Family Support Act of 1988 and, 78
  Nancy Kassebaum and, 121
  Patsy Mink and, 147
  poverty and, 179, 181
  Smith-Hughes Act of 1917 and, 213
  Effiegene Wingo and, 242
John Birch Society, 68
Johnson, Andrew, 117, 118
Johnson, Anna, 192
Johnson, Claudia Alta ("Lady Bird"), 30, **117**
Johnson, Eddie Bernice, **117**
Johnson, Eliza McCardie, **117**
Johnson, Lyndon B.
  affirmative action and, 9
  appointments of, 12–13, 124
  Corrine Boggs and, 22
  Liz Carpenter and, 30
  Lillian Carter and, 30
  Civil Rights Act of 1964 and, 37
  Executive Order 11375 and, 71
  Betty Furness and, 89
  Sarah Hughes and, 113
  Claudia "Lady Bird" Johnson and, 117
  Esther Peterson and, 171
  Presidential Advisory Council on the Status of Women, 109
  women's rights and, 53
Johnson, Martha, 118
Johnson, Nancy, 43
Johnson, Nancy L., **118**
Johnson, Paul, 118
Johnson, Sharon, 118
Johnson v. Transportation Agency, Santa Clara County, California (1987), 10, **118**, 208
Johnson v. University of Pittsburgh (1973, 1977), **118**
Johnston, J. Bennett, 125
Joint Economic Committee, 108
Jones, George, 119
Jones, Mary Harris ("Mother"), **119**
Jones, Paula Corbin, **119**
Jones v. Clinton, **119**
Jordan, Barbara Charline, **119**
Joslyn, Helen Leslie, 90
Joslyn, Hezikiah, 90
Journal of Politics and Public Opinion Quarterly, 160
Journal of the American Medical Association, 141
Judicial reform, 112
The Jungle (Lewis), 186
Jury service, 112, 182, 189
"Just Say No" campaign, 189
Justice Department
  abortion and, 194
  Civil Division, 109
  domestic violence and, 57
  Jamie Gorelick and, 97
  Margaret McKenna and, 139
  Virginia Military Institute and, 229
  Webster v. Reproductive Health Services and, 235
Kahn, Alfred, 75
Kahn, Florence Prag, **121**
Kahn, Julius, 121
Kahn, Kim Fridkin, xxiv, 160
Kaid, Lynda Lee, 160
Kaiser Aluminum and Chemical Corporation, 10
Kamerman, Sheila, 75
Kansas, 161, 177, 232
Kansas Freedmen's Relief Association, 43
Kaptur, Marcy, **121**
Kassebaum (Baker), Nancy Landon, 86, **121**
Kathlene, Lyn, xxvii
Katzenbach v. McClung (1964), 37
Kay, Herma Hill, 118
Kean, Tom, 240
Kee, John, 122
Kee, Maude Elizabeth, **122**
Kefauver-Harris Drug Amendment, 222
Kelley, Florence, 113, **122**, 173, 186, 207, 229
Kelly, Edna Flannery, **122**
Kelly, Sue W., **122**
Kennedy, Anthony M., 10, 110, 173
Kennedy, Caroline, 165
Kennedy, Edward, 10, 121
Kennedy, Jacqueline. *See* Onassis, Jacqueline Lee Bouvier Kennedy
Kennedy, John F.
  affirmative action and, 9
  appointments of, 53, 97, 113
  Corrine Boggs and, 22
  Rachel Carson and, 30
  Citizens Advisory Council on the Status of Women and, 36
  Civil Rights Act of 1964 and, 37
  Equal Pay Act and, 67
  Executive Order 10980 and, 70, 182
  Florence Harriman and, 102
  Jacqueline Kennedy Onassis and, 165–66
  Esther Peterson and, 171
  President's Commission on the Status of Women and, xviii, 67, 182, 207, 217, 222
  Helen Thomas and, 223
  women's vote and, 53
  Molly Yard and, 251
Kennedy, John F., Jr., 165
Kennedy, Patrick, 165
Kennedy, Robert, 166
Kennelly, Barbara Bailey, **122**
Kentucky, J, 68, 174
Kentucky Education and Humanities Cabinet, 41
Kerber, Linda, xiv
Kershner, Jacob, 97
Key Issues Committee, 189
Keys, Martha Elizabeth, **122**
Khouri, Callie, 222
Kilpatrick, Carolyn Cheeks, **123**
Kilpatrick, James J., 45
King, Coretta Scott, **123**
King, Martin Luther, Jr., 123
King v. Smith (1968), 237
Kingston, Paul, 75
Kirkpatrick, Jeane J., 45, 46, **123**, 194
Klein, Herbert, 240
Knauer, Virginia, **123**
Knox, Henry, 202
Knutson, Coya Gjesdal, **124**
Kohl, Herb, 33
Koontz, Elizabeth Duncan, **124**
Koop, C. Everett, 194
Korean War, 52, 145
Korn/Ferry International, 96

Military service (continued)
military academies and, 144, 146
Persian Gulf War and, 146, 170
President's Commission on the Status of Women and, 182
Tailhood Scandal and, 220
Vietnam War and, 145, 205
Women's Equity Action League and, 245
women's issues and, 144–46
Milk, Harvey, 79
Mill, John Stuart, 128
Millender-McDonald, Juanita, **147**
Miller, Elizabeth Smith, 22
Miller, Emma Guffey, **147**
Miller, Frieda Segelke, **147**
Millet, Kate, 49, **147**, 184
Minimum Wage Act of 1918, 8
Minimum Wage Board, 8, 19
Minimum wage/maximum hour laws, **147**. *See also* specific laws
Clara Beyer and, 19
Shirley Chisholm and, 36
Equal Rights Amendment and, 67
Muller v. Oregon and, 151
as protective legislation, 147, 185
Rosenfeld v. Southern Pacific Corporation and, 198
women's issues and, 147
Mining and Metallurgical Society, 111
The Minister's Wooing (Stowe), 218
Mink, Patsy, **147**
Minnesota, xvii, 43
Minnesota Women's Campaign Fund, 300
Minor, Francis, xvi
Minor v. Happersett (1875), xvi, 232
Minor, Virginia Louisa, xv–xvi, **148**
Minorities
"Get Out the Vote" and, xxii
glass ceiling and, 95, 96
Eddie Bernice Johnson and, 117
Sheila Lee and, 126
Cynthia McKinney and, 139
Carrie Meek and, 143
National Women's Conference and, 158
suffrage and, 232
Maxine Waters and, 235
welfare and, 237
Ellen Wilson and, 242
The Miracle of Living (Balch), 17
Mississippi, 42, 68, 174
Mississippi University for Women v. Hogan (1982), **148**, 208
Missouri, xvii, 6, 235
Missouri Woman, 21
Missouri Woman Suffrage Association (MWSA), xvi
Missouri Woman's Committee, Council of National Defense, 21
Missouri Women's Action Fund, 300
Mitchell, George, 213
Mitchell, John N., 149
Mitchell, Martha "Bunny," **149**
Mobilizing Woman-Power (Blatch), 21
Mofford, Rose, **149**
Mohr, Richard, 75
Molinari, Susan, **149**
Mommy track. *See* Family leave/mommy track
Mondale, Walter, 12, 79, 82–83
Monroe, Elizabeth Kortright, **149**
Monroe, James, 149
Montaigne, Michel de, 75
Montana State Federation of Negro Women's Clubs, **149**
Moral consensus, 128
Moral Majority, 68
Morella, Constance A., 87, **149**
Morgan, Anne, 48
Morgan, Robin, 151
Mormon Church, 68
Morrill Act of 1862, 213
Morse, Wayne, 132
Moscone, George, 79
Moseley-Braun, Carol, xxii, **150**
Moskowitz, Belle Lindner Israels, **150**
Mother Earth, 97
Mothers' Aid Law, 75
Mothers' Pensions programs, 11, 237
Motor Voter Law, xxii
Mott, James, 150, 205
Mott, Lucretia Coffin, **150**
abolition and, 81
Declaration of Sentiments and Resolutions and, 51, 150, 216, 258
National Woman's Rights Convention and, 157
Philadelphia Female Anti-Slavery Society and, 171
Seneca Falls Convention and, 205, 245, 248
sex discrimination and, xiv
suffrage and, 150
Mount Holyoke, 61, 206
Mount Rushmore Memorial Commission, 99
Ms. Foundation for Women (MFW), 221, 290
Ms. magazine, 76, **150**, 217
MTV, J
Mujeres Activas en Letras Y Cambio Social (MALCS), 290
Muller v. Oregon (1908), 75, 147, **151**, 185, 207, 209
"Multiple Risk Factor Intervention Trial," 141
"Murphy Brown," xix, **151**
Murray, Patty, J, **151**, 159
Murray, Pauli, 81, **152**
Muskie, Edmund, 12
MW (Media Watch), 290
MWSA (Missouri Woman Suffrage Association), xvi
"My Day" (Roosevelt), 198
My Life with Martin Luther King (King), 123
My Turn (Reagan), 189
Myers, Betsy, **152**
Myers, Dee Dee, **152**
Myers, Sandra L., 160
Myrick, Sue, **152**

NAACP (National Association for the Advancement of Colored People), 108, 122, 149, 168, 222, 239
NACW (National Association of Colored Women), 19, 40, 153, 155, 159, 222, 226
NACW (National Association of Commissions for Women), 291
NAFE (National Association of Female Executives), 291
NAFMW (National Action for Former Military Wives), 291
NAFTA, 70
Naisbitt, John, 77
Nashville Gas Company v. Satty (1977), **153**, 182
Nathan S. Kline Medal of Merit, 31
Nation, 159
National Abortion and Reproductive Action League (NARAL), 291
National Abortion Rights Action League (NARAL), xx, 5, 173
National Academy of Sciences, 118
National Action for Former Military Wives (NAFMW), 291
National Advisory Committee for the White House Conference on Aging, 101
National Advisory Committee for Women, 6
National Advisory Council on the Education of Disadvantaged Children, 124
National American Woman Suffrage Association (NAWSA), **153**
American Woman Suffrage Association and, 13, 14–15, 20, 153, 161
Alva Belmont and, 19
Cable Act of 1922 and, 29
Carrie Chapman Catt and, 246
Congressional Union and, 43
creation of, xvi
Abigail Duniway and, 59
Helen Gardner and, 90
Mary Hay and, 105
Jessie Hooper and, 111
National Woman Suffrage Association and, 156, 161
Alice Paul and, 169
political participation and, xvi–xvii
Jeannette Rankin and, 188
Anna Howard Shaw and, 210
state campaigns of, 153, 169
Lucy Stone and, 218
suffrage and, 81, 153, 248
Martha Thomas and, 223
Sue White and, 240
Woman's Journal and, 243
National American Women Suffrage Alliance, 8
National Association for the Advancement of Colored People (NAACP), 108, 122, 149, 168, 222, 239
National Association of Colored Women (NACW), 19, 40, **153**, 155, 159, 222, 226
National Association of Colored Women's Clubs, 41
National Association of Commissions for Women (NACW), 291
National Association of Female Executives (NAFE), 291